Reward Management

5th edition

Reward Management

Alternatives, consequences and contexts

Sarah E Jones
Stephen J Perkins

CIPD

KoganPage

Third edition published by the Chartered Institute of Personnel and Development 2016
Fourth edition published in Great Britain and the United States in 2020 by Kogan Page Limited
Fifth edition 2024

2nd Floor, 45 Gee Street
London
EC1V 3RS
United Kingdom

8 W 38th Street, Suite 902
New York, NY 10018
USA

4737/23 Ansari Road
Daryaganj
New Delhi 110002
India

www.koganpage.com

Kogan Page books are printed on paper from sustainable forests.

ISBNs

Hardback 978 1 3986 1291 4
Paperback 978 1 3986 1289 1
Ebook 978 1 3986 1290 7

British Library Cataloguing-in-Publication Data

A CIP record for this book is available from the British Library.

Library of Congress Control Number

2023951850

Typeset by Integra Software Services, Pondicherry
Print production managed by Jellyfish
Printed and bound by CPI Group (UK) Ltd, Croydon, CR0 4YY

CONTENTS

LIST OF FIGURES

LIST OF TABLES

BOOK PLAN

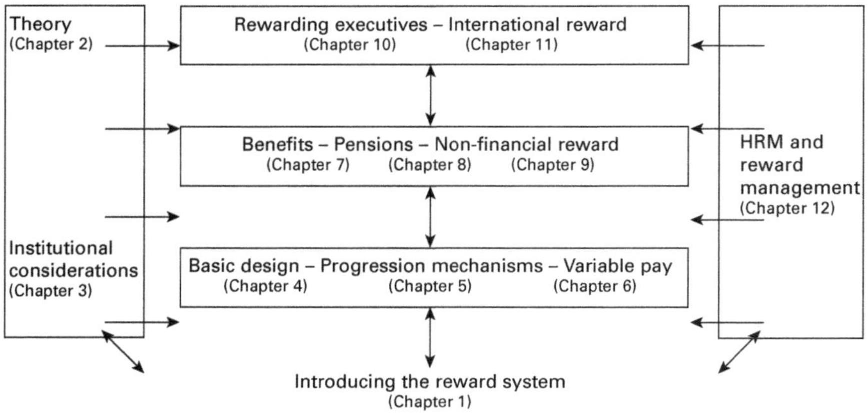

Theory
(Chapter 2)
Institutional considerations
(Chapter 3)
Rewarding executives – International reward
(Chapter 10) (Chapter 11)
Benefits – Pensions – Non-financial reward
(Chapter 7) (Chapter 8) (Chapter 9)
Basic design – Progression mechanisms – Variable pay
(Chapter 4) (Chapter 5) (Chapter 6)
HRM and reward management
(Chapter 12)
Introducing the reward system
(Chapter 1)

CIPD QUALIFICATIONS MAP

If you are studying the CIPD Advanced Qualification module Reward Management, the following table may be useful in mapping learning outcomes to the chapters of this book.

Number	Learning Outcome	Mapped to chapters in *Reward Management*
1	Analyse the relationship between the environment, strategy and systems of reward management.	**Chapter 1** Introducing the reward management system **Chapter 3** The legal, employment relations and market context **Chapter 5** Pay setting, composition and progression **Chapter 6** Variable pay schemes **Chapter 12** Reward management within 'HRM'
2	Explore the conceptual apparatus and theoretical debates informing reward management.	**Chapter 1** Introducing the reward management system **Chapter 2** Conceptual and theoretical frameworks **Chapter 12** Reward management within 'HRM'
3	Critically discuss traditional, contingent and knowledge bases for transactional and relational rewards.	**Chapter 4** Base pay structures and relationships **Chapter 5** Pay setting, composition and progression **Chapter 6** Variable pay schemes **Chapter 7** Benefits **Chapter 8** Pensions **Chapter 9** Non-financial rewards
4	Design internally consistent reward structures that recognise labour market and equity constraints.	**Chapter 3** The legal, employment relations and market context **Chapter 4** Base pay structures and relationships **Chapter 5** Pay setting, composition and progression **Chapter 7** Benefits **Chapter 9** Non-financial rewards **Chapter 12** Reward management within 'HRM'
5	Analyse executive and expatriate rewards in an international context.	**Chapter 10** Rewarding directors and executives **Chapter 11** International reward management
6	Critically evaluate key issues in reward management.	**Chapter 1** Introducing the reward management system **Chapter 2** Conceptual and theoretical frameworks **Chapter 3** The legal, employment relations and market context **Chapter 4** Base pay structures and relationships **Chapter 5** Pay setting, composition and progression **Chapter 6** Variable pay schemes **Chapter 7** Benefits **Chapter 8** Pensions **Chapter 9** Non-financial reward **Chapter 12** Reward management within 'HRM'

FOREWORD BY CHARLES COTTON, SENIOR REWARD AND PERFORMANCE ADVISER, CIPD

It would be fair to say that a lot has happened since my foreword for the fourth edition of this book was published back in January 2020. In the UK, workplaces have been buffeted by such events as Brexit, the global pandemic, the shift to hybrid working, the cost-of-living crisis, so-called culture wars and the healthcare crisis. But what have been the responses in terms of pay and benefits, and will these responses last or fade away?

And what about the future? For instance, how will generative AI shape the world of work, and how will it influence what reward professionals do? Given that my previous foreword only mentioned one of these events, I'll refrain from making predictions about the possible global events that will shape our future. Instead, I'll look at how reward professionals have been responding to some of what's been happening since the start of 2020 and where we could be headed.

As our research noted in 2020: 'Given the impact of the pandemic, the subsequent restrictions on business activity and calls for employers to build back better, we might have expected most employers to have responded by changing how they manage fixed pay and/or variable reward and recognition.'

Yet our research finds that despite the calls for employers to use the pandemic as an opportunity to revisit how they managed their pay and benefits, most workplaces didn't see a change. If there were changes, then they were temporary and targeted at some workers. It seemed that 'business as usual' trumped 'build back better'.

To be fair to reward and people professionals during this period, most had been so busy responding to these events that they rarely got the chance to reflect on whether they were rewarding the right people, for the right reasons, in the right way and at the right time. Many thought that they would have this opportunity once things had begun to settle down.

Only things didn't settle down. We went from a pandemic to acute labour and skills shortages as the world economies reopened from their lockdowns. The UK witnessed widespread vacancies in such sectors as transport, leisure, hospitality, public services and caring. And such occupations as HGV drivers, delivery employees, abattoir workers, bar staff and consultants.

In response, employers started to offer higher salaries and signing on bonuses to attract staff. They introduced referral bonuses to incentivise their existing workers to encourage their friends and family to apply for jobs. Some employers made multiple pay awards to keep their pay rates competitive, while many also resorted to counteroffers to persuade their staff to remain rather than leave. Others tried to tempt staff to join or stay with flexible working opportunities.

Other organisations were busy trying to get more of their staff back into the office. However, few did this either by offering staff more money if they returned or proposing to reduce their pay if they remained at home. A combination of a tight labour market, administrative complexity and legal repercussions put many employers off from doing this. Instead, the focus was on tempting workers back by offering new and enhanced perks, such as free food, an onsite gym or refurbished office space.

While tactics were busy trumping strategy, the next crisis was ambling into view. The recovery of the global economies was putting pressure on the supply of goods and services and shortages were pushing up prices. In addition, energy costs were starting to climb, not only resulting in higher bills but leading to various UK energy suppliers going bust. Finally, Ukraine was invaded, resulting in even higher energy costs and food prices. Inflation increased to levels not seen for a generation and many people faced a cost-of-living crisis. And just when things couldn't get worse, accommodation costs shot up with employees having to spend even more on rents or mortgages.

Inflation and labour shortages forced many employers to make the size of pay rises not seen for over twenty years. Even then, the increase in earnings lagged behind the increase in inflation and real wages slumped back to where they had been in the late 2000s. Rather than just increasing base pay, many employers gave cost-of-living supplements to help their staff, especially lower-waged workers. However, the combination of salary increases and supplements began to have an impact on receiving state benefits. Some reward professionals found out that among the skills required to do their job a new one to add to the list was a knowledge of the interaction between reward and state benefits, such as Universal Credit or Child Benefit.

The cost-of-living crisis has not only seen a jump in the number of workplaces signing up to become a real Living Wage employer, but also an increase in the number adopting a formal employee financial wellbeing policy. Employers looked at their reward package to see how well it protected their employees from either falling into financial difficulty or, if they did, how well the package helped them get out of their financial difficulty. The CIPD responded by launching resources helping those employers wanting to assist their staff deal with the cost-of-living crisis.

Various new initiatives came into being, such as earned salary access schemes or payroll autosaving, while existing ones were promoted more to staff, such as debt advice or cycle-to-work schemes. Some benefits, which some had regarded as being consigned to the dustbin of reward history, such as the staff canteen or the hardship fund, were making a comeback. However, to try and recruit staff, we saw the phenomenon of perk-washing, offering benefits that in practice were hard to access due to work constraints.

Underpinning the emphasis on benefits was a focus on communicating to employees about how the package could help them cut their living costs, how it could help protect them against financial stress and how it could help them if they got into money problems. There was a focus on tackling the workplace stigma around admitting that you had got money problems, highlighting that employees wouldn't be judged if they asked for help and highlighting sources of independent and confidential financial guidance.

And employers weren't only having to flag how the reward package could support their employees' financial welfare, but also their health and mental wellbeing as healthcare systems started to buckle under the strain of labour and skills shortages. Reward professionals were helping their employers look for ways to help keep their staff healthy, as well as helping those who did become physically or mentally ill.

In addition to responding to various pressures to look at better ways to communicate the value of the reward offering, reward professionals were also under external and internal pressure to be more open and transparent about how reward decisions were made and the outcomes of those decisions. Externally, some investors and customers were concerned whether the money they were spending or investing was promoting good people management practices, such as non-bias pay. Internally, management saw that an important part of the employee experience was people understanding what behaviours and performances the organisation was prepared to reward, and why.

Consequently, as well as disclosing pay gaps by gender and CEO pay ratios, some organisations started to do the same by ethnicity, age and socioeconomic background. They also checked whether their employees understood how reward was being managed and the rationale behind this. As well as being transparent about pay arrangements with existing staff, many employers were also being open about remuneration in their job advertisements.

However, having the data and systems that allow reward professionals to be transparent about pay is crucial. If reward professionals haven't got modern HR information systems, or they lack the skills to interrogate the data on them, then being able to explain what compensation and benefits decisions have been made, and why they've been made, is going to be hard.

Especially, when such stakeholders as investors or the senior leadership team want this information rapidly. In the past year, a lot of attention has been given to the impact of AI innovation in large language models. Not only should this technology make such reward processes as the annual pay review or the creation of the annual gender pay report quicker, but it should also be able to help make predictions about the possible impact of such decisions as a 6 per cent pay rise will have on employee commitment. How rapid the take-up of AI is in pay and benefits management will depend on the case for investment made by reward professionals.

This book provides excellent grounding for students to explore all the reward options that are available, how to evaluate the ones that are most appropriate for their context, and the issues to consider when introducing a new initiative or revising the existing arrangements.

While I said I wouldn't make predictions about the future, if I had to, I would say that reward transparency and fairness will be key drivers in the next three years. Not least because these trends became evident over the past decade. And that AI will be a key driver in how reward is managed and designed.

WALKTHROUGH OF TEXTBOOK FEATURES AND ONLINE RESOURCES

This volume has been designed with students and their tutors in mind. You'll see from the contents that it is structured into **four complementary parts**. The book plan on page xii shows diagrammatically how the various elements complement one another interactively.

Part One starts with the fundamentals of placing contemporary reward management into context; the narrative reflects the kinds of expectations that the CIPD has set out to guide the development and accreditation of *thoughtful professionals* in HRM generally and reward management specifically. As we introduce the volume, we show how in each chapter links are made to current CIPD-related learning outcomes; and these are summarised in the CIPD Qualifications Map on page xiii.

Once these principles about choices, consequences and contexts are set out and related to systems thinking, along with the multidisciplinary sources of theory to guide thinking and evidence-based practice, and our subject field placed within its institutional setting, we move in **Part Two** to describe the key building blocks for understanding and critically engaging with reward management.

Part Three naturally leads in to description and analysis of factors recognised as representing reward management in its wider contexts, including non-financial elements that are important when thinking strategically about engaging people to bring about managerially intended outcomes. In so doing we remember the need for a careful balance between what organisation management may regard as priorities and employee perceptions about the way their skills and experience may be willingly deployed and recognised in ways they value and regard as fair.

Part Four concludes by drawing some overarching principles together about the intellectual and practical location of reward management within wider strategic management policy and the institutional policies against which these may be regulated. Before that summing up, this part takes a deep dive into areas that have proved complex and controversial – executive remuneration and reward associated with managing people internationally.

Throughout the text there are plenty of mini case studies and questions for self-reflection as well as group activity within and beyond the classroom.

Turning to the complementary materials for **access online**, we have produced a set of model lesson formats in the shape of slide decks that tutors may draw on in organising lectures, seminars and assessment activities for their students. These also may provide a short-form ready reference that students may find helpful when reflecting back on the programme of study they are following, including during assessment-related revision times. In addition, both within the text (after each chapter's summing-up box) and through links within the book's online reference pages, suggestions are made, with hyperlinks wherever possible, to online sources comprising blogs, guides and reports, in particular via the CIPD website – some of which we have researched and written – that will take the kinds of argument and evidence set out in the book into more detailed areas of knowledge as applied in practice.

PART ONE

In Part One we introduce the volume and our rationale for it, and then engage with concepts, theory and the institutional context for reward management alternative approaches and consequences. We review the range of theory that informs ideas and practice on reward management, to help students grasp frameworks likely to be of assistance when addressing subsequent aspects of the book's coverage. We devote a chapter to issues that help locate contemporary reward management systems within institutional contexts.

01
Introduction: Reward management systems

CHAPTER LEARNING OUTCOMES

At the end of this chapter you should understand and be able to explain the following:

- How to use this book as a guide to concepts and themes encountered when navigating this complex, contested field of study.
- Definitions of employee reward and its management.
- Reward management alternatives and consequences flowing from the strategic choices made, conceptualised in 'systemic' terms, situating 'effort–reward' bargaining in its various contexts.

CIPD STRATEGIC REWARD MANAGEMENT MODULE (7HR03) LEARNING OUTCOMES

Learners will be able to:

1.1 Examine the key factors influencing the design of reward strategy and policy frameworks.

> **1.2** Discuss the importance of aligning the reward framework to the wider organisational context and strategy, so as to understand effective reward strategies and policy frameworks.

This book is intended to help guide people learning about and practising 'reward management' (defined below). We set out to share insights into what's involved and how to approach an area of people management that is as complex as it is fascinating. As media headlines daily attest (Key Issues in Reward Management 1.1), it is a controversial field. It attracts a welter of academic analysis and advice from popular commentators. More than 'just pay', to the layperson, the range of reward management alternatives may be bewildering. And like any other area of people management, while on the face of it self-evident, it's worth remembering that the focus of attention is *people*. Diverse people – managers, employees, and those who regulate and represent them – who interpret and act on their interpretations and ways of bringing order to the socio-economic institutions of work and organisation, influenced, in turn, by their unique and evolving character and circumstances.

The book's structure aligns with the CIPD's Strategic People Management framework; in particular, the Strategic Reward Management unit 7HR03. Each chapter's learning outcomes map to the requirements specified within that framework. This is the fifth edition of our textbook and, while as we show in the unfolding text, there are various commonalities in reward management, the dynamics of organisations and people and their interactions mean there are changes to reflect on. When asked, our Foreword writer, Charles Cotton, CIPD Senior Advisor for Reward & Performance, was readily able to list novel contextual features for managing reward observable since the fourth edition was published in January 2020!

For example, the implications for reward management of:

- the shift to hybrid working;
- the so-called 'great resignation';
- the loss of over 55-year-olds from the labour market;
- the cost-of-living crisis;
- the cost-of-doing-business crisis;
- the greater focus on the 'S' in ESG by investors, customers, and employees (e.g. good work, EDI, tackling in-work poverty, etc);
- AI innovation in large language models such as Bard, ChatGPT and similar, and of course;
- calls for greater pay transparency driven not only by UK developments but also by those in the USA and the EU, putting pressure on large UK employers.

(Cotton, 2023, personal correspondence)

We have kept those and other developments in mind while revising the text. We have also kept the focus on perennial themes involved in creating and sustaining reward management systems (defined below) as a strategic endeavour. We encourage our readers to adopt a critical stance when faced with ideas that academic and practitioner literature on our topic puts forward. There is no denying that much proverbial ink has been spilled on describing what may be referred to as a 'normative viewpoint', i.e. advocating the use of specific reward plans and practices on the basis that choosing these will achieve managerial priorities. Almost a quarter-century ago, a pair of US-based authors and management consultants used the phrase *Pay People Right!* (Zingheim and Schuster, 2000) as a call to action by employers. Subtitling their volume 'Breakthrough reward strategies to create great companies', they argued that 'pay is a powerful communicator of values and directions' (2000: xv).

Removing the hyperbole, the imperative here is to ensure reward management systems align with an organisation's strategic goals. In other words, leadership teams need to decide how best to apply their organisation's resources, including investment in employee pay and benefits, to enable outcomes the organisation is required to achieve to fulfil its purpose. That may be profitability, public service provision or charitable endeavours. A decade earlier still, the same authors introduced another question to guide reward management: 'how can we find ways in which the workforce can share in the organisation's success?' (Schuster and Zingheim, 1992: xv). They argue that it is 'part of the formula people look for' (xv) when evaluating whether or not to work for an employer (and by extension whether to stay with it and to work in ways aligned with the employer's expectations).

We share the view that the choices employers make between the reward management alternatives open to them – explicitly and implicitly – have the potential to signal managerial priorities and intentions to all stakeholders in formal organisations. That includes at least implicitly communicating the assumptions shared by organisational leaders and those to whom they are accountable (whether these are governments, private investors or trustees) regarding the role and nature of the people wanted to perform work to fulfil the corporate purpose and the basis on which value created will be distributed.

A requirement for Boards of Directors to ensure that reward management is 'designed to support strategy and promote long-term sustainable success' has been included in corporate governance regulations (discussed at some length in Chapter 10). Executive remuneration 'should be aligned to company purpose and values and be clearly linked to the successful delivery of the company's long-term strategy' (FRC, 2018: 13). Echoing the transparency point in Charles Cotton's list above, the Board is required additionally to state how employment conditions (including rewards) applicable to other employees in the organisation have been taken into consideration when setting 'top pay'. This includes whether and how employees other than directors have been consulted when drawing up policies for executive director reward management, making reference to any comparative indicators setting the overall context for this corporate activity (KPMG, 2013).

The term 'reward management' itself is significant, implying an active role for employers; standing in contrast to views in which it is external forces of supply and demand in jobs and workers that regulate employment. We will see in the next chapter, when we discuss theoretical approaches to help evaluate reward management ideas and action, that thinking varies over the role if any for line managers in determining wages and other payments to people related to employment. Caution is needed to avoid reading too much into rhetorical statements to the effect that adopting the 'right' reward practices will produce outcomes that are equally universal in the perceived benefits to the various parties. Even Zingheim and Schuster add the caveat that applying a reward-business process accelerator 'isn't a quick fix' (2000: xvi). They suggest that: 'Much of the popular literature on management ... avoids issues of pay, perhaps because it's harder to address than many of the gentler and less powerful change tools' (2000: xvii). Note here the implication that reward management is associated with progressiveness: travelling from one organisational state to another. Critics of so-called 'new pay' discourse (i.e. writing intended to persuade the reader to adopt normative policies, in place of those shaped by a plurality of interests and contexts) have argued that advocates' practices may be associated with psychological outcomes of the very sort Zingheim and Schuster (2000), for example, say they wish to eradicate. In particular, a sense of personal anxiety when faced with pay that remains permanently 'at risk' (Heery, 1996).

The remainder of this introductory chapter is organised to satisfy three main objectives. First is to clarify meaning(s) attached to employee reward management and the links with relations around employment, accounting for orientation(s) towards the workforce. Secondly, to scrutinise references to 'reward systems', and then to appraise the utility of long-standing 'systems' thinking to help assemble and interpret material on the alternatives, consequences and contexts for contemporary reward management. Thirdly, it fleshes out the 'plan of the book' diagram [located on pxii], to outline the structure and content of the subsequent four parts arranged over the subsequent 12 chapters.

KEY ISSUES IN REWARD MANAGEMENT 1.1

According to Torsten Bell, Chief Executive of the Resolution Foundation, a 'think tank', while soaring inflation in 2022–23 has adversely affected workers' real wages, Britain's pay problems – and the stagnation in living standards they have contributed to – go much further back. If wages had continued to grow as they were before the financial crash of 2008, earnings controlling for inflation would be around £11,000 higher annually than they currently are. He calls this 'a 37 per cent lost wages gap':

> The gap between typical UK household incomes and those of comparator countries has also widened. In the period running up to the financial crisis, German households were better off than British households by £500 per year, but that has since increased to £4,000. The toxic combination of low growth and high inequality mean that poorer households in Britain are most exposed to this stagnation. While typical households in the UK are 9 per cent poorer than their equivalents in France, low-income households are now 22 per cent poorer.

(**SOURCE:** www.resolutionfoundation.org/press-releases/15-years-of-economic-stagnation-has-left-workers-across-britain-with-an-11000-a-year-lost-wages-gap/)

Reward dispersion

In September 2022, Kwasi Kwarteng, briefly Chancellor of the Exchequer, said that the UK would remove the cap on bankers' bonuses it had inherited from EU banking provisions. While relatively few of the other proposals announced at that time survived the change of administration, this proposal was adopted by his successor, Jeremy Hunt, for incorporation into regulatory frameworks.

(**SOURCE:** www.shlegal.com/insights/first-formal-steps-towards-removal-of-the-bonus-cap-in-uk-banks)

Median FTSE 100 CEO pay at the beginning of January 2023 stood at £3.41 million, according to the High Pay Centre. This figure was 103 times the median full time worker's pay of £33,000. It represented a 39 per cent increase on median CEO pay levels as of January 2022, while the median worker's pay had only increased by 6 per cent over the same period. In the view of High Pay Centre Director, Luke Hildyard, 'In the worst economic circumstances that most people can remember, it is difficult to believe that a handful of top earners are still raking in such extraordinary amounts of money.'

(**SOURCE:** highpaycentre.org/high-pay-hour-how-quickly-ceos-earn-the-uk-median-wage)

Pay and employment relations disputes

In Spring 2023, the BBC reported hundreds of thousands of workers taking part in strikes or planning to. Trade unions were calling for wage rises to keep up with rising prices. Strike action involved ambulance workers, civil servants, nurses, junior doctors, postal workers, rail workers, school teachers and university staff.

(**SOURCE:** www.bbc.co.uk/news/business-62134314)

EDI and pay

Shell in the UK publishes its gender and ethnicity pay gaps. For 2022, the company's mean gender pay gap ranged from 11.7 per cent to 20.7 per cent, while its ethnicity pay gap ranged from 1.5 per cent to 12.6 per cent. Shell says it is committed to closing these gaps and is taking steps to address the issue, including unconscious bias training and providing more flexible working arrangements.

(**SOURCE:** https://www.shell.co.uk/about-us/careers/about-careers-at-shell/we-are-one-team/diversity-inclusion/diversity-pay-gap-report.html#:~:text=Our%20gender%20pay%20gap%20continues,of%20this%20range%20was%2054.9%25)

Pensions in crisis?

Growing numbers of workers are cutting their workplace pension contributions or opting out of schemes entirely because they cannot afford payments – prompting calls for employers to increase the amounts they pay in.

With real wages falling and bills rising sharply, people across the country are looking for ways to reduce spending and supplement their incomes, and the TUC said it was hearing about staff in both the public and private sectors who had concluded they could not afford to save for retirement at the moment.

(**SOURCE:** www.theguardian.com/business/2022/aug/31/more-people-leaving-workplace-pension-schemes-tuc-warns)

Employee reward and wellbeing

In its 2022 reward survey report the CIPD said:

... although some employers are making a much-valued difference to the financial wellbeing of their workforces, others are falling short of employees' expectations. One in four employees say money worries impact their ability to do their job; with the cost of living soaring in the UK, it's likely that more and more people will experience poor financial wellbeing and face impossible decisions about money. In the worst cases, they may not be able to heat their homes, pay rent, or buy essentials. Employers and practitioners, alongside policymakers, will need to take urgent action to ensure they support workers' financial wellbeing and that in-work poverty does not become more widely entrenched.

(**SOURCE:** www.cipd.co.uk/knowledge/strategy/reward/surveys)

Stories like those above, taken from a brief window of media coverage, exemplifies the sense that reward management, whatever else it may be, isn't easy. The astute HR professional will appraise 'solutions' with a critical eye. Effort-reward bargaining as a socio-economic process requires people to work it out. That may be through formalised negotiations in collective settings with intermediaries acting for management and workforce; or in day-to-day interactions between the supervisor seeking to motivate one or more subordinates to 'perform' to achieve the supervisor's goals; or even for the individual working out mentally what and how much to do. It also involves a diverse array of stakeholders making judgments and drawing their own conclusions on how reward management outcomes impact their own interests. To guide critical (reflexive) thinking about the diverse range of reward management 'issues', Chapter 2 summarises the work of theorists from a variety of disciplines that we argue help interpret problems and help frame practical solutions HR professionals are expected to craft and advise on.

1.1 Reward management ideas and practices

Looking at the basics, we briefly discuss the terms 'employee reward' and 'reward management'. Employee reward represents one of the central pillars supporting the employment relationship (Kessler, 2005). As illustrated in Key Issues in Reward Management 1.1, its management is likely to influence the character and quality of that relationship and its outcomes.

DEFINITIONS

Employee 'compensation', 'remuneration' or 'reward' (terms that may be used interchangeably in the literature) may be defined as 'all forms of financial returns and tangible services and benefits employees receive' (Milkovich and Newman, 2004: 3).

'Work under an employment relationship is undertaken in return for pay' (Rubery and Grimshaw, 2003: 12). But the nature of this 'exchange relationship' (Steers and Porter, 1987: 203, emphasis in original) implies more than an economic transaction. Classically, employee reward and its management may be perceived as an 'effort-bargain' (Behrend, 1957; Baldmus, 1961) between the parties to the employment relationship, needing to be continuously renewed on either side.

Employee 'reward(s)' may, however, be differentiated between:

extrinsic, tangible or 'transactional' reward for undertaking work in employment, on the one hand, and

intrinsic reward derived from work and employment, on the other hand.

Extrinsic reward – in the form of salary, incentive pay and benefits – serves the purpose of directly recognising the comparative value of organisational roles and the contribution individuals may make in performing them. Extrinsic employee benefits and 'perks' delivered in a non-cash form (e.g. company cars, paid holiday and health care), or 'deferred remuneration' (e.g. occupational pension benefits or equity share-based rewards that may be financially realised at a future date) may reflect managerial efforts to keep rewards competitive, intended to recruit and retain sufficient employees of the right calibre, and to secure work accomplishment for the organisation. Benefits may also reflect an employer's interest in employee wellbeing. The nature and combination of extrinsic reward is dynamic: for example, present-day contributions to an employee's 'portable' retirement income fund (or 'defined contribution' pension scheme) are increasingly offered in place of a 'company – defined benefit – pension', reflecting the increasingly 'flexible' employment relationship. We discuss such complexities in Chapter 8 on pensions.

Intrinsic reward may be further subdivided (Kessler, 2001). On the one hand, 'environmental rewards' may be manifested in the physical surroundings in which work is performed, combined with other factors, such as the values displayed in the workplace by organisational leaders and work supervisors, and perceptions of their leadership quality. On the other hand, 'development-oriented rewards' that tend to be more individually directed may be offered to recognise employee aspirations to receive learning and development opportunities, and to gain acknowledgement of outstanding work and build feelings of accomplishment – wherever possible consolidated tangibly through career advancement (Milkovich and Newman, 2004). It is argued that extending the features of employee reward beyond those specified in the 'economic contract' may help to secure employees' discretionary effort (Wright, 2005: 1.2.2). This 'intrinsic' or 'psychological' contract in work relationships (Levinson et al, 1962; Schein, 1965; Rousseau, 1995) forms the basis of the 'total reward' proposition (see Chapter 9). Attention to ESG considerations and openness to hybrid work arrangements may be viewed as part of what today's managements may be expected to factor in to such a proposition, reflecting employees' own checklists in the post Covid-19 pandemic years.

1.2 Employee reward levels vs 'labour costs'

The *rate* of employee reward is not the same as the *cost* of employing someone. It is possible to pay higher rates of reward to employees compared with a competitor and yet have employment costs – as a proportion of the total costs of running an organisation – that are relatively lower (Pfeffer, 1998a). The key ingredient is *productivity* – that is, what the employer is able to achieve in terms of efficient and effective output from the workforce for each component of a person's capacity to work. Context is also key: labour costs will also vary depending on whether the organisation is capital or labour intensive.

For example, compare two microprocessor producers where one pays higher wages than the other but keeps the overall cost of employment at a managerially acceptable level by requiring significantly fewer person-work hours to create a similar number of microchips.

Following a similar logic, cutting salary and wage rates is no panacea for reducing labour costs:

> I may replace my $2000 a week engineers with ones that earn $500, but my costs may skyrocket because the new lower-paid employees are inexperienced, slow, and less capable. In that case I would have increased my costs by cutting my rates.
>
> (Pfeffer, 1998a: 110)

Initiative is needed organisationally to ensure that employee reward is not just specified and determined. Active management is also required to ensure all parties interested in the effort-reward bargain understand what intentions follow from what is on offer and what this implies in what will be rewarded and how rewards will be delivered.

> Reward management may thus be simply defined as the combined actions an employer may take to specify at what levels employee reward will be offered, based on chosen criteria and data; how the offer will be regulated over time; and how both the intended links between organisational goals and values should be understood and acted on by the parties to the employment relationship.

1.3 Situating reward management systemically

In this book, the reader is offered a way of situating 'the problem of reward management' (by which we mean patterned activity to be specified and understood, to inform action) within the context of argument and evidence related to the *employment system*. In fact the 'system' is multidimensional: it is at the least one that reflects the national and international environment within which employees are contracted to work and employers need to manage their activities. By definition that 'system' is diverse; and we should not assume that it is immune to effects from beyond the immediate arena of organisation and employment. Wider economic, political, social and technological phenomena – set within a historical period, itself affected by the past – create a dynamic setting that employers, and the people management specialists who advise them, need to take into consideration when evaluating the alternative approaches to managing employee reward and the expected return on investment and other consequences that follow. And employment systems will be encountered at a variety of levels below the macro level – e.g. industry sector, organisation, workplace, each of which is likely to be just as diverse, reflecting the range of people and situations involved. We discuss the dynamic contexts for reward management in greater detail in Chapter 3.

A report published by the CIPD in 2023 drawing on empirical data from 1,500 non-HR business leaders as well as HR specialists draws attention expressly to the need for HR professionals to be 'systems thinkers' (CIPD, 2023d: 71) going behind dashboard-style intelligence provision to decision-makers to locate strategy recommendations in context.

The human resource management literature frequently refers to reward (or compensation, pay or remuneration) systems (e.g. Boxall and Purcell, 2003; Heery and Noon, 2017; Kessler, 2005, 2007; Marchington and Wilkinson, 2005; Milkovich and Newman, 2004; Ulrich, 1997). But as Robert Persig observes in his classic text *Zen and the Art of Motorcycle Maintenance* (1991): 'There's so much talk about the system. And so little understanding.' We can find little in the published debates among commentators in the field that explicitly justifies why a 'systems' view of employee reward is appropriate, or using ideas that have their roots in 'general systems theory' (von Bertalanffy, 1969). This is despite the fact that, as Meadows and Wright (2008: xi) point out, 'Today it is widely accepted that systems thinking is a critical tool in addressing the many environmental, political and social, and economic challenges we face around the world.'

While pursuing a search for underlying regularities that characterise the world in general Ludwig von Bertalanffy, a biologist and the founding father of general systems theory, adopted the 'system' as 'an organising concept' to help overcome differences between different academic disciplines (Burrell and Morgan, 1979: 58).

A system is formed from 'elements and parts that are organised and interdependent' (Holmwood, 2006: 587). Systems can be either 'closed' or 'open' (Daft and Marcic, 2020). Closed systems are exemplified by conventional physics that isolates systems from their environments; for example, the 'controlled experiment' where phenomena are exposed to testing but isolated from the places in which such phenomena naturally occur. Closed systems, von Bertalanffy (1969) argues, will by definition become independent from their environment, but this will undermine attempts to understand the system as a dynamic phenomenon in continuous interaction with other, contextually linked, systems. Such reductionist thinking may lead to perverse outcomes. Haines (1998) cautions against isolating the elements of a system for analysis to their most basic trait and then reassembling the 'answer' without consideration for the inevitable 'infection' that will affect the phenomenon once returned as a whole to its environment. In effect, one system colliding with other systems. For example, if we offer short-term cash incentives to financial services executives (see Chapters 6 and 10) it may be assumed that their resultant behaviour will benefit the firm. However, without moderating factors including acknowledging the time lapse between apparent outcomes and actual value creation or destruction, such hermetically sealed incentive programmes may encourage individuals to act in ways that, when ignoring risk becomes endemic to this category of employee, may risk plunging the whole system into crisis. As discussed in Chapter 10, corporate governance has evolved into a risk-based approach to reward management due to such evidenced concerns.

In direct contrast to a closed system, an 'open systems' approach draws attention not just to the structure or substance of phenomena but to the processes that impact on the system, and its impact in turn on those other systems with which it interacts. Open systems 'engage in transactions with their environment, "importing" and "exporting" and changing themselves in the process', continuously 'building up and breaking down ... component parts' (Burrell and Morgan, 1979: 59). Thus, open systems theory offers a route for studying 'the pattern of relationships which characterise a system and its relationship to its environment in order to *understand* the way in which it operates' and so to 'discern different types of open system in practice' (Burrell and Morgan, 1979: 59, emphasis in original).

Controversy regarding the use of incentives to reward certain employees in financial services illustrates the potential hazards of regarding a reward system as 'closed' or self-contained. As will be discussed in Chapter 2, classical economics theory on wage determination assumes away environmental factors (or context), to consider employment market transactions in the abstract, using the 'all other things being equal' caveat. And ideas from psychology such as Vroom's 'expectancy theory' (also considered in Chapter 2) may be seen as drawing on the systems input-transformation-output-feedback model: an incentive system may be designed on the basis of assuming that desired behaviour will result provided the individual can 'see' what is expected, the extent to which achievement is realistic given available resources, and whether they find the incentive offered of sufficient value to them. But again, there is a need for caution in extrapolating from such theorising reduced to the individual disconnected from the wider social context. For example, conditioning what is deemed valuable and the degree of 'contribution' required and the trust the individual has in managerial representatives to honour the bargain, derived from prior interactions with peers and superiors.

> The conceptual lynchpin of systems thinking... is that all systems are circular entities. This concept, which is based on the actual nature of systems, is integral to the input-transformation-output-feedback model that forms the framework for systems thinking...
>
> ... In viewing our organizations... as levels of systems within, and colliding with, other systems we align ourselves with the principles of openness, interrelation, and

> interdependence, and so cement the systems concept. When problem-solving, we look for patterns of behavior and events, rather than at isolated events, and we work on understanding how each pattern relates to the whole. We begin to see how problems are connected to other problems – and are forced to look at solving those problems in a new light. In fact, the solution to any systems problem is usually found at the next highest system.
>
> (Haines, 1998: 283-91)

Mindful of the importance of paying attention to the hierarchy of systems (or the environment) within which they function, interpreting reward management systems as 'open' may be more realistic in the context of the contemporary economy. Organisations and their sub-systems interact with an increasingly interconnected division of labour across a capitalist 'world system' (Wallerstein, 1983), in which organisations of different sizes and stages of development enter into a diversity of employment relationships with people in locations that are also at various stages of development and change.

Consistent with the integrationist 'HRM' approach we discuss in Chapter 12, within the organisation itself reward management systems may be deliberately located in continuous interaction with internal 'environmental conditions' derived vertically from corporate strategies and horizontally from other people management structures and processes, not to mention the interactions with regulatory system expectations introduced to the organisation from the external 'political economy' (i.e. the intersection of political and economic systems). Depending on the viewpoint of the commentator, the direction of influence vertically and horizontally is debatable. Nonetheless, ideas from open systems theory may help encourage reflexivity around employee reward. Whether or not specifically goal-directed, a reward system may evolve, regress or disintegrate, not only experiencing change itself but also possibly influencing changes to an organisational environment (Daft and Marcic, 2020) and spilling over into an external employment and business system in the process.

An example of this may be the arrival of a large multinational corporation in a developing or transforming economy, where the inward investors and their managerial agents may introduce practices that begin to reshape a competitive environment for effort–reward bargaining. Choosing between a closed or open systems perspective has important consequences for the underlying assumptions accompanying the theories that help to interpret and understand how and why reward systems function. Theorists debate alternative explanations for adaptation within and between non-static systems, including provisions for addressing conflict and creating consensus among the actors within the system, underscored by the institutional context for reward management (see below).

1.3.1 Criticisms of systems thinking

Despite the influence that the 'systems approach' has had on various branches of management and social science since the mid-twentieth century, systems theory may be criticised when its users do little more than propose the reduction of complex phenomena to elements that may be observed and where possible experimented on, while promising not to forget that in reality the parts need to be considered 'holistically' and in 'interaction' (Burrell and Morgan, 1979).

Within the social sciences 'grand theory'-building attempts to explain modern society in systems terms, such as by American sociologist Talcott Parsons in the 1950s, have been criticised for the implicit assumption of converging values among populations which, given the diversity of people within and across the world's nations, lacks empirical grounding (Abercrombie et al, 2000). A prediction that societies would come to mirror the industrial and employment system characteristic of the USA (Kerr et al, 1964) has remained controversial. Important criticisms are associated with the potential of analysts to confer a self-determining (or 'reified') status on socio-economic systems, over-emphasising *systems* while neglecting *action* (Holmwood, 2006). In Chapter 2, for example, we take a critical look at the classical labour economist's view that vests ultimate authority in market forces in regulating the employee reward system.

Another important criticism has been the argument that social systems theory is couched in conservative ideology and lacks the capacity to deal adequately with the presence of conflict and change in social life (Mingers, 2015). This latter point may be answered to some extent by reference back to the more sophisticated project on which von Bertalanffy embarked. Attention may be paid to sources of influence, for example, in settling the terms of the effort–reward bargain. The necessity for individuals to interpret aspects of both the extrinsic and intrinsic employment relationship implies that, while management – as the 'keepers' of organisational and employment resources – may enjoy a 'dispositional' advantage in framing the offer (Edwards, 1986, 2003), the position remains indeterminate (Shields, 2007). Managers may not be assumed to act consistently, and employees may interpret their roles in ways that have unforeseen consequences neither with the intended business nor HRM strategy.

In shaping discussion in this volume, while not ignoring the limitations of a systems perspective as this may be applied to reward management, it seems appropriate to remain sensitive to the ways in which elements interact with one another, and with other systemic features observable at various levels of environmental analysis. For example, those connected with managerial strategy and with other human resource management designs and activity inside the organisation, as well as with economic markets, and other institutions, such as the law, shareholders, trade unions, etc, located externally. In 'voluntary associations of purposeful members who themselves manifest a choice of both ends and means' to achieve organisational outcomes (Gharajedaghi, 1999: 12), the parties may be viewed as seeking to regulate the effort–reward bargain, processing information and learning from powerful feedback loops within an open system setting which may either amplify or dampen change (Haines, 1998; Wheatley, 2020), to modify and refine their orientation to the employment relationship. For example, if a reward system is designed to reward employees for meeting certain goals, this could lead to a positive feedback loop. This loop could encourage employees to work harder and to achieve even more goals. On the other hand, if a reward system is designed to reward employees for seniority, this could lead to a negative feedback loop. This loop could discourage employees from taking on new challenges and from learning new skills. It is our contention that the thinking HR performer (a concept incorporated into CIPD professional standards since the early 2000s) will benefit from bearing this in mind when reflecting on theory and practice in connection with reward management systems.

In summary, we have chosen to focus on 'open', dynamic systems within which reward management is practised (i.e. not regarding reward systems as sealed vacuums to be acted on as though in laboratory settings) so as to help readers grasp the fact that more is in play than a process with predefined outcomes.

> **STUDENT EXERCISE**
>
> Discuss the benefits of approaching the analysis of reward management systems as proposed above. Considering the criticisms we have sketched, why do you think a systems approach may have been popular among social analysts?

1.4 Rewarding the employment relationship

A fundamental principle associated with designing and administering employee reward is that these activities are undertaken within a complex set of people and organisational interrelationships – a series of interconnecting systems coinciding around the employment relationship. Recently, recognising the political context within which reward outcomes are determined, especially concerning the controversy around the widening pay gap between executives in organisations and other employees, reward management is considered a feature of corporate governance (e.g. Perkins and Shortland, 2022, Aleweld et al, 2015). Managerially the intention may be to design reward so that it acts, in alignment with other features of human resource management, to secure the strategic intentions of the employer: to get things done through securing and deploying the capacities of the workforce. The social context for managing employment relationships and the reward dimensions, however, may mean that, while the intent may be strategic, the diversity of people and settings logically gives rise to risks that the outcomes desired by senior management may not automatically appear in practice. As discussed later in this volume, our research for the CIPD has sought systematically to evaluate claims regarding efforts by organisations to match corporate strategy and systematic reward management (e.g. Jones et al, 2015; Perkins et al, 2019; Cotton et al, 2021; 2022).

While organisation leaders may deploy what management guru Peter Drucker called their 'theory of the business' (aka strategy), managers at each level between corporate and 'front line' and, in turn, employees may apply their own criteria to work out how to engage with it. And it would be unwise for any manager to assume that the 'engagement' is unfailingly consistent with corporate intentions. A complex mix of demographic, economic, social and related circumstances – including feelings towards co-workers and managers, and occupational and professional allegiances – act as prisms through which people view what's on offer and what's expected of them in return. As we will see throughout the book, interpersonal-organisational comparative factors impact on sense-making. Prominent among these are considerations of equity ('does how I'm treated feel fair?'), associated with factors such as ethnicity and gender, and cultural norms and values across social and geographical spaces internationally ('how does my world-view interact with the employer and other key stakeholders?').

The Annual Survey of Hours and Earnings, published by the UK's Office for National Statistics, indicated that in April 2022 annual earnings for the bottom 10 per cent of full-time employees in the UK was approximately £19,500 (ONS, 2022). This figure contrasts with the position at the opposite end of the earnings spectrum, whereby the top 10 per cent of full-time employees earned around £62,500. There were variations by region. While the median annual earnings in the country as a whole was £33,000 in 2022, the figure ranged from around £29,500 in the North East of England to approximately £41,900 in London.

Summary trends illustrated in the same survey report include:

- An increase in average hourly pay in 2022 for full-time employees for all percentiles year-on-year, but with a larger increase in the lower deciles. Part-time jobs at the fifth percentile saw the largest increase in hourly pay.
- Based on hourly pay levels, there was a reduction in the proportion of low-paid employee jobs: from 14.3 per cent in 2021 to 10.5 per cent in 2022, the lowest since the ONS began reporting this series in 1997, with the proportion of high-paid employee jobs falling 0.7 percentage points on-the-year to 23.7 per cent in 2022.
- The ONS found that the lowest-earning employees tend to be part time, younger (aged between 16 and 21 years) and in the elementary occupations or in the hospitality industry.
- The highest-earning employees are concentrated in the managerial and professional occupations, aged between 35 and 49 years, or working in the information and communication, and finance and insurance service industries.
- The number of jobs paid below the National Minimum Wage and National Living Wage is 509,000 (1.7 per cent) employee jobs.

The ONS (2022) point out that employees working more than 30 paid hours per week (or 25 or more for the teaching professions) are categorised as full-time. Low pay is defined as two-thirds of median hourly earnings; high pay is defined as 1.5 times median hourly earnings.

KEY ISSUES IN REWARD MANAGEMENT 1.2

Which are the highest and lowest paid jobs in the UK?

Below are shown the highest and lowest paid occupations median full-time annual earnings, according to the 2022 Annual Survey of Hours and Earnings.

Highest paid

Chief executives and senior officials £121,434
Marketing, sales and advertising directors £95,818

Financial managers and directors £91,853
Specialist medical practitioners £83,482
Information technology directors £82,363
Functional managers and directors £80,411
Legal professionals £79,818
Air traffic controllers £77,819
Aircraft pilots and flight engineers £74,570
Senior police officers £74,232
Financial institution managers and directors £73,307
Natural and social science professionals £72,817
Human resource managers and directors £72,215
Senior professionals of educational establishments £71,845
Electrical engineers £70,964
Production managers and directors in manufacturing £70,834
IT specialist managers £70,725
Senior officers in protective services £70,522
Engineering professionals (excluding electrotechnology) £69,747
Sales accounts and business development managers £69,239

Lowest paid

Retail cashiers and check-out operators £20,592
Packers and bottlers £20,592
Care escorts £20,592
Kitchen assistants £20,592
Fitness instructors £20,592
Security guards and related occupations £20,592
Hospital porters £20,396
Cooks £20,253
Bar and catering supervisors £20,245
Collector salespersons and credit agents £20,038
Playworkers £20,033
Early education and childcare assistants £19,577
Beauticians and related occupations £19,211
Cleaners £17,077
Retail workers £17,077
Hairdressers £17,077
Teaching assistants £17,077
Waiting staff £16,568
Leisure and theme park attendants £14,064

(Office for National Statistics (ONS) (2022))

Figure 1.1 Labour is losing out: The share of national income paid to workers has been declining in many countries (evolution of the labour share of income, per cent)

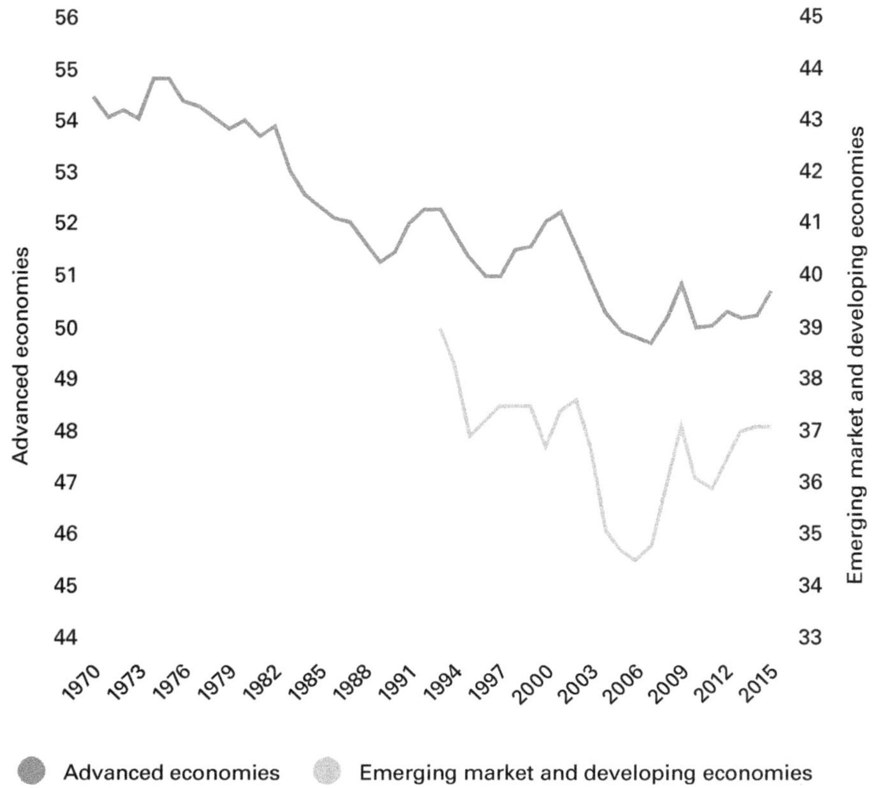

SOURCE: International monetary Fund, April 2017 – World Economic Outlook

Adopting a longer term, international perspective according to research for the International Labour Organisation (ILO) (Stockhammer, 2013), the share of wages in national income has declined across the developed world over the past several decades with similar patterns emerging in the developing economies. Distribution has become more polarised in most OECD countries (OECD, 2011), with the very top income groups increasing their income shares substantially in the Anglo-Saxon countries, in particular in the USA. Overall, real wage growth has lagged behind productivity growth since around 1980 and this constitutes a major historical change as wage shares had been stable or increasing in the post-war era. The ILO report found strong negative effects of 'financialisation' as well as negative effects of welfare state retrenchment and globalisation on the wage share. While technological change has had a positive impact on wage shares in developing economies, in advanced economies in contrast it has had a (modestly) negative impact. The research also found that globalisation (in production) had had robust negative effects, even in developing economies. Another explanatory factor for the decline in wage share is seen as the decline in organised labour market institutions such as trade unions and collective bargaining. Consequences arising from the economic impact of policies adopted during the Covid-19 pandemic may augment these trends.

What are the social justice implications for what is referred to as pay dispersion within the economy? A high level investigation commissioned by the UK government, led by a well-known economist, Will Hutton, explored questions specifically intended to set some standards for judging 'fair pay' nominally in the public services, although expected to influence practice more generally (Hutton, 2010, 2011). In the face of the continuing gap between levels of pay enjoyed by members of the UK workforce based on their demographic characteristics (see Chapters 3 and 4) employers have been required to become more transparent using equal pay audits. Undertaking its 'first ever' equal pay audit in 2008, the University of Kent stated that:

> The purpose of the Audit was to help the University identify any pay inequities arising because of gender. Future Equal Pay Audits will have a wider scope to also include race and disability. The recommendations from the report will be used to assist in reviewing our practices in relation to pay and grading policies and procedures.
>
> (University of Kent, 2008)

CIPD research examining barriers to employees improving their level of earnings over time (or 'pay progression') indicates that changes to the composition of job types in the UK economy are inhibiting movement 'up the ladder' (CIPD, 2015). A squeeze on traditional 'middle tier' jobs is apparently disabling significant numbers of people in full-time employment moving off the bottom rung of the ladder, even if they have capabilities and are willing to work hard. And the research evidences findings that 'the likelihood of being "stuck" is strongly correlated with being female and increases with age' (CIPD, 2015: 4).

Another growing influence on reward management in the UK, at least for the lowest paid, is the popularity of the 'living wage' concept. Originally a device to encourage employers to voluntarily adopt rates of pay required to provide a minimum living standard, this campaign has seen strong growth in the number of employers signing up as accredited employers (see Chapter 3 for more details). Indeed, a former Chancellor of the Exchequer, George Osborne, acknowledged its success in naming his new higher national minimum wage rate for those over 25 a 'national living wage'.

The scope for what Knights and McCabe (2000) label an 'interpretative gap' between reward management designs and how people interpret and react to them is likely, even if at face value the managers and employees espouse a strong sense of what academic commentators have labelled organisational membership (or commitment to corporate aims) and citizenship behaviours (helping those with whom they interact in an unselfish way). People's orientation to work – why they work and the values they bring to the employment relationship – and their sense of vested interest in accepting the offer of an employment contract is at root 'indeterminate' (Marsden, 1999).

Managing people purposively in organisations, under an employment relationship, reflects what well over half a century ago economist Hilde Behrend (1957) described as an 'effort bargain'. While the formal agreement to work for an employer may specify explicit terms, and may be accompanied by statements that describe the job to be performed, the way the bundles of tasks should be approached, and the performance expected, in practice a negotiation is taking place. That negotiation may reflect the employer's strategic expectations. But it also will be influenced by the employee's interpretation of what is offered – implicitly as well as explicitly, accounting for psychological, social and economic exchanges. For example, the extent to which employees judge the 'deal' to be worth it as a just return for the commitment and capability to work they are investing, in turn needs to be taken into account in designing the 'reward proposition' and how it is administered across the variety of people and settings within which employment (and reward) relationships are to be found.

We explore the 'reward proposition' over the course of this volume, culminating in a discussion in Chapter 9 on so-called 'total rewards'. The implication is that, while these days reward management choices are fairly extensive, there are limits to the 'packages' and 'modes of delivery' to select from. The variety of characteristics attributable to the managers who oversee them and the employees who are targeted for such 'interventions' (characterised e.g. by age, ethnicity, gender, bodily status and orientation), and the sectoral, national, regional and global settings inhabited, are in contrast potentially limitless. Recognising this gives pause for serious reflection. What may work to produce specific outcomes among one group and in one setting may result in a completely different set of interpretations and outcomes, and be accompanied by the need for variation in how to approach the effort-reward bargaining process, when transplanted to people and settings elsewhere.

1.5 Influences on employee reward thinking

Much of the literature concerning employee reward is informed by the twin disciplines of economics and psychology (reviewed in depth in Chapter 2). Our introductory remarks, however, signal the presence not only of phenomena concerned with macro-economic market transactions and/or individual micro-perceptions and responses but also of ethical, moral, political, social and technological factors – as well as managerial strategies and responses from the parties to the employment systems. These parties include finance capital investors, governments, trade unions and other 'stakeholders', not least employees. Interest groups may adopt a variety of starting points in their approach to employee reward management and the way it can be objectively described and determined, or subjectively interpreted and socially constructed and deconstructed. The consequence of this is that not only do reward systems designers and decision takers find themselves confronted with conflicting prescriptions on how to derive effective consequences from investment decisions; they also encounter alternative ways of thinking about the subject – whether these feature explicitly in the commentary or lurk implicitly below the contextual surface.

Given the range of factors complementing and supplementing economic and psychological issues, the search for guidance on how to navigate potentially conflicting, sometimes contradictory, 'best practice' techniques may be usefully supported by literature drawn from employee relations and HRM, political science, sociology, strategic management and so on (also reviewed in Chapter 2). These ideas and concepts will need careful interpretation and critical evaluation. But they may help to situate alternative reward management principles and practices within the particularities of the context in which they have been fashioned and in which they will be implemented.

That is the case whether the context is spatial and/or temporal, related to organisation and workforce – as well as managerial – characteristics, and cultural and/or institutional factors, not forgetting philosophical considerations that set the scene for what decision-makers and their advisers think is being observed and acted on, and how knowledge to inform the process is itself constituted. Observing these principles, it seems to us, the reader will be able to adopt a thematic and theoretically grounded orientation to the subject, rather than one overly reliant on 'techniques' (even when technical commentary is informed by reports of what 'works' and what does not, gathered in 'real world' settings).

1.6 Reward and the employer–employee relationship

Three basic reasons are generally given for rewarding employees, namely to:

- secure;
- retain; and
- motivate.

(CIPD, 2006)

Employers, or managers and supervisors acting on the employer's behalf, whether they are in 'for-profit' organisations, government agencies or other 'not-for-profit' enterprises, offer reward(s) that may be counted as representing the 'price' for employing 'labour', moderated by particular economic market conditions. But the employment relationship has a complex character. Employees are not selling 'their souls' as a labour market commodity (Rubery and Grimshaw, 2003: 2), but a capacity for and willingness to work. The relative value of economic recognition it is deemed legitimate for an individual to expect in employment is mediated through principles of fairness, equity, justice and respect for the human condition, expressly surfaced in Hutton's (2011) analysis.

Because reward is about a relationship, the outcome of which is open to the striking of a bargain (Kessler, 2001), the phenomenon is dynamic and not wholly subject to unitary managerial design or control (Marsden, 1999). A formal contract may be entered into between the parties – effort for reward – but the precise details of whether and to what extent employee effort matches managerial expectations remain unpredictable. Managerially, 'performance management' arrangements may be introduced to try to order the process, but the extent of employees' willingness to co-operate in terms of not only 'membership behaviour' (a decision to join and stay with an employer), but also 'task behaviour' (complying with managerial expectations over completing assigned work tasks) and 'organisational citizenship behaviour' (voluntarily and altruistically acting in ways that exceed membership and task compliance) is ultimately a function of employee choice (Shields et al, 2021).

As we saw in the opening section, influential voices in reward management have argued that reward management needs to complement and reinforce a 'new logic' of organising (e.g. Lawler, 2000). Under this reasoning, reward management needs to match the criteria for judging an organisation as 'effective' (i.e. that it achieves a fit between the need for capabilities in co-ordinating and motivating behaviour matched to economic market demands, on the one hand, and competencies that distinguish the organisation from its competitors, on the other). Simultaneously, effectiveness implies that reward management policies and processes are attuned to environmental conditions (contextual influences) while also retaining a focus on enactment of a specific corporate strategy.

SELF-ASSESSMENT EXERCISE*

Draw up a list of factors that employers and employees may hold in common in terms of reward management, and highlight areas where interests may also diverge. What are the implications for day-to-day effort–reward bargaining?

* This is the first in a series of two types of activity we invite *Reward Management* readers to engage in, to help them in actively thinking through and assessing the argument and evidence presented. This 'self-assessment exercise' is something that may be undertaken as part of private study. A second set of themes presented at various points throughout the book under the heading 'STUDENT EXERCISE' may be appropriate as a classroom session or, outside the formal learning environment, informally in conversation with peers or 'learning sets'.

1.7 Orientations towards employees

To develop proficiency in thinking about and practising reward management, it helps to make connections systematically between the alternative approaches available to practitioners and the consequences of the choices exercised, within the context in which decisions will be taken and acted upon. Given the need to continuously renew the 'effort bargain', as defined above, one contextual influence on choices between alternative reward approaches and their consequences concerns the dynamic interaction between expectations among those involved regarding the character of their relationships. Explicit and implicit managerial orientations towards workforce members signal to employees how to perceive how their employer regards them. While it is possible the approach may be standardised across an organisation, it is likely that it will differ to some extent at least between different workforce segments/locations/times. For example, when there are certain skills at a premium in jobs markets, at different hierarchical levels or between certain functions. Or perhaps in specific locations where an organisation operates, or during the various phases in an organisation's lifecycle from start-up to maturity and possible retrenchment. Table 1.1 works through these basic orientations, suggesting possible consequences for the managerial rewards agenda.

The commentary in Table 1.1 illustrates the nature and implications of regarding workforce members as assets or liabilities on a 'human capital balance sheet'. It also casts them in the guise of 'customers' for the 'employment propositions' an

Table 1.1 Orientations towards the workforce: Reward management implications

Interpretation	Issues	Reward management agenda
'Employees are "our greatest asset" ... they need to be used effectively'		
Employees are valuable objects, but devoid of feeling, which are operated by the owner or agent for maximum utility.	How do we source compliant objects? How do we keep them in prime shape to do our bidding? Pump-priming, instrumental relationship.	Buy on 'contingency terms'. Service regularly (by service agent?). Run to breakdown: refurbish or write off and replace. Utility (exploitative) orientation?
Employees are a liability ... they need to be controlled'		
Employees are 'debts' for which one is liable, or troublesome responsibilities, and therefore need to be limited, assiduously policed or expunged.	How do we minimise our 'debts'? How do we keep them under close surveillance? Wary, possibly antagonistic relationship.	Minimise cost of 'debt'. Arm's-length relations. Ensure ability to write off liability at earliest opportunity. Resigned-utility orientation?
'Employees are "customers" ... understand and serve them'		
Employees are independent beings; they exercise choices based on logic and emotion. They will offer loyalty to a 'supplier' of employment/reward if they believe the promise and see results.	What 'customers' do we want? What can we (afford to) supply? What are the alternatives? Active supplier role to continuously renew an employee-centred relationship.	Understand 'customer' preferences. Honest and transparent response with specification available. Regular client relationship review. Service orientation?
'Employees are "corporate allies" ... develop a mutual success agenda'		
Employees are independent beings; they exercise choices based on logic and emotion. They will offer commitment to organisational partners if they believe in them and see results in the substance and process of the effort–reward bargain.	What allies do we need and desire? What can we (afford to) trade? What are the alternatives? Active partner role to continuously renew a mutually profitable employment relationship.	Understand allies' needs and priorities. Honest and transparent response: accommodation available? Regular alliance relationship dialogue. Reciprocal commitment orientation?

SOURCE: Adapted from Perkins (2000)

organisation might market, or potential allies in a reciprocal partnership (even if in the final analysis the employer retains residual rights over the economic value created).

In the first two orientations, employees appear to be viewed either as emotionally inert, despite recognised potential to add value to organisational activity. Or they are perceived as a source of unwelcome intrusion into an organisational model that management would rather do without – perhaps to replace workers with mechanisation through investment in technology, such as the announcement by BT that it may adopt artificial intelligence in place of some 40 per cent of its workforce by 2030 (Sweney, 2023). A third orientation follows the conceptual thread that if people really do represent 'our greatest assets', the consequence is that the employer needs to find ways of 'selling' an employment 'brand', implying that employees hold the upper hand in the transaction. A fourth orientation towards the workforce signals that, while the employer recognises the latent value in people who may be persuaded to work for the organisation – still carrying a risk that the relationship may become employee-dependent (see e.g. Pfeffer and Salancik, 2003) – both parties have alternative pathways open to them.

A mixture of economic and socio-psychological factors may condition the choices. The rhetoric of extrinsic or intrinsic contractual promises may fall short of the reality. Unplanned circumstances such as changes in investment or trading conditions might undermine 'ability to pay'. Rather than risk this, an employer may signal an orientation in which each party to the employment relationship focuses on the process of reaching an accommodation, involving continuous and transparent mutual focus on reaching an holistic 'deal'. As Herriot and Pemberton (1995) argue, this may in turn require a 'renegotiate or exit' orientation on the part of the employee. But the task open to managerial initiative is one of setting clear 'rules of engagement' and, by actions rather than words alone, communicating the potential for an employment relationship, founded on mutual trust and respect. Such 'employment alliances' imply the scope for conflicting positions to arise between the parties – perhaps acknowledged as inevitable – with a willingness to explore the room for compromise and trade-off initially to secure the long-term benefits with which the 'partnership' ideal is imbued by stakeholders.

This may all sound rather esoteric: fine in principle – but what about the practice? Two examples below may help illustrate issues to be weighed in considering alternatives and consequences in employer orientations towards employees.

CASE STUDY 1.1

Periphery to core

One of the authors served on a large UK National Health Service Trust board of directors, overseeing a new hospital building project under public/private partnership commercial terms. To the great concern of employees working in 'support' services associated with keeping the hospital running day to day (catering staff, 'domestics' and other ancillary workers), the project plans involved the TUPE-transfer of their employment to the new private management partner. A potentially damaging employment relations dispute was averted when the senior hospital administrators explained to groups of employees affected that, being honest, they would always find themselves as peripheral workers – in effect, 'liabilities' or 'second-class', when viewed against the Trust's clinicians and nursing professionals. Without necessarily compromising the psychological contract they believed they had entered into in joining the NHS, they would remain members of a 'healthcare partnership', but enhanced by transition to 'core workforce' status in their new employment relationship.

The implication was a basis for effort–reward bargaining where their interests were potentially advanced, not only in extrinsic reward but also in terms of scope for recognition, personal and career development, and the sense of 'involvement'. The point is that an employer may find decisive action – in this case transferring a workforce segment into an outsourced arrangement – a more satisfactory option on both sides of the effort bargain than one hampered by half-hearted in-house managerial commitment.

Promise meets practice

The same author undertook an enquiry for a sub-set of the European partners of a large professional services firm. During the transformation the organisation was undergoing at the time, an announcement was made by its corporate leadership with great fanfare on both sides of the Atlantic that, to create conditions in which the firm's managerial and professional employees would adopt the highest quality service orientation towards clients, the firm would treat its people as 'clients' too in their employment relationship. The investigation involved focus group discussions with a cross-section of managers and professionals across a fairly wide geographical base, one telling remark from which might be interpreted as necessitating caution when top managers consider 'talking up' the employment promise. The partners 'treat us as no more than money-making machines', the researchers were told. Clearly, although no doubt well-intentioned from the 'bridge', at 'deck' level 'crew members' received a distorted 'orientation signal'.

SELF-ASSESSMENT EXERCISE

Two case cameo illustrations have been provided covering the 'liabilities' and 'customers' segments in Table 1.1. To test your understanding, search for some company annual report and accounts statements in which the seemingly ubiquitous 'people as greatest assets' statement appears in the chair's statement or similar commentary. Then look for statements embedded in reports, or in other sources of corporate information (e.g. company websites and/or analysts' appraisals). To what extent do you find these consistent with the 'assets' principle, or are there indications of more partnership orientations? You might conduct a similar 'audit' of your own organisation or one known to you.

We have signalled that management faces a series of alternatives for approaching reward management – as do employees. Various consequences follow on from adopting one or other mode of engagement with this complex aspect of organisation and people management. The consequences flowing from reward management choices, whether conditioned by tradition or alternative logic for organising, may be viewed in terms of the nature of expectations the parties hold, the quality of the relationships and the underlying principles regulating their interaction.

1.8 A few words on our tripartite taxonomy

This book reviews theory and practice associated with reward management systems as these interact with the employment relationship and effort–reward bargain. To create a thematic focus for the discussion of the material assembled, the emphasis throughout is on the alternatives that call for decision-making, carrying consequences in each case, which may be interpreted in and conditioned by particular and changing contexts. Before concluding the chapter with a summary of the book's overall content and structure, at this point a short statement is appropriate on what we intend to convey through our 'alternatives, consequences and context' refrain.

An **alternative** is located in a proposition containing two (sometimes more) statements, or offer of two (or more) things, the acceptance of one of which involves the rejection of the other(s). Alternative possibilities, alternative statements of some position, may exist, open to the exercise of choice by social actors. Decision-takers are required to make selections between alternatives, electing for one course of action over one or more alternatives. The act of choosing involves preferential determination between things proposed. A choice may be exercised managerially, for example, to reward employees for time they commit to the employer or on their performance outcomes, including the ways these are achieved. Each of the parties has a choice of how to approach the effort–reward bargain, and this is likely to be influenced by the assumptions and priorities they bring to the interaction and the nature of the relationship involved.

Being positioned to exercise choice locates decision-takers relative to other social actors and implies, among other things, making judgements to secure the most favourable (or fit-for-purpose) outcome, to attain something that is worthy of being chosen, having special value relative to other available options. Choices are logically followed by consequences: it is an open question whether or not the decision-takers base their selection between alternatives either on logically conjectured projections or by reference to empirical evidence of past outcomes, to assist the process of judgement in pursuit of a preferred outcome (i.e. one that is anticipated and accords with the project being pursued by the chooser). Actors called to exercise choices in terms of the effort–reward bargain (managers and/or employees) may be influenced by reference to 'benchmark' data on practice reported elsewhere or experience over time during the course of a particular employment relationship or employment relations in general. They may also be faced by ideas from advisers and other opinion-formers about what is deemed fitting or cost-effective in the circumstances.

A **consequence** may be described as something that follows as an action or condition, effect or result, from something antecedent to that consequence. A consequence following a particular act of choosing may be considered as predetermined (i.e. located within a cause-and-effect relationship). Where social relations are involved, as in the case of weighing alternatives in effort–reward bargaining, the situation is unlikely to be so clear-cut. While consequences may form a logical sequence starting with a specific choice, opening them to logical deduction from certain premises, a caveat is necessary. The consequence of an action, or decision to act, being logically inferred (involving the exercise of judgement) is suggestive of a position where absolute certainty may be open to question. Hence, logical deductions may usefully be tested drawing on an existing pool of relevant empirical knowledge.

Adopting an alternative definition, choices may lead to outcomes that are 'of consequence': that is, they are endowed with importance (assumed consequentiality). They have an impact (positive or negative) on the people and circumstances in which the choice plays out. The corollary of this assertion is that scope for systematic reflection on inferred consequences – prior to action – merits the attention of parties involved in effort–reward bargaining, and those whose role is to advise them, whether as employees, managers, national/supranational government policy-makers or other stakeholders in the complex field of employee reward. At minimum, systemic-looped feedback reflection and learning may help improve the quality of judgement exercised under dynamic conditions.

Selection decisions between alternative effort–reward bargain approaches do not occur in isolation. In systems terms, the selections between alternatives by groups of decision-takers interact with the choices exercised by others, and in each case their choices may be viewed as reflecting particular interests. For example, managerial decisions to select one reward management strategy and thus reject others will interact with decision-taking by other groups of managers, as well as employees who may be the targets of such decision-taking. How alternatives are weighed and acted on, and the consequences that follow, are open to influence from the context (or environment) in which organisations are situated and how it is interpreted by the parties to the effort–reward bargain.

Interaction between the elements perceived as systematically regulating the employment relationship and effort–reward bargain may be theorised as context-bound or context-free. Reference to context describes action to weave or sew together contextualised phenomena to facilitate interpretation and possibly explanation. If something is contextual the implication is of a situation belonging to the context – if not standing in a dependency relation with then at least influenced systematically by the context.

The context for reward management and the alternatives and consequences associated with its determination may be framed in terms of corporate, national and international systems. Managerially, the scale and sector of an organisation, its predominant technological make-up (affecting the balance of emphasis in the capabilities required to resource operations), its history and the predisposition of those who lead and make up the general membership may be viewed as bounding to some extent employee reward policy alternatives deemed legitimate. Adopting an open systems perspective, external to the organisation, context is likely to reflect the nature of its ownership, and the influence of the various stakeholders and other institutions with whom the organisation's members may be perceived to have a relationship – such as business partners, investor groups, state regulators representing a 'public interest', trade unions and so on. Also, the competitive environment, for sources of investment and revenue (not forgetting employee talent), is likely to influence profitability and the disposition of management to invest in the effort–reward bargain.

Looking beyond the internal organisational setting and its immediate context, as noted earlier, an increasingly significant influence on organisation systems, and on HRM and reward management systems, is attributed to the 'global context' (Franklin, 2006). A recurring theme in the literature is the question of whether or not approaches to employment regulation are converging internationally or whether they remain divergent, owing to the influence of culture and institutional factors within particular national systems (Anakwe, 2002; Katz and Darbishire, 2000; Sparrow, 1999).

Whether or not the organisation employs people across geo-ethnic borders, it may be argued that regional and global employment systems need to be factored in to attempts to evaluate the alternative ways of approaching the effort–reward bargain. A common governance architecture for contemporary 'business systems' may be assumed (Whitley, 2000): capitalist principles inform the basis on which actors will seek to arrange the affairs of organisations and those of the national and international systems within which they are situated (Coates, 2000; Furåker, 2005).

Even if it is accepted that capitalism provides the dominant organising logic, however, alternative 'varieties of capitalism' (Albert, 1993; Hall and Soskice, 2001) have been postulated, reflecting the institutional basis for reaching 'social peace' as an antecedent of successful economic production (Roe, 2003: 1). Although a 'directional convergence' around particular sets of policies and practices for the management of organisations, including effort-bargaining orientations, may be open to perception, 'final convergence' may not be reliably assumed (Tregaskis and Brewster, 2006). Detailed policies and practices may reflect different interpretations of the opportunities and limitations of the global, national and organisational settings in which choices between alternatives are being made. The accent may vary according to the systematic interaction between economic, historical, legal, political, social and technological factors, in turn affected by cultural and psychological factors – that is, the influence of socialisation on decision-makers' interpretations of perceived opportunities and limitations.

The institutional context for reward management is discussed in Chapter 3 and, specifically in the case of executive reward, in Chapter 10. In-depth treatment of the transnational context for corporate governance and knowledge mobilisation features in Chapter 11. While the latter chapter deals with the topic specifically, given its overriding influence on reward management considerations an eye for the international dimension remains open throughout the volume.

In short, it is our position that understanding reward management will be assisted by attention to themes systematically arising as the parties evaluate and act on the range of alternative courses of action open to them and reflection, conceptually and empirically, on consequences that may follow from these choices. In the case of both alternatives and consequences the influence of the open systemic context in which alternatives occur and are weighed and consequences are played out is something that needs to be accounted for in drawing conclusions, which may in turn inform policy and practice.

STUDENT EXERCISE

Consider the argument that, owing to the scale of western multinationals, their preferences for determining reward management systems will tend to prevail across the countries in which they set up operations. To what extent can you build an alternative, or 'divergent', perspective? Are the tendencies polar opposites?

1.9 Conclusions and key learning points

In this chapter, we have defined employee reward and reward management, reflecting on their various manifestations, and introduced the concept of the effort–reward bargain and the consequences of applying this theoretical notion when trying to make sense of interaction between the parties to the employment relationship. We have introduced a model encouraging reflection on the orientations employers may adopt towards their employees when evaluating reward alternatives and the consequences implied, positing four possible scenarios. We have also briefly appraised the merits and criticisms of applying systems thinking when conceptualising reward management. Commentary on developments in the corporate, national and international context for reward management has been briefly reviewed to situate alternative reward management designs and the consequences that may follow from selected applications.

For postgraduate students following a specialist Reward Management module, the book can be used sequentially. Chapters have been written mindful of the CIPD's Strategic People Management framework focusing on the Strategic Reward Management unit 7HR03. We have designed the content and style of the book as a text to support CIPD-related students in particular. But we hope the volume will be of relevance to other readers interested in this important subject associated with people at work and their management. Students of general management and those following final-year undergraduate and postgraduate HRM programmes may find it beneficial initially to engage with Part One, in order to locate selective engagement with subsequent content, depending on specific interests or assigned work. Throughout the book, commentary is illustrated using Key Issues in Reward Management extracts and calls for 'self-assessment' and other exercises, to inform discussion of issues raised. The intention is also to assist readers' preparation in addressing summative assessment questions. Case study material appears at various points to illustrate how conceptual arguments relate to practice. To conclude this chapter, a summary follows setting out a plan of the overall text.

1.10 Overview of the book

The book is structured in four parts over 12 chapters, including this introduction.

Part One deals with concepts, theory and the institutional context for employee reward management alternative approaches and consequences.

While conceptual and theoretical frameworks inform the treatment of reward management throughout the book, in **Chapter 2** particular attention is devoted to the principal attempts to theorise the subject. Acting as a reference point for what follows in subsequent chapters, models may be identified drawing on a multidisciplinary academic literature: principally (labour) economics, industrial/organisational psychology, employment relations, management strategy, and the sociology of organisations and work. Emerging themes include the extent to which employee reward is something open to 'management'; assumptions about people and work motivation under conditions of employment; and the social and political interactions around the effort–reward bargain. The content of this chapter also enables us to signal themes traced throughout the volume related to how notions of equity and social justice, diversity and its management, and the possible implications of a 'global' economy interact with ideas and practices making up the reward management field.

A complementary foundational discussion – this time covering the legal, employment relations market and geopolitical environment – is presented in **Chapter 3.** The material includes the impact of principal legislation and related regulatory developments affecting reward management, beyond economic market influences, along with the role of collective bargaining where applicable. The dynamic nature of transnational institutional environments for managing reward cannot realistically be ignored. The future post-Brexit, post-Covid and post-renewed war on the European mainland remains an open question. The chapter also considers the impact of the labour market on reward decisions and pay determination.

Part Two introduces and evaluates structures and processes for extrinsic reward management, describing some of the practicalities of their design and operation.

The basic architecture of pay systems is the focus of **Chapter 4.** Descriptions of and arguments for applying 'pay structures' are examined, including alternative types of pay structure, and conditions affecting their design and operation. Many pay structures are underscored by an aspiration to create the conditions for 'internal equity'. The objective has become even more important with the development of anti-discrimination regulatory frameworks. The concept, role, alternative approaches and administration of 'job evaluation' are discussed together with the impact on pay structures. Debate surrounding 'job' or 'role' analysis as the basis for structuring pay, as well as questions and practicalities regarding alignment of pay structures with external markets for jobs and people, is appraised.

Payment methods, salary progression management and their consequences are reviewed in **Chapter 5.** Wages systems and salary systems are compared, as are 'seniority-' or 'service'-related pay versus pay 'contingent' on inputs (e.g. skills) or outputs (e.g. pre-set target achievement) or combined under the rubric of 'contribution-based pay'. The critical part played by 'performance management' and the centrality of line managers to the process of managing contingent pay systems is reviewed. The role of 'compensatory payments' for working 'flexibly', in particular beyond contracted 'basic' hours, such as overtime, shift and call-out payments, is assessed. The practice of augmenting pay using concepts such as 'premiums' related to specific employment locations is also discussed.

Beyond time-based systems, the notion and variety of 'variable pay' (as a performance-motivating 'incentive' or 'reinforcement' device) is reviewed in **Chapter 6.** Short-term and long-term, individual, team and organisational 'bonus' payments, including profit-related pay and profit sharing, gain-sharing, as well as equity (share) based 'financial participation' initiatives that may be applied to some or all workforce segments are described and evaluated. The discussion includes 'sales bonuses' and other incentives for particular workforce segments.

Part Three reviews principles, policies and frameworks for 'non-cash benefits', 'deferred remuneration' and 'intrinsic rewards' and alternative routes to managing them.

Employee benefits and allowances, and policies for their application, are the subject of **Chapter 7**. Typologies of benefits – 'welfare', 'compensatory' or 'status'; types of benefits; 'single status' and 'harmonisation', flexible (or 'cafeteria') systems – are appraised. The principal employee benefits that may be applied beyond salary and wages and their roles (e.g. legal minima versus 'perks') are discussed. The interrelationship between employee benefits and taxation and social insurance systems – which vary significantly according to the national context – is reviewed.

Given an increasingly contentious and 'strategic' role within employee reward, **Chapter 8** is devoted to debates around pensions – a 'deferred' form of remuneration. Consideration begins with a discussion of the development and role of 'superannuation schemes', situating the topic in historical perspective, moving to examination of the contemporary and contested role of the state vs employers vs private insurance providers in employee 'retirement' provision. The main types of pension scheme are introduced, linked to their role within a reward management programme. Government policy intervention affecting future pensions provision is also analysed.

The increasing attention directed towards forms of 'non-financial reward' focuses discussion in **Chapter 9**. The concept is defined and related to notions of 'total reward', the 'employment proposition' and ideas around 'employee engagement', aligning extrinsic reward management with management of the 'psychological contract'. The question of why this factor may be of increasing importance in reward management is investigated, accounting for issues such as 'employee recognition', 'workforce diversity' and its consequences, as well as 'career management' and 'employee involvement' initiatives.

Part Four gives specific attention to rewarding employees who have a direct influence on corporate governance, as well as the employee reward implications of organisational expansion requiring transnational knowledge mobilisation. Finally, attention turns specifically to questions around alignment between organisational strategy, HRM and employee reward management.

Rewarding corporate executives and directors is discussed in **Chapter 10**. Ideas on the composition and management of reward for employees occupying senior managerial roles are reviewed. This discussion is complemented by engagement with the corporate governance and increasingly emotionally charged 'top pay' debate, including the role of remuneration committees and advisers; 'executive incentives' (short-term and longer-term approaches, cash- and/or equity-based); executive benefits and perquisites; contractual conditions; compliance and public disclosure requirements. Attention is paid to corporate governance developments reflecting unabated controversy around incentive pay and regulatory efforts to address public concern about excess, with requirements for more disclosure locating executive remuneration in the context of how others are rewarded, requiring a more active role by corporate shareholders.

Developments in international reward management are critically reviewed in **Chapter 11**. Factors impacting on the design of transnational reward management systems are assessed. Questions around 'globalisation' and corporate structure propositions, focused on 'knowledge mobilisation', are considered, along with the extent to which these give rise to standardisation in reward management practice across 'multi-local' environments, as well as the part played by reward management systems in supporting employee expatriation programmes. Expatriate–local reward management opportunities and threats in the competitive climate for multinational enterprise are also critically reviewed. The role of information technology in communicating and calibrating international reward practice is introduced.

To conclude the book on an integrative and thematic note, **Chapter 12** covers the reward management-HRM axis. The importance of a strategic approach to people management in general, and reward management in particular, is highlighted, with a focus on vertical integration along one dimension, complementing horizontal integration along another, to ensure consistency across the range of people management policies and practices. Contested literature, where universal 'best practice' thinking meets 'contingency-based' and 'critical' commentary, is reviewed. Roles attributable to the parties to employee reward management systems, in particular the interface between specialists and line managers under the HRM rubric, are appraised.

Explore further

For a discussion comparing and contrasting prescription, empirical evaluation, critical materialist and post-structuralist commentary, see Shields, J, Brown M, Kaine, S, Dolle-Samuel, C, North-Samaradzic, A, McLean, P, Johns, R, O'Leary, P, Plimmer, G and Robinson, J (2021) *Managing Employee Performance and Reward: Concepts, Practices, Strategies*, 2nd edn, Cambridge: Cambridge University Press.

For a critical appraisal of debates around the imperatives of 'reward strategy' as though this were an alternative to managing equity-based factors implicit in the effort–reward bargain, see Kessler, I (2007) Reward choices: strategy and equity, in Storey, J (ed.), *Human Resource Management: A Critical Text*, 3rd edn, London, Thompson, pp. 159–76.

For a treatment of employment systems contexts, see Rubery, G and Grimshaw, D (2003) *The Organization of Employment: An International Perspective*, Basingstoke: Palgrave Macmillan.

For research and commentary on a range of relevant topics intended to help professionals learn how to implement a reward strategy that supports organisational objectives, the reward strategy section of the CIPD's Knowledge Hub may be accessed at www.cipd.co.uk/knowledge/strategy/reward.

02 Conceptual and theoretical frameworks

CHAPTER LEARNING OUTCOMES

At the end of this chapter you should understand and be able to explain the following:

- Approaches to help theorise reward management to enable critical evaluation of choices and consequences in context(s).
- Ways of conceptualising and theoretical debates informing reward management.

CIPD STRATEGIC REWARD MANAGEMENT MODULE (7HR03) LEARNING OUTCOMES

Learners will be able to:

1.1 Examine the key factors influencing the design of reward strategy and policy frameworks.

1.4 Critically evaluate the impact of organisational reward strategies to attract, motivate and retain talent.

4.4 Explain the merits and impact of transparency and fairness in approaches to reward.

2.1 Introduction

The idea of an 'effort–reward bargain' (introduced in Chapter 1), gives rise to some basic questions between the parties to the employment relationship.

Adopting the **employee's** viewpoint, the issues include what return can be obtained for making available to an employer skills and experience (or 'human capital') – as well as time and contribution to value-creating activities – that is both fair and equitable. Thus, both practical and ethical considerations apply.

This book is concerned with managing employee reward and, drawing on Milkovich, Newman and Gerhart (2020), from the **employer/managerial** perspective two strategic questions call for answers:

1. How do we set the *necessary* level of expenditure on rewarding employees? and
2. How can the substance and process of employee reward be used, if at all, to influence individual and collective employee work attitudes and behaviours?

To describe something as 'strategic' implies that it involves the exercise of *choice* among alternatives, where limited resources are being committed, with consequences that are likely to apply beyond the short term. Applying our 'systems' conceptualisation, in this chapter we examine alternative approaches to interpreting and addressing these basic reward management questions, and the consequences of choosing between the alternative explanations on offer.

There is, of course, a danger in addressing the 'applied' problems associated with employee reward at levels abstracted from 'real-world' contexts. Theoretical frameworks can give no more than a partial picture of the world; and 'seemingly neutral concepts may carry hidden value assumptions' (Furåker, 2005: 2). We briefly discuss below, therefore, the reasons why theorising reward management is important. We also explore the assumptions and frames of reference informing ideas about 'reward strategies' and their expected outcomes. In this regard, we seek to avoid a trap highlighted by Kessler (2007): some commentators describing a shift to a 'strategic reward management paradigm' have positioned the demands of corporate strategy as though necessarily in competition with considerations of external and internal equity in the way reward is distributed and the outcomes derived from the process (e.g. Gomez-Mejia and Balkin, 1992).

The presence of ethical as well as practical considerations is not an exclusively employee concern. If only to avoid the kinds of criticisms, for example, associated with the idea of a 'bonus culture' in financial services, and consequent social inequity and the encouragement of perverse behaviours, those responsible for reward management may wish to explore the logic of strategies that stakeholders will judge to be legitimate in a more holistic sense than may be inferred from exhortations to use reward to 'drive a performance culture' (Hutton, 2011). The complexity of culture, or institutionalised ways of organising social interactions, is such that without some effort to understand what is involved there is a high risk of unwelcome or unintended consequences. The means is therefore required to help in the process of interpretation and understanding.

2.2 The importance of theory in reward management

Responses to the basic questions about reward management posed above are likely to be influenced by whom you ask. How we theorise socio-economic situations is not value neutral. Over the years, debate on employee reward and its management has been 'heavily informed and structured by conceptual, analytical and theoretical frameworks from various disciplines' (Kessler, 2001: 206). The ways questions are framed and answered reflect the contrasting assumptions and priorities of these disciplines, as well as debates among commentators within them. Practising managers, who have their own assumptions and preoccupations in relation to employee reward, may find the resulting outpouring of commentary – whether normative (prescribing how we should determine employee reward) or analytical (how do we actually determine it according to empirical research) – confusing and/or downright irritating.

In the face of all this inconclusive discussion, it seems reasonable to ask, 'why get involved in theory at all?' Reward management is an applied field – whether the interested parties are employers or employees, or their representatives, or regulators. Why not simply follow 'practical' steps to work out what is the best course of action based on trial and error? Indeed, it could be argued that people management practice in Britain largely gets along without explicit models and frameworks to guide people management. For example, the WERS 1998 study found only 14 per cent of workplaces applied the 'HRM model' (e.g. that outlined by Guest, 1987) comprehensively (Cully et al, 1999). Currently the last in the WERS series, based on 2011 data, showed that the level workplaces covered by a formal strategic plan for key HRM considerations (diversity, development, job satisfaction) had not altered significantly since previous findings were published (van Wanrooy et al, 2013).

From the viewpoint of the HR 'thinking performer', however, wishing to adopt a systematic approach mindful of the complexity involved as sketched above, it may be wise to treat handling the effort–reward bargain as an exercise in risk management. Managing risk necessitates grasping both positive and negative consequences associated with the likelihood of an occurrence – and where negative consequences are predictable to focus on prevention and mitigation of harm (Institute of Risk Management, 2002). In addressing this risky reward management 'puzzle', 'there is nothing so practical as a good theory' (Lewin, 1947, cited in Caldwell, 2006: 49) on the basis that:

> Theory deals with concepts and their interrelationships and is aimed at helping us understand and explain how and why things happen in the world.

Unpacking this a little further, while theory involves simplification so as to abstract from the complexities of the empirical world, it does offer ways systematically to weigh how to engage with specific contexts in all their diversity. In using theory of course, consistent with an open systems perspective, it is important to remember that not only are contexts for practising reward management complex, but they are also ever-changing, as the economic and organisational environment changes, in turn. Working at a level abstracted from specific contexts, the practitioner is, however, enabled to surface assumptions about, say, the character of the employment relationship and its openness to management. Those assumptions are important in critically appraising ideas about how to 'do' reward management, reflecting on the extent to which the assumptions built into ideas are consistent with those based on observing a specific organisational setting. For example, one might read an article in an American management journal describing a particular approach to linking, say, pay and performance. Before trying to follow this approach in a different location or at a different time, there is a question of assessing the extent to which the assumptions embedded in the approach derived from the specificities of the business system in the USA will apply in a different setting. Theorising the problem of reward management also enables specification of testable propositions and criteria for evaluating them. This is important not only for those conducting academic research. Management practitioners may also wish to pilot test predicted outcomes against observable practise before choosing to commit significant scarce organisational resources: an evidence-based risk management in the reward domain is thereby made possible.

2.3 Managing the effort bargain – theoretical pillars

Approaches to reward management are accompanied by underlying assumptions about the nature of people and organisations, about how social and management science may be mobilised to 'know' those environments, and about the methodologies for gathering and interpreting data to develop that knowledge (Burrell and Morgan, 1979). Assumptions underlying alternative theories for making sense of reward management systems extend to the expectations of the parties, and the legitimacy with which their relationships may be regulated. Like other systems, 'systems of thought' evolve, regress or disintegrate, importing and exporting ideas and organising models within and between them. Thus, the student of reward management should not be surprised to discover a range of theory which is subject to debate and disagreement among commentators. To help put some boundaries around the approaches and debates, what follows is an overview that is discipline-based, acknowledging the themes placed centre stage given the preoccupations of specific intellectual communities.

Academic disciplines through which reward management may be theorised include economics, industrial (or employment) relations, occupational psychology, political science, organisational sociology and strategic HRM. Each of these emphasise different aspects of the reward relationship between employers, employees and other stakeholders (such as the state and its regulatory agencies). For example:

- An economist might concentrate on how 'market forces' bring employers and employees into contact and sanction wage rates. The emphasis tends to be on determinants rather than consequences of employee reward: an economist's question might be, why do wage differentials exist?
- A traditional industrial relations focus might be on how wage rates may be 'marked up' owing to the presence of institutions such as employer associations and trade unions, engaged in forms of collective bargaining.

- The occupational psychologist might direct attention to the human 'drives' or internalised preferences leading people to seek out extrinsic and intrinsic forms of reward and recognition, or processes by which an individual's motivation to work may be influenced positively or negatively.
- Those interested in political forces at play in work organisations might position the analytical spotlight on the relative power to extract effort and to establish the criteria for reward distribution among individuals and groups within economic value-creating environments.
- Organisation and work sociologists might encourage exploration of the values and orientations employees bring to the workplace as both individuals and groups, and the likely impact on how they perceive the fairness or 'equity' of the employment relationship. Culture formation may be emphasised in the process, as well as the need to pay attention to similarities and differences between groups (ethnicity and gender, for example) impacting on reward outcomes and how they may be explained.
- Strategic HRM commentators might seek to identify and measure the systematic alignment of reward management designs with business aims, other people management practices and organisational performance.

These varying agendas mean that explanations and priorities may be in competition with one another for decision-makers' attention. The law (e.g. on minimum wage levels and on equal pay for work of equal value) also has a role to play in approaching reward management policy and practice, as discussed in Chapter 3. The 'systems orientation' selected also may be seen as influencing priorities for specifying and answering questions. Closed system thinking may pay little attention to the behaviour of individuals and groups, saying markets or instincts will settle pay outcomes and associated behaviour. More open systems analysis, in contrast, may offer increased scope for goal-directed managerial interventions in employee reward. This may, however, be more historically or more future-focused, more individual- or more group-oriented, or accented more towards manipulation or regulation of the reward relationship.

The 'basic' questions with which we began this chapter may thus be approached in a variety of ways. Different theoretical approaches to managing employee reward may be grouped in terms of either their emphasis on structuring reward, on the one hand, and on the process of reward determination, on the other. A long-standing debate exists too around whether or not extrinsic reward (a term defined in Chapter 1) will directly influence work behaviour or is merely one among a number of influences. Kohn (1993), in fact, sets out 'the case against rewards', at work and in other environments (e.g. at school), which he regards a form of bribery, with the consequence that 'people who are trying to earn a reward end up doing a poorer job on many tasks than people who are not' (1993: 49). Table 2.1 summarises the ways alternative theories derived from various disciplines may be used to address the basic reward management questions we posed at the start of the chapter. The range and interplay of theory around these issues is explored in detail over the following sections of the chapter.

Table 2.1 Reward theory and the 'basic questions': A selective overview

Issue	Theory	Source	Comment
	'Necessary' expenditure on employee reward		
Labour market allocation and associated wage-level determination	Market clearing	Neoclassical economics	Closed system model – external influences are regarded as 'noise'
Employee attraction and retention in high-skill contexts	Human capital	Institutional economics	Premium attracted by valuable experience/ skills
Secure control over employee labour power and retain core skills	Exchange theory Efficiency wages	Institutional economics	Bargains to limit instrumental behaviour by employees that carries greater costs to employers
Maintain stability of production and avoid spot market 'deals' (financed by monopoly profits)	Internal labour market Rent-sharing/gift exchange Wage-gap/union mark-up	Institutional economics Industrial relations	Generally a feature of large private firms or public sector organisations
Create an incentive for those at or close to top of hierarchy	Tournaments and winner-takes-all regimes	Management economics	Assumes top talent creates supernormal corporate profits
	Managerial influence on work attitudes and behaviour from investment employee reward		
Job/role design to delimit employee discretion	Role	Sociology	Predictive capacity limited by interpretative complexities
Managerial control	Agency	Labour economics/ strategy	Align employee/ employer interests – monitor activity
Employee needs satisfaction	Drive theories (for example two-factor theory, hierarchy of needs theory)	Managerial psychology	Research bias undermines reward-related validity; more useful in focusing attention on job enrichment programmes
Harnessing ability to learn	Reinforcement theory	Managerial psychology	Sensitivity required to avoid harming implicit contract

(*continued*)

Table 2.1 (Continued)

Issue	Theory	Source	Comment
Providing incentive for future-facing effort	Goal theory Expectancy theory	Managerial psychology	Care needed that signals are perceived as informational rather than attempted control
Controlling or informational signals to employees	Cognitive evaluation theory	Managerial psychology	Adults in work environments engage reflexively with their supervisors in continuous effort–reward bargaining
Fair returns for investment of human capital with an employer			
Perceptions of organisational justice	Distributive justice Procedural justice Interpersonal justice	Political science/ sociology	Attention to process as much as the substance of employee reward
Trust in employer to respect implicit expectations	Psychological contract theory	Managerial psychology	Care needed to avoid damaging employees' implicit expectations

2.4 Labour market theory

A major concept the reward management student needs to understand from the start is the concept of a 'labour market' within a monetary economy (Blanco et al, 2022). This term implies that there is competition for labour in the same way that, within a capitalist society, goods and services are traded for monetary payment in a 'market'. Hence employers seek to purchase labour at the best price and workers seek to sell their labour within this market at the best price. Below we consider the main economic theories concerning reward. We begin by looking at classical labour market theory, which has dominated management thinking for over two centuries.

2.4.1 Classical labour market theory

The notion of rational choice by the parties to the effort–reward relationship underpins 'classical' labour market theory. The assumption is that pay will be fixed in the labour market where the demand for workers equates exactly to the supply, known as 'market clearing' (Black, 2002). So, when the supply of labour meets employers' demands, employers will have to offer work at that price and workers will have to accept work at that price: this is the 'value of the marginal product of labour' (see Figure 2.1). Taken to its logical conclusion, this theory suggests that there is little point in employers attempting to differentiate themselves from their competitors by paying different (higher) wages as, in the final analysis, everyone has to pay the same as everyone else. 'The only "effective" policy is to pay what others do' (Gerhart and Rynes, 2003: 15). And since the theory indicates that pay policies will always tend towards equilibrium (or a state of balance), there is little point investigating what other employers do in setting their pay policies and practices. Essentially, employers should expect to pay, and employees should expect to obtain, wages for labour determined by an external market. Theoretically, the market regulates the employment relationship: employees make a rational choice to forgo leisure to make themselves available for work. Labour is perceived as a commodity that has a price just like any other.

This self-regulating model of the employment system – attributed to eighteenth-century Scottish economist Adam Smith – and its 'neoclassical' restatements by late nineteenth-century European economists such as Jevons, Menger and Walrus (Watson, 2005) – assumes that each of the parties is free to choose between work and leisure (employees) and to hire or not (employers). Employers will compete for labour with other employers, and employees will compete for paid work with other employees. It is also assumed that each party will be comprehensively informed ('perfect information', in the economist's jargon) about the present state of the market. For employees this means knowing about where work is available and the rewards on offer. For employers this means knowing how many and where the employees are available to work and the 'price' at which they are being acquired. The parties will, it is assumed, instinctively seek to maximise their individual interests, with supply and demand across the labour market tending to be stable over time, all other things being equal.

Rationally seeking 'maximum utility', employees will assess jobs by weighing the overall economic merits of different jobs. Thus, jobs that are less pleasant than others, or those that carry more risk, or that are more difficult to attain mastery of,

Figure 2.1 Wage determination in a perfectly competitive employment market, balancing supply of workers willing to sell a capacity to accept employment (S) with employers' demand for labour (D)

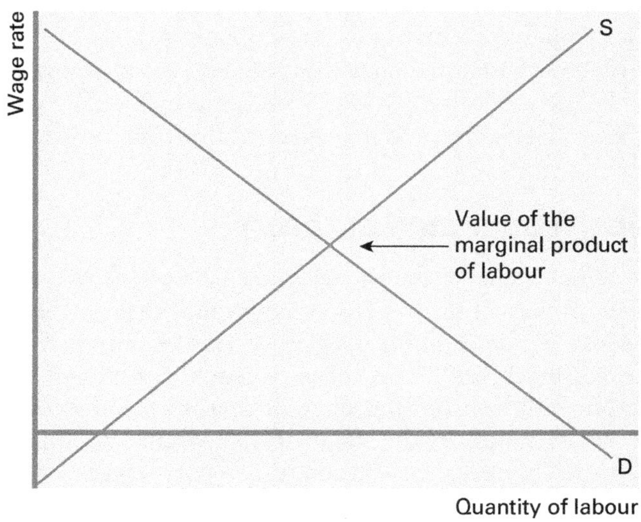

will require higher pay than those whose characteristics are the reverse. The model indicates limited discretion for employers in wage setting, as short-run attractiveness will tend to be eroded over the longer term, as abstract 'market forces' compel employers to offer jobs of roughly similar attractiveness or else fail to secure the labour to resource their organisations. Employers who pay above the market rate will be forced to charge higher prices for their goods which, if not matched by competitors, it is predicted will lead to reduced revenues as customers buy more cheaply elsewhere. The result will be either bankruptcy for the employer or cuts in costs – specifically wage costs or reduced employment.

Even neoclassical labour economists recognise, however, that such a theory may be too simplistic. They sound a note of caution regarding the effects of 'market distortions' arising from political interventions in the labour market. For example, state regulations governing minimum wage levels, or the presence of employees acting collectively through trade unions, may act to disrupt the natural order of the market. Provided such distortions are minimised (and this is a job the neoclassical school allocates to governments), then even though from time to time there may be a shift in labour wage rates, this will be temporary. Any change in wage rates may be attributed to rises and falls in labour supply and demand, or to changes as new employers and/or employees enter the market or existing employers and/or employees exit. Instrumentally oriented, the tendency will be for the parties to conclude that 'marginal utility' derived from the employment exchange relationship (the additional unit of labour power exchanged in return for each small increase in compensation for lost leisure opportunities) is best maximised by compliance with the 'free' functioning of market forces.

2.4.2 Criticisms of the classical labour market

Since the middle of the twentieth century, research has indicated that the labour market does not operate in such a simple fashion as advocated by classical economics. Nonetheless, the influence of neoclassical labour economists on reward systems thinking has been remarkably durable. As Gerhart and Rynes (2003) argue, apologists for alleged excesses in executive reward have pointed to the effect of 'market forces'. Executives are simply being paid what the market demands (see Chapter 10 for a detailed discussion). The economic purist will argue in defence of criticism that any departure from market 'norms' will be self-adjusting over time. Or it may require the removal of 'market distortions' – e.g. co-operation by members of an employers' association in fixing rates of pay for an industry sector; or by political administrations setting minimum wage rates for the economy; or through employees combining in trade unions to improve wage rates relative to other groups of workers.

That defence notwithstanding, it is controversial to assume that employees have 'perfect' knowledge of competing types of work, and that the socio-economic costs for employees to transfer between employers are not prohibitive. Once the neoclassical assumptions are compared with social and political, let alone economic, reality the model becomes less reliable as a basis for predicting labour allocation. For example, Rees (1973) points out that the 'competitive model' uses the individual as its unit of analysis. Employment systems may be regulated in part by factors that locate individuals in their wider social context – as members of a household where, for example, domestic commitments limit availability to participate in the labour force as an employee, or as individuals undergoing education and other forms of 'work'. Such phenomena may inhibit the rational decision-making implied under the neoclassical economic model.

The notion of a self-regulating employment system is undermined by the fact that it is not limited to the actions of current and prospective employees. Employers, for example a multinational joint venture company, may be able to dominate certain employment systems, with the resources to outbid local firms for labour on terms that are attractive to the employer compared with relative rates of pay in the employer's country of origin. A specific longstanding example of this phenomenon, known by economists as 'monopsony' (i.e. there is effectively only one buyer in the market), has been the National Health Service in the UK. Even though some health care employers trade as private companies, and there are instances of outsourced support functions or public-private partnerships, the NHS is by far the major employer of occupational groups such as doctors and nurses. If such health professionals wish to work at their chosen occupation, they may have little choice, in the final analysis, in who employs them or the pay levels on offer (which are set nationally). Under such circumstances the only alternative is to seek promotion to improve individual pay or to change occupations. Although there are so-called pay review bodies whose role is notionally to inform pay determination in government-funded sectors such as the NHS, as a briefing from NHS Employers in May 2023 indicates, frustrations around this particular labour market have bubbled to the surface in largely unprecedented ways – see www.nhsemployers.org/articles/confirmed-industrial-action-strike-days.

Decisions to recruit or supply labour, including decisions between competing employment opportunities, are, therefore, more complicated than simple decisions around trading paid work for leisure, and vice versa. In summary:

> The more a firm or a business sector approaches the conditions of full and effective competition, the more likely it is that the competitive theory will provide useful pointers. But where competition, whether in the product market or in the labour market, is restricted, the greater the departure from competitive theory that is required to explain empirical observations or to analyse the consequences of alternative strategies for remuneration.
>
> (Beaumont and Hunter, 2000: 46)

In fairness to Adam Smith's original conceptualisation, the influence of 'total net advantage', not price alone, on an employee's choice to enter or remain outside the labour market, and to move between employers or stay put, has been set aside by subsequent economic theorists. To locate pricing of labour in the economic market, other economists have assumed away all non-pecuniary aspects – premised on 'all else being equal' (Rottenberg, 1956, cited in Gerhart and Rynes, 2003). And, as Watson (2005: 64) puts it, in pursuit of elegant conceptual models, neoclassical economists set aside 'the learning processes through which actual conduct is formed' – habits acquired through repeated human interaction. The influence of history and learning is emphasised by postclassical social science theorists, as we shall see when discussing psychological theory below.

Whether or not to supply their labour to employers is not the sole economic issue for the employee. There is also the question of the amount of effort individuals will make available to the employer, once employed (Rees, 1973). Over the years average hours of work in industrialised economies have declined substantially. Employers set hours of work and in theory employees have to accept these. Those employees with domestic responsibilities, a consideration that may be viewed as particularly affecting women, however, have demonstrated their willingness to opt between employments where hours of work are more in keeping with other demands on their time. And individuals may be willing to make trade-offs between more acceptable hours and the level of pay or 'work-life balance available'. (We take up this discussion in Chapter 9 related to the notion of 'total reward'.) Of course, legislation, as well as market forces, may affect the hours of work undertaken by workforce participants. Introducing a comparative dimension, in countries where there are traditional family-related calls on individuals' time – e.g. where agriculture remains a significant family concern – there may be seasons where employers have difficulty in securing the required supply of labour. Their employees may absent themselves to undertake work that cannot be delayed, such as the annual olive harvest in countries on the southern periphery of the European Union. Institutional factors merit attention, therefore.

SELF-ASSESSMENT EXERCISE

Can you explain the continuation of the classical labour market model of pay determination, despite the evidence from the real world of employment?

2.5 Alternative economic theories of reward management

There are a number of alternative economic theories to the classical labour market approach. **'Institutional labour economics theory'** redefines the market-clearing model in order to explain differentials between wage levels, contingent on institutional factors (Martins, 2021). While the general assumption is kept that employers' and employees' expectations will rest on maximising their economic interests, a more open systems view is evident. Factors arising from the environmental and organisational context are introduced (e.g. culture and values, initiatives by governments and other organisations and interest groups), which may be associated with differential employee reward levels across the labour market. Such 'contingencies' may result in employment relationships that still tend towards a primarily individualised orientation, or they may open the way for bargaining activity along a collective dimension. Substantive labour market contingencies may be cited, such as the scale of organisations, the industry sector or the stage of economic development in a particular employment system. Economists have cited these contingencies as one explanation for what has been termed 'stickiness' in wage levels: if market-clearing theory applies, why in practice do wage levels rarely appear to fall?

This reframing of external labour market-clearing systems thinking opens the potential for employers to seek positive answers to the second basic reward management question: how can reward investments enable managers to influence employee attitudes and behaviours in the workplace? The scope is introduced for a 'strategic' regulatory role for management to act in ways that compensate for market imperfections (at least in the short run). Vertical alignment between business strategy focused on competing for revenue through product or service quality, or on price alone, may be cascaded into decisions to offer a wage premium or on efforts to achieve pay compression (i.e. the narrowing, over time, of pay differentials between people in the same job or between people in different, usually adjacent, grades).

The assumption of perfect information on the part of employers and employees influencing labour supply and demand is discarded within institutional economics theorising in favour of more 'bounded rationality'. In particular, in assessing how individual workers perceive the overall attractiveness of employment opportunities in a labour market, the institutional economist may consider that employees may find it more rational to ignore higher short-term rewards in favour of longer-term considerations, such as the social costs of changing employers (e.g. loss of workplace environment, contacts, knowledge of an organisation's production system, etc). In terms of strategic initiatives, theorists such as Williamson (1975) have suggested that managers enter into contracts designed to minimise the economic costs of organising productive activity – including putting labour power to work to create value in the most efficient way. Rationality and instrumentalism between the parties in the nature of their expectations and underlying relationship remain important **transaction cost theory** assumptions. In other words, both employers and workers make complex decisions about the employment relationship weighing up the scope for trade-offs between multiple issues affecting their interests in the transaction.

The **resource-based theory of the firm** (Barney et al, 2001) carries an assumption that economic efficiency and effectiveness will be achieved through managerial initiatives to take advantage of distinctive organisational resources (combining people with physical resources and processes to create valuable outcomes). Employee reward horizontally aligned into unique bundles with other HRM practices (Kessler, 2001; Purcell, 1999) is deployed to help form and sustain a distinctive organisational culture. While a managerial emphasis on 'resource leverage' may be advocated as more rational over simple cost containment, Kessler (2001) points to tensions at the heart of the resource-based view. This relates to the problem of disentangling the complex series of steps to achieving effective vertical and horizontal bundling processes, making the cause–effect linkages somewhat problematic.

Instead, a **new institutional approach** to strategizing (Kozenkow, 2013), paying attention to the various political and social pressures confronting people in organisations, both internal and external to the organisational system, may facilitate more effective reward management decision-making. Over time, employers and employees in specific contexts may build a shared history of effort–reward determination. This may involve accumulated learning on how to interpret factors such as internal norms and values, as well as external indicators (e.g. comparisons with other employers, from state legislation and from trade union interventions). The common understandings reached carry with them a shared legitimacy regarding employee reward-setting processes and outcomes. Underlying differences of interest may be held in check (Rubery, 1997) as the parties trust one another given common experience to follow 'rules of engagement' that are slow to change.

STUDENT EXERCISE

Discuss the factors managers need to weigh in attempting to create alignment vertically between corporate strategy and reward management, and horizontally between reward management policies and processes and other HRM initiatives.

2.6 Human capital theory

Another economic theory relevant to reward management is **human capital theory**. This approach theorises that individuals accumulate human capital by investing time and money (including deferred earnings) in education, training, experience and other qualities, that increase their productive capacity and thus worth to an employer (Abercrombie et al, 2000). While all employees bring some skill and experience to the performance of their tasks, accumulated educational attainment and experience give rise to differentiation in the level of reward necessary to secure and retain certain people. Competition among organisations across national boundaries – as more goods and services contain a higher marginal labour value content in terms of the skills, knowledge and accredited specialist experience needed – introduces a need for reward management system regulation beyond simple market-clearing mechanisms.

> The proposition that a trained worker, like a machine, represents a valuable investment is a very old one in the history of economics. In both cases making the investment requires a sacrifice of current consumption in order to increase future output.
>
> (Rees, 1973: 35)

Human capital theory (developed by Schultz and Becker in the 1960s) distinguishes between expenditures on labour representing consumption and those representing investment in (human) capital. Human labour is, however, unlike capital equipment in that it is not generally sold but 'rented out for work' (the exception is work relations based on slavery). The market is for the services of the capital, not the capital stock itself.

Hendry (2003: 1433) argues that to satisfy a universal imperative to secure skills cost-effectively, managers must balance 'two considerations involving skills and costs…'. Managerial discretion may be exercised in various ways to create employment systems. First, to achieve the basic HRM tasks of getting, keeping, motivating and developing people. Secondly, to 'secure skills' also implies controlling them in different ways and to different degrees depending on how important they are to being able to achieve organisational goals.

Exchange theory is premised on the notion that, under capitalist relations of production, employers and employees enter into an agreement whereby the employer contracts to pay wages or other extrinsic rewards to the employee in return for a willingness on the part of employees not only to give up their right to leisure but also to accept the direction of the employer over the application of their labour capacity.

Within this reciprocal relationship (Molm, 2010), the employer then has to convert rented labour power into labour that has an economic value. For both parties the issue is to weigh potential risk and reward within the social exchange relationship. Issues around the relative value of different skills and the transaction costs in harnessing them partly explain workforce segmentation into core and peripheral 'employment systems' (Atkinson, 1984; Kalleberg, 2003). Employers will generally invest more in the 'core' permanent workforce than the 'peripheral' workforce that can be dispensed with when times are hard.

2.7 Efficiency wage theory

A related line of argument within the institutional economics tradition is the idea of **'efficiency wage'** payments: a managerial strategy to achieve more 'efficient' employment contracts over the medium term (Altman, 2020). If employers assume that employees will use their human capital to secure alternative work at enhanced pay rates, but their loss to the employer would incur transaction costs greater than paying above market rates, paying higher reward levels is a rational employer response to sustain an ongoing relationship. Efficiency wages are thus an investment in firm-specific or idiosyncratic skills and knowledge, to maximise loyalty and minimise opportunistic employee behaviour.

The exercise of managerial discretion to regulate reward levels may also be a function of firm size. If the organisation is more complex to monitor, higher levels of reward are offered to employees in the expectation that people will see it as an incentive to perform better than the (possibly underperforming) external market norm. As noted above, the market-clearing mechanism takes no explicit account of the amount of effort individuals will supply to transform their labour power into organisationally valuable outputs.

Efficiency wage theory also indicates a potential disciplinary aspect, addressing what economists have labelled 'soldiering' (withholding full effort) on the part of the employee. The argument is that, if people feel better paid, they will not only be inclined to work harder but also their performance will be conditioned by a fear of losing employment with above-market pay. Here the transaction focuses on offsetting higher wages against the possibility of incurring replacement costs due to voluntary employee resignations (or 'wastage' effects). More positively, efficiency wage levels may theoretically introduce a 'sorting effect'.

Organisations whose operating strategies require higher human capital levels may find it more efficient to use above-market wage levels to signal their wish to attract above-average quality workers. The need for close supervision within the system may be reduced. This relates to the **'responsible autonomy'** approach identified by Friedman (1977, 1984), where management perceives the need to respond to inherent limitations on their ability to exercise 'direct control' over some occupational groups and turn to alternative strategies intended to align employee effort with managerial priorities. Internalised discipline on the employee's part, reinforced by above-market reward for the core workforce, may be a less costly option than funding additional supervision (Rubery, 1997). There is particular relevant when employing 'knowledge workers'.

Efficiency wages may be consistent, for example, with the bundles of HRM practices accompanying resource-based strategy. By contrast, given the emphasis in strategic approaches informed by transaction cost theorising to minimise organisational costs, paying an efficiency wage may be criticised as carrying an inherent risk. Assumptions may be misplaced that employee compliance will follow above-market reward investments. While a resource-based orientation may assume unity of interests between employers and employees, under transaction cost theory – consistent with a rationale of economic self-maximisation on either side – the nature of the employment relationship is viewed as one in which the principal party (the employer or management representative) assumes that the agent it employs will pursue interests that inherently differ from those of the principal. More explicit monitoring controls over employee effort, or tangible incentives that limit the principal's risk, may logically follow.

2.8 Principal–agent theory

Also known as 'agency theory', this introduces the notion of *deferred* payment mechanisms. Rynes and Gerhart (2000) identify agency theory as having emerged within economics and management as the dominant basis for examining pay determination processes and outcomes. Pay rates may be set below 'market-guaranteed' levels but workers are offered the opportunity to earn above-average total remuneration, contingent on higher performance. An agency-based approach to reward strategy may be associated with notions of incremental pay progression as individuals ascend internal job ladders, reasoning that the expectation of earning a full return on their human capital investment only over a lengthy employment career will encourage people to stay beyond the below-market paid phase in the early period of employment. Assuming organisational stability, an investment in seniority-building increases the individual's economic worth to the employer, while acting to mitigate divergence in the interests of employees and other stakeholders over the longer term. Approaches to pay progression are considered in detail in Chapter 5.

Alternatively, particularly where stable employment relationships may not be assumed, agency-based theorising may emphasise outcome-based deferred rewards such as profit-sharing, gain-sharing and long-term, stock ownership-based incentive plans – especially those designed for senior staff (see Chapters 6 and 10 for empirically informed discussion). The size of the deferred reward offered may be linked to the level of complexity (and associated transactional cost to principals) in monitoring agents' behaviour. Gaining prominence in recent years, alongside corporate governance reforms, agency theorists (e.g. Jensen and Meckling, 1976; Jensen and Murphy, 1990; Jensen et al, 2004) reason that alignment of interests between employed agents and other stakeholders (and shareholders, in particular) will require employees to share the risks associated with the organisation. This risk-sharing can be achieved by making a significant amount of employees' potential total earnings dependent on their own contribution to the organisation's financial success. The banking crisis of 2008–09 and its aftermath has led to challenges that offering large incentives to employees has resulted in a 'bonus culture' within which insufficient attention has been paid to the risks involved to financial investors and beyond, where governments have initiated 'rescue' operations to mitigate the impact of 'bank failures' on the wider economy. In autumn 2010 the report of a review led by Sir David Walker called for the mix of any financial incentives to be oriented towards longer-term performance outcomes, rather than short-term risk taking, with two-thirds of any cash bonuses deferred so that returns to investors could be validated before payments to the employees. The application of agency theory to executive reward management is discussed in Chapter 10.

Forms of contingency or 'at risk' pay administered on a short-term basis are not new, of course. Piece-rate forms of payment were associated with manual work before the industrial revolution. They have been in use since the sixteenth century and were associated with the rise of merchant capitalism and home-working/cottage industry (Smith, 1989). Transforming practice into theory, the 'scientific management' approach of early American management consultants, such as FW Taylor (1911), emphasised the role of the 'piecework bonus' as a motivational financial reward which, combined with a paternalistic management style, was intended to sustain labour productivity levels and to discourage workforce unionisation.

Managerial discretion to pay differentially may also be linked to job or – in more flexible work contexts – role design. Roles have been important constructs for sociologists in analysing organisations. Roles are viewed as socially determined signals to individuals about what is expected of them. They form the collective basis of institutions such as workplaces. And, as bundles of socially defined attributes and expectations, theoretically these elevate the role beyond the characteristics of the individual. The idea is that people will conform to what is expected of the position that they occupy. **Role theory** is applied to predict how behaviour is socially influenced (Anglin et al, 2022). Thus, an engineer in a firm is likely to behave in ways expected of the role of engineer rather than the individual role occupant. There remains an interesting balance to be struck in how a role is 'priced' and how the individual's contribution to organisational performance is reflected in reward. Playing a systemic role, pay rates based on the job or role contain signals of how individuals are expected to align themselves with the overall work system (see Chapter 4 for a detailed discussion of the issues involved).

The problem of unravelling the complexity inherent in organisation-people 'resource bundles', and the 'agency' problem of monitoring behaviour, were raised above. The socially determined effort–reward assumptions within role theory as a source of managerial control may be questioned in each of those contexts. For example, to what degree is individual performance important: what messages will be given to direct and reinforce the way the individual should behave in discharging responsibilities rather than simply executing the role 'objectively'? Is the level or role-position in the hierarchy important? How free is the worker under the organisation's operating rules to innovate and be creative? Is such creativity predominantly inward-facing (say, in the R&D environment) or required of even the most junior, customer-facing, role?

Extrinsic reward for performing job tasks strictly to the role description may send messages that may be inappropriate to a position that requires the exercise of discretion. How do organisations communicate the correct balance of informational and controlling signals through reward policies and practices? Is role-making a function of prescription – where behaviours are explicitly signalled in job design – or something that emerges through the process of trial and error as the individual interacts with peers and supervisor(s) to secure understanding of what is deemed to be value-added, reinforced over time through reward outcomes? It may be hypothesised that process issues may be as important as substantive ones.

2.9 Internal labour markets

Where organisations seek a stable relationship with their workforces, a 'structured **internal labour market**' (ILM) (Kerr, 1954, cited in Hendry, 2003) may be created and maintained to insulate some or all the organisation's employees from the vagaries of external market forces impacting on an organisation's ability to retain its employees. Doeringer (1967: 207, cited in White, 2000) comments that:

> The theoretical construct of the internal labour market... may be more precisely defined as an administrative unit within which the market functions of pricing, allocating and often training labor are performed. It is governed by a set of institutional rules which delineate the boundaries of the internal market and determine its internal structure. These institutional or administrative hiring and work rules define the 'ports of entry' into the internal market, the relationship between jobs for purposes of internal mobility, and the privileges which accrue to workers within the internal market.

Entry portals from the labour market are restricted, limiting access to 'career ladders' (Doeringer and Piore, 1971; Thurow, 1975). Some current examples of internal labour markets would be the armed forces or the police where entry is restricted to particular grades (e.g. private and lieutenant for the armed forces and constable for the police service). It is not possible to enter the organisation at other levels than those proscribed (e.g. one cannot join as a sergeant or major in the armed forces or a superintendent in the police). Contrasting with reliance on sourcing employees based on external labour market competition, an ILM affords management greater knowledge about candidates. It also substitutes for potentially costly 'spot bargaining' or haggling over wage rates with individuals about their market value. It has also been deployed defensively as a union avoidance strategy.

In the United States the development of internal labour markets dates from after the First World War and was a product of both demands for equity from trade unions and the development of modern personnel management with its emphasis on long-term planning (Cappelli, 1995). In Britain, in contrast, it has been noted that 'most British employers did not build strong internal labour systems but relied more on market mechanisms for obtaining labour' (Gospel, 1992: 179). In systems terms, rather than being a theoretical assumption, ILMs represent an intended strategy with consequences including transaction costs. The question of the affordability of ILM-based reward management, and recent countervailing tendencies, is discussed below.

Under ILM, wage rates are attached to jobs rather than to workers (Williamson, 1975). Employees are rewarded by clear, long-term and guaranteed career trajectories rather than purely financial incentives. Labour pricing and allocation are governed by corporately determined rules and procedures (Gerhart and Rynes, 2003), whereby jobs are arranged hierarchically, and reward rates are attached to jobs rather than to individuals (Beaumont and Hunter, 2000). An ILM may be a response to adoption

Figure 2.2 A multifaceted pay-setting framework

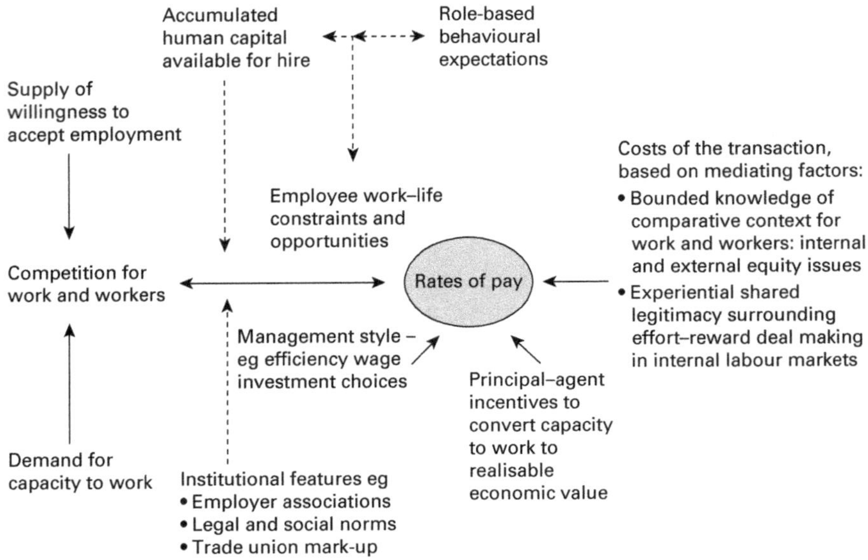

of a resource-based strategy: seeking to preserve the idiosyncratic collection of skills and related processes internal to the organisational system as a basis for sustainable competitive advantage. In terms of employee expectations and the character of the relationship offered by management, a reputation for internal promotion signals an incentive and retention effect – at least to those classified as part of the 'core' workforce. The downside, of course, is sacrificing access to a wider talent pool.

ILMs are, on the face of it, expensive fixtures: the question arises of how employers can afford to commit to insulating segments or all workforce members from external market-clearing processes. So-called **'rent-sharing'** or **'ability-to-pay' theories** have been advanced to address this issue. An 'economic rent' is a return for doing something (selling a good or service, for example) based on the perceived value to the user that they are willing to pay to the current holder of a resource that is 'in excess of the minimum needed to attract the resources to that activity' (Milgrom and Roberts, 1992, cited in Gerhart and Rynes, 2003). In other words, firms making above-normal profits, whether owing to monopoly power or effective competitive organisation, may share these 'rents' with employees in the form of above-market-clearing rates of reward. Transaction cost assumptions may apply, as in efficiency wage theory: the ILM-determined employment rates are intended to reduce risks to continuous production by the workforce.

An alternative but not dissimilar theoretical approach may be perceived in the **gift-exchange** variant of institutional economics (Dhami et al, 2023), whereby the employer gifts to employees higher than market average rewards, signalling a relationship regulated by a mutual expectation of reciprocity (i.e. that employees will 'gift' discretionary effort to the organisation in return). A link may be posited here with the notion of a 'psychological contract' discussed later in the chapter. Employer 'gift' wages may be funded by supernormal profits, or forward investment in anticipation of limiting future transaction costs through unplanned employee turnover, shirking or possible trade union encroachment on managerial discretion. Whether these theoretical assumptions are borne out is an open empirical question. As with the resource-based strategy position, internalised labour market system complexities are difficult to unravel analytically in pursuit of cause-and-effect associations.

2.10 Wage-gap (or union mark-up) theory

Rent-share funding for ILMs associated with a business strategy based on consistent, high-quality production, attracting premium product prices/revenues, may be reversed under price-sensitive, low-pay strategies. The capacity of workers, however, to use 'episodic advantage' (e.g. skilled labour shortages in particular locations) around the 'frontier of control' over workplace relations (Edwards, 1990), and to 'hold other stakeholders hostage' in terms of halting production, has attracted the attention of industrial relations writers seeking explanations for the differences in average wage levels between unionised and non-unionised workplaces (Gerhart and Rynes, 2003).

While ILMs may feature in a trade union avoidance strategy, another neo-institutionalist approach, **'wage-gap theory'**, attributes agreement by employers who enjoy some degree of monopoly power in their product markets to share part of the higher-than-normal profits with the workforce, in return for agreement by employee representatives for continuity of production. The outcome is a 'trade union mark-up' over competitive market rates (see Heery, 2000a). Zweimüller and Barth (1992) investigated indications that wage rates across six OECD countries (Austria, Canada, Germany, Norway, Sweden and the USA) remained similar, controlling for labour quality. Efficiency wages paid in response to human capital factors were found to be less significant than the incidence of trade unions and collective agreements. In particular this reflected co-ordinated bargaining across industries, where differentials between wage payments across the industry sectors surveyed reflected a union mark-up.

A summary illustration of the ways in which neoclassical wage determination modelling may be expanded, drawing on the range of neo-institutional theory discussed in this section of the chapter, influencing the character and outcome of reward systems, is presented in Figure 2.2. While lacking the parsimonious elegance of the neoclassical model (Figure 2.1), it may offer a more accurate reflection of the dynamics encountered by managers and employees in practice.

2.11 Criticism of neo-institutionalist arguments

Rubery (1997) criticises the attribution of a functional role to employee reward structures and levels in mainstream social science theorising (whether at economy or organisational level). She argues that, as management has sought to regulate employment relationships on more 'flexible' terms (e.g. shifting the risk from employer to employees through performance-contingent forms of pay), to support business product market-competitive strategies and/or to maximise the investment returns to shareholders, income has been redistributed in favour of the higher paid (see the Annual Survey of Hours and Earnings (ONS, 2022) data presented in Chapter 1).

During the 1980s and 1990s, institutional processes designed to reward people with 'fair wages' and alignment with reward levels enjoyed by workers of similar productivity (the 'going rate') were substantially reduced, encouraged by government exhortations that pay should be based simply on firms' ability to pay. This change may also be attributed to the decline of trade union power and the prevalence of collective bargaining (Chapter 3). If internalising reward determination within the organisation was 'developed to overcome various forms of market failure, might it not be that, as the labour market itself undergoes change, this device will be less important?' (Beaumont and Hunter, 2000: 54).

Existing reward determination theory is found deficient in its overriding emphasis on stability and consensus-building, even where a plurality of interests in the employment relationship is recognised. Rubery (1997) argues for labour market regulation theory to be reconsidered. She argues that more attention should be paid to the potential for conflict, as value is redistributed between organisational stakeholders to privilege finance capital over human capital – and the scope for discretionary, random or opportunistic decisions on the part of the principals to the effort–reward relationship. Expectations between the parties, the nature of their relationships and the balance of regulatory influence have decisively shifted in favour of management, amplifying tendencies already inherent in the substance and process of reward management. While these trends may be significant, Rubery (1997) emphasises the social nature of wage markets, in which employers cannot legitimately act in ways that wholly ignore social expectations, even though former checks and balances associated with private-sector collective wage bargaining may have been eroded. This topic is one to which we return when considering variable, pay-for-performance approaches (Chapter 6).

2.12 Tournament theory and winner-take-all regimes

Where managerial 'cadres' are needed to support strategy execution, introducing 'tournaments' and 'winner-take-all' regimes may be preferred to opening up the system to the discipline of the external market. The theory is that discipline from the outside product and investment markets is imported to ILMs. Contrary to the original ILM approach, where pay progression over the course of a career is offered to motivate employees to remain within an organisation, tournament theory focuses attention on jobs and the relative gaps between the reward attached to particular jobs. In place of steady upward progress, careers are perceived to involve 'kinks', where promotion between hierarchical levels is the defining feature, with major 'prizes' for 'winners'.

As further discussed in Chapter 10, however, empirical evidence of the operation of tournaments usually comes from the arts and sport, such as the argument that networked TV enables widely dispersed populations to watch the 'world's best' without ever having to share the same physical space. Those who are the greatest draw will attract the largest 'prize money'. The 'war-for-talent' argument has extended the analogy into the conventional business world, but evidence of theory-in-practice is limited.

'Prize' amounts vary between levels in the hierarchy, increasing in value the higher individuals progress up the organisation. This reflects the reduction in the remaining progression opportunities (Conyon and Peck, 1998; Lazear, 1995, 1999). Messages regarding orientation towards particular individuals and workforce segments are conveyed from this structuring of pay within the organisation. Management may choose either to compress reward hierarchies, indicating a more collective orientation to performance achievement, or to reverse the principle, based on the view that a few stars are likely to produce most value and therefore need higher extrinsic signals that the organisation wishes to recognise and retain them. Rather than emphasising group co-operation, individuals are encouraged to compete for prizes under winner-take-all rules of the game.

Under **winner-take-all theorising** (broadly similar to **tournament theory**), it is assumed that defining differences exist between the very best and next best (Frank and Cook, 1995). Small differences in 'core talent' ability may be worth a lot to employers, and the argument is made that market forces tend to reward these differences handsomely. The top job (CEO) arguably needs the highest relative reward, with the largest gap over subordinate roles, given that there is nowhere else to go internally. This does not imply intent to motivate CEO performance: arguably, high performance by the individual is not important. Instead, the idea is to encourage subordinate levels to continue to compete in the earlier 'elimination rounds'.

To sum up at this point, the basic questions, presented in economic terms, of how much an employer needs to pay, and what expectations employees may realistically hold on their ability to secure returns on their human capital, may be addressed in a variety of ways. Once exclusively market-regulating approaches are confronted with institutionally sensitive frameworks (i.e. a more open systems orientation), alternatives for gaining some 'employer leverage' on their reward investment aligned with various strategic considerations come into consideration. In drawing on economics and sociology of work theory it should be clear from the range of approaches discussed that there is no generally accepted 'one size fits all' answer. And more radical evaluation indicates that basic assumptions regarding the functional consequences of mainstream thinking may be open to challenge from a variety of directions as employment systems continue to evolve.

In the next part of the chapter we consider theories associated in particular with psychological 'motivation' to perform in work situations. We also turn attention to the processes impacting on whether employees perceive their reward from work as fair, equitable and just.

STUDENT (GROUP) EXERCISE

Discuss the possible relationship between human capital assumptions, efficiency wages and internal labour markets. Would employers be more or less likely to establish and maintain an internal labour market where collective bargaining relations contribute to a 'mark-up' on the external rate for the job?

What might be the consequences of attempting reward system 'reform' following a tournament approach?

2.13 Alternative perspectives on employee motivation and reward

It may appear self-evident that, in the words of Bowey and Thorpe (2000: 81), 'To be effective, remuneration systems need to be based on a sound understanding of how people at work are motivated.' But motivation theory has been dogged by popularisation of conclusions from laboratory or pseudo-experimental research designs, as well as an 'open systems effect' derived from the influence of the prevailing management and political ideologies and philosophies of particular eras. Moving between a variety of fairly extreme positions, the search continued throughout the twentieth century for 'one-best-way' to address the second and third questions cited at the start of this chapter, namely, the role of reward as a managerial 'lever' for employee performance, and the sense individuals might share of receiving 'just reward' for their skills and effort. The result has been faddishness in the adoption and discarding of policies intended to offer incentives and recognition for workers, possibly based on what Pfeffer (1998a) labels 'dangerous myths'.

Bowey and Thorpe (2000) argue that the low level of understanding of how reward systems affect employee behaviour can be blamed on a combination of factors: the degree of opposition between theoretical positions; conflicting real-life examples of what seems to work; and poorly disseminated research findings (see Guest's (2007: 1020) evidence-based discussion of 'the challenge of communicating scientific knowledge to practitioners'). Although psychologists and other social scientists may dismiss ideas as unsubstantiated, certain nostrums have passed into individuals' experience portfolio and into general management folklore. Hence, organisation leaders may be seen confidently acting in a manner explicitly or implicitly informed by simplistic motivation theories (or simplistic interpretations of them). In short, much 'old' motivation theory has not 'died and gone away ... the great majority of managers in Britain, the United States and, quite worryingly, Central and Eastern Europe (as well as other developing countries) believe there is one best way to motivate employees to work well' (Bowey and Thorpe, 2000: 81–83).

2.14 Definitions of motivation

Ideas surrounding motivation – a word derived from the Latin movere, 'to move' – have their roots in 'hedonism' in ancient Greek philosophy: that is, the principle that humans seek to maximise pleasure and minimise pain. Movere is also credited as the Latin source of the modern English word 'emotion' – clearly a mainstream interest for psychologically inclined investigators.

Although consensus around the precise meaning of the term is elusive, even between psychologists (Kleinginna and Kleinginna, 1981), human motivation can be broadly defined as stimuli acting on, or within, a person that cause the arousal, direction and persistence of goal-directed, voluntary effort. In other words, motivation is concerned with what gets someone to make a choice to act, selecting between alternatives (including no action), and the sustained focus of that action. Motivation theory is thus, in general, concerned with explaining why and how behaviour is activated and sustained. If this understanding can be ascertained, it follows that, in relation to employee motivation, better-informed performance and reward management may be undertaken (Antoni, 2022).

Hedonism is not something that is easily subjected to objective measurement – and, indeed, most aspects of motivation have to be inferred from observable behaviour (assumed to be in response to some actual or perceived energising force(s) external to the individual). When psychology began interacting with management science, psychological investigations that had previously concentrated on experimental situations involving animals stood in contrast to some of the underlying theories that appeared to guide managerial practice (and still do in some cases).

Early theorising on motivation, frequently informed by laboratory experiments using animals, concentrates on 'content' aspects (or perceived 'needs' – see below) or **what** motivates somebody. An accent on 'process' aspects – **how** people are motivated – becomes more pronounced when psychological theorising interacts with other thought systems such as anthropology, sociology and political science, as perceptions of equity and social justice in human relationships are factored in.

Thematically, discussion has included attempts to distinguish between intrinsic and extrinsic human motivation. Herzberg's **two-factor theory** (alternatively referred to as the **'motivation-hygiene' theory**) argues that intrinsic and extrinsic factors are wholly separate phenomena (Kohn, 1993a), arranged by Maslow (1954) as a **hierarchy of needs** (Fish, 2022). Once a fair level of pay is established, for example, money ceases to be a significant motivator for long-term performance. Factors such as salary levels and working conditions demotivate (by being poor) rather than motivate (by being good). While two-factor theory was discredited as an academic theory relevant to employee performance management four decades ago (House and Wigdor, 1967, cited by Rousseau, 2006), this distinction has had important consequences for reward management systems design. Emphasis on extrinsic aspects (such as pay and other tangible employment benefits) has been juxtaposed with intrinsic sources of motivation (such as feelings within the person or group when participating in inherently satisfying work). Discussion on the design and application of pay progression systems, variable pay and incentive plans (Chapters 5 and 6), as well as the 'executive incentives', informed by agency theory presupposing the salience of economic motivators (Chapter 10), should be read mindful of this disputed psychologically grounded territory.

The psychological motivation literature shifts the emphasis on economic incentives and penalties found in economic theory towards biological and psychological 'predispositions' and to 'drives', to 'working environment' and to the quality of social relationships around production – in each case with recipes for managerial action. While trailblazers of particular approaches may appear to have great success in applying their prescriptions, subsequent empirical evidence indicates a more mixed scorecard (Fish, 2022). More reflexive motivation theory has lessened tendencies towards a binary (either/or) emphasis, putting the individual subject of motivation back in, as an active participant in design and application of organisational policies and practices with non-static and diverse characteristics. Thus expectations of each of the main parties to the effort–reward bargain have been more equally placed in the foreground, and relationships and regulatory processes refocused along the lines of active and reciprocal co-determination.

The implications of themes within motivation theory may be traced in a similar way to approaches within economic theory. These range from closed systems reasoning where scope for managerial initiative is constrained, to more open systems logic that accounts for institutional factors. The prescriptions vary between an accent on modifying employee behaviour to one in which it is the organisational environment that managers should act upon, to enable employee potential to be released. In the first case the assumption is that individuals need to be persuaded to perform; in the second case, that people enter the work relationship actively wishing to do a good job. These ideas are 'unpacked' below.

2.15 Instincts, learned behaviours and expectancy

In psychology, the 'scientific' assumption is that human motivation should not be perceived simply based on individuals rationally pursuing self-interest. Instead, writers such as James and McDougall argue that internal cues lead individuals to behave in certain ways owing to 'automatic predispositions' (cited in Steers and Porter, 1987). The problem with substituting instinct for hedonistic rationality to explain human motivation is the number of discernible factors that may apply. Lists of instincts can grow into the thousands (Steers and Porter, 1987). And their variation in intensity and motive may not always lead to action/behaviour.

Freudians (i.e. those following the teachings of neurologist Sigmund Freud, 1856–1939) argue that such instinctive forces may be unknown even to the individual – they are a product of the subconscious mind. Given a stance not unlike the closed system economists, an emphasis on the inner aspects of the individual psyche and notions of predisposed unconscious behaviour leaves little room for positive managerial intervention. Individuals striving to fulfil unconscious desires that are unknown to them are unlikely to be discernible during normal manager–employee interaction.

If instinctive or objectively rational behavioural tendencies are deemed inadequate in explaining human motivation, attention turns to the capacity of humans to learn from experience. Active managerial interventions may be premised on the theory that 'history counts' (Perkins and Shortland, 2022), and if people have learned that needs will be satisfied arising from certain types of behaviour and its outcomes, active steps can be taken to reinforce the attractiveness of reproducing activities consistent with managerial goals.

Drive and **reinforcement** theories take up the notion of learning over instinct, so that subjects find themselves motivated to behave in certain ways owing to habit.

Allport (1954) used the term 'historical hedonism' to describe this form of motivation. This argument follows the logic that subjects learn from the consequences of their actions and tend to repeat those that attract positive outcomes and abandon those that result in negative consequences. Woodworth (1918) introduced the notion of physiological 'drives' – specific 'energisers' such as thirst, hunger, reproduction, etc – towards or away from certain goals. Cannon (in the 1930s) used the term 'homeostasis' to describe a situation where arousal is triggered and the subject is driven to satisfy it, thus restoring equilibrium: e.g. a feeling of thirst motivates the subject to drink. Cannon assumed that organisms exist in a permanently dynamic state, their drives changing in response to 'disequilibriums' in their environment. Certain drives may come to the surface at various times and, once satisfied, decline. An individual who is out of work, for example, may be driven (or energised) to restore equilibrium in having the means of financial self-support by seeking out employment, based on previous experience that this attracts payment – that is, the means of achieving the goal of restoring equilibrium of being financially secure (Steers and Porter, 1987). Maslow (1954, cited in Hollyforde and Whiddett, 2002) contends that not satisfying employee expectations of a fair return on human capital may inhibit 'higher order' motivation taking place.

In response to criticisms that historical hedonism is insufficient to explain human behaviour that involves conscious choice, a further factor has been added, namely, that subjects require a psychological incentive to influence their expectation of what will occur in the future. This may be different from and not just a repetition of past outcomes (Hull, 1952). The anticipated effect on behaviour of the size of reward anticipated is thus factored in.

Reinforcement theory (Skinner, 1953) extends notions of learned behaviour and locates it in social encounters. Under this conceptualisation, the managerial role becomes central in motivational encounters ('social learning'). The assumption of this theory is that people seek positive reinforcement for their actions. Reinforcement theory may in fact be viewed as less a motivational theory and more concerned with subjects' responses to social encounters. Managers 'educate' employees in what is required to secure the desired reinforcement for their actions, and the task of management is to find out what will act to reinforce desired behaviour among subordinates and then monitor and appraise accordingly. Under this theory, differentiating between employees' individual performance outcomes will reinforce the learned connection between action and reward. Under reinforcement theory, people's mental state is ignored (Steers and Porter, 1987). The emphasis is on learning about how particular ways of 'operating on the environment' (another way of describing behaviour) lead to rewarding outcomes, reinforcing the aim for favourable rewards to be achieved and to avoid situations that carry penalties.

An alternative, 'cognitive' approach to motivation theory – where it is assumed that employees are thinking individuals who make rational choices based on experience – offers a corrective to instinct and drive-based theory. Here, rather than 'hedonism of the past', grounded in habit, a form of 'hedonism of the future' is postulated. Employee behaviour may be perceived as purposeful and goal-directed, grounded in beliefs and expectations surrounding future events. **Goal-setting theory** (Locke et al, 1981) and **expectancy theory** (Vroom, 1964) influence thinking about employee performance management (Mabey et al, 1998). Instead of understanding

Figure 2.3 Valance-instrumentality-expectancy (VIE) model developed by Porter and Lawler, displayed by Pinder (1987)

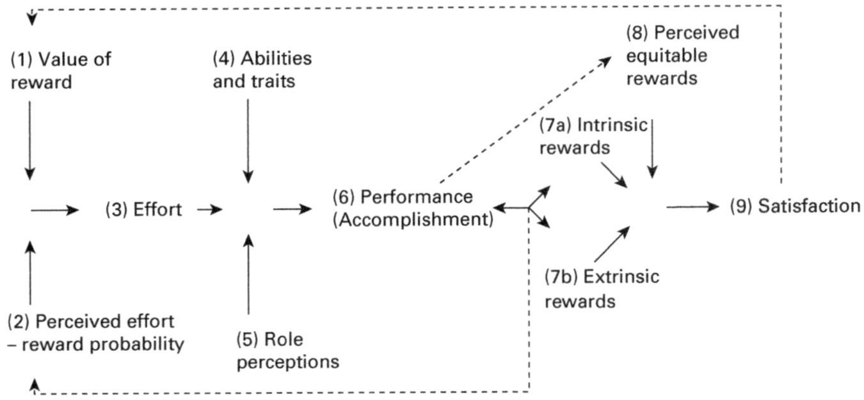

SOURCE: Pinder, 1987. Reproduced by kind permission of McGraw-Hill

human motivation in terms of stimulus–response, the focus becomes human subjects' conscious evaluation of courses of action, to select the one that is most valued by the individual. Past events are not discounted entirely. However, they are perceived as only important as influences on today's values and expectation – they are not directly linked to behaviour, as the drive theorist would contend.

Although distinguishing between notions of 'general excitement' triggering behaviour and selectivity towards the 'positively valant', Atkinson (1964) argues that theories of motivation based either on learned habits or on goal-directed behaviour share many of the same concepts. Both anticipate the presence of some reward or outcome that is desired and sought. And 'both theories include the notion of a learned connection between the central variables; drive theory posits a learned stimulus–response association, while cognitive theories see a learned association between behaviour and outcome' (Steers and Porter, 1987: 14).

Goals pursued by employees may play an important role in motivating superior performance in that, while following them, employees examine the consequences of their behaviour (Locke, 1968, cited in Mabey et al, 1998). If their estimation is that current behaviour will not support goal attainment, people are likely either (a) to modify their behaviour, or (b) to choose more achievable goals. Managers and supervisors may engage with employees in the goal-setting process to facilitate the best way to enlist employee co-operation in ways likely to serve organisational aims. Building on a theory of 'path-goal' approaches to work performance, developed by Georgopoulos et al (1957, in Mabey et al, 1998), Vroom's (1964) approach may be perceived as interfacing with goal theory, highlighting perceptions of future events as the basis on which performance is governed – that is, future expectations influence current behaviour. Perceptions among workers that high productivity will result in personal goal achievement are hypothesised as resulting in highly productive workers, with the reverse also being true.

Identification of these influences by work psychology researchers led to a specification of expectancy theory based on a combination of three factors (Galbraith and Cummings, 1967, cited in Mabey et al, 1998: 130–1):

1 The 'expectancy' factor, or an individual's own assessment of whether performing in a certain way will lead to a measurable result;
2 The 'instrumentality factor', or perceived likelihood by a person that such a result will, in turn, presage the attainment of a given reward; and
3 The 'valance' factor, or the individual's assessment of their likely satisfaction with the reward obtained.

Expectancy theory indicates that, 'if a person sees that performing in a certain way will bring about a reward which he or she values, then this individual is more likely to attempt to perform in that way than if the relationship between effort and measured performance, or measured performance and rewards, is slight or uncertain' (Mabey et al, 1998: 131). The model was further refined in the light of research by Porter and Lawler (1968, cited in Pinder, 1987), to include the motivational influence of active self-reflection on the individual's abilities and other traits, the perceived nature of the role to be performed and the degree of equity attributed to both extrinsic and intrinsic reward likely to result from the endeavour. The nine-factor 'VIE' position is summarised visually in Figure 2.3.

In empirical tests of goal setting and expectancy theories, evidence suggests that, to achieve predicted outcomes, goal specification is all-important. This places significant demands on managers to establish relatively small numbers of fairly concrete objectives. In practice, in today's fast-moving multifaceted organisational climate, this exhortation may prove difficult to comply with. Also, as Whittington (2001) has pointed out, drawing on the work of writers such as Henry Mintzberg, advance planning and goal specification frequently give way to forms of strategy that are emergent, where aims and objectives (especially at the level of the individual employee) are liable to modification as people and organisations and socio-economic open systems environment interact. Vertical and horizontal alignment of people and performance initiatives are discussed in Chapter 12.

2.16 The psychological contract and reward

Critical evaluations of goal setting and expectancy theories draw attention to the notion of a **psychological contract**, a phenomenon that reflects the package of reciprocal obligations implicitly constituting an employee–organisation exchange relationship (Antoni, 2022). The psychological contract has been defined as 'a set of beliefs about what each party is entitled to receive, and obligated to give, in exchange for another party's contributions' (Levinson et al, 1962, cited in Morrison and Robinson, 1997: 226). For Rousseau and Tijoriwala (1998: 679) it constitutes '... an individual's belief in mutual obligations between that person and another party such as an employer (either a firm or another person)'. Drawing inspiration

Figure 2.4 A model of the psychological contract

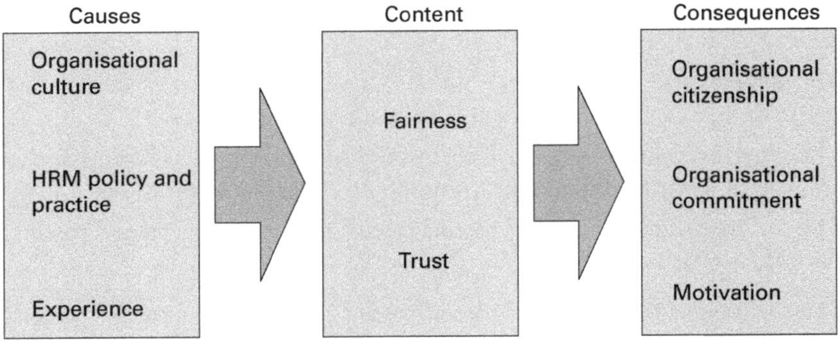

SOURCE: Based on Guest and Conway, 2004

from psychology and organisational behaviour rather than economics, the emphasis of psychological contract theory is that employment is a relationship in which the mutual obligations of employer and employee may be imprecise but have nevertheless to be respected. According to the CIPD (2003), which has sponsored surveys of 'the state of the psychological contact' in UK workplaces starting in the mid-1990s (see Guest and Conway, 2004), 'the price of failing to fulfil expectations may be serious damage to the relationship and to the organisation'.

There is evidence that reward management system designs have consequences for the organisation–employee psychological contract (Guest, 2004; Rousseau and Greller, 1994). If this is the case, the argument runs, it should also have an impact on the type of the psychological contract. Rousseau (1995) differentiates between 'relational', that is, open-ended employment relationships characterised by a high mutual interest, and 'transactional' psychological contracts, encapsulated in the statement: 'A fair day's work for a fair day's pay' (Rousseau, 1995: 91).

Described by Mabey et al (1998: 133) as 'a rich and nuanced collection of shared understandings built up over time', containing 'subtle structures of tacit but critical employee commitment', psychological contracts are at risk of being undermined by managerial interventions that emphasise a limited number of performance dimensions only. If the theoretical assumptions hold, it may be reasoned that insensitive handling of the psychological contract may encourage individuals to focus on instrumentally prescribed task activity (i.e. 'working to [explicit] contract'), sacrificing whole-job pride, to the detriment of long-term contribution to overall organisation performance.

The summary psychological contract dynamics in Figure 2.4 illustrate a systems orientation: contract inputs or 'causes', which are in turn affected by open system factors such as expectations and experience of work and alternative employment opportunities beyond the organisation, interact as throughput institutionalised in terms of inter-party trust and perceived fair dealing in both substance and process. In turn, system outputs follow – not only motivated performance, but also 'citizenship' behaviours beneficial to the organisation (i.e. working 'beyond contract', in Fox's (1974) phrase), accompanied by employee satisfaction and sense of wellbeing at work. Specific applications of the psychological contract notion are discussed in Chapters 9 and 12.

STUDENT EXERCISE

Debate the arguments that managers may need to evaluate when considering competing motivation theories. Is it necessary to decide between either extrinsic or intrinsic approaches to motivating employees? Does reward have a large or a limited role to play in aligning the workforce with managerial objectives?

2.17 Individuals, institutions and strategic alignment

Psychology-inspired theorising about managing reward has been criticised for remaining overly focused at the micro (organisational) level. The risk is that the 'brokering role' between academic debate and managerial practice will become detached as practising managers focus their interests on developments in the strategy literature (Kulik, 2001). Guest (1997) contends that, in place of reliance on normative commentary on specific 'low-level' behavioural theories, further attention is needed on the more sophisticated (strategic) interplay between the multiple factors involved (an implicit argument for open systems thinking). Taking just one example, expectancy theory should be perceived not as a theory of motivation alone. Theoretical links need to be made between motivation and performance.

Guest (1997, 2001) puts forward 'HRM', with its emphasis on aligning every aspect of organisation and people management, as a candidate for a theoretical framework to link behavioural theories and HR practices, with the emphasis on performance. He advocates attention to contingencies. In linking with strategy, it is necessary to be able to theorise when HRM matters most in achieving business goals. For example, service sector business environments may require a greater strategic emphasis on HRM factors. As previously indicated, the accent is on alignment at both the vertical and horizontal levels – that is, between people management and corporate goals, and between the elements of HRM policy and practice, reflecting holistic systems thinking. (We explore these issues in detail in Chapter 12.)

The 'traditional' managerial approach to motivating workers may be described as fear of punishment. However, such an orientation has tended to be associated with work relationships based on some sort of mutual obligation between the parties, as under feudalism, for example. Emerging in the era of late industrialisation, **'scientific management'** may be perceived as a critique of inefficient managerial organisation rather than of the workforce. Taylorism is complemented by a moral view that fair treatment of workers will (and should) be achieved by specifying precisely what tasks are to be performed, and how they are to be performed, and training the workforce accordingly. Reward is to be tied to task/output attainment, provided this is exactly in accordance with managerial specifications. It is an open question as to how theory informing scientific management may be extended to help explain the reward implications of AI-worker interaction in emerging white collar techno workplaces.

In contrast with economics-based motivation under scientific management theory, what became known as the **'human relations'** school of thought, popularised by Elton Mayo (1945), adopts a more holistic view of the person performing a job. The source of employee satisfaction derives from the social relations surrounding work. Instead of simply specifying fragmented job tasks, the managerial role is to make employees at work feel important – by permitting some limited task discretion and by enhancing manager–employee communications. Some recognition is also given to teamwork rather than the atomised individual – in pay system terms reinforcing this with 'gain-sharing' and similar collectively based variable pay plans (see Chapter 6). But the human relations school faces criticism that the work design itself remains 'deskilled', and the emphasis is still on ensuring direct compliance with managerial authority. Motivation is socially located with the intention of securing managerial aims without attention to aligning these with the goals of workforce members themselves.

'Human resources' models have been articulated as the basis on which, while retaining the unitarism of human relations thinking, more satisfying work itself may be designed by management, for example McGregor's classic **'Theory X – Theory Y'** perspective (Lawter et al, 2015). Theory X, conditioned by ideas from the scientific management school (not unlike the agency theory featuring in mainstream corporate governance-linked executive reward initiatives discussed in Chapter 10), charges management with actions intended to modify the worker, on the assumption that this is the only way to enlist employees in productive activity. The more employee-centred Theory Y approach to work design and motivation (which assumes that the average person likes work and wants to contribute to performing job tasks) contrasts with scientific management work design, not adequately corrected for the limited discretion offered under human relations management. Again, a parallel might be drawn with the 'stakeholder' variant of agency theory advanced by Buck et al (1998): see Chapter 10.

Human resources models tend to see motivation as driven by a complex amalgam of interrelated factors, such as money, need for affiliation, need for achievement and desire to find meaning in work activities (Fish, 2022; Miles, 1965). Under this view, rather than being reluctant workers, needing incentives to trade leisure for work, employees are perceived as talent reservoirs that management has to engage (Steers and Porter, 1987). Employees, it is assumed, are 'pre-motivated' to perform positively in pursuit of satisfaction in the work they undertake and the self-esteem that may be obtained by recognition for a positive contribution to organisational success.

As Steers and Porter comment: 'In contrast to the traditional and human relations models, management's task is seen not so much as one of manipulating employees to accept managerial authority, as it is of setting up conditions so that employees can meet their own goals at the same as meeting the organization's goals' (1987: 18). Employees are recognised and rewarded for their ability and willingness to make significant and rational decisions previously reserved to management.

Contingency theory (e.g. Child, 1975; Donaldson, 2003) draws attention to the structural context for managerial action, rather than encouraging the importation of universal (one-best-way) ideologies. Following this logic, managers should make judgements about which approach or combination of approaches intended to motivate a diverse workforce best fits with the observable organisational circumstances. Under a contingency approach, ideas about employee motivation from the scientific management, human relations and human resources schools of thought may all be used at one time (Steers and Porter, 1987).

The manager's task is to diagnose the situation to be managed and, not swayed by particular 'solutions' for application organisation-wide, apply the approach that appears most likely to align with the prevailing combination of organisation, technology, competitive and people conditions, context by specific context. Reward management becomes a more finely tuned signalling feature within the vertical and horizontal alignment matrix. Its use is neither to induce the theoretically 'self-maximising' economic agent to concentrate on exceeding production quotas nor to relegate it to the status of a 'hygiene factor', sharply differentiated from 'motivators' implicit in the work itself (Fish, 2022).

Managerially, it is not an 'either-or' situation, rather one of combination and balance: working out which situation calls for which blend of extrinsic and intrinsic motivational factors. Developments in **cognitive evaluation theory** indicate that, while prior commentary argued that managerial attention to extrinsic reward gave subjects the wrong signals, the position is subtler than that (Gerhart and Rynes, 2003). Subjects of early cognitive motivation experiments – frequently children – lacked maturity. Adults in work/employment environments have a more refined capacity – based on experience – to read the signals from those overseeing their work and its recognition. Likely to be aware of attempts to exercise control over their endeavours, positive informational indicators help individuals in judging to what extent pursuit of their goals (and hence performance) will be in tune with organisational expectations of them.

Carefully managed extrinsic rewards may therefore serve as signals that individuals may use to guide their own behaviour, potentially increasing intrinsic interest in work. The risk of manipulation remains, but active engagement in the effort–reward bargaining process as a dynamic exercise between the parties, where self-evidently the individual has an influence on outcomes, implies a more balanced relationship around productive activity. The model illustrated in Figure 2.3 may be revisited bearing this in mind.

The strategic alignment orientation among HRM theorists stresses the need for greater managerial attention to the diverse reactions (as well as dynamic priorities associated with work and reward) among employees. Based on the premise that employees make sophisticated judgements about the messages being signalled to them through reward, and other HRM initiatives, the focus shifts from one of structure to one placing greater stress on processes. In particular, in place of top-down initiatives, this involves employees as active participants in reward design, and the capacity to draw on a flexible range of extrinsic combined with intrinsic sources of reward and recognition as part of what Herriot and Pemberton (1995) label 'new deals'.

Individuals may focus less on the content of reward and more on comparing the informational signals regarding relative recognition they receive against organisational peers (Chen et al, 2002). Equity and comparability are factors that may not actively motivate – but they may be anticipated to have a depressing effect on the motivational influence associated with extrinsic rewards for employment and performance in the job if mismanaged.

Distributive justice theory – how people assess the relative outcomes of reward allocation among peers – and **procedural justice** – how the process is managed, including the capacity of the individual to have their voice heard in reward system design and application – are also factors flagged for management attention (e.g. Cox, 2004). 'Decision-making is said to be procedurally just when those affected have an opportunity to influence decisions and when they are treated with neutrality, trustworthiness, and respect' (Tepper et al, 2006: 103). When the reverse situation is observable, targets of procedural injustice may be motivated to retaliate against those who are seen as blameworthy, based on a sense of resentment.

Additionally, some organisational justice theorists draw attention to **interpersonal justice** – the way that the interaction between the superior and subordinate, the quality of the relationship they enjoy and its perceived character relative to other organisational members, is handled (Olkkonen and Lipponen, 2006). Smith (2005: 6) thus encourages the location of extrinsic reward within 'a complex web of relationships'. In short, socio-psychological contract quality may be expected to modify employee perspectives on management in particular settings, positively or negatively influencing work orientations and pre-motivation to perform, with consequences for managerial potential to achieve corporate goals.

SELF-ASSESSMENT EXERCISE

What are the main cognitive processes by which employees may be expected to evaluate extrinsic reward opportunities, and how do these interact with intrinsic factors that are expected to lead to job satisfaction and motivation to exercise discretionary effort on the employer's behalf? In what ways may managers influence the processes positively or negatively?

2.18 Conclusions and key learning points

Theory underlies action, whether implicit or explicit. To undertake systematic consideration of the alternatives, consequences and contexts of reward management, a grasp of the range of theories that have developed from within the social and management sciences is a prerequisite. Analytical models and prescriptions addressing the propensity of individuals and groups to make their labour power available, and to accept direction and commitment to managerial aspirations, are available in abundance. As discussed in this chapter, some approaches privilege material factors – where it is assumed that employment relationships, expectations among the parties, and regulation of reward systems may be investigated and understood primarily in terms of factors associated with economic exchange. Others may place greater emphasis on behavioural and ideological phenomena, taking intrinsic dimensions into account:

- Economics theory may be abstract in the extreme, adopting a closed systems perspective, and in a similar vein psychological theory may concentrate attention on more biological factors, where managerial intervention may be regarded as of limited influence on outcomes.
- More institutionally inclined economics theory and similarly institutional and more cognitive approaches to psychology articulate roles for active managerial initiatives, alternating between efforts intended to modify employee behaviour or to create the environmental conditions in which employees may direct their own efforts to act in ways that may satisfy managerial goal-directed aspirations.
- Managerial practice may appear to the casual observer to be reliant on a non-theoretical approach, or at least theory that is unarticulated and may be almost subconscious, based on practitioners' socialisation and habit. More clearly developed thinking may be discerned, however, impacting on the ways alternative approaches and their anticipated consequences are weighed. In some cases, this means adopting a position that managerial practice in the efficient pursuit of employee co-operation may best be served by matching the approach to the environmental contingencies observable in particular cases. This may involve mixing and matching thinking and concomitant approaches to reward management (aligned to people management more generally), perceiving available policy and practice as situated along a range or spectrum, rather than assuming a polarisation of approaches to choose from, in pursuit of universal 'best practice'.

Reflection on these considerations may help to inform HR thinking performers and general managers alike in gaining a better understanding of the possible courses of action at the effort–reward nexus. In order to innovate further in applying scientific thinking to reward management among other aspects of the people professional's tasks, the CIPD has advocated use of 'people analytics', also known as HR analytics.

> People analytics uses both people-data, collected by HR systems (such as payroll, absence management) and business information (for example, operations performance data). At its core, people analytics enables HR practitioners and employers to gain insights into their workforce, HR policies and practices, with a focus on the human capital element of the workforce and can ultimately inform more evidence-based decision making.
>
> (CIPD, 2018a)

Explore further

To gain an appreciation of economic theory as this contributes to the understanding of reward management, see Beaumont, P and Hunter, L (2000) Labour economics, competition and compensation, in Thorpe, R and Homan, G (eds.) *Strategic Reward Systems*, London: FT-Prentice Hall, pp. 45–62.

For an overview of applying psychology-informed theory, see Antoni, C (2022) Psychological perspectives on reward management, in Perkins, SJ (ed.) *The Routledge Companion to Reward Management*, London: Routledge, pp. 16–24.

For a US-derived sense of direction for reward balancing the academic and theoretical with the administrative and practical as technology interfaces with behavioural phenomena, see the article by Scott, D and Jordan, D (2018) The future of work and rewards, *World at Work Journal*, Q3, vol. 27.

An easily digestible collection of theory-based mini-articles, including coverage of some key reward topics, is offered in Hutchings, K, Michailova, S and Wilkinson, A (eds.) (forthcoming, 2024) *A Guide to Key Theories for Human Resource Management Research*, Cheltenham: Edward Elgar.

A detailed overview of research in behavioural science and its role in making reward management practices more effective is accessible in the CIPD report Show me the Money: The behavioural science of reward, www.cipd.co.uk/knowledge/culture/behaviour/reward-report#. It is also worth visiting the CIPD Learning Hub 'Essential Insights': Exploring Reward course pages.

03 The context of reward management: Legal frameworks, market conditions and employment relations

CHAPTER LEARNING OUTCOMES

At the end of this chapter, you should understand and be able to explain the following:

- The importance of both legal and employment relations regulation in the design of reward systems.
- The major employment laws governing the reward relationship.
- The role of the labour market in determining pay.
- The role of collective bargaining as a means to joint regulation of the reward relationship.

CIPD STRATEGIC REWARD MANAGEMENT (7HR03) LEARNING OUTCOMES

Learners will be able to:

1.1 Examine the key factors influencing the design of reward strategy and policy frameworks.

1.2 Discuss the importance of aligning the reward framework to the wider organisational context and strategy.

1.3 Critically justify the value of reward benchmarking exercises and the main methodologies organisations use to gather data.

1.4 Critically evaluate the impact of organisational reward strategies to attract, motivate and retain talent.

4.1 Critically discuss the key legal requirements relating to pay and reward and the implications of non-compliance.

3.1 Introduction

Any strategic approach to reward management has to be placed within the context of the legal, employment relations and labour market environment within which the organisation operates. Indeed, with the increasing globalisation of business, human resources professionals not only need to know the details of their own country's regulatory framework and labour market, but also those of other regions. In most developed industrial economies, the employment relationship is governed by both specific legislation and a framework of accepted social norms governing the employment relationship, including acceptance of the employees' right to trade union membership and recognition for the negotiation of pay and conditions. However, even between economically developed countries there is considerable variation in the extent of employment regulation (OECD, 2019). In more recently developed economies, especially those without the benefits of democratic political systems, employment rights may be more minimal for employees, and trade unions may be banned or state-controlled. Even in developing economies, however, there are often minimum rights, such as limits on working time, minimum wage laws and the prohibition of child labour. Most countries have at least some legislation affecting pay and conditions of employment, usually setting out minimum standards that constrain employers in designing their own reward systems.

National culture may also play a vital role in the design of reward systems, although the balance between national and organisational cultures may differ according to circumstances. We deal in more detail with the issue of international reward management in Chapter 11 and the influence of organisational culture in Chapter 2, but it is important to say here that the legal, employment relations, cultural and market contexts can vary greatly between countries, especially between developed and developing economies.

Reward in organisations is shaped and constrained by the environment in which it operates. This includes:

- external factors – the legal regulation of pay terms and conditions and labour market conditions;
- internal factors – voluntary agreements to jointly regulate the relationship via the process of consultation and negotiation with trade unions known as 'collective bargaining'.

In this chapter we consider both the external and internal factors shaping strategic reward management; the major legal, market and employment relations constraints concerning reward matters upon employers, employees and trade unions in the UK.

Since the 1970s, external factors, such as employment law, have become much more important than internal factors, such as collective bargaining, as the major form of regulation of the reward relationship between employers and workers. Before the 1970s there was relatively little legislation governing pay and conditions of service in the UK, but by the end of the twentieth century a raft of new protective legislation had been passed. These new laws, some, but not all, originating from EU Directives, covered a range of rights to pay equity, minimum wages, sick pay and holiday entitlement, working hours and time off work, and rights to trade union recognition for collective bargaining purposes.

We begin by examining this development of a regulated reward relationship before going on to consider how pay is determined in terms of the external labour market. Lastly, we examine the uses and processes of collective bargaining.

3.2 Legal regulation of reward systems

The basis for the design and maintenance of any reward system in any country is the underpinning legal framework. While employers may wish, as far as possible, to create reward strategies for their own particular circumstances, the starting point will always be what the law allows or requires. In this section we examine the major areas of UK legislation affecting the reward relationship between employer and employee.

The major areas of UK law affecting pay and reward are as follows:

- contracts of employment;
- the National Minimum Wage and National Living Wage;
- hours of work, holidays and paid time off;
- unfair discrimination in pay and conditions on the grounds of protected characteristics such as sex, race or age, or because of employment status. This includes:
  - equal pay for work of equal value;
  - gender pay gap reporting.

Each of these areas of employment law and how they shape reward systems will be examined in turn in this chapter.

For further information on the legal regulation of share ownership and profit-sharing schemes see Chapter 6; for employee benefits packages including statutory benefits see Chapter 7; and for laws affecting pension schemes see Chapter 8.

3.2.1 Contracts of employment

> **KEY LEGISLATION**
>
> Employment Rights Act 1996 (and amendments)

As discussed in Chapter 1, the exchange of money for work is the central feature of the employment contract. If no money changes hands, it is highly unlikely that a contract of employment will exist. A contract of employment exists as soon as an employee accepts the offer of employment (see Lewis and Sergeant (2017) for a fuller explanation of the contract of employment). A contract of employment does not need to be in writing, and in the past the details of payment might have been purely verbal. However, employers are required to state the terms on which the contract is made. The Employment Rights Act 1996 (ERA) requires employers to provide 'a written statement of particulars of employment' (Legislation.gov.uk, 2023a). These include (among other requirements) the following:

- the rate of remuneration, how it is calculated and the interval at which it is to be paid;
- the terms and conditions relating to hours of work, holidays and holiday pay, and sick pay;
- terms relating to pension arrangements; and
- details regarding any collective agreements that directly affect the employee's terms and conditions of employment.

For the purposes of the ERA, 'wages' are defined as including 'any fee, bonus, commission, holiday pay or other emolument"' (Legislation.gov.uk, 2023b) referable to in the contract of employment, whether payable under the contract or otherwise. Certain other payments are also covered by this definition of 'wages', such as statutory sick pay and statutory maternity pay, but pension payments and redundancy pay are expressly excluded. Taxable benefits (e.g. company cars) are not treated as 'wages', except where they can be exchanged for money, goods or services (such as vouchers or stamps).

The Employment Rights Act 1996 requires employers to provide an itemised pay statement (i.e. a pay slip) to all workers and also provides certain other protections. Employers are constrained by the law in what can be deducted from an employee's pay. In general, the only deductions that an employer has an absolute right to deduct from a worker's wages or salary are those required by statute, such as income tax and National Insurance contributions.

3.2.2 *The National Minimum Wage and National Living Wage*

> **KEY LEGISLATION**
>
> National Minimum Wage Act 1998 (plus 2015 amendment to introduce the National Living Wage)

Figure 3.1 UK wage growth 1978–2018 by hourly pay percentile

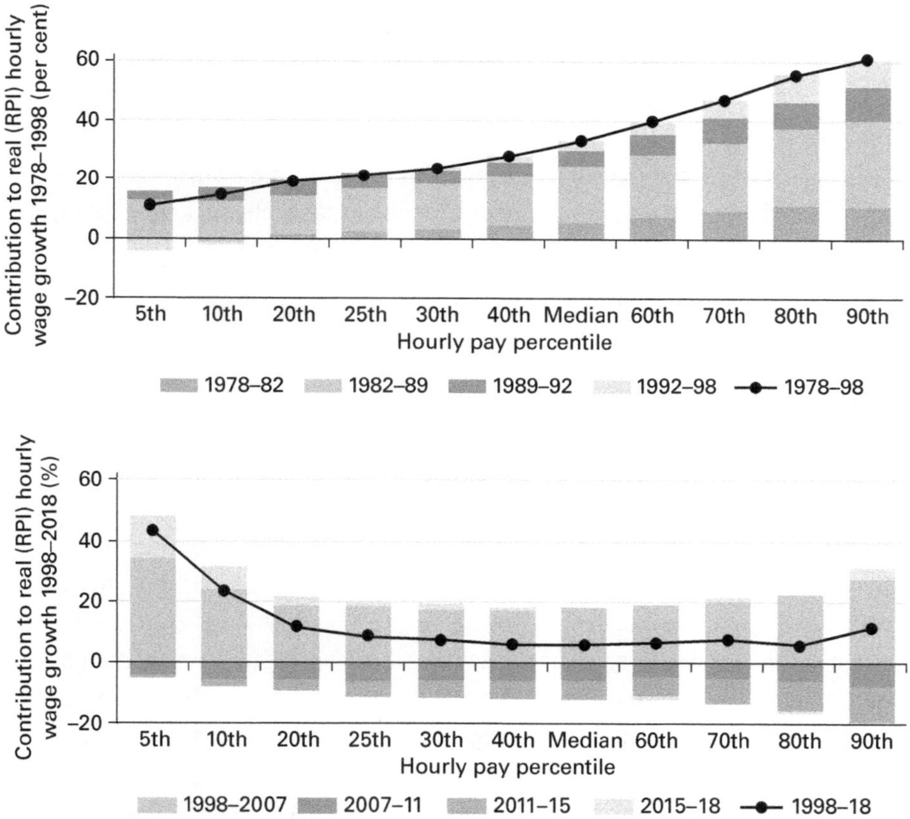

SOURCE: Low Pay Commission (2019)

In the UK, before the passing of the National Minimum Wage (NMW) Act in 1998, there was only limited legal control of wage levels in specific industries where Statutory Wages Councils attempted to ensure that pay levels could not fall below a legal minimum in sectors where it was felt that employees did not have the protection of collective agreements through trade unions, e.g. 'sweated' industries.

Since 1999, all employers in the UK have had to pay at least the national minimum wage to their employees. Before the NMW was introduced, fears were expressed that setting such a floor to pay would lead to increases in unemployment, increased price inflation and increased overall earnings growth. However, these fears were not realised. Indeed, on the twentieth anniversary of the NMW, in 2019, research by the Low Pay Commission (LPC) found that the minimum wage has reversed the pre-1999 trend of pay growth inequality and that lowest paid workers have seen their hourly pay grow faster than all other workers (see Figure 3.1). They also found that lowest-paid workers earn £5,000 a year (for a full-time worker) more in real terms than if there had been no minimum wage and that 30 per cent of workers have benefited either directly or indirectly from the minimum wage. Overall, the LPC did not find any significant negative effects on employment from introducing and raising the minimum wage (Low Pay Commission, 2019).

KEY ISSUES IN REWARD MANAGEMENT 3.1

National Minimum Wage and National Living Wage: Key facts

The minimum wage is calculated as an hourly rate based on a worker's pay over a fixed period (the 'pay reference period') divided by the number of hours worked. There are currently five main rates based on age in years:

- Apprenticeship rate (aged under 19 or in first year of apprenticeship)
- Under 18 rate
- 18 to 20 rate
- 21 to 22 rate
- 23 and over – National Living Wage (NLW) rate

The National Minimum Wage and National Living Wage apply throughout the UK, and there are no variations or exclusions based on region, size of employer, occupation or industry. The definition of earnings for the NMW is that all 'standard' pay (i.e. basic pay plus all payments based on output, productivity and performance, including bonuses, performance-related pay and tips paid through the payroll) can count towards the calculation of the wage. This definition excludes all premium pay (such as overtime, shift and special allowances and pay supplements), and all benefits (including benefits-in-kind with the exception of a maximum offset for those employees receiving free accommodation). Since October 2009 no service charges, tips, gratuities and cover charges can be counted toward the National Minimum Wage.

The NMW and NLW do not apply to members of the armed forces, self-employed workers, volunteers, family workers and au pairs, share fishermen or students on placements of up to a year.

> The NMW and NLW are reviewed annually and any changes take effect from 1 April each year.
>
> Full details of the requirements of the National Minimum Wage and National Living Wage Regulations are laid out in the Guide, available online at www.gov.uk/national-minimum-wage.

The minimum wage is up-rated periodically by the LPC, an independent body set up by the government to make recommendations on the level, detail and enforcement of the minimum wage. The Commission is constituted on a tripartite basis, with representatives from employers, trade unions and independent academics. Since its first report in 1999, the LPC has produced a report each year following periodic consultations.

When the NMW was introduced in April 1999 there were two rates: the adult rate (22+) was set at £3.60 per hour and the 18–21 rate was set at £3.00. Since then, a 16–17 rate was introduced in 2004 followed by an Apprenticeship rate in 2010. While increases in the rate were kept more or less in line with the growth in average earnings from 1999 to 2001, from 2002 the LPC pushed the rate ahead of average earnings. In 2015 the then Chancellor of the Exchequer announced a higher 'living wage' rate would be incorporated within the national minimum wage legislation. The National Living Wage was introduced on 1 April 2016 at a rate of £7.20 per hour for those aged 25 and over. The government's stated target was for the NLW to reach 60 per cent of median earnings which was achieved when the NLW reached £8.72 in 2020. In April 2021, the age threshold for the NLW was lowered to 23 and a new target for the NLW to reach two-thirds of median earnings by 2024 has been set.

Deliberate refusal to pay the NMW is a criminal offence. There are six criminal offences relating to the NMW, with a fine for each:

- refusal or wilful neglect to pay the NMW/NLW;
- failing to keep NMW/NLW records;
- keeping false records;
- producing false records or information;
- intentionally obstructing an enforcement officer;
- refusing or neglecting to give information to an enforcement officer.

In 2015 the Government announced a package of measures to enforce the NMW and NLW, including doubling the penalties for non-payment of the statutory rates from 100 per cent to 200 per cent of the arrears owed to workers. Unusually, compared to other UK employment law, enforcement occurs through two mechanisms. As with many employment protections, employees can enforce the law themselves through application to an Employment Tribunal. In addition, HM Revenue and Customs has a team of enforcement officers whose role is to both investigate complaints and to pro-actively target employers where there is deemed to be a high risk of

Figure 3.2 The National Minimum Wage and National Living Wage 1999–2019

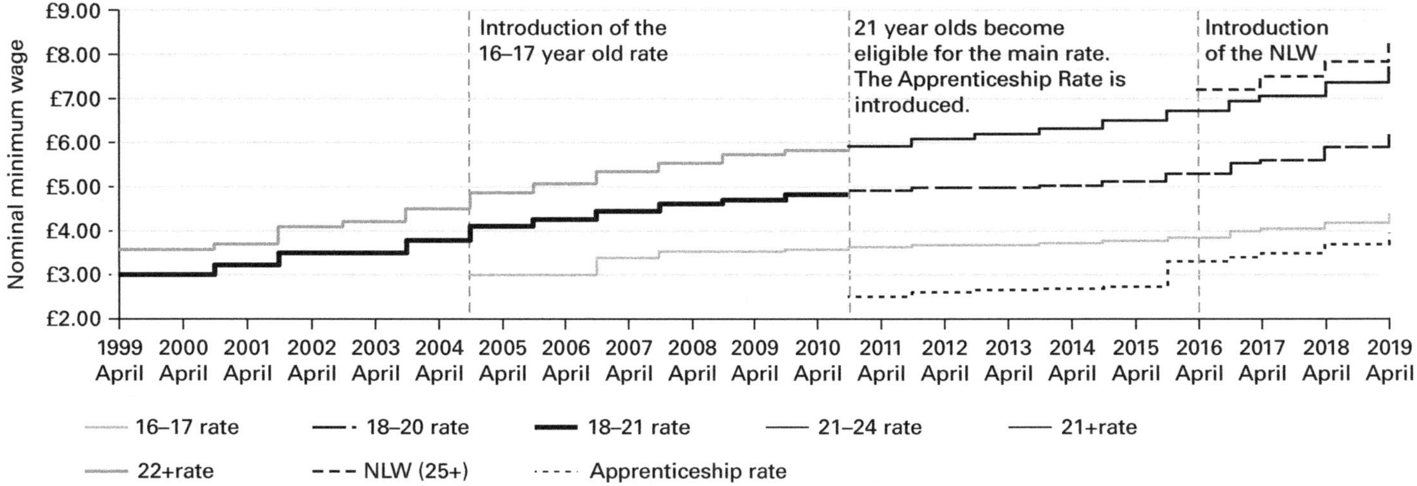

SOURCE: Low Pay Commission (2019)

Figure 3.3 Income inequality measures from 1977 to financial year ending 2022

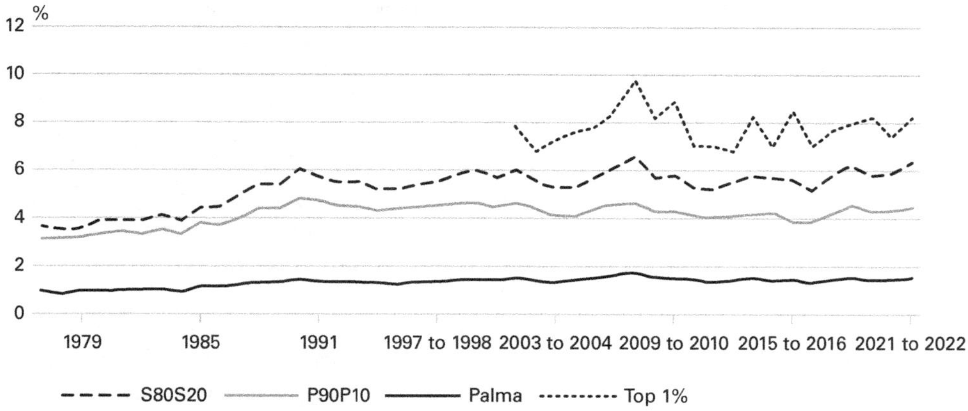

SOURCE: Office for National Statistics, Household Finances Survey (ONS, 2023a)

non-compliance bringing criminal prosecutions against employers for deliberate non-compliance. In 2019/20, HMRC completed over three thousand investigations of potential minimum wage underpayment, of which 1,260 resulted in arrears being repaid to workers. Despite these mechanisms, the Low Pay Commission estimates that approximately 440,000 individuals a year continue to be underpaid (Low Pay Commission, 2021).

Although non-compliance with NMW legislation has the potential to distort competition and threatens the continued success of minimum wage policy, on the whole the policy continues to be successful. As the minimum wage has been increased it has increasingly become the lowest grade rate in many sectors. While in 1999 the level of the wage set affected only the very lowest-paid workers, it now has a major influence on pay levels in many sectors. Many employers do not wish to be seen as 'minimum wage' employers and hence increase their minimum rates to stay just ahead of the statutory minimum.

Wage inequality

The introduction of the NMW and NLW is set against a background of growing wage inequality in the UK. By the end of the 20th century, inequality between the highest and lowest paid had widened to reach the highest levels experienced in a hundred years (Machin, 1999: 185) and the introduction of the NMW was, in part, intended to counter this trend. However, figures from the Office for National Statistics (ONS, 2023a) based on ratios between high and low earners indicate that in the 10-year period up to 2022 income inequality in the UK widened further (see Figure 3.3) with overall income inequality in the UK sitting at 50.2 per cent (with 0 per cent indicating complete equality). For more information on measures on income inequality used by ONS, visit their website at www.ons.gov.uk.

Wage inequality in the UK has been largely fuelled by above-inflation earnings growth among the highest paid, increases in the gap between the wages of the skilled and unskilled, the decline of trade unionism, technological changes and greater female participation in paid work over time (Institute for Fiscal Studies, cited by

ONS, 2007). However, recent research in 20 OECD countries including the UK also suggests that wage-setting practices by organisations have a significant effect on wage inequality, with roughly one-third of overall wage inequality being accounted for by the differences in wage-setting practices by organisations for workers with similar skills. These wage differentials are primarily due to productivity differences as well as differences in the extent to which firms pass on productivity benefits to workers in the form of rewards (Criscuolo et al, 2022). The authors suggest that in order to reduce wage inequality, government policies should focus on reducing productivity gaps between firms and promoting job mobility as well as containment of wage-setting powers of organisations through minimum wages and collectively negotiated wage floors (Criscuolo et al, 2022).

One of the stated aims of the NLW introduction was to raise UK workers' productivity alongside pay and the Low Pay Commission has recently consulted employers on this issue. ONS (2022) figures suggest that productivity has returned to pre-Covid-19 levels, but no further, as of early 2023.

In the UK the Living Wage Foundation has been campaigning for fair wages in relation to the cost of living since 2001. The Real Living Wage rate campaigned for is based on the amount an individual needs to earn to cover the basic costs of living according to region (London and the rest of the country) as calculated by the Resolution Foundation overseen by the Living Wage Commission. In 2022, the Real Living Wage was calculated to be £11.95 per hour (London) or £10.90 per hour (outside London). While still some way below the Real Living Wage rate, the NLW is deemed to be on target to converge with the current outside London rate by 2024 according to LPC (2023). The Living Wage Foundation continues to campaign for the Real Living Wage and points out that approximately 6 million jobs in the UK pay less than the Real Living Wage based on what people need to meet their basic needs and fully participate in society (Living Wage Foundation, 2016). Employers can seek accreditation from the Living Wage Foundation to become a Living Wage Employer. The 2021 CIPD Reward Management Survey shows 55 per cent of employers are either already accredited Living Wage Employers (18 per cent), are planning or considering accreditation (19 per cent) or already pay the Real Living Wage but don't see the need for accreditation (18 per cent).

STUDENT EXERCISE

In a group of three to four students, undertake some desktop research into National Minimum Wage enforcement in the case of Leicester garment manufacturers in 2020. This case hit the news headlines for multiple reasons including potential for modern slavery, worker exploitation and poor compliance with Covid-19 restrictions. The garment manufacturers formed part of some large and well-known retailers' supply chains which further heightened the public's interest in the case.

One aspect of the case involved apparent breaches of NMW regulations which are detailed in the Low Pay Commission's report published in 2022: Compliance and Enforcement of the National Minimum Wage: The case of the Leicester textiles sector.

You should focus your research on a number of key questions:

- How did non-compliance with NMW manifest in this case? What were employers doing to circumvent the regulations?
- Why were these workers reluctant to report these breaches of NMW?
- Is there evidence of improvement since 2020? And if so, what has been most influential, NMW enforcement teams or the role of the retailers?
- Based on this case, what should organisations do to ensure their suppliers are compliant with NMW?

Present your findings to the rest of your class.

3.2.3 *Unlawful pay discrimination and protected characteristics*

KEY LEGISLATION

Equal Pay Act 1970

Equal Pay (Amendment) Regulations 1983

Employment Equality (Age) Regulations 2006

Equality Act 2010 (plus 2017 amendment Gender Pay Gap Information Regulations)

A major change in the regulation of reward systems has been the increasing concern to make various forms of discrimination unlawful. There has been particular focus on sex discrimination as well as the rights of part-time workers, fixed-term contract workers and agency workers. Laws against discrimination on grounds of protected characteristics have also had effects on some aspects of reward systems.

The Equality Act 2010 came into force on 1 October 2010 and introduced the requirement for pay transparency. This means that it is unlawful for an employer to prevent employees discussing whether differences in their pay are due to protected characteristics and any employment contract that requires pay secrecy is unenforceable. In more general terms, the Equality Act, and much of the legislation it replaced and consolidated, makes it unlawful to treat people less favourably because of nine protected characteristics: age, disability, gender reassignment, marriage and civil partnership, pregnancy and maternity, race, religion and belief, sex and sexual orientation. In reward terms, this means that any pay decisions cannot be directly or indirectly discriminatory, although it is noted that age-related pay differentials up to the age of 22 are legal providing NMW levels are met (see above). For women who are pregnant or on maternity leave, the test is not whether the woman is treated worse than someone else, but whether she is treated unfavourably because of her pregnancy or maternity leave and paying a reduced salary during a leave period is not considered unfavourable.

Within the nine protected characteristics there are three specific areas that have particular implications for reward systems: age discrimination; sex discrimination – equal pay for equal value and the gender pay gap; and race discrimination – increasing attention on the ethnicity pay gap. Each of these will be examined in detail below.

Age discrimination

Discrimination on the basis of age has been unlawful in the UK since 2006 (Employment Equality (Age) regulations), further consolidated by the Equality Act, 2010. This legislation has some important implications for reward systems, not least the use of age-related pay rates and service-related entitlement to benefits. The Regulations may also affect the use of long, seniority-based pay scales.

A number of areas of potential unlawful pay discrimination on the basis of age have been identified. These include the common practice of setting recruitment salaries in line with the new postholder's previous salary. While this may be an intuitive response to secure the desired candidate, in terms of job weight, there may be no difference between the job of the new recruit and those already employed, or others being recruited. This is a particular problem if those benefiting from a premium from their previous salary are largely men and those not benefiting are women, but it may also pose a problem in terms of older versus younger workers. In this circumstance there is a clear risk of gender and/or age discrimination. Starting salaries therefore need to be set in line with objective and justifiable criteria and any anomalies dealt with. An audit or review of the distribution of salaries within each grade by gender and age will be one method of checking on this. How these factors interact with a face-paced, tight labour market where managers are under pressure to make quick decisions to appoint is a critical question for people professionals.

A second potential problem is the linking of salary level or benefits entitlement to service (for example, where pay progression is based on annual increments or where holiday entitlement increases with service). The regulations allow for a five-year exemption period for such service-related rewards, so that service up to five years can be counted as a criterion for either incremental movement through a grade or for benefits entitlement. Service-related entitlements beyond five years need to be justified in terms of a business need. Rewarding experience or encouraging loyalty may well be considered justifiable, but a clear case would need to be made here. Clearly, long-service requirements can discriminate against younger employees and many women, who may be more likely to have shorter periods of service due to time out of the labour market.

The Cadman judgment from the European Court of Justice (ECJ) in 2006 set out some principles for service-related pay in relation to equal pay. Cadman, who worked for the Health and Safety Executive (HSE), brought a claim under the Equal Pay Act after discovering that four of her (male) colleagues in the same grade were paid more than her. This was because, although carrying out the same level of work, the males had longer service and hence were ahead of Ms Cadman in the service-based incremental scale. The HSE argued that longer service equated to more experience. In dismissing Cadman's claim, the ECJ ruled that service was an appropriate criterion for rewarding experience but went on to warn that such service-based progression needed to be objectively justified, particularly where an employee provides evidence raising serious doubts about the utility of such a criterion. There is no doubt that a victory for Cadman would have placed the continued use of service-based incremental pay progression in jeopardy.

Equal pay for work of equal value

Until the passing of the Equal Pay Act in 1970 it was perfectly legal to pay women less than men for doing the same job. The gap between the average earnings of full-time men and women workers was 31 per cent in 1970 and the Act was a major breakthrough in the journey towards greater equality between men and women. Since then, the law covering equal pay has become increasingly complex. Equal pay law is now consolidated into the Equality Act 2010 and a raft of case law has set precedents for how these cases should be ruled on.

The Equal Pay Act 1970 outlawed unequal pay for men and women doing the same jobs. Employers were given a five-year period in which to bring women's pay up to the same level as men's. This measure did not take account, however, of the fact that women's employment tends to be concentrated in particular sectors and occupations, and that their pay was therefore usually lower than for jobs of the equivalent value for men. This was because their jobs were seen as 'women's work' and hence innately inferior to men's work, rather than based on any genuine assessment of their content and value.

To deal with this inequality of treatment, the concept of pay for equal work of equal value was born. This concept originated in European Union legislation and was brought into UK law by the Equal Pay (Amendment) Regulations (1983). These Regulations require employers to ensure that their pay structures do not discriminate in terms of valuing the work of men and women employed by them. In order to defend themselves against equal-pay claims, employers must be able to prove that their grading structures are based on the principle of equal pay for work of equal value. This means that different jobs within the grading system must be equally valued according to the content of those jobs rather than the gender of the person doing them. While the law does not require this, the orthodox method of ensuring this is through job-evaluating all jobs.

DEFINITIONS

Equal work counts as either:

Like work – work where the job and skills are the same or similar.

Work rated as equivalent – work that is rated as equivalent, usually using a fair job evaluation. This could be because the level of skill, responsibility and effort needed to do the work are equivalent.

Work of equal value – work that is not similar but is of equal value. This could be because the level of skill, training, responsibility or demands of the working conditions are of equal value.

> Some jobs can be classed as equal work, even if the roles seem different. For example, a clerical job and a warehouse job might be classed as equal work.
>
> (ACAS, 2023a)

In the Equality Act all contractual terms are covered by the equal pay provisions, not just those directly related to pay (EHRC, 2016) and equal pay will therefore include:

- basic pay;
- non-discretionary bonuses;
- overtime rates and allowances;
- performance-related benefits;
- severance and redundancy pay;
- access to pension schemes;
- benefits under pension schemes;
- hours of work;
- company cars;
- sick pay;
- fringe benefits such as travel allowances; and
- benefits in kind.

In order to bring a claim for equal pay to an employment tribunal an applicant must be able to identify a comparator of the opposite gender working or having worked for the same employer and who is paid more or has more beneficial terms and conditions of employment than the person bringing the claim. Employers can defend an equal pay claim if they can show that the reason for the unequal pay is due to a 'material factor' (for example payment of a London weighting allowance). But a 'material factor' defence can only work if the material factor itself does not put one gender at a disproportionate disadvantage and it has to be objectively justifiable. It is particularly difficult where the comparators are doing different jobs. Historical reasons for the different pay levels are not sufficient to establish a defence. However, labour market reasons may be advanced as a defence (such as a skill shortage in a particular job or for working at unsocial hours).

Equal pay for work of equal value has become a major issue in strategic reward management, especially in the public services where the risk of claims has been one of the driving forces behind 'pay modernisation' agreements in local government, the NHS and higher education (Bach, 2010; Perkins and White, 2010). Equal pay is particularly an issue in the public services for three main reasons: because reward practices are generally more transparent compared to the private sector; because government has encouraged the public services to set an example of good practice; and because there have been clearly identified cases of gender discrimination in pay practices (e.g. males in jobs such as refuse collection having access to significant incentive earnings whereas female cleaners and catering staff have not, despite being on the same grade).

The problems in the public services demonstrate the impact that legislation can have on reward practice. The major issue in the public services is retrospective compensation for past inequality. Where, under job-evaluation exercises as part of 'pay modernisation', women are found to have been discriminated against they can claim retrospective 'back pay' for up to six years, adding considerably to the cost of implementing new 'equality-proofed' pay structures.

However, as the case study below highlights, in recent years, private sector companies have also experienced high-profile equal pay claims and although these might prove difficult for claimants to pursue, the ultimate costs for respondent organisations could run into billions.

CASE STUDY 3.1

Asda workers' equal pay claim

The class action equal pay claim of tens of thousands of Asda supermarket shopfloor workers demonstrates the stages necessary in pursuing an equal pay claim as well as the length of time these cases can take to resolve.

To bring a successful equal pay claim, claimants must establish three main arguments:

1. the job roles are comparable;
2. the job roles are of equal value;
3. there is no justified reason for paying these job roles unequally.

A Manchester Employment Tribunal heard the first stage of the claim, supported by the GMB Union, starting in June 2016. The claimants were mostly women working in shop-based roles on the shopfloor, counters and checkouts. They argued that their roles were comparable to those of the mostly male-dominated warehouse roles in distribution centres. The Tribunal decided that the roles in question were comparable in October 2016. Asda appealed the decision which was heard by the Employment Appeal Tribunal (EAT) in August 2017. In 10 points of dispute, they argued that no comparison between the two groups of workers was possible. The argument centred on the operational separation between the stores and the distribution centres which meant there were different methods of pay-setting in each workplace. The EAT found these arguments unsuccessful and ruled in favour of the original tribunal decision. Asda then further appealed this decision to the Court of Appeal which they subsequently lost in January 2019. The company then sought permission to appeal to the Supreme Court, which was granted. In March 2021 the Supreme Court ruled that the shopfloor workers rules could legitimately be compared to workers in the distribution centres. The first stage of the claim has therefore been decided in the claimants' favour

In the meantime, the second stage of the claim began in 2019, with the Employment Tribunal considering evidence of the 'equal value' of shop-based and distribution centre-based roles. There has been no further official updates in this second stage of the claim but if successful, the tribunal will then have to decide whether there is a justifiable reason for the store workers to earn typically between £1 and £3 an hour less than the warehouse/distribution workers. Only once these points have been successfully made will the equal pay claim succeed.

However, if this case does succeed, according to representing solicitors Leigh Day, it paves the way for successful outcomes in other ongoing claims against other big retailers: Sainsburys, Morrisons, Tesco, Co-op and Next. The total value of claims brought against the big four supermarkets, assuming all 500,000 eligible store staff claim and win, could be over £8 billion.

(**SOURCES:** Faragher, 2019; Leigh Day, 2019; Osbourne, 2016)

CASE STUDY QUESTIONS

What do you think are the reasons for differentials in pay between store-based and distribution centre roles? Think broadly: some of these reasons could be internal to the organisation, some may well be about societal perceptions of gender roles.

What actions can employers take to ensure they have evaluated their job roles fairly and accurately? And how can employers design out wider gender bias from these evaluations?

Gender pay gap reporting

While there is common conflation of equal pay and the gender pay gap, the two deal with related, but different, things. Equal pay is the legal requirement to pay employees doing the same, similar, or equal work the same amount of pay, while the gender pay gap refers to the difference in average earnings between all men and all women (ACAS, 2023b). The 'gap' refers to the difference between men's and women's pay as a percentage of men's pay (i.e. a gender pay gap of 15 per cent would mean that women, on average, earn 15 per cent less than men). Gender pay gaps can be negative or positive. A negative gap would mean that women are paid, on average, more than men.

Although it was debated through development of the bill, the 2010 Equality Act did not make the reporting of gender pay gaps by employers mandatory and instead a voluntary scheme was initiated (Government Equalities Office, 2011). By 2016, a mere five organisations (AstraZeneca, Friends Life, Genesis Housing, PwC and Tesco) had voluntarily published their gender pay gap data and it was clear that the voluntary approach would not be effective. In 2017 therefore, the Equality Act 2010 (Gender Pay Gap Information) Regulations 2017 were introduced which made it mandatory for all private and voluntary-sector organisations employing more than 250 people in any part of a year to publish their gender pay gap data. Public sector organisations were also required to publish this data under the Equality Act 2010 (Specific Duties and Public Authorities) Regulations 2017. The first data was published in 2018 based on a 'snapshot date' of 31 March 2017 (for the public sector) or 5 April 2017 (for the private and voluntary sectors) and has been published each year since.

The emphasis on mandatory gender pay gap reporting as an approach has been criticised for failing to directly address the deep-seated problems of gender inequality in employment, i.e. women being unable to progress in their careers and being over-represented in low paid, often part-time, low-prospect jobs (Dalingwater, 2018). However, it was broadly welcomed by equal pay campaigners such as the Fawcett Society as a step towards gender equality at work.

KEY ISSUES IN REWARD MANAGEMENT 3.2

Mandatory gender pay reporting: Key facts

Employers with 250 or more employees on the 'snapshot date' of 31 March (public sector) or 5 April (private and voluntary sectors) must publish the following calculations:

- percentage of men and women in each hourly pay quarter;
- mean (average) gender pay gap for hourly pay;
- median gender pay gap for hourly pay;
- percentage of men and women receiving bonus pay;
- mean (average) gender pay gap for bonus pay;
- median gender pay gap for bonus pay.

The data must relate to employees (using the wide definition provided by the Equality Act 2010 which includes workers and some self-employed groups) and be published within a year of every 'snapshot date'.

The data can be accompanied by a narrative that comments on the challenges faced by the organisation regarding gender pay gap issues and any successes they may have had in closing the gap. They may also wish to comment on their long-term plans for further closing the pay gap.

The pay data (plus narrative if included) must be published on the employer website and the government's gender pay gap service website which also allows public access to the data.

If employers do not report on time, or report inaccurate data, the Equality and Human Rights Commission (EHRC) may take enforcement action which can lead to court orders and fines.

Figure 3.4 Gender pay gap for gross median earnings (excluding overtime), UK, April 1997–2022

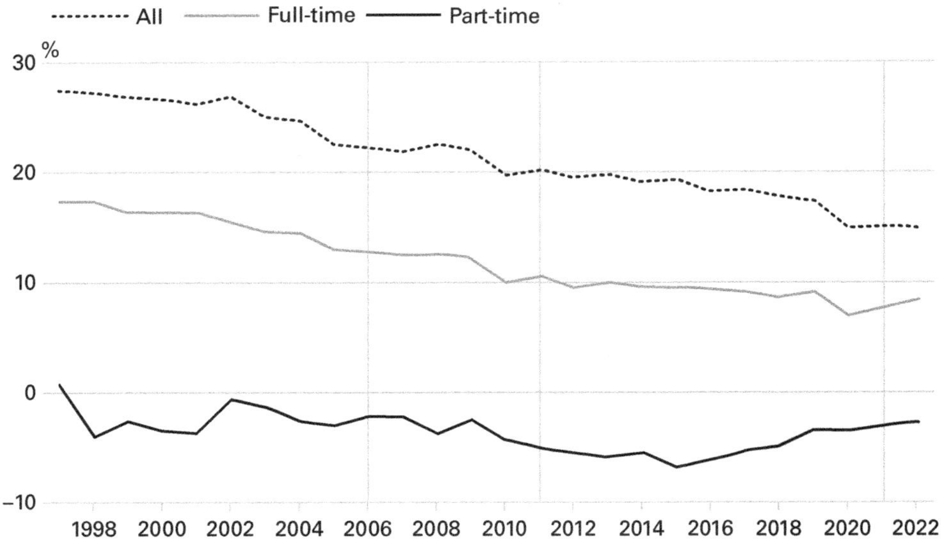

SOURCE: ONS (2023a)

Recent Office for National Statistics (ONS) data from the Annual Survey of Hours and Earnings (ASHE) shows that the gender pay gap for full-time employees (based on median hourly earnings excluding overtime) was 8.3 per cent in 2022. This is slightly up from the previous two years (7 per cent in 2020 and 7.7 per cent in 2021) although ONS urge caution due to uncertainties in the dataset due to the effects of the Covid-19 pandemic such as furlough and disruption in data reporting. The longer-term trend shows the gap narrowing from 17.4 per cent in 1997 to 8.3 per cent in 2022 (ONS, 2023a) (see Figure 3.4). However, the picture is a complex one. The pay gap for all employees stands at 14.9 per cent yet for part-time employees there is a negative gap; part-time women are paid 2.8 per cent more than part-time men. These counter-intuitive figures are explained by the greater numbers of women working in part-time jobs which tend to be lower paid than full-time work. It is easy, when comparing like-for-like, to miss the bigger picture that overall there is still a very significant pay gap between most women and most men.

Figure 3.5, also derived from ONS data, demonstrates that the scale and direction of the gender pay gap varies according to age. Young women, from 18–39, in full-time work, experience a very low or even reversed gender pay gap but the gap opens up from age 40. This reflects the fact that from the age of 30 many women take time out from the labour market to take the primary role in caring for children; they are both more likely to work part time thereafter and suffer reduced opportunities on their return to work, taking less-senior or lower-paid roles (Fawcett Society, 2015).

Traditional explanations for the gender pay gap have used the 'human capital' model of Becker (1957) and Mincer and Polacheck (1974) (see Chapter 2). Human capital models use observable characteristics such as level of education or part-time working to 'account' for elements of the gender pay gap, with what is 'left over' often seen as due to discrimination. This approach has been criticised for three reasons.

Figure 3.5 Gender pay gap for full-time median gross hourly earnings (excluding overtime), by age-group, UK, April 1997–2022

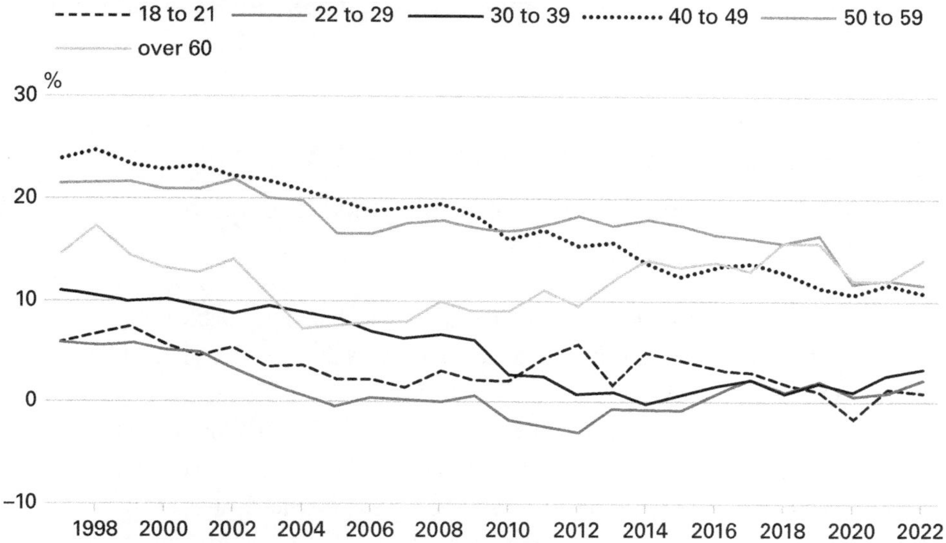

SOURCE: ONS (2023a)

First, the various explanatory variables, such as differing behaviours and work patterns, that some human capital models use to 'explain away' the gender pay gap are founded on an underlying notion of rational choices made against the backdrop of a gender-neutral playing field which is deeply flawed (Lips, 2013). Second, apportioning the residual component as due to direct discrimination may overestimate the effects of discrimination. Thirdly, the model fails to recognise the structural elements in the labour market. For example, differences in gender pay gaps between countries can be attributed to differences in the labour market context such as the presence of unions, collective bargaining and shifts in returns to skills rather than differences in the characteristics of women in the workplace (Blau, 1996).

A number of causes of the gender pay gap in UK have been identified. Walby and Olsen (2002), Olsen and Walby (2004) and Olsen et al (2010) found that these include: differences in the patterns of male and female employment (i.e. differences in the jobs they do); their previous employment histories; levels of qualifications; and unequal pay where it exists (i.e. the extent to which women are being treated unfairly, and not being paid the same amount for the same, similar or equal-value jobs). The research identified the most important factors behind the gender pay gap as discrimination and other factors associated with being female (29 per cent of the problem) and the years of full-time employment experience (26 per cent). Interruptions to the labour market owing to family care accounted for 15 per cent, and occupational segregation (i.e. the different patterns of employment for men and women) for 13 per cent. More recently, using British Household Panel Survey data up to 2015, Costa Dias et al (2018) find that differences in working experience can explain up to two-thirds of the gender pay gap for graduates 20 years after childbirth, and that the gap is largely driven by differences in working hours. For women with no college education, the role of working experience is less pronounced, but it can still account for one-third of the gender pay gap 20 years after childbirth. These findings strongly suggest both a part-time penalty and motherhood penalty is associated with the gender pay gap.

KEY ISSUES IN REWARD MANAGEMENT 3.3

Artificial intelligence (AI) reinforcing gender occupational segregation and pay inequity

A widely reported case in October 2018 highlights the challenges in breaking the established gender biases in occupational patterns that would be needed to achieve gender pay parity.

Reuters reported that Amazon had developed an experimental recruitment algorithm that 'learned' from the previous 10 years of CV screening to penalise candidate CVs that contained the term 'women's' (as in 'women's chess club captain') and even attendance at women-only colleges in USA. This disparity was most pronounced in technical roles such as software developers. The technology also reportedly favoured candidates who described themselves using verbs more commonly found on male engineers' CVs, such as 'executed' and 'captured'. In effect, the recruitment engine had learned that women were less desirable candidates for jobs because of the embedded male dominance in these highly paid occupations.

As the Reuters report noted, this case serves as a salutary lesson for companies seeking to automate their recruitment processes (Dastin, 2018). AI is not an inherently unbiased and objective tool and long-standing gender inequalities are difficult to shift.

For employers and HR professionals seeking to ensure equal pay and tackle the gender pay gap in their organisations, being faced with the array of deep-seated historical and societal causes for gender pay inequality is no doubt dispiriting. However, the EHRC (2016) provides a comprehensive code of practice on establishing and maintaining equal pay through using transparent, bias-free job evaluation systems; minimising managerial discretion in pay decisions and conducting regular equal pay audits (see Chapter 4 on equity audits and base pay structure design).

SELF-ASSESSMENT EXERCISE

Conduct a mini survey of the gender pay gaps in organisations with which you are familiar by going to gender-pay-gap.service.gov.uk/.

Are you surprised by the results?

What are the implications for the employer brand of these organisations?

It should be noted that at present the legislation on equal pay and gender pay gap reporting refers to 'men' and 'women' only with no reference to transgender or non-binary employees. This could be challenging for employers in terms of both accurate mandatory reporting and dealing sensitively with staff on this matter. It also has the potential to mask other significant pay equity issues because these groups of employees are potentially hidden in pay gap reporting through misidentification or absence of reporting (Christen, 2018).

Ethnicity pay gap reporting

It was widely anticipated that mandatory ethnicity pay gap (EPG) reporting would be introduced following government consultation which closed in January 2019. As of 2023 no such action has been forthcoming despite submission of a petition calling for EPG reporting with over 130,000 signatures as well as widespread public condemnation of racism and discrimination by many organisations following Black Lives Matter protests in 2020. This has led CIPD to urge employers to voluntarily compile ethnicity pay reports as a step to improving inclusion and tackling racism, publishing a guide for organisations in 2021 (CIPD, 2021a), and the government have published guidance for employers on reporting ethnicity pay (Gov.uk, 2023)

Compiling good data on ethnicity pay gaps is cited as one of the challenges employers may face in EPG reporting. The Resolution Foundation (Henehan and Rose, 2018) analysed UK pay data to test for differences in hourly pay between ethnic groups of employees and caution that the results require careful interpretation. Personal and work-related characteristics of different ethnic groups in the UK vary widely, and many influence pay, often pulling results in opposing directions. Nevertheless, findings (controlling for age, region, qualification, occupation, industry, employment mode and contract type, tenure and whether a person was born in the UK) show that:

- Most ethnicity groups experience pay penalties in excess of 5 per cent.
- Penalties are largest for black male graduates (17 per cent) and for Pakistani/Bangladeshi non-graduate men (14 per cent).
- There is less variation in the size of penalties that exist between graduates and non-graduates than there is between different ethnic groups themselves.
- Penalties tend to be smaller among women than among men.
- Penalties have remained stubborn for graduates but moved in different directions for non-graduates.

(Henehan and Rose, 2018)

ONS data published in 2020 presented a similarly heterogeneous picture, emphasising that there is substantial variety within the pay experiences of different ethnic groups in the UK. Findings included:

- Employees from the Chinese ethnic group had median earnings of 23 per cent more than White British employees.
- Employees from the Pakistani ethnic group had median earnings of 16 per cent less than White British employees.
- The percentage difference in median hourly pay between people of a White ethnicity and all those who belong to an ethnic minority group is largest in London at 23.8 per cent.

- The existing pay gap between White British and other ethnic groups is generally smaller for younger employees than it is for older employees.

(ONS, 2020)

The ONS (2020) data also showed that the ethnicity pay gap between White British employees and most other ethnic groups narrowed once other characteristics such as education and occupation were taken into account. Nevertheless, significant gaps remained, in particular for those born outside of the UK.

For employers, ethnicity pay gap reporting is likely to prove more challenging than gender pay gap reporting. For one thing, many organisations do not regularly capture ethnicity data on their employees, and according to a report by PwC, many employers have concerns around associated legal restrictions and GDPR compliance (Brown, 2019). However more recently, 56 per cent of organisations responding to the 2021 CIPD Reward Management Survey said their employers would find it 'easy' or 'very easy' to comply with mandatory ethnicity pay gap reporting (CIPD, 2021b).

3.2.4 *Hours of work, holidays and paid time off*

KEY LEGISLATION

Working Time Regulations 1998

Most employment contracts stipulate some, at least notional, hours of attendance despite some workers being paid entirely by output, and others working on professional contracts requiring them to work flexibly, without fixed hours of work. Many workers are paid an hourly rate or weekly wage, while those on annual salaries will have their pay divided up into monthly instalments. Working time is therefore vital in calculating an employee's pay. Because pay and time at work are so intrinsically linked together, any legislative framework affecting reward is likely to include some limits on working time and rights to holidays and time off. In general, manual workers have traditionally worked longer hours than non-manual, but this pattern has been changing in recent years. There has been a move to harmonise the working hours of all employees within an organisation, and of course there has been a trend towards increasing unpaid working time for many professional staff.

Working time is regulated through the Working Time Regulations 1998 (WTR) which lay down a maximum working week of 48 hours (averaged over a 17-week period) with stipulated rest breaks. Many collective agreements (and even some employers who are not party to such agreements) stipulate that workers should be compensated for working additional hours or unsocial hours, such as shift working or at night. Some workers, such as key maintenance personnel, may also be paid for being 'called out' from home to deal with urgent work problems or may be given an 'on-call' payment for being available out of normal working hours. There is no legislation in the UK requiring an overtime premium, a shift premium or an 'on call' or 'call out' payment.

Until the passing of the WTR in 1998 there was no statutory entitlement to any paid holiday in the UK. Such entitlement was purely down to the individual contract of employment. Holiday entitlement has increased since then to the statutory minimum of 28 days (including the eight statutory 'bank holidays') for full-time employees. This minimum statutory entitlement is not service-related and begins on day one of employment. More detailed coverage of non-statutory holidays is provided in Chapter 7 on benefits.

Employees are also entitled to time off work for other reasons. These include:

- maternity leave;
- paternity leave;
- adoption leave;
- parental leave;
- parental bereavement leave;
- time off work to look after dependants;
- time off work for public duties;
- time off work for trade union duties.

Some of this leave is paid (at least at minimum rates and/or for minimum periods), but in some cases this is not required. In recent years there has been a significant improvement in the provision of such special leave for family-friendly reasons. See Chapter 7 for further details.

3.3 The impact of the labour market

The second constraint on the reward system is the labour market. As discussed in Chapter 2, while employers may attempt to defend themselves against competition for their labour through asserting internal labour market principles, with emphasis upon equity and fairness, the external market for labour always exerts a countervailing pressure. While job evaluation may help to provide a 'felt fair' hierarchy of jobs within the organisation, under which jobs of equal weight are graded the same, there are always different market rates for different occupations and skills.

This tension between establishing internal differentials for different jobs, on the one hand, and ensuring that specific occupations or skills can be recruited from the external labour market and retained, on the other, is a constant threat to any attempt at rationality in pay structures. The price of labour in the external market, which will depend on both broader economic conditions and the individual stocks of particular skills and occupations available, is a key constraint on what an organisation does internally. As Kessler (2007: 167) states, 'external equity is an organisational imperative'; put simply, if employees can see that they can earn more elsewhere, many will leave, so it is important for organisations to maintain competitive pay to retain workers. In this way, internal comparison becomes secondary to external considerations and pay is largely (if not exclusively) determined through market surveys and benchmarking (Mitra, Gupta and Shaw, 2011).

The notion of market pay is well-established, reflecting the shift to more individualised payment systems and growing emphasis on the external market, rather than internal equity. Annual surveys of reward practice by the CIPD have consistently shown that achieving and maintaining market competitiveness is a key objective for organisations; 47 per cent of organisations in 2019 (Marriott and Perkins, 2019). Linking salary levels to what other organisations in the same labour market are paying is nothing new, but the shift to more market-related pay-setting has been connected with tighter labour markets when unemployment is low and employees can move easily between employers.

Benchmarking of hourly rates, salary structures and individual salaries against external market comparators is essential in determining the market rate. This might be the mid-point of a salary band, the 'market median' or 'market indicator' (IDS, 2004). This normally refers to the rate for the job at full competence and should be distinguished from a 'market supplement' paid on top of base salary as a recruitment and retention device in tight labour markets. Under market-based pay, the market rate determines the level of base pay and informs pay increases (see Chapter 4 for further information on benchmarking and Chapter 5 for market-based pay).

Research indicates that 'the extent to which market benchmarking determines pay levels and their subsequent up-rating can be very different' (IDS, 2004: 8). In some cases, employers will use market benchmarks alongside other factors such as inflation, performance, skills or experience to set the pay level, but in other cases, employers set their pay levels almost entirely in line with market medians. The latter approach is often associated with broad-banded pay structures or job families (dealt with in Chapter 4). In smaller organisations, with less formalised pay structures, setting pay for individual workers through reference to external pay rates for the same job is common.

This growing emphasis on the external market and decentralised pay decision-making has led to a rapid growth in the amount of information relating to pay and benefits levels and practices (White, 2009). There is a wide range of salary surveys from various providers available to pay and benefits professionals.

3.4 Collective bargaining

In the preceding sections we laid out the framework of UK law regulating the reward system and the impact of the labour market in determining pay-setting and pay increases. But, as mentioned earlier, regulation of the reward system is not done entirely through external factors. In many organisations, the design and outcomes of the reward system are shaped through the process of collective bargaining. In this section we define collective bargaining and consider its advantages and disadvantages as a means to determining pay. We also look briefly at the coverage of collective agreements and how this has changed in recent years. We also consider the levels at which pay determination may take place.

Gennard et al (2016: 27) define collective bargaining as 'a system of industrial governance whereby unions and employers jointly reach decisions concerning the employment relationship' including the setting of 'pay and conditions on behalf of the workers for whom they are recognised'. In practice, collective agreements are applied to all employees, whether union members or not. It is also the case that organisations that do not recognise trade unions may still follow the collective agreement applying to workers in their sector or industry (e.g. in the construction and printing industries). For this reason, collective bargaining covers a larger proportion of the workforce than trade union membership.

3.4.1 Why use collective bargaining?

A major decision for employers is to decide the scope for, if any, employee involvement in the reward determination process – so-called 'employee voice'. Employers may choose to consult with individual employees or groups of employees about the design and any changes to the reward system, or they may decide that it is management's prerogative to decide on these matters. On the other hand, where an employer recognises a trade union this normally implies that there will be a more formal relationship, including collective bargaining over pay and conditions. Indeed, formal recognition of a trade union by an employer for collective bargaining purposes will imply negotiations over pay and conditions. Even in workplaces without any formal employee representation or consultation arrangements, however, the reward system remains a contested area of the employment relationship, and any changes will require careful handling by the employer.

The logic behind collective bargaining – from the trade union perspective – is that, because the employment relationship is an unequal one between the buyers and sellers of labour, individual employees are stronger when able to negotiate as a group, rather than as individuals. There are, however, also advantages to employers in determining pay through collective bargaining. In the UK the agreements reached through this negotiating process are non-legally binding contracts between the parties, unless the two parties expressly agree that such agreements are legal contracts. The content of such agreements, however, can be incorporated into individual contracts of employment that then become legally binding.

Gennard and Judge identify four prerequisites for collective bargaining (2002: 272):

- There must be organisation on the part of the employers and employees.
- There must be a substantive agreement to enter into collective bargaining.
- There must be a procedural agreement.
- Both the employer and employees must be able to impose sanctions (costs) upon each other so that they can reassess their positions towards each other in terms of the demands they make of each other.

At the extreme, this final prerequisite may mean the temporary withdrawal of all or part of their labour by employees (known as industrial action or a 'strike') or a 'lock out' by employers where the employer tells staff not to come to work unless prepared to work normally. There is some protection for employees taking industrial action in that they may not be dismissed when taking industrial action for the first 12 weeks of the dispute. Employers also cannot selectively dismiss workers taking action. It is worth noting here that since 2011 the top reason for employees taking industrial action is over pay and conditions, with 83 per cent of working days lost due to disputes over pay in 2018 (ONS, 2019). In the last few years, due to a complex set of political and economic conditions, not least a severe cost of living crisis, industrial disputes and strike action has markedly increased, with pay and pension issues sitting at the heart of most disputes. ONS (2023b) report that in December 2022 a total of 843,000 working days were lost due to labour disputes, which was the highest recorded monthly total since November 2011.

The choice for employers in whether to bargain collectively with trade unions is often circumscribed. In certain parts of the economy, especially in the public sector, trade unions are well represented among the workforce, and even managers may be union members. In certain cases, union representation in the pay determination system is embedded and accepted, even if not welcomed, by management. In the public sector, trade unions are an accepted part of the independent Pay Review Body system (discussed in Chapter 5), with evidence being submitted by and discussed with the unions.

Elsewhere, the decision to recognise unions may not be an employer's choice. Where unions use the union recognition rights under the Employment Relations Act 1999 to claim representation on behalf of the workforce, there are legal duties placed on employers. If the unions can demonstrate that 40 per cent of those in the 'bargaining unit' (the group for which recognition is sought) wish to be represented, then the recognition is automatic. With recognition rights goes the duty of the employer to engage in negotiations with the union about pay and conditions.

But many employers voluntarily recognise trade unions for collective bargaining purposes. There may be advantages in having reward determined formally through the process of negotiation with employee representatives. In general terms, some employers welcome the opportunity to involve their staff in decisions about reward – even if these are limited to the composition of the pay package and the processes of reward rather than the levels of pay. We discussed in Chapter 2 the more general advantages of having employee voice in the reward design process, especially the legitimacy conferred on decision-making by mutual agreement.

One significant advantage for employers of collective bargaining over individual negotiation is that a collective agreement can avoid having to reach a separate agreement with each employee. Under the employment contract, once terms have been agreed through the process of collective bargaining, any pay changes can be incorporated into individual terms and conditions without having to seek individual agreement with each worker. This can make pay determination and indeed other changes in terms and conditions considerably simpler in the longer term. However, many employers experiencing the wave of industrial action across sectors such as transport, education and healthcare in 2022/23 will also have recognised the disadvantages of the collective bargaining system when agreements on pay and conditions cannot be reached.

SELF-ASSESSMENT EXERCISE

Write down a list of advantages and disadvantages for having collective bargaining in an organisation. Consider how these might affect the reward system in your own organisation or one with which you are familiar.

3.4.2 Centralisation of pay determination

There are important issues for employers about the level at which pay is determined. Where collective bargaining exists, there have been important debates, in terms of management strategy and economic outcomes, about whether centralised bargaining (at industry or sector level) is better than decentralised (at organisation or workplace level) (see Arrowsmith and Sisson, 1999; Brown et al, 2009; Calmfors and Driffill, 1988; Purcell and Ahlstrand, 1994; White, 2009).

The issue of centralised bargaining in the public sector has been an ongoing political issue for government. Both Conservative and Labour governments have argued for more regional determination of pay in the public services, proposing that public organisations need to reflect regional variations in labour markets in their pay-setting mechanisms. A counter-argument has been that pay variations are small outside the regions clustering around London (largely London and the South East) and that regional pay-setting would be too simple a tool to deal with complex local, regional and national labour markets for public servants (IDS, 2006a).

Evidence suggests that where employers are engaged in collective bargaining, negotiations are most likely to take place at sector or industry level and then at single employer level. Bargaining at workplace level was least common. However, this picture was almost entirely influenced by the prevalence of large sector-wide agreements in the public sector. In the private sector it is much more common for employers to bargain at organisational or workplace level.

The arguments about whether to centralise or decentralise collective bargaining levels may be of reducing interest (except perhaps in the public sector) as coverage declines. But there are still important strategic issues for all employers about where decisions are taken about pay matters, irrespective of whether or not they have collective bargaining.

3.4.3 The declining coverage of collective bargaining

Since the 1980s, there has been a significant decline in the use of collective bargaining as the major method of pay determination, reflecting large-scale changes in the labour market and industrial relations landscape. In 2021, the pay and conditions of 26 per cent of UK employees were agreed by collective bargaining between employers and trade unions down from 36 per cent in 1996, although there was significant variation between sectors with 58.2 per cent of public sector employees covered by collective agreements compared to just 13.7 per cent in the private sector (BEIS, 2022).

Collective bargaining coverage also varies between industrial sectors (see Table 3.1). Coverage is highest in the public sector; electricity, gas, steam and air conditioning supply; transportation and storage; and water supply. It is lowest in accommodation and food service activities. There is some indication that pay in workplaces covered by collective bargaining (the so-called 'union mark-up) is higher than elsewhere although this premium appears to be diminishing, at least in the private sector (BEIS, 2022; Blanchflower and Bryson, 2010). In terms of outcomes, workplaces covered by collective bargaining appear to have more compressed pay distribution (i.e. a smaller gap between the lowest and highest paid). Employees covered by collective agreements are also less likely to be low-paid (Kersley et al, 2006). In general, workplaces with collective agreements also tend to provide better

Table 3.1 Trade union membership as a proportion of employees, union presence and coverage of collective agreements between employers and unions, 2018 (% not seasonally adjusted)

	Union density	Trade unions present in workplace[2]	Employee's pay affected by collective agreement between employer and union[3]
All employees	23.4	48.2	26.0
Sector			
Private	13.2	32.3	14.7
Public	52.5	87.7	58.9
Industry[1]			
Agriculture, forestry and fishing	*	15.9	*
Mining and quarrying	16.6	45.5	14.2
Manufacturing	17.1	41.3	20.5
Electricity, gas, steam and air conditioning supply	35.2	69.6	48.4
Water supply, sewerage, waste management and remediation activities	28.8	62.1	39.6
Construction	11.9	31.2	13.4
Wholesale and retail trade; repair of motor vehicles and motorcycles	11.9	30.5	14.7
Transportation and storage	36.1	62.8	41.0
Accommodation and food service activities	3.3	9.6	3.5
Information and communication	7.8	26.8	11.5

Financial and insurance activities	12.7	36.4	17.7
Real estate activities	12.5	27.5	8.5
Professional, scientific and technical activities	7.0	23.4	9.3
Administrative and support service activities	10.0	25.3	10.8
Public administration and defence; compulsory social security	45.4	81.2	57.3
Education	47.6	82.2	48.4
Human health and social work activities	38.1	66.1	36.5
Arts, entertainment and recreation	14.9	35.9	18.6
Other service activities	10.2	22.7	12.6

SOURCE: Labour Force Survey, Office for National Statistics (BEIS, 2019a)

NOTES: 1. Based on Standard Industrial Classification 2007; 2. The proportion of employees whose workplace has some employees who are union members; 3. The proportion of employees whose pay and conditions are agreed in negotiations between the employer and a trade union.

basic conditions of service such as holiday entitlement, pensions and sick pay (Forth and Millward, 2000) and reduce wage inequality (Hayter, 2015).

It is worth noting here that the decline of collective bargaining in the UK has been mirrored in several other developed countries; the share of employees covered by collective agreements in OECD countries fell from 45 per cent in 1985 to 32 per cent in 2016 and was most noticeable in Central and Eastern European countries as well as in Australia and New Zealand (OECD, 2017). However, coverage has been relatively stable in many European countries where it remains the most important determinant of pay and conditions (OECD, 2017).

This variation in collective bargaining coverage largely reflects the differences in economic and political agendas between those countries that espouse the 'social market' and those that favour economic liberalism (Hall and Soskice, 2001). Countries which adhere to the concept of 'social partnership' between the major stakeholders in society – the government, employers' and workers' representatives – are likely to have higher rates of collective bargaining. These nations generally believe that it is the role of government to ensure that inequalities of wealth are kept to a minimum; that citizens have certain rights to consultation over their employment conditions; and that both employers and trade unions have a role to play in the management of national economies. This belief is often manifested in national constitutions and national labour codes that lay down the rights and duties of employers and workers (e.g. France and Belgium), enforceable through labour inspectorates, although there are examples where this is achieved more through collective agreements than through law (e.g. Denmark). While it is true that this model has come under increasing strain since the European recession from 2008 and associated political upheavals (see Vaughan-Whitehead, 2015), certain aspects of the model remain visible.

In contrast, in liberal market economies a limited regulation of the labour market is favoured with the emphasis upon the rights of individual employers and workers, rather than statutory collective rights and protection (e.g. the USA, and the UK). In the USA, the doctrine of 'employment at will' predominates (i.e. the legal presumption is that the employment relationship is voluntary and indefinite for both employer and employee, and either side can end the relationship with impunity). This means that there are few laws protecting workers from wrongful dismissal or workplace unfairness in the USA.

3.4.4 Alternative pay determination methods

According to WERS, by far the most common form of pay determination at workplace level in 2011 was unilateral pay-setting by management (van Wanrooy et al, 2013a), with some 87 per cent of workplaces setting pay in this manner. Other methods include negotiation with individual employees or through consultation and information (but not negotiation) with employees (e.g. via a company council). Some 13 per cent of workplaces set pay through individual negotiation with employees. The CIPD Reward Management Survey (Marriott and Perkins, 2019), using a slightly different framework, found that the most utilised factors in base pay-setting were: ability to pay (used by 35 per cent of organisations), market rates using

Table 3.2 Factors most important in setting salaries within organisational pay structures (% of organisations)

	Ability to pay	Market rates using JE	Market rates not using JE	Collective bargaining	Cost of living
2019	35	34	26	21	17
By sector					
Manufacturing and production	12	17	21	10	14
Private sector, of which:	20	22	19	6	9
Retail, hospitality, catering, leisure and cleaning	27	22	27	5	8
Legal, financial, technology and other professional services	19	20	15	5	10
Other private sector	18	25	20	8	8
Public services	21	16	7	44	7
Voluntary, community, not-for-profit	47	29	7	2	14

SOURCE: CIPD Reward Management Survey data (Marriott and Perkins, 2019)

job evaluation (34 per cent), market rates not using job evaluation (26 per cent), collective bargaining (21 per cent) and cost of living (17 per cent), although there was considerable variation according to industry sector (see Table 3.2). CIPD have focused their survey questions in different areas since 2020 in response to the seismic effects of Covid-19 and economic upheavals, so we do not have comparable data. We might, however, expect to see cost of living issues taking a much higher priority for employers as they decide on pay increases in a period of high inflation, while also being constrained by ability to pay as costs increase across the board.

In the public sector a common method of pay determination for major groups of public servants (such as school teachers in England and Wales, doctors and dentists, NHS staff, the armed forces and the prison service) is the independent Pay Review Body (PRB). These review bodies provide evidence-based advice to the government on levels of pay for the various groups.

> In making recommendations, review bodies need to consider:
>
> - the need to recruit, retain and motivate suitably able and qualified people
> - the financial circumstances of the government.
>
> (OME, 2012)

The government is not, however, bound by PRB's recommendations, which are passed to government for consideration and implementation. This said, in recent commentary about industrial action in the public sector (NHS workers, school teachers), there have been questions raised about the extent to which PRBs can remain truly independent when the government sets them such a tight remit within the constraints of departmental spending plans, inflation targets and the like (Giles, 2022). According to WERS 2011 (van Wanrooy et al, 2013a), in the public sector, PRBs accounted for pay determination for at least some employees in 35 per cent of workplaces.

SELF-ASSESSMENT EXERCISE

How is pay determined in your organisation or one with which you are familiar? At what level are decisions taken about the structure of reward and the pay levels for particular jobs?

Is there any consultation with employees about either the pay system or increases in pay?

3.5 Conclusions and key learning points

In this chapter we have considered the major regulatory and contextual limits on the design of the reward system. Clearly, an employer's options for alternative reward strategies will be limited by these constraints. While employers have little choice in whether to follow legal requirements, there are very real alternatives available in terms of other forms of regulation. There are also clear consequences that arise from these alternatives. Collective bargaining has explicit consequences in terms of sharing reward decisions with employees through their trade union organisations. But the limitations of the labour market will also have implicit consequences. Failure to respond to labour market changes will leave organisations at a disadvantage competitively, while trying to 'buck the market' may also have risks.

As we have noted, the law plays an increasingly important role in reward management. HR professionals need to continually keep up to date with legal changes in the field. In many ways, these legal limits have increasingly circumscribed the freedom of employers within the EU to design reward systems along American 'new pay' lines, but this may change depending on the extent of regulatory changes post-Brexit, which as of 2023 have not been apparent, and will vary according to the type and size of organisation. Certainly, in the public sector and among larger private sector employers, issues of equal pay and discrimination are being taken increasingly seriously – partly in response to national and international expressions of discontent about injustice but also because of the very high financial liabilities that can accrue from getting it wrong, either legally or reputationally. Clearly, a major skill for reward specialists is being able to implement reward strategy within the constraints of the law.

At the same time, other forms of regulation are in decline, especially the use of collective bargaining to determine pay systems and levels. Nonetheless, pay-setting through negotiation with trade unions remains important for many large organisations, especially in the public sector. Even in workplaces where unions are not recognised, these agreements may have an important influence upon pay levels because they may set industry 'norms'. Reward specialists also need to be aware that the use of collective bargaining varies substantially between countries and, particularly where global reward strategies are being considered, the role of unions can be very important.

The final environmental constraint on employers is the state of the wider economy, especially the cost of living and the labour market. Market pay, whereby individual pay levels are linked to the external market value of particular jobs alongside notions of internal equity, has become the norm. And it is clear that inflation, whether high or low, and the pay increases awarded by competitors in the same labour market, remain key factors in pay decisions.

Explore further

The details of employment legislation change fairly frequently, so the best way to check current requirements is the government website www.gov.uk/browse/employing-people.

An alternative source is the ACAS website: www.acas.org.uk/pay-and-wages.

To obtain a fuller understanding of the theory underpinning employment regulation and the content of the law in the UK, see Lewis, D and Sergeant, M (2017) *Essentials of Employment Law*, 14th edn, London: Chartered Institute of Personnel and Development.

For a fuller understanding of the role of collective bargaining, see Williams, S (2014) *Introducing Employment Relations. A Critical Approach*, Oxford: Oxford University Press.

For a review of progress with equal pay, see Rubery, J and Grimshaw, D (2015) The 40-year pursuit of equal pay: a case of constantly moving goalposts, *Cambridge Journal of Economics*, vol. 39, no. 2, pp. 319–43.

For an exploration of ethnicity pay gap issues, see Brynin, M and Güveli, A (2012) Understanding the ethnic pay gap in Britain, *Work, Employment & Society*, vol. 26, no. 4, pp. 574–87.

PART TWO

In Part Two structures and processes for extrinsic reward determination are introduced and evaluated. Practicalities surrounding their design and operation are sketched. Over three chapters, first, basic employee reward architecture is described; second, pay determination and systems for pay 'progression' are specified; and third, notions of variable pay – contingent on factors such as competence, skill, performance and summative 'contribution' – are reviewed.

04
Base pay structures and relationships

CHAPTER LEARNING OUTCOMES

At the end of this chapter, you should understand and be able to explain the following:

- The importance of pay structures in framing pay decisions balancing internal equity and external market competitiveness.
- The various types of pay structures in use and their relationship to organisational needs.
- The use of job analysis and job evaluation as mechanisms to apportion value to jobs while also protecting organisations from legal challenges.
- The emergence of more flexible and person-based reward structures.
- The use of pay intelligence sources to update reward systems.

CIPD STRATEGIC REWARD MANAGEMENT (7HR03) LEARNING OUTCOMES

Learners will be able to:

2.2. Analyse the role of base pay in attracting and motivating employees.

3.1. Evaluate pay structures and their suitability in different organisational contexts.

4.2. Critically evaluate the role job evaluation plays in formulating reward decisions.

4.1 Introduction

Two major components of any reward system are, on the one hand, a pay structure and, on the other hand, methods for rewarding an employee for growth or contribution in the job or role – known as 'pay progression'. Issues concerned with pay progression are treated in the next chapter. Here we consider the former aspect: pay structures designed to meet both the requirements for equity and fairness between employees internally, and to monitor the structure's continuing alignment with external comparators.

> There is a tension between seeking coherence and equity in pay and grading structures on the one hand and seeking to change occupational pay relativities on the other.
>
> (IDS, 2006a: 4)

For reward practitioners these twin requirements, and the fact that they are often perceived to be in conflict, is a major strategic and operational issue. How does one meet the needs for fairness and equity within the organisation while at the same time recognising that the external market for those jobs may differ substantially for different occupations and roles? The issue, moreover, is subject to legal regulation through the requirement to ensure equal pay for work of equal value between males and females (see Chapter 3). As Jeffery (2019: 35) argues:

> ... left to develop organically, pay structures are often simply inoperable... Whether driven by transparency, gender pay – and the forthcoming ethnicity requirements* – or just a general desire for fairness [salary structures] are a reaction to the pay inflation and resentment that can arise when managers are left to make decisions unchecked, free to exercise bias.

*In the spring of 2023, while ruling out mandatory reporting, the UK government issued long-awaited guidance to employers on voluntarily declaring any gap between the pay of their workforces along ethnic lines as part of an 'inclusive Britain' initiative.

(www.lewissilkin.com/en/insights/ethnicity-pay-gap-reporting-guidance-published#:~:text=The%20government%20has%20ruled%20out,report %20on%20a%20voluntary%20basis.)

The job grading and pay structure underpins the architecture of a reward management system and sets the framework for base pay allocation. This chapter will consider the rationale for grading systems and the various options available. The major method for attributing value to jobs within organisations – job evaluation – is discussed. Finally, how such pay structures are related to the external labour market and the various methods for benchmarking the value of individual posts against competitors are reviewed.

4.2 Grading structures

Grading structures are the core building blocks of any organisation's human resource management system, not just for pay but underpinning management of conditions of service and career development as well. Small organisations (and even some larger ones), however, may not have any formal organisational structure. As such they may choose to pay their staff individual salaries or wage rates completely at management discretion (known as 'spot rates'), based on the owner's or manager's view of the relative merit and market value of each individual member of staff. But generally, as soon as organisations begin to grow, the need for some sort of formal organisational structure, complete with job or 'grade' levels, becomes apparent. This is especially the case where the owner of the business devolves operational oversight of the enterprise to a manager and hence no longer has sustained direct access to evidence of individual employees' strengths and weaknesses.

Even if a formal grading structure is not acknowledged by management or communicated to staff, in reality some sort of employee 'hierarchy' will usually exist. This is because few employers have complete freedom to pay individuals simply what they wish. Pay structures are de facto created in these situations because different jobs usually attract different rates of pay according to their value in the external market and because employees doing higher-level work will expect to be paid more than those doing lower-level work.

DEFINITION

A grouping of jobs with equivalent demands which are offered the same rate or range of pay. Jobs are often allocated to grades through a formal process of job evaluation. A pay structure will typically comprise a hierarchy of grades with less demanding jobs occupying the lower grades and more demanding jobs occupying the higher.

(Heery and Noon, 2017)

The creation of grading structures is closely linked to the desired shape of the organisation. Child (1984) suggests that there are two major decisions to be taken in the design of organisations. The first is the vertical dimension – the length of the organisational hierarchy – and whether the structure is tall or flat. Organisations must decide on what degree of vertical differentiation there should be between people and jobs. The second dimension is the degree of horizontal differentiation between groups and sections, departments and divisions. Research indicates that these organisational dimensions tend to reflect the 'span of control' – the number of staff managed by a supervisor or manager. For example, if many people are doing basically the same function, they can be grouped under a single manager or supervisor, leading to a flat structure. If, on the other hand, there are many specialised sections or departments the dissimilarity between functions and the greater need for co-ordination between these different sections will mean that each requires its own specialist supervisor or manager. This in turn leads to fewer spans of control, greater numbers of managers and a longer vertical hierarchy.

Major questions thus arise about how organisations group together employees of similar and different functions or on what basis an organisation should be specialised. Grading structures and 'job' or 'career' families therefore relate closely to the shape of an organisation. For example, an organisation such as a fast-food company will tend to have large numbers of people doing the same or similar type of work, and hence these organisations will have fairly flat grading structures. In contrast, a large bureaucratic organisation (like a local council, a university or a hospital) will tend to have a wide range of functions, and hence grading structures will tend to be both taller and more differentiated on the horizontal level.

Figure 4.1 graphically portrays four types of organisational shape. The first example is the traditional hierarchical pyramid, in the past often found in manufacturing, with the numbers of people in each grade reducing the higher one rises up the structure. The second example represents, perhaps, a more modern structure where most of the staff will be found in the central part of the grading hierarchy. This is more likely in knowledge-worker-type organisations where teams of professional staff are supported by fewer, lower-grade, numbers of administrative and clerical staff. The third example is a typical flat, service-type organisation, such as a fast-food company. Here there are large numbers of fairly low-skilled workers working in a small number of grades in the restaurants but managed by a central HQ of higher-paid administrative and management staff. The fourth example is a job family structure where staff are organised in vertical silos depending on their function. Each silo will have its own hierarchy, but at the highest (management) levels roles may become more generalist and interchangeable.

Organisational shape can even vary between organisations within the same field. For example, in his report on the use of incentive pay in the civil service, John Makinson (2000) examined the organisational shape of four departments and agencies. Looking at the spread of staff by pay level, there were significant differences in shape between the four, reflecting the different vertical and horizontal influences at

Figure 4.1 Types of organisational structure

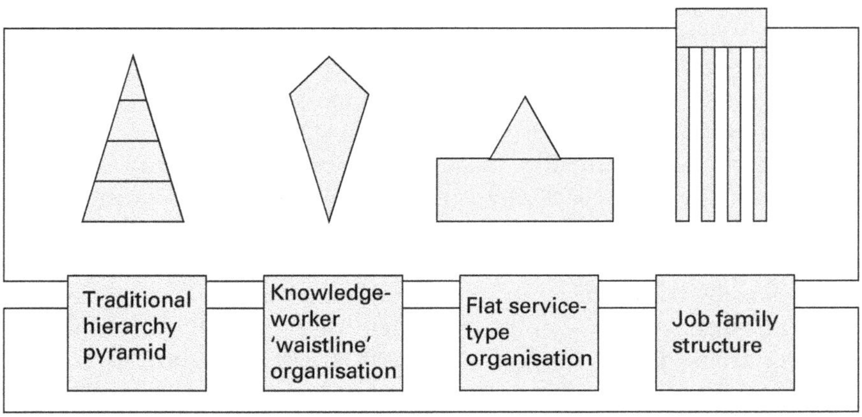

work. For example, before the two were amalgamated, the Inland Revenue exhibited a traditional hierarchical pyramid – with decreasing numbers of staff the higher the level one goes. On the other hand, Customs and Excise appeared to be a 'waist-line' organisation with the majority of its staff located in the middle of its structure. It would be interesting to see how the organisation now merged to form His Majesty's Revenue and Customs (HMRC) is reflected in its new shape and consequent grading structure.

SELF-ASSESSMENT EXERCISE

Compare three different types of organisations – a manufacturing company, a retail chain and a university – and think about what the vertical and horizontal organisational shapes might look like.

Grading also usually reflects the value of jobs as related to the level of skill, difficulty or responsibility required for a particular task. This will often reflect the amount of investment in education and training required for the job. For example, it has been calculated that there is a 'lifetime pay premium' for those who undertake university education, whereby the investment in education at an early age positions the graduates for higher-paid jobs throughout their working careers. Armstrong and Stephens (2005) comment that a grading structure only becomes a pay structure when pay rates or ranges are attached to grades. The hierarchy of grades or different job families may therefore also reflect the demand and supply of those particular attributes in the external labour market.

How one ascribes value to a job or role is a major decision for organisations but is no easy task. Adam Smith, the father of classical economics, commented in 1776 (1776: 134):

> There may be more labour in an hour's hard work than in two hours' easy business; or in an hour's application to a trade which cost ten years' labour to learn, than in a month's industry at an ordinary and obvious employment. But it is not easy to find any accurate measure either of hardship or ingenuity.

The value of a particular job within society, moreover, can change over time and vary between different types of society. Technological change can rapidly change the value of a particular occupation or skill (Braverman, 1997). For example, in the past the skills of the typesetter in the printing industry were very well rewarded, but the advent of new computer-based technology largely de-skilled these jobs, with resulting reductions in the value attributed to them. In general, unskilled manual labour is perceived today to be of much less value than in the days when manufacturing and the extractive industries relied on large numbers of such workers. An important aspect of this variation in the value given to different jobs in different societies and historical epochs has been the consistent undervaluing of jobs done predominantly by females (Hastings, 2009). For example, while in the past both typesetters and typists used the same keyboard technology, the typesetting role was overwhelmingly performed by males and was paid at a higher level than that of typists (Cockburn, 1991).

Another key reason why employers establish pay structures is the rational need for employees to know why they are paid at the levels they are paid. If reward practices are to be seen as equitable, fair and consistent, employees must be able to see how their position within the organisation relates to that of others. The traditional key to this process has been the definition of the 'job' – what is required of the employee by the employer. But in more recent times there has been decreasing emphasis upon the details of the work carried out as such and more upon the *role* played by the employee within the organisation. As the 'new pay' writers emphasise, there has been a shift away from 'pay for the job' to 'pay for the person' (Schuster and Zingheim, 2000).

More importantly, grading structures usually provide the organisational framework for managing the employment relationship, such as recruitment entry points and career development pathways. They also indicate the wider social values that are placed on particular occupations. Grading structures therefore have much wider functions than simply providing the basis for paying staff and deciding the range of benefits on offer.

4.3 The historical development of grading structures

Pay structures in the UK have traditionally been separate for manual and non-manual workers. The origins of manual worker grading structures can be found in the systems established under the medieval craft guilds and perpetuated through the development of trades unions, apprenticeship schemes and collective bargaining in the 19th century (Hastings, 2009). Non-manual grading structures developed at a later stage in the growth of capitalism. These reflected the growth of the administrative and technical functions in the enterprise and the creation of new bureaucratic structures within organisations.

Manual work has traditionally been divided between skilled and unskilled. Skilled workers normally served an apprenticeship or training period before being allowed to join the craft guild or trade organisation. In contrast, employment of unskilled workers, such as labourers who required no training, was not regulated and most manual workers were employed on a casual, often daily, basis. The pay of skilled workers was determined through formal procedures (initially craft guilds but later through agreements between employers and unions) and was based on notions of exclusivity and restrictions on the supply of their skills. The level of skill required for the job, therefore, largely determined pay rates. In time, gradations of skill level led to the development of semi-skilled and unskilled rates. As Hastings (2009) indicates, this social construction of skill usually discriminated against females, who did not have access to guild or craft training (and initially to trade union membership) and whose jobs were considered unskilled on the ground that they did not require physical strength.

In contrast, non-manual workers' grading systems developed with the growth of large administrative activities such as finance, the railways and the public services. Unlike manual workers, such 'white-collar' professionals had career and status expectations. To this end, non-manual grading structures tended to be more complex and incorporate the notion of career (and hence pay) progression, both within a grade and between grades, in line with growing experience and service.

In recent times, the decline of manufacturing and its associated manual labour has led to an erosion of the 'class divide' in grading structures. The creation of more 'single status', 'integrated' or 'harmonised' pay structures for all workers within an enterprise has been noted, with the inclusion of manual workers alongside other staff (Russell, 1998). This was particularly driven by the perceived success of Japanese firms, which operated 'single status', in the 1980s and 1990s. Despite this trend, there continue to be separate grading structures for manual and non-manual workers in many organisations. More importantly, most organisations retain separate pay and grading arrangements for their senior executives and managers (see Chapter 10) and sometimes for key functions (such as sales staff).

4.4 Pay structures and equal pay for work of equal value

Over time, increasing attention has been paid in the design of pay structures to the issue of gender discrimination. As detailed in Chapter 3, there has been a substantial growth in both the content of equal-pay legislation in the UK (and Europe generally) and in case law. Reporting now required by law on the gender pay gap (Brown and Rickard, 2019) shows that despite over 35 years of equal-pay law, pay inequality between men and women continues. For this reason, the gender discrimination potential of any pay and grading system needs to be considered carefully.

Job evaluation (JE) has become the major tool for ensuring equity of treatment in valuing jobs or roles. An analytical job evaluation scheme (explained later in this chapter) has become the major defence for employers facing equal-pay challenges. Some writers, however, have questioned the efficacy of JE in resolving equal-pay issues (Arnault et al, 2001; Figart, 2001; Gilbert, 2005; Madigan and Hoover, 1986; Wagner, 2022). The critique of JE as a tool for dealing with equal pay is discussed later in this chapter.

Any choice of pay structure will require careful consideration of the equal-pay implications, bearing in mind also that equal pay and the gender pay gap are different, the latter being the difference between men's and women's average earnings (Saari et al, 2021). Fuller details of the statutory requirements in the UK for equal pay are provided in Chapter 3. For up-to-date guidance on employers' legal responsibilities see the Equality and Human Rights Commission (EHRC) web pages: www.equalityhumanrights.com/en/our-work/equal-pay.

KEY ISSUES IN REWARD MANAGEMENT 4.1

Will government guidance on ethnicity pay reporting create more equal workplaces?

Susannah Bottriell, an employment law solicitor at Fieldfisher, considers whether official advice on how voluntary publishing of pay data should be conducted will help close remuneration gaps.

Following the UK Government's commitment in March 2022 to issue guidance to assist employers in calculating ethnicity pay and take meaningful action to close any gaps, in April this year it published its guidance on ethnicity pay gap reporting. Employers may assume they have freedom to decide on pay levels for their workers, but, in reality, this freedom is constrained by market forces, legislation and guidance.

There has been a growing trend over a number of years for the government to encourage or mandate pay transparency, including through public reporting mechanisms.

Pay reporting in the private sector principally began in 2017 when mandatory gender pay gap reporting was introduced for certain employers. Since that time, various events have increased awareness of discrimination and inequality in the workplace and society as a whole. The government has therefore made certain commitments as part of its strategy to improve equality and fairness, which has included issuing guidance on ethnicity pay reporting. Critics of pay reporting, however, note that reporting alone may not be an effective tool in reducing pay gaps.

The guidance

Unlike gender pay gap reporting, ethnicity pay reporting is voluntary. Some companies already publish data regarding ethnicity pay gaps.

Many elements of the government's guidance align with existing gender pay gap reporting guidance, particularly the calculations methodology. It acknowledges that ethnicity pay reporting is more complex than gender pay reporting; for example, ethnicity pay reviews can involve many ethnic groups. The guidance allows employers to decide the best process for combining certain groups to ensure reliable results and confidentiality.

Split into five sections, the guidance contains a number of helpful recommendations, including:

- The best way to collect ethnicity data is to ask employees to report their own ethnicity. There should always be a way to opt out of responding. Calculations should be made about the proportion of employees who did not disclose their ethnicity, as this is a measure of engagement levels.
- Employers should use detailed ethnicity classifications wherever possible. A list of categories in England and Wales has been provided, which is the same categorisation as is used in the census.
- The guidance recommends how to choose which ethnic groups to include in the calculations, including minimum category sizes in each ethnic group. This will vary depending on whether the results will be published or merely analysed internally.

- These recommendations aim to ensure employee confidentiality and statistical robustness.
- To maintain confidentiality, in some cases businesses may only be able to report pay gaps between two groups ('binary' reporting). The government strongly discourages this in isolation, as it will disguise details, which are necessary to understand pay gaps.
- Employers should examine any gaps and formulate appropriate actions. The government has provided questions to consider when seeking to understand causes of pay gaps.

The guidance has also left some areas open to organisations; for example:

- There are different ways to aggregate ethnic categories that contain fewer individuals than the minimum category size. The guidance does not directly explain how to do this, though it does provide some considerations. It explains that this necessitates understanding and judgement of the ethnicity of the workforce.
- Employers may want to publish an action plan to address how the organisation will tackle pay gaps. However, the guidance provides high-level information only as to what this should contain.

Effectiveness of pay reporting

The advantages of promoting an inclusive and diverse workforce are well established and the guidance is a welcome attempt to shine light on an area of diversity equality, which currently is not particularly clear. It should help employers prepare accurate calculations in a consistent way. However, it will be interesting to see how many employers choose to report voluntarily, given the complexities involved.

Mandatory reporting of the gender pay gap has been in place for six years, but so far there is little indication that it has been a particularly effective tool for creating change. A study by PwC in 2022 found that, while the average gender pay gap is slowly narrowing, the gap will not disappear until 2151 at the current rate of progress.

Calls have been made for obligations to go further than data reporting. The Fawcett Society suggests that all employers should be required to submit a mandatory action plan on the improvements they will make to gender equality. In addition, the Equality and Human Rights Commission is responsible for enforcement, and some have commented that this is weak. This means employers that do not comply may face few repercussions in practice. Consequently, businesses can comply with gender pay gap reporting, but if they are unpersuaded or apathetic about the benefits of having a diverse and equal workplace, they have no obligation to create meaningful change.

Reporting at least encourages employers to consider the issues, but this is just the first step. It will not be sufficient solely to calculate the gap. To make meaningful changes, employers need to scrutinise the data comprehensively, determine actions, consult and engage with their workforce, and review and amend their action plan.

Next steps

Various organisations have called for ethnicity pay reporting to be mandatory, including the Trades Union Congress, Confederation of British Industry and Equality and Human Rights Commission. However, the government has so far not indicated any plans to take this step.

On the same day as publishing its ethnicity pay reporting guidance, the government also published guidance on positive action in the workplace. Certain positive action can be used in recruitment and promotion, so may be relevant to addressing pay gap concerns. The government is also set to launch an 'inclusion at work' panel in 2023. This will provide advice on actions to take to progress fairness and inclusion.

(Susannah Bottriell, *People Management*, 12 June 2023)

SELF-ASSESSMENT EXERCISE

Look at the EHRC online guidance cited above. What are the key requirements for equal pay, and how would they apply in your own organisation or one with which you are acquainted?

4.5 The objectives of grading structures

As described above, an organisation's shape, in terms of the deployment of its people, is a key determinant of its grading structure, but this is not to imply that the design of such structures is mechanistic or deterministic. Organisations may redesign grading structures as a proactive device in changing or developing their human resource strategy. In doing this, various objectives are often considered, not just those associated with reward.

To paraphrase Armstrong (2002), criteria to be examined when designing pay structures include:

- the issue of the pay relationships between staff and the achievement of equity, fairness and consistency;
- the relationship of the internal structure to the pressures arising from the external labour market;
- the degree of operational flexibility and continuous development envisaged;
- the scope for rewarding performance and increases in skill and competence within the structure;
- the clarity of reward and career paths;
- the ease with which they can be communicated; and
- the degree of control over pay that the structure provides to management.

The emphasis that different organisations place on these different criteria will determine the form of such structures.

As noted above, however, organisations face a continuous tension between, on the one hand, the need for internal equity, fairness and consistency in motivating staff and, on the other, the need to meet the demands of the external labour market in recruiting and retaining staff (IDS, 2006a).

4.6 Types of pay structure

Organisations can operate a single, integrated pay structure for all employees within the enterprise (so-called 'single status'), or there may be separate structures for different groups of employees or occupations. To repeat, a traditional divide has been between manual (often hourly-paid wage) workers and non-manual salaried staff (Hastings, 2009), but elsewhere the structures may reflect different professional or occupational job or career 'families' (e.g. finance, marketing and sales, research and development). Another important factor in the past has been the influence of trade unions and collective bargaining whereby different trade unions organised different groups of workers, each with their own pay structure.

There are several types of pay structure. In general, the differences revolve around whether they are individual or collective and whether they are narrow or wide in scope. The types include:

- individual 'spot rate' or rate for the job;
- individual job ranges;
- narrow-graded structures;
- service-related pay spines;
- broad-banded structures;
- 'job families' or 'career grades'.

In 2019, the CIPD Annual Reward Management Survey (Marriot and Perkins, 2019) found that 60 per cent of organisations use pay structures; but there is great variation

Table 4.1 Use of pay structures to organise base pay (% of respondents)

	Yes	No
All	60	40
By sector		
Manufacturing and production	47	53
Private sector, of which:	51	49
Retail, hospitality, catering, leisure and cleaning	63	38
Legal, financial, technology and other professional services	43	57
Other private sector	53	47
Public services	93	7
Voluntary, community, not-for-profit	72	28
By size		
SME (<250)	46	54
Large (250–9,999)	79	21
Very large (10,000+)	92	8

SOURCE: Marriot and Perkins (2019)

Table 4.2 Basis for structuring base pay

	Individual rates/spot salaries	Narrow-graded pay structures	Incremental salary progression	Job family	Broadbanded pay structures
2019*	49	38	37	42	28
2017*	41	34	30	35	25
2014*	50	32	31	29	26
2013*	49	37	32	30	29
2012*	47	29	29	25	27
2011*	53	21	30	28	35

SOURCE: Marriot and Perkins (2019)

among the sectors and sizes of organisations. Public services are markedly most likely to use such structures (93 per cent), with the voluntary sector also reporting their use in 72 per cent of cases. The 'legal, financial, technology and other professional services' sub-sector is least likely to do so (43 per cent), only just exceeded by the manufacturing and production sector (47 per cent). The use of such structures increases notably with an increase in organisation size, from 46 per cent among SMEs up to 92 per cent in large organisations.

The survey found that, although the incidence has varied over recent years, the most common structures are individual pay rates/spot salaries (49 per cent). But the situation is dynamic: all categories of pay structures have seen a rise in percentage over previous years, indicating that respondents are selecting a wider range of options. Job families continue to become more widely used, at 42 per cent, having risen from 28 per cent of organisations in 2011. Narrow graded pay structures also continue to increase at 38 per cent, rising from 21 per cent in 2011.

Research for the Office for Manpower Economics (the body that administers the UK Pay Review Bodies and Police Negotiating Board) on developments in occupational pay differentiation points to two parallel developments. These are a growing emphasis upon job evaluation and job weight to design equal-pay-proofed structures, on the one hand, and a renewed emphasis on market testing of pay levels through benchmarking, on the other. The source of these developments is attributed to the de-layering of organisations in the early 1990s and the creation of so-called 'broad-banded' pay structures. These broad-banded structures gave employers much more freedom to place and progress employees through the pay range (OME, 2006). The job or career family concept represents another means to respond to external labour market pressures.

4.6.1 'Spot rates' or 'rate for the job'

Smaller organisations may not have formal grading structures as such but will pay each individual worker a separate wage rate or salary. This is sometimes referred to as a 'spot rate'. Each job rate will be reviewed periodically, but no guaranteed progression is provided within the grade. Traditionally, such single pay rates have been most common at the very bottom of organisational structures (for manual workers) or at the very top (for chief executives and senior managers – see Chapter 10).

The BMW Oxford pay structure shown below is an example of such a single rate system for manual workers in a manufacturing environment.

4.6.2 Individual job ranges

A development of the individual 'spot rate' is the provision of a pay range for each member of staff. This may just be a minimum and a maximum for the grade. It

Table 4.3 BMW Oxford pay structure (1 January 2014)

Grade	Job examples	£ per annum	£ per hour
2	Track assembler	26,944	14.00
3	Rectifier, relief operator	28,194	14.65
4	Craftsman (single skill), team co-ordinator	29,353	15.26
5	Multi-skilled craftsman	30,723	15.97
6	Logistics officer, technician	32,297	16.79
7	Production area manager	33,817	17.58

SOURCE: IDS Pay Report 1126, July 2014.

provides the employee with some expectancy of pay progression (on top of any cost-of-living increase), but movement through the range may not be formalised or it may be based on some measure of the employee's performance or seniority. What is different about such individual job ranges in contrast to narrow grades or broad bands is that there is still no collective structure as such – each individual employee will have his or her own range.

4.6.3 Narrow-graded structures

Once organisations move beyond informal, individualised pay structures, they have a choice in the degree of flexibility they wish to introduce. The 'narrow-grade' pay structure is the traditional form of grouping employees according to their skills, competencies and responsibilities. In some cases, especially in the public services, these grades may be attached to a common pay spine. Under a narrow-grade structure, a 'career ladder' or 'staircase' of grades exists, each grade having its own 'scale', with usually a number of pay 'increments' (in the case of a pay spine these will be points on the spine) to allow pay progression. These narrow grades may or may not overlap. Where they overlap this allows employees to continue to progress up the pay scale without having to be promoted to a higher grade (see Figure 4.2). The grading structure for NHS nurses and other health professions is a good example of a typical narrow-grade structure with overlapping grades (see Table 4.4).

Figure 4.2 A typical narrow-graded structure

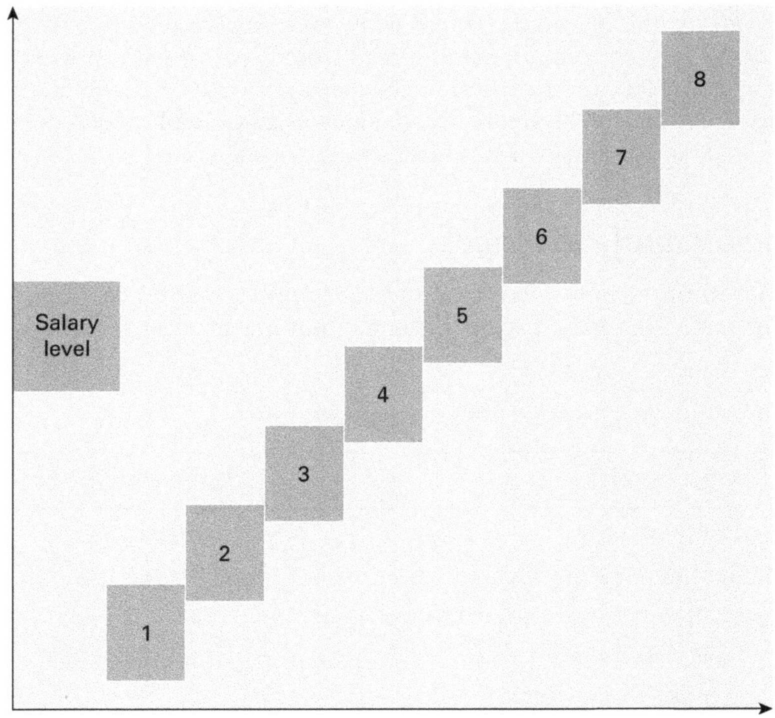

Table 4.4 Pay structure for NHS nurses and other health professions (England, 1 April 2014)

Band	Minimum £ per annum	Maximum £ per annum	Spine points	Job examples
1	14,294	15,013	1–3	Healthcare science support worker (entry level)
2	14,294	17,425	1–8	Clinical support worker, healthcare science support worker (stage 2), phlebotomist
3	16,271	19,268	6–12	Anatomical pathology technician – mortuary (entry level), clinical support worker (higher level), dental nurse, health improvement resource assistant, healthcare science support worker (higher level)
4	18,838	22,016	11–17	Ambulance practitioner, anatomical pathology technician – mortuary, assistant/associate practitioner, cytology screener, dental nurse, health improvement resource assistant (higher level), medical engineering technician (entry level), nursery nurse, occupational therapy technician, optometrist (entry level), pharmacy technician, play specialist
5	21,478	27,901	16–23	Ambulance practitioner specialist, assistant practitioner (higher level), biomedical scientist, chaplain (entry level), clinical psychologist, counsellor (entry level), dental nurse specialist/ team leader, dental technician, dietician, healthcare scientist practitioner, medical physics technician, midwife (new entrant), nurse (qualified), occupational therapist, orthoptist, pharmacist (entry level), physiotherapist, podiatrist, radiographer, speech and language therapist, theatre practitioner
6	25,783	34,530	21–29	Ambulance practitioner advanced, arts therapist (entry level), chaplain, clinical psychology trainee, counsellor, dietician specialist, district nurse, healthcare scientist specialist, health visitor, midwife, pharmacist, sexual health adviser, specialist medical photographer, specialist nurse, trainee clinical psychologist

(continued)

Table 4.4 (Continued)

Band	Minimum £ per annum	Maximum £ per annum	Spine points	Job examples
7	30,764	40,558	26–34	Arts therapist, clinical psychologist, dietician (advanced), health visitor specialist, midwife (higher level), nurse team manager, orthoptist (advanced), radiographer advanced/specialist/ team manager, registered clinical scientist, specialist counsellor, sexual health advisory service manager
8a	39,239	47,088	33–38	Dental laboratory manager, midwife consultant, modern matron, nurse consultant, occupational therapist consultant, pharmacist advanced, principal clinical psychologist, principal clinical scientist
8b	45,707	56,504	37–42	Consultant clinical psychologist, principal clinical scientist
8c	54,998	67,805	41–46	Consultant clinical scientist
8d	65,922	81,618	45–50	–
9	77,850	98,453	49–54	Head of service

SOURCE: NHS terms and conditions of service handbook. The NHS Staff Council.

The number of grades or bands in a narrow-banded structure can vary but usually consists of more than four grades to accommodate the full range of jobs and levels in an organisation. The number of increments within each scale may also vary, although in recent years many organisations have reduced the number of points in each scale. This has been partly to simplify structures but has also reflected equal-pay concerns about the potential gender discrimination risks of having very long scales (i.e. where women take career breaks to have children they may return to a point where their male colleagues have already moved ahead). We discuss this issue in Chapter 5.

4.6.3 Pay spines

Pay 'spines' (or a column of pay points) are common in the public services. These spines provide the 'backbone' to local grading structures and are often a way of linking local pay structures to some national pay structure. Under the Framework Agreement for Pay Modernisation in Higher Education, for example, a 51-point spine provides the starting point for local institutions to create their grading structures (see Figure 4.3). The uplift to the pay spine remains subject to national pay negotiations between the employers and trade unions, but which spine points are used for particular job levels is left to local determination. A model grading structure was provided at national level as a guide but locally employers have adapted this model to varying degrees or ignored it altogether.

Figure 4.3 Higher education pay spine and model grading structure

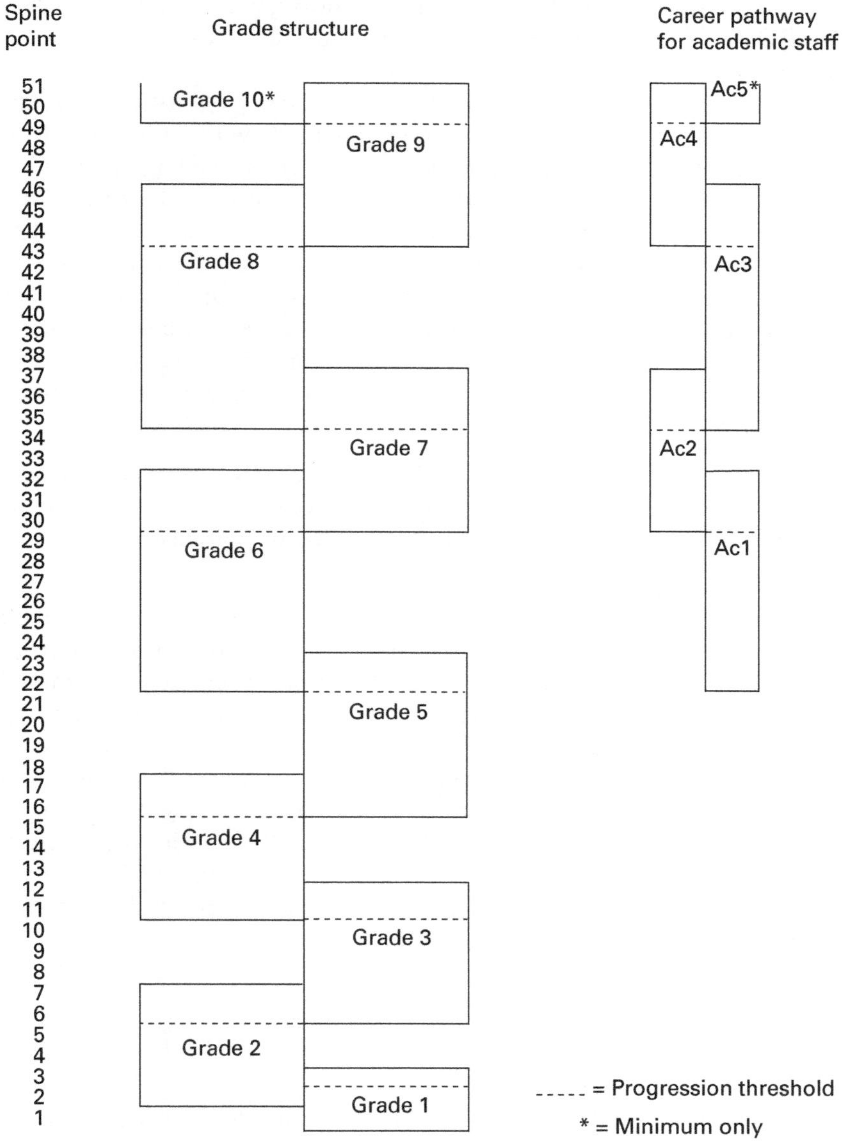

SOURCE: Joint Negotiating Committee for Higher Education Staffs 2004

4.6.4 *Broad bands*

The main alternative to narrow grades is so-called 'broad-banding'. Under a broad-band structure, employees are grouped into a small number of (normally no more than five) pay bands. In each band the span between the floor and ceiling of each band is wide (perhaps the maximum salary point will be between 70 and 100 per cent or more of the minimum). The concept originated in the USA and was seen as a more flexible system than the rigidity of narrow grades (Gilbert and Abosch, 1996; Leblanc, 1992). It grew out of the 'downsizing' of organisations in the 1980s and early 1990s when hierarchical layers were stripped out of companies, reducing the scope for employee advancement through promotions.

Broad bands have been seen as more flexible than narrow grades in that employees can continue to be rewarded for growth in their role without necessarily having to be promoted into a higher grade. Such structures also provide managers with both more flexibility in progressing individual employees through the career structure and greater discretion in setting appointment salaries. They have been particularly useful where performance- or competence-based progression has been adopted as they provide a wide range within which individual contribution can be recognised. It has been argued that broad bands reflect the new, more flexible, career structures found in the flatter hierarchies in many organisations. This enables lateral career moves to take place more easily than in traditional 'narrow-grade' structures. IDS (2006b: 4) comments:

> In theory, broad-banded structures provided vast distances between salary minimums and maximums and individuals could be placed more or less anywhere on the scale. Management was therefore able to exercise some degree of individual differentiation within non-transparent structures.

The CIPD (2001) points out, however, that the term is often used loosely. Some organisations claim to have broad bands, even when they have seven or more grades and spans of only 40 to 50 per cent. The IPD (2000) suggested that these latter structures might be better called 'fat grades', while those that are truly broad-banded could be termed 'career-based' structures. The latter term is seen as appropriate because many of the organisations reporting having such pay structures claim that they are as much about career development as the delivery of pay. Armstrong (2012) distinguishes between 'broad grades' and 'broad bands'. The former is defined as a sequence of between six and nine grades with fairly broad pay ranges (between 40 and 50 per cent) while 'broad bands' are defined as a series of five or six bands with wider pay ranges (between 50 and 80 per cent).

DEFINITION

Broad-banding is the replacement of a graded structure comprised of multiple short grades with a small number of broad pay 'bands', usually four or five in total.

(Heery and Noon 2017)

In the example in Figures 4.4 and 4.5, a traditional nine-grade structure with grades spanning 40 per cent of base salary could be converted into a structure with three 100 per cent spans as shown.

Over 20 years ago, a survey of broadbanding (IPD, 2000) found that such structures varied in practice between different organisational levels. Broad-banded structures with three or fewer bands were most common for senior executives,

Figure 4.4 Traditional graded structure – 40 per cent grade width

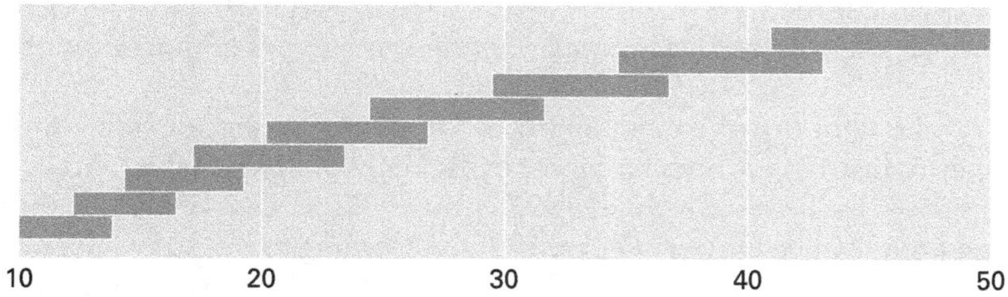

SOURCE: IPD (1997)

Figure 4.5 Broadbanded structure – 100 per cent band width

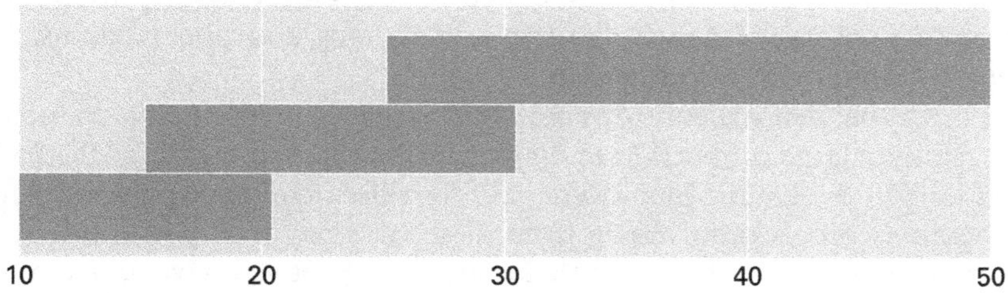

SOURCE: IPD (1997)

Table 4.5 Reasons for introducing broad bands

Objectives	% of respondents
To provide more flexibility in reward	29
To reflect changes in organisational structure	18
To provide a better base for rewarding growth in competence	14
To replace an over-complex pay structure	12
To devolve more responsibility for pay decisions to managers	11
To provide a better basis for rewarding career progression	11
To reduce the need for job evaluation	8
To simplify pay administration	7
To eliminate the need for job evaluation	2

SOURCE: IPD (2000)

whereas those with six to nine bands were most common for staff. The width of grades also varied: the most common spans were between 50 and 79 per cent. In terms of usage, the CIPD (2001) summarises various surveys of practice with broad bands.

The prevalence of broad bands ranged between 49 per cent (of staff) in the IPD 1999 survey to just 12 per cent in a survey by IRS in 2000 (IRS, 2000a). According to a sample survey, by Towers Perrin in 1997, around 32 per cent of UK organisations were using broad bands (Towers Perrin, 1997). According to the 2019 CIPD Reward Management Survey (Marriot and Perkins, 2019), broad bands are the fifth most common form of grading structure (28 per cent) but popularity had fallen since 2011.

Reasons given by employers in the IPD (2000) survey for adopting broad bands are shown in Table 4.5.

The IPD (2000) survey found that most employers felt that their objectives for broad bands had been broadly achieved. Where they had failed the most common reasons were poor performance management systems and poor training of line managers to administer the new system.

While broad-banded structures were initially seen as an alternative to job evaluation, in reality a large proportion of employers continue to use JE as the basis for assigning jobs to the bands. Employers have also been concerned about the threat of unlimited pay progression arising from these wide pay spans. As a result, many have inserted performance bars into their bands while others have adopted 'zones' within bands that indicate the normal range of pay for a particular job or role (see Figure 4.6). These zones often reflect the external market reference or anchor points for a fully competent individual and are often aligned to the comparator rates in the external labour market.

The advantages and disadvantages of broad bands have been summarised as follows (IPD, 1997). Advantages are that such structures allow an employer to adjust the pay of an individual more easily. This includes more freedom to set pay levels for new employees and to progress staff through a pay range without having to frequently promote them to a new grade. Such structures also allow organisations

Figure 4.6 A broad-banded structure with zones for individual roles

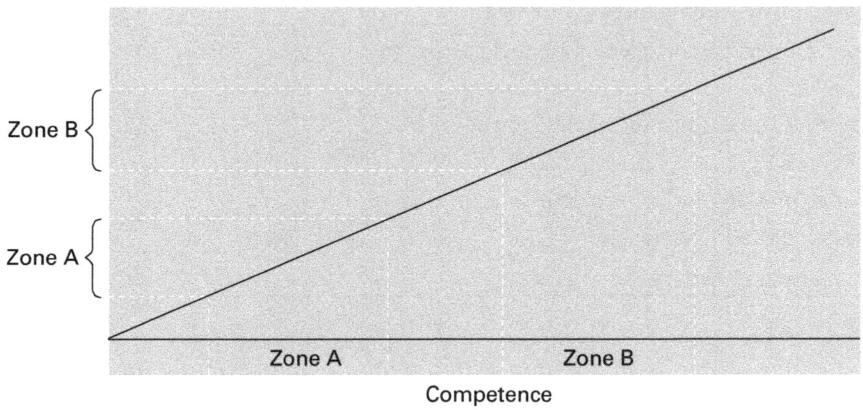

SOURCE: IPD (1997)

to reward lateral career movement, continuous learning and the achievement of high levels of competence and contribution.

A major disadvantage identified, however, is that broad bands may restrict promotion opportunities for employees, with resultant effects upon morale and motivation. Furthermore, those in higher grades who see their jobs 'collapsed' into new broad bands may feel that their work has been devalued. The wide pay spans may raise employee expectations that cannot in practice be realised. The possible employee perception of lack of clarity in the structure – with no clear 'career signposts' – may also concern employees. This potential lack of clear criteria for progression may lay the organisation open to the risks of discrimination and inequity.

This is exemplified by the case of the Biotechnology and Biological Sciences Research Council, which was one of the first organisations to conduct an equal-pay audit. It found that broad pay bands and low pay increases since the organisation moved away from the previous civil service pay system meant that women were clustered at the bottom of pay bands. By introducing faster progression and reducing the link between recruitment salaries and an applicant's previous salary (which had led to gender discrimination in the past) the organisation was able to make its pay system fairer (Allison et al, 2002). Most importantly, there may be a very real risk of pay 'drift' if progression through the bands is not closely controlled.

According to IDS (2006b: 5), 'Pure broad-banded structures had weaknesses from the start. They were harder to manage than narrower graded structures and made considerable demands on line managers who found it difficult to explain salary levels and limits on progression.' A major issue is whether broad bands match the culture of the organisation – broad bands may not suit very hierarchical organisations. Despite this, it is worth observing that, according to CIPD annual reward survey results, broad bands have been adopted in almost a third of public service organisations (Marriot and Perkins, 2019).

Some evidence indicates that broad-banding has become more 'structured', with a return to more transparency and easily understood principles for band allocation and progression. Armstrong (2012: 222) claims that the 'original notion of unstructured broad bands is now no longer commonly practised in the UK'. This is because the original concept of unstructured bands and flexible progression based on individual performance was too vague, too open to pay drift and too open to equal pay challenges to work at the operational level. Both employees and their managers often felt the system lacked coherence and transparency. More structure was therefore introduced into the bands through the use of reference points. And job evaluation placed yet more constraints on flexibility in starting salaries and progression. 'Broad-banding in its original sense is therefore not the panacea it was once thought to be' Armstrong (2012: 227).

SELF-ASSESSMENT EXERCISE

What are the advantages and potential disadvantages of broad bands? What mitigations might be applied to overcome perceived disadvantages?

4.6.5 *Job families/career grades*

Another recent reward phenomenon has been the growth of 'job families' or 'career grades'. In some ways these reflect the need for organisations to link the pay of a particular occupational group (e.g. information technology) or business process (e.g. customer services) to different external labour markets. Job or career families are especially useful where the alternative would be a single structure with various ad hoc market allowances or supplements to reward particularly hard-to-fill jobs. This trend towards job families could be seen as constituting a retreat from attempts to create single, harmonised pay structures and a return to the occupational segregation of the workforce described earlier in this chapter. This may well, however, make pay progression easier for employees to understand. Moreover, unlike traditional segregated pay structures based on different 'bargaining groups' for different occupations, job families can form part of a single, integrated pay structure and can sit within job-evaluated structures or a single pay spine. IDS (2012: 3) observes that 'A well-designed job family structure... can ensure that employees performing roles of comparable value are equally rewarded, while providing scope for differentiating the pay for certain groups of staff according to the market.'

DEFINITION

A job family is a set of jobs based around common activities but conducted at different levels of the organisation. For instance, a finance and accounting job family could embrace junior finance officers, senior accountants, and the finance director of the enterprise. A job family may form the basis for an integrated pay structure, such that all jobs within the family are managed using a common set of rules and procedures.

(Heery and Noon 2017)

IDS (2012) distinguishes between job families and career families. Both systems group together jobs with similar characteristics, but a career family structure generally has a common pay and grading structure while a job family structure may have separate arrangements for each family. But the terms are often used interchangeably by practitioners.

4.6.6 *How do job families work?*

Each job family has its own number of levels with different pay ranges. The band/role/grade width may even vary within the job family. But in some job family structures all families have the same number of levels. Some organisations only operate job families for specific occupational groups – often those that attract a high market premium (such as IT) – while others have applied the concept to their whole workforce.

Table 4.6 Objectives for job families

Objectives	% of respondents
To map out career paths	28
To achieve more flexibility	24
To identify market groups	22
To provide for rewards to be based on personal contribution and progress	21

SOURCE: IPD (2000)

Organisations may establish their job or career families on the basis of clear functional groups – e.g. HR, IT, finance or marketing – or they may reflect broader organisational divisions, such as administration, customer services or support services. Each job or career family will then be divided vertically into levels or grades, reflecting levels of experience, knowledge, skills and/or competencies. An example given by IDS (2012) is SSI UK, which has five levels across three families – manufacturing and production, engineering and technical services and corporate functions. A feature identified by IDS of such systems is that there may be fewer levels than in traditional grading structures. Such systems may also allow greater lateral movement between job families, especially where levels are broadly comparable.

Although research by the IPD (2000) found that job family structures then existed in only 16 per cent of organisations, 17 per cent were planning to introduce them within the next two years. A high proportion of the survey respondents had fitted their job families into common broad-banded pay structures and had allocated levels in their job families by using job evaluation. A smaller proportion based their levels on competence or skill. The trend towards job families in that research carried out in 1999 has been confirmed in more recent research.

Table 4.6 summarises IPD research into the main objectives of organisations in using job families.

Research by IDS (2012) suggested that the key reasons for using job families were to ensure consistency of treatment for employees doing comparable roles, the scope available to vary pay for each group according to the market, to clarify career paths and to integrate reward with other HR aspects.

Commenting on its research, the IPD suggested that the introduction of job families into broad-banded pay structures reflected the need for organisations to find ways of demonstrating career and pay progression opportunities for staff in increasingly opaque grading systems. However, as Wright (2004) has argued, job families can be seen as divisive in organisations seeking greater teamworking between different occupational groups and may create risks of gender pay discrimination if the job families are made up predominantly of one gender or the other. If a job family approach is adopted, regular external benchmarking is required to justify paying some jobs more than others – particularly where they are broadly comparable in terms of job size and accountability.

SELF-ASSESSMENT EXERCISE

What are the benefits of a job family system and what might be the potential problems?

To summarise, the alternatives available to employers in creating a grading and pay structure are many, and each will have its own advantages and disadvantages to be considered. Employers have sought to move away from traditional grading systems based on hierarchy towards more flexible systems such as broad bands and job families. In the public services, however, there have been contrary moves towards simpler, harmonised pay structures that bring different occupational bargaining groups together on to single pay spines. The consequences of decisions about organisational structure are far-reaching, not just in relation to reward.

4.6.7 Research findings on how organisations match jobs, people and pay

The 2019 CIPD Annual Reward Survey report (Marriot and Perkins, 2019) reveals that almost all organisations cite 'knowledge and skills required' as a factor in decisions regarding pay grades; the complexity of the job and amount of judgement or decision making are also seen as important by a large number of organisations. The pace of the job, physical skills required, and scope of the role are seen as least important. Analysis of the data is summarised in Table 4.7.

The 'legal, financial, technology and other professional services' sub-sector and the voluntary sector are least likely to cite 'knowledge and skills required' as being a factor, while public sector services are most likely to do so.

The 'retail, hospitality, catering, leisure and cleaning' sub-sector are just as likely to consider the 'complexity of the job' as they are to cite 'knowledge and skills required', while other sectors, notably the public and voluntary sectors, use this much less often. The public and voluntary sectors are both more likely than others to consider the 'amount of strategy and planning' involved.

Unsurprisingly, the manufacturing sector and the 'retail, hospitality, catering, leisure and cleaning' sub-sector are more likely than any other to cite the 'physical skills required'. Within the private services sector sub-sectors, the 'impact of the job on the organisation' is seen as particularly important in the 'retail, hospitality, catering, leisure and cleaning' sub-sector but less so in the other sub-sectors. This same pattern is seen in 'responsibility for financial resources' which are cited by over half of the 'retail, hospitality, catering, leisure and cleaning' sub-sector, but around a third of the other sub-sectors.

'Knowledge and skills required' and 'complexity of the job' are decreasingly likely to be used as criteria as the organisation size increases. Conversely, the 'amount of judgement or decision-making', the 'amount of strategy or planning', 'responsibility for financial resources' and 'number of direct reports' all become more frequently used as the organisation size rises. 'Knowledge and skills required' are seen as particularly

Table 4.7 Responses to CIPD 2019 reward survey question: 'Which of the following factors does your organisation use to decide which jobs go within which pay grades/bands?'

	Knowledge and skills required	Com-plexity of the job	Amount of judgement/ decision-making	Impact of job on organisation	Amount of strategy/ planning	Responsi-bility for financial resources	Number of direct reports	Interper-sonal skills required	Pace of the job	Physical skills required	Scope of role
All	92	72	71	60	57	44	35	32	21	20	11
By sector											
Manufacturing and production	94	74	80	71	51	31	49	20	29	37	14
Private sector, of which:	91	79	64	62	49	38	29	39	25	22	16
Retail, hospitality, catering, leisure and cleaning	95	95	57	76	48	52	29	43	24	38	5
Legal, financial, technology and other professional services	86	81	62	62	51	32	27	35	30	14	16
Other private sector	92	70	68	56	48	36	30	40	22	22	20

(continued)

Table 4.7 (Continued)

	Knowledge and skills required	Com-plexity of the job	Amount of judgement/ decision-making	Impact of job on organisation	Amount of strategy/ planning	Responsi-bility for financial resources	Number of direct reports	Interper-sonal skills required	Pace of the job	Physical skills required	Scope of role
Public services	97	63	84	51	65	54	35	27	11	14	2
Voluntary, community, not-for-profit	89	64	64	60	69	56	40	31	18	9	11
By size											
SME (<250)	93	75	68	65	56	41	31	36	26	21	13
Large (250–9,999)	93	71	74	55	57	46	37	28	16	19	10
Very large (10,000+)	80	50	80	70	70	60	50	40	20	10	0
By employee category											
Management/ professional	76	50	61	48	55	41	27	10	3	3	9
Other employees	90	61	46	41	19	20	20	29	20	19	6

SOURCE: Marriot and Perkins (2019)

important for 'other' employees, where it is seen as a factor in nine-tenths of cases as opposed to only just over three-quarters for management/professional employees. The 'complexity of the job' and 'interpersonal skills required' are also cited more often for non-management/professional employees.

Factors used more often in the case of management and professional employees are the 'amount of judgement and decision making', the 'impact of the job on the organisation', the 'amount of strategy and planning' and 'responsibility for financial resources'. The 'pace of the job' and 'physical skills required' are much more common among 'other' employees while they are hardly seen as a factor for management and professional employees.

4.7 Job evaluation

As mentioned earlier, job evaluation (JE) has become the major mechanism for valuing the content of jobs or roles. Despite criticism by the 'new pay' writers as old-fashioned and bureaucratic, there is no sign that its popularity in the UK is diminishing. This is demonstrated by major JE exercises in the public services in the 1990s and 2000s – for example, in local government, the NHS and higher education. Reward consultancies, such as Korn Ferry (Hay Group), also continue to make good business from their JE guide charts. It is no panacea, however.

Acas (2014a) sum it up in terms of 'considerations and risks': making a success of any JE scheme will involve commitment by senior managers, transparency and cost as organisations will need to be able to pay for any grading structure.

Widely used as the basis for creating a grading structure, JE helps to establish the relative value of different jobs or roles within an organisation. It is informed by a process of job or role analysis, whereby the key aspects of the work are analysed. According to Hills (1989: 3–32), four basic assumptions underpin the use of JE:

- Jobs differ in terms of the various required contributions from the employee (e.g. in terms of skill, responsibility, effort etc).
- Employees will accept the criteria used to assess job worth.
- JE plans assume that equity perceptions lie in the eyes of the beholders, i.e. the employees.
- Organisations assume that equity criteria remain stable over time.

JE is primarily used to inform decisions about pay and grading, but increasingly has found other purposes. Many organisations use JE to underpin the revision of existing pay and grading structures, but it can also be a tool to assimilate new jobs into existing structures. Research by IDS (2013a) found that JE was used where there was significant change in the organisation of work, when an organisation was going through a period of rapid growth or as a 'housekeeping' exercise. Mergers of organisations were another example of JE usage when two pay structures had to be harmonised. JE was also used when skill levels changed following an upgrade or new technology was introduced. In the public sector, the major pressure for the use of JE has been equal pay legislation. IDS (2007a: 5) notes that 'One by-product of analytical schemes is that the factors they employ can be used to produce job profiles. These can then be used to show staff how their current position differs from or is similar to other roles in the organisation and how they might therefore progress to the next level. In flatter organisations, this can also be useful for encouraging employees to make lateral movements across the structure.'

DEFINITION

Job evaluation is a procedure for assessing the relative demands of jobs with a view to allocating jobs to positions within a pay structure. Job evaluation involves job analysis, the production of job descriptions, and an assessment of the 'size' of jobs (i.e. how demanding they are) so that they can be placed in rank order and divided into grades. The latter will thus consist of jobs with equivalent demands, which will receive the same basic rate of pay or be allocated to the same salary scale or pay range.

(Heery and Noon 2017)

4.8 The development of job evaluation

Given criticisms of JE by 'new pay' writers, it is worth looking at its origins and the reasons why it became so popular. Job evaluation was closely identified with the development of 'scientific management' and the rise of mass production industries (Figart, 2001). As Mahoney (1992: 338) comments, 'the concept of job was the unifying concept in the scientific management approach to organisation and management'. JE offered an apparently 'rational' management technique for distinguishing between the value of different jobs in handling the distribution of pay within the organisation.

The earliest record of job evaluation is the introduction of a job classification system by the Commonwealth Edison Company of Chicago in 1909, although even earlier, in 1902, the US Civil Service Commission had recommended the reclassification of pay rates on the basis of the 'duties performed' (Hills, 1989). In the USA, four major JE techniques had been established by 1926 – ranking, grade description, factor comparison and points factor. The points factor system of Edward Hay became the most common method, and the Hay system remains the pre-eminent JE scheme in the world today.

While JE was originally focused largely on establishing internal pay differentials, it was also viewed as a strategy for controlling pay costs (see Figart, 2001 for an interesting account of the history of JE). Edward Hay (cited in Figart 2001: 410) argued that 'job evaluation permits considerable control over salary costs'. From its inception it was also seen as a method for constraining the effects of collective bargaining on pay levels. JE provided a seemingly scientific method of allocating value to jobs and hence could counter the pressures exerted by trade unions representing particular well-organised groups of workers. On the other hand, Mahoney

(1992: 338) argues that such job-based pay structures led to the concept of 'job ownership expressed in the labor movement and collective bargaining'. Unions were therefore ambivalent about JE. JE was also seen as a means of reducing pay disparities between departments and divisions and hence lessening employee grievances and escalating wage costs through competition between groups of employees or individuals within the same enterprise.

It is interesting to note that, at the time of its introduction, economists were concerned that job evaluation would reduce the effects of the market in pay-setting and hence undermine the natural working of the labour market. While collective bargaining outcomes were considered, at the end of the day, to be susceptible to the natural pressures of the labour market, JE was not. While in recent times JE has tended to be used more for non-manual jobs than manual, it was originally seen as a device to deal with the growth of non-craft jobs as mass production replaced craft manufacture. Whereas craft workers were seen to have individual value according to their skills (i.e. the person), unskilled workers were seen as more easily dealt with on a 'job' basis. This provides an interesting context for today's criticisms of job evaluation that it rewards the 'job' rather than the 'person'.

Job evaluation grew rapidly during the Second World War, especially in the USA where a freeze on pay increases meant that the only way to obtain a pay rise was to be regraded. In the post-war period JE became an integral part of many large corporations' remuneration practices, reinforcing the internal labour market and 'lifetime' employment practices of the period. There was a further growth in the use of JE in the 1960s and 1970s. Jacques (1964) developed a method based on the theory of the 'time span of discretion', under which jobs are ranked according to the maximum period of time a person was expected to work on their own before becoming accountable to a manager.

Pritchard and Murlis (1992) make the interesting observation that the 1960s and 1970s was a period when UK government incomes policies led to a strong concern for internal equity rather than market competitiveness. Because in reality the only form of pay progression allowed on top of the incomes policy pay limit was fixed incremental progression, organisations exercised little difference in practice between high and low performers. Therefore, in many organisations pay was almost entirely JE-driven, with annual uplifts to the pay structure in line with the government-decreed incomes policy pay limit. The major way to obtain a real pay increase was to be regraded under the JE scheme.

4.9 The critique of job evaluation

In recent years, however, JE has been subjected to criticism (Livy, 2020). Critiques have come from both the normative 'new pay' literature in the USA and academic research. As mentioned earlier, however, criticism of job evaluation is not new. Criticism of JE from management writers has focused on four issues (CIPD, 2001). First, JE can be highly bureaucratic and paper-intensive, as well as inflexible, 'time-wasting' and costly. Secondly, it reinforces the concept of a rigid hierarchy that is not in accord with the ways in which de-layered and process-based organisations function. Thirdly, it inhibits flexibility in making pay and grading decisions.

Fourthly, it is inconsistent with the ways in which work is now carried out – it is important to pay for the person rather than the job.

According to Lawler (2000: 109), 'Even when job evaluation is used in conjunction with a traditional top-down approach to management, it has a number of problems. These include the fact that "job worth" can be hard to communicate and that people find the value system that underlies job worth difficult to accept because they think of *themselves* as having value to the organisation, not the work they do.' Lawler argues that the message from tying pay and benefits to job size is that higher-level individuals who hold highly evaluated jobs are the ones who matter; 'thus the key to being a success is moving to bigger and bigger jobs'. This may suit traditional hierarchical organisations but may not be appropriate where the most valuable staff in an organisation do not supervise many people and may not have responsibility for large budgets. Moreover, because job evaluation links an individual with a 'job' or 'role', it becomes difficult to change those jobs or roles if the outcome is a reduction in JE points. Staff may also see JE as a route to promotion and hence higher pay, so that regrading appeals become a constant feature of the system. Lastly, JE can create its own internal bureaucracy, with a team of staff permanently employed in keeping the JE system up to date. For Jeffery (2019: 37), while some organisations 'still rely on the notion of job evaluation, others are moving beyond simple ideas of input and output'.

The 'new pay' writers (e.g. Lawler, 1990; Mahoney, 1992; Schuster and Zingheim, 1992) generally see JE as a barrier to strategic reward and an obstacle to more variable and individual forms of reward. For these writers, internal equity is about individual performance and contribution, rather than job size. Research by McNabb and Whitfield (2001) gives some support to this critique. Using two large UK datasets – the Workplace Industrial Relations Survey and the employer Manpower – they found that there was a weak link between JE and 'high performance' work practices. Organisations using the full range of high-performance work practices were, in particular, less likely to have analytical JE schemes. Organisations that had both analytical JE and high-performance work practices had significantly worse financial performance than those that had one or the other of these, but not both.

The other critique of JE has come from an equal-pay perspective. Figart (2001: 405) argues that while JE has traditionally been about establishing pay equity, the 'process of reconciling equal pay as ideology with pre-existing gender wage disparities resulted in a narrow definition of equal work'. While JE has become the major practical tool for combating gender pay discrimination in the workplace, some writers suggest that the use of JE is problematic in dealing with equal value (or 'comparable worth' in the USA).

Research undertaken in the 1980s (Madigan and Hoover, 1986) subjected 206 job classifications to evaluation using six different JE schemes. The study found wide differences in the value allocated to the same job under the different schemes. Similarly, an experiment by Arnault et al (2001) rated the same set of 27 jobs, using three different JE schemes. The results were again different for each job. The research indicates that the choice of job evaluation method significantly affects decisions on job hierarchies and pay equity, and that attempts to promote equal value may be quite sensitive to the JE scheme chosen. Gilbert (2005), in a review of the use of JE in UK employment tribunal cases about equal pay, concludes that in some cases JE has been used as a barrier or weapon against those making such a claim.

Quaid (1993: 239), an ex-JE consultant, argues that job evaluation is in fact a 'myth' because 'it is a process based on widely held beliefs that cannot be tested objectively'. An article by Gilbert (2012: 137), reviewing 40 years of UK equal pay legislation, concludes that 'the standards for selecting job evaluation and the obstacles of introducing job evaluation have significantly changed over the period, leaving little promise of an extension of its use to achieve equal pay'.

SELF-ASSESSMENT EXERCISE

Thinking about the various objectives of job evaluation described above, which of these objectives do you think is most important for (1) employers and (2) employees? Are they the same?

4.10 The types of job evaluation

As already mentioned, there are fundamentally two types of JE – analytical and non-analytical – but there are various types of scheme under both headings (Livy, 2020). Non-analytical schemes evaluate 'whole jobs' as opposed to analytical schemes that break down jobs into factors or component elements such as the points factor method. Non-analytical schemes may use simply job titles or simple job descriptions to compare job content. While such schemes are simpler, more flexible and cheaper to implement than analytical schemes, they are also more open to charges of subjectivity and inconsistency, mainly because it is difficult for the job analyst to distinguish between the job content and the performance of the jobholder. For this reason, non-analytical JE schemes are not generally defensible against equal-pay challenges.

Analytical schemes, on the other hand, are seen as a potential defence against claims for equal pay for work of equal value because such schemes are seen as more rigorous in their analysis of job content, but this would depend on the validity of the methods used. Analytical JE schemes can still be challenged on the basis that they are in some way flawed in the factors used.

4.10.1 Non-analytical schemes

The main types of non-analytical JE scheme, according to Armstrong and Baron (1995), include the following:

- job ranking;
- paired comparison ranking;
- job classification;
- internal benchmarking.

These will be considered in turn.

Job ranking

Job ranking is the simplest form of JE and consists of comparing jobs with one another to produce a rank order or hierarchy. As Armstrong and Baron (1995) comment, in one sense all JE schemes are about ranking jobs, but the difference between non-analytical and analytical schemes is that the latter attempt to quantify the judgments made. A list of criteria may be used in job ranking, but the weight that individual job analysts give to these criteria will differ, creating problems of consistency and uniformity.

Paired comparison ranking

An alternative to simple job ranking is a system known as 'paired comparisons'. This is similar to job ranking but involves an element of points-scoring to give an indication of the relationship between two different jobs. Pairs of benchmark jobs are compared with points being allocated to each role according to whether the job is of

Figure 4.7 Example of a paired comparison ranking form

Company: XYZ Ltd		Division						Headquarters					
Evaluator		Name: J. Smith											
		Job title: Company secretary											
Job letter		a	b	c	d	e	f	g	h	i	j		
Job letter	JOB TITLES	Accounts assistant	Bought ledger controller	Computer operator	Customer service officer	Marketing assistant	Personnel officer	Postroom assistant	Receptionist	Sales executive	Secretary	TOTAL SCORE	OVERALL RANKING
A	Accounts assistant		0	1	0	1	0	2	2	0	0	6	8
B	Bought ledger controller	2		2	2	2	0	2	2	0	2	14	3
C	Computer operator	1	0		1	1	0	2	2	0	0	7	7
D	Customer service officer	2	0	1		2	0	2	1	0	1	9	4=
E	Marketing assistant	1	0	1	0		0	2	2	0	2	8	6
F	Personnel officer	2	2	2	2	2		2	2	0	2	16	2
G	Postroom assistant	0	0	0	0	0	0		1	0	0	1	10
H	Receptionist	0	0	0	1	0	0	1		0	0	2	9
I	Sales executive	2	2	2	2	2	2	2	2		2	18	1
J	Secretary	2	0	2	1	0	0	2	2	0		9	4=

SOURCE: Armstrong and Baron (1995: 57)

less, similar or more importance than the other (i.e. with a score of 0, 1 or 2 accordingly). The scores for each job are then added up to produce an indicative rank order. Such paired comparisons may be used in small organisations but would not provide an effective defence against an equal-pay challenge as there is no detailed evidence of why one job is considered more important or demanding than another.

Job classification

Job classification begins from a different perspective. Unlike job ranking and paired comparisons, where the grading structure emerges from the spread of job levels identified through the JE exercise, under job classification the grading structure is designed first, along with job descriptions for each grade or level. Several representative (benchmark) jobs are then compared against these job descriptions to validate the structure, and the remaining jobs are then slotted into the predefined grades. Unlike job ranking and paired comparisons, job classification does lay down basic principles for comparing jobs based on the skills, effort and responsibility laid down in the job descriptors. But, unlike analytical schemes, it does not quantify these differences. The problem, again, is that too much subjectivity in deciding the level of job is left in the hands of the analyst. For this reason, such schemes would not normally provide a defence against an equal-pay challenge.

In the past some proprietary job classification schemes were available; for example, the one provided for clerical and administrative staffs by the Institute for Administrative Management (IAM). But the development of equal-pay law has led to these being no longer considered commercially viable.

Internal benchmarking

Armstrong and Baron (1995) comment that internal benchmarking has never been dignified as a formal type in the textbooks on job evaluation but is probably what people often do through intuition when valuing jobs. It is about comparing the job under review with any similar internal benchmark jobs that have already been properly graded. The job is then slotted into the appropriate grade. This comparison is usually made on a 'whole job' basis without analysing the job factor by factor, although this fact leaves the decision open to challenge under equal-pay law.

In some ways internal benchmarking is like job classification in that the job is compared against an existing grading structure, but it is different in that the existing grading structure is likely to be based on analytical methods. Armstrong and Baron (1995) say that internal benchmarking is perhaps the most used method of informal or semi-formal JE. It is sometimes used after a formal analytical JE process has been completed to slot in similar jobs to grades without having to evaluate every single job.

4.10.2 Analytical schemes

As mentioned earlier, the key difference between analytical and non-analytical schemes is that the former breaks down individual jobs into component parts rather than using the 'whole job' as in the latter.

The main types of analytical JE scheme are as follows:

- factor comparison;
- points-factor rating;
- competence-based job evaluation.

These will be analysed in turn.

Factor comparison

The factor comparison method was one of the earliest JE schemes invented (by Eugene Benge in 1941). In a traditional factor comparison scheme, jobs are broken down into their component elements or 'factors' under five headings: mental requirements, skill requirements, physical requirements, responsibilities and working conditions. The main difference between traditional factor comparison schemes and points-factor schemes is that, in the former, monetary values are related directly to factor scores. Under the points-factor method, only points are attached to factors.

Traditional factor comparison schemes are little used today but a variant – 'graduated factor comparison' – is often used in equal-value cases. This variant requires comparisons to be made on a graduated scale (e.g. low, medium, high), but the factors are not weighted. This can be especially useful when comparing just a few jobs (as in an equal-value case), and in some ways is a rather more sophisticated form of non-analytical job ranking.

Factor comparison entails comparing an individual job directly with another in terms of a defined factor. The rate of pay of each benchmark job is broken down and distributed among the factors, based on the relative importance of the factors. This means that the selected benchmark jobs used to arrive at the price of the various factors must be properly paid to start with.

Another method is analytical factor comparison. This technique compares the content of jobs against a set of descriptions for each factor. These are arranged in order of difficulty, but with no number score, allowing the job grade to be deduced from the overall results.

Points-factor rating

The points-factor rating method was the first quantitative form of JE and was invented by Lott in 1924. Many standalone, internally designed JE schemes are of this type. Points-factor rating breaks down each job into several factors, which are scored against a numerical scale. The sum of the factor scores gives the total job size.

The method works as follows. A number of job factors are selected and defined (e.g. skill, responsibility and effort). Such factors must be common to all jobs in the organisation or to clusters of jobs in job families. The levels or degrees to which each factor is present in the organisation are then defined. Each factor may be assigned a weighting, and this is translated into a maximum point score that can be given to each factor. The sum of the scores for each factor indicates the maximum score that can be given to any job.

The maximum points for each factor are then distributed between the levels or degrees of each factor. Each level thus has its own score or range of points. Benchmark jobs are then analysed in terms of the factors, and the level at which each of the factors is present in the benchmark jobs is determined by reference to the factor plan. Scores are given for each factor in line with the factor plan and added together to produce a total score for each of the benchmark jobs. This in turn produces a rank order of jobs. A grading structure is then developed from the rank order, with each grade defined in terms of the range of points attached. The job grades are then priced according to external market rates and/or existing rates of pay and relativities. The job content for each factor is usually described, and the job analyst selects the factor level most appropriate to the job.

STUDENT EXERCISE

Look at the examples of factor plans below. Why do you think the public sector schemes generally have more factors than the proprietary schemes? Which do you think is better, simplicity or the full range of potential criteria?

To summarise, points-factor rating has three main components:

- the factors;
- the number of levels in each factor;
- the score for each factor level.

The choice and number of factors is crucial to the success of the scheme. The number of factors will depend to a large extent on the type of organisation and the range of occupations, but the minimum number would be three and the maximum probably fewer than 20. The types of factors used will vary from scheme to scheme, but they should cover all the significant features of the workforce, be acceptable in terms of equal-value considerations and avoid double-counting, omission or combining of features.

The EHRC (2014) has published guidance on the factors possibly open to gender bias. For example, length of service, experience, heavy lifting and physical hazards tend to favour male jobs while caring, dexterity and typing/keyboard skills will tend to favour females.

The number of levels for each factor is also an issue. Having the same number of levels for each factor may not be appropriate. Some factors just have a larger range of levels to be analysed and measured.

Competence-based job evaluation

Skills- and competency-based pay schemes emerged during the late 1980s as one strand of the movement from industrial relations-oriented people management to one driven by the HRM paradigm. One key proposition put forward was that

Table 4.8 Some examples of points-factor JE schemes

Some examples of factor plans

Hay Guide Chart-Profile Method

- I Know-how
- I Problem-solving
- I Accountability

KPMG Equate

- I Accountability
- I Job impact
- I Thinking demands
- I Communication demands
- I Knowledge, skills and experience

PA

- I Judgement
- I Planning and management
- I Communication
- I Job impact
- I Theoretical knowledge and application
- I Skills acquisition and practice
- I Effect of errors
- I Manual dexterity and effort

PricewaterhouseCoopers

- I Responsibility
- I Knowledge
- I Mental skills
- I Physical skills
- I Environmental conditions

Higher Education Role Analysis

- I Communication
- I Teamwork and motivation
- I Liaison and networking
- I Service delivery
- I Decision-making processes and outcomes
- I Planning and organising resources
- I Initiative and problem-solving
- I Analysis and research
- I Sensory and physical demands
- I Work environment
- I Pastoral care and welfare

(continued)

Table 4.8 (Continued)

- I Team development
- I Teaching and learning support
- I Knowledge and experience

NHS Agenda for Change

- I Communication and relationship skills
- I Knowledge, training and experience
- I Analytical and judgement skills
- I Planning and organisational skills
- I Physical skills
- I Responsibilities for patient/client care
- I Responsibilities for policy and service development
- I Responsibilities for financial and physical resources
- I Responsibilities for human resources
- I Responsibilities for information resources
- I Responsibilities for research and development
- I Freedom to act
- I Physical effort
- I Emotional effort
- I Working conditions

*Local Government Single Status**

- I Knowledge and skills
- I Effort demands
- I Responsibilities
- I Environmental demands

perceived weaknesses with the application of job evaluation methodologies was an inability to match more 'flexible' business, organisation and employment environments. The proposition was therefore to shift the focus from jobs to people – whose contribution was to be evaluated and rewarded according to the skills and competencies that they can demonstrate. Pritchard and Murlis (1993) argue that the appeal of such approaches is that they offset the limitations of traditional pay structures and their analytical foundations by paying greater attention to the importance of the people who occupy – and contribute or perform in – jobs within the workplace. This shifts recognition towards acquisition of new capabilities (competencies and skills) to make job flexibility and multitasking work in practice.

The argument attracted three principal lines of critique:

1 Organisational effectiveness is ultimately concerned with outputs. There is a risk that an over-emphasis on employee competencies and skills could encourage an 'input culture' at odds with the requirements of organisations competing for customers and/or making use of charitable or publicly funded resources to meet corporate aims.

2. A policy of evaluation based on acquisition of skills and competencies is likely to raise expectations that pay levels will increase, raising concerns about increasing organisational costs. As a minimum, it puts a strong onus on managements to ensure that the skills and competencies paid for are the ones required. In fast-moving or 'agile' organisational environments there is a danger that time to develop these capabilities will result in potential obsolescence as the demand moves on, but with the locked-in cost burden of employee expectations.
3. Comparability is challenging. Much of the work to develop skills/competency based analytical evaluation schemes has been with relatively homogenous groups. In cases where the population is not homogeneous it is necessary to break it down into sub-segments or 'families'. And while skills/competency assessment and grade/salary progression may be achieved within these groups, the approach is less conducive to making inter-group comparisons (say, in an industrial setting comparison between plant operation families and craftsperson families); comparing groups where skills/competency based evaluation applies and those elsewhere in an organisation subject to more traditional job evaluation practices; and increasingly significant as organisations move beyond internally oriented employment markets to external comparisons for the purpose of pay regulation, say, between different locations.

Competence-based evaluation in practice has tended to be associated with setting and regulating the basis for progression through broad-banded salary structures.

4.11 The prevalence of job evaluation in the UK

Despite criticism of job evaluation beginning in the 1990s from both the 'new pay' writers and feminist critics, job evaluation continues to be commonly used in the UK. Although the 2011 Workplace Employee Relations Survey did not ask a question about the use of job evaluation, the 2004 survey found that 25 per cent of workplaces with 25 or more employees had a job evaluated pay structure. It established that such schemes were more common in larger workplaces and organisations, workplaces that were part of a wider organisation and workplaces in the public sector (Kersley et al, 2006 and Table 4.9). Three-fifths of workplaces in the public administration sector had formal job evaluation schemes compared with one-tenth in the private construction sector. JE was also more likely to be found in unionised workplaces and in workplaces where most staff were female. There was also a strong correlation between the use of JE and the presence of formal policies on equal opportunities or managing diversity.

Almost three-fifths of the workplaces with JE schemes used analytical points-rating schemes. These were particularly common in larger workplaces and organisations, and within the public sector.

The WERS survey in 1998 did not contain questions on job evaluation but earlier versions did, allowing some longitudinal analysis of trends. Between 1980 and 1990 there was a rise in the prevalence of JE from 21 per cent of workplaces to 26 per cent. A key change since 1990, however, has been the continuing increase in JE in the public

Table 4.9 Presence of a JE scheme, by workplace characteristics

	Job evaluation scheme (% of workplaces)
All workplaces	20
Workplace size	
10–24 employees	17
25–49 employees	22
50–99 employees	23
100–199 employees	35
200–499 employees	36
500 or more employees	54
All workplaces with 25 or more employees	25
Organisation status	
Standalone workplace	7
Part of a larger organisation	27
Organisation size	
10–99 employees	9
100–999 employees	21
1,000–9,999 employees	30
10,000 employees or more	34
Sector of ownership	
Private	16
Public	42
Industry	
Manufacturing	14
Electricity, gas and water	(43)
Construction	10
Wholesale and retail	17
Hotels and restaurants	13
Transport and communications	15
Financial intermediation	42
Other business services	16
Public administration	59
Education	25
Health	28
Other community services	23
Union recognition	
No union recognised	12
At least one union recognised	41

SOURCE: Kersley et al (2006: 245)

sector (up from 27 per cent in 1990 to 44 per cent in 2004). This has been mirrored by some decline in the use of JE by the private sector (down from around a quarter of all workplaces in 1990 to a fifth in 2004) (Kersley et al, 2006).

Research for the Office of Manpower Economics on private sector pay systems (OME, 2014) found that job evaluation was used by 25 per cent of respondents to a survey but it was more common for those with incremental scales (36 per cent) than those with salary ranges (21 per cent).

4.12 Choosing a job evaluation scheme

In choosing which type of JE scheme to use, organisations have some choice. The main options are buying 'off the shelf' from a provider of one of the proprietary schemes (e.g. Korn Ferry/Hay) or designing one's own, although there is the possibility of adapting an existing proprietary scheme as well. In recent times there has been a trend towards schemes specifically designed for a particular sector, especially in the UK public sector. Examples include the NHS Agenda for Change scheme, the HERA scheme used in much of higher education and the local government 'Single Status' scheme. All these sector-specific schemes had to deal with issues arising from the harmonisation of different occupational 'bargaining' groups on to single pay spines. Because of the range of jobs and roles covered, it was felt that 'off the shelf' schemes would not be able to reflect the wide range and scope of the organisations' functions.

More importantly, remedying cases of gender discrimination was central to these exercises, and again it was felt that only a bespoke approach would work in dealing with this issue. In the NHS, the use of the Agenda for Change scheme is mandatory, but in both local government and higher education organisations are free to choose their own schemes. In some cases, this has meant that proprietary schemes have been selected. Berrocal et al (2018) carried out research to identify empirical evidence regarding possible differences resulting from the influence the evaluation method used. Their conclusion was that, comparatively, methods classify and order roles in a very similar way (and their research was in line with prior studies). However, variation was perceived when drilling deeper into the data, depending on factors used and weightings attached to them when JE is applied to jobs located at the extremes of grade or band boundaries. Berrocal et al (2018) argue as a result that when choosing a JE method not only the objectives of the exercise but also the characteristics of the organisation need to be accounted for. Overall, they argue that to ensure acceptance of JE outcomes by groups most affected, especially when evaluations are taking place in the context of organisational changes – e.g. automation, flexibilisation, virtualisation – such employees need to be actively involved in the JE process. In other words, 'The administrative and political realities of each organisation' must be considered (Berrocal 2018: 127).

A first stage in any process of selecting a JE scheme is the establishment of a project team to assess the project, set the timetable and compare the various schemes available. The information collected by the project team can be used to make informed decisions about which product is most appropriate for the organisation or indeed whether a bespoke scheme needs to be designed in-house.

Project teams will often include representatives of the workforce, as well as HR staff. In unionised environments, trade union representatives are often invited to join, but even in non-union environments it makes sense to involve staff from various levels of the organisation. Their expertise can help in making the right decisions about the choice of scheme. Also, such staff participation helps achieve staff 'buy-in', building confidence in and assisting acceptance of the final outcomes from the scheme. The degree of staff involvement will vary from organisation to organisation, but the larger the project the larger the chances of staff involvement.

Clearly, if staff are involved, they will need to be given time away from their normal duties to take part in the process. This may mean providing facility time to staff representatives and may also suggest that realistic timescales are required. In addition to the actual project team (of which there may be sub-committees dealing with specific tasks), there may be a steering committee of senior managers to monitor and oversee the process.

Organisations often use external HR consultants to assist either in the selection of an appropriate JE scheme or in the design of an in-house scheme. Acas (2014a) has produced a useful guide to job evaluation while the EHRC (2014) has produced guidance on equal pay that covers issues relating to job evaluation.

STUDENT EXERCISE

Thinking about the grading system in your own organisation or one with which you are familiar, what would be the major issues in taking a decision to select a JE scheme?

4.12.1 The design stage

Deciding on the factors to be used to evaluate jobs or roles is the key decision. As mentioned earlier, this is increasingly important if the scheme is to satisfy the requirements of equal-value legislation. According to IDS (2007a), the factors used in JE schemes can be divided into four broad categories:

- Inputs – what contributions are jobholders required to make?
- Processes – how are jobs done?
- Accountabilities – for whom is the jobholder responsible?
- Impact – what is the job's overall influence on the organisation's activities?

As shown in Table 4.8 summarising the range of factors used in different schemes, the number of factors can be as few as two or as many as 15. Often broad categories are broken down into sub-factors.

Organisations use a number of criteria in making a choice about the number and types of factors to be used. Factors need to be measurable, comprehensive, not unfairly discriminatory and balanced across the whole job population covered. IDS (2007a) says that employers will need to decide whether the factors to be used will help reward the inputs and outputs identified, and whether they will be happy to live with any consequences in terms of potential pay costs.

To make the factors clear to both staff and evaluators, there is usually a set of descriptions alongside each factor to explain the criteria to be used in judging them.

As mentioned earlier, factors may be weighted so that some are more important than others. These are usually expressed as percentages, which are used to calculate the total scores for each job or role. This may mean deciding whether a factor is 'essential' or 'desirable' for the job. If an organisation chooses to use a proprietary scheme the weightings will already be decided in many cases, but in the case of 'in-house' schemes decisions about weighting will usually be taken by the project team or steering group. It is at this stage in the process that the potential for gender discrimination is most apparent. If the factors themselves or the weighting applied to them is biased in favour of male occupations, the scheme may well not meet the test of an Employment Tribunal.

4.12.2 *Job or role analysis*

Having decided on the shape of the scheme, the factors to be used and the weighting (if any) to be applied to them, the next stage is beginning analysis of jobs or roles. Job or role analysis is a methodology for developing an understanding of the content of a job or role. Its outcome has traditionally been a job description, but increasingly it is a role profile.

DEFINITION

Job analysis is the process of analysing the content of jobs in order to guide recruitment and selection, identify training needs, or for the purposes of job evaluation.

(Heery and Noon, 2017)

The difference between job descriptions and role profiles is as follows.

A **job description** typically provides an overview of the job and its place in the organisational structure, a detailed description of the duties and responsibilities of the job and a commentary matching the various JE factor headings. Job descriptions, however, require regular updating to reflect any changes in the work of the jobholder as they are fundamentally prescriptive documents detailing what the employer and employee expect to be accomplished. In that sense, job descriptions have a quasi-contractual nature, and some writers have commented that this tends to limit employee activity to the contract, rather than encouraging employees to work flexibly 'beyond contract'.

A **role profile**, in contrast, is seen as more flexible in that it perhaps provides a more 'psychological' approach. Role profiles are more about the type of personality required for the task and are more focused on outputs and inputs, the knowledge and skills required and expected behaviours. As Armstrong et al (2003: 94) comment, the concept of role focuses on 'what is needed to deliver organisation objectives, by setting out the behavioural expectations as well as the expected outcomes, rather than the minutiae of how the work needs to be done'.

An advantage of a role profile is that it does not need regular change, as there is no detailed description of how the work should be done. Role profiles are much more about setting out how the employee is expected to contribute and behave, rather than the detailed requirements of the particular job. The use of role profiles also enables a more generic approach, reducing the number of documents that need to be kept – unlike job descriptions, where there might be a separate document for every job in the organisation.

Such job or role analysis is used not just for job evaluation purposes but for a range of other HR applications, including job-matching against the external market, pay structure design, recruitment and staff development.

There are a number of techniques for conducting job or role analysis. These include interviews with jobholders and supervisors, observation of work activity or the completion of job-analysis questionnaires by the jobholder. Interviewing jobholders, though the most thorough way of collecting information, is onerous and time-consuming (IDS, 2007a). For this reason, the method is often limited to particularly complex jobs or roles or where only a few jobs or roles are being considered. Instead, employers are increasingly using questionnaires to gather information, often in line with the factor plan being used in the JE scheme. This more quantitative approach has the advantage that large amounts of information can be collected rapidly and in a consistent manner. Its disadvantage, as with other quantitative research techniques, is that it may miss subtle differences between jobs or roles and there is reduced opportunity to clarify ambiguities in responses. Of course, if there are existing job descriptions or role profiles these can be used in the JE exercise, but it is essential that such documents are up to date, and they may not be designed to match the factor plan.

While in smaller organisations it may be possible to evaluate all posts, in larger organisations it is usual that only a series of 'benchmark' or typical jobs or roles are analysed. Once these have been evaluated, other jobs or roles are compared with the benchmark job descriptions or role profiles and matched to the appropriate level. It is therefore vital that the benchmarks cover a fair range of jobs or roles and be selected to avoid any bias, especially in terms of gender and other protected characteristics.

STUDENT EXERCISE

What is the difference between a job description and a role profile? Which would you say is the method used to describe grade content in an organisation you know?

4.12.3 Scoring the jobs or roles

Once the information about the benchmark jobs and roles has been collected and validated – usually by a supervisor and/or senior manager – the evaluations can be completed. If an analytical JE approach is being used, 'scores' or 'ranks' are usually assigned to each of the factors. These scores are then analysed using relevant software to calculate a total score for the job or role. According to the total scores, all the jobs can be ranked to produce a 'league table' of jobs or roles in the organisation. Using software usually makes the calculation of scores very easy as these can instantaneously produce the weightings and apply any complex algorithms required for different factors.

The next stage is to set grade or band boundaries around this hierarchy of jobs or roles. It is usual in any point-factor scheme for scores to cluster around certain points in the hierarchy. These usually indicate where the grade or band 'break points' should be. Today most organisations use pay-modelling software to review the different outcomes and costs for different grade boundaries. Some organisations may opt to set the grade or band boundaries first and then allocate jobs/roles based on their scores or by comparing them to generic role profiles for each grade or band.

This stage is most important as where the grade or band boundaries fall can have a dramatic effect on the cost implications of any new grading structure for the employer. This depends on the number of employees that will benefit from the new structure (referred to as 'green circled') and the number who will be disadvantaged (referred to as 'red circled'). By moving grade or band boundaries, the numbers of these 'green' and 'red' circled staff can be reduced or increased. Clearly, the more 'green' outcomes there are, the higher the likely costs as these staff will have to be promoted or moved up the grade. But 'red circled' staff are also problematic. Apart from any motivational issues associated with being 'downgraded', there is usually a period of pay protection for these employees, which can also be costly. Keeping the number of red and green circles to a minimum, with most staff moving across on their existing level, is clearly the objective for many employers.

Once a grading structure has been agreed, the next stage is to allocate pay ranges to each grade or band. These are often set in line with external market rate reference points. Where a proprietary JE scheme is used, one advantage may be that the consultant may be able to provide such reference points from their own pay information database. In other circumstances, employers may well need to conduct an external pay benchmarking exercise to decide on the grade or role minima and maxima. In some of the large-scale JE exercises in the UK public services, there has been a pay spine of incremental points against which organisations have been able to plot their grade boundaries.

4.12.4 The implementation stage

Once the JE outcomes and any new grading scheme have been agreed, the final stage is implementation. The big problem here is that there will undoubtedly be winners and losers from any JE exercise. Given the fact that most employees are particularly sensitive to their place in the organisational hierarchy, and that any changes may impact on longer-term earnings potential (including for pension benefits accrual), changes in their rank or place in the hierarchy of jobs/roles can be very disturbing. It is at this stage that JE ceases to be a 'technical' exercise, and the employee relations aspects of reward come to the fore. All the skills of reward practitioners have to be deployed to handle the disappointments that may result from a JE exercise.

The key issues here involve communication of the results to staff, some protection arrangements for those downgraded, and the avenue for individual appeals against the results. Many organisations stress the importance of openness and transparency when carrying out a JE exercise (IDS, 2007a). Often staff representatives are directly involved in the process alongside HR and other managers. But the amount of information that is shared with the workforce varies. It is usual for staff to be told about why the exercise is happening; what and whom it will involve; when it will take place and when results will be expected; the implications for staff; and any appeals process. Individual members of staff may be given their overall JE score, although in some cases they will only be told in which grade they have been placed. It is rare for employers to give out individual factor scores as these are seen as both too complex and potentially contentious where an individual just misses a grade by a few points.

Communication

The main methods of communication with employees are those usually utilised in the workplace, for example in-house magazines, email bulletins, staff presentations and briefings by managers and supervisors, help desks, videos and written guidance often posted to organisation intranets. Line managers need to be especially well-briefed to be able to explain any individual grading decision. It is usual to write to all staff individually with their own result.

Upgrading, downgrading and pay protection

Staff who are upgraded ('green circled') in the JE scheme are usually moved into the most appropriate pay band for the score achieved but at the minimum point of the scale (unless the grades overlap, and the individual is already within the next grade range). There is usually a date agreed when all staff are assimilated to the new structure.

The situation with downgraded employees ('red circled') is more difficult. Generally, employers guarantee that nobody will receive an immediate pay cut because of job evaluation. Those jobs found to have been over-graded are usually moved down to the new grade, but their pay level is protected for a time. During this period of protection, employees may be encouraged to undergo training and development to ensure that they can meet the needs of their old grade (by expanding their duties or role) and hence be reinstated in their old grade. Normally pay is protected at the old pay level for a period of years, usually no more than three. Protection may involve a pay freeze, or it may allow for cost-of-living increases but no pay progression within the grade. If, after the protection period expires, the employee has been unable to be redeployed or upgraded, they will revert to the salary of the grade they were originally allocated to under the JE exercise. Because there is a risk that indefinite pay protection agreements may become discriminatory over time, indefinite pay protection arrangements are generally considered to be contrary to good practice and should be for as short a time as possible, but each case will depend on circumstances, details of which may only be resolved through judgements in legal cases.

Figure 4.8 Job evaluation process flowchart

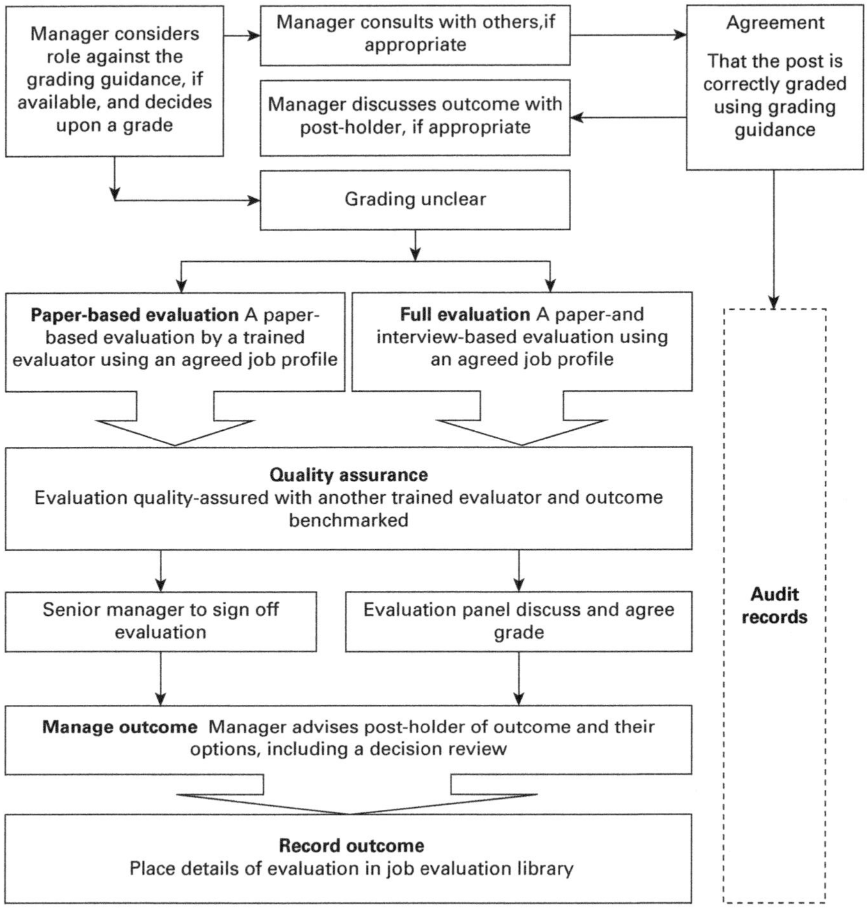

Appeals

Natural justice dictates that individuals should be able to appeal against a JE decision. A formal process is normally established whereby an employee can appeal against the grade or banding allocated to them. Certain guidelines normally exist to control this process. Appeals may only be possible if the individual can prove that there was something wrong with their job or role description, or because the process was implemented unfairly. A deadline for appeals is usually set. As with other grievance procedures, the appeals process usually starts with an informal stage of a meeting between the individual and their line manager and an HR officer. At this stage, misunderstandings can be cleared up and minor complaints dealt with. The next stage is normally a formal appeals panel, chaired by an independent manager. Where an appeal is successful the job or role is usually re-evaluated by a different analyst or scoring panel.

> **STUDENT EXERCISE**
>
> Make a list of the key issues to consider when implementing a JE scheme. Rank these in the order you consider to be most important.

4.13 Aligning pay with the market

As discussed at the beginning of the chapter, there is a continuing tension within organisations between the internal need for equity and the demands of the external market for labour. On the one hand, a pay structure needs to be fair, consistent and transparent in terms of the internal ranking of jobs if it is to satisfy employees. On the other hand, this equity and rationality is not normally reflected in the external labour market. In the external market, the value of jobs is much more likely to reflect the supply of, and demand for, different skills and the relative power of different occupational groups to control the price of their labour. As mentioned earlier in the book, such factors change over time and may be subject to subjective perceptions. Even where employees organise themselves into trade unions to enforce equity upon employers, the pressures of the labour market will often dictate the relative power of different unions and different bargaining groups.

In this section we consider how organisations manage this tension and what sources of information they use as evidence to support their decisions. While employers often refer to the 'market rate', really there is no such thing. While economists may speak of the point where supply and demand curves meet and the market-clearing rate is set, there may be a number of 'market rates' for the same job. As Armstrong (2012: 178) states, 'People often refer to the market rate, but it is a much more elusive concept than it seems.'

Organisations can respond to the demands of the external market in various ways. In Chapter 2, we discussed the important concept of the 'internal labour market' and how employers may seek to protect themselves from the vagaries of the external market. Prior to the 1980s, the relative global economic stability meant that many organisations, especially larger ones, could defend themselves from external competition for their labour by creating strong incentives for staff to remain loyal. These incentives included 'lifetime careers', strong grading and career development structures, pay and benefits systems that rewarded service and loyalty, and the development of firm-specific skills that were not easily transferable to other employers.

From the 1980s, however, the much more competitive global economic environment has weakened such systems so that today much more emphasis is placed on 'employability' than 'lifetime employment'; reward systems are linked to individual performance and acquisition of skills rather than service; and pay levels are benchmarked against external comparators rather than internal equity.

Market pricing of jobs involves collecting pay and benefits data for equivalent jobs to establish their market rate or price, the speed at which rates are changing and the direction of any changes. In considering the external market for a particular job, employers must decide on the segment of the labour market in which such jobs are to be found. In general, there are three main segments:

- the immediate local labour market surrounding the workplace (the town or suburb);
- the regional labour market (the geographical region or travel-to-work zone);
- the national (or, indeed, international) market.

In general, lower-level jobs (e.g. manual and clerical) are found in the local labour market; medium-level jobs (e.g. administrative and technical posts) in the regional market; and senior jobs (senior managers and the professions) in the national or international market. This is a generalisation, of course, and some industries recruit their manual workers from much wider labour markets (e.g. construction and hospitality workers are highly mobile, even across national frontiers). Employers also distinguish between sectors and industries as the same role may be paid differently in different contexts. Again, it is more likely that sectoral data will be more important for some jobs than others. Some occupations are transferable across sectoral or industry boundaries while others only exist in particular types of workplaces. The size of the organisations compared will also be an important issue in benchmarking.

The advantages of market-based pay are that it allows employers to respond flexibly to changes in the labour market and to target pay according to external value. It can be particularly appropriate where organisations adopt a job or career family structure, and therefore need to apply different levels of pay to different occupational groups. Research on pay structures (OME, 2014) found a clear difference in practice between those organisations using 'spot rates', where 93 per cent used market rates, those using salary ranges (86 per cent) and those using incremental scales (56 per cent). This survey found that the majority of respondents who used market rates set the rate at the midpoint of the pay range. However, those using incremental scales tended to set their rates higher up the scale, so it took longer for employees to reach their market rate than in those organisations those using pay ranges. This largely reflected the fact that most organisations using incremental scales tended to start employees at the bottom of the career scale and progress them to the fully competent rate over several years.

But linking pay too closely to market comparisons may be problematic. It can undermine internal relativities and teamworking across different occupations. It can also break down harmonised pay structures and can lack transparency. Following the market can also create an upward spiral in pay as employers compete to stay 'ahead of the pack'. Not least, such systems can create very real problems of unequal pay where external values for occupations simply reinforce traditional pay gaps.

It should also be remembered that the market is only one consideration when setting pay levels (see Chapter 3). External comparisons may be irrelevant if either labour turnover reveals no problem with recruitment and retention or if the employer's ability to pay more is limited anyway by the financial resources available.

Six ways of differentiating between different groups of employees to match the market are described by OME (2006):

- interim ad hoc payments for specific groups;
- market supplements (this is most common in the public sector);

- separate pay structures for different groups of staff;
- job or career family structures;
- skills-based approaches whereby organisations address skill shortages by developing their own staff;
- using grading structures and/or actively encouraging grade drift (i.e. regrading staff where there are recruitment and retention issues).

KEY ISSUES IN REWARD MANAGEMENT 4.2

Why we need to overhaul our approach to compensation

It's time to retire unfair 'methods' of pay and reward in favour of ideas that fit how 21st-century employees want to work, says Josh Bersin

Attracting the new people we need, as well as keeping the ones we already have, often comes down to the compensation we're prepared to offer them. In 95 per cent of organisations, the answer almost certainly centres around outdated concepts like 'salary bands' and 'job levels' – ideas established decades ago that simply aren't a good fit for the complexities of today's employment landscape.

This is because corporate pay practices have not caught up with the new world of work. This issue comes to light in recent research my team carried out that highlights how broken the pay and benefits model is right now. For example, we found pay and rewards are now the top drivers of employee experience, with 44 per cent of workers believing they are underpaid, but a mere 5 per cent of organisations have a defined clear strategy for implementing a skills-based pay regime.

What's really important about that last finding is that the firms that do have a defined strategy in place for skills-based pay are twice as likely to innovate.

The 'total rewards' concept is no longer fit for purpose. We have to totally rethink compensation. The way we're going to achieve this is to replace the 'total rewards' concept line managers think is the only way to execute promotions and pay grades. In a total rewards model, every job has a company secret 'level'. Within that level, there is a salary band that employees advance through via a performance management process until they reach the top.

The issue is that while we continue to rely on this old linear process, the world of work is completely changing around us. We are seeing massive demand for enhanced employee wellbeing, extended benefits and flexible work arrangements.

There are also big skills gaps as new technologies and business models are invented. We have to pay premium compensation to attract individuals with those rare skills, but this poses a problem for resourcing and can leave existing employees feeling undervalued.

We've created a landscape riddled with inequities and inconsistencies in pay. As a result, the total rewards system is at the point of collapse.

The benefits of 'systemic rewards'

Fortunately, there is a new, super-rational and data-driven successor waiting in the wings, which we term 'systemic rewards'. A systemic rewards philosophy better reflects evolving workforce requirements and balances pay equity and pay for performance. Our research has revealed that organisations embracing this approach are 3.1 times more likely to excel in innovation and 2.4 times more likely to be acknowledged as a great place to work compared to businesses still stuck on total rewards.

Under a systemic rewards approach that emphasises proper implementation of pay for performance, we have found that organisations are 2.7 times more likely to engage and retain their key people effectively. The 9 per cent of organisations that excel in this area also enjoy Glassdoor ratings of almost 15 per cent above average.

These ideas emerge from conversations with systemic rewards pioneers we spoke to, including Salesforce, Schneider Electric, American Airlines and Unilever. But how do you catch up? It requires concerted effort and close collaboration with colleagues from L&D, your talent acquisition team, your equality, diversity and inclusion specialists, and your employee experience people.

Implementing a systemic rewards approach that truly aligns with a company's goals and values requires a strong philosophical foundation starting in the C-Suite. It is essential to address challenging but necessary questions such as: 'How do we define and measure performance here? How are we going to communicate performance metrics and goals clearly across the organisation so people feel that it's fair?'

Clearly, moving beyond total rewards needs a comprehensive discussion about what performance truly entails within your environment. That conversation needs to extend beyond performance management and delve into the question of what aspects of performance we need to be rewarding: Collaboration? Innovation? Profitability? Some other facet of contribution?

While the transition to systemic rewards may present challenges, it is nonetheless essential for modern organisations to make the move. 1970s pay and benefits structures just won't meet the needs of today's workforce, nor the complexities of today's business landscape.

(Josh Bersin, *People Management*, 22 June 2023)

STUDENT EXERCISE

Informed by the consultant's manifesto laid out in Key Issues in Reward Management 4.2 calling for a radical overhaul of pay structures, set alongside the foregoing assessment of how they tend to be designed and enacted currently, summarise for a hypothetical client the risks and benefits of evolutionary versus the promise of transformational change. You may wish to compare Josh Bersin's use of the phrase 'total rewards' with its definition in Chapter 9 to inform your assessment of the issues in play.

4.14 Market benchmarking

While job evaluation can be used to match jobs against the market using a consultancy's pay database, in general market pricing is seen as an alternative method for fixing pay levels. Market pricing exercises usually involve some method of job matching against comparable jobs in the external labour market. This can range from basic analysis using job titles or job descriptions through to the use of bespoke analytical job evaluation exercises.

The types of benchmarking data available to employers include the following: information on pay awards (whether negotiated or not) and actual salary scales; company-specific data; commercially produced salary surveys or pay databases held by consultants; and pay 'clubs', which share information between participants. In addition, some organisations analyse job advertisements. Such data can be broken down into two forms, non-analytical and analytical. In general, non-analytical information means data collected based on job titles only or where the survey asks respondents to match their jobs to short 'capsule' descriptions of levels and functions. The former is clearly problematic in that a single job title can cover a range of different job descriptions and pay levels. The latter enables more accurate comparisons to be made but is still based on fairly 'broad brush' criteria. Comparisons can also be made using 'whole job' comparisons or measures of responsibility.

According to IDS (2013b) there is little published information in either the practitioner or academic literature on organisations' market pricing practices. In general, private sector employers tend to benchmark against their own industry or at least against similar companies. In some cases, the collected data will date from different survey periods and hence some work is needed to ensure the data are aged to overcome these disparities. Some companies use management consultancy databases or commission bespoke exercises from consultants. The following types of sources of information were identified by IDS (2013b):

- general surveys;
- occupational surveys;
- sector-specific surveys;
- membership surveys;
- local surveys;

- salary guides;
- pay clubs;
- bespoke surveys.

Basic information about pay levels for particular job titles can be found in a range of published sources. Earnings data by occupation is available in various UK government statistical series, such as the Annual Survey of Hours and Earnings and the Labour Force Survey, while more specific information on named organisations is available from commercial providers such as XpertHR and the Labour Research Department (LRD). In some cases, wage rates agreed in national agreements for specific occupations and levels may form the benchmark for those occupations. A good example is the national rates agreed for electricians under the Joint Industry Board in the electrical contracting industry – these rates are not just followed by electrical contractors but often set the level for electricians employed elsewhere.

In contrast, the analytical job-matching method uses analytical job evaluation techniques to determine 'job size' comparisons, in which jobs are broken down into factors and points and each benchmark scored against the factor points scale. The total score gives the 'size' of each job being compared. Undoubtedly analytical comparisons are the most accurate, but such an approach can be lengthy, labour-intensive and expensive. Where employers already use a patented JE scheme, comparisons with the external market may be made easier through access to the consultant's database of JE outcomes. Unfortunately, this can limit the type of comparisons available to those organisations using that particular JE scheme.

ONS (2006) research on market pricing came to three main conclusions: first, in pricing their jobs organisations rely on more than one source of data; secondly, reading across to data based on analytical job evaluation techniques is only part of the exercise and often is not used at all; thirdly, data-gathering exercises are ongoing and the results implemented annually, or within the year if recruitment and retention problems are severe.

4.14.1 *Salary surveys*

Surveys of pay and conditions form an important source of intelligence for organisations. The number of surveys has grown considerably over the past few decades, and the IDS Guide to Salary Surveys listed almost 300 such sources. They fall broadly into two main types: those available to anybody for a price and those only available to participants (often known as 'pay club' surveys). The type of survey available to non-participants is normally organised by job title or generic job description/level. Participants in such surveys are asked to match their own jobs to the survey level and function descriptors. The problem with such surveys is the big range in quality between survey providers and the need for rigorous analysis of the data if the results are to be meaningful. Those surveys based on job evaluation generally provide better results, but they can be very expensive and are normally only available to the consultants' clients.

Another important issue to consider when judging the relative merits of surveys is the purpose for which they were designed. Many professional institutions run their own membership surveys as a means to inform their members of their potential value. These surveys are often 'self-reported' by members and can therefore suffer from inaccurate reporting. In contrast, surveys where results are submitted by employers and based on actual payroll information are likely to be more accurate.

A key issue in considering the potential value of surveys is the sample size, as variations in sample sizes for competing surveys in the same field can lead to quite different results. As a general rule, the larger the sample the better will be the survey's accuracy. Employers also need to know about the sample organisations – their size, sector and geographical spread. Clearly, a sample based on just large organisations in the financial services sector in London would provide a very limited picture if one were seeking general data on clerical staff salaries. Difficulties in interpreting the results of any survey indicate that employers should never rely on a single source of pay data but always 'triangulate' one source with a couple of others (IDS, 2013b). Where the post is particularly special or unique, employers may commission their own 'bespoke' survey from a consultant.

Another problem is the issue of 'matched samples'. If a survey is conducted every year, it may well be the case that the number of participants will vary from year to year. Moreover, within each participating organisation there will be turnover of individual staff throughout the year, with some staff leaving and others arriving. These changes can have considerable statistical effects on year-on-year comparisons. To ensure there is a comparison of the same organisations and same individuals year on year, some surveys provide a constant or 'matched' sample whereby data is provided that makes comparisons on exactly the same basis as the previous year's survey.

Surveys can provide a range of data on various aspects of reward. The most common data definitions are: base pay; cash bonuses; short-term incentives; long-term incentives; total earnings; employee benefits; and total remuneration.

Having collected sufficient market data to make a comparison, employers have to decide at what level in the range or distribution of salaries they wish to pay. This is termed 'market position' and can apply either to the whole pay structure or may be varied according to job family or even individuals. In any aggregate set of data it is normally assumed that the market rate is the median or midpoint, but most organisations claim to be in the 'upper quartile' (top 25 per cent). As IDS (2013b) says, this is intriguing because some organisations must form the 'lower quartile'. Most surveys will also provide an arithmetic average or 'mean', but generally employers prefer to use the median as it cannot be distorted by extreme 'outliers' (either a few very high-paid or very low-paid staff). The UK government statistical service, the Office for National Statistics, has been keen to use the median as its benchmark, rather than the mean, and especially when making comparisons of earnings by gender. However, the mean is used in European data on the gender pay gap.

Another useful statistic is the 'inter-quartile range'. This measures the range between the 25th and 75th percentile. Employers may also use the data to decide both starter rates for new recruits and target salaries after a number of years' service.

In order to check whether internal pay levels are in line with the market, employers can calculate a 'compa-ratio'. A compa-ratio of 'one' shows that the internal level and the market level are equal. A ratio of less than one would indicate that the internal level was below the market, and a ratio of more than one would indicate it was above the market.

A 'salary policy line' may also be drawn. This can be a curve or a straight line that relates internal salary points to the chosen survey target levels. A regression or 'best fit' line may then be constructed, and salary ranges constructed around this.

A key point is that medians and means should not be confused with salary mid-points. Means and medians can be lower than mid-points because either promotion, transfer or resignation leaves the remaining postholders concentrated at the bottom of the pay range or low turnover means that the majority of postholders reach their maximum point.

4.15 Equal pay reviews

Given the importance of grading structures in ensuring equity of treatment and given the increasing importance of equal pay for work of equal value legislation, regular auditing of the outcomes of an organisation's pay structure has become highly advisable. Such equal pay reviews (sometimes called equal pay audits) are recommended by the Equality and Human Rights Commission (EHRC). There had been provision for compulsory equal pay audits for all employers with more than 250 staff under the Equality Act 2010, but the UK coalition government elected in May 2010 decided initially that such audits would remain voluntary. However, following a further consultation in 2013, the government decided that from 1 October 2014, employment tribunals have the power to order mandatory equal pay audits.

An equal pay review allows an employer to identify any situations where males and females receive different levels of pay for reasons that cannot be explained by anything other than by gender. It can therefore be an important means to avoid the risk of equal pay legal challenges. The EHRC makes clear, however, that such reviews cannot directly address other reasons for inequality such as occupational segregation or the absence of flexible working in higher paid jobs, both of which have been identified as causes of the gender pay gap.

Research for the EHRC in 2008 (Adams et al, 2008) found an increase in equal pay reviews since 2005 with 17 per cent of organisations having completed a review, 5 per cent having reviews in progress and a further 17 per cent planning to conduct a review. Reviews were most commonly being carried out in the public sector with 43 per cent of organisations having either completed a review, having one in progress or planning to conduct one. This compared to 23 per cent in the private sector. This difference is explained by the EHRC in terms of workforce composition – women being the majority in the public sector but a minority in the private sector – but it also probably relates to the fact that reward systems are much more likely to be the result of collective bargaining in the public sector and hence more transparent. The one sector where there had been a decline in the proportion of reviews was manufacturing. The survey also found that the incidence of equal pay reviews increased with size of organisation.

In March 2023, the CIPD published a guide on gender pay gap reporting. Introducing the guide, the Institute makes the point that 'Thanks to sophisticated payroll software, it is relatively easy for organisations to collect and publish the pay data required for gender pay gap reporting.' Employers are told: 'What you do with the figures afterwards may require much more skill from people professionals.

Although not compulsory, it's important to create a narrative, putting the figures into context for your customers, your employees and other stakeholders, and set out the action you plan to take to address the gap' (CIPD, 2023a). Since gender pay gap reporting was introduced, the UK government has consulted on mandatory reporting of ethnicity pay data and, although not presently a legal requirement, some organisations are already reporting. The CIPD strongly encourages organisations to report on ethnicity pay gaps as well as those in respect of gender. The CIPD guide on Ethnicity Pay Reporting offers more information (CIPD, 2023b).

4.15.1 Why do employers conduct equal pay reviews?

The EHRC research found that some 37 per cent of organisations stated that they had an objective of closing the gender pay gap. Again, however, there was a significant difference in responses from the public and private sectors. Around two-thirds of public sector organisations had this stated objective, compared to 35 per cent of private sector (Adams et al, 2008).

The most common reason cited for conducting an equal pay review was that it was 'good business sense' and the desire to be seen as a 'good practice employer'. The most common reason given why the organisation had not conducted a review was that it already provided equal pay. Just under half of those who had conducted or were conducting an equal pay review planned to do this every year while around a fifth planned to conduct one every two years and a further fifth every three years.

In the 2019 annual reward survey the CIPD asked respondents to comment on steps taken to ensure fairness in pay decisions and processes. And also to indicate whether or not the results had been shared with the workforce.

A gender pay gap report is by far the most common means organisations have taken to ensure fairness, 60 per cent of organisations having done so, although 19 per cent have not shared the findings with employees. An equal pay audit has been undertaken by just over a third of organisations (39 per cent) but of those who have done so, more than half have not shared the findings.

A survey about pay fairness, of employees or line managers, is used by between a fifth and a quarter of organisations and the findings of these surveys are more likely to be shared with employees. For example, 23 per cent of organisations have undertaken a survey of employee views on the fairness of pay processes and only 5 per cent have not shared those findings. An ethnicity pay report and a CEO pay report have been undertaken by 17 per cent of organisations, but only 8 per cent have shared the findings of an ethnicity pay report with employees and only 7 per cent have done so in the case of a CEO pay report.

A disability pay report, LGBT pay report or report on employees with care responsibilities is much less likely to be undertaken; the proportions of organisations having done so are 9 per cent, 8 per cent and 4 per cent respectively.

In comparison, when as part of the same survey exercise the CIPD collected data on employee attitudes, only 24 per cent of respondents reported that they were aware of a gender pay gap review or audit being carried out; 54 per cent were unaware of such a report, and a further 22 per cent said that they did not know if they had been told about one or not. This contrasts with the figure above from the survey of management, where 41 per cent of respondents reported that gender pay gap findings had been shared with employees.

Table 4.10 Organisations with stated reduction in gender pay gap objective

	GB	Manufacturing	Construction	Private services	Public sector	All private sector
Yes	37	31	36	35	63	35
No	62	69	64	64	34	65
Don't know	1	1	1	0	4	0
Base	866	213	206	217	230	636

SOURCE: Adams et al (2008: 22)

Table 4.11 Steps taken to ensure fairness in pay decisions and processes (% organisations)

	Yes, findings shared with employees	Yes, findings not shared with employees	Yes, either	No
Equal pay audit	17	22	39	61
Gender pay gap report	41	19	60	40
Ethnicity pay report	8	9	17	83
CEO pay ratio report	7	10	17	83
Disability pay report	5	4	9	91
LGBT pay report	5	4	8	92
Pay report of employees with child/elder care responsibilities	2	2	4	96
Survey of employee views on the fairness of pay processes	18	5	23	77
Survey of employee views on the fairness of pay outcomes	19	7	25	75
Survey of line manager views on the fairness of pay processes and outcomes	14	6	20	80

SOURCE: Marriot and Perkins (2019)

Figure 4.9 Has your organisation told you that it has published a review of what men and women in your organisation typically earn?

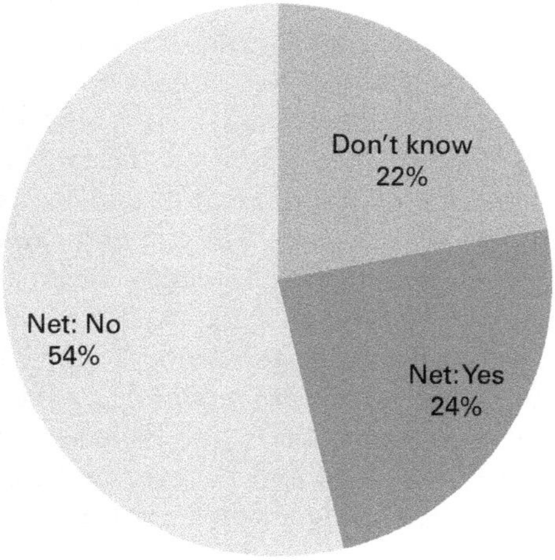

SOURCE: Marriot and Perkins (2019)

4.15.2 EHRC observations on action-oriented equal pay auditing

The EHRC states that an 'equal pay audit involves comparing the pay of protected groups who are doing equal work in your organisation, investigating the causes of any pay gaps by gender, ethnicity, disability or working pattern and planning to close any gaps that cannot be justified on grounds other than one of those characteristics' (EHRC, 2010: 1). It goes on to say that an equal pay audit is not simply a data collection exercise but also entails a commitment to put right any unjustified pay inequalities. The Commission lays down five benefits from an equal pay audit:

- Complying with the law and good practice.
- Identifying, explaining and eliminating unjustifiable pay gaps.
- Having rational, fair, transparent pay arrangements.
- Demonstrating to employees and to potential employees a commitment to fairness and equality.
- Demonstrating organisational values to those it does business with.

The Commission recommends its five-step equal pay audit model. The five steps are as follows: 1) deciding the scope of the audit and identifying the data needed; 2) identifying where employees in protected groups are doing equal work; 3) collecting and comparing pay data to identify any significant pay gaps; 4) establishing the causes of any significant pay gaps and deciding whether these are free from discrimination; and 5) developing an equal pay action plan and continuing to audit and monitor pay.

4.15.3 *Public sector equality duties*

Particular duties are placed on public sector employers relating to equality issues. These duties cover three areas: race equality, disability equality and gender equality. The first of these duties – race equality – was introduced following the Macpherson Report on the murder of Stephen Lawrence which revealed institutional racism in the Metropolitan Police. Prior to this legislation the emphasis of existing equality law was on rectifying cases of discrimination and harassment after they had occurred, rather than preventing such cases. The aim of the new duty was to shift the onus from the individual to organisations, placing for the first time an obligation on public organisations to positively promote equality, not merely to avoid discrimination. Further duties concerning disability and gender followed.

As part of these duties, public bodies are required to conduct an equality impact assessment (EIA) to ensure that their policies, and the way they carry out their functions, do what they are intended to do and for everybody. Carrying out an EIA is about systematically assessing the likely effects of policies on people (public clients and employees) in respect of disability, gender, race and, where they choose, wider equality areas. This includes reviewing opportunities to promote equality that may have previously been missed or could be better used, as well as negative or adverse effects that can be removed or mitigated where possible.

The importance of these duties and, in particular EIAs, in relation to reward management is clear. Any major decisions on changes to pay and benefits systems will probably require such an impact assessment to ensure that none of the proposed changes have equality implications. Further information on EIAs can be found on the EHRC website: www.equalityhumanrights.com/en/advice-and-guidance/equality-impact-assessments.

STUDENT EXERCISE

Download EHRC guidance on what equal pay means and review how this guidance might apply in your organisation or one with which you are familiar: www.equalityhumanrights.com/en/advice-and-guidance/what-equal-pay.

STUDENT ACTIVITY

Designing a professorial pay structure at Woburn University

Woburn University is located in the English Midlands and has over 25,000 students and around 4,000 staff. There are approximately 75 professors in the institution and there are plans under the current three-year strategic plan to expand this number to 150.

Background

For many years the professorial pay structure at Woburn University comprised a standard single grade pay scale, with no set definitions on where an individual should be assimilated onto the grade or how they would progress. It was decided in consultation with a representative group of key stakeholders that a more structured system was needed. The main drivers were a desire to link professorial activity to the University's strategy and also to introduce a more transparent system which linked contribution to pay progression.

A new three-banded pay and grading system was therefore introduced comprising two sets of eight drivers – one set applied to 'research' and the other 'teaching and learning'. Depending on the focus of activity, a professor would be reviewed against one set of drivers for the purposes of assimilation into the new system. Descriptors for each driver set out the expected activity level for the three bands within the system. For example, drivers under the 'research' heading included a professor's publication record and contribution to securing research funding. Professors were then assessed against the relevant set of drivers and received a score for each driver of 0, 1, 2 or 3. Certain key drivers attracted a weighted score, and by factoring this in, total scores were arrived at which correlated to one of the three pay bands. Assimilation to the new system progressed relatively smoothly and appeared to have successfully delivered on the project aims.

The current professorial structure

The professorial salary grade is comprised of three pay bands, as shown in the tables below. Pay progression mechanisms for each band reflect a combination of factors including market norms, individual development and contribution. Pay progression within the normal zones of all three bands is automatic and applied annually in August.

Figure 4.10 Professorial pay bands

Band 3	
Spinal point	**Salary £s**
614	£91, 757
613	£88, 228
612	£84, 834
611	£81, 571
610	£78, 434
609	£75, 418
608	£72, 517
607	£69, 728

Band 2	
Spinal point	**Salary £s**
608	£72, 517
607	£69, 728
606	£67, 046
605	£64, 467
604	£61, 987

Band 1	
Spinal point	**Salary £s**
603	£59, 604
602	£57, 312
601	£55, 106

Bands 2 and 3 have contribution zones which can be accessed through a successful recommendation or self-nomination for contribution increments.

At present, 50 per cent of professors are located within band 1 and 25 per cent each in bands 2 and 3.

In all bands of the professorial grade, pay progression is subject to professors demonstrating normal (good) performance and participating in an annual performance and career development review (PDCR). Professors must be in post for a minimum of six months to be eligible for progression. A successful recommendation for a contribution award will result in either accelerated progression within band, access to the contribution zone in bands 2 or 3 or movement to an upper band.

Once a professor has accessed the contribution zones in bands 2 or 3, there are no automatic annual increments but pay is consolidated and cannot move down within the band.

A professor may be recommended or can self-nominate to move between bands, if it can be evidenced that their contribution meets the requisite driver descriptors for the relevant upper band.

The professorial pay structure (band minima, maxima and incremental points), shown in Figure 4.10, is reviewed on an annual basis. General pay uplift awards are determined following negotiation at the University's Heads Information, Negotiation and Consultation Forum. The review takes account of:

1 any change in the cost of living;
2 the economic circumstances of the University;
3 experiences in the recruitment and retention of professors;
4 any available market pay data.

The need for review

The main problem was that the system did not take into account the fluctuations and timescales which affect a professor's work output. For example, a professor spending five years writing a book would score highly in the year the book was published but hardly at all in the other four years.

Questions

1 You have been charged by the university's leadership team with re-designing the professorial pay structure to better reflect the work of professors.
2 Is the current grading system for professors fit for purpose? Is the existing narrow grade structure (with consolidated increments) right for these staff? Would you want to make any changes and if so what?
3 Are the three levels of professor within the structure right? Should there be greater or less differentiation?
4 Does the current incremental system allow sufficient flexibility in progression within

the grade? Should there be automatic progression within the lower half of each grade?

5 Should contribution-based increments be consolidated as at present?

6 Does the current professorial grading structure allow sufficient flexibility to reflect the external market value of each individual? How might such flexibility be introduced to the pay structure?

7 In terms of criteria for grade allocation and progression, what do you think should be the major indicators of professorial performance?

8 Given the observation on the long-term nature of academic results, how might this problem be addressed in any pay for contribution system?

4.16 Conclusions and key learning points

In this chapter we have covered the purpose of grading and pay structures. It is important to remember that grading structures exist for a range of organisational reasons, not simply reward, but they only become pay structures when pay is allocated to a grade. Pay structures form the foundations for any reward system by creating the architecture for all the other aspects of the system. As discussed, there is a range of pay structures available from which employers can choose – from quite simple and individualised systems to complex job-evaluated structures.

But employers do not have total freedom in this choice. These different structures usually reflect important contextual issues, not least the type of organisation, the range of employees employed and the span of management control. And, of course, the need to comply with relevant external regulation. The degree to which reward is bargained is also vital. For example, where trade unions are present there is normally a stronger emphasis on internal equity, the 'rate for the job', a concern for promotion opportunities for all and less emphasis on individualised pay. In non-union settings, in contrast, employers may have more freedom to move individual employees through the grading structure as they see fit.

The consequences of these decisions also vary. While some employers have sought to move away from traditional hierarchical structures using more flexible broad bands and job families, other employers have sought to simplify and rationalise their pay structures. More flexible organisational structures may offer employers greater discretion, but the consequences may be an absence of coherence and hence employee dissatisfaction.

The continued popularity of job evaluation is reinforced by the general acceptability of JE to trade unions and the legal requirements to ensure that pay structures are free of gender bias. While traditional job evaluation techniques have been criticised from both the managerial and academic perspectives (Wagner, 2022), they continue to provide the major mechanism for assessing the value of individual jobs.

One consequence, however, is that an employer will have less discretion over how employees are valued within the organisation.

Whatever grading structure is adopted, there will be always be some degree of tension in maintaining the equilibrium of this structure against the external market. As we have explained, jobs that may have the same value within the internal structure may not have the same value when compared with the external market. Benchmarking the pay of job or career families, or indeed individual jobs, against the external market may assist with recruitment and retention but may lead to the entrenching of traditional pay hierarchies and can simply produce chronic 'pay drift' as employers chase their competitors.

Most importantly, grading structures of any kind can only attempt to weigh the value of one job against another – they cannot provide a means to reward the individual effort bargain. The major ways in which employers adjust the levels of pay to reflect the individual effort bargain are through the concept of pay progression and contribution, on the one hand, and various forms of variable pay additions, on the other. In Chapter 5, the various forms of pay progression within and between grades are discussed, before turning in Chapter 6 to the various forms of variable pay.

Explore further

A CIPD Fact Sheet on pay structures and pay progression, published in December 2022, outlines the purpose of pay structures (it also addresses pay progression): www.cipd.org/uk/knowledge/factsheets/pay-structures-factsheet/.

For a fuller exploration of job evaluation techniques and equal pay, see Armstrong, M, Cummins, A, Hastings, S and Wood, W (2005) *Job Evaluation. A guide to achieving equal pay*, London: Kogan Page.

See also Livy, B (2020) *Job Evaluation: A critical review*, London: Taylor and Francis (Google Books) and guidance produced by Acas Job Evaluation; Considerations and Risks, available to download from the Acas website at: www.acas.org.uk/job-evaluation-considerations-and-risks-advice-booklet.

For a discussion and critique of the equality issues arising from grading structures, see Hastings, S (2009) Grading systems, estimating value and equality, in White, G and Druker, J (eds) *Reward Management: A critical text*, London: Routledge. See also Gilbert, K (2012) Promises and practices: job evaluation and equal pay forty years on, *Industrial Relations Journal*, vol. 43, no. 2, pp. 137–51. And for analysis that concludes placing stress on the need for greater awareness on the value of feminised work within organisations, see Wagner, I (2022) Equal pay for work of equal value? Iceland and the Equal Pay Standard, *Social Politics: International Studies in Gender, State & Society*, vol. 29, no. 2, pp. 477–96.

For a discussion of market-based pay structures and the techniques used to compare pay levels, see IDS (2006) *Developments in occupational pay differentiation. A research report of the Office for Manpower Economics*, October 2006, London: Incomes Data Services.

For a fuller discussion of job family structures, see IDS (2012) *Job Families*, HR Studies 972, August, London: IDS.

05 Pay-setting, composition and progression

CHAPTER LEARNING OUTCOMES

At the end of this chapter, you should understand and be able to explain the following:

- The setting of pay levels for individual jobs, grades or roles.
- The composition of reward and the differences between basic pay, earnings, total remuneration and total reward.
- The difference between wages and salary systems and the frequency with which reward is delivered.
- The different methods by which employees can progress through a pay structure and the various criteria used to make decisions about progression – service, skill or knowledge acquisition, competence, performance or by reference to market rates.
- Compensation for particular forms of work – for example, overtime and shift premiums, call-out and on-call pay, location allowances and market supplements.

CIPD STRATEGIC REWARD MANAGEMENT (7HR03) LEARNING OUTCOMES

Learners will be able to:

2.2. Analyse the role of base pay in attracting and motivating employees.

3.2 Analyse the advantages and disadvantages to organisations of using incremental pay scales.

3.3 Assess the benefits and challenges of using performance appraisal to guide pay progression decisions.

5.1 Introduction

As we discussed in the previous chapter, the grading structure provides the overall architecture of the reward system and usually relates closely to organisational structure. But grading structures only provide a mechanism for allocating staff to an appropriate level within the organisational hierarchy. This process does not tell an employer what pay level to assign to any grade or band or how to reward the individual effort bargain. Deciding what and how to pay the employees in these various grades or roles is a further reward decision. Pay levels have to be attached to the grades or bands to create a 'pay structure', and decisions must be made about whether, or on what basis, employees will progress through the pay structure.

Gerhart and Rynes (2003: 115) argue that 'There are several reasons to believe that the decisions of organisations regarding *how* to pay are in some sense more strategic and more important to performance outcomes than decisions about *how much* to pay.' One reason is that organisations are probably more constrained in pay-level decisions – because of market comparisons – than how they pay. Research indicates that organisations differ more in how they pay than how much, and also that the differences in type of pay (e.g. pay based on performance rather than not) have a stronger relationship with organisational performance than pay levels alone. In this chapter, we therefore consider the various criteria used to progress employees through the pay structure.

Most employees today have some form of pay progression built into their pay structures. CIPD (2022a) define pay progression as the method of moving an individual to higher pay levels within a grade, distinct from pay increases that are linked to either cost of living or formal promotion to a higher grade. Movement *between* grades is normally through the process of promotion, although in rare circumstances promotion between grades may be automatic after a period of service, probation or induction. In many professional or skilled occupations, employees expect to move up the pay hierarchy over time. Progression *within* the grade can be contingent on a range of criteria – by service, age, performance, competence, acquisition of skills and qualifications or, in many cases, simply a comparison with external market rates.

Although published some time ago, a report by the CIPD on the lack of pay progression for the low-paid remains relevant in an era increasingly defined by concerns about pay equity and wage inequality. The report identifies a number of reasons for the lack of pay progression in low-paid workers, including a lack of opportunities to improve skills, and argues that 'Low-paid workers need opportunities to progress to a higher-paying job without leaving their employer and HR has a role to play in delivering it, especially in supporting and challenging managers in the creation of meaningful progression pathways for people wanting to work part-time' (CIPD, 2014a).

It is also important for the student of strategic reward management to understand some basic concepts about the composition of pay (see box below), pay progression and the different approaches to reward systems in different sectors and for different occupations.

ISSUES IN REWARD MANAGEMENT

Composition of pay

An important concept in reward management is the difference between base pay, earnings, total remuneration and total reward. We provide some definitions below, but students should also see Chapter 9 where we discuss the 'total reward' concept (see Figure 9.1).

1 *Base pay* is the fixed part of the remuneration package and is usually the guaranteed and contractual part. This can be the hourly basic pay rate (often expressed as a weekly wage) or an annual salary.
2 *Earnings* include base pay and all the payments made in addition to this basic wage or salary. These may include such additional payments as bonuses, overtime pay, shift pay, market or location pay supplements, compensatory payments for on-call working or call-out, and any additional allowances for holding particular skills or working in particular circumstances.
3 *Total remuneration* will include base pay, all other earnings plus the various benefits provided such as holidays, sick pay and pensions.
4 *Total reward* includes both financial and non-financial rewards. This will include basic pay, all additional earnings, benefits and the wider non-financial rewards available in the workplace (such as recognition schemes, the work environment, etc).

A key issue for HR professionals is the gap between base pay levels and actual earnings, known as 'pay drift' or 'wage drift'. Pay drift can be caused by payment of non-guaranteed pay, such as overtime, shift and incentive bonuses which has traditionally formed a substantial part of the pay packet for workers in manual occupations. In comparison, non-manual workers have traditionally tended to have little in the way of additions to their base salaries, but this position is now changing. With the increasing spread of more variable pay systems (see Chapter 6), non-manual earnings may be subject to more variation from month to month and therefore also subject to pay drift. Pay drift can become problematic for organisations when it is necessary to fix or predict pay costs, either because of budget restrictions or where there are tight profit margins.

Research on pay drift in the UK is rare, but one study by IDS for the Office of Manpower Economics (IDS, 2006c) found considerable differences between the private and public sectors in terms of pay drift. First, private sector pay drift was higher overall than in the public sector. Second, in the private sector, pay drift was largely the result of performance-related progression through the grade whereas the pay drift in the public sector was more likely to be related to seniority or service-related incremental progression through the grade. Indeed Collins (2019) reported that NHS pay reforms have been increasingly focused on removing this type of pay drift. In the UK economy as a whole, ONS and IDS data shows that in the years preceding the pandemic the rate of pay drift was typically between 0.5 per cent and 1 per cent (MacQueen, 2022). However, the post-pandemic period has seen dramatic increases in the rate of inflation with wage increases lagging behind. Some employers may well be seeking to 'correct' this by using non-consolidated payments such as bonuses which could widen the pay drift effect. In summary, both pay progression as well as non-consolidated payments can have a substantive impact on labour costs and reward professionals need to understand these mechanisms and how to control them.

5.2 Wages or salary systems?

Before going on to examine the different types of pay progression, it is worth noting that there are different systems for paying employees. The difference between manual and non-manual work has traditionally been designated by the terms 'wages system' and 'salary system'. 'Wage' normally refers to a system of single pay rates for each grade or role (e.g. £10 per hour) whereas 'salary' implies an annual payment (e.g. £25,000 per year). While salaries are normally stated as annual amounts, in reality the salary is normally delivered in 12 monthly instalments. A salary also often implies some progression opportunities, with employees moving up through the grade or range from a minimum to a maximum.

The big difference between wages and salary systems in the past was that waged workers tended to have less security of income and more fluctuating pay levels, with large amounts of incentive pay and/or overtime or shift pay on top of low hourly rates. In contrast, salaried workers had more secure and guaranteed incomes, but little in the way of incentive pay. This situation is now less clear cut, with smaller numbers of manual workers being paid by their output and a lot more non-manual workers now being paid according to their performance (Druker, 2009). Data from the April 2017 Annual Survey of Hours and Earnings (ONS, 2017) indicates that the vast majority, 84.6 per cent of employees in the UK, are paid monthly or four-weekly, 13.6 per cent are paid weekly and just 1.7 per cent are paid fortnightly which suggests that the salary system may be more prevalent.

As we mentioned in Chapter 4, some employees – often those in 'broad-based', non-specialist roles – have single wage rates or 'spot' salaries, that is, single pay points for each job, with no provision for rewarding growth in the job or role. For example, workers in a fast food or retail outlet are often paid on a single hourly grade rate (with their pay calculated on the number of hours worked). They may in some cases be paid a different hourly rate according the 'zone' or location in which they work (and in some cases may be able to move to a higher rate on the basis of their performance), but in general there is only one rate for each grade and there are few additions to the basic rate.

In a typical narrow-grade structure, or where a pay spine exists, employees will usually progress through the grade in steps, or 'increments', as these are often called. These increments can be valuable additional elements to the annual cost-of-living rise and can lead to significant pay drift. In broad-band structures, however, there may not be any increments as such, and employees may move between the minimum and maximum by percentage increases based on criteria such as merit, skill acquisition or the measurement of competence. In other words, increasingly there is no guaranteed progression to the maximum of the grade.

In addition to progression 'within grade' there is also progression 'between grades'. Normally this indicates promotion to a larger job or role. In some cases, pay grades or bands overlap so that progression can continue within the grade or role without the necessity for promotion.

SELF-ASSESSMENT EXERCISE

Ask your friends, fellow students and family members about **how** they are paid. What jobs are paid through wages systems and what sort are salaried? What does this tell us about the value placed on these jobs?

5.3 Pay contingencies – job, person, performance

It can be argued that there are three 'contingencies' in making decisions about pay – the job role, the personal attributes held by the individual and their performance (Mahoney, 1989). The first of these, pay based on job-role, often determined by a job evaluation process, was covered in Chapter 4. In this chapter we consider the other two contingencies – pay based on criteria related to personal attributes such as skills (person-based pay systems) and pay based on performance-related criteria such as sales or profits (performance-based pay systems) (Casey et al, 1991). As Kessler states (2013: 247): 'If "job" is the basis for establishing the grading structure, a pay system is the mechanism driving pay movements once the post has been allocated to a grade.'

Table 5.1 shows the range of options available within the person- and performance-based systems. As can be seen, as well as age and seniority, other forms of

Table 5.1 Categories of pay system

Person	Performance
Age	*Individual*
Seniority/experience	Sales (commission)
Qualifications	Goods (piecework)
Competence	Objectives (IPRP/merit)
Behaviour/traits	
Attitudes	*Group*
Knowledge	Profits (profit-sharing)
Skills	Value added (gain-sharing)
	Team target (team pay)

SOURCE: Adapted from Kessler (2013)

person-related progression might be based on criteria such as the acquisition of skills or knowledge (often in the form of qualifications) or the development of competencies. This might be categorised as 'pay for development' or 'pay for the right attitudes'. Apart from individual performance-related pay as a form of pay progression, we deal with all the various performance-based systems in Chapter 6 on variable pay.

The 2019 CIPD Reward Management survey (Marriot and Perkins, 2019) found, consistent with previous years' surveys, that the most popular criterion used in progressing pay within a pay scale was individual performance with 75 per cent of organisations using this approach. However, differences between sectors continue to be evident, with the public sector more likely to use competencies (51 per cent) and service-related pay (48 per cent) and manufacturing and production being far more likely to use individual performance (91 per cent) and skills (75 per cent).

SELF-ASSESSMENT EXERCISE

Looking at Table 5.1, which categories of pay system are used in your organisation (or one with which you are familiar)?

Based on your experience of these pay systems in practice, identify advantages and disadvantages for the employer and the employees.

5.4 Pay for time, performance or output?

Brown (1989) argues that pay systems have been subject to two basic criteria: time and performance. In other words, employees may be paid for the time they spend at work (or the time taken to undertake a specific task), or they may be paid according to the quantity or quality of the work produced. The big question is how to value the work in terms of the time taken to perform a task. For a professional sportsperson or entertainer (or indeed a management consultant), the value of several hours' work may be very high while for the lowest-paid workers, an hour's work may be measured in a few pounds or dollars. The alternative, payment by performance – whether quantity or quality of work produced – poses other problems, not least the issue of how to measure individual input or output.

Time-based pay systems normally reward the worker for their attendance at the workplace, through payment of an hourly rate. Such systems have had the advantage of predictability for both the employer and the employee – the employer can easily calculate wage costs and the employee can easily calculate their potential weekly pay. Where additional hours are required of employees by their employers, overtime payments can be used, where workers are paid a higher hourly rate for each additional hour worked on top of the contracted hours. Similarly, in order to incentivise employees to work unsocial working hours (i.e. those outside the normal working hours such as night shifts), employers often pay additional premiums for working shifts or rotas.

During the Covid-19 pandemic many countries, including the UK, experienced restrictions on travel and being in close contact with other people. During this time, only essential 'frontline' services and production were permitted to remain in operation and large swathes of the working population were either furloughed or were asked to work from home. For the first time for many employers and employees, there was no monitoring of when people were working or, indeed, how many hours they were working. Early indications from research, including by Barabaschi et al (2022) in Italy, suggests that remote working had positive relationships with productivity, autonomy, motivation and trust. And the findings suggest that physical attendance at a workplace is not as important for performance as having objectives which are shared and agreed upon. The unique circumstances of the pandemic may have played a role here, but it may be seen that these mass experiences of remote working will give rise to much more flexibility in both working location and time. Certainly ONS (2022) data suggests that nearly one-quarter of workers considered themselves to be 'hybrid' working in May 2022.

However, as Kessler (2013) points out, it is difficult to completely separate time and performance in pay systems. A pay system driven by time can incorporate all three pay contingencies – job, person and performance – in the sense that progression within the grade (job) often operates on the basis of service (person) and service is seen as some measure of performance. It is assumed in such systems that the longer a person occupies a job or role, the more skills and knowledge will have been acquired. Such systems can also act as a retention device – employees are paid for their loyalty in staying with the organisation. On the other hand, as discussed above, equal pay and age discrimination legislation have increasingly provided challenges to seniority-based systems of pay progression. But while seniority-based pay may pose equal-pay risks, it should be noted that individual performance or merit can still be rewarded on top of seniority or service-based pay progression. In some organisations, the highest increments in each grade may be reserved for high performers, or merit may be rewarded through one-off bonus payments rather than through the progression system.

Additionally, time can be used as a form of performance measure. While some employees are paid entirely by their output (e.g. traditional payment by the piece), most piecework systems today are based on how long a particular task takes to complete. A standard time will be agreed for the typical worker and extra pay provided if the work can be completed in less time. And even when employees are paid according to their performance, their pay is still usually related in some way to the time spent working. With the growth of part-time and casual work, and particularly zero-hours contracts, many employees continue to be paid by the number of hours worked each week, rather than a fixed amount.

SELF-ASSESSMENT EXERCISE

What are the main advantages and disadvantages of time-based pay systems as opposed to those based on output? Are there particular circumstances where an organisation may choose such a reward system?

In the next part of this chapter, we consider the various criteria used for pay progression. These include the following:

- service- or seniority-based pay;
- age-related pay;
- performance-related pay;
- competency-based pay;
- skills-based pay;
- market-based pay.

Table 5.2 Pay progression criteria, by sector (% organisations)

	Manufacturing and production	Private sector services	Voluntary and not-for-profit sector	Public services
Individual performance	84	75	60	56
Market rates	72	70	54	37
Competencies	75	68	56	57
Skills	83	64	46	45
Employee potential/ value/ retention	73	66	28	27
Length of service	20	33	30	53

SOURCE: Marriot and Perkins (2019)

The 2019 CIPD Reward Management survey (Marriot and Perkins, 2019) indicates the prevalence of these various methods of pay progression. As can be seen the rank order varies between sectors. In manufacturing, private services and the voluntary sector the most popular form of progression is individual performance, but in the public services it is competencies. As can be seen from Table 5.2, progression based on service is much more common in the public and voluntary sectors than the private. Individual performance is also the most common criterion for all the four occupational groups used in the CIPD survey.

5.5 Pay progression and equal pay issues

As we discuss in Chapter 3, a key aspect of any reward system is the necessity for it to meet legal requirements, especially those relating to equality law. Pay progression systems, as with the design of grading systems, present employers with risks of equal pay and age discrimination challenges if they do not meet certain criteria. As Thompson (2009: 137) argues, 'societal values around equity and fair treatment, articulated through legal codes, have shaped the administrative rules governing salary progression systems'. The notion of progressing pay through seniority or service was once accepted as a fair, transparent and non-discriminatory way of rewarding experience and stability of employment within organisations (OME, 2018). In the last two decades, however, as social norms have perhaps shifted, this method of progressing individuals through their pay scale has been legally challenged. A number of cases illustrate the key issues:

Case 1: The Advisory, Conciliation and Arbitration Service (ACAS) moved to shorten their pay scales in 2001 after losing an equal pay case. *In Crossley and Others v. ACAS* (Birmingham Employment Tribunal, 1304744/98 20.12.99), the Employment Tribunal (ET) found in favour of the Applicants that the ACAS pay system, which rewarded length of service, was indirectly discriminatory and hence in breach of the Equal Pay Act (cited in Thompson, 2009).

Case 2: In *Cadman v. Health and Safety Executive*, which went to the European Court of Justice ([2006] IRLR 969) for a ruling, the need for pay progression systems to be objectively justified was emphasised. Cadman brought the original ET claim on the basis of a comparison with four male comparators who were paid between £4,000 and £9,000 more than her. Each comparator was in the same band as her and doing work that had been rated as equivalent under a valid job evaluation study. The comparators were paid more than her, however, because they had longer service (OME, 2018).

Case 3: In *Wilson v. Health and Safety Executive* ([2010] IRLR 59, Court of Appeal) a similar claim to that of Cadman was brought and succeeded, again emphasising that a pay progression system which took employees 10 years to rise from the bottom to the top of the salary scale could not be objectively justified (OME, 2018).

In these and similar situations, women may be doing exactly the same level of work as men but are paid less on the increment scale simply because they have taken time out of the labour market due to childcare, noting that only 27.8 per cent of women are in full-time work three years after childbirth, compared to 90 per cent of new fathers (Harkness et al, 2019). While it may take four to five years to learn some jobs, longer service periods probably do not accurately reflect an ongoing 'learning curve', and some jobs may well be mastered in under five years. In addition, the Equality Act (2010) specifically highlights the issue of age-related pay differentials accruing over time. Schedule 9, Para 10 of the Act stipulates that it is not age discrimination to pay less based on shorter length of service (despite younger employees clearly being more likely to have shorter service than older employees). However, the Act also says that where a disadvantaged employee has more than five years' service with an employer it is up to the employer to show legitimate belief that the disadvantage 'fulfils a business need' (OME, 2018). The inference is that pay scales with more than five annual increments risk attracting claims for age discrimination.

5.6 Service- or seniority-based pay

The traditional method of pay progression within grade for many employees has been according to length of service or seniority. The assumption is that length of service equals improved knowledge and experience, and hence improved performance. Historically, such systems were the product of strong internal labour markets and were designed to provide rewards for loyalty to the organisation. Such systems are also seen as having the potential to enhance employee commitment (Benson, 1995; Cappelli, 1995; Shaw and Gupta, 2007), potentially leading to higher productivity, better quality and customer service, and lower levels of staff turnover.

Seniority-based systems operate on the basis of fixed steps or 'increments' on a scale from the minimum to the maximum of the grade. Under such progression systems, increments may be withheld for poor performance or employees may be fast-tracked up the grade by jumping increments, but the expectation of most employees is that progression to the maximum is guaranteed. Some scales have a bar under which employees may have to meet certain criteria to progress further – for example, merit or competence.

As shown by the CIPD (Marriot and Perkins, 2019) data, such service-related progression is still common in many parts of the public services and voluntary sector, but is increasingly absent from the private sector. The data also makes it clear that many organisations will use a number of different criteria to progress pay. While incremental systems can co-exist with performance, contribution or other forms of pay progression, IDS found that 57 per cent of those using such systems see service as the primary factor, and 41 per cent said that progression to the maximum was automatic (IDS, 2010a: 5). For example, the Department for Health and Social Care acknowledges that pay progression remains 'near automatic' in most NHS organisations (Collins, 2019) despite repeated attempts by successive governments to reform these pay practices in the public sector.

Service-related progression systems have generally been popular with trade unions because they provide automatic and guaranteed progression to the maximum of the grade for all staff – and because this does not normally involve the line manager in pay decisions. Such systems can be popular with line managers too for the same reason – they do not have to become involved in individual pay decisions. Such systems also have the advantage that pay costs are relatively predictable. As long as the employer knows how many staff are located on each salary point, he or she can calculate the cost of annual progression fairly easily. On the other hand, a downside to such systems is that in hard times an organisation's pay bill will continue to increase, even if there is no annual cost-of-living increase, because of the cost of increments. IDS (2010a) found that even where there was a freeze on general pay awards, the great majority of organisations continued to pay increments.

Such service-based systems have traditionally been unpopular with reward writers and many senior managers because they are seen as inequitable, inflexible and encourage 'time-serving' behaviour among employees. The criticism is that poor performance is treated equally with good performance, so there is no incentive to improve. Such reward writers have also pointed out that the assumption that length of service implies more experience and hence higher performance is unproven. In times of low staff turnover, such systems can also become expensive as every employee moves to the maximum of the grade. Indeed, one reason why performance-related progression became so popular in the 1980s was that employers wanted to release pressure at the maximum points of grades without necessarily having to reward all staff in the same way.

As mentioned earlier, in recent years such systems have also been criticised from a gender and age discrimination perspective (also see Chapter 3). In 2010, before the Equality Act came into force IDS found that the number of steps in incremental pay scales varied between 2 and 15, with a median of 5 (2010a: 4). The EHRC (2020) recommends a number of pay progression practices to mitigate against unequal pay including:

- guaranteeing that employees will reach the maximum pay point in their pay band within a reasonable timeframe;
- setting time limits within which employees will reach each pay point;
- setting target pay points for all staff to reach within a specific time;
- setting competency and experience criteria for workers to reach each pay point;
- having shorter pay scales, which accurately reflect the time needed to become fully competent at a job, or
- giving those at the bottom of the pay band a higher percentage pay increase than those at the top.

The original aim of rewarding loyalty through such systems, moreover, seems less important to organisations today. According to Lawler (2000: 122), seniority-based pay best suits the traditional internal labour market – or 'develop and build from within' – human capital approach. It also fits organisations that are relatively stable and need to have a long-term committed workforce. Lawler, writing more than 20 years ago, cites such stable, capital-intensive organisations where stability of employment and long-term employment relationships are required to develop an in-depth understanding of the business. But these organisations seem increasingly rare in rapidly changing business environments where there needs to be equally rapid changes in workforce capabilities. According to Lawler, 'the seniority approach is likely to retain all employees, not just those required to deal with new technologies, markets and businesses' (2000: 122). Moreover, 'it does nothing to facilitate the departure of employees whose skills and knowledge are no longer needed'. Lastly, Lawler argues that seniority-based rewards can contribute to an 'entitlement-oriented culture', 'in which individuals feel they are owed something simply because they are long-tenure employees'. Armstrong and Brown (1999: 235) echo the concern that in service- or seniority-based pay systems, 'people are rewarded for being there and not for the value of their contribution'.

5.7 Age-related pay

A linked form of pay progression to seniority is progression based on age, whereby pay rates are attached to specific ages. Age is different to seniority in that it normally provides the progression route for younger workers, and such pay progression was traditionally linked to periods of training or apprenticeship. Age-related pay progression is now rare, largely owing to the high numbers of young people going into higher education and a decline in apprenticeship-type training programmes. The National Minimum Wage in the UK, however, does mean that some organisations have separate 'youth rates' and the NMW retains separate hourly rates for under 18 year olds, those between 18 and 20 and those between 21 and 22 with the adult National Living Wage rate starting at 23. The main reason that the Low Pay Commission has continued to advocate age-related rates is because of concerns that paying the 'adult' rate to workers under 23 would lead to higher levels of unemployment among younger age groups (see Chapter 3).

Those employers with age-related pay for younger workers argue that the lower pay levels reflect the employers' cost in contributing to training and also the 'market value' of such workers in the external labour market. Other employers, however, argue that age-related progression is contrary to concepts of pay for performance or contribution. Age discrimination law, moreover, has placed a question mark over relating pay to age, although the minimum wage regulations currently allow such differentiation (see Chapter 3).

SELF-ASSESSMENT EXERCISE

Prepare a briefing paper on the advantages and disadvantages of (1) service-related pay and (2) age-related pay.

5.8 Individual performance-related pay (PRP)

Performance-related pay (PRP) is defined by CIPD (2022a) as 'a way of managing pay by linking salary progression to an assessment of individual performance, usually measured against pre-agreed objectives'. This type of pay progression is sometimes known as merit pay and is often dependent on some evaluation of a worker's performance by a line manager, usually through the performance management and appraisal systems.

While many pay-for-performance schemes link pay to progression through the grade or band, some schemes provide annual 'one-off' merit bonuses that do not relate to pay progression and are therefore not consolidated into base pay. In this chapter we consider reward for performance only as a mechanism for progression through the pay and grading system. Incentive pay, merit bonuses and other forms of variable pay are covered in Chapter 6.

DEFINITIONS

The terminology associated with pay and performance can be confusing with different terms used to refer to the same or very similar pay schemes:

Merit pay: 'An individualized system of payment in which earnings are related to an assessment of employee performance in the job. Merit pay is also known as appraisal-related and individual performance-related pay and is usually based on a system of annual performance appraisal, which is used to allocate employees to one of a small number of performance bands. The level of performance rating then determines either the award of cash bonuses or salary progression through a scale or range.'

Performance-related pay: 1) 'The broad class of payment systems which relate pay to some measure of work performance. As such, it can embrace profit-sharing, merit pay, gain-sharing, piecework, sales incentives, and other output-based pay systems.' 2) 'Individualized systems in which salary increases are related to the results of performance appraisal.'

'This latter usage corresponds to appraisal-related pay or merit pay. To avoid confusion, some writers refer to individual performance-related pay (IPRP).'

(Heery and Noon, 2017)

There has been a lengthy and wide-ranging debate among both HR practitioners, reward consultants and academic commentators about the advantages and disadvantages of individual performance-related pay. In both the USA and the UK there has been conflicting research evidence about whether such systems work. The differences between economic and psychological theories were discussed in Chapter 2, but it is worth remembering here that psychological theory places much more importance on individual differences to explain differences in performance than does economic theory. While economists recognise the role of ability in performance (in efficiency wage theory), psychologists have found many more variables to consider, such as personality, the need for achievement and self-esteem. Gerhart and Rynes (2003) suggest that economists (and many managers) may find this complexity inconvenient, but argue that ignoring the individual and contextual differences may impede managers in seeking to improve performance. Finally, psychologists are interested in the meaning of money to employees and the part it plays in their lives. Money often provides an important measure of an individual's success and status when comparing themselves to other workers. A belief that one is not being treated equitably, furthermore, is an important factor in working life, and pay is an important mechanism for signalling value and achievement. OME (2014), considering evidence from the UK public sector, noted that theoretical critiques of IPRP centre on the idea that 'the economic logic behind PRP cannot fully capture the range of factors which motivate an employee. Peer effects, perceptions of fairness and intrinsic motivation will all affect an employee's performance – and pay schemes will necessarily interact with these factors. Disregarding them may therefore subvert desired outcomes or lead to unintended consequences.' The most important motivational theories underpinning performance-related pay are expectancy theory, goal-setting theory, equity theory, attribution theory, agency theory and tournament theory (see Chapter 2 for a discussion of relevant theory).

5.8.1 Framing PRP

Kessler (2013) points out that any typology of performance-pay systems must address three questions. These are:

- What is being assessed?
- How is it being measured?
- How is it being rewarded?

The first of these questions concerns the unit of performance. Are we assessing the individual, the team or the organisation? While historically much of the emphasis on incentives has related to individuals, there is increasing interest in group or organisational incentives for performance (Conroy and Gupta, 2015; Jones et al, 2021; Park and Kin, 2022). The main advantage of such collective incentives is seen as their potential to foster co-operation between group members. On the other hand, Gerhart and Rynes (2003) provide both theoretical arguments and research evidence that there may be efficiency losses under such group schemes. For PRP purposes, the individual only is assessed, but we will return to group-based incentives in the next chapter.

The second issue is whether pay is to be based on inputs (e.g. behavioural criteria) or outputs (e.g. results). In general, it is easier to measure results than behaviours, and there is evidence that organisations have moved towards greater use of results-based plans – or 'contracts', in agency theory terms (Gerhart and Rynes, 2003). This growth is explained by the spreading of results-based pay plans down from senior management to other staff. It is also explained by changes in the labour market towards more flexible employment relationships, such as outsourcing, temporary employment and individual contracting. Outputs are usually defined in quantitative terms, such as the number of sales, productivity increases, quality improvements or profit growth.

Inputs are more difficult to measure as they are generally more qualitative in nature and are therefore more likely to be individual targets rather than group or organisation. Inputs may be framed as behaviours (what people do) or traits (personality characteristics) or indeed 'behavioural traits' (see section 5.9 Competency-based pay). According to Heneman (1992), behaviours have two advantages over traits – first, they are more easily defined, and second, the employee has more control over them because performance expectations are usually more explicitly defined. Research has shown that the decision to base pay on results instead of behaviours or traits can have a substantial effect on the rank ordering of employees for pay purposes (Gerhart and Rynes, 2003: 167). This suggests that results and behaviour-based systems yield different and often conflicting information about individual performance.

The third question relates to the performance–pay link. This can be automatic, for example, where the achievement of target results leads to the automatic payment of an agreed pay increase, where some judgement has to be made about the performance achieved and the level of reward deserved. The latter normally involves some form of individual appraisal of the employee's performance by their line manager which can be either an informal system (without any employee involvement) or, increasingly in many organisations, a formal part of the performance management system where both manager and employee meet to discuss the issues (see Jones and White, 2021 and also section 5.8.5 below).

5.8.2 Arguments in favour of PRP

Lawler (2000) identified the following advantages of performance-related pay progression. First, he argues that basing individual pay on performance has a strong motivational effect by allowing 'an almost perfect line of sight' between the behaviour of individuals and their rewards. Lawler argues that, 'with an effective individual pay-for-performance system, the potential exists to create a highly motivated workforce in which employees see a close relationship between how well they perform and how much they are paid' (Lawler 2000: 149). Secondly, IPRP enables organisations to retain high performers, who will have a higher market rate in the external labour market than average performers. Thirdly, IPRP can help remove poor performers from the organisation (so-called 'crowding out') because, as their relationship to the external market falls (through zero or minimal pay increases), they will not be able to afford to remain as employees.

These tenets of PRP have largely been taken up by reward commentators and are frequently referred to in modern textbooks, such as Armstrong and Brown (1999), which advocate recognising achievement with a financial, tangible reward. According to CIPD (2022a) the objectives of PRP can include motivation of staff by explicitly linking their pay with performance, embedding entrepreneurialism or 'high-performance-working' in the organisation and fairly recognising higher performance with greater rewards. And there appears to be some compelling evidence that these objectives can be realised by organisations. Shaw and Gupta's (2015: 281) essay, including meta-analysis of research papers, finds that 'financial incentives relate positively to performance, do not reduce intrinsic motivation, and, in general, are more effective than… thought'.

5.8.3 Arguments against PRP

There is, however, a long-standing critique of PRP in the academic literature. Kohn's much-cited article for the *Harvard Business Review* (Kohn, 1993b) argued that incentive schemes fail for the following reasons:

- pay is not a motivator;
- they punish staff who do not receive them, leading to demotivation;
- they rupture relationships through competition and undermine teamwork;
- they are used as an alternative to managing staff performance properly;
- they discourage risk-taking; and
- they undermine intrinsic interest in the work.

Heneman (1992) similarly identified a number of potential pitfalls with PRP. Most important is the decrease in intrinsic motivation identified by Deci (1972) and popularised by Pink (2009), but he also identifies decreased co-operation between employees, decreased self-esteem and decreased equity. Pfeffer (1998a), a strong proponent of the 'best practice' school of HRM, has argued strongly against PRP, arguing that such schemes have been plagued by a number of problems. First, subjectivity and 'capriciousness' among managers has tended to reward employees' political skills or 'ingratiating personalities', rather than their performance. Secondly, individual PRP has undermined teamworking by emphasising individual success, sometimes at the expense of peers. Thirdly, Pfeffer argues that there is often an absence of concern for organisational performance so that individual objectives ignore wider organisational needs. Fourthly, PRP encourages a short-term focus among employees and discourages long-term planning. Fifthly, there is a tendency for such systems to produce a climate of fear in the workplace. Finally, and most importantly, Pfeffer (1998s: 204) argues that 'by making pay contingent upon performance (as judged by management), management is signalling that it is they – not the individual – who is in control'. As a consequence, 'performance-related pay may lower the individual's feelings of competence and self-determination, and run counter to an intrinsic reward policy'.

Lastly, there is a view that placing emphasis on individual performance is unethical (Heery, 2000b). Heery argues that IPRP is unethical because:

- it poses a threat to employee security (by putting their income at risk) and hence undermines employee commitment;
- it is potentially unjust in both terms of procedural and distributive justice, leading to possible gender and other forms of discrimination; and
- it is undemocratic in that it leaves little scope for collective employee involvement in pay decisions.

Criticism of IPRP has not just come from academic writers. Two UK government reports also concluded that IPRP had not worked well in the civil service (Bichard, 1999; Makinson, 2000). Bichard concluded that there was little evidence that the existing civil service pay arrangements had helped to confront poor performance, and that the 'performance pay system is not perceived to offer significant rewards for excellence'. Belle (2015), finding that performance-related pay for nursing staff adversely affected motivation, and Bryson et al's (2017) research also conclude that PRP is unsuitable for public sector 'prosocial' working environments.

SELF-ASSESSMENT EXERCISE

What are the arguments for and against individual performance-related pay? Which of these arguments do you find most convincing? What do your fellow students think?

5.8.4 What does the research evidence tell us about PRP?

Several large-scale research projects in the USA have indicated that financial incentives can have a substantial impact upon employee performance (Shaw and Gupta, 2015). According to Gerhart and Rynes (2003), however, many studies have tended to be primarily focused on employees carrying out relatively simple work tasks and were conducted at the level of the individual rather than the organisational level of analysis. Moreover, most of the empirical research on the relationship between pay and performance outcomes has concentrated on how pay influences the attitudes and behaviours of individual employees (e.g. the motivational effects). There has, however, been some limited research on how pay can have a 'sorting effect' alongside an 'incentive effect' by influencing the ability and characteristics of an organisation's workforce through improved recruitment, retention and turnover. Trevor et al (1997) in a study of voluntary turnover and job performance find high performers are less likely to leave if their pay growth is commensurate with their performance. Work by Nyberg (2010) supports these findings in a study of insurance workers as does that by Shaw et al (2009) showing 'expectation-enhancements', including performance-related pay, are negatively related to high performers' quit rates and positively related to poor performers' quit rates suggesting a sorting effect in the organisations studied. And Gerhart and Fang (2014) find evidence of higher performing employees self-selecting into jobs in which they can earn more through performance incentives.

Gerhart and Rynes (2003: 122) point out that the relationship between incentives and performance is complex and relates to many moderating factors, such as goal difficulty, task complexity, work interdependence and individual self-efficacy. Recent research by Fang and Gerhart (2012) has challenged Deci's view that pay for performance diminishes intrinsic reward and they argue that intrinsic interest may actually rise under PRP because it focuses employees' attention more on their role.

Milkovich and Newman (2008), in their review of a range of research studies about the effects of linking pay to employee behaviour, cite Huselid's (1995) study of HR practices in over 3,000 companies. This found a clear correlation between organisations that had IPRP and those that had higher annual sales per employee. They also cite Heneman's (1992) review of research on PRP, which reported that 40 out of the 42 research studies examined found that performance increased when pay was tied to performance. A study of 200 companies by Gerhart and Milkovich (1990) found a 1.5 per cent increase in return on assets for every 10 per cent increase in the size of the bonus. Furthermore, they found that the variable portion of pay had a stronger impact on individual and corporate performance than did the level of base pay.

Almost all of this research on the beneficial effects of PRP comes from the USA. This might be explained by the fact, as Lawler (2000) has argued, that PRP is more acceptable in a strongly individualistic national culture such as the USA than in more collectivist cultures. It is interesting to note that there are few similar large-scale studies of IPRP in the UK, Europe or elsewhere that have found such strong links between IPRP and corporate performance. Research by Dickinson (2006), however, on employee preferences for the bases of pay differentials identified three major elements – responsibility, qualifications and performance. Dickinson comments that the level of support found for performance as a criterion in her research was surprising, given the association of PRP with variability in pay and problems with performance assessment.

In the UK, much of the academic research on IPRP has been critical. In particular the UK research looking at employee attitudes to IPRP, as opposed to management perceptions of its effectiveness, has found little evidence of any motivational effect (see Heery, 1998; IRS, 2000b; Kessler and Purcell, 1992; Marsden and Richardson, 1992; Thompson, 1993). Marsden and French's large-scale study of various PRP schemes in the public services found that PRP had failed to motivate many staff and was seen as divisive (Marsden and French, 1998). On the other hand, they identified a paradox that, despite the negative views of employees, productivity seemed to improve.

A review of the literature on PRP in the public sector in the USA (Perry et al, 2009: 43) argued that, 'at the aggregate level, our analysis finds that performance-related pay in the public sector consistently fails to deliver on its promise'. Similarly, a literature review on PRP in the public sector (OME, 2014: 10) found that, while PRP schemes 'can be effective in improving outcomes... a central conclusion is that the outcomes from PRP are mixed, dependent upon organisational and occupational context and scheme design and implementation'.

All the earlier UK studies of IPRP were conducted in the public services – probably because it is easier for researchers to access public sector employees than those in the private sector and, to some extent, the premise of PRP in public sector work has been more controversial (Bajorek and Bevan, 2015). Kessler (2000) has argued that this concentration of UK PRP research in the public sector may have biased the overall picture towards this negative outcome, as such pay systems are more likely to be problematic in a public service culture than in the private sector. This is partly because such systems often challenge collectively bargained pay arrangements and, as we discussed in Chapter 3, the public sector is much more likely to negotiate pay with unions than the private sector. It has also been argued that PRP, and its emphasis on extrinsic monetary reward, is incompatible with the type of obligation-based, intrinsic motivation most often encountered in public sector work (Bajorek and Bevan, 2015). It is perhaps surprising that so little research on performance-related pay has been conducted in the private sector in the UK, where one might expect the climate and circumstances to be more congenial to such pay systems.

Given this bias to the public sector, much of the UK research has found that, while in general employees favour the concept of being paid according to their individual performance, the actual experience of working under such systems for the majority of workers had been negative. In a review of research papers on PRP in the public sector, Bajorek and Bevan (2015) find that while PRP schemes can be effective across the public sector (health, education and the civil service), findings were mixed, with

PRP effectiveness often dependent on scheme design and organisational context. Moreover, where any positive effects were found, these were often small and short lived.

The major problems identified with PRP processes revolve around three major operational issues:

- the setting of appropriate performance measures;
- the evaluation of performance; and
- the linking of performance appraisal outcomes to pay.

Kessler (2000) points out the problems of setting performance targets, particularly for less-skilled jobs or for certain professional jobs. He also notes concerns about subjectivity in the evaluation process and the reluctance of line managers to differentiate between employees. Research cited by Kessler also found that a large majority of managers surveyed said that their employees distrusted line managers to make judgements on their performance. Finally, Kessler identifies problems with the amount of performance pay being delivered as insufficient to motivate individuals. Small amounts of IPRP are particularly a problem during periods of low inflation.

One of the few studies of IPRP in the private sector (Lewis, 1998) looked at three financial services organisations. This research suggests that, even if the pay element of the performance management cycle is not accepted by employees, if conducted effectively the processes that determine the reward may 'mitigate the unacceptable impact of the pay element'. Lewis concludes that the effectiveness of the IPRP process cycle is central to the acceptance by employees of this form of payment, and that key to this are the skills and attitudes of the line managers in the process.

The link between organisational culture and IPRP is also a key variable (although little researched) in its success. In some organisations the introduction of IPRP has failed because the concept does not fit easily with organisational culture. A good example is the research by Randle (1997) on the use of IPRP in a pharmaceuticals research environment. This research questioned the appropriateness of such pay schemes in a 'knowledge worker' environment. While the scientists broadly accepted the fairness of pay for performance, it was one of the 'most consistently disliked management practices' (Randle, 1997: 198). As Randle suggests, 'Measuring the quality of ideas, a crucial aspect of individual performance in research, presents huge problems for managers.'

IPRP has also been used as a tool to change organisational cultures. Brown and Armstrong (1999) argue that IPRP played a particularly important role in the UK in the development of the 'reward management' paradigm, marking an important shift in the UK away from 'passive, reactive pay administration to active, strategic reward management' (1999: xii).

Marsden (2004), revisiting his earlier research on IPRP in the public services, considers the paradox that IPRP has led to performance improvements despite employees' evident distaste for the process. He states that much of the literature on IPRP misses this point in focusing on its role as an incentive. Much of the research has therefore concentrated on whether employees feel better motivated, rather than whether performance improved as a result. Its role as a means to renegotiate performance 'norms', he argues, has been largely neglected. The use of IPRP in the UK public services, argues Marsden, has actually been primarily about renegotiating the 'effort bargain' between employers and employees in order to reassert management's control, rather than seeking ways to improve motivation. As Marsden (2007: 108) states: 'Procedural justice is an important support for effective renegotiation of performance goals and standards, but the associated procedures will work better if their design fits with management's underlying agenda of change.'

5.8.5 PRP and the performance management system

As indicated above, the PRP system has always been closely linked to an organisation's performance management system. This requires clear processes for establishing what performance measurements are to be used; how performance is to be measured; and how any resulting performance rating or 'score' is to be linked to pay. It also involves important decisions about who is to undertake the measurement and when.

A useful theoretical frame for understanding the importance of the performance management process is the concept of 'procedural justice' versus 'distributive justice' (see Chapter 2). Procedural justice is defined as the fairness of the procedures for allocating rewards, while distributive justice is defined as the fairness of the actual rewards received (Folger and Cropanzano, 1998). In general, where procedures are operated fairly there is more likelihood that employees will accept the actual rewards on offer. As Marsden (2007: 111) states: 'The processes associated with performance appraisal, and the design and allocation of associated rewards all fall under the umbrella of procedural justice, and, it is argued, employees are likely to withdraw performance if they feel that management violate procedural justice norms when operating their reward systems.' In other words, employees are likely to feel that distributive justice has not been achieved if they perceive that procedural justice has been violated. This failure can result from a variety of operational problems: the inability of managers to set attainable goals and review employees' performance accurately; if managers are not acting in good faith; if the performance criteria contradict employees' own professional values and experience; and if management's concept of motivation is not in alignment with the employees' sense of value and achievement. Procedural justice is therefore not just about having the right procedures, 'but rather of having procedures that are sufficiently well-informed to lead to decisions that are considered fair' (Marsden, 2007: 112).

According to Bach (2013), with the increasing recognition of the problems that permeate many organisations' performance appraisal systems, there has been a shift from performance appraisal alone to the wider concept of performance management. This has focused attention on the broader organisational context in which appraisal takes place and the key role of the line manager, rather than the HR department, in managing individual performance. As Bach (2013: 221) indicates, 'it remains important, however, to differentiate between the two concepts rather than assume that performance appraisal has been replaced by performance management'.

Boswell and Boudreau (2000) identify two main functions for appraisal systems – evaluative and developmental. The evaluative approach uses performance appraisals to fix salary levels, decide about promotion, make decisions about recruitment and retention, recognise good performance and identify poor performers. In this approach the appraiser acts as judge and the primary purpose is to differentiate between individual employees. In contrast, the developmental approach includes the identification of training needs, providing feedback on performance and the identification of individual strengths and weaknesses. In this approach the appraiser takes the role of mentor or coach and focuses primarily on the individual. In general, the linkage of appraisal to reward outcomes is an example of the evaluative approach.

The CIPD (2016) suggest that performance management is broadly defined as activity that:

- establishes objectives through which individuals and teams can see their part in the organisation's mission and strategy;
- improves performance among employees, teams and ultimately organisations;
- holds people to account for their performance by linking it to reward, career progression and termination of contracts.

Although previous research by the CIPD (2009a) and WERS (van Wanrooy et al, 2013), indicated that there had been a marked increase in the number of organisations using a formal system of performance management over the preceding years, in recent times there appears to have been a push back against overly formal performance management and especially the idea of a fixed, annual cycle culminating with a performance appraisal:

> Common practice in performance management has remained broadly stable for two or three decades, but the last few years has seen a proliferation of popular articles challenging the received wisdom. The broad thrust is that traditional practices – in particular the dreaded annual appraisal – are outdated, if indeed they ever worked.
>
> (CIPD, 2016: 5)

The traditional performance management cycle has been comprised of three stages (see Figure 5.1).

The first stage is *performance planning* where objectives are agreed between the manager and employee. The performance plan, agreed by both the employee and manager, establishes the framework for the process. According to IDS (2007b),

Figure 5.1 The performance management cycle

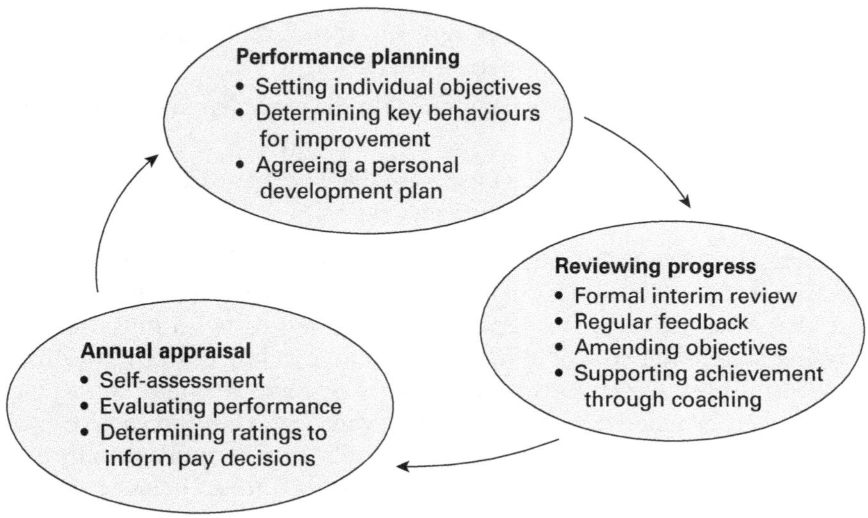

there are three core elements to this plan: individual objectives; competencies and behaviours; and personal development plans.

The second stage of the process is about *reviewing progress*. This entails formal interim reviews, regular informal feedback to the employee by the manager and, if necessary, changes to the performance plan to reflect any changed circumstances.

The third stage is the *annual appraisal*. This requires the collection of evidence, both by the employee and the manager, to prepare for the meeting. This evidence can include feedback from colleagues and clients or customers and self-assessment by the employee. The meeting between the manager and employee will then take place to review the evidence. As mentioned earlier, it is easier to evaluate performance against 'hard' quantitative measures of achievement of tasks or project-oriented goals than against competencies or behaviours. Evaluation of competencies or behaviours is primarily based on the managers' own observations or those of colleagues, but organisations often provide a checklist for this purpose. An outcome of the appraisal is the 'rating' of individual performance. This stage is especially important if the outcomes of the appraisal are to be linked to pay progression or reward. IDS (2007b) found that there are essentially three core levels of performance rating used in organisations, between which there may be further 'shades' of performance. These three are:

- 'exceptional', or 'exceeds expectations';
- 'effective', or 'meets expectations';
- 'not effective', or 'below expectations'.

In some cases, there may be separate rating scales for achievement of objectives and for competencies exhibited. Some organisations have absolute measures of performance against which an 'effective performer' is measured while others allow assessment against performance relative to other staff. To ensure that different managers are not applying different standards, organisations may use a 'grandparent' system whereby each appraisal has to be signed off by a more senior manager. This may be followed up by a more formal evaluation of the overall outcomes of the process through an audit by the HR department.

The major ways pay progression and individual performance are linked are as follows:

- Through the award of additional 'performance-related' increments on top of an essentially service-based progression system.
- Through all incremental progression within the grade based on performance ratings.
- Through 'all merit' annual pay increases where the increase will range in size according to the individual performance rating.

Clearly, there also have to be some controls over 'pay drift' under an PRP system. If all managers choose to award high performance ratings – and there is research evidence that line managers are often reluctant to award low ratings for fear of antagonising staff – the cost of IPRP can escalate quickly. For this reason many IPRP systems operate a 'forced distribution' whereby there are limits on the number of staff who can be entered under each rating category. This 'forced distribution', however, can also create further problems because it may be seen as unfair by staff who exceed their targets but are not selected for the top rating. A classic example of this issue was the so-called 'stack ranking' system at Microsoft, which was widely detested by both managers and staff (Eichenwald, 2012) and finally abandoned. There will also be audits of each manager's ratings to ensure that consistent standards are being applied across the workforce. Another feature of many PRP systems is that merit increases may be larger at the bottom of the pay range and smaller at the top. This reflects that view that performance improvements are most obvious when staff are starting in their roles and become less clear as their experience grows.

CASE STUDY 5.1

From annual increments to PRP, evaluating teachers' pay reform

The government has introduced substantial reforms to the pay of teachers in the English local authority (LA) maintained sector, to give schools greater freedom to decide how much they pay teachers and how quickly their pay progresses. The new system was introduced in September 2013 and affected pay decisions in LA maintained schools from September 2014 (changes were voluntary in academies). A central feature was the abolition of automatic progression for all classroom teachers, and the introduction of performance-related pay (PRP). Schools also now have more flexibility to decide starting salaries when recruiting teachers, and are no longer required to match teachers' previous salaries.

The study set out to identify what reforms schools were making, what influenced their decisions and the perceived implications for staff and schools.

The study comprised five strands of activity:

1. a literature review;
2. a headteacher survey;
3. a teacher survey;
4. case studies in eight schools;
5. analysis of administrative data from the School Workforce Census (SWC).

Key findings

Adoption of pay reforms

- The surveys with headteachers undertaken in spring 2015 revealed that almost all (99%) of LA maintained primary and secondary schools and a majority (62%) of academies had implemented pay reforms.
- The most common reforms to classroom teachers' pay were: to relate all progression to performance; to enable teachers to progress at different rates; and to abolish automatic pay progression on the main pay range.
- The interviews with staff in case-study schools revealed that a number of changes had been introduced to schools' performance management processes. The main changes related to objective setting, evidence use and progression pathways. Performance management processes were reported to be more transparent, robust and rigorous as a result.

Implementation of pay reforms

- The surveys with headteachers undertaken in spring 2015 as part of this research revealed that the most common types of evidence used by schools to assess teacher effectiveness were: pupil progress; classroom observation; teacher standards; measures linked to the school improvement plan; and pupil attainment. Most schools were using these measures prior to the introduction of the pay reforms.
- The main challenges associated with the pay reforms, as reported by case-study interviewees, were: the additional staff time involved in collecting and reviewing evidence for performance reviews; the pressure on teachers to meet pupil outcome targets; and the challenge of applying a school's pay policy fairly in certain situations, such as job shares.

Teachers' views of pay reforms

- The teacher survey found that two thirds (66%) of teachers felt they understood their school's pay policy and about half (52%) felt they had received adequate training on the policy. However, less than a quarter (23%) felt they had had a meaningful opportunity to contribute to their school's pay policy before it was introduced.
- A majority of teachers had positive attitudes towards the implementation of their school's pay policy. Over half of respondents agreed that it: treated all staff equally without favouritism (60%); was clear and easy to understand (57%); and was applied consistently across all teachers (52%).
- Fewer teachers were convinced of the motivational nature of their school's pay policy. Just over a quarter (27%) agreed that it

Table 5.3 School teachers' (E&W) pay ranges, 1 September 2018

Main pay range 2018–annual salary				
	England and Wales (excluding the London area) £	**Inner London area £**	**Outer London area £**	**Fringe area £**
Minimum	23,720	29,664	27,596	24,859
Maximum	35,008	40,372	38,963	36,157
Upper pay range 2018–annual salary				
	England and Wales (excluding the London area) £	**Inner London area £**	**Outer London area £**	**Fringe area £**
Minimum	36,646	44,489	40,310	37,758
Maximum	39,406	48,244	43,348	40,520

(**SOURCE:** DfE (2018) School teachers' pay and conditions document 2018 and guidance on school teachers' pay and conditions, September 2018, www.gov.uk/government/publications/school-teachers-pay-and-conditions)

helped motivate underperforming teachers and 38% agreed that it helped their school to further motivate teachers who were already performing well. Only 34% agreed that it resulted in a fair allocation of pay for staff in the school.

- A majority of teachers (66%) thought that their school's current pay policy had added to their workload and 58% thought that it had made no difference to the way they worked.

National trends in pay of teachers and school leaders

Analysis of national data from the SWC investigated changes between 2010 and 2015:

- Many schools, when they did increase teacher pay, were still awarding annual increases in line with the previous (now reference) spine points, though this practice varied across LA areas. The increased variation in annual pay awards around reference spine points suggests that at least some schools had moved away from using this benchmark.
- There was some evidence of increased flexibility in progression from the main to the upper pay range, with a greater proportion of those below the top of the main pay range progressing to the upper pay range following the reforms (2.7% between 2010 and 2011, compared with 7.8% between 2014 and 2015).

(**SOURCE:** DfE (2017) Evaluation of Teachers' Pay Reform Research brief, October 2017, www.gov.uk/government/publications/teachers-pay-reform-evaluation)

NOTE: *the above is based on selected extracts from the evaluation report. The full research brief contains further findings and information.*

CASE STUDY QUESTIONS

1 Based on the evidence presented in this case study, what do you think have been the positive aspects of teachers' pay reform? Which groups do you think have benefited most?

2 What have been the negative effects of pay reform? What implications might these have for the teaching profession?

The case study mentions the use of 'reference spine points', the previous pay scale framework. Go to the teacher union websites (neu.org.uk/advice/teachers-pay-structure or www.nasuwt.org.uk/advice/pay-pensions/pay-progression.html) to find out more about the these 'reference' scales. Why do you think the trade unions continue to publish them, and what effect might this have?

As highlighted by CIPD (2016), there has recently been a shift away from the sort of formalised, cyclical performance management process described above. This has been epitomised by high-profile, large US organisations such as Deloitte, Microsoft, Adobe and even GE (the original 'rank and yank' corporation), abandoning performance management approaches that use the appraisal-rating system. There appear to be a number of reasons for this so-called 'performance management revolution'.

Cappelli and Tavis (2016) in *Harvard Business Review* cite criticisms surrounding bureaucracy, restrictions on creativity and innovation, and the near-universal unpopularity of appraisals with managers and employees alike. More important, the authors claim, are the negative effects of the end-of-year accountability model; financial reward or punishment based on past performance rather than future-focused growth and development.

While ratings can send important messages to staff about their performance, they have also been recognised as potentially demotivating and subject to manager bias. One way of combatting this potential for bias has been the growth of multiple stakeholders in the appraisal process (so-called '360 degree' appraisal), following widespread usage in the USA (Bach, 2013). The involvement of not just line managers in the process but also colleagues and even clients is intended to provide a more rounded view of individual performance, less subject to personal bias. This form of multi-source feedback may involve a combination of information from self-appraisal, subordinate appraisal, peer appraisal and feedback from other internal and external customers (Silverman et al, 2005).

KEY ISSUES IN REWARD MANAGEMENT 5.1

Rewarding performance without ratings?

Appraisals gave managers a clear-cut way of tying rewards to individual contributions. Companies changing their (performance management) systems are trying to figure out how their new practices will affect the pay-for-performance model, which none of them have explicitly abandoned.

They still differentiate rewards, usually relying on managers' qualitative judgments rather than numerical ratings. In pilot programmes at Juniper Systems and Cargill, supervisors had no difficulty allocating merit-based pay without appraisal scores. In fact, both line managers and HR staff felt that paying closer attention to employee performance throughout the year was likely to make their merit-pay decisions more valid.

But it will be interesting to see whether most supervisors end up reviewing the feedback they've given each employee over the year before determining merit increases. (Deloitte's managers already do this.) If so, might they produce something like an annual appraisal score – even though it's more carefully considered? And could that subtly undermine development by shifting managers' focus back to accountability?

(**SOURCE:** Cappelli and Tavis, 2016)

As Cappelli and Tavis (2016) point out (see Key Issues in Reward Management 5.1), organisations replacing their formalised rating-appraisal performance management systems with more regular, informal conversations or 'check-ins' will have to decide whether to continue linking performance to pay and, if they do, how these decisions will be made. The pattern of linking performance management systems to pay in UK is unclear although there is evidence that it had been increasing in the past two decades. In 2009 (CIPD, 2009a), less than a third of respondents linked their performance management system to pay. In contrast, the most recent WERS (van Wanrooy et al, 2013) found that the percentage of workplaces directly linking pay to the outcomes of appraisal rose between 2004 and 2011, with a quarter of workplaces partly determining non-managerial pay in this way, up from 16 per cent in 2004. Similarly, a survey by e-reward (e-reward, 2014) found that almost 60 per cent of its survey respondents linked an overall performance rating to pay. In 2019 the CIPD (Marriot and Perkins, 2019) Reward Management Survey shows 75 per cent of organisations using individual performance as a criterion for pay progression, although not necessarily as a result of ratings and often in conjunction with other criteria. It remains to be seen what the effects of the 'performance management revolution' will have on PRP as a means of pay progression.

SELF-ASSESSMENT EXERCISE

From your own experience of being appraised – or indeed given feedback on your academic performance as a student – what do you think are the major obstacles to a fair and consistent system of assessing your performance? How might these be overcome? What do your fellow students think?

5.9 Competency-based pay

As doubts have increased in recent times about the effects of PRP, there have been moves either to change the process – through improving the design of schemes – or shift to new methods of individualised pay progression. Under these alternative systems, progression still relates to assessment of the individual worker rather than everybody having guaranteed progression to the maximum of the grade or band as under a traditional seniority-based system. The criteria for progression are entirely linked to input-based factors rather than target outputs. There is some evidence that competency-based progression systems are more popular among employees (and trades unions) than PRP because they incorporate a notion of employee development into pay progression. Not only are workers encouraged to develop their skills, but they are also rewarded for doing so. Whereas IPRP can appear to be simply a punitive system to penalise workers, competency-based systems can in contrast appear positive for employees' own career development.

The growth of competency-based HR systems has partly been attributed to the changing nature of white-collar work. As Mayhew and Keep (1999) argue, non-manual work is increasingly as much about behaviours and attitudes displayed at work as the possession of any particular analytic skills or skills based on understanding theoretical concepts. This change has been driven particularly by the growth of the service sector, where competitiveness is highly dependent on the social skills of the employees (Thompson, 2000). These 'people skills' are found in both private services such as retail, finance and hospitality and in traditional public services such as health and education. Such 'interpersonal skills' are often difficult to measure under traditional output-based PRP schemes, and employers have become increasingly interested in 'competency-based' approaches. Traditional PRP schemes have been observed to create a 'tunnel vision' situation where employees focus only on what is required to be achieved at the expense of how it is achieved. They have also, as we have seen, been criticised for undermining teamwork. Competency-based pay, in contrast, rewards behaviours and attitudes such as co-operation, courtesy and communication.

Another attraction of competency-based pay is that it can form part of a much wider competency-based HR system, with the same competencies being used for other HR functions. Research by XpertHR (2014a) found that competencies were commonly used for performance management, training and development, recruitment, succession planning and capability and redundancy procedures as well as pay.

DEFINITION

A payment system that relates salary progression or a cash bonus to the display of 'competencies' by individual employees. Systems originate in the identification of competency, understood as the key attributes and behaviours of employees that underlie good performance in a particular organisation or job.

(Heery and Noon, 2017)

The growth of competencies or 'behavioural traits' as the building blocks for HR systems began in the 1980s and developed through the 1990s. Boyatzis (1982), for example, argued that it was possible to identify and define the behaviours that good performers display and hence these could be codified and used to evaluate and develop such behaviours across an organisation. Lawler (1990) claimed that the use of competencies reflected the shift away from HR systems built on the traditional concept of 'job' with fixed duties, accountabilities and responsibilities towards more fluid and developmental approaches. As Thompson (2000: 142) indicates, 'under these new structures, the job paradigm is seen as less effective because it leads to inflexibility, and creates a mindset that resists managerial objectives to adapt continuously to changing organisational circumstances'. According to Lawler (1996: 76), the 'challenge in a competency-based organisation is to focus on what individuals need to be able to do in order to make the work processes operate effectively'.

Competency-based systems are also often linked to the introduction of broad-banded grading systems (see Chapter 4) as they enable the absence of vertical career progression to be replaced by a new language of performance and development within the role that is not necessarily linked to promotion. It can also provide more lateral flexibility to move employees across career boundaries as progression is no longer linked to specific skills and knowledge but to abilities and behaviours. Brown

(2001) makes the point that competency measures are often combined with more traditional performance measures, and hence a more suitable term might be 'competency-*related* pay'.

5.9.1 Competence or competency?

A key issue is one of definition. Woodruffe (1991) suggested that there is a difference between '*competence*' and '*competency*'. **Competence** refers to the areas of work in which the employee is competent (measurable skills). **Competency** is a wider concept and refers to the behaviours that underpin competent performance (i.e. an assessment of the employee's attitudes and behaviour). In a similar fashion, Armstrong and Brown (1999: 235) identify a distinction between 'technical competencies' – which refer to the knowledge and skills employees need to do their job – and 'behavioural competencies', which refer to the personal characteristics that employees bring to their work (e.g. teamworking, strategic perspective, leadership and achievement-orientation). Research by Rickard et al (2012) on pay progression conflates competencies with skills as a single method of progression with the distinguishing features being that skills measurements tend to apply to manual workers while competencies apply more to non-manual workers, but in some cases organisations may use a combination of both observable skills and work behaviours.

Under competency-related progression individual employees will still be subject to a performance review, but the issues addressed will be the extent to which they have met or exceeded the expected level of competency for their role. Such systems can look, on the surface at least, very similar to traditional PRP ratings, and there is some variation between organisations in terms of the mix of skills and behaviours required. Some competency-based schemes may emphasise the acquisition and use of particular skills (such as knowledge of particular computer software systems) more than the behaviours and attitudes required. Most competency-based pay (CBP) systems will refer both to inputs (e.g. knowledge, skills, attitudes, attributes and abilities) and outputs (measurable achievements), but there may also be an emphasis on process – how the work is carried out.

The incidence of CBP is unclear, largely because it is often used in combination with other pay progression criteria rather than alone. According to the most recent 2019 CIPD Reward Survey (Marriot and Perkins, 2019), 62 per cent of respondents based progression on competence to some extent. This was most common in the professional service sector (legal, financial, technology, etc) with 72 per cent of organisations using this approach; and least common in the public sector (51 per cent). Research by XpertHR (2014) found that 6 in 10 respondents used competencies for designing grading structures and over half used them as part of the pay progression system. A survey of private sector pay progression practices for the OME (2014a) found 38 per cent used behavioural competencies as part of their progression criteria. The practice appeared to be more common among those with salary ranges (41 per cent) than those with incremental scales (33 per cent).

An argument can be made in favour of competency-related pay on the grounds that it can encourage the development and improvement of desired competencies, facilitate lateral career moves and encourage staff to take an interest in their own development, moving away from PRP towards organisational competencies

(Rickard et al, 2012: 35). However, according to Milkovich et al (2014), there is little empirical research on the use of competency systems. They argue that it may be more appropriate to pay people according to what they are actually doing rather than according to what they are capable of doing, which then blurs the line between competency pay and PRP.

Sparrow (1996) argues that there are two levels of competency – one that is trait-based and not amenable to change (e.g. it concerns the individual's own personality), and one that is open to change. Most competency-related pay schemes, he argues, are not robust enough to be able to distinguish between these two. Sparrow also casts doubt on the ability of managers to measure and evaluate complex issues like human behaviour. Strebler et al (1997) have also raised issues about the desired behaviours used in competence schemes, not least the risk of gender and ethnic stereotyping of the desired personality traits. Lawler (1996) too questions the ability to measure an individual's ability to perform a task, and argues that core competencies may not be relevant in assessing individual roles arguing that they need to be combined with other criteria for to make progression decisions.

More recent data bears out some of these concerns. Research by XpertHR (2014) reported that around 40 per cent of respondents to their survey had experienced problems with competencies, the most important being an understanding of the system among the users of the system (67 per cent). This would suggest that overly complex competency systems can be self-defeating. Milkovich et al (2014: 179) point out that because 'competencies are trying to get at what underlies work behaviours, there is a lot of fuzziness in defining them'. Another problem found by XpertHR was identifying the appropriate performance levels for particular individuals' roles.

SELF-ASSESSMENT EXERCISE

Consider the advantages and disadvantages of competency-related pay progression, how such schemes differ from PRP and whether they are preferable.

5.10 Skills-based pay

Another way of linking pay increases to individual employees is through skills-based assessment. Such schemes link progression – either through the grade/band or through promotion to a new grade/band – to acquisition of designated skill levels. Such systems are also sometimes known as 'pay for knowledge' or 'knowledge-based pay'.

Skills-based pay (SBP) has been seen as promoting workforce flexibility through rewarding individuals for the type, number and depth of skills held. However, the way SBP systems are designed and structured is very much context-and industry-dependent (Lockey et al, 2017). SBP also includes 'competencies' where these are defined as skills or knowledge rather than behaviours. While prevalent in manufacturing and engineering industries, SBP is also found in academia as well as retail, distribution, catering and other private services.

Lockey et al (2017) give three prerequisites for an effective SBP system:

1 skills should be clearly defined;
2 a training system that allows employees to seek and acquire the desired skills should be available;
3 a formal competency testing system to ensure the mastery and maintenance of the desired skills should be implemented.

DEFINITION

Skill-based pay is an input-based payment system in which employees receive increases in pay for undergoing training and adding to their range or depth of skills.

(Heery and Noon, 2017)

Such systems have often been used in organisations that use self-managed work teams. In these organisations, individuals are required to learn a range of skills in order that the team can operate with a minimum amount of supervision and control. According to Lawler (2000: 131), such schemes were first used in the late 1960s in both the USA and Europe, 'and they remain the system of choice in manufacturing and service environments that use self-managing teams'. It has also been observed that SBP plans often require fewer classifications and grades than traditional reward systems (Recardo and Pricone, 1996). Skills-based pay systems are normally founded on the view that employees are only paid for the skills and knowledge the organisation needs them to acquire and that they are willing and able to use. Such schemes therefore normally provide guidance on what skills are required and for what purpose.

Five types of SBP plans have been identified by Recardo and Pricone (1996), which can be categorised as follows:

- *Vertical skill* measure the acquisition of input/output skills within a single job (e.g. a press operator acquiring preventive maintenance skills).
- *Horizontal skill plans* reward the acquisition of complementary skills across several jobs (e.g. an individual learns how to do both accounts payable and accounts received).
- *Depth skill plans* reward skill specialisation (e.g. a computer programmer specialising in databases).
- *Basic skill systems* reward employees for developing expertise in the basic skill areas (mathematics, reading, writing and speaking English).
- *Combination plans* reward any of the skills above.

Most SBP systems are of the last category.

Recardo and Pricone also point out that SBP systems normally require the redesign of jobs by shifting away from traditional Taylorist job design and towards more socio-technical approaches that 'focus on the completion of a discrete piece of work, foster task variability, promote task significance, provide on-going "realtime" feedback, and enhance decision-making autonomy' (Recardo and Pricone, 1996: 17). Once the work has been redesigned, tasks are then reconfigured into 'skill blocks'. The number and sequence of skills that an employee can learn vary significantly between organisations. In some manufacturing environments employees may have the opportunity to learn all the jobs required within a 'cell'. Learning may be accomplished through job rotation, and there are normally a minimum number of skills that an employee must acquire within a specified period. Acquisition of the required skills is rewarded by progression – either through an additional increment or pay increase or, in some cases, regrading.

Many SBP systems require some form of certification of skills. This requires clear measures of demonstrable ability, and evaluation is normally conducted through observation, oral or written tests or on-the-job performance. Workers may also be required to undergo periodic recertification, with failure possibly leading to reductions in pay.

It is easy to see why proponents of SBP claim that it promotes flexible working practices achieved partly through fewer and simpler job classifications and partly through the employee involvement that such systems encourage. Such systems could also improve operational problem-solving and cut the cost of supervisory and administrative overheads. In addition they may provide pay progression routes for manual workers who traditionally may have been paid on single 'spot rates', thereby opening up opportunities for earnings growth. SPB has also been seen as a more equitable pay system because it is argued that it rewards demonstrable increases in the value of the worker to the employer.

Most of the benefits of SBP discussed above, however, link to the promotion of more flexible, less Taylorist, methods of job design. The real question is whether the linkage to pay is necessary as an incentive for employees to adopt such practices. Armstrong and Stephens (2005) are critical and argue that SBP is expensive to introduce and maintain. They state that 'Although in theory a skill-based scheme will pay only for necessary skills, in practice individuals will not be using them all at the same time and some may be used infrequently, if at all' (2005: 249).

Lawler (2000), however, concludes that paying for skills can be an effective approach to determining base pay. But, like Armstrong and Stephens, he also sees SBP as relatively high-maintenance because skills need continuous updating as the technology and structure of the organisation change and individuals change their ability to perform tasks. A big question is: what happens when a worker has learned all the skills required? Lawler (2000) argues that skills-based pay, because it does not pay for ongoing performance, also needs to be combined with some form of performance-related pay if it is to be effective. He also comments that SBP may help to retain the most skilled workers because they become highly paid relative to the market rate for their jobs and because the specificity of the skills learned makes it difficult for them to find other jobs.

IDS (2010a) found that around 14 per cent of organisations were using skills acquisition as the most important factor in determining individual pay increases. The Reward Management Survey (Marriot and Perkins, 2019) reported that progression based on skills was found in 56 per cent of organisations and that it was most common in manufacturing and production (75 per cent) and private sector services (63 per cent).

Research on skills-based pay has found that such systems are generally well accepted by employees because 'it is easy to see the connection between the plan, the work and size of the paycheck' (Milkovich et al, 2014: 175). The systems therefore provide a strong incentive for employees to improve their skill levels. There is also evidence of benefits to workers in terms of workforce productivity and attitudes (Mitra et al, 2011). Lockey et al (2017) also cite a number of studies which find evidence of SBP creating positive workplace attitudes (improved employee satisfaction and commitment) and flexibility (greater adaptability of employees in meeting production needs, and increased work team effectiveness) which led to improvements in the relationship between pay plans and workplace productivity.

5.11 Market-based pay

Another method of individual pay progression considered in this chapter is market-based pay. As we discussed in Chapter 3, all pay structures have to be kept in line with the wider economy – either in terms of the pay levels of competitors or keeping the purchasing power of pay in line with inflation. Research by XpertHR (2012) found that pay benchmarking was used by over 94 per cent of respondents to a survey on market-based pay. The survey found that the main purposes of market benchmarking were to conduct spot checks on current salaries (85.4 per cent), to support the pay review process (78.1 per cent), to set salaries for new recruits (71.5 per cent) and to set salary rates within a grading structure or spot rates system (64.2 per cent). We looked at these pay alignment issues in Chapter 3. Employers use a wide range of market benchmarking tools to ensure that both the whole pay structure is kept competitive within the external labour market and in setting individual salary levels. Gathering pay intelligence, such as salary survey data and relevant economic data, has become a major and ongoing exercise for the reward manager.

In this section, however, we discuss briefly how organisations use pay and benefits data to design individual pay packages and to govern the rate of progression through the grade or band. Pricing a particular job for both recruitment and retention purposes requires a clear understanding of the value of particular occupations in various labour markets (local, regional, national or international, depending on the level of the job). As we have already indicated earlier, there is in all organisations a constant dynamic tension between meeting the demands of internal equity (so that staff feel fairly paid in comparison to their colleagues) and the needs of the external labour market. These two pressures can, in reality, yield very different outcomes. For example, under job evaluation an accounts manager and a marketing manager may score at the same level in terms of job 'weight' (and hence be graded in the same grade or band). But when external comparisons are made it may well be found that accounts managers are paid considerably more than marketing managers. There may also be significant differences in pay level for the same role both between organisations in the same field, in different geographic locations and between sectors or industries.

As is also discussed in previous chapters, to research the market for particular jobs, employers use a range of benchmarking tools, the main one of which is the salary survey. As has been argued (White, 2009), over the last few decades there has been a dramatic increase in the number and range of salary survey sources available to the reward practitioner. Sources include:

> **Published data** from pay surveys and similar organisations can give some indication of going rates. The degree to which it's useful is limited because of problems in comparing like with like, but they can help with periodic 'reality checks' on levels and movements and are useful sources of data on specific occupations or localities.
>
> **Pay clubs** – employer groups that regularly exchange pay information. These generally only allow participants to access the data.
>
> **Special surveys** funded by individual organisations from specialist pay consultancies, but access is usually limited to the contractor and participants.
>
> **Consultants' pay databases** containing data collected on a systematic or ad hoc basis that they relate to the results of their job evaluation schemes to compare pay rates across organisations on a common basis: this ability is one of the attractions of job evaluation for many organisations. To be viable it is important that the factors measure common job/role characteristics and can enable comparisons to be made across different jobs/roles and organisations; the data is based on an adequate sample; and the job analyses are carried out systematically and conscientiously.
>
> (SOURCE: CIPD, 2022b)

This increase in benchmarking partly reflects the diminishing importance of industry-wide pay agreements (where all employers in a sector pay the same for the same jobs) as collective bargaining has declined as the major form of pay determination. It also reflects the increasing individualisation of reward systems, with greater emphasis on the performance or competence of the person in the role, rather than the 'rate for the job'.

Research on private sector pay progression for the OME (2014) found differences in the use and positioning of market rates, with organisations operating salary ranges much more likely to use market rates (66 per cent) than those using incremental scales (56 per cent). Most employers set the 'market rate' at the midpoint of the range but those using incremental scales were more likely to set this at a higher level. The research demonstrates a key difference between the type of progression associated with pay ranges and that associated with incremental scales. Those with the latter tend to recruit staff at the bottom of the scale and move employees up to the 'market rate' once competent in the role while those using ranges tend to recruit higher up the range but progression slows once employees have reached the 'market rate' (OME, 2014).

In some cases, the provider of a job evaluation system will also provide an annual pay benchmarking exercise for its clients. By accessing salary data collected from all its clients, the JE provider can provide a good gauge of pay levels for jobs of similar weight in different organisations. The sample, however, is clearly limited to those organisations using that particular JE scheme.

One problem identified with market pay is the potential lack of transparency for employees. Employees must take on trust the benchmark estimate of the value of their job in the external market. Benchmarking the particular job will depend on the availability of good comparator data, but there will be some jobs where data is sparse and others where the data is inconclusive. In addition, the employer then needs to communicate the outcome in simple terms to the employee. In smaller organisations, individual pay levels may be set and updated solely in line with market information about the particular job or role. Others may have job families (see Chapter 4), which allow the employer to distinguish between different occupational groups in terms of their wider market value.

There are, of course, implicit dangers of gender discrimination in this process, particularly if one occupational group (e.g. HR) is predominantly female and another (e.g. finance and accountancy) is predominantly male. If the data used by employers is not sound, or indeed merely reflects occupational pay inequities, employers may leave themselves open to equal-pay claims. Equal-pay legislation does, however, recognise the 'market' as a defence for inequality in particular circumstances.

An alternative method of dealing with the market is to have market supplements for particular jobs or roles. These additions to base pay are often paid to compensate staff where their grade or band allocation under a job evaluation scheme places them at a disadvantage within the wider labour market. For example, IT specialists may be graded alongside other technical and administrative staff but may require a market supplement if their pay is to stay in line with the external market for such staff. Such supplements need to be regularly reviewed as the external market can change and employers can end up paying for shortage skills that no longer exist.

5.12 Pay for contribution

Given the range of methods of linking pay to progression discussed in this chapter, the HR professional may well be bewildered. Each method has its own advantages and disadvantages, and the choice of system, at the end of the day, is contingent on the strategy, circumstances and culture of the organisation. What has appeared in more recent times is a more 'blended' approach to reward design. This approach has been designated 'pay for contribution' by Armstrong and Brown (1999). In their book, *Paying for Contribution*, they set out a new approach to pay design in which no particular progression system is advocated. Rather, they propose a return to contingency theory (see Chapter 2) and a 'pick and mix' view of reward design. This is partly a defence of individual-based reward systems in the face of strong criticism of traditional PRP systems – and to a lesser extent competence and skills-based systems – and partly a call for a more strategic approach to the design of reward systems that emphasises strategic fit rather than best practice.

Armstrong and Brown (1999: xiii) argue that their approach is a 'manifestly distinct approach', characterised by the following:

- paying for how results are achieved as well as the results themselves, thus paying for competence as well as performance;
- paying for those skills and behaviours supporting the future success of the individual and the organisation, not just immediate results;
- rewarding a combination of organisation, team and individual performance, rather than concentrating wholly on the latter;
- the use of a wide variety of reward vehicles;
- a long-term evolutionary approach, incorporating a variety of HR systems and processes, rather than attempting a pay 'quick fix';

- addressing all aspects of reward strategy: the objectives and goals, the design and systems, the implementation and operation, rather than just focusing on the design mechanics.

These authors argue that this return to contingency is happening because:

> Traditional categorisations such as paying for the job or paying for the person; paying in fixed base pay or paying in variable bonus; paying for the team or paying for the individual's performance; and paying for results or how those results are achieved... are increasingly being broken down as companies develop a series of tailored and hybrid approaches, which themselves are subject to regular modification and change. Changing a pay or bonus plan after a year of operation used to be seen as an admission of failure... now it is increasingly regarded as obvious and essential.
>
> (Armstrong and Brown, 1999: 415)

They continue:

> As the research and our experience have illustrated, there is no universal set of success criteria, just as there are no 'right' or 'wrong' types of scheme. Success is totally dependent on your pay and reward scheme objectives, and on the environment and circumstances in which you introduce and operate it. The same scheme can work brilliantly in one setting and fail disastrously in another.
>
> (1999: 416)

They identify three main features of their 'pay for contribution' paradigm:

- An acknowledgement that 'pay is potentially a highly powerful management tool'.
- An aversion to 'off-the-shelf, merit pay systems'.
- An acknowledgement of 'a strategic approach to reward.

They also provide five 'practical pointers'. These are:

- Contribution-based pay is particularly appropriate in sectors where it is recognised that employee skills and behaviours are the key to competitive success.
- Pay generally supports the move towards a more competence- and contribution-focused organisation, rather than leading the change.
- All aspects of pay and reward need to be integrated (i.e. a 'total reward' approach).
- In the majority of organisations, there is still the need to consider job content and results achieved as well as competencies, base pay as well as bonus, individual as well as teams, when paying for contribution.
- Keep it simple.

There does seem to be some empirical support for Brown and Armstrong's view that organisations are using more 'blended' pay progression systems, rather than relying on one method. A survey for the OME (OME, 2014: vii) on private sector pay progression in the UK found that the 'majority of organisations base progression on

Table 5.4 Comparison of 1980s-style pay-for-performance approaches with pay for contribution

	Pay for performance	Pay for contribution
Organising philosophy	Formulas, systems	Processes
HR approach	Instrumentalist; people as costs	Commitment; people as assets
Measurement	Pay for results, the 'whats', achieving individual objectives	Multi-dimensional, pay for results and 'how' results are achieved
Measures	Financial goals Cost-efficiency	Broad variety of strategic goals: financial, service, operating, etc Added value
Focus of measurement	Individual	Multi-level: business, team, individual
Design	Uniform merit pay and/or individual bonus approach throughout the organisation	Diverse approaches using a wide variety of reward methods, to suit the needs of different areas/staff groups
Timescales	Immediate past performance	Past performance, and contribution to future strategic goals
Performance management	Past review and ratings focus Top-down Quantitative	Mix of past review and future development 360-degree Quantitative and qualitative
Pay linkage	Fixed formula, matrix	Looser, more flexible linkages, pay 'pots'
Administration	Controlled by HR	Owned/operated by line/users
Communication and involvement	Top-down, written	Face to face, open, high involvement
Evaluation of effectiveness	Act of faith	Regular review and monitoring against clearly defined success criteria
Changes over time	Regarded as failure; all or nothing	Regular incremental modification

SOURCE: Brown and Armstrong (1999)

a combination of criteria and the survey showed a common hybrid research is to use performance alongside skills, competencies and behaviour'. Only 17 per cent used a single method. The latest CIPD Reward Management Survey (Marriott and Perkins, 2019) results also indicate that organisations do not use pay progression criteria in isolation and a 'blended' approach appears to be common.

SELF-ASSESSMENT EXERCISE

Is the 'contribution-based pay' concept just 'old wine in new bottles', or do you think it is really new? To what extent do you think such a contingency-based approach is required, or do you believe that the 'best practice' approach of writers such as Jeffrey Pfeffer is more convincing?

Table 5.5 summarises many of the types of pay progression dealt with in this chapter.

Table 5.5 Progression types

Type	Description	Advantages	Pitfalls
Pure Types			
Service	Annual increments based on time spent in grade – still common in not-for-profit and public sectors. In private sector, likely to be modified by performance requirements	Highly transparent, with clear career paths for staff, usually based on experience	Can be a source of discrimination if scales are long, as women tend to have breaks in service
Performance	Appraisal-based payments consolidated into basic salary, on basis of overall 'pot', with individual increases varying according to performance. Commonplace for white-collar staff, much less so for manual workers	Can improve staff motivation and retention	Associated with low transparency; can demotivate, especially in periods of low inflation
Competency	Dimensions of behaviour that an employee must display in order to perform capably in their role in the workplace, for example analytical thinking, communications skills. Some schemes mix behavioural elements with more objective measures of skill level	Often more acceptable to staff and unions than merit-based approaches	Complex – link to pay not straightforward
Skills	Extra pay for completing each skill module in a sequence. Grew out of traditional approaches for manual and craft workers, for example apprenticeships, but now applied to lower-level white-collar staff as well	Pay differentiated more objectively, on basis of skills or experience	Need to ensure skills are being used in the job; updates necessary as work processes change

(continued)

Table 5.5 (Continued)

Type	Description	Advantages	Pitfalls
Market	Linking salary levels to what other organisations pay for similar jobs. Exact applications vary, from 'market anchors' with no floors/ceilings, to using market rates to define progression within ranges	Can assist with retention, especially in tight labour markets	If market static, no progression, which may demotivate; issues around transparency, and data availability (specialised jobs)
Contribution	New concept, sometimes defined as performance plus competency, which measures employees' achievement against both objectives and competencies	Provides ability to influence employees' behaviour	Most suited to senior management roles; needs to fit with company culture
Hybrid types			
Service plus performance	Most common hybrid – progression according to annual increments, subject to satisfactory performance. More rapid progression possible, subject to budgets	Flexibility to withhold or accelerate increments	Stronger links to performance constrained by budgets
Performance plus market	Various systems that provide accelerated progression to a market rate or zone, with slower progress once this has been achieved. Commonplace in finance	Said to speed progression to target rates, with added openness about ways pay is managed	Staff dislike lack of progression above market rates; not always as transparent as claimed
Performance plus skills or competency	Progression accelerated or withheld on basis of performance, but also link to skills acquisition. Common among call centre employers and some electronics manufacturers, for example Motorola	Flexibility for employers; can aid staff retention	Need to focus on use of skills, not simply on their acquisition

SOURCE: IDS (2006c: 15–16)

5.13 Compensatory payments

Finally, in terms of the composition of pay, this section deals with special 'compensatory payments' to employees working in particular circumstances. These tend to be applied to all staff in a grade or role, irrespective of their individual performance or market rate. The main examples of compensatory payments are: location allowances; overtime premiums; shift premiums; and call-out and standby payments. There are also some particular allowances paid to manual workers in particular industries – for example, tool allowances for engineering and construction crafts. While location allowances may apply to all levels of staff, overtime, shift and call-out payments are usually limited to lower-grade employees. Furthermore, in recent years there has been a concerted effort by many employers to move away from a plethora of separate allowances and premiums towards so-called 'clean remuneration' whereby these allowances are integrated or 'consolidated' into base pay.

5.13.1 Location allowances

Location allowances originally emerged in London in the 1970s to compensate workers for the higher cost of living within the metropolitan region. Such allowances continue to feature in many organisations' reward systems in order to be able to recruit and retain staff within the city. Moreover, within the tight labour market of the 1990s, such allowances began to spread out beyond London to the so-called 'Roseland' area (Rest of South East) and further.

Originally such allowances, or 'weightings' as they are often known, were designed to provide 'cost compensation' to staff for living and working in London (and were based on government indices showing changes in costs published for this purpose). Because of the indices, allowances tended to be similar across organisations. In more recent times, however, such allowances have become more associated with recruitment and retention issues (because the London and South East regions in the UK have the tightest labour markets) and hence become more market-based and differentiated. Employers have also moved away from flat-rate allowances (e.g. £3,500 pa) paid to all staff irrespective of grade level towards percentage allowances or simply to regional pay bands. IDS notes a range of other methods of dealing with the London labour market (IDS, 2010b). These include:

- separate, higher, London salary scales or ranges;
- zonal pay systems, with particular locations moving from one zone to another according to local labour market conditions;
- nationwide, broad-banded structures, providing scope to vary pay levels according to 'market salary guides';
- various forms of 'recruitment and retention' or 'hot spot' supplements; and
- the use of grading flexibilities within existing pay spines.

A survey in 2013 (XpertHR, 2013) of location pay and allowances found that over half the respondents (54 per cent) use market-based or market-linked pay scales to respond to geographic differences in supply and demand for labour. A third (31 per cent) use specific London allowances as an addition to basic salaries and a fifth (19 per cent) make location payments to employees working outside the capital. Fewer than 16 per cent of respondents use location pay scales such as a separate London scale. Some 70 per cent of respondents make their allowances pensionable. Where location allowances are paid, they apply to all employees in 60 per cent of organisations, while a fifth target them at particular job roles or employee groups.

Figures produced by IDS (cited in Hirsch, 2016) on London allowances show the wide range of amounts provided in allowances with workers within the Energy and Water sector in Central/Inner London being paid 10 times the allowance of workers in the retail sector in the London Fringe/South East. Hirsch (2016), in a report for charity Trust for London, calls for a fresh approach to location allowances, looking closely at what Londoners need to spend to reach a minimum living standard compared to elsewhere in the UK factoring in the additional costs of housing, childcare and public transport of working in the capital city.

5.13.2 Overtime premiums

Compensation for working more than the contractual hours for the job is often paid through an overtime premium. These premiums may vary between the times when the extra hours are worked, with higher compensation for working weekends and bank holidays than weekdays. There are legal limits on working hours in the UK (the Working Time Regulations), but there is no legislation laying down the overtime rates to be paid (unlike employees in the USA covered by collective agreements with trade unions). These rates are decided at industry or organisation level. Typical overtime premiums paid may be one and half times the basic hourly rate for weekdays and Saturdays (known as 'time and a half') and double the hourly rate for working on weekends (known as 'double time'). Such premiums have been most commonly found in manufacturing and the public services and among lower-grade manual and clerical staff. Eligibility for overtime pay may differ between manual and non-manual staff, with white-collar grades often having a cut-off point above which overtime premiums are not paid.

Recent statistics on overtime working (ONS, 2018b) show that since 1997, basic paid hours have increased slightly from 37.8 to 38.2 hours per week, whereas overtime hours have decreased, falling from 2.2 hours to just 1 hour per week in 2018. The figures also show that overtime makes up 2.5 per cent of mean gross weekly earnings (3.2 per cent of male earnings and just 1.3 per cent of female earnings).

Some employers have sought to reduce the cost of overtime working by introducing so-called 'annualised hours' systems where employees are contracted to work flexibly within an overall annual limit (with any hours beyond the limit being paid extra). The annual hours total typically comprises a high proportion of 'rostered' hours and a small number of flexible hours, which are worked as and when required. Under these schemes, overtime premiums are consolidated into enhanced basic salaries.

5.13.3 Shift premiums

As well as compensating employees for working additional, overtime hours many organisations pay compensatory payments for working other unsocial hours such as shifts. In some occupations, 24/7 working is essential (i.e. in many continuous process industries and the public services), but elsewhere shift working may depend on demand for the goods or services. The most common shift pattern is a two-shift system (two eight-hour shifts over 24 hours). Shift systems that involve a mix of day and night work are the second most common, closely followed by three-shift working (three eight-hour shifts over 24 hours).

Shift premiums vary according to the type of shift worked (e.g. time of shift, length of shift, extent to which night or weekend working is required). The most recent earnings and hours statistics (ONS, 2018b) indicate that shift premiums only made up 0.9 per cent of full-time mean weekly earnings.

5.13.4 *On-call and call-out pay*

A final common form of compensatory payment is that given for being on standby or 'on call' at home or in the workplace, and for being called out to work outside normal working hours. In many sectors, key workers may need to be available 24/7 in case of emergencies or mechanical/production breakdowns. This is most common in manufacturing and the public services, but even in other sectors there may be key workers required to be available at short notice to deal with specific contingencies – such as IT failures, security issues, etc.

5.14 Conclusions and key learning points

In this chapter we have explored the various methods of linking pay levels to grades or bands to create pay structures. As we have seen, pay structures are dynamic and progression through the structure can relate to various factors (see Table 5.5 for overview). While seniority-based pay was traditionally the most common form of pay progression, at least for non-manual workers, this picture changed dramatically in the 1980s and 1990s. While initially there was a strong shift to individual performance-related pay (PRP), in more recent times employers have sought to find alternative, more transparent and manageable systems of pay progression. These have included competency-based, skills-based, market-based and contribution-based. The last of these provides a blended approach where different factors are combined to reflect different aspects of an employee's contribution. One thing is clear: pay progression systems have become more varied and individualised. Even in the UK public services and the not-for-profit sector seniority-based pay is now being replaced by more individualised progression based on blends of performance, competencies or skills acquisition.

As we have discussed, the major issue to be addressed is the extent to which progression is guaranteed and to what extent it is contingent on some form of individual appraisal or review of the employee's progress. Seniority-based systems have traditionally offered both employers and employees stability and predictability. Once other criteria are used to judge employee progress, there are clear consequences in terms of frequent renegotiation of the effort bargain; the requirement for robust systems of evaluation; and a strong reliance on line managers to make good decisions.

Clearly, context plays a key role in the selection of a pay progression system. The predictability of seniority-based systems, both for employer and employee, coupled to resource constraints, has until recently limited the spread of alternative progression systems in the public and not-for-profit sectors. The presence of trade unions has also acted as a barrier to change. In contrast, the private sector has had both the resources to finance new initiatives in pay progression and, in many workplaces, greater discretion to experiment. The effects of alternative progression systems will vary according to the system adopted. But these consequences are also likely to reflect the context in which the progression system is introduced. The process is vital. For this reason, robust performance management systems are a prerequisite for any contingent form of pay progression.

Explore further

For a consideration of the evidence-base for the efficacy of financial incentives as well as practical guidance from CIPD, see www.cipd.org/uk/knowledge/evidence-reviews/evidence-financial-incentives/.

06 Variable and contingent pay schemes

CHAPTER LEARNING OUTCOMES

At the end of this chapter, you should understand and be able to explain the following:

- The concepts of variable, contingent and incentive pay.
- The various types of contingent payment system: short-term and long-term; individual, team, and collective.

CIPD STRATEGIC REWARD MANAGEMENT (7HR03) LEARNING OUTCOMES

Learners will be able to:

2.3 Analyse a range of contingent pay schemes, including the advantages and disadvantages for organisations.

4.3 Examine the potential ethical issues arising from the use of contingent forms of reward.

6.1 Introduction

In the previous chapter we discussed how employers set pay levels and how, for the majority of employees, there is some form of base pay progression through the grade or band. In this chapter we consider the alternatives to paying a fixed basic wage or salary by adopting various forms of 'contingent' or 'variable pay'. These pay components often co-exist alongside base pay, but in recent years there has been a growth in the variety of such payments, particularly for non-manual employees.

A number of reasons why employers use variable or contingent forms of remuneration have been identified: to elicit greater work effort (input) or output from workers, to enhance employees' commitment, to attract better-quality workers, to retain workers when labour markets are tight, to introduce a stronger element of fairness into remuneration practices or to act as a substitute for direct monitoring of worker performance by management (Pendleton et al, 2009). Research by IDS (2010c: 2) found that organisations adopted incentive or bonus schemes for the following reasons:

- to improve business performance (e.g. sales, productivity or profits);
- to focus employees' efforts on a number of important areas (e.g. safety, quality or customer care);
- to motivate staff by establishing a clear link between pay and performance and allowing them to share in the success of the business;
- to assist recruitment and retention by forming a key attraction of the reward package on offer;
- to help build the desired workplace culture by promoting certain behaviours, such as teamwork or good attendance.

A strong message from the New Pay writers in the 1990s was that base pay should form a diminishing part of the overall remuneration package and that reward should be composed of various separate elements, each of which should be based on specific measures of performance (Schuster and Zingheim, 1992: 154). The pretext for this view is that if reward is to be genuinely strategic in purpose, the system must reflect the various strategic priorities and psychological levers available to the employer. Such variable payments may be individual, group or organisation-wide.

This shift to variable pay may, however, have important implications for both employers and employees. As discussed in Chapter 5, there has been a strong critique of the notion of linking pay to performance (e.g. Kohn, 1993b; Pfeffer, 1998; Pink, 2009). The consequences of placing stronger emphasis upon 'variable pay' which is contingent upon the employee meeting specific criteria implies a shift in the employment relationship towards one where the employees carry more risk (Heery, 2000b). On the other hand, they may also have the capacity to increase control over their own reward outcomes. It is also worth remembering that such variable pay systems (which have always existed for manual workers) have a history of industrial conflict and unforeseen consequences, not least in terms of loss of management control, as employees learn to 'work the system'.

The use of variable pay has changed significantly in the UK in recent years. This change has been attributed to a number of factors, including the decline of collective determination of pay, the rise of the human resource management paradigm, the intensification of product market competition, the globalisation of production and changes in the political landscape (Pendleton et al, 2009). In this chapter we consider the context for this new emphasis upon variable, contingent pay, the degree to which pay has become more variable, the various alternative forms of variable pay available and their particular purposes, and the consequences of such developments.

Despite the existence of a range of critical research, both theoretical and empirical, about the motivational effects of pay (see Chapter 2 for the debate on this issue), many organisations base their reward philosophy on the view that money motivates. They continue, therefore, to design their remuneration systems around the concept of rewards for those who achieve specified targets and penalties for those who do not. Basing pay on the level of output or production has been a part of payment systems for many hundreds of years, even in pre-industrial times. As described earlier in this book, manual workers' earnings have traditionally fluctuated from week to week, according to both the effects of incentive pay and enhanced base pay for working extra and/or unsocial hours. For this reason, incentive pay has been a long-standing and contested area of the employment relationship.

In contrast, the use of incentives for non-manual employees has been a more recent phenomenon but has grown rapidly over the last few decades. The large annual bonuses paid by finance and legal firms in the City of London attract critical press attention and have a major impact on the government's average earnings index. Incentive pay is now common for non-manual employees in the private sector. The crisis in the banking sector in 2008/09 led to a review of the use of incentives to drive performance, with new attention focused on the perverse outcomes which may result. In both the USA, the UK and in the EU there have moves by central governments to put in place new regulatory measures to control the operation of bonuses for executive and senior staff (see Chapter 10).

From the discussion in Chapter 2, students will be aware that the first key text advocating incentives to improve productivity is the work of Taylor (1911), the father of 'scientific management'. The history of incentives, however, goes back at least to the beginning of the Industrial Revolution and even to ancient history. Most early work on the effects of incentives tackled productivity improvements in manufacturing environments and among manual workers. Only with the growth of the sales function in organisations in the twentieth century did the concept of financial incentives start to be applied to non-manual occupations.

Overall, in the past, variable contingent pay has been more likely to be found among male occupational groups than female and the potential for gender discrimination in such schemes has been a common criticism (Koskinen Sandberg, 2017). Many of the equal pay problems in the public sector have arisen from both occupational segregation (where jobs are considered to be 'better suited' to men or women) and the widespread use of bonus schemes for male manual workers (such as refuse collection and road maintenance) which are not available to female workers on the same grade (such as care workers or school meals staff).

Chapter 2 provides a discussion of the motivational theory underpinning the concept of pay for performance and this chapter should also be read in conjunction with Chapter 5 on pay progression systems because the conceptual differences between incentive pay, variable pay, performance-related pay and 'pay for contribution' can be confusing to the student of reward management. We begin this chapter by unpacking some of these terms.

6.2 Some key concepts

The traditional terminology used to describe payment systems designed to secure high levels of output or performance has been 'incentive scheme' or 'payment by results' (PBR). These terms were commonly used in the past to describe payment systems for manual workers in the manufacturing and construction industries (Smith, 1989). In recent times, however, incentive pay has become much more common for all types of employee. Heery and Noon (2017) define an incentive as 'a cash payment or some other reward that is offered to employees, conditional on an improvement in performance'. They go on to say that the 'purpose of an incentive is to induce motivation'. In a sense, all of the payment terms listed below refer to various forms of 'variable pay'. Whereas some, however, embrace both forms of pay progression within a grade or band and standalone payments, others are clearly only applicable to additional payments that are not consolidated into base pay.

The central proposition of the incentive effect is that pay influences the level or intensity of individual and group motivation and therefore output (Gerhart, Rynes and Fulmer, 2009). Armstrong and Murlis (2007) argue that incentives are 'forward-looking' whereas rewards are 'backward-looking' or retrospective. In other words, an incentive is designed to provide direct effect – 'Do this and you will receive this'. Incentives are therefore normally based on some form of target.

In contrast, argue Armstrong and Murlis, financial rewards are more indirect in motivational effect and more about recognition of employee efforts, rather than tied to some measurable target. They state, for example, that a bonus is a financial reward, rather than an incentive. This distinction relates to the differences between expectancy and reinforcement theory (see Chapter 2). Expectancy theory views motivation from a forward-looking perspective whereby expectations of reward are set in advance while reinforcement theory is more about retrospective recognition of past performance. In practice, however, the terms 'incentive' and 'reward' are often used interchangeably and often describe exactly the same type of payment.

Pendleton et al (2009), in their review of British practice since 1984, define contingent pay as 'those systems where some or all of employee remuneration is dependent (contingent) on some measure (objective or subjective) of output or performance' (Pendleton et al, 2009: 257). Armstrong and Murlis (2007: 297), in contrast, define contingent pay as 'payments related to individual performance, contribution, competence or skill or to team and the organisation'. Shields (2007: 348) observes that it may also be inappropriate to classify skills-based or competency-related pay systems as performance-related rewards because they focus on rewarding employees' productive inputs, rather than work behaviour or outputs. These types of individual pay relate more to forms of pay progression within base pay than incentive pay as such. Armstrong and Brown (2019), however, include both skills-based and competency-based rewards within their concept of 'pay for contribution'.

A more useful term for these types of reward may be 'variable pay'. In the UK Workplace Employee Relations Survey (WERS) 'variable pay' is defined as having three main forms: performance-related pay, profit-related pay and employee share schemes. WERS defines performance-related pay ('also known as incentive pay') as payment-by-results, 'in which the level of pay is determined objectively by the amount of work done or its value' and merit-based systems, 'in which pay is related to a subjective assessment of performance by a supervisor or manager' (Kersley et al, 2006: 191). For Armstrong and Brown (2019), variable pay is 'pay at risk' and Armstrong and Murlis (2007) argue that variable pay, unlike base pay, has to be re-earned and is not consolidated into base pay. This is articulated by Heery and Noon (2017) as payments that 'vary upwards or downwards, depending on performance, and that... are discrete: after payment, the slate is wiped clean and employees have to earn their commission, profit share, or bonus afresh'.

In this chapter we have decided to use the term 'variable pay' as an overarching concept covering all forms of 'unconsolidated' pay separate from base pay usually contingent upon achievement of certain performance-related criteria. It is important to note, however, that we have not included in this chapter some forms of pay variation (as opposed to variable pay), such as location allowances or enhancements to the hourly rate for working unsocial hours, as forms of compensatory payments within base pay (see Chapter 5 for more on these forms of payment).

DEFINITIONS

At-risk pay: 'Proportion of remuneration which is contingent on a measure of employee, workgroup, or organizational performance and which has to be "re-earned" in each pay period.'

Bonus: 'A payment that is made in addition to the basic wage or salary and which, in most cases, is linked to the achievement of a performance target or behavioural standard of some kind. The defining feature of bonuses is that they are supplementary payments, usually in cash, which are not consolidated into the basic salary or wage; that is, they have to be re-earned afresh in each bonus period by the employee.'

Contingent pay: 'Pay that is linked to measures of individual, group, or company performance. Contingent pay is used as a means of incentivizing workers and promoting shared interests in higher output, productivity, customer satisfaction, and other indicators of business success.'

Incentive: 'A cash payment or some other reward that is offered to employees conditional on an improvement in performance. The purpose of an incentive is to induce motivation.'

Payment by results (PBR): 'A system of payment in which earnings are tied to estimates of worker output or performance. There are various forms of PBR, including piecework, work-measured incentives, and appraisal-related pay.'

Performance-related pay: 1) 'The broad class of payment systems which relate pay to some measure of work performance. As such, it can embrace profit-sharing, merit pay, gain-sharing, piecework, sales incentives, and other output-based pay systems.' 2) 'Individualized systems in which salary increases are related to the results of performance appraisal. This latter usage corresponds to appraisal-related pay or merit pay. To avoid confusion, some writers refer to individual performance-related pay (IPRP).'

Sales commission: 'A bonus proportionate to the financial value of sales.'

Sales incentive:'An output-based payment system that is widely used in retail and other sectors and which links the remuneration of sales staff, either individually or collectively, to the value of sales. Sales incentives take a number of different forms, including 'commission-only' schemes, in which all earnings are dependent on sales, and schemes that offer bonuses and commission on top of a basic salary.'

(Heery and Noon, 2017)

SELF-ASSESSMENT EXERCISE

What are the key aspects of 'variable pay' in its widest definition? What are the various forms of variable pay?

6.3 The dimensions of variable pay

There are five major dimensions in the design of variable pay components. These are:

- What is being measured? Inputs or outputs?
- What period of performance does the payment reward? Short-term (i.e. 12 months or less) or long-term (over a year)?
- Does the payment reward an individual's performance, or does it relate to team or organisational success? Or does it operate at all three levels?
- Is measurement based on a single factor or multiple factors?
- What form does the payment take? Cash, company shares or non-financial?

The first important dimension in designing variable payments is whether they will reward outputs from the work or inputs by the employee. In general terms, it is easier to measure outputs (where these are concrete products or cash outcomes) than inputs (which tend to be more based on behaviours and attitudes to work). Financial incentives are therefore more likely to be found in industries and occupations where individual or team performance can be most easily identified and measured. Schemes that measure individual inputs or behaviours are more likely to be found in sectors and occupations where performance measures are less tangible (e.g. for health workers or in a research and development environment).

KEY ISSUES IN REWARD MANAGEMENT 6.1

Gamification of variable pay

A *People Management* article draws attention to an emerging trend in the management and communication of variable pay schemes:

> Over three-quarters of employees would welcome the introduction of a gamified rewards system by their managers. Out of 1,000 employees polled, 79 per cent said they would like to see a gamified bonus system introduced in which achievements or good behaviours are reinforced by giving out points or small rewards.
>
> However, experts said this might be an indication that employees want more feedback and recognition of their contributions and their efforts rather than any particular type of incentive package.
>
> The survey, conducted by One4all Rewards, found half of employees had any form of gamification in their workplace, and that less than half of employers (48 per cent) currently offer gamified rewards or incentives to their employees.
>
> Gamification is a management style where elements of competition and rewards are built into the role to motivate and incentivise employees. Traditionally, this is through non-cash incentives, such as virtual prizes, progression up leaderboards or other gifts, but can also be part of a cash bonus scheme.
>
> The report claimed organisations were deterred from using these sorts of incentives because of their added complexity.
>
> Alan Smith, UK managing director at One4all Rewards said: 'Some companies shy away from rewards systems based on gamification; however they are not only incredibly powerful, but they can be quite cost effective as they rely on giving out small rewards rather than large bonuses.'
>
> He added it was understandable that companies used to making one-off bonus payments at the end of the financial year would be hesitant to introduce a more complex system, but said there were a number of ways managers could manage the introduction of a gamified system.
>
> The report said communication was key when rolling out a gamified benefits system, with one in four (25 per cent) of respondents saying they would want clear communication about the system from the start.
>
> However, Charles Cotton, CIPD senior performance and reward adviser, said the research might indicate employees more generally might be looking for more feedback and recognition of good work.

'What's important is employees being rewarded and recognised for their contributions in a frequent and supportive way,' Cotton said.

'Gamification is one way of doing that, but there are others, and what the organisation should be thinking about is "how can we be better at recognising the contribution and achievement of our employees in ways that add value to our organisation" – then think about what means they should go down.'

He added that gamification had its pitfalls, and suggested businesses consider it as an incentive tool to be used in specific situations and to be constantly monitored.

One such concern would be 'crowding out', where employees become so concerned with winning incentives that other business objectives fall by the wayside. 'It's important for the organisation to think, if this was to happen, what could be the unintended consequences,' said Cotton.

'What research seems to indicate is, to work, games need to be designed to build in scope, autonomy and control. If it's quite controlling and people don't have much autonomy then it probably isn't going to have as much impact as would be hoped.'

He added that the power of a lot of incentives, both cash and non-cash, can erode very quickly as employees get used to them, so businesses need to think about adapting their processes.

(Churchill, 2019)

QUESTIONS

Thinking about an organisation with which you are familiar, what would be the benefits of gamifying rewards in the way described by this article?

Can you think of any disadvantages of the gamification of variable pay in addition to those mentioned above?

The second dimension to consider is whether the incentive will be short-term, so that the reward follows closely behind the achievement, or long-term, where the reward may require a much longer time period of measurement. Some have argued that incentives will only work in behavioural terms if the reward is made close in time to the achievement of the performance. Longer-term incentives have been seen as having a less powerful motivational effect. For example, work-measured incentive schemes usually relate to individual output over fairly short periods (a shift, a working day, a working week or a month) while schemes that relate the incentive to company performance targets or profitability will probably provide annual payments. Share ownership schemes (through share bonuses, share options or share purchase) will require even longer time periods to yield results. These longer-term forms of variable pay might be seen more as a manifestation of agency theory (linking the employee's interest to that of the owner or manager).

The third dimension is whether the incentive will relate to individual performance, group or team performance, or to some measure of organisational or corporate performance, all of which are discussed below. The latter two types – group and organisation-wide schemes – focus on achievement of collective objectives rather than individual ones. Collective rewards are designed to encourage socially integrative behaviour (i.e. collaboration and co-operation), rather than the self-assertive tendencies (i.e. competition) found in individual approaches (Wilson and Bowey, 1989). In some organisations pay will vary according to all three of these measures. Individual workers may receive a personal bonus, a team bonus based on the success of the group or team in meeting their targets, and perhaps an annual bonus based on profits or achieved targets of the organisation. These three incentives may all be paid at the same time but more normally they are based on different frequencies of payment. In general, it is thought that the closer the performance unit to the employee, the more effective will be the link between the reward and the outcome. Individually based systems are therefore perceived as having the strongest incentive effects whereas those systems based on collective performance run the risk of 'free-riders' – those less effective workers who coast along on the efforts of their colleagues. On the other hand, individual rewards are more likely to give rise to perverse effects such as restriction of output, conflict between workers and management and the pursuit of goals contrary to the organisation's intended outcomes (Pendleton et al, 2009). Indeed, the unintentional ill effects of poorly designed performance-related pay schemes have come under increasing scrutiny as contributing to unethical and dysfunctional behaviour (Transparency International UK, 2016). There is also some evidence that employees prefer collective forms of incentive, rather than individual (Conroy and Gupta, 2015).

The fourth dimension relates to whether the incentive is based on a single target or objective or several factors. Single-factor schemes can be useful in focusing employee effort on a key objective such as profitability or productivity. Indeed, research by IRS (2011) identifies both as commonly cited bonus factors alongside the more generic 'performance'. Other single-factors include 'sales', 'attendance' and 'completion of projects'. Far more common, however, are multi-factor schemes which combine, as described above, individual objectives with business unit or organisational performance. Whilst some are 'soft' competency-type measures such as 'team-working' and 'customer service', the majority are harder metrics: 'year-on-year profit growth', 'complaints', 'health and safety record' and 'sickness absence' (IRS, 2011). This may prompt the critical HR professional to question the validity of some incentive schemes which although they may be promoted as using more 'objective' measures may well be driven by ease of measurement rather than factors, albeit subjective ones, which might be more relevant to good performance.

The fifth dimension relates to what form the incentive will take. Although the most common form of incentive is a cash payment, in some cases the reward takes the form of shares in the organisation or some non-financial reward (e.g. a gift or free holiday) (see Chapter 9). Payments may also be differentiated on the basis of an

Figure 6.1 Types of variable pay

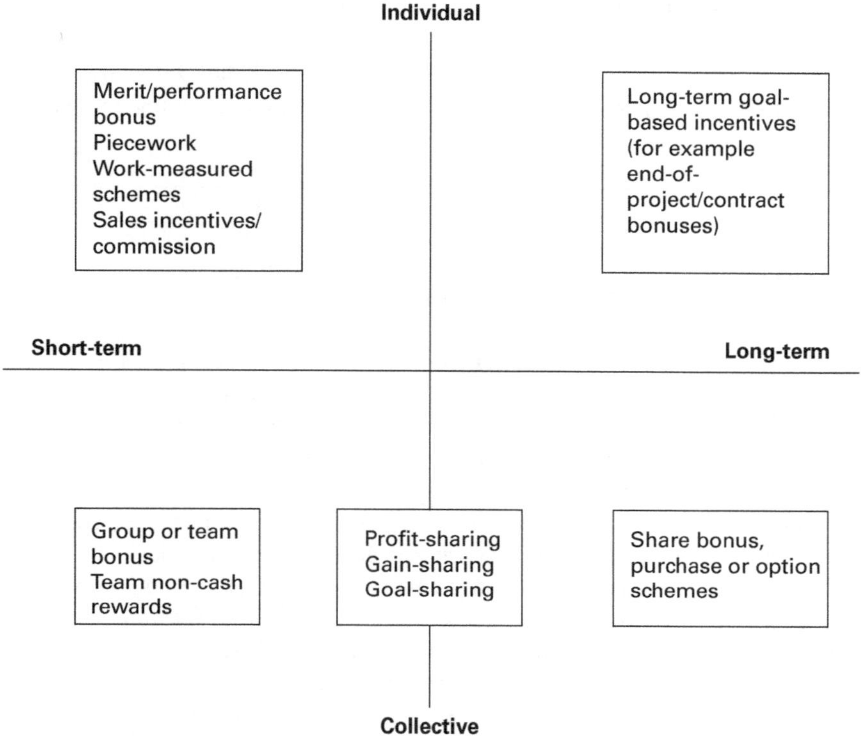

employee's job level. While a chief executive will typically receive a bonus equating to 47.2 per cent of basic salary, this drops markedly to 11 per cent for department managers and just 4.1 per cent for entry-level staff (Attwood, 2015). Paying a percentage also clearly benefits the higher-paid, rather than a flat-rate amount across all employees.

Figure 6.1 illustrates the various types of variable payment available in terms of two of these dimensions – short-term or long-term, and individual or collective.

The major categories of variable pay are:

- individual results-based schemes (e.g. individual bonuses, sales commission and traditional piecework/work-measured schemes);
- group- or team-based rewards;
- collective short-term incentives (e.g. gain-sharing, goal-sharing, profit-sharing);
- collective long-term incentives (e.g. employee share schemes and employee ownership).

Each of these categories is dealt with in turn below.

SELF-ASSESSMENT EXERCISE

What are the major dimensions to be considered when designing variable payments? How do these relate to the context of your own organisation (or one with which you are familiar)?

6.4 Individual variable pay

Individual results-based or performance-based rewards are probably the most common form of variable pay. At their most basic, in smaller organisations they may simply be one-off cash sums paid out by the owner of the business to individuals considered to have done a 'good job'. In larger organisations, however, there is usually a more formalised and structured approach.

The major forms of results-based incentive schemes are bonuses, commission, traditional piecework schemes and work-measured schemes. The latter normally relate the incentive in some way to output. For non-manual workers, more common are sales commission or customer service incentives, although these reflect more the 'value' of the output than the output alone. As CIPD (Marriot and Perkins, 2019) data shows, the most common individual results-based rewards are non-consolidated cash bonuses that relate the incentive to some measure of individual achievement of target goals (used by 62 per cent of organisations). These differ from merit pay schemes that are more likely to measure behaviours through combining output/input in a 'contribution' model (Brown and Armstrong, 1999).

Traditional output-based schemes began to wane in the 1960s, partly because they were seen as encouraging 'pay drift' (i.e. earnings increased faster than base pay rises) and because of the industrial relations climate that they engendered. Research by IDS (2007c) found that organisations in the engineering industry largely moved away from these individualised schemes towards schemes related more to collective performance in some form, such as company-wide profit-sharing or other profit-based systems. Three-quarters of the bonus schemes examined in the research were based on company-wide performance targets rather than individual output. Elsewhere, manual workers are now subject to appraisal-based pay systems, and criteria such as training targets, safety or quality are widespread. Where individual bonus schemes exist, they may be designed to reward corporate or plant-level targets or new ways of working. Attendance bonuses – which reward target levels of attendance at work – are also common in manufacturing. These trends reflect both the shift of employment away from traditional manufacturing and extractive industries, where output was more easily measured, and the increasing focus in many manufacturing firms on quality, flexibility and efficiency rather than quantity of output. Such individual output-based schemes are therefore much rarer today but can still be found in some sectors.

The following sections outline each of the major areas of individual results-based schemes, starting with individual bonuses, commission and piecework.

6.4.1 Individual bonuses

Individual bonuses can help focus the employee on the desired results or behaviours, but they are only likely to work where those results or behaviours can be easily measured. Individual bonus schemes are therefore more commonly found where hard financial or output targets can be set, such as in sales, production, manufacturing and logistics (IDS, 2007d: Marriot and Perkins, 2019). Schemes can have perverse effects, however, when employees are encouraged to compete rather than co-operate. They are therefore sometimes seen as inappropriate for professional or more knowledge-based occupations where the sharing of information is key. There may also be, in line with expectancy theory, an issue about the size of the reward, with a clear link between the desired results and the amount of bonus paid. Such schemes have been found to work best where individuals or groups are able to control their own work and are thus able to vary their performance or levels of output.

The individual bonus has now become common for managers and other professional occupations but also for other employee categories (Marriot and Perkins, 2019). Despite the negative press the operation of these sorts of bonuses have given rise to in the past few years, research by Attwood (2019) has shown the median incentive-based payment for professional employees is just 8.4 per cent of base salary which is far from the 'fat cat bonus' image sometimes portrayed in the media. That said, there is clearly continued concern that bonuses can lead to undesirable behaviours. CIPD (2018b) cites the Financial Services Authority's (FSA) view that these types of variable pay mechanisms were 'contributory factors' in precipitating the financial crisis of 2008/09. The FSA suggested that practices in investment banking tended 'to reward short term revenue and profit targets' and, in so doing, 'gave staff incentives to pursue unduly risky practices' (CIPD, 2018b).

6.4.2 Sales incentives and commission

Commission on sales or customers served is one of the oldest and simplest forms of individual incentive used to motivate non-manual workers. Commission schemes are designed to motivate the worker to increase individual output. So, for example, a typical sales commission scheme might pay a 10 per cent bonus (i.e. 10 per cent of base salary) for every 100 sales achieved. In an estate agency, commission may be paid according the value of the property sold over a particular period of time. In hairdressing, stylists are often paid on the basis of commission on the amount of money generated by the salon each week (including both customers served and sales of haircare products).

Some jobs are rewarded entirely by commission on sales (i.e. there is no base salary), although employers must pay at least the National Minimum Wage. It is more common, however, for commission to be paid on top of base salary. Rates of commission will also need to be set at levels that ensure they are affordable. Where commission accounts for a very high proportion of total earnings, there may be resultant problems with employee behaviour. For example, sales staff may prioritise particular products where commission is highest or may indulge in 'hard sell' tactics that endanger good customer relations. As Shields (2007: 408) states: 'Commission payments may encourage aggressive, deceptive and negligent selling practices, including the sale of goods to consumers who may be unable to service a consumer credit or loan debt.' This is a good example of the unintended consequences that can arise from ill-conceived rewards.

The 2019 CIPD Reward Management Survey data in Figure 6.1 indicates that among organisations using variable pay, nearly half (46 per cent) use sales commission schemes and these are more common in manufacturing and production (55 per cent) as well as private sector services, particularly in retail and associated industries (61 per cent).

6.4.3 Individual piecework and work measured schemes

Under individual piecework systems, employees are paid per unit of production. Employees are therefore paid according to the number of items they produce or process, so pay is directly related to results. Thus, if the piece rate is £1 per item, production of 100 items will yield £100 in pay. Such work is now largely limited to low-paid and often 'hidden economy' jobs, especially home-workers in clothing and toy manufacture, and workers in agriculture and food processing. The most recent CIPD data finds just 5 per cent of organisations operating variable pay schemes use piece rates with the vast majority in the manufacturing and production sector (Marriot and Perkins, 2019). This decline in piecework largely reflects the fact that technological changes in manufacturing mean that workers now have little control over their own pace of work and that employers are today often more interested in quality than quantity.

Most schemes provide a minimum earnings guarantee or 'fall-back' rate, and there may be allowance for 'downtime' caused by machine failure, maintenance or shortage of materials. Under the National Minimum Wage (NMW) Regulations, employers must determine a 'fair' piece rate for each piece or task accomplished, by reference to the rate of the average worker, ensuring that most workers will achieve the NMW.

It is often said that piecework is an ideal form of incentive because of its simplicity and the clear link between output and pay. It is also effectively 'self-supervising' in that it is in the employees' interest to keep busy and manage their time effectively. Employees can also easily calculate their pay from the price per piece and set their own pace of work to match their aspirations. The reason why the incidence of traditional piecework has diminished so much is that it has serious disadvantages. Taylor (1911) identified two main problems with piecework: the tendency for employees to hoard work and restrict their output, and the tendency for employers to cut the rate if production levels rise, so defeating any motivational gain. For employers these are also potential problems with quality (because the emphasis is on output). For employees there can be problems in predicting longer-term earnings levels in the absence of a guaranteed weekly income.

In work-measured schemes the job, or its component parts, is timed and a standard time for completion of the task established. The incentive is related to exceeding this standard time target for the task. In other words, if the task can be completed in less than the standard time, the employee's pay will increase in proportion to that standard. The advantage of work-measured schemes is therefore that performance is linked to the hourly rate of pay. Under such schemes workers can often earn an extra third in pay for exceeding the standard time for the job. The downside is the potential work intensification that may result for the worker and the risk that quality of work will suffer.

The advantage of work-measured incentives for employers is that they are a more effective method of measuring employee performance on the job than simply counting the number of pieces produced or processed. Such schemes are best suited to short-cycle, repetitive work where changes in the work are infrequent. Such schemes, from a management perspective, may also require rigorous supervisory management if workers are not to manipulate schemes to their own advantage. Strong quality control mechanisms are also essential.

Lastly, technological changes in manufacturing have made it much more difficult for employees to influence the speed of production. Manufacture technology means that many of the production jobs once done manually by people are now performed by workplace robots or other automatic processes. Manufacturing systems based on 'just-in-time' philosophies, where stock is kept to a minimum, also mitigate against these schemes, which emphasise output (and thus the amount of stored stock) over quality.

SELF-ASSESSMENT EXERCISE

What are the major types of individual variable pay? Why have they fallen from favour in some industries but gained favour elsewhere?

6.5 Team-based variable pay

One alternative to individual results-based incentives is a group or team reward. Under such schemes the reward is distributed between the members of the work group or team rather than different rewards being received by members of the same team. Team incentives for manual workers have existed for some time, but they became popular in the 1990s for non-manual workers too as employers sought new ways to encourage collaboration and knowledge-sharing between employees (Heneman and von Hippel, 1995). In some cases, team rewards were seen as an alternative to individual performance-related pay and, in the UK civil service, there was active encouragement of and experimentation with such approaches in the 1990s (Makinson, 2000). Experiments were run in the Benefits Agency, the Inland Revenue and Customs and Excise. The Institute of Employment Studies and Hay also ran a major project on teamworking in the National Health Service.

Shields (2007) states that most team-based schemes are adaptations of multi-factor business unit gain-sharing or goal-sharing plans (see later in this chapter) and that their emergence coincided with the development of high-involvement or high-performance 'best practice' models of HRM, of which teamworking is one example. The 2011 WERS (van Wanrooy et al, 2013) found that 8 per cent of employees are paid PBR based on group results (in comparison with 13 per cent for individual results and 11 per cent for organisational results). As with other forms of PBR, schemes based on group results are more common in the private sector (9 per cent) than the public sector (2 per cent). The CIPD Reward Management Survey published in 2019 results indicate that profit-sharing schemes are the most common group reward scheme, operated by 51 per cent of organisations using performance-related reward. However, team bonuses are nearly as common (47 per cent) followed by schemes based on goal-sharing (33 per cent) and non-monetary group- or team-based schemes (30 per cent) (Marriot and Perkins, 2019).

DEFINITION

Team pay links payments to members of a formally established team to the performance of that team. The rewards are usually provided in the form of a cash bonus and are shared among the members of the team in accordance with a published formula. Rewards for individuals may also be influenced by assessments of their contribution to team results.

(Armstrong, 2019: 224)

The rationale for team-based reward is to encourage the behaviours that encourage effective teamworking. It is often seen as an alternative to individual performance-related pay, which, it is argued, encourages individuals to focus on their own targets to the exclusion of wider priorities, and discourages managers and supervisors from developing teams (Armstrong and Murlis, 2007). Research by Thompson (1995) found that the main advantages of team pay were that it rewards teamwork and co-operation, encourages the group to improve work systems, increases flexibility and the ability to respond to changing needs, encourages information-sharing and communication, and helps to focus people on the wider organisation.

Teamworking is not, however, problem-free. There is clearly the issue of the 'free-loader' who does not perform his or her share of the team's work but is still eligible for the reward. For this reason, managers may need to ensure careful supervision. Research by Kinnie et al (1998) found clear evidence of improvements in productivity from teamworking but also commented on the possible negative aspects. These included reduced quality of working life for workers, because of greater pressures to perform and the close monitoring of work required, and the potential for social pressures on members of the team to conform to group norms, with the possibility of harassment of weaker members of the team. An evaluation of an experiment with team-based reward within the UK civil service (Burgess et al, 2004) found that team incentives worked well for small teams but not for larger ones. It also found that the team incentive had a major effect on the quantity of work produced, but not quality.

Armstrong (2019) argues that team pay works best where teams are easily defined and of relatively long standing. He also argues that it can be demotivating for staff who prefer to be rewarded individually and that it can be problematic to distinguish the contributions of individual team members. As mentioned above, group norms can also lead to undesirable effects in terms of social cohesion in the work group, and uncooperative attitudes can be spread from individuals to the wider team, leading to barriers to flexibility and change. Research on team-based pay is far less established than individual performance pay and there are a number of different factors that are significantly affect the design of such schemes. According to Conroy and Gupta (2015) these include: the level of interdependence within groups or teams; the measurement of performance (at individual and team levels) and the unique influences on team dynamics (e.g. stage of team development and composition).

6.5.1 Types of teamworking

Like all reward initiatives, both the context and form of team reward influence its acceptability and success. Shields (2007, 2015) points out that the decision whether to use group incentives as opposed to organisation or department-level rewards depends on the degree of inter-team dependence. Where teams operate more or less autonomously it is easier to identify individual team performance, but where teams are highly dependent on other teams, broader incentives may be more appropriate. Team rewards will also relate closely to the form of teamworking adopted by organisations. Academics have broadly identified two types of teamworking (Gallie et al, 2012; Thursfield, 2015):

- **Self-directed or self-managed teams** which have control over work activities (work effort, the choice of tasks, the methods of carrying out tasks and quality standards) as well as the composition of the team and even its leadership. These teams are characterised by high commitment and levels of autonomy.
- **Semi-autonomous teams** which have some control over work activities only and will have far lower levels of autonomy, greater surveillance and lower skills levels.

6.5.2 Measuring team performance

As with measuring any employee performance, there are a number of dimensions to consider. Measurement may be (a) behaviour or results based, (b) objective or subjective, (c) relative or absolute (Conroy and Gupta, 2015). The measures for team pay will vary according to the type of team. Those for manual workers will probably reflect both quantity and quality of output, and may also reward initiative and a good safety record. For non-manual teams the measures may include sales, accuracy and customer satisfaction. Measurement of team performance may be based on a single factor or on multiple factors. Single-factor schemes tend to focus on labour productivity or labour cost savings.

6.5.3 Team-based pay allocation

A major decision to be taken in group or team reward systems is how to distribute any rewards. Two main approaches are prominent in paying teams, equality (i.e. paying the same for all) and equity (i.e. differentiated based on individual contribution) (Conroy and Gupta, 2015). And Shields (2007, 2015) identifies four main methods of distribution:

- each member of the team receives the same cash sum;
- team bonuses are paid as a percentage of individual base pay;
- individual awards are based on individual appraisal ratings;
- non-cash recognition awards.

Clearly, the first of these takes an egalitarian approach, but is more likely to be used where members of the team are all on the same grade and thus closer together in terms of base pay levels. The second allows the differentials manifested in the grading system to be reflected in the team reward. The third approach allows individual performance ratings to be reflected in the distribution, but this may contradict the objective of creating team cohesion. Non-cash awards can be a valued alternative and can be tailored to meet specific team needs (see Chapter 9). Lawler (2000: 218) suggests that organisations should be quite clear about what they are seeking to reward through team pay and only types of work that are interdependent and performed in collectivist cultures should be rewarded by team pay.

SELF-ASSESSMENT EXERCISE

What are the perceived advantages and disadvantages of team- or group-based variable pay? In what environments have such schemes been found to work best?

6.6 Collective short-term variable pay

Collective short-term rewards are those that apply at organisational level and normally deliver the reward within a year or less. Clearly, collective rewards are quite different from individual-based systems, and the decision to share the reward between employees, rather than target incentives on individual performance, is normally based on the context and objectives of the organisation or workplace. Where organisations wish to encourage knowledge-sharing, co-operative behaviour and collaboration, collective rewards may be more appropriate than individual ones. They may also be more suited where the nature of the work or occupation means individual performance is difficult to measure or where intrinsic rewards may be more important.

Collective rewards are usually more acceptable to trade unions because they are normally based on organisation-wide results rather than individual outcomes, and may allow the reward to be subject to the collective bargaining process. On the other hand, such collective rewards may also exist alongside individual (and team) rewards and, indeed, collaborative behaviour may be rewarded as part of an assessment of individual performance.

There are two main forms of short-term collective variable pay: profit-sharing and gain-sharing.

6.6.1 Profit-sharing

Profit-sharing has a long history, the earliest examples appearing in the mid-19th century. In its early incarnations it fulfilled three key objectives:

- First, financial participation was seen as a useful response to unions' demands for a role in management decision-making through co-determination.
- A second objective was to avoid unionisation altogether through binding workers' financial interest to their employer, rather than through a trade union.
- A third objective was to improve efficiency – it was thought that workers who had a financial stake in their employer's business were less likely to shirk, so economising on supervision (Mitchell et al, 1990).

In the USA in the 1980s, Weitzman (1984) argued that where companies adopt profit-sharing, changes in product demand would be met by adjustments in pay and not through job losses (although this premise was based on the idea that the profit share would form part of base pay rather than be paid on top of base pay). He argued from research evidence at the level of the firm that there was a clear link between profit-sharing firms and higher productivity. Profit-sharing is also common in many other developed countries, not least Japan. In France, profit-sharing is common because it is mandatory to provide such 'participation' schemes in companies employing more than 50 employees.

In the UK, in the 1980s and 1990s, profit-sharing and share ownership were encouraged as key to reducing labour market rigidity and improving flexible working. In order to encourage such financial participation schemes legislation was passed offering tax advantages to such schemes. The main vehicle to encourage profit-sharing was cash-based, profit-related pay. By 1997 some 14,500 schemes were active, but the loss of income tax that resulted led, in time, to a reversal of government policy, with no further tax relief available after 2000. There was little evidence of any benefit from the scheme in terms of employment or wage flexibility (Hyman, 2000). This again perhaps demonstrates the problem of unintended consequences in adopting ill-conceived variable pay systems.

According to Armstrong and Murlis (2007) and Armstrong (2019), the objectives for profit-sharing include the closer identification of employees with their employer through a common concern for its progress and as a means to raising employee interest and understanding of the firm's business. These authors also see profit-sharing as a means to better co-operation between management and employees, with employers demonstrating their goodwill in concrete terms. Armstrong (2019), however, is cautions that the links between individual effort and collective reward may be too remote for there to be a direct incentive effect.

6.6.2 Types of scheme

There are two main types of profit-sharing schemes: cash schemes and stock schemes. Under a cash scheme a proportion of profits is paid direct to employees, whereas under a stock scheme a proportion of profits is paid as shares in the company. The most common form is the cash scheme.

Most profit-sharing schemes are open to all employees, although there is often a service requirement before the employee becomes eligible. The 2011 WERS (van Wanrooy et al, 2013) found that profit-related pay coverage of non-managerial employees rose between 2004 and 2011 with 10 per cent of workplaces having 100 per cent coverage of non-managerial employees in 2011. The 2019 CIPD Reward Survey, however, finds management and professional employees are more likely to be covered by profit-sharing schemes (51 per cent of organisations using a performance-related reward scheme use profit-sharing for these employees) than non-managerial/professional employees (39 per cent) (Marriot and Perkins, 2019).

Three main approaches to calculating the share of profits have been identified (Armstrong and Murlis, 2007):

- a fixed percentage of profit based on a predetermined formula;
- the amount of profit share is determined at the discretion of the board of the organisation;
- a combination of the first and second approaches – a profit threshold is fixed below which no payment is made, and maximum limits placed on the proportion of profits to be distributed.

A fourth method is for payments to be 'smoothed'. Under this arrangement, the formula produces an annual sum that is added to the profit share pool. A fixed proportion is then distributed, and the balance carried forward to future years. This enables the scheme to pay out similar amounts each year, irrespective of the actual annual profit. Of course, this method may well defeat the purpose of linking the reward to company performance, and might not really be considered a short-term reward but rather a retention or goodwill measure.

There are several mechanisms for distributing the profit shares: as a proportion of base pay with no increment for service; as a proportion of earnings with the reward linked to service; or in proportion to pay and some measure of individual performance, although this is uncommon. The percentage of pay paid out can vary between 2 per cent and 20 per cent or more (Armstrong, 2012) but, according to Armstrong and Murlis (2007), ideally the share should be between 5 per cent and 10 per cent – this is meaningful but at the same time will not build up too much reliance on the payment or substitute variable pay for base pay.

6.6.3 The incidence of profit-sharing

The 2011 WERS (van Wanrooy et al, 2013) found that 29 per cent of workplaces had some employees in receipt of profit-related pay largely unchanged from all workplace results in 2004. Incidence of profit-sharing in the private sector also remained steady; from 34 per cent in 2004 to 33 per cent in 2011. In the public sector, however, a clear increase in incidence is apparent; from 1 per cent of workplaces using profit-related pay in 2004 to 5 per cent in 2011.

Some years later, the CIPD Reward Management Survey (Marriot and Perkins, 2019) results show substantially higher rates across the board (although sampling differences should be noted). Some 51 per cent of organisations with performance-related reward use profit-sharing; 55 per cent in private sector services, 50 per cent in manufacturing and production, 33 per cent in the voluntary and not-for-profit sector and 29 per cent in the public sector.

Internationally, the rates of profit-sharing vary significantly by country. In Taiwan there is a statutory requirement for companies to have a profit-sharing plan in place, (Hsu and Liao, 2013) so presumably nearly all firms operate some form of profit-sharing. In other countries, the highest rates are in France (35 per cent) and Canada (32 per cent) with the lowest rates in Portugal (3 per cent) and Greece (2.9 per cent) (Hambly et al, 2017).

6.6.4 The effects of profit-sharing

There is as yet little academic consensus on the effectiveness of profit-sharing, despite a large volume of research having been conducted. Early research (e.g. Blanchflower and Oswald, 1987, 1988) established no significant link between business performance and firms with profit-sharing schemes. However, a study of the effects of profit-sharing on employee attitudes conducted for the UK Department of Employment in 1986 (Poole and Jenkins, 1990) found clear evidence of a link between such schemes and a positive set of attitudes in employees on a wide range of aspects of company policy. Similarly, research by Coyle-Shapiro et al (2002) found that favourable perceptions of profit-sharing served to increase organisational commitment. As Hyman (2009: 215) comments, profit-sharing 'in association with other progressive human resource policies may well act as a positive incentive and can improve productivity'. Nyberg et al (2018) also find finds positive organisational performance outcomes relating to collective performance-related schemes such as profit-sharing.

6.6.5 Gainsharing

Gainsharing is a form of collective short-term incentive whereby the organisation seeks to share the financial benefits of any improvement in productivity or performance with its workforce. Gain-sharing differs from profit-sharing in that the latter is based on a wide range of factors that contribute to improved profitability (such as depreciation, tax and bad debt expenses), many of which the individual employee will have little control over. In contrast, the factors used in gain-sharing are likely to be more limited and be much more closely linked to the employees' ability to affect outcomes.

Gainsharing plans have four defining features (Shields, 2007: 421):

- a focus on measurable results that are within the employees' collective control;
- the specification of a historical baseline of financial performance against which subsequent gains can be measured;
- the use of a predetermined formula for sharing the monetary gains between the organisation and participating employees; and
- a formal system for employees to make suggestions and decisions about ways to improve performance.

Armstrong and Murlis (2007) and Armstrong (2019) argue that fundamental to gain-sharing is a sense of ownership and involvement in the scheme by the workforce. Good communications are therefore essential.

Gainsharing is well established in the USA. There are two main types of gain-sharing plan: traditional single-factor schemes and multi-factor schemes. Traditional single-factor schemes focus on a single issue (such as labour cost reductions or productivity improvements) and are usually self-financing. In other words, the monetary gain is generated from efficiency savings. The second type, multi-factor schemes, combine a number of measures such as sales value, productivity and savings on material wastage. Such schemes can also include non-financial measures – for example, customer satisfaction or improved safety compliance – although the inclusion of factors like these rather negates the concept that the reward has to be generated from direct monetary savings.

The three, traditional gain-sharing plans are the Scanlon Plan, the Rucker Plan and Improshare. The Scanlon Plan measures employment costs as a proportion of total sales. The Rucker Plan is similar in measuring employment costs against sales, but less the costs of materials and supplies. The rationale for this is that it measures 'value added' by employees and that materials and supply costs are independent variables over which the employees have no control. Improshare is based on an established standard that defines the expected hours needed to produce an acceptable level of output, based on work-measurement techniques. Any savings from the achievement of greater output in fewer hours is then shared between the firm and its employees according to a predetermined formula. Payments are made on a monthly, quarterly or annual basis. The CIPD Reward Survey makes no distinction between different types of gain-sharing plan but finds 20 per cent of organisations with some form of performance-related reward operating gain-sharing (Jones et al, 2015).

The advantages of gain-sharing are that rewards are closely related to monetary gains that employees can directly influence. Such schemes may also improve employee commitment and reduce supervision needs. The fact that they are usually jointly administered means that they fit well with a unionised environment. The research evidence on the effects of gain-sharing is quite positive (Shields, 2015). Zondo (2018) found specific positive effects of gainsharing in the South African automotive parts manufacturing industry where it not only improved productivity but also reduced spoilage and absenteeism rates.

A variant of gain-sharing is goal-sharing, whereby a set of goals is established against which collective performance is measured and a monetary reward attached to the outcomes. A series of goals is set, and a predetermined amount is paid for each goal achieved. In a sense, this is simply a collective form of the individual results-based incentive scheme. It is different from gain-sharing, however, in that payments are linked to future targets rather than based on benchmark historical data. Payments can be flat-rate or there may be a scale of payment according to how well the target is achieved. Such schemes, like gain-sharing, usually pay out on a monthly, quarterly or annual basis. But, unlike gain-sharing, which relies on any rewards being self-financing, the money for goal-sharing schemes has to be found from other sources.

SELF-ASSESSMENT EXERCISE

What are the major forms of short-term collective variable pay? Consider each in turn and weigh the advantages and disadvantages of such schemes in relation to your own organisation or sector.

6.7 Collective long-term variable pay and employee ownership

Collective long-term incentives are defined as those that reward organisational performance but where the receipt of the reward takes longer than 12 months (Shields, 2007). The main form of collective long-term reward is the employee share ownership scheme where workers own shares in their employing organisations. Such schemes usually provide shares in one of two ways: either employees are given shares in their company, or they purchase shares over time from their own funds or through a fund established by the company. In the USA such schemes are more likely to be known as stock option schemes.

Share option schemes have many of the same objectives as profit-sharing or gain-sharing schemes, and are also a form of employee financial participation. They therefore reflect the principles of agency theory in attempting to bring into alignment the aims of the principal (the organisation) and the agent (the worker). Under the share option approach, however, workers actually take a stake in the ownership of their employing organisation. In such schemes employees have a personal financial investment that is missing from most profit-sharing or gain-sharing schemes. Whereas a profit-share scheme may yield nothing in a year when the organisation has a poor performance, a disastrous fall in the share price may well wipe out any accumulated gain for the employee. The reward is therefore much more 'at risk' than short-term collective payments.

Research for the HMRC (Kerr and Tate, 2008) found that the principal motivations for setting up all-employee share schemes were to enable employees to participate in the ownership of the organisation and to encourage employees to acquire shares in the organisation. Increasing employee commitment and motivation were also cited as reasons for introducing a scheme.

As Hyman (2000: 180) notes, both supporters and critics of share employee share schemes tend to adopt similar arguments but from opposing perspectives. The first argument is that employee share schemes offer 'property rights' to participants. For supporters this is seen as a device to encourage popular belief in capitalism, whereas critics see the schemes as obscuring the true nature of the relationship between capital and labour in society by creating a 'false consciousness' among workers.

The second argument is that the property nexus positively influences the behaviour of the employee towards the organisation, reinforcing identification with the employer's interest and loosening collectivist ideology. For employers, the associated benefits are assumed to be greater organisational commitment; easier recruitment of scarce staff; and better retention of employees through the fact that full tax-free benefits only accrue to employees after a qualifying period.

The third argument is that there is unilateral management control over the scheme (as opposed to profit-sharing and gain-sharing, where it may be more likely that managers and workers have joint control).

The advantages of such schemes to employees may include the fact that, as shareholders, employees will gain a better understanding of the company's performance and directly benefit from any success (especially where the shares are provided free). Such schemes also provide a tax-efficient method of saving and an income from dividends or capital gains if the shares are sold.

In contrast, the disadvantages are that the employees become financially dependent on their employer – if the company closes down, they may not only lose their jobs but the value of their savings as well (high profile examples of these cases include Marconi, Northern Rock Building Society and HBoS). Such schemes also require a reasonable length of service to see any real benefit, so employees who leave after a few years' service may not see any benefit. These schemes may not therefore be appropriate where there is high turnover of staff.

A review of the research evidence (Hyman, 2009) generally reports positive effects of employee share ownership on company performance. Conyon and Freeman (2004) also found positive productivity effects, especially for share option schemes. A survey of employers for the HMRC (Kerr and Tate, 2008) found that employers reported a positive effect on the organisation as a whole, with improved relations between the organisation and its employees, but there were mixed views about the effects on productivity, around 45 per cent reporting that there was no effect. The survey of employees found that having a share scheme had encouraged employees to accept job offers and almost half of respondents said that the schemes had encouraged them to stay with the organisation. Loyalty to the organisation was also found to be stronger among participating employees as opposed to non-participants. The major reasons for employees participating in the share schemes were that they were an 'easy way to save', followed by 'a way to make money'. More recently, Blasi, Freeman and Kruse (2016) find that employees in organisations that use collective variable pay (including employee share ownership and stock options) extensively participate more in decisions, have greater information sharing, trust supervisors more and report a more positive workplace culture than in other companies.

However, as Hyman (2009) points out, there are issues of causality – we cannot be sure that employee share ownership is the key variable to explain the success of the enterprise. It may also be that successful firms are more likely to introduce such schemes than less successful – because they can afford to. Hyman also makes the point that few studies have been conducted on the effects of failing performance on employee ownership schemes. There is also little evidence that employee attitudes and behaviour are affected by such schemes. Numerous studies have failed to find any a causal link between share ownership, employee attitudes and behaviour and organisational performance (McHugh et al, 2005, cited in Hyman, 2009).

Evidence also indicates that the value of shares owned by employees does not tend to be high and that they are not retained for long periods (Hyman, 2009). This might suggest that the use of such schemes to build employee loyalty might be misconceived and that employees take a much more instrumental attitude towards such rewards. The small relative value of the shares may mean that employees see them as a form of bonus or gratuity rather than creating a sense of co-ownership of the enterprise. There is also a view that such schemes provide rewards so distant from individual employee performance that they serve no real incentive value. The size of worker share holdings is also probably insufficient to give them any real participative role in the firm's governance.

Perhaps because of some of these concerns, there has been a renewed growth in interest in more meaningful employee ownership models in recent years. Following the 2012 Nuttall Review, in 2014 the Finance Act introduced a new form of tax advantaged statutory trust, the Employee Ownership Trust (EOT). While share plans allow employees to participate in the financial wellbeing of their organisation, employee ownership implies a much more significant involvement in shaping organisational decisions and direction.

6.7.1 Types of employee share schemes and employee ownership

In the UK, the following schemes can confer partial or total company ownership by employees:

- Share Incentive Plans (SIPs);
- savings-related share option schemes (also known as Save-As-You-Earn (SAYE) or ShareSave schemes);
- Enterprise Management Incentives (EMIs) and other executive share plans;
- Company Share Option Plans (CSOPs);
- employee shareholder status – an employment status that gives the right to a minimum value of company shares in exchange for decreased employment rights;
- Employee Ownership Trusts – a trust which owns the controlling (more than 50 per cent) shareholding on behalf of employees.

HMRC (2022) data gives the total number of companies operating employee share schemes in 2021 as 16,330, an increase of 6 per cent on the previous year and an 88 per cent increase on 2010. However, the data also shows that this huge increase in numbers of schemes has been almost entirely driven by EMIs which allow companies to offer share options up to the value of £250,000 in a three-year period; a much higher amount in comparison with other schemes. The incidence of the more broad-based share schemes has fallen during this period despite SAYE schemes remaining the largest in terms of the value of options granted.

In times of economic uncertainty, the attraction of ShareSave plans (SAYE and SIPs) may be diminished, particularly when share prices fall lower than the option price. In these circumstances, employees in schemes approaching maturity may decide to take their savings and bonus as cash rather than exercise their option to buy shares. On the other hand, when share prices are low, employees may consider it an ideal time to contribute to a scheme and potentially gain from any market recovery in future. This chapter concentrates on broad-based schemes. See Chapter 10 for executive share schemes.

Estimates of the number of employee-owned organisations in UK put the figure at approximately 1300 at December 2022 which represents a doubling of such organisations in the past three years, largely driven by the EOT model (Employee Ownership Association, 2023).

6.7.2 Share incentive plans

Share Incentive Plans (SIPs) were introduced in the Finance Act 2000 and replaced the former AESOP (all-employee share ownership plan). The SIP is a tax-advantaged all-employee scheme that gives employees the opportunity to own shares in the company they work for. HMRC outlines the four types of plan are available: free shares (up to £3,600 a year per employee); partnership shares (employees can use up to £1,800 a year to buy shares from gross salary); matching shares (a maximum ratio of two free shares for each partnership share purchased); and dividend shares (additional shares may be invested in the plan as dividend shares if employer scheme allows) (Gov.uk, 2019a). The SIPS must be set up under a trust that holds the shares for the participating employees. Shares must be offered to all employees who are eligible under the legislation, including part-time employees. A qualifying period of service can, however, apply.

6.7.3 Savings-related share option schemes

Savings-related schemes, better known as Save-As-You-Earn (SAYE), or ShareSave schemes, were introduced under the Finance Act 1980 as all-employee share schemes. These allow employees to be granted an option to buy shares in their employer's company at a fixed price. Shares can be purchased through amounts set aside under an SAYE contract. The price of the shares is set by the market price at the date of the grant and may be discounted by up to 20 per cent.

Employers can offer options that can be exercised in three, five or seven years from the date of grant. A tax-free bonus is paid at the end of the savings contract, when the employee has the choice of whether or not to purchase the shares. If the share price is below the exercise price, the employee can choose to keep the savings and tax-free bonus. If the employee takes the share option, they are subject to capital gains tax but may transfer shares to a spouse or to an ISA to shelter the capital gain. There is a maximum savings amount of £500 a month.

6.7.4 Enterprise Management Incentives

Enterprise Management Incentives (EMIs) were introduced under the Finance Act 2000 with the aim of encouraging small independent firms to utilise share ownership as a means to attract, retain and reward their staff. EMIs do not require HMRC approval in advance, although unlisted firms must submit a share valuation. Up to £250,000 worth of shares can be bought by the employee in a three-year period and any gains are exempt from tax and NI contributions although Capital Gains Tax may be payable if the shares are sold (Gov.uk, 2019b).

A research project on EMIs for the HMRC (Ipsos Mori, 2008) found that employee retention was the key reason employers had introduced a scheme although the associated tax advantages for employers were also mentioned. The report also noted that EMI did not feature very highly as a deciding factor among employees as to whether or not to work for the company.

6.7.5 Company share option plans

Company share option plans (CSOPs) were introduced under the Finance Act 1996. Under this scheme employees are given a share option but not an obligation to buy a certain number of shares at a fixed price at a particular time. This type of scheme is mainly used for senior managers, although some employers offer the scheme to all employees. The aggregate value of all outstanding share options must not exceed £30,000 at the market value at the time of the grant (Gov.uk, 2019c).

6.7.6 Employee shareholder status

In 2013 the UK Growth and Infrastructure Act allowed employees and employers to agree a new form of employment status: 'employee shareholder' (ESS). People working under an employee shareholder contract could receive a minimum of £2,000 worth of shares in the employer's company with no set maximum value. As part of the contract, the employee shareholder loses certain employment rights including unfair dismissal rights (unless the dismissal is automatically unfair or related to discrimination or health and safety reasons); rights to statutory redundancy pay and the right to request flexible working. Other employment rights such as the National Minimum Wage, TUPE, minimum notice periods and working time rights would still apply (BIS, 2014).

While the purpose of introducing employee shareholder status was largely understood to be aimed at stimulating recruitment, productivity and economic growth by reducing the burden of employment legislation for employers and giving employees a greater stake in the success of their companies, there was widespread opposition to these measures from trade unions and the House of Lords as well as some employers. Opponents claimed that this initiative represented a threat to long-fought-for employment rights. However, the take up was far lower than the government anticipated with only 350 employers agreeing share valuations with HMRC for the purpose of such agreements two years after its introduction (Moss, 2015). Specific tax relief was removed in 2016 for anyone who became an employee shareholder after this date, effectively rendering the ESS over.

6.7.7 Employee ownership trusts

> Employee ownership can take one of three forms:
>
> Direct employee ownership – using one or more tax advantaged share plans, employees become registered individual shareholders of a majority of the shares in their company,
>
> Indirect employee ownership – shares are held collectively on behalf of employees, normally through an employee trust,
>
> Combined direct and indirect ownership – a combination of individual and collective share ownership.
>
> (Employee Ownership Association, 2023)

EOTs provide employees with an indirect way of owning their company, holding the shares in trust, on their behalf and distributing cash bonuses with advantageous tax relief. This is often referred to as the 'John Lewis' model because the well-known retailer uses a similar arrangement.

CASE STUDY 6.1

Employee ownership benefits at Purcell

Purcell – our EO story: 'Community of many voices' strengthened and empowered

Purcell is one of the world's leading design practices with more than 70 years' experience as architects, master planners and heritage consultants operating across regions of the UK and Asia Pacific.

Currently with 236 employee owners, the AJ100 architectural practice has provided expert services as architects, designers, heritage and specialist consultants on many of the UK's best-known buildings.

Overview

The retirement of several co-owners between 2016 and 2018 left the remaining two owners of Purcell responsible for a global team and facing an existential crisis. The resulting shockwaves brought into question a previously secured ownership contingency model, with the immediate need to protect the organisation's independence, ownership and – above all – people, now brought to the fore.

Over seven previous decades, Purcell had cultivated a unique place in the industry and a reliable reputation around the world, but the remaining owners recognised that opportunities to simultaneously reinvent, adapt and safeguard a practice are rare.

With an enthusiastic, highly specialised and extraordinarily talented workforce facing a prodigious level of uncertainty and inevitable change, its leadership embarked on a consultation process aimed at breaking down barriers of accountability and transparency, incentivising its employees and giving them a substantial – even personal – stake in the company's performance.

The lengthy process that led us to employee ownership (EO) has been enduringly positive, with strategic and financial benefits becoming almost immediately apparent: employee engagement is up significantly, and financial communication and awareness have notably increased, with profits to the half-year point almost double the profit for the full year to April 2019.

The need for transformation

Purcell's architectural legacy, created by founder Donovan Purcell in 1947, was threatened by quick and unforeseen ownership changes, leaving two remaining co-owners accountable for the whole body of staff, spread regionally and internationally across 16 studio locations. Their clear desire not to sell to an external buyer was tempered by the acknowledgement that a pivotal change to operations was needed to continue the future of the practice.

Exploring methods of leaving a legacy for a new generation of owners without putting financial strain on the company or its working capital, the owners focused on creating a culture that drove results and a solution that would endure through employees' emotional engagement. Creating a clear line of sight between employees' individual actions and the cumulative impact Purcell's bottom line – and with that our own rewards – would ensure Purcell could thrive and operate in perpetuity.

Enhancing engagement

Insights from our staff were fundamental to our transition – without their wholehearted buy-in, EO would be unviable. Through a series of 'Roadshows', CEO Mark Goldspink visited each studio to articulate his vision: intrinsically linking the needs of both the company and the individual employees, empowering each of them to be accountable for our success or failure.

The unanimous agreement to move to the EO model meant an opportunity to clarify the kind of culture we wanted to build and to understand the specific behaviours that entailed.

To re-establish our organisational capability through a shared mindset, staff members volunteered to create Purcell's new values and behaviours. Drawing on ideas and consultation from all levels and regions of the business, as well as gaining thoughtful insight from some of our longest-serving clients, staff became united by a sense of common purpose and began encouraging the notion of ownership to less engaged colleagues.

Translating this to a set of day-to-day actions was the first step in tangibly linking our strategic goals to how they should be delivered under the new model. To provide a clearer means of communication between employees and the new board, and to give employees the opportunity to raise concerns or ideas, the Purcell Voice was established. This ongoing forum continues to act as a powerful mechanism for reminding all Purcell's people of their responsibility to act as owners and make a difference.

Our next step was the launch of Purcell's Collective Ambition. This document sets out our five-year business plan in line with our principal objectives, aspiring to underpin the daily actions of all employees, and with key performance indicators to provide measures for holding the board to account.

Integrating EO's participatory culture meant fresh thinking for our operational model and structure. With a stringent focus on our clients' needs, we re-organised our studios into regional groups, paving the way for more focused leadership, management and work-winning strategies. This has contributed to overall growth through the regional integration of resources, offering frequent opportunities to create efficiencies and share knowledge.

Our evolution from Donovan Purcell's philosophies was outlined in our final key document, the Purcell Constitution. Though still inextricably bound to the original ethos and philosophy, the constitution highlights both the process and practicalities of our reinvention; now thriving within a fairer, grassroots-driven structure that corresponds to the practice's developing ambitions and central to our identity.

Strategic and financial results: What was achieved?

EO has transformed employee engagement culture in our organisation; encouraging employees to take control of their own learning and development journey, deepening scrutiny in our everyday business decisions, creating distinctive local identities for their studios, significantly increasing costs awareness and contributing to increased inter-regional collaboration and success.

A new generation of owners has found their voice, playing an active role in leading the business to greater successes. The extensive commitment and effort put into realigning our culture has already started to pay off – as demonstrated through responses to our employee engagement surveys, where 72 per cent of our staff shared the belief that the board and partners are taking the business in the right direction to achieve success; 79 per cent agreed that Purcell provides equal opportunities for all; and 69 per cent advocated our new ownership structure.

Our employee trust now owns 70 per cent of the business, with the remaining 30 per cent transferring from May 2026. With the metrics of our Employee Inform surveys showing marked increases this year – including engagement up 8 per cent, belief in the board to achieve success up 34 per cent, trustworthiness of leadership up 7 per cent and employees' sense of importance up 31 per cent – there is significant confidence amongst those who matter most that EO is bringing tangible benefits and an optimistic future.

Our profitability is improving, with a profit at the end of our first EO year of £2 million, compared to annual profits of £1.3m (2021 and 2020) and £720,000 (2019). Revenue is now back to pre-pandemic levels and our bank balance has tripled in the last two years, despite making significant repayments to our former owners since May 2021 as part of our move to EO. Our bank balance and net assets value have already returned to nearing pre-EO levels.

Our journey has reinvented and enhanced the collaborative approach that we have perpetually strived for in the way we work. Purcell's identity is unchanged, but our community of many voices – who come together with enthusiasm to support each other in achieving and celebrating collective success – is undeniably strengthened by our new sense of participation and self-empowerment.

(Employee Ownership Association, 2022)

QUESTIONS

In summary, what are the key benefits of employee ownership experienced by this company?

What contextual aspects of the company's characteristics might have made employee ownership so successful for them?

Thinking about your own organisation, or one with which you are familiar, do you think employee ownership would be as successful there? Justify your response.

6.8 The incidence of variable pay

While it is widely accepted that there has been a substantial increase in the use of variable pay in developed economies since the 1980s, there is also evidence for a more recent levelling off, or even decline, in the incidence of some performance pay schemes.

The growth of variable pay has taken different forms in different countries, with a strong emphasis upon employee financial participation schemes (organisation-wide profit-sharing or share ownership schemes). In some countries, such as France, profit-sharing has been compulsory for some years in firms above a certain size. The growth of individual incentive schemes has been more patchy, but, over the long-term, there has been a clear increase in such schemes in the USA, Canada, Australia and the UK. A 2002 survey by Lowe et al (2002) of 770 North American organisations found that more than two-thirds operated variable pay plans of some sort. A study of performance pay plans in Canada and Australia (Long and Shields, 2005) found that the great majority of firms in both countries utilised at least one performance pay plan for their non-management employees.

In the UK, the most recent Workplace Employee Relations Survey, in 2011, confirmed a substantial increase in the use of performance-related pay in the two decades up to 2004 but found a levelling off since then (van Wanrooy et al, 2013). The survey found that just over half (55 per cent) of all workplaces use at least one incentive pay scheme, while one-fifth (20 per cent) of employees received payment by results (PBR) in addition to their fixed wage; 3 per cent were solely reliant on PBR and the remaining 77 per cent were on a fixed wage only. The WERS data shows the influence of sector on the prevalence of incentive pay. It is more common in the private sector (60 per cent of workplaces) than in the public sector (22 per cent) (van Wanrooy et al, 2013).

Since 2011, research using Office for National Statistics data and looking at the incidence and size of bonus payments in the UK over the 2000s finds that there has been no substantial increase in performance-related pay and, if anything, the incidence of these schemes has fallen (Forth, Bryson and Stokes, 2014).

This apparent decline in the use of variable pay schemes is supported by the most recent findings from CIPD's Reward Management Survey (Marriot and Perkins, 2019) which suggest a steady downward trend in performance-related reward schemes since at least 2012 (see Figure 6.1). The report notes that just 44 per cent of organisations responding to the survey are operating at least one scheme in comparison to 65 per cent in 2012. Continued uncertainty in the economic environment may be causing some organisations to either put their bonus payouts on hold or shift reward packages away from variable pay perhaps indicating unwillingness to risk paying out unless overall organisational performance is stronger (Jones et al, 2015). Although some of the widely reported downsides of individual performance-related schemes highlighted earlier in this chapter may also be having an effect here.

Table 6.1 Proportion of organisations operating one of more performance-related pay scheme

Year	%
2019	44
2017	48
2015	49
2013	55
2012	65

SOURCE: Marriott and Perkins (2019)

6.9 Conclusions and key learning points

This chapter has covered the range of variable pay options. We discussed how the terminology can be confusing and how there are various terms used for these forms of reward. We explained that we have adopted the term 'variable pay' to denote all the alternative methods of paying employees by unconsolidated forms of contingent reward – either as an alternative to or as an addition to base pay. We also discussed the traditional divide between manual and non-manual workers' variable pay systems and how there have been countervailing trends in recent years. Pay for manual workers has increasingly moved away from individualised systems, such as piecework and work-measured schemes, towards more collective forms of reward, such as team-based reward and profit-sharing. A major reason for this shift in emphasis has been for employee relations reasons – employers were losing control of individualised reward systems – but it also reflects the economic and social changes in the workplace in recent times. The decline of manufacturing and changes in production methods have also driven these changes in payment systems.

In contrast, for non-manual workers there has been a strong shift towards more variable pay systems, with the traditional 'commission' payments made to sales staff being spread more widely to other groups of staff. There has also been a large growth in individual bonus schemes, especially in the financial services industry although levels of scrutiny in this area has increased. These observations reinforce the importance of context in designing such schemes. What may work in one environment or for one part of the workforce may not work for another.

We identified the various dimensions of variable pay – both in terms of individual, team or collective rewards and in terms of short-term or long-term focus. As we noted, there have been recent moves away from individualised forms of variable pay and towards team or other collective rewards. This change has reflected changes in context for organisations, with increasing emphasis on the need for teamwork, knowledge-sharing and quality improvement. Individual competitive behaviour may no longer be appropriate in many organisations, and so individual forms of reward no longer work.

There has also been a growth in more long-term forms of reward. These new forms have often sought to increase employee engagement with business objectives rather than simply seeking to motivate them to increase productivity or profits. Several of these collective forms involve employee participation, where employees have a level of financial ownership of the organisation, although such moves raise questions about employees' control over organisational strategy. In some cases, employee financial participation has been extended into full employee ownership models where employees have a genuine voice in organisational strategy, rather than simply a financial stake in the organisation's future.

Although some employers use only one form of variable pay, many are using several types at individual, team and organisational levels. Clearly, the consequences of using variable pay are diverse, and the research evidence provides both support and a critique for such practices.

Explore further

For a more detailed discussion of the various forms of variable pay, see Shields, J (2015) *Managing Employee Performance and Reward. Concepts, practices, strategies*, 2nd edition, Cambridge: Cambridge University Press.

For an overview of up to date research on behavioural approaches to variable pay (and other elements of reward) see CIPD (2015) *Show me the money! The behavioural science of reward*, London, CIPD.

For more information on employee ownership, its forms, benefits and organisations following this approach, see the Employee Ownership Association website at employeeownership.co.uk/.

PART THREE

In Part Three we review principles, policies and frameworks for non-cash benefits, deferred remuneration and 'intrinsic' rewards. The three chapters in this part cover, respectively, non-cash employment benefits and their delivery; managing retirement pensions; and the significant field of non-financial rewards, combining with cash remuneration, deferred compensation and material benefits under the rubric of 'total reward'.

07 Benefits

CHAPTER LEARNING OUTCOMES

At the end of this chapter, you should understand and be able to explain the following:

- The purpose of employee benefits within the reward system.
- Benefits strategy and the role of taxation in the design of benefits.
- The various types of employee benefit and their different roles.
- The major benefits provided.
- Flexible or 'cafeteria' benefits.
- Voluntary benefits.
- Salary sacrifice schemes.

CIPD STRATEGIC REWARD MANAGEMENT (7HR03) LEARNING OUTCOMES

Learners will be able to:

2.4 Evaluate different types of employee benefits and their suitability in different organisational contexts.

7.1 Introduction

Employee benefits (or 'conditions of service' or 'fringe benefits', as they are sometimes termed) are those additional parts of the remuneration package that are not cash pay. Although these benefits may not be part of the monthly or weekly pay statement, they clearly have a cost to the employer and a value to the recipient. It is often estimated that employee benefits can comprise up to 40 per cent of the costs to organisations of employing staff. In some cases, despite being seen as non-cash items, they are received in cash form (such as sick pay, maternity pay or redundancy pay). In the case of pensions, they are often viewed as a form of 'deferred remuneration' in that the employee saves part of their annual income towards a guaranteed future income when retired. We deal with pensions, which are of increasing importance within reward systems, in Chapter 8.

In this chapter we consider first the current absence of both theory and research on employee benefits before proceeding to look at the contextual issues driving benefits provision. We then consider a number of typologies of benefits to enable some theoretical analysis before reviewing the decisions required of managers. We go on to examine three main categories of benefit: welfare, work-related and status. Finally, we look at three developments in benefit practice: flexible or 'cafeteria' benefits, voluntary benefits and salary sacrifice systems.

The role of employee benefits within the reward system varies between countries. In some countries, such as the USA, the absence of a 'welfare state' has meant that employers have been expected to bear the burden of employee healthcare, whereas in many European countries the state plays a much more central role in the provision (and regulation) of benefits. Another key variable is the tax regime used in each country, which can affect the value of the benefit to both employer and employee. As we outline in Chapter 3, in many countries there are legal minima set for certain benefits that have to be provided by employers (e.g. leave entitlements) and the provision of benefits may also be governed by discrimination law. For example, in the UK the advent of age discrimination law raised issues about service-related benefits which may benefit older workers more than younger (although currently these are exempt if there is no more than a five-year service requirement).

Although benefits have been a growing part of the remuneration package in the UK since the mid-20th century, there have been some significant developments in recent years, especially in the provision of pensions and 'family-friendly' benefits reflecting wider changes in society. There has also been increasing employer concern about the escalating costs of such benefits and a perception that employees do not always recognise the value of what is on offer but take such benefits for granted. This in turn has led to both a 'budget' approach to benefits based on the concepts of flexibility and choice and to an increasing emphasis on the 'total reward' concept (see Chapter 9), by which employers talk about the value of the whole pay and benefits package.

This has shifted the rationale of many employers' benefits policies from an emphasis on the welfare 'safety net' nature of the benefit to an emphasis on the 'value for money' approach. Increasingly, employers are seeking to discover whether benefits can play a more strategic role in wider human resource policy, such as recruitment, retention, motivation and performance. On the other hand, legislation is also playing an increasing role in defining both the content and the boundaries for employee benefits.

DEFINITION

'Employee benefits or 'fringe benefits' form part of remuneration and consist of a broad range of additions to an employee's income… An important function of benefits is to provide for employee security in the event of disruption to regular earnings, while in other cases benefits may confer status or serve as an aid to recruitment and retention.'

(Heery and Noon, 2017)

7.2 An absence of theory

Many employers view benefits as a key part of the employment contract, and a number of objectives are often mentioned as the explanation. For example, Armstrong and Murlis (2007) argue that benefits increase commitment, provide for the actual or perceived personal needs of employees, can add to the 'employer brand', attracting and retaining staff, and provide a tax-efficient method of remunerating staff. Unfortunately, unlike some other components in the reward system, there has been scant research or development of theory concerning benefits. In most cases we simply do not know if benefits work or not.

It has been argued that the 'benefits construct' is ambiguous and definitions lack consensus. Some authors include in their definitions only those items that are legally required or have a direct cost to the employer, while others take a broader viewpoint. One thing is clear: benefits are 'not wages for time worked, nor are they normally viewed as performance-contingent' (Lengnick-Hall and Bereman, 1994: 102).

As Milkovich and Newman (2008) point out, there are no clear answers to the questions of whether effective benefit management contributes to organisational effectiveness and performance or whether benefits impact upon an organisation's ability to attract, retain and motivate employees. They say that a 'similar lack of research surrounds each of the other potential payoffs to a sound benefits programme' (Milkovich and Newman, 2008: 399). Employer strategy in the past has been largely reactive, either to particular labour market pressures or to legislative requirements.

It is also apparent that spend on benefits as a proportion of the overall wage bill can vary widely with estimates of benefits as a proportion of total labour costs ranging from 15 per cent to 40 per cent in OECD countries (OECD, 1997, cited in Wright, 2009). In the UK, CIPD's 2013 Reward Management Survey (Jones et al, 2013a) found that 43 per cent of firms spend 10 per cent of the total employee reward package on benefits, 26 per cent spend 20 per cent and 10 per cent spend 30 per cent of the total package on benefits. However, there were 15 per cent of employers who claim to spend nothing on benefits and 100 per cent of their reward spend on pay.

Pendleton (1997) argues that variations in the use and form of benefit provision between organisations are systematically related to the organisational, institutional and contextual differences between firms but, as Robinson and Hudson (2008: 213) note,

> there is no over-arching, coherent, theoretical approach to work in this area and this gives rise to the need to use empirical evidence to validate or reject theoretical hypotheses about the use of benefits.

Wright (2009) suggests two theoretical perspectives for benefits policy: economic and psychological. Forth and Millward (2000) indicate that from the economic perspective, some employers may choose to provide more generous benefits to compensate for lower base pay and earnings levels. This is partly confirmed by the fact that many public service employers provide more generous benefits than their private sector competitors in the labour market to compensate for less competitive salaries for similar jobs. Indeed, as one of the panel participants in the CIPD (Marriot and Perkins, 2018: 44) Reward Management Survey discussion puts it: 'My organisation is never going to be a high payer, but what we can do is look after our people.' On the other hand, research has found that benefits tend to be better in higher-paying organisations than lower-paying (Dale-Olsen, 2005). In other words, the entire pay package is pitched at a more competitive level.

Research has also shown that low-paid workers are likely to have fewer and less generous benefits than the higher-paid (Forth and Millward, 2000). Forth and Millward (2000: 50) suggest that efficiency wage theory (see Chapter 2) may also be of relevance. Better benefits and higher wages may go together as part of a policy to elicit worker loyalty and effort. Or it may be a result of unions pressing for benefits as well as higher wages. Forth and Millward comment that in representing the preferences of their typical members, unions tend to favour the preferences of older, relatively permanent workers who have a greater desire for fringe benefits, especially those that increase with service. Recent data from CIPD's Reward Management Survey 2022, suggests that low-paid workers (in this case those earning less than £20,000 per annum) are indeed less satisfied and feel they have less access to benefits in comparison with higher-paid employees (see Figure 7.1)

Barringer and Milkovich (1998) suggest that institutional theory, resource dependency theory, agency theory and transaction cost theory might all be useful avenues to explore the effects of benefits on employee behaviour (see Chapter 2 for explanations of these theories), but that as yet there has been little attempt to explore the field using such theory. Robinson and Hudson (2008) posit several theoretical positions to explain how employee benefits might impact at the level of the employee. On the one hand they might be seen as encouraging and safeguarding investments in valuable human capital and creating commitment and loyalty to the organisation. On the other hand, they might be seen as a form of 'efficiency wage', increasing the level of total rewards above the market clearing rate to retain productive labour. As they state (Robinson and Hudson, 2008: 213):

> In this sense benefits may offer a potential solution to the broader agency problem that underpins the employment relationship by encouraging some alignment of goals between parties. Benefits might also motivate workers to volunteer additional effort and free up private information, especially where workers' actions are unobservable or not easily measured and consequently the potential for opportunism is high.

A third approach is through the functioning of internal labour markets by which workers are motivated by the wage increase they would earn if they won a promotion through competition with other workers. By extending this concept to total

Figure 7.1 Low-paid employees least likely to have access to strong benefits package

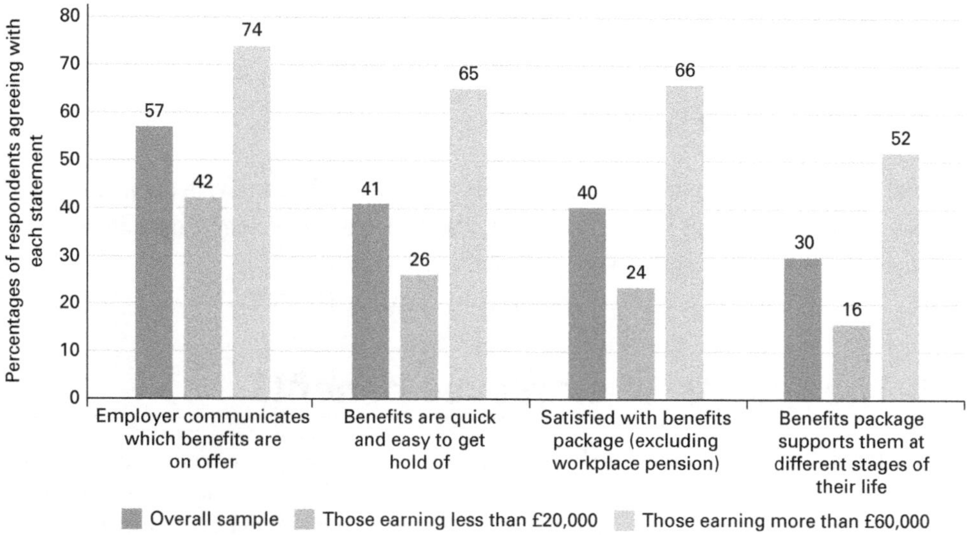

SOURCE: CIPD (2022c)

reward – including benefits – 'workers will behave as predicted so long as the firm operates a hierarchy of benefits' (Robinson and Hudson, 2008: 214). On the other hand, employees in firms which operate a 'single status' system may be motivated by the more equitable distribution of benefits.

Milkovich and Newman (2008) refer to two US studies that support the view that benefits reduce the mobility of staff (Mitchell, 1982; Schiller and Weiss, 1979). But more detailed studies (Evan and Macpherson, 1996; Mitchell, 1983) found that in reality this was due to just two benefits: pensions and healthcare. More recently, Ko and Hur (2014) find no relationship between traditional employee benefits and turnover but they do find that satisfaction with family-friendly benefits is negatively related to turnover intention, i.e. employees satisfied with family friendly benefits were less likely to leave the organisation. There is little research evidence to date to support the view that benefits contribute to improving employee performance and thus the company 'bottom line'. There is, however, some indication that employers who provide work–life balance benefits have experienced improved productivity (Lambert, 2000).

In terms of psychological theory, Cole and Flint (2003) use organisational justice theory to investigate employee perception of flexible benefits compared to traditional benefits systems. Through testing the self-interest and relational models of organisational justice, they found that employees with flexible benefits systems had significantly higher perceptions of procedural justice than those in traditional systems, although there were no significant differences in perceptions of distributive justice between the two plan types.

Finally, Balkin and Werner (2023) use organisational support theory and equity theory, seen through the perspectives of social and economic exchange relationships, to predicting a positive relationship between discretionary benefits (i.e. those that are not legally required) and individual performance.

> **SELF-ASSESSMENT EXERCISE**
>
> What is the role of employee benefits? To what extent do they motivate staff, or are they just tools to recruit and retain staff? If you think they are indeed motivational, which benefits would motivate you to higher performance?

7.3 The growth of employee benefits

In the UK, the development of welfare provision in the workplace went hand in hand with the development of the personnel function in the final decades of the century. It was enlightened employers such as Rowntree, Cadbury and Lever Brothers who were the first to develop on-site healthcare facilities, sick pay, subsidised meals and housing. The provision of such benefits was partly driven by philanthropic, 'moral' motives and partly by the view that such welfare benefits would yield a healthier and thus more productive workforce. They were also regarded as important elements in employer strategies to resist trade union organisation in their workplaces.

The company pension began in the second half of the 19th century, some schemes being established for clerical staff in the civil service, banking and the railway companies. State pension provisions and other large employer pension schemes were developed through the first quarter of the 20th century with company schemes given further impetus following the industrial conflict between employers and unions of the 1920s, when employers sought to insulate themselves from union organisation through adopting more humane conditions for workers. It was not, however, until the election of a Labour government following World War II in 1945 that the 1946 National Insurance Act introduced a universal contributory state pension for all citizens.

State sickness benefit, paid to workers unfit for work through accident or ill health, had been introduced through the National Insurance Act of 1911, but paid maternity leave did not arrive until the 1975 Employment Protection Act. Paid holidays were rare until the Holidays with Pay Act 1938, which gave workers covered by collective agreements and wages boards the right to holidays. The growth of holiday entitlement followed the spread of collective bargaining between employers and unions, and holiday entitlements were incorporated into collective agreements. It was not until the 1998 Working Time Regulations, however, that for the first time there was a statutory holiday entitlement for all workers in the UK.

As this short history of the development of benefits shows, the growth in the range of employer-provided benefits has largely been driven by responses to external initiatives. Growth in both the range and level of benefits provided has been strong since the 1960s. Between 1964 and 1981 benefits in UK manufacturing industry increased from 11 per cent of average pre-tax remuneration to 19 per cent (Green et al, 1985). As Smith (2000: 166) notes:

> Uneven distribution of these benefits – with high-paid employees receiving absolutely and proportionately much more than the low-paid – has been a consistent characteristic for decades. Until the 1970s the provision of benefits to manual workers was unusual, apart from annual holiday entitlement and some compensatory payments (ie for travel and subsistence).

Several factors have changed this situation. In the USA, Milkovich and Newman (2008) identify five such factors: wage and price controls, labour unions, employer initiatives, cost-effectiveness and government policy.

In the UK, as we have seen above, there were similar developments to those in the USA. Smith (2000) argues that there were two key developments in the UK. The first was the passing of the 1975 Social Security Pensions Act, which allowed employers and employees to 'contract out' of the state secondary pension and join employers' schemes. The second was the repeal of the Truck Acts in 1986, which led to manual workers moving on to salary systems and paved the way for the 'harmonisation' of their benefits with other staff.

In the 1980s, there was a big growth in the range of benefits provided as employers sought to profit from the tax advantages of providing certain benefits (e.g. company cars) as opposed to the cash alternative. A large industry of benefits consultants developed to advise employers on how best to use the tax and National Insurance rules to their advantage. In the 1990s these tax and National Insurance loopholes began to be closed by the UK government and the emphasis shifted to cost containment. While there are still avenues to explore in terms of 'tax efficiency', some employers today have cut back their entitlement to a range of core benefits and prefer to emphasise the cash part of the total reward package, especially where large bonuses are available. One avenue to reduce the cost of benefits that has emerged is the availability of 'salary sacrifice', whereby employees can give up part of their taxable pay in return for a non-cash benefit that is treated in a more beneficial manner in relation to taxation (see later in this chapter).

As we will see in the following sections, the range of available benefits continues to grow, with a vast array of benefits being offered to employees in various forms. However, a very recent trend has apparently emerged from the combined effects of the Covid-19 pandemic and the cost of living crisis in the UK. First, there is a renewed emphasis on work–life balance benefits, such as flexible or hybrid working seemingly in response to employee demand. And second, the potential for employee benefits to be aimed at contributing to employees' financial wellbeing by offsetting the so-called 'poverty-premium' – the additional costs incurred by those on low incomes for accessing basic goods or services (e.g. paying bills on receipt rather than by direct debit arrangements or using pre-payment meters for electricity). We will explore both of these in more detail later in this chapter.

STUDENT EXERCISE

Discuss the following question in groups:

How far are employee benefits a 'moral' issue for your organisation (or one with which you are familiar)?

Which benefits offered by this organisation could be classed as meeting the 'moral' obligations of an employer?

7.4 Typologies of employee benefits

As mentioned above, there is now a wide range of benefits provided to employees by employers. The major ones are listed in Table 7.1. But different benefits have different organisational objectives:

- some are required by law (e.g. minimum holiday entitlement, statutory sick pay);
- some are provided to compensate employees for expenditure incurred in the performance of their work or to assist in that work, often known as 'expenses' (e.g. travel and subsistence expenses, essential user company cars or vans);
- some are welfare benefits designed to retain employees, manage wellbeing or create a positive employer brand;
- some are 'status' benefits provided as 'perks' to retain and incentivise more senior staff (e.g. non-essential user company cars).

In some cases, it is not easy to classify the purpose of a benefit easily. For example, private healthcare can be seen as both a 'welfare' benefit and a 'status' benefit because it is usually only available to higher-paid employees. Similarly, a company car might be seen as essential in some cases (such as mobile sales staff and maintenance engineers) but as a 'status' benefit where it is non-essential to carry out the job.

Table 7.1 The major types of benefit

Sick pay	Personal accident insurance
Holidays	Travel and subsistence
Private health care	Permanent health (long-term sickness) insurance
Life assurance	Season ticket loans
Maternity leave	Discounts on company goods or services
Paternity leave	Sports or social club membership
Compassionate leave	Subsidised canteen or luncheon vouchers
Pensions or 'superannuation'	Health screening
Childcare vouchers	Above statutory redundancy pay
Counselling (career, financial or personal)	Company loans (for example for computers)
Subsidised mortgages	Company car
Relocation expenses	Car mileage allowance
Long-term disability/permanent health insurance	Sabbaticals
Parental leave	Pre-retirement planning
Adoption leave	Early retirement options
Career breaks	Company credit cards
Training and education fees	Work clothing allowances and laundering
Time off work for public duties, trade union duties and so on	

Table 7.2 Typologies for categorising benefits

Author(s)	Typology
Armstrong and Murlis (2007) – seven categories	• pensions • personal security (for example health insurance and redundancy or life insurance) • financial assistance (for example loans, relocation expenses) • personal needs (for example holidays, childcare, retirement counselling) • company cars and petrol • other benefits (for example subsidised workplace restaurants or meal vouchers and gym membership) • intangible benefits (for example pleasant working environment, easy access to transport and shops)
Hume (1995) – three categories	• financial security (pensions, life assurance, personal accident insurance, above statutory sick pay, private health insurance, above statutory redundancy pay) • financial assistance (subsidised mortgages, company loans, relocation expenses, company cars) • personal needs (annual leave, maternity/paternity leave, career breaks and sabbaticals, counselling, medical services, childcare, subsidised catering, sports and social facilities, clothing/laundry services, training and education)
Smith (1983) – three categories	• security (for example pensions, sick pay, life insurance) • goodwill (for example holidays, early retirement, relocation) • performance (for example company cars, health insurance)
Wright (2004) – four categories	• personal security and health (for example pensions, above statutory sick pay) • job, status and seniority-related (for example cars, holidays above statutory minimum) • family-friendly (for example childcare, elder care, above statutory maternity/paternity leave) • social or 'goodwill' or lifestyle benefits (for example subsidised catering, sports/social facilities)

There have been a number of attempts to create a typology of benefits (see Table 7.2). For example, Armstrong and Murlis (2007) suggest that benefits can be divided into seven categories: pensions schemes, personal security, financial assistance, personal needs, company cars and fuel, 'other benefits', and intangible benefits. In contrast, Smith (1983) suggests just three categories: security, goodwill and performance. Hume (1995) also suggests just three main categories: financial security, financial support and personal needs. Wright (2004) provides four categories, adding a category for family-friendly benefits separate from goodwill or personal needs.

Smith (2000) has also attempted to analyse the impact of various benefits on organisations by considering them under three headings: contribution to the HRM function, contribution to performance/goodwill/security and role as motivator or 'hygiene' factor. Smith sees some benefits – such as enhanced leave, sick pay and life insurance – as 'hygiene' factors; that is, their presence may not motivate but their absence may have a negative effect. In contrast, he sees such benefits as pensions, cars and expenses as motivators. Smith argues that some benefits will have a more direct impact upon motivation than others, but that the majority of benefits can have implications for performance and motivation. Perkins (1998) argues that benefits will only link to company performance if the workforce values them.

A very different approach to categorising benefits is adopted by Flannery et al (1996). These Hay consultants suggest that benefits can be categorised according to the type of organisation in which they are found. From a strategic perspective, the Flannery et al typology makes some sense, with its emphasis upon contingency theory. It is worth remembering, however, that employers in the USA – the context for Flannery et al – have more freedom in the design of benefits packages than in Europe, first because of the different tax regimes, and second because the requirements for statutory benefits are fewer in the USA.

Flannery et al's model envisages four main types of organisational culture: functional, process, time-based and network. **Functional cultures** are highly organised and bureaucratic, with clear lines of authority and accountability. They provide secure employment and have a strong sense of equity. The benefits of a functional culture are epitomised by the values of longevity and security, reflecting the aspirations of the career-focused employees employed. There is a strong emphasis on generous pension entitlement, and life and health insurance.

In contrast, although security is still important for **process-based cultures**, the performance of the team or group is more important. Pensions in process cultures may be linked to profit-sharing plans tied to organisational performance. Healthcare and life insurance benefits are less important, reflecting the fact that there is less expectation that employees will stay with the organisation in the long term, and there may be more choice in benefits than in a functional culture.

A **time-based culture** aims to maximise the return on fixed assets and requires flexibility and technical agility. Employees are encouraged to be multi-skilled and are often engaged short-term. In time-based cultures the emphasis is on portability of benefits, because employees tend to move around a lot, sometimes from team to team but also from one business unit to another. Benefits therefore tend to be highly flexible and movable, with lots of choice for employees. Employees may also be expected to share the cost of their benefits.

Finally, in the **network culture** work is designed around alliances for specific projects. Such organisations are propelled 'by innovation, mobility and market creation and penetration' (Flannery et al, 1996: 39). Benefits in such organisations tend to be very dissimilar to those of other cultures. In general, there are far fewer benefits and those that do exist tend to be very flexible. Employees are also expected to shoulder a significant share of the cost of their benefits.

SELF-ASSESSMENT EXERCISE

To what extent do you think the various categorisations of benefits make sense in practice? What do your fellow students think? Thinking about your organisation – or one with which you are familiar – try to apply these models.

7.5 Employee attitudes to benefits

Research has indicated that equity is an important consideration among employees in relation to benefits. For this reason, an employer policy that bases the allocation of benefits upon individual performance or contribution is very rare. Even where there is individual choice available to employees, it is unlikely that overall entitlement will vary for those on the same grade or pay range. Trade unions will tend to hold the view that all staff should have the same entitlement and range of benefits, irrespective of status or rank.

Another way of assessing employee view on benefits is to conduct some analysis of their preferences. It is often assumed that these preferences will relate to demographics, younger workers having different preferences from older ones, and males different from females, married people different from single, and manual workers different from non-manual. Research from the USA, however, appears to show that this is only partly true (Milkovich and Newman, 2008). Whereas there is evidence that older workers have a stronger preference for pensions and those with families for family benefits, differences based on gender, marital status and social class seem less important. In contrast, there was a great deal of similarity across these groups in terms of preferences. The most popular benefits were health/medical insurance and stock plans, and the least favoured were options such as early retirement, profit-sharing, shorter hours and counselling services.

However, UK research by PricewaterhouseCoopers (PwC) surveying 2,423 employees has shown that while there are commonalities in preferences – for discount shopping vouchers, access to lower mortgage rates and additional holiday for example – there are differences in preference between genders as well as career stage (Lewis, 2015). While women responding to the survey were more likely to value medical insurance and childcare vouchers, men valued company cars, pensions and workplace share schemes more highly than women. The research also indicated that younger workers (18–24 year olds) were more likely to value company cars and developmental benefits such as training programmes than older workers. PwC suggest that benefits should not be designed on a 'one size fits all basis'; individual preferences and different segments of the workforce should be catered for if employers were to retain diverse talent (Lewis, 2015).

Taking a different approach, de la Torre-Ruiz et al (2017) in their survey of 874 Spanish workers found evidence that the personality type of employees had an effect on their satisfaction with flexible benefits plans. First, there was a clear indication that greater benefits flexibility had a generally positive effect on how satisfied employees were with how their benefits were determined. However, those employees with a low internal locus of control were much less satisfied with inflexible benefits plans. The authors suggest that this is because, unlike those with a high internal locus of control who perceive their choice of benefits to be an entitlement, for those who do not feel they can control a broad array of factors in their lives, the opportunity to exercise choice in benefits provision is more highly valued.

The practical challenges of tailoring benefits to employee preferences is one question employers face when formulating their benefits policies. As people professionals become more attuned to the greater breadth of employee needs in diverse workforces, it makes sense that employee flexibility to select the benefits they value most is a logical solution.

7.6 Benefits policies and decisions

Like all aspects of reward, many employers have clear and transparent policies concerning entitlement to benefits, although in smaller businesses these may be less formalised. Some organisations choose to operate a 'single status' policy whereby all staff receive the same range of benefits. Even in single status or harmonised workplaces, however, some status benefits such as company cars will be limited to senior staff. Other employers offer different benefits for different groups of staff, the range and/or value of the package normally increasing for higher grades within the organisational hierarchy. In some cases, these variations may reflect different collective agreements for different groups of employees.

Milkovich and Newman (2008) provide a useful list of issues that have to be considered when designing a benefits package. They are:

- Who should be protected or benefited?
- How much choice should employees have?
- How should benefits be financed?
- Are the benefits legally defensible?

The first decision to be taken is the **range of benefits** to be offered to staff. Some benefits are now expected by prospective employees (such as pensions and season ticket loans) and are seen as a hygiene factor in recruitment and retention, whereas others are required by law (such as sick pay and maternity leave). Will all staff receive the same range of benefits, or will some be available only to certain levels of staff? What will be the implications in terms of both cost and employee relations?

Second, employers have to decide on the **scale of the benefits** provided. What values will they attach to each benefit, and what will be the cost of each? Increasingly, employers are seeking to use a budget approach to benefits and to control the amounts they are prepared to pay for particular benefits. This is particularly important if an employer wishes to introduce an element of choice of benefits or benefit scale. Some benefits are linked to seniority or service – for example, annual leave often increases with service. Although this might be seen as a breach of age discrimination law, the Equality Act 2010 includes an exemption for all 'benefits' awarded by service as long as the service period required is five years or less. Employers who wish to have a service period longer than five years must demonstrate a 'business need'.

Third, employers will have to decide on the **overall 'spend' on benefits** compared to total remuneration. How much of the total pay costs will benefits account for? Clearly, the costs will be more significant in labour-intensive organisations than in capital-intensive, where labour costs form a minor proportion of total costs. Some organisations have adopted a 'total remuneration' approach and will only discuss the total spend with employees rather than the value of basic pay alone. Emphasising the value of the benefits on offer, however, is particularly difficult where pay levels are negotiated separately from local conditions of service (as in some industry-wide collective agreements).

In the USA, there is an increasing tendency for employees to make a contribution to the cost of their benefits. This is viewed as advantageous in two ways: first it makes employees more aware of the cost and so they place greater value on the benefits provided, and second, employees are more likely to control their use of the benefits if it affects their cost. In the UK, however, the only major benefit to which employees are expected to make a contribution is pensions, although sometimes the benefit entitlement can be increased by employees' making additional contributions (e.g. where employees make contributions to private medical insurance plans to cover their family members). Voluntary benefits, where employees can purchase additional benefits out of their own income, are also now available (and 'salary sacrifice' allows employees to gain tax advantages from this choice).

The fourth decision is **how benefits are allocated** to staff. Will all staff be treated the same, or will there be a hierarchy of benefits according to grade? Employers should be aware that the benefits provided for a particular grade or level of worker, however, cannot vary according to whether they are full-time or part-time. In the UK and Europe employees working on permanent part-time contracts are entitled to the same benefits (pro rata) as full-time. Clearly, those on short-term contracts may not be eligible for those benefits where there is a service requirement, but once they have completed the required service period, they must be offered the opportunity to join. The other issue is whether there will be 'single status' whereby all employees receive the same benefits, or whether there will be different arrangements for different groups of employees.

'Harmonised' approaches to managing human resources were particularly popular in the 1980s and 1990s when an influx into the UK of Japanese companies – in which single status is the norm – led to a growth in single status (Druker, 2000; Price and Price, 1994; Russell, 1998). In recent times, however, this trend has slowed and organisations have been more interested in containing the costs of the existing arrangements rather than incurring additional costs by extending some benefits to lower-level staff. Where harmonisation has been implemented it has been more to do with mergers and acquisitions – the need to bring the reward systems of two separate organisations together – rather than between different groups of workers in the same organisation. Concerns about the status divide between manual and non-manual employees appear less important today, probably because they are often less likely to be different in practice.

A fifth and final consideration is the **degree of employee choice** in the allocation of benefits. A recent trend has been towards 'cafeteria' or 'flexible benefits' whereby each employee is given a personal budget to spend on a 'menu' of possible benefits. We consider flexible benefits later in this chapter.

Whatever decisions are made by employers on the benefits provided, external comparisons with the market will be essential to ensure that the level of benefits on offer is, and remains, competitive. This involves careful research on market comparisons. As Armstrong and Murlis (2007) indicate, however, in some cases the principle of equity of treatment may be abandoned because of the requirement to provide key staff with particularly attractive benefits. There are considerable variations in benefits practice between organisations, and particularly between sectors or industries. In general, the private sector tends to provide more 'status' benefits, such as company cars, than the public sector, but increasingly, the public sector tends to provide more generous pensions, holiday entitlement and family-friendly benefits.

7.7 Benefits provisions in the UK

Information about benefits provision in UK workplaces is available from the regular CIPD Reward Management Survey which surveys both employers and employees. The last survey to look at benefits in detail, in 2021, set out to capture:

- the types of benefits employers provide, and who's receiving them;
- any changes being planned for 2022;
- how the benefits landscape has evolved since 2018;
- the impact of the pandemic – and skills and labour shortages – on the benefits package;
- employer attitudes and responses to financial wellbeing and in-work poverty.

The survey focuses on key areas of benefit provision:

- career and wellbeing benefits;
- financial wellbeing and organisational support;
- social, family and technology benefits;
- in-work poverty and financial support;
- benefits, homeworking and recruitment.

Figure 7.2 shows the most commonly offered universal benefits in organisations responding to the CIPD (2022) Reward Management Survey (Cotton et al, 2022). Perhaps surprisingly given the challenges faced by many employers in 2020–21, in the three years since the previous survey focusing on benefits provision, the incidence of the most common benefits offered to all employees has risen. This may be due to a different sample of employers responding to the survey or could reflect employer responses to the tighter labour market conditions following Brexit and the Covid-19 pandemic in a move aimed at attracting and retaining staff. Another possibility is that employers are looking to reduce complexity of benefits plans by offering benefits across the board rather than restricting them to certain groups.

These types of drivers and the strategic responses they elicit were considered in the 2013 CIPD Reward Management Survey Report supplement. The research finds that organisations pursuing a cost-focused business strategy are more likely to use 'recognition' benefits (e.g. vouchers, gifts, discounted goods, etc) as well as voluntary/affinity benefits whereas organisations pursuing a quality-focused

Figure 7.2 Ten most common benefits provided to all staff (%)

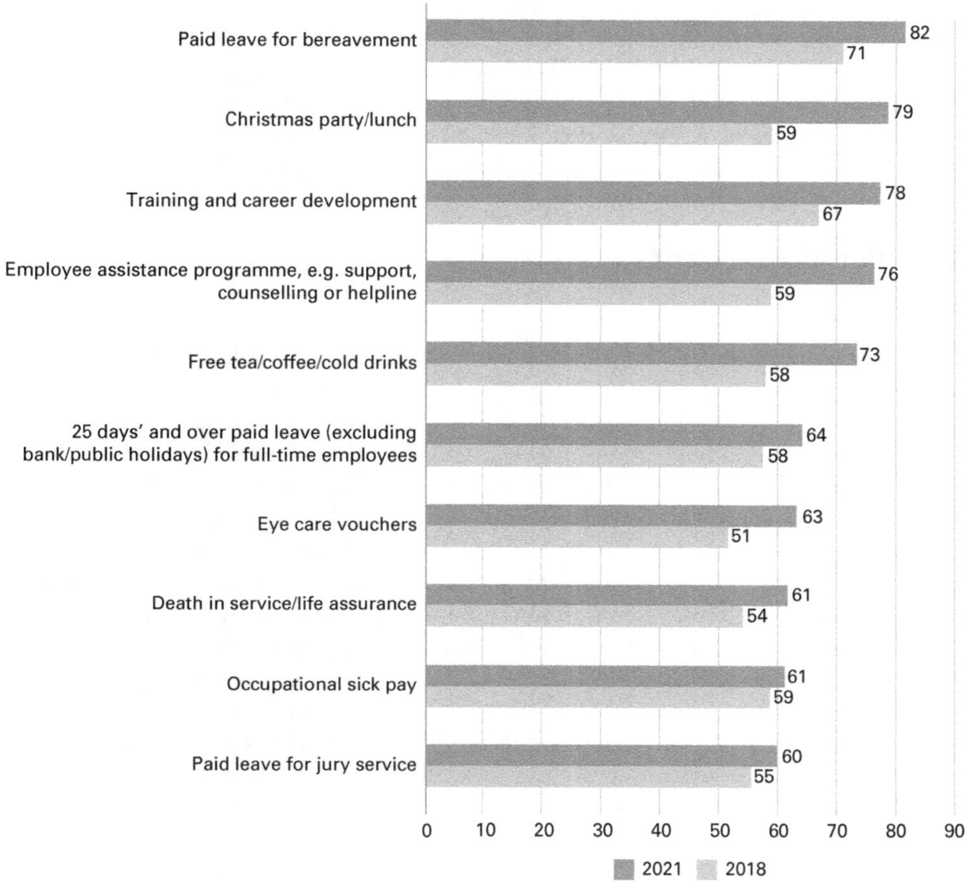

SOURCE: Cotton et al (2022)

strategy were more likely to offer a large range of different benefits, 'developmental benefits and benefits with a financial equivalence (e.g. pension scheme, company car, etc) (Jones et al, 2013b). The research also finds that certain key HR outcomes in the workplace (such as employee relations climate, labour productivity, employee recruitment, retention, absenteeism and pay discontent) are associated with different benefits management practices. Overall, the report offers evidence that employee benefits choices can be informed by strategic business orientation and indeed that the consequences of these choices can have an impact on employee outcomes and behaviour.

SELF-ASSESSMENT EXERCISE

Thinking about your own organisation (or one with which you are familiar) what are the issues driving the provision of benefits? How do the benefits fit with the business strategy of the organisation?

In the section below, we review some of the major benefits available. First, we consider the 'welfare' benefits, those expected by employees and often where there is a statutory minimum entitlement fixed by the government and those that explicitly address the wellbeing of staff. We then consider those benefits provided to attract applicants for jobs and to enable employees to undertake their jobs (recruitment and retention measures or compensatory benefits), which we term 'work-related benefits'. Finally, we consider status or 'perk' benefits (e.g. company cars).

7.7.1 *Welfare benefits*

Holidays

Since 2009 workers in the UK have been entitled to 28 days' holiday per year (including the eight statutory or 'bank' holidays), based on a five-day working week.

The CIPD Reward Management Survey (Cotton et al, 2022) shows that 64 per cent of respondent organisations offer all of their staff more than 25 days' holiday in addition to eight bank holidays per year (see Figure 7.2). This is in line with previous research from XpertHR (2015a) which shows the median number of days annual leave (excluding bank holidays) for employees with more than a year's service is 25 days, holiday entitlement at the lower quartile is 23 days and at the upper quartile is 28 days. The minimum amount of holiday entitlement (excluding bank holidays) is 20 days and the maximum is a whopping 82 days.

XpertHR (2015a) also found that 39 per cent of organisations have the same annual leave arrangements for all employees; 35 per cent have two groups with different entitlements; 14 per cent have three groups with different entitlements; and the remaining 12 per cent of employers have three or more variations. Presumably these different groups related to either seniority or were service-related.

The management of holidays is a major issue for managers in order to ensure that on the one hand there is equity of treatment in allocating holidays in the annual rota, and that on the other not all staff take holidays at the same time. In some cases, however, employers may decide to fix the weeks of holiday and close the plant or offices for that period. This not only overcomes the problem of holiday rotas but also allows the employer time to carry out essential annual maintenance work on the plant.

There are also various provisions in many organisations for special leave. This is most commonly for compassionate leave for close relatives who are bereaved. It is normally paid leave for a fixed period, with the option of further unpaid leave if necessary. Special leave may also be granted for other reasons, such as time off for public duties, to carry out trade union duties or to deal with urgent family commitments. In the UK, there are statutory rights to particular types of special leave.

Sick leave

Since 1983, employers have been required to pay Statutory Sick Pay (SSP) for most employed people. This change was largely driven by the government's wish to transfer the financial burden of sickness benefit from the public purse to employers. Employers used to be able to recover some of the SSP paid out if they qualified but this provision ended in April 2014. In 2019 the government held a consultation to explore making statutory sick pay more flexible, in part aimed at preventing long-term ill health causing people to lose their jobs. Part of the consultation considered re-establishing an SSP rebate for small businesses which help employees return to work (Webber, 2019). However, given the Covid-19 pandemic, the government have decided that it is not yet the right time to make changes to the system although have indicated SSP will remain under review (Brione and Powell, 2022).

The full weekly SSP rate from April 2023 is £109.40. Employees qualify if they have been sick for at least a period of four calendar days and have reached a threshold average weekly earnings. SSP is payable for up to 28 weeks.

Employers can choose to provide occupational sick pay schemes equal to or above the SSP rates. A survey by XpertHR (2015b) found the following:

> Three-quarters (74.4%) of respondents offer all employees occupational sick pay schemes that are more generous than statutory sick pay (SSP).
>
> One-third (32.1%) of organisations that provide occupational sick pay do this from the first day of employment.
>
> Entitlement to occupational sick pay increases with length of service in almost two-thirds (63.5%) of organisations that offer it.
>
> (XpertHR, 2015b)

The same research found that occupational sick pay was much more common in the public sector where all of the respondents in this category offered occupational schemes more generous than SSP alone (at least to some employees), compared with 94 per cent in manufacturing and production and 93 per cent in private sector services (XpertHR, 2015b).

XpertHR (2015b) also found that of organisations offering an occupational sick pay scheme after a year of service, nearly 9 out of 10 provide a period of full pay. Table 7.3 provides full details.

Maternity, paternity and parental benefits

Statutory leave and pay provisions for employees becoming parents have increased substantially in the past 30 years. At present the rights for eligible employees include: maternity leave up to 52 weeks (regardless of service), maternity pay for 39 weeks, rights to two paid weeks' paternity leave, paid adoption leave, the right to request flexible working arrangements, the right to unpaid parental leave to care for a child and the right of all employees to take time off to care for a dependant, including elderly relatives. Most recently the Shared Parental Leave Regulations (2014) has moved towards allowing eligible mothers, fathers, partners and adopters to share time off from work in the early months of child-rearing and provide flexibility to take time off in blocks interspersed with returns to work rather than having to take leave in one long chunk. The extension of provisions has been welcomed by many and employers clearly have both obligations to comply with these provisions and choices about whether and how to offer benefits in excess of statutory requirements.

Many UK employers do provide maternity and paternity leave in excess of statutory requirements, known as 'occupational' maternity or paternity leave, especially in the public services.

Table 7.3 Periods of full pay for sick leave

Length of time on full pay (having completed one year of service)	% of organisations
Less than 4 weeks	25.9
4 weeks	22.8
More than 4 weeks but less than 8 weeks	7.6
8 weeks	18.0
More than 8 weeks but less than 3 months	5.5
3 months	11.9
More than 3 months but less than 6 months	1.9
6 months	6.4

SOURCE: Data from XpertHR (2015b)

The 2022 CIPD Reward Management Survey found 49 per cent of employers offering enhanced maternity/paternity leave (Cotton et al, 2022) overall. Some 68 per cent of public sector organisations offer occupational maternity pay in excess of statutory maternity pay, followed by 53 per cent in the voluntary sector, 44 per cent in private sector services and only 38 per cent in manufacturing and production (Cotton et al, 2022).

While the complexity and proliferation of statutory regulation on employee rights to leave and pay on becoming a parent can cause headaches for employers, particularly small organisations without specialist HR functions, there is also a key retention opportunity for some in enhancing maternity/paternity benefits. This has been recognised by some high-profile employers, particularly in the US where statutory provisions are far less generous than in the UK. *People Management* magazine reported in August 2015 that the video streaming company Netflix was following other Silicon Valley employers Uber and Reddit in offering unlimited paid leave for new parents. Chief Talent Officer, Tawni Cranz is reported as blogging:

> Parents can return part-time, full-time, or return and then go back out as needed. We'll just keep paying them normally, eliminating the headache of switching to state or disability pay. Each employee gets to figure out what's best for them and their family, and then works with their managers for coverage during their absences.
>
> (*People Management*, 5 August 2015)

The article notes that the attraction and retention of talent is a clear driver of this policy. Whether or not mainstream employers will ever go quite this far in extending maternity and paternity provisions is debatable but there are indications that this is an area of employee benefits that can provide employers with opportunities to aid recruitment and retention, particularly in knowledge-based economies.

STUDENT EXERCISE

What are the maternity, paternity and other parental benefits offered by your organisation (or one with which you are familiar)?

How far do they go above and beyond statutory requirements?

How far do they aid recruitment and retention?

Is there more the organisation could do to encourage new parents to stay with the organisation besides what is currently offered?

Childcare

An increasingly popular benefit among employees is employer assistance with childcare. There are currently three types of employer-supported childcare: childcare voucher schemes, direct payments to childcare providers/a childcare allowance and workplace childcare provision. All three of these methods can attract exemptions from tax and NI contributions. Employees pay no tax or NICs on the benefit, and employers pay no NICs. The amount depends on the type of support provided – whether it is in addition to or instead of the employee's salary. The latter is known as salary sacrifice, whereby the employee forgoes part of their salary in exchange for this non-taxable benefit. With workplace provision (e.g. nurseries or creches) the saving for employers and employees can be much higher because the exemption is on the whole of the subsidy.

From autumn 2015, however, the government began to phase out tax arrangements for employer-supported childcare with the childcare voucher scheme closing to new entrants in October 2018. Instead 'tax-free childcare' has been introduced that is not dependant on employer support, i.e. parents with children in childcare settings will be able to take advantage of tax-free childcare costs without the employer providing access to vouchers or other childcare support.

Cotton et al (2022) found 53 per cent of employers responding to the CIPD Reward Management Survey offered childcare vouchers for those enrolled in pre-2018 schemes. However, on-site nurseries or creches continue to be rare with just 5 per cent of organisations offering this benefit.

Death in service/life assurance

While there is no statutory requirement to provide life assurance, many employers choose to do so. This can be provided either as part of the pension scheme benefits or separately. It normally provides for a multiple of the employee's salary (e.g. up to the HMRC limit of four times the annual salary) in the event of death-in-service. The CIPD reported 61 per cent of employers offering this benefit in 2021 (Cotton et al, 2022) and XPertHR (2019) found 76 per cent of organisations offered death-in-service benefits. Entitlements may vary between different categories of employee. This is a relatively cheap benefit because it only becomes a cost to the employer if the employee dies in service. Benefits are normally free of income and inheritance tax.

Permanent health insurance

Permanent health insurance (PHI) is often provided to cover employees who are long-term sick or injured, when their sick leave entitlement ends. It is normally payable after the first six months of sickness absence. Cover can be provided either through the pension scheme or through a separate insurance policy. There are usually substantial discounts from insurance companies for group schemes – where there is a guaranteed number of staff covered – and it can be much cheaper than individual employees insuring themselves. Employees are only taxed on the benefits in payment and not on any premiums paid by the employer. CIPD research shows 34 per cent of employers offering PHI in 2021 to some or all staff (Cotton et al, 2022).

Extra statutory redundancy pay

Although employees are entitled to a minimum level of statutory redundancy pay if they are dismissed due to an end to or diminished requirement for their work, many employers provide additional compensation. This is sometimes referred to as a 'severance package'. It can be set down in a policy or provided on an ad hoc basis in particular circumstances. Such extra-statutory compensation may cover additional service-related payments (e.g. two weeks per year of service instead of the statutory one), or paying above the statutory maximum weekly pay limit. It may also involve ex gratia payments – so-called 'golden handshakes'.

7.7.2 Work-related benefits

Flexible/hybrid or homeworking

The rise of flexible working as an employee benefit has long been recognised, and in the wake of the Covid-19 pandemic, the option to routinely or permanently work from home or from any place away from the traditional office has rocketed up the list of desirable, and even expected, employee benefits. CIPD include 'a compressed working week, job-sharing, part-time working, term-time working, homeworking, flexitime' within a definition of 'flexible working' which is offered by 85 per cent of employers to some or all staff (Cotton et al, 2022). For many employees, the flexibility to work at different times and places is a highly valued aspect of an employer's offer. A recent Hays report finds that 62 per cent of employees would consider changing job if they could choose how often they were in the workplace when working in a hybrid way. Hays also found that among professionals planning to change career in 2023, 50 per cent plan to find a job that is 'more of a mix of hybrid working', and 24 per cent plan on finding a role that's based completely remotely (Hays, 2023).

Accommodation

Some employees may be required to live 'over the shop' or in company-provided housing. Such employees include caretakers or janitors, publicans and hotel staff, and those working in residential care homes. In some cases, accommodation may only be provided when the employee is required to be on site (such as doctors in hospitals). In other cases, the accommodation is provided so that the employees can be close to their jobs (e.g. in agriculture). Such accommodation can be a substantial benefit to the employee, either in areas of high-cost housing (e.g. London) or in rural areas where work is located a long way from areas of habitation. But it also provides a substantial benefit to the employer in having staff readily available on site.

Under the National Minimum Wage legislation, employers are entitled to offset the cost of accommodation provided for employees against the calculation of entitlement to the minimum wage, but only up to a statutory limit. Research for the Low Pay Commission (White et al, 2007) found that in fact low-paid employees are less likely to be found in 'tied accommodation' than higher-paid employees. The LPC research found that in 2005 around 290,000 people were living in tied accommodation (1.1 per cent of all employees). The sectors where such accommodation is most likely to be found are agriculture, hospitality, retail, social care and leisure, travel and sport.

Employers may also provide subsidised or free catering services for employees in the workplace but, unlike tied accommodation, such subsidies cannot be offset against the national minimum wage. In some organisations the employer provides vouchers which can be exchanged in particular restaurants and outlets.

Mortgage assistance, loans and discounts

A key benefit to attract and retain employees is assistance with home ownership. An alternative to tied or subsidised accommodation may be assistance with house purchase. Subsidised mortgages are a considerable benefit, although they are largely confined to the finance sector. The subsidy is usually limited to a particular level of subsidy but tends to be available to all staff, irrespective of grade, service or age. Housing assistance can also be given in the form of bridging loans or a guaranteed selling price, sometimes as part of a relocation agreement.

In recent years the tight labour market in London, the South East and East of England has led to problems of recruiting key workers into the public services (e.g. teachers, NHS staff and police officers). This in turn saw the government introducing housing assistance schemes for 'key workers' such as the Key Worker Living Programme (2004) and First Homes (2021). These type of schemes provide help with home ownership for those who are eligible. There are a number of 'products' available for key workers including equity loans for the purchase of homes, shared-ownership of newly built homes and intermediate renting at subsidised levels.

Organisations can also provide smaller loans interest-free or at favourable interest rates. These can be used for specific purchases such as personal computers or can be made to help employees in financial hardship. HMRC places a limit on when such loans can be tax-free. Repayments are normally made through payroll and are normally interest-free. Other common loans are the season ticket loan for commuters and cycle-to-work scheme loans. CIPD (Cotton et al, 2022) finds that these types of loans are among the most common types of employee benefits offered with 51 per cent of employers offering cycle-to-work scheme loans and 30 per cent offering season ticket loans for public transport.

Relocation

Another important benefit necessary to recruit and retain staff is relocation expenses. Where employees are required to move from one part of the country to another by the new employer, the employer often provides a subsidy towards this cost. This normally covers the costs of moving as well as some contribution to legal and estate agent fees. HMRC places a tax limit on what can be provided tax-free. According to CIPD (Cotton et al, 2022) 13 per cent of organisations offer relocation assistance to all employees and a further 25 per cent of organisations offer it as a benefit dependent on grade/seniority.

Travel and subsistence

Most employers will provide reimbursement of reasonable travel and subsistence costs incurred by employees in carrying out their work. This can apply to flights, rail and bus journeys, hotel charges and meals taken en route. Organisations normally have policies setting out the monetary limits on what can be claimed. There may also be clothing allowances and laundry tokens for those who are required to wear a company uniform.

SELF-ASSESSMENT EXERCISE

What are the major forms of work-related benefits? What is the purpose of such benefits in the reward system?

7.7.3 Status benefits

Company cars and car allowances

Although the great majority of company-owned cars are found in the private sector, in recent years some public sector employers have begun to provide cars through leasing or assisted purchase schemes. Armstrong and Murlis (2007) comment that the company car appears to be a rare phenomenon that is found in Britain but few other countries. There are basically two types of provision: for staff who require the use of a car (or van) to undertake their work, such as travelling sales staff and mobile maintenance engineers; and as a status symbol for senior staff.

The CIPD Reward Management Survey (2021) finds that the popularity of the company car is 'undiminished' in the UK with 37 per cent of employers providing company cars to some or all employees and 47 per cent providing a car allowance (Cotton et al, 2022). In both cases the majority of employers providing these benefits do so depending on grade, seniority, location, job and so on and we might expect that company cars are still seen as a status symbol to some extent.

Company car policies are driven by three key factors: cost containment, health and safety, and environmental considerations (IDS, 2010d). There are onerous administrative systems necessary to operate a company car fleet, which is why many organisations outsource this job to an external provider.

With increasing use of flexible or 'cafeteria' benefits policies (see below), some employers are leaving the choice to employees of whether they have a car or take another benefit or cash instead. Cars provided are usually taxed, insured and maintained by the employer. Clearly, where employees are expected to travel between work locations on a regular basis (e.g. to visit clients or customers), and particularly where the employee has to carry a large load (e.g. tools, parts or samples), cars are usually provided from within a fleet and may not be personally allocated. Where they are provided as a status benefit, the employee is often given some choice of vehicle within a specified budget, although in some cases companies will specify a particular make and model.

The value of a company car as a benefit can be high but the advantage to the employer of providing such a status benefit is that cars are a highly visible reward and can therefore play an important role in the recruitment and retention of staff. It was also, until the mid-1990s, a relatively cheap benefit to provide when the tax and NI implications were taken into account. Since then, the government has closed various tax loopholes for company cars, partly to collect more revenue and partly as a measure to discourage the use of cars for environmental reasons.

The advantage to the employee is also less now than it was some years ago because the tax treatment for the employee has changed. There is, however, still a financial advantage to having one's car insured, taxed and maintained by one's employer. A company car can also be a very visible sign of status. For this reason, organisations trying to develop a more harmonised or 'single status' culture may decide not to provide such a benefit.

Most company car policies stipulate when and to whom the entitlement applies, the rules governing the use of company vehicles, and the choice of the make and model of car provided. Company cars today are generally leased, rather than purchased, but some companies still prefer to purchase the vehicles and may allow the employee to buy it when its period of use is over. In some cases, employees may be allowed to add their own cash to purchase a higher-specification model. Cars are commonly replaced after three or four years or 80,000 miles, whichever comes first. Clearly, essential user cars will probably experience more wear and tear than status vehicles, and so may be replaced earlier.

One alternative to car leasing is the personal contract plan (PCP). This entails the employer's making regular payments over an agreed period to finance the car, with the option of final purchase at the end of the contract or returning the car and starting a new plan. Some of these plans include insurance and maintenance costs. PCPs can be offered to the whole workforce or limited to particular levels or groups of employees.

Another alternative is the employee car ownership scheme, whereby the employee enters into an agreement with a leasing firm for the purchase of the vehicle, rather than the employer, over an agreed period or mileage. This allows the employer to transfer ownership of the car to the employee so that the employer is not taxed on the benefit as a company car.

When considering the provision of company cars it is imperative to decide whether fuel will also be provided for private use. If this is the case, there are further tax implications. Since April 2003, the tax on car fuel benefit has been based on the carbon dioxide emissions of the car.

Where employees use their own cars for work purposes, they must be insured for this purpose. Car mileage allowances are usually based on some assessment of the maintenance, depreciation and other running costs as well as reimbursement of the actual cost of the fuel used. There may be a ceiling on the mileage allowed for any single journey to encourage the use of public transport for longer journeys. Car mileage allowances are usually expressed in pence per mile.

Other status benefits

Employers may also provide credit cards or fuel cards if employees are expected to make purchases on the employers' behalf. In addition, where employees are engaged on international assignments (see Chapter 11), the organisation may pay the fees for the private education of an expatriate manager's children. One could also consider private medical insurance a status benefit as it is usually limited to more senior levels of staff.

> **SELF-ASSESSMENT EXERCISE**
>
> What are the main forms of status benefits? What purpose do they serve, and to what extent do they conflict with other reward principles such as transparency, equity and performance?

7.8 Flexible benefits

While some organisations have always allowed some limited degree of flexibility in the employee's choice of benefits, it is only over the last few decades that flexible benefits programmes have begun to develop in the UK. Flexible benefits schemes are systems that allow employees to vary their pay and benefits package to meet their personal requirements.

The concept, like so many reward ideas, is an import from the USA where the first plans were introduced in the 1970s. It is generally believed that the incidence of flexible benefit plans in the USA remains ahead of the UK; this is partly explained by the more benign attitude towards such flexibility by the US Internal Revenue than by the UK HMRC.

> **DEFINITION**
>
> Flexible benefits arrangements (known also as 'cafeteria benefits' or 'flex plans') allow staff to vary their package to meet their own needs. The dividing line between pay and benefits is less fixed and employees are able either to retain their existing salary while changing the mix of various benefits they receive or move their salary up or down by taking fewer or more benefits.
>
> (CIPD, 2023a)

Heery and Noon (2017) identify two main forms of flexible benefits. The first is 'within benefit' flexibility, which allows employees to take more of a particular benefit by surrendering cash rewards and vice versa (e.g. better holiday entitlement). The second form is 'across-benefit' flexibility, also known as 'cafeteria benefits', by which an employee is given a personal budget or points and then asked to select the benefits he or she wants from a menu (up to the maximum points or budget ceiling).

Armstrong and Murlis (2007), indicate that UK employers have adopted any of three approaches to flexible benefits:

- the introduction of new 'voluntary' or discounted benefits funded by the employee out of post-tax income or by salary sacrifice (we deal with these approaches later in the chapter);
- variation in the level of existing benefits with a compensatory adjustment to cash pay;
- defining the benefits package in terms of a 'flex fund' to be spent as the employee wishes.

7.8.1. Meeting employee needs or cutting employer costs?

The concept of flexible or 'cafeteria' benefits schemes as it originated in the USA was an employer response to the escalating cost of benefits, especially private healthcare. The concept also fitted well with the American 'new pay' paradigm, with its advocacy of more individual-oriented reward systems, and with discussions about the need for more variable pay. Giving employees some choice in their benefits was seen as both meeting changing demands from employees and assisting in limiting the cost of benefits provision. Flexible benefits have also been promoted as a good recruitment and retention measure and as part of a wider 'employee value proposition' (Naylor, 2014).

7.8.2 Advantages and disadvantages of flexible benefits

A number of advantages (and disadvantages) of flexible benefits have been identified. Heery and Noon (2017) cite both the emphasis on choice in these schemes and its accommodation of the needs of a more diverse and individualistic workforce as well as the facility to enforce tighter control over benefit costs.

The advantages of flexible benefits include:

- Employees choose benefits that they want and value, rather than having to accept unwanted and under-valued benefits.
- If a budget system is adopted, the cost of benefits is better controlled.
- Employers and employees share the responsibility for benefits.
- Employees can change their benefits as their lifestyle changes (e.g. from single to partnered status, from childless to family-oriented and from family- to retirement-oriented).
- Employees participate in the design of their reward package.
- Couples or households can avoid duplication of benefits.
- Employers are seen as responding to employee demands for flexibility.

The disadvantages of flexible benefits are:

- Such schemes can be complex and difficult to administer because records of the benefits selected must be kept on each individual employee and updated regularly.
- Employees need good financial counselling to ensure that they do not make financially risky decisions (e.g. choosing to withdraw from a pension scheme).
- Discounts on some benefits may be lost if coverage ceases to be blanket and employees withdraw from schemes (and so costs may rise).
- Employees may feel that a budget system limits the value of what is on offer, and unions may claim that the scheme is designed to cut costs rather than assist employees.

(adapted from CIPD, 2007a)

External benefits consultants, who may design and administer the scheme on behalf of the employer, can supply 'off-the-shelf' flexible benefits systems. This can reduce the amount of onerous administration required and reduce costs.

To avoid employees taking risky decisions, many organisations insist that certain core benefits are not flexible below a certain level. Some employers will structure flexible benefits plans so that core benefits can be adjusted but cannot be removed from the package. Core items might include pensions, life assurance, critical illness insurance and holidays. In addition, non-core benefits can be chosen which might include health, financial and lifestyle benefits such as dental insurance, household insurance, gym membership or childcare schemes.

7.8.3 The incidence of flexible benefits

The 2021 CIPD Reward Management survey (Cotton et al, 2022) found that a quarter of employers offer a level of choice in benefits provision. Of these, 45 per cent offer flexible benefits to employees, up from 37 per cent in 2018. It also found that such benefits were more common among large organisations and in the private sector. XPertHR (2019) finds only 6 per cent of organisations offer a full flexible benefits scheme whereas 33 per cent offer some form of flexibility in benefits provision with the benefits most likely to be available on a flexible basis being annual leave (buying/selling) (71 per cent), cycle to work loans (68 per cent) and childcare vouchers (55 per cent).

7.8.4 Introducing flexible benefits

Most flexible benefits schemes are initially based on an organisation's existing benefits provision, but the range of benefits on offer may either be reduced or increased once the scheme is in operation. Some employers prefer to exclude certain flexing of benefits, such as sick pay, maternity leave and pension entitlement.

The employee is given a menu of benefits from which to make a choice. There is usually a budget limit on what can be flexed and some baseline provision that must be taken (such as a minimum level of life cover and permanent life insurance). In the case of holidays, employees cannot flex their entitlement below the statutory minimum required. In some cases, employers provide their menu in cash terms, showing the cost of each benefit so that employees can calculate the impact of any choices. This helps to convey to employees the cost (and value) of their benefits, but can also have the disadvantage that employees are encouraged to think they are spending their own money, rather than the employer's. In other cases, employers use a points system for allocating choices. Regardless of which method is used, all schemes make a clear distinction between notional salary and the final value of the salary actually paid.

Schemes have to be costed on the basis of predicted take-up of particular benefits. To stop employees making 'adverse' selections, the relative values of benefits are usually set so as to avoid too many such choices.

Employers report a number of common barriers to implementation including cost of implementation (reported by 64 per cent), complexity of administration (49 per cent), getting approval for business case (41 per cent), ongoing costs of flexible benefits including technology (40 per cent) and updating existing technology (such as HR and payroll systems) (32 per cent) (Employee Benefits/Towers Watson, 2014)

As flexible benefits schemes appear to be increasingly popular in the UK, the CIPD's expressed view broadly welcomes this trend, seeing flexible benefits as:

> ... an ideal way of addressing employee diversity, cost-effectiveness in benefits provision and of harmonising reward practices, especially during merger and acquisition. However, they are not a 'magic' solution and need to be managed as part of an integrated reward strategy with clear goals and excellent support processes. Scheme communication and administration should build on insights from behavioural science about how people react to choice and make decisions.
>
> (CIPD, 2018c)

As with employee benefits generally, academic research on the effects of flexible benefits schemes on employees, as opposed to descriptions of how schemes operate, is sparse in the UK, and most of the research has been conducted in the USA.

KEY ISSUES IN REWARD MANAGEMENT 7.1

Benefits for a hybrid workforce

Where season ticket loans, company pensions and cycle-to-work schemes were once among the flagship features of an employee benefits package, these may no longer be enough – or even appropriate – for the hybrid workforce.

Of the many things to come out of the Covid pandemic, perhaps one of the most unexpected was the rise of a new hybrid workforce. A survey by Webex shows that 57 per cent now expect to be in the office for 10 days or less each month, while Atlascloud research found that 84 per cent of UK office workers would like to be able to work from home at least some of the time going forward.

This new, flexible way of working is having a positive impact on employees' health, wellbeing and work–life balance, however it does bring with it some challenges for the senior leadership team and HR.

When a large percentage of staff were in the office every day, there was a definite sense of community amongst employees. They saw each other daily, caught up on news and felt that they were seen and heard by their superiors. It was easy to communicate with staff, hold meetings and keep everyone up to date on company business.

Now that large numbers of staff are rarely in the office and some team members only work on alternate days, it is down to the HR team to find new ways of building a sense of inclusion and engagement. According to McKinsey, not feeling a sense of belonging was one of the most frequently cited reasons for leaving a job in the past six months, which shows just how important it is for companies to get this right.

Rethink your benefits

This is where employee benefits packages come in, as they can help employees feel valued and appreciated. But where private healthcare and a company pension were once enough, things have moved on and now employees expect to receive a whole range of benefits including salary loans, holiday trading, electric car schemes, tech schemes and so much more.

The challenge for businesses now is how to make these benefits relevant for all employees, no matter where they are working, whether they are in the office or at home, and what stage they are at on their life journey.

We would rather avoid benefit mismatches like offering a company car to a non-driver, or providing a season ticket loan to someone who is working from home full-time. The very best employee benefits programmes offer a degree of flexibility so that each employee can pick and choose their own portfolio of benefits that work perfectly for them.

By allowing employees to build their own individual benefits package, they immediately feel valued, which in turn helps keep them engaged and motivated.

There are many different companies offering flexible benefits options for employers... which [bring] together a wide range of pre-selected benefits all in one place. This not only makes it easy for employees to craft their own rewards package but also makes coordinating the packages much more efficient for the HR team.

Use tech to keep in touch

Technology is key to improving communication with a remote or hybrid workforce. By using an app-based system... employers can schedule regular messaging straight to an employee's smartphone or computer. Employees can always see a complete overview of their chosen package, view the progress of an application or adjust their choices. They do not need to be in the office to do this.

By offering a flexible benefits solution that is managed and run through a single platform, it is easier for employers to add different benefits to the mix.

Employee surveys can also be a valuable way to gain feedback on the benefits that are available and what future benefits employees would like to see. This helps ensure that employees are happy with what is being offered and that the offer remains relevant to their working arrangements. This in turn keeps usage and engagement up.

An extract from 'How to ensure your benefits are fit for a hybrid workforce' by Julie Stayte, Personnel Today, *1 March 2022.*

STUDENT EXERCISE

Read the extract above from *Personnel Today* magazine's 'How to ensure your benefits are fit for a hybrid workforce'. Working with fellow students, complete the following task.

The article emphasises the value of flexible benefits for employees who are working flexibly. Using this as a starting point, prepare a short presentation making the case for flexible benefits to be presented to the senior executive team.

7.9 Voluntary and discount benefits

Voluntary and discount benefits are a low-cost method of enhancing the benefits on offer to employees. These types of benefit appear to be increasingly popular for those employers offering choice of benefits to their employees. Crucially, the difference between voluntary benefits and 'core' benefits is that the employee pays rather than the employer.

DEFINITION

Both discount benefits and voluntary benefits allow employees to buy discounted products or services through their employer out of their own taxable pay or via a salary sacrifice arrangement. Voluntary benefits are more formal. They are often

> arranged by a benefits provider, and purchases are made via the payroll. Discount benefits are less formal, with employees making purchases from their bank account. While the employer does not pay for the benefits provided under both types of schemes it may incur research, administration, and communication costs.
>
> (CIPD, 2023a)

Employers can either negotiate directly with the supplier of the service or product, or they can outsource this role to a third-party organisation. Increasingly organisations are signing up to pre-arranged benefits packages, via online platforms or apps. Some of these external providers charge an annual subscription fee for access, while others offer free access and make their money from advertising and commission on sales.

The range of typical voluntary benefits products includes financial products (such as personal loans, mortgages and childcare vouchers), holidays and travel (discounted flights and holiday packages, travel insurance), health (healthcare cash plans, dental plans, optical care, gym/health club membership), motoring (car purchase, rental, insurance, breakdown cover), home and garden (discounts on garden equipment), entertainment (reductions on tickets for events and entry charges at a range of attractions) and gifts (jewellery, confectionery, floral gifts).

Of the 25 per cent of respondents to the CIPD Reward Management Survey 2021 offering some level of choice in benefits provision, 73 per cent said they offered discount benefits while 61 per cent offered voluntary benefits.

XPertHR (2019) find that most employers using voluntary schemes use a third-party supplier, others provide a combined offering between themselves and the third-party supplier and the minority administer the scheme entirely in-house. The same survey finds that the benefits most likely to be offered through a voluntary benefits scheme are:

- retail discounts/vouchers (64 per cent)
- gym membership (51 per cent)
- healthcare cash plan (44 per cent)
- health screening (32 per cent)
- dental insurance (31 per cent)
- private medical insurance (31 per cent)

(XPertHR, 2019)

7.9.1 Salary sacrifice schemes

One adjunct of a flexible or voluntary benefits scheme may be salary sacrifice arrangements. Salary sacrifice schemes have allowed employees to give up part of their taxable pay in return for a non-cash benefit that is treated in a more beneficial manner for tax and/or National Insurance contributions (NICs) purposes (IDS, 2010d). Both employer and employee agree in writing to such an arrangement. Following any amendments to the employment contract, the employee becomes liable for tax and NICs on the lower salary and any non-cash 'benefit-in-kind' (BIK). Because many of the benefits offered through such schemes have been wholly or partly exempt from tax and NICs, there has been a clear incentive to enter into such an arrangement for both parties.

There have, however, been some recent changes to HMRC rules regarding salary sacrifice, with the range of benefits falling into advantageous tax and NICs category being restricted. Lewis (2017) reports that from April 2017, health checks, gym memberships, car parking near the workplace, technology, accommodation, school fees and cars can no longer be offered with such advantages. Some benefits including pension contributions, employer-supported childcare, cycle-to-work schemes and ultra-low emission vehicles are unaffected by the changes (Lewis, 2017)

There are clearly important issues to be considered by both employer and employee under such arrangements, and employers may provide financial counselling for employees to explain the details. One important point is that employees cannot reduce their pay below the national minimum wage through such schemes.

7.10 Benefits communication

Recent commentary on employee benefits has suggested that many employers may be missing an opportunity to engage employees because of poorly communicated benefits schemes. Baska (2018) cites research by independent financial and corporate adviser Chase de Vere who found that 41 per cent of companies do not provide regular updates to employees on the benefits available to them, leading the author to conclude that money spent on benefits is potentially 'not being appreciated or valued' by employees.

The 2021 CIPD Reward Management Survey Report (2022: 22) also emphasises the danger of failing to properly communicate benefits provision for employers:

> If employees don't know what's being provided and why, or how to access those benefits and which ones could be of use to them, they won't fully appreciate the benefits on offer and how they meet their needs. This could have an impact on their decisions to stay and perform.

The survey found that 58 per cent of respondent organisations are open with employees about pay/benefits on offer, why they are provided, and what people need to do to receive them, but only 18 per cent actively tests the understanding of staff about the pay and benefits on offer. This suggests that many employers are missing opportunities to fully communicate the value of their benefits offer to their employees.

Some of the issues around benefits communications are closely linked with the 'total rewards' approach and we will explore this further in Chapter 9 on non-financial reward.

7.11 Conclusions and key learning points

In this chapter we have considered a further component within the reward system: employee benefits. As we have discussed, the major reasons for the growth of such benefits were external pressures from government and from the labour market, but such rewards have been perceived as important for recruitment and retention as well. Government regulation remains an important driver for occupational benefits policies in terms of requiring minimum levels of benefits. Research on benefits is sparse, and what exists is inconclusive as to what effects such rewards have upon employees, either in terms of loyalty to the organisation, in motivational terms, or on organisational performance.

We identified three main categories of benefits: welfare benefits, work-related benefits and status benefits. Each of these categories serves a different function within the reward system. As we discussed, the range and level of benefits offered by employers varies between sectors and between organisations. In general, the higher paid the employee, the more likely they are to have more generous benefits. Attempts to reduce the status divide between manual and non-manual workers through 'harmonisation' or 'single status' were common in the 1980s and 1990s, but these moves appear to have slowed as other management priorities have come to the fore – not least, the growing cost of benefits.

Employers' concerns about the increasing cost of benefits have led them to increasingly consider a 'budget' approach, rather than blanket provision, and to launch new communications initiatives aimed at making employees more aware of the value of the benefits provided. The major initiative has been the development of flexible or cafeteria benefits, and while the spread of such schemes remains slower in the UK compared to the USA, not least because of the tax implications of swapping one benefit for another, flexible benefits are now a key feature of UK employee benefits. We also noted both the growth of discount and voluntary benefits, whereby employees contribute towards the cost of their benefits, and the option of salary sacrifice schemes, which, despite current changes, still offer employees tax and NIC reductions.

The communication of benefits policy and schemes remains vital. The alternative forms of benefit available to organisations provide a large range of options, but the consequences of each need careful consideration. This is particularly important where employees are being required to make financial decisions such as over flexible benefits and salary sacrifice schemes.

Explore further

For a practical look at employee benefits and reward communications in general see Rose, M (2018) *Reward management: A practical introduction*, 2nd edn, HR Fundamentals, London: Kogan Page.

Baska, M (2018) Businesses 'throwing money down the drain' by not communicating employee benefits, *People Management*, 27 July.

CIPD (2023) *Employee Benefits: an introduction.* Factsheet. Available at: prod.cipd.co.uk/en/knowledge/factsheets/benefits-factsheet/.

08
Pensions

CHAPTER LEARNING OUTCOMES

At the end of this chapter, you should understand and be able to explain the following:

- Purpose and role of pensions in employee reward systems.
- Origins and development of pension schemes.
- Different types of pensions and their respective advantages and disadvantages to employers and employees.
- Main provisions of a workplace pension scheme.
- Factors affecting choice of scheme.
- HR's role in administering and managing pension choices.
- Current trends in pension provision and debates about the future provision of workplace pensions.

CIPD STRATEGIC REWARD MANAGEMENT (7HR03) LEARNING OUTCOMES

Learners will be able to:

2.4 Evaluate different types of employee benefits and their suitability in different organisational contexts.

4.1 Critically discuss the key legal requirements relating to pay and reward and the implications of non-compliance.

8.1 Introduction

Workplace pensions (the term used by the UK government to describe occupational retirement pension arrangements set up by employers) are a material element of organisations' employee reward packages. Management of pensions became a strategic 'benefits' issue for employers from 2012, when a requirement for automatic enrolment was introduced by the UK government. Data published by the Office for National Statistics indicated that between 2012 and 2019 there had been a 29 percentage point increase in the number of UK employees enrolled in a workplace pension scheme (ONS, 2019a). By April 2021, the workplace pension participation rate in the UK stood at 79 per cent (22.6 million employees); the gap in employee workplace pension participation rates between the public (91 per cent) and private sectors (75 per cent) was among its lowest levels, mainly driven by increased participation in the private sector, up from 32 per cent in 2012 (ONS, 2022).

Britain's pension system is unique within Europe, and the legal and tax constraints on the design and running of schemes are stringent. As the CIPD observes (CIPD, 2019b), 'Pensions are a complicated subject and no action should be taken without professional guidance.' This is an area where the expertise of human resources professionals alone may be insufficient; however, it remains an important area of knowledge for those specialising in reward management. All HR staff should understand at least the basic architecture of pension schemes, the major options available to employers and the underlying legal requirements.

DEFINITION

A workplace pension is a pension which is provided or facilitated through a workplace, principally for employees. It includes both occupational pension schemes and all forms of group personal and group stakeholder pensions.

(ONS, 2022)

Figure 8.1 Workplace pension participation trends 1997–2021

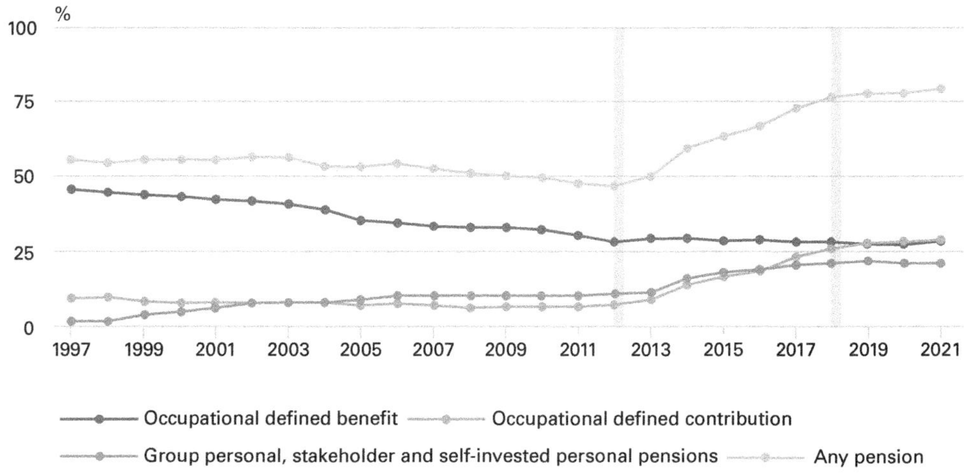

SOURCE: Office for National Statistics - Annual Survey of Hours and Earnings (ASHE)

For employees, pensions represent 'deferred pay': employers set aside some of the regular pay otherwise received by the employee for the future payment of an income when they retire. In some cases, the employer does not require a contribution from the employee, but in most schemes the employee is required to make a (usually smaller) contribution to the pension fund. Because pensions are seen as part of reward, or the 'wage-effort bargain' as theorised in Chapter 2, even if the reward is deferred until after the employee retires from working, it is a contested area and, where trade unions are present, they will see pension provision and contributions as a negotiable item. Recent years have seen many examples in the UK of industrial action by trade unions concerning changes in their members' pension entitlements (e.g. in airports, local government, schools, universities, Pfizer, United Utilities and even among the Beefeaters at the Tower of London).

Over the past decade there have been major changes in both the legal requirements concerning UK workplace pensions and in employer practice in terms of types of provision offered. Indeed, most developed countries are facing a pensions crisis, because of demographic changes, which is leading to a radical overhaul of existing provision. We are devoting a separate chapter to pensions because of the significance of the political debate about their future, setting the context (Chapter 3). As expressed by the CIPD (2019b): 'Since automatic enrolment, the decision regarding workplace pensions comes down to how much the employer should contribute.'

This chapter describes the origins and development of pensions in the UK and their purpose and role within an organisation's reward management system, along with the different roles of the state and occupational schemes. The main types of pension, their tax treatment and respective advantages and disadvantages to employers and employees are introduced, along with the major elements provided and methods of funding. Consideration is given to debates about the future of workplace pensions and the role of human resources specialists in administering and communicating about this challenging, important area of reward management.

8.2 The origins and development of UK pension schemes

Given their legal underpinning, our focus in this text is pension provision in the UK jurisdiction. Even in pre-industrial times there were local funds available to citizens who fell upon hard times: local community relief funds for the elderly, the sick and destitute were recorded during the 14th-century reign of Richard II (Smith, 2000). The first real workplace pension scheme to provide lifetime pensions on retirement due to old age was that provided for navy officers in the 1670s. From the 17th century pensions were also made available to senior civil servants. This initiative was followed by private firms associated with the government, such as the Bank of England in 1739. From the mid-19th century, railway companies began establishing pension schemes for their employees, and were followed by large private sector firms such as Reuters (1882), WH Smith (1894) and Colmans (1899). Public sector schemes came into force from the 1890s including teachers and the police in 1890 and in 1922. These early occupationally linked pensions ranged in benefit structure from flat cash amounts to pensions based on career average or final salary.

The schemes were primarily provided for managers and clerical staff; manual workers were not usually included. For this reason, another source of early financial provision in retirement was the friendly societies and trade unions established by workers in the 19th century. Some trade unions continued to provide this benefit until quite recently. It was unusual for women to be included, mainly because they were expected to give up work when they got married, but this often led to unmarried women being without any pension income in retirement. This together with the relative rarity of spouse pension provision contributed to poverty among widows as they tended to live longer than men but could not rely on their husband's pension to provide them with an income for the remainder of their lives.

It was not until the start of the 20th century that the state began to provide some minimum pension entitlement for citizens (who met certain eligibility criteria). The first, non-contributory, state scheme in the UK was introduced by the Liberal government in 1908 and was payable from age 70. However, it was means tested and subject to a 'character' test. It was then improved in 1925, when a contributory scheme was introduced for manual workers and others earning up to £250 a year which was payable from age 65 and included maintenance for widows. As a result of the growing awareness of levels of poverty among older women, the State Pension age for unmarried women was reduced to age 60 from 1940. It is interesting to note that, at the time, average life expectancy had risen to 63 for women but was only 58 for men (ONS, 2015). For the first time a majority of the poorest two-thirds of the UK population could contribute to and draw a pension (Smith, 2000).

This development was followed by many large private sector companies introducing their own workplace pension schemes, especially once tax relief was granted on contributions to such schemes from 1921. The introduction of such schemes was partly an attempt by employers to move away from the 'hire and fire' employment methods of the 19th century to an approach that emphasised the need for employee loyalty and retention. Pensions were seen as a useful method to attract good workers and assist in creating a compliant and happy workforce. It was also a move intended to counter trade union organisation in their workplaces.

Not until after the Second World War, though, were pensions provided for all citizens. The Labour government of 1945 introduced a contributory flat-rate pension scheme for all workers under the 1946 National Insurance Act which retained the existing State Pension ages of 65 for men and 60 for women. This remained the major source of retirement income for most workers until a second, additional State Pension based on individual earnings (known as graduated pension) was introduced under the 1959 National Insurance Act. The next big change was the Social Security Pensions Act 1975 (the so-called 'Castle Plan', after the then Labour minister Barbara Castle). This Act introduced the State Earnings-Related Pension Scheme (SERPS) and allowed employers and employees with occupational schemes to 'contract out' of the state scheme under certain circumstances and pay lower National Insurance contributions. In return the pension scheme was required to pay a level of benefit which was the equivalent to that provided by SERPS. This is known as the Guaranteed Minimum Pension (GMP).

The cost of pensions to both the state and employers has always been an issue, and in 1980 the then Conservative government sought to reduce the cost of the state scheme. It did this by cutting the link between increases in the State Pension and increases in average earnings, linking them to price inflation instead (although from

2010 the coalition government introduced the so-called 'triple lock' whereby State Pensions currently increase annually by inflation, earnings growth or 2.5 per cent, whichever the greater). In 1986 the government also sought to reduce costs by making it easier for workers to opt out of SERPS into a private pension. The 1990s saw both a major pensions scandal at the Mirror Group of newspapers and a pensions 'mis-selling' scandal among private pension providers, the latter partly consequent on the 1986 changes, which encouraged the growth of the private pensions industry and led to many employees choosing 'defined contribution' (DC) pensions over more valuable 'defined benefit' (DB) pensions. (The terms DC and DB are explained later in the chapter.) As a result, there was a significant tightening up of UK pensions legislation. The 1995 Pensions Act set up regulatory and compensation schemes for those whose pension schemes go into liquidation, including the Occupational Pensions Regulatory Authority (later the Pensions Regulator) and the DB minimum funding requirement. The 2004 Pensions Act built on this and led to the creation of the state-backed Pension Protection Fund (PPF), established in April 2005 as a lifeboat for defined benefit pensions when the sponsoring employer becomes insolvent. The PPF was much in the news in early 2019, in the light of a potential transfer of the Carillion pension scheme consequent on that company's financial collapse.

In relation to the issues noted above, together with the introduction of personal pensions and the removal of the ability for employers to make occupational pension scheme membership compulsory from 1988, there was a significant reduction in the number of employees saving in a workplace pension scheme from 1995 – down from 40 per cent in 1995 to 32 per cent in 2005 (Government Actuary's Department, 2006: 9; Pensions Commission, 2004: 81). Following increasing concern about this decline and the rising cost of pensions at the start of the 21st century, major reports were published between 2004 and 2006 by the government-appointed Pensions Commission, chaired by Lord Adair Turner. As a result pensions reform moved to the top of the government agenda with changes to both the State Pension system and a new requirement on employers to provide all workers aged between 22 and the State Pension age, meeting a minimum annual earnings threshold (currently £10,000) and not participating in a workplace pension scheme, with the opportunity to join a pension scheme. Starting in October 2012, with gradual introduction by 2018, all UK employers now have a duty to automatically enrol eligible employees into a qualifying pension scheme and to make contributions on their behalf. Minimum contribution levels were also introduced, in a phased process, with full implementation also by 2018. In order to meet the legal requirements, from April 2019 minimum contributions of 8.0 per cent of an employee's qualifying earnings must be made, of which at least 3.0 per cent must come from the employer. There were government-commissioned reports on public sector pension schemes in 2010 and 2011 by the Independent Public Service Pensions Commission, chaired by Lord Hutton, which led to the reform of those schemes, notwithstanding fierce opposition and industrial action by the trades unions (Hutton, 2010, 2011).

The UK pension system is rather different from that of most other developed countries. The countries most similar are Ireland and the Netherlands. Workplace pension schemes are quite rare in most European countries and, where they exist, they tend to be exclusive to senior staff. In Europe, reliance on state provision of pensions is more common for most employees. The USA, in comparison, has been more aligned with the UK, with a minimum state provision and DB and DC employer-sponsored occupational schemes, including those provided for federal and state employees. In Australia, there is a means-tested pension provided by the state, but from the 1990s compulsory DC private pensions have been required for everyone earning more than a fixed monthly amount. Employers are obliged to pay contributions into these private pensions (to which employees are encouraged to contribute through tax incentives). Most schemes in Australia are run on an industry basis, rather than at company level (Schifferes, 2005).

8.3 UK workplace pension schemes today

Trends in active membership of both private and public sector workplace pension schemes since the requirement on employers under the Pensions Act 2007 to automatically enrol employees into an occupational pension scheme (AE) is captured in the ONS's occupational pension schemes survey database. Since 2013, the trend-line showing growth in active membership of workplace pension schemes in the private sector has been especially steep, levelling off after 2018 (see Figure 8.2).

Digging into the detail, a significant trend in membership of workplace pension schemes is in the type of benefit – or 'pension promise' on offer. The Pensions Schemes Act 2015 categorises private workplace pensions into three broad types: defined benefit (DB), defined contribution (DC) whose definition may be extended to incorporate group personal or group stakeholder schemes, and shared risk (also known as 'defined ambition') schemes. DB schemes are usually workplace pensions arranged by the employer who generally manages the scheme via trustees elected in part from the active or retired workforce, siting together with managerially designated trustees accountable for scheme oversight, including investment strategy. Sometimes DB

Figure 8.2 Eligible employees participating in a workplace pension

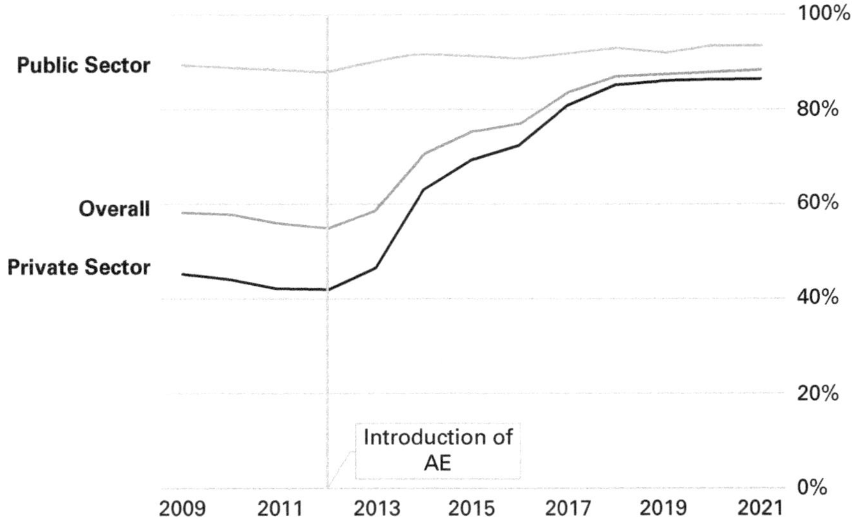

SOURCE: Office for National Statistics/HMG DWP

schemes are called 'final salary' or 'career average' pension schemes. The value of pensions in payment depends on the scheme's rules, not on investments or how much members have paid in. The employer's pension promise is to pay a certain amount each year when the scheme member retires. Amounts are usually based on a number of things, such as the beneficiaries' salary and how long they worked for the particular employer. The average value of a DB pension is typically larger than a DC pension.

DC schemes, sometimes called 'money purchase' pension plans, allow employers to save money on behalf of employees, setting aside a specific amount of an individual's annual earnings. Employees may be allowed to contribute as well, with the combined funds accumulating over time as a 'pension pot' put into investments intended to provide income in retirement. Unlike DB schemes, they offer no guaranteed annual pension amount. The pot and thus the pension in payment can decrease as well as increase depending on the performance of the investments. To reduce risk, as individual members move closer to when they wish to activate the pension some schemes will move funds into lower-risk investments (but remember there is no longer a fixed retirement age). As noted, the term DC also covers group personal and group stakeholder pension schemes. But the key difference is that the pension provider is not the employer but an outside organisation such as an insurance company, which makes the pensions promise to individual contributors.

In the case of shared risk (intended to move from the traditional DB-DC binary divide), schemes offer a promise while members are saving for their pension about some, but not all, of the outcome from the scheme. According to government information, for example, shared risk schemes might promise some, but not all, of the income the member will receive; the size of the savings they will accrue based on a contribution level; and the rate of income their savings will buy them. Shared risk schemes offer more certainty to members about the outcome while they are saving than a DC scheme does.

Figure 8.3 illustrates savings levels in all pension scheme types in 2021.

Towards the end of the 1990s across all categories of membership, ONS records show DB pension schemes accounted for approaching half of the numbers involved. By 2021, DB pension membership levels had fallen to around 28 per cent; DC had increased to a level beginning to overtake DB membership, with group personal or group stakeholder schemes at around 24 per cent of active pension members across the UK workforce (see Figure 8.1). The position is further defined taking account of organisational sector. The ONS, reporting in April 2019, sum matters up as follows:

> In 2018, public sector employee pension memberships were predominantly in occupational defined benefit pension schemes (93%), unchanged from 2017. Conversely this pension scheme type was not common amongst private sector pension members with just over one in nine (12%) private sector pension memberships being in occupational defined benefit schemes.
>
> The majority of workplace pensions in the private sector were of occupational defined contribution schemes, which accounted for nearly half of all employee private sector pension memberships (48%) in 2018, an increase of 3 percentage points since 2017.
>
> (ONS, 2019b)

Figure 8.3 Amount saved by eligible employees in 2021

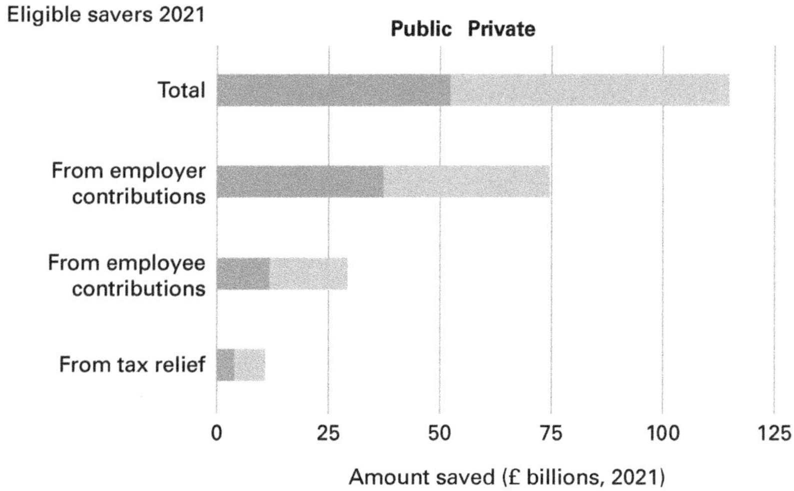

SOURCE: DWP estimates derived from the ONS ASHE, GB, 2009 to 2021

The dramatic fall in DB scheme membership reflects employer reaction to increasing costs of these schemes, largely because of demographic change – greater longevity and hence longer periods of pension liabilities. The rise in DC membership is likely to have been caused by the workplace pension reforms – DC arrangements (including group personal pensions) were seen as the most prudent approach for employers to meet their new obligations under automatic enrolment, because there is no guaranteed pension amount. Since auto-enrolment began, various master trust arrangements have also become important players in the pensions market – again with provision typically on a DC basis. Master trusts involve a single provider managing a pension scheme for multiple employers under a single trust arrangement and include the National Employment Savings Trust (NEST), which was set up as a DC scheme. NEST is a qualifying pension scheme, established under the Pensions Act 2008, to support the introduction of automatic enrolment.

There are wider considerations impacting on the future administration of occupational pension schemes taking account of changes in the social landscape. The Pensions Regulator published guidance in March 2023 on equality, diversity and inclusion (EDI) for scheme-governing bodies and employers. Following the guidance is voluntary, but the Regulator is hoping that it will be used by schemes and employers to improve their decision making.

8.4 The UK State Pension scheme

All UK citizens are entitled to the full basic State Pension if they have built up enough qualifying years during their working life. The State Pension in the UK is unfunded. An unfunded scheme has no underlying fund of assets, so current workers pay the pensions of those that have already retired. Therefore, this type of scheme represents an intergenerational transfer between workers and pensioners. Membership of the basic State Pension scheme is compulsory for all employed and self-employed workers with earnings above the Lower Earnings Limit, and contributions are collected through the government's national insurance system.

Until April 2016 the state scheme consisted of two elements: a basic State Pension based on national insurance contributions and the number of qualifying years and an additional pension based on the average earnings level during the working career. For those in a good occupational pension there was also the opportunity to 'contract out' of the state additional pension and pay lower national insurance contributions.

From 6 April 2016, however, a new flat rate, single-tier State Pension has applied to all men born on or after 6 April 1951 or women born on or after 6 April 1953. The new flat rate State Pension is a single weekly amount subject to annual review. To receive any new State Pension an individual must have at least 10 qualifying years of National Insurance contributions and to receive the full pension requires 35 qualifying years. 'Contracting out' from the second State Pension, abolished under the new arrangements, also ceased from 6 April 2016, so that both employers and employees with contracted-out schemes now have to pay increased national insurance contributions (DWP, 2018).

On 6 April 2010 the State Pension age for women started to increase gradually from 60 to 65, to match that applicable to men. Under the Pensions Act 2011, it was decided that women's State Pension age would increase more quickly to 65 between April 2016 and November 2018. From December 2018 the State Pension age for both men and women began to increase to reach 66 by October 2020 and, from 2026 to 2028, the State Pension age for both men and women will start rising to 67. The government is planning to review the State Pension age every five years. Any changes will not affect the timetables for moving the State Pension age to 65 or to 66 or 67, but it could mean changes for younger people. In 2013 the Chancellor of the Exchequer said future generations could spend up to a third of their adult life in retirement. Based on this, the DWP (2016) produced indicative tables on how entitlement to the State Pension could move from 67 to 68 from the mid-2030s and to 69 in the late 2040s. An initial target of 70 is pencilled in for the 2060s, but if life expectancy and improving mortality rates continue at their current levels, the State Pension age could hit 77 by the mid-2070s.

8.4.1 Fiscal and communications issues

The UK government Chancellor's Spring Budget 2023 announced the most significant pensions tax changes for many years. The most fundamental shift was to change the limits on how much individuals can save into their pensions – both the amounts permissible in a given year and over the course of their working lives. After several years of gradually reducing these limits, this is viewed as a partial U-turn, principally it seems to encourage older people back to the workplace. The Chancellor's key aim was to ensure that highly skilled individuals, particularly senior National Health Service staff, would not be disincentivised from rejoining the workforce. The changes will have also wider implications for many employees, pension scheme trustees and employers alike. The lifetime allowance (LTA) charge disappears from April 2023, and the LTA itself will be abolished from April 2024. Other allowances were increased, most notably the Annual Allowance which will be £60,000 from April

2023. Those likely to benefit the most from the Chancellor's reforms will be high earners and older individuals wishing to return to the workforce. But impacting the UK workforce more widely, the new regime will reduce the circumstances in which pension savings pots are taxed both on contributions in as well as benefits paid out.

Turning to regulatory changes impacting on what employers must do to communicate to employees on pensions benefits, from 1 October 2022, where a DC scheme is used for auto-enrolment of UK employees, a 'simpler' annual benefit statement to all of an occupational pension scheme members (except pensioners) has been required. Trustees must consider the needs of disabled people when deciding on the format to use, but the statement must not exceed one double-sided sheet of A4 when printed and can be provided in hard or electronic copy. It must be provided within 12 months of the end of the scheme year. Statutory guidance published alongside the amending regulations includes an illustrative template of the two-page statement. Trustees may use their own branding, but this should not undermine information provided or increase beyond the permitted length of the statement. The Secretary of State for Work and Pensions is to assess the effectiveness of the new requirements and will publish a report within five years of 1 October 2022, and five-yearly after that.

In respect of DB schemes, in July 2022 the Department for Work and Pensions opened consultation on the draft Occupational Pension Scheme (Funding and Investment Strategy and Amendment) Regulations 2023. On 16 December 2022, the UK Pensions Regulator published its second consultation on the long-awaited draft DB Funding Code, running until the end of March 2023. The current funding regime is subject to a major overhaul, with changes expected to come into force in October 2023.

In summary, according to consultancy Norton Rose, the draft Regulations require DB schemes to have a 'journey plan' aiming for 'low dependency' on the sponsoring employer by the time they reach 'significant maturity'. Trustees need to develop a 'funding and investment strategy' and to submit a 'statement of strategy' to the Regulator. By 'significant maturity', assets should be invested in a 'low dependency investment allocation' and the scheme should then be fully funded on a 'low dependency funding basis'. For the first time, the draft Regulations set out how the strength of the employer covenant is to be assessed and they stipulate that scheme deficits must be recovered 'as soon as the employer can reasonably afford'.

(Source of the latest developments reported: Norton Rose Fullbright Pensions Hub, nortonrosefulbright.com/en/knowledge/publications/22a4f011/essential-pensions-hub)

KEY ISSUES IN REWARD MANAGEMENT 8.1

Only a third (29 per cent) of organisations check whether their defined contribution (DC) pensions schemes are delivering value for money for its employees every one to three years, according to the CIPD's Spring Labour Market Outlook (LMO) 2023.

The survey of 2,019 organisations, conducted on behalf of the CIPD by YouGov, found just under a third (27 per cent) also review whether it's delivering value for money for the organisation.

The data also found people professionals 'simply were unaware' if the workplace had ever reviewed the DC scheme's value for money – either from its members' (30 per cent) or employer's (33 per cent) perspectives.

Sam Holmes, head of financial coaching at financial wellbeing and coaching specialist Bippit, said that despite workplace pensions being the most expensive employee benefit an employer can provide, it is often the benefit that gets 'the least attention from a HR perspective'.

Holmes said this is likely because of the regulatory and compliance requirements that come with a pension.

'This pensions compliance angle usually takes priority for HR teams and senior leaders, finding comfort in the knowledge that their scheme is legally and tax compliant. The fear being that any change could cause issues later down the line,' said Holmes.

'But with workplace pension compliance dominating HR bandwidth, the focus gets lost when it comes to the efficacy of pensions in relation to employee wellbeing, retention of talent, financial efficiency, employee engagement and education with reference to their longer term financial planning.'

The survey also found that 15 per cent of HR professionals had noticed an increase in staff cutting contributions since the start of 2022, with a third (33 per cent) saying that if an employee left the pensions scheme they would keep the contribution.

The CIPD is encouraging employers to review how they could support those temporarily opting out of pension saving due to the cost of living crisis, and suggested this could be done through financial wellbeing benefits and the option to reduce their contribution rather than fully opting out.

A spokesperson for The Pensions Regulator (TPR) – which launched a joint consultation into a new Value for Money (VfM) framework for those who run pension schemes with the Financial Conduct Authority (FCA) and Department for Working Pensions (DWP) – said that while auto-enrolment is a great way to save for retirement, it recognises that the cost of living crisis has an impact.

'For some people, stopping contributions could have a serious impact on their retirement living standards,' they warned.

'We encourage employers to signpost savers who are considering opting out of their pension to first contact MoneyHelper, the government-backed service which gives free and impartial advice and will help them make the best decision.'

Similarly, Justin Corliss, senior pensions development manager at Royal London, said good value is beneficial to both employers and employees – as workers get the 'best possible pension outcome' and it can act as a good staff recruitment and retention tool.

He also suggested: 'Competitive pressure among providers can result in reduced costs over time, and regular reviews will identify this. It is important, however, not just to look at the cost, as services such as communication and engagement and the investment proposition can also make a big difference.'

Additional tools offered by schemes such as employee wellbeing initiatives are 'continuously evolving' and reviews can ensure the best value is achieved from an employee benefits perspective, Corliss added.

Action points for HR

Charles Cotton, senior adviser for performance and reward at the CIPD, advised HR teams to focus on the following areas to determine whether their organisation's pension plan is delivering value for money:

- How the scheme is being governed.
- What retirement outcomes are being achieved.
- How the plan compares to schemes offered by other providers through such measures as net promoter scores, employer and employee cost, and scheme features.

(**SOURCE:** Elizabeth Howlett, *People Management*, 14 June 2023)

8.5 Why do employers provide pension schemes?

The introduction of employer-sponsored workplace pensions is closely linked to the development of human resource management. As suggested above, the growth of pension schemes was intrinsically linked to changes in employment practices at the start of the 20th century. Employers viewed pension schemes as a useful aid to reward the loyalty of those staff they wished to retain – initially managers and white-collar senior staff but later other workers. Pensions developed hand in hand with the concept of an internal labour market (see Chapter 2), in which employers sought to protect themselves from having their employees recruited by competitors. As discussed in Chapter 7, pensions are one of only two benefits identified in the US literature as being closely correlated with retention and staff satisfaction, the other being stock options. Providing access to a pension, and especially an employer contributory scheme, has been seen in the past as 'good employer' branding. A survey by the CBI (CBI, 2011) found that the major reasons given for offering a workplace pension were: the business case for pensions rather than higher pay; aiding recruitment and retention; because employers should assist employees to plan for retirement; because they enhance corporate reputation; and because employers feel a paternalistic obligation to employees. HM Revenue and Customs-approved pension schemes also provide a very tax-efficient method of saving for employees.

A review of the econometric research on the effect of pensions (Taylor, 2009) argues that all the studies show a close correlation between membership of an employer-sponsored pension scheme and low labour turnover but that this is questionable. Taylor (2000) argues that it may not be the pension scheme as such that causes retention, but rather some other independent variable, such as higher pay or better HR management, that often correlates with those organisations providing pensions. Taylor also points out that most of these studies pre-dated legislation that stopped schemes having rules that heavily penalised early leavers. Provisions on pensions vesting (i.e. when employees accrue rights to pensions benefits), first introduced in April 2006, were designed to prevent employers using vesting periods as a device to 'trap' employees into staying longer than they wish to. Under the 2015 Act, deferred benefit entitlements were introduced to bring workplace pensions into line with personal pensions.

Research by the NAPF, renamed as the Pensions and Lifetime Savings Association (2010), found that staff increasingly view pensions as the best way to save for retirement and the most important employee benefit on offer. But they have become less confident that their schemes will deliver when they reach retirement age. And anyway, pensions are seen as confusing, information provided to active members something to put in a drawer for another day. Perhaps the 2022 pensions communications regulations will address this – but it remains a moot point. The underlying ambition prompting these changes can be seen in observations by the PLSA's George Currie in a June 2019 blog post:

> The PLSA firmly believes both the Government and the pensions sector must do more to ensure everyone has an adequate income in retirement. To do that the industry must do all it can to communicate its messages to savers more effectively... It's for that very reason that the PLSA is working with the Association of British Insurers (ABI) to promote the Simpler Annual Statement (SAS)... [While], on its own, the SAS is not a panacea... it would form part of a suite of initiatives that sit alongside the creation of the Money and Pensions Service (MAPS) and our very own Retirement Income Targets. These initiatives will make it easier for savers to engage with their pensions and gain a greater understanding of their future retirement income.
>
> (PLSA, 2019)

In terms of the effect of pensions as recruitment devices there is even less research evidence. Research by the NAPF (2007) indicates that while a pension scheme can be attractive to job candidates and act as an important element in their decision to apply for jobs, there seems to be less concern about the type of pension on offer. Moreover, research for the CIPD (2009b) indicates that the shift from the more generous DB schemes to the less generous DC schemes has had no obvious impact upon labour turnover in the private sector. The closure of DB schemes has not led to any observable increase in employee mobility. Research by Loretto et al (1999), looking at undergraduate student views on pensions, found that many, especially males, did not rate pensions highly in terms of employment choice, preferring individual decisions on how to spend their money. Similarly, research by Hales and Gough (2002) on employee perceptions of occupational pensions found that the attraction of these schemes was not the security they provided but rather the opportunity for cost-effective saving and the possibility of early retirement. Hales and Gough concluded that company pension schemes are seen more as contingent private transactions than as part of long-term stable commitments by – and to – an employer.

A further factor which encouraged the implementation of workplace pensions, particularly DB pensions, is their use as a workforce management tool. Most DB pension schemes have provision for ill health pensions or early retirement pensions and are often included in redundancy or severance policies with a pension enhancement being offered to those employees meeting the relevant criteria. This enables employers to offer generous terms to those employees affected which in turn encourages employees to leave the business, for example by opting for voluntary severance schemes or redundancy exercises as they can see that they will continue to receive an income after leaving their employer. This, together with relatively high funding rates in DB schemes in the 1980s, led to an increase in employees retiring early (in their 50s). The increased cost of providing these enhanced benefits in DB schemes and the move to DC has led to these exercises being curtailed in today's economic climate and a move away from such high levels of early retirement.

A final factor that may influence employer provision of pensions is the presence of collective bargaining. In other words, through their unions, employees demand the establishment and/or continuation of good pension schemes. The 2004 WERS (Kersley et al, 2006) found that core employees in workplaces with some collective bargaining were significantly more likely to be entitled to an employer pension scheme than those not covered by collective agreements. This held true both for the whole economy and the private sector data. It is also interesting to note, however, that entitlement to an employer pension scheme was associated with lower pay satisfaction. This suggests 'either that employees face a pay penalty in order to obtain pension rights or else that, when offered as a supplement to pay, employees may prefer a cash equivalent' (Kersley et al, 2006: 201).

SELF-ASSESSMENT EXERCISE

To what extent do you think employees value an occupational pension? From discussion with colleagues and friends, do you think employees prefer to have a larger disposable income than a smaller income and a guaranteed pension on retirement? Does this vary based on demography (age, ethnicity, gender, etc)?

8.6 Categories of pension scheme

Pension schemes (as distinct from state retirement pension) can be categorised in a variety of ways and some are specifically defined in the pensions tax legislation. Very broadly the three main types are:

- occupational pension schemes;
- public service pension schemes; and
- personal pension schemes.

An occupational pension scheme is one set up by an employer (a private sector employer often referred to as the sponsoring employer) to provide benefits for or in respect of its own employees. Occupational pension schemes may also provide benefits to individuals who are connected to employees of any employer in the scheme, for example, spouses or children. As discussed above, occupational pension schemes can be either DB- or DC-based but are usually funded and administered under trust law, with the control of their funds sitting with a board of trustees. This is designed to ensure some independence from the employer and has become even more important as a safeguard following the Mirror Group pensions scandal cited earlier. Trustee boards have significant obligations under the law and the trust deed and rules of the pension scheme. The advantages of setting up a scheme under trust law are that: HM Revenue and Customs approval of schemes is dependent on this; the assets of the scheme are separate from those of the employer; and it provides protection for those beneficiaries who are not employees (i.e. spouses and dependants). UK trust-based schemes are overseen by the Pensions Regulator.

One particular form of occupational pension scheme is a master trust. The original trust-based schemes were developed in the 1950s by insurance companies and were set up to avoid the costs associated with an employer running its own trust-based scheme. This approach was also used to set up a number of non-insured multi-employer schemes based around industry sectors, such as construction. Changes in tax law have enabled master trusts to become much more flexible and in recent years these have been used as auto-enrolment solutions, particularly for smaller employers who may not have the resources to run their own pension scheme. A master trust is a multi-employer occupational scheme where each employer has its own section within the master arrangement. There is one legal trust and therefore one trustee board. The trustee retains decision making independence on things such as investment and service providers under a trust-wide governance structure. The decisions over benefit and contribution levels typically reside with the employer. Master trusts offer a viable route for those employers who want the benefit of a governance function (albeit without their having direct control) but with pooled (lower) operating costs and greater simplicity than a single employer scheme.

The alternative to a trust-based scheme is a contract-based pension scheme, which is usually a DC arrangement and can be set up on an individual or group basis; for example, a Group Personal Pension. The main difference is that instead of being run by a board of trustees on behalf of the employer, a contract-based pension is set up by the employee contracting with the pension provider directly, often an insurance company. This means that the governance burden on the employer is significantly lighter than under a trust-based scheme. However, this can lead to a weaker relationship between the employer and the pension provider, with employees having to take greater responsibility for their own pension provision.

A public service pension scheme is a scheme which is established by or under an Act of Parliament, specified in an order made by the Treasury, or approved by a Minister of the Crown or an appropriate UK, Scotland, Wales or Northern Ireland government body or department. Examples of public service pension schemes include pension schemes for the civil service, the armed forces, NHS and local government. The main public service schemes are unfunded with pensions being paid directly by HM Treasury. Therefore, the main issue for these schemes is one of cash flow; if the contributions paid in by current members do not equal the amount that needs to be paid out to existing pensioners then the Treasury has to make up the difference out of tax revenue. In contrast, an example of a funded public service pension scheme is the Local Government Pension Scheme, which is run as 89 separate funds in England and Wales, 11 in Scotland and one in Northern Ireland that invests contributions paid in, to accumulate the means to cover the cost of pensions in payment.

Personal pension schemes are DC schemes (which can also be known as 'money purchase' schemes) normally set up by a financial institution, such as an insurance company, that are open to individuals including employees and the self-employed. It is possible for someone to participate in an occupational and personal pension at the same time. These are contract-based pensions and it is unusual for an employer to contribute to an individual's personal pension.

A pension scheme is defined in UK tax legislation as 'a scheme or other arrangement(s) that can provide benefits to a person/in respect of a person in any of the following circumstances: retirement, death, having reached a particular age, serious ill-health or incapacity, or similar circumstances' (HMRC, 2015). A pension scheme does not have to provide benefits in all of these situations. For example, if a scheme provides only death in service benefits it would still fall within the definition of a pension scheme.

By way of a segue into discussion of tax treatment of workplace pensions, attention is needed to the category of registered pension scheme: a pension scheme that is registered under Chapter 2 of Part 4 of the Finance Act 2004 because either an application to be registered has been made and the scheme has been registered by HMRC, or the scheme is treated as automatically registered. The main benefit of a pension scheme being registered is the availability of certain tax reliefs and exemptions, such as being able to provide lump sums free of tax (up to certain limits).

In contrast, non-registered pension schemes, known as employer-financed retirement benefit schemes (EFRBS), are schemes that can pay certain retirement or death benefits for employees or former employees. EFRBS do not get any of the explicit tax advantages that registered schemes receive, such as tax relief on employee contributions or investment income. Under an EFRBS, an employer makes a contractual promise to an employee (or group of employees) to provide pension benefits to nominated beneficiaries (employees, former employees or their dependants). EFRBS can be either funded or unfunded and are often expensive to set up. They are often used to provide top-up benefits for executives and other high earners to compensate them for the restrictions on the amount of pension saving that can be made to tax registered schemes due to the annual allowance and the lifetime allowance. In 2011 HMRC deliberately made funded EFRBS less tax efficient by introducing new tax and national insurance charges on employer contributions or accrual under them from 6 April 2011. This limited the use of funded EFRBS. HMRC subsequently reviewed unfunded EFRBS to ensure employers and employees are not using them as tax avoidance schemes. HMRC labels EFRBS as disguised remuneration schemes and the provisions, so far as they relate to pensions, are designed to ensure that it is not more tax efficient to save in a non-registered pension scheme than it is to have savings above the annual allowance in a registered pension scheme.

8.7 Tax treatment of pensions

The tax legislation covering pensions categorises the type of benefits a pension scheme can provide into the following four types (two of which we described above):

- Defined benefit (DB) schemes that should provide an amount of benefit based on a known formula, where the benefit does not depend on how much money is within the scheme, i.e. the same amount is payable regardless of whether the scheme is in surplus or deficit. Final salary and career average schemes are both examples of DB scheme structures.
- Defined contribution (DC), also known as 'money purchase' schemes. The amount of pension is not known in advance as it will depend on how much money is in the scheme member's 'pot'. The size of the member's pension pot in the scheme will depend on the amount that has been contributed to the scheme, the investment return received on those contributions and the charges that are deducted.
- Cash balance schemes work in much the same way as DC schemes, but with some features of a DB scheme: the defined benefit is a lump sum expressed as a formula linked to the member's final salary. The contribution rate may be set as a proportion of salary or it may include some minimum levels of guarantee, such as a guaranteed minimum investment return. The difference between pure DC and cash balance is that the size of the member's pension pot is not only dependent on the contributions that have been paid into the scheme. However, for the purposes of providing member benefits the rules are generally the same as for DC benefits.
- Hybrid schemes which may provide either defined benefit, money purchase, cash balance or a combination of these benefits.

(HMRC, 2015)

The taxation of registered pension schemes and their arrangements can broadly be divided into three stages: contributions, investments and benefits. Contributions are made into a fund by individual members and often by their employer too with tax relief generally available on those contributions, providing an incentive to save for retirement. The fund into which the contributions are paid is invested with the aim of generating income and capital investment returns in order to provide retirement benefits at the relevant time. In DC arrangements the investment risk is borne entirely by individual members, whereas in DB arrangements it is borne by the employer. Individuals then take their benefits from the fund when they reach retirement.

Historically, benefits have often been taken as a tax-free lump sum and regular income payments that are either paid by the scheme or through an annuity purchased from an insurance company. From 6 April 2015, however, the way in which individuals may access their DC pension savings changed. The Taxation of Pensions Act 2014 made a number of changes to existing pensions tax legislation relating to how registered DC pension schemes can provide benefits to members. These changes give individuals greater flexibility with how they can take benefits from their DC arrangements from age 55 (often referred to as pensions freedom or flexibility). From 6 April 2015, individuals who have reached the normal minimum pension age (age 55) can access as much of their pension savings in DC arrangements as and when they want. Where individuals do take advantage of the new flexibilities and withdraw any taxable amount from their DC fund, they will trigger the money purchase annual allowance (MPAA) rules and will be subject to a £10,000 money purchase annual allowance in respect of any future savings in DC arrangements. The new arrangements mean that from 6 April 2015 benefits from a DC arrangement under a registered pension scheme can be taken from age 55 by choosing one or more of the following options: taking an annuity; designating some or all of the DC funds to provide a drawdown pension; a scheme pension; or taking an 'uncrystallised' funds pension lump sum (UFPLS). The first three options require that the pension payments are taxable, and the member can also choose to take a tax-free pension commencement lump sum when they first start their pension.

Tax relief is available on individual and employer contributions to registered pension schemes. Tax relief on individuals' contributions is available at their marginal rate and employees are not taxed on their employer's contributions as a benefit in kind. Therefore, employer contributions are not subject to income tax or corporation tax. Most investment growth of the assets held within registered pension schemes is also exempt from income and capital gains tax. Members of registered pension schemes can make unlimited contributions in a tax year but there is a limit on the amount of contributions that will receive tax relief. This is based on two criteria:

- Employees can only receive tax relief on an amount of contributions up to their taxable income. If the individual has no or low taxable income, then they can contribute up to £2,880 per year and receive tax relief, creating an effective contribution to the pension pot of £3,600.
- Their pension input amount as tested against the Annual Allowance. In a DC scheme the pension input is simply the cash amount of employer and employee contributions paid into the scheme. In a DB scheme the pension input is the increase in value in the pension over the pension input period. Since April 2016 the annual allowance has been restricted further for those employees whose total taxable earnings (including salary, investment income, rental income and pension contributions or accrual) are over £150,000. In these cases, the annual allowance is tapered by £1 for every additional £2 of income. The application of the tapered annual allowance is particularly complex, but more information is available on the HMRC website, www.gov.uk/government/publications/pensions-tapered-annual-allowance.

Unlike members, there is no set limit on the amount of tax relief an employer may receive on its contributions. Tax relief on employer contributions is provided by allowing them to be deducted as a business expense (although not automatically), therefore reducing the employer's taxable profit.

Most payments to scheme members (i.e. the retirement benefits) are liable to income tax but members have the option of taking up to 25 per cent of their pension pot as a tax-free pension commencement lump sum with the remainder as taxable pension. For members of DC schemes, the post-2015 pension flexibilities mean they could also opt to be paid an 'uncrystallised' pension lump sum: normally 25 per cent of this is tax-free with the remainder liable to income tax.

There is no limit on the amount of pension saving an individual can build up in a registered pension scheme nor is there an absolute limit on the amount of benefits such a scheme can provide. However, the lifetime allowance limits the total amount of benefits an individual can draw from all registered pension schemes in their lifetime without being subject to an additional tax charge. The lifetime allowance stands at £1,073,100. As with the annual allowance the way benefits are tested against the lifetime allowance depends on the type of pension scheme. For a DC scheme it is the amount in the member's pension fund at retirement, including investment returns. For a DB scheme the pension that goes into payment is calculated and multiplied by 20 and then any tax-free lump sum is added. If the pension value exceeds the lifetime allowance the member has to pay additional tax of 55 per cent if the excess is taken as a lump sum and 25 per cent if the amount is taken as pension (plus income tax on the pension in payment).

8.8 Comparing main pension scheme types

There are advantages and disadvantages for both employers and employees in the two main types of pension scheme. In a DB scheme, contributions are made by employers, employees or both into a pension fund (although in some public sector schemes there is no actual fund), which is then invested, and pensions paid out of the investment income. When a scheme member retires, his or her pension is calculated on the basis of the number of years' membership of the scheme and their salary. The pension can be based on some proportion of the final salary or earnings received, or the best year's earnings of the most recent service period (normally three years) but could also be a 'career average revalued earnings' (known as CARE) calculation. CARE pensions provide members with an amount of annual pension accrual as a proportion of their earnings in that year. Each year's accrual is then revalued annually, usually by an index linked to inflation. The sum total of all of the years of accrual is the pension payable in retirement. In both final salary and CARE schemes the resulting pension depends on the level of annual accrual, the length of service and salary of the member. In cases where the salary increases in line with inflation, final salary and CARE produce similar results in terms of retirement pension. Therefore, CARE may benefit lower-paid workers, or those whose earnings peak mid-career, and final salary may benefit those who expect their highest earnings capacity to be at the end of their career. CARE is also generally fairer for those with a broken service history, such as women who have taken time off work to care for children, as final salary sees these members lose out more in terms of drop in retirement income over the missing period of service.

DB schemes also usually come with a package of benefits such as death in service cover, dependants' pension and ill health cover. In addition, if the member leaves before their retirement age the pension they leave behind will be 'deferred' and receive inflation linked increases until they retire. The pension in retirement is also usually increased annually in line with inflation. These are fixed benefits which are provided at substantial cost which is reduced due to the pooled nature of the pension fund investments.

The reason such schemes are known as 'defined benefit' schemes is because the retirement benefit is calculated based on a known formula so the employee (and employer) are able to forecast, assuming the requisite number of years' service will have been completed on retirement, the amount of the final benefit to be received (calculated at today's value). This amount of pension is payable to the employee at retirement regardless of the funding level of the scheme at that point. In this way the retirement benefit that has accrued is 'guaranteed'. In a DB scheme any funding shortfall is the responsibility of the sponsoring employer and this provides a valuable level of security to DB members.

A DC scheme also operates on the basis of employer and employee contributions paid into a fund, which is then invested until the member retires. Under a DC scheme, employees usually have the option to decide where their fund is invested, whereas under a DB scheme the fund is centrally controlled and invested usually under the scrutiny of a group of fund trustees, some of whom are elected to represent employee member interests. Employer contributions can be a fixed percentage of salary or the contribution may increase with service. An alternative is that the employer agrees to match whatever the employee puts in (or may agree to a multiple of the employee contribution). Automatic enrolment legislation requires employers to pay a minimum contribution (3 per cent of qualifying earnings from April 2019). ONS research found fewer than 1 in 10 employees (9 per cent) with an occupational DC pension receiving a contribution of at least 12 per cent of their pensionable earnings from their employer in 2019. The majority (70 per cent) of employees with a pension of this type received between 2 per cent and less than 8 per cent of their pensionable earnings from their employers (ONS, 2020). At retirement, due to the introduction of the new 'pensions flexibilities', DC members have a number of choices to make regarding their benefits which can range from taking the whole amount as a cash lump sum (an UFPLS) to buying an annuity.

However, unlike a DB scheme, the value of the benefits they will receive at retirement age from a DC scheme is not known in advance. The amount of pension will be based on the level of contributions paid in, the charges deducted and the return on investment on the individual's pension 'pot' at the time of retirement, which cannot be accurately predicted. Therefore, a DC pension provides less security to the member in relation to their income in retirement. Since April 2015 DC members no longer have to choose to buy an annuity – they can instead keep their fund invested and draw down income directly from their pot. However, if the member decides to buy an annuity, they can choose which provider they wish to buy an annuity from. They do not have to use the same provider that they invested their DC pot with. This is called taking an Open Market Option and all pension providers need to communicate this option to members at retirement. Members also have a choice between a number of different types of annuity such as single life or joint life (joint life would include payment of a spouse pension when the member dies), flat rate or increasing in line with inflation, fixed term or for life. They could also obtain a better annuity rate if any health conditions or lifestyle issues, such as smoking, are taken into account. This is called an enhanced annuity. These have increased in popularity as the cost of buying annuities has increased because it enables the member to get a better annuity rate and therefore a higher pension in retirement. It should be clear from this summary description that DC pension planning is not simple; beneficiaries may be wise to take financial advice or access free guidance from the government's Pension Wise service.

As referred to above, the size of a member's DC pot at retirement depends on three things: the contributions made, the investment returns achieved and the charges deducted. To promote value for money for DC scheme members the government has introduced a cap on the charges that can apply to default funds. A default fund is the investment option which must be offered to scheme members who do not wish to make their own investment choice and it is often the most common investment fund used by DC scheme members. Since April 2015 annual administration charges and management fees charged by a pension provider have been capped at 0.75 per cent for any default fund used by a DC scheme that qualifies for auto-enrolment. At the same time, applicable from April 2016, the government enacted legislation to prevent higher charges being applied to member pots once the employee has left the employer (DWP, 2016).

The original employer justification for DB schemes was that they helped to recruit and retain good staff. They also had the benefit of fixing a retirement age so that employees could both be encouraged to stay until the scheme retirement age was reached, but no longer, thus dealing with any possible declining performance issues (Taylor, 2009). However, in 2011 this changed with the removal of the default retirement age which means that employees could no longer be forced to retire at 65, and the removal of the rule that employees had to draw a pension by 75.

The main disadvantage of a DB scheme for an employer is that they have to take responsibility for any risk that the fund will not be sufficient to pay the benefits that have been built up by scheme members. The liabilities of a DB scheme may exceed its assets if salaries grow faster than expected, the age at which pensioners die increases (because the pension has to last for longer), or the fund investments do not perform as well as projected. This can lead to a deficit in the pension scheme which ultimately has to be paid off by the employer out of their existing resources and may mean the employer has to provide a substantial additional contribution to keep the scheme solvent. On the other hand, if the fund is in surplus, the employer can stop making contributions on the employee's behalf until the fund is in balance again (as many employers did in the 1980s and 1990s in order to reduce scheme surpluses and potential tax charges).

Clearly, the great advantage of the DB scheme for employees is that their future retirement income is funded and backed by the sponsoring employer. Final salary pensions tend to reward those employees who receive promotion through their career, particularly towards the end, but the disadvantage of this is that such schemes were designed to reward loyalty and service with a single employer. If the employee does not work for that employer for his or her entire working career, then the resulting pension will be smaller than the maximum entitlement (e.g. an employee who worked for five years may only receive 5/60ths of their final salary). Moving a DB pension entitlement from employer to employer is administratively difficult, can take a very long time, and the amount of pension payable by the receiving scheme will depend on the factors used in the calculations by both schemes which may include a reduction in the transfer value if the scheme is in deficit. For these reasons, final salary DB schemes do not suit those who regularly change their employer. The pension can be deferred (i.e. left in the scheme but not collected until retirement age), but the deferred pension may only increase in line with the legal requirement for protection of the value of the pension. Under the Pensions Act 1995, schemes are obliged to provide for an annual inflation-related increase in deferred pensions, although the trustees may have the power to pay higher increases at their discretion.

CARE schemes are slightly different in that they are seen as providing a fairer distribution of benefits across staff at all salary levels. Those employees who have rapid promotion through their career may not benefit as much from a CARE scheme as they would from a final salary scheme, but all employees receive a more comparable share of benefits from the fund. Also, in a CARE scheme the annual pension is revalued in line with inflation whether the member is still employed or has deferred their benefit so the loss on leaving the employer is less severe. Therefore, CARE schemes may be better overall for employees who leave with short service or move employer frequently.

In the case of DC schemes, the advantage to the employer is that, there being no defined pension promised at retirement, there cannot be a deficit which they have to make good. All the employer needs to maintain is their level of contribution, not the final benefit. DC relies on the employee taking greater responsibility for their income requirements in retirement as it is the contribution rate and investment returns which are the key drivers of the size of fund which the member will have to rely on when they retire.

The advantage to the employee of DC pension benefits is that they are usually much easier to transfer to another employer as one is simply transferring a sum of money, not a specific level of pension. The disadvantage for the employee is that they will have no clear idea of what the pension fund will yield in the final pension amount until they get close to retirement (although schemes usually provide projections based on current fund performance and various investment return scenarios).

Together with more stringent regulation and governance requirements, the increasing risk falling on employers due to the escalating cost of DB schemes has led to a substantial decline in employers offering such schemes, illustrated in the material presented earlier in the chapter. Even in the public sector, where such schemes have been common, there have been government reforms to change the basis of calculation from final salary to career average (see below).

SELF-ASSESSMENT EXERCISE

What are the major advantages and disadvantages of defined benefit and defined contribution pension schemes for 1) employers and 2) employees? What policy choices face employers, and what communication implications flow from them?

8.9 Retirement and pension age

While UK equalities legislation now incorporates age discrimination, and hence an employee cannot be dismissed simply on having reached a particular 'retirement age', pension schemes still use the term 'pension age' and there is normally a minimum age at which benefits can be taken. Pension age is the age at which pension benefits can be taken from a registered pension scheme. The rules of a scheme will determine the minimum and maximum ages at which benefits can be taken from that scheme.

Registered pension schemes cannot normally pay any benefits to members until they reach normal minimum pension age. UK tax legislation states that from 6 April 2010 normal minimum pension age is age 55 (before 6 April 2010 it was age 50). Prohibition on registered schemes to have a normal minimum pension age lower than age 55 applies equally to individuals in occupations that usually retire before 55 (for example, professional sports people or those in hazardous occupations). The UK government's intension is that the minimum age at which people can access their private pension under the new tax rules will increase from 55 to 57 in 2028 and will then track at 10 years below State Pension age.

8.10 Equality issues

Data from the UK government's Department for Work and Pensions Family Resources Survey, reported in August 2019 by the Korn Ferry Institute, show that British women will receive pension payments that are 40 per cent lower than those of men. The difference means women get around £7,000 less in pension payments a year than do men. Similar results are reported applying to the European Union countries. The pension gap is more than double the so-called gender pay gap, where men typically get paid more than women.

This suggests that, despite recent attention to gender pay gap issues, the implications for pensions are harder to resolve. Twenty years ago, the UK Pensions Commission (2004) found that women pensioners in the UK are significantly poorer than men. Explanation is found in the fact that females have a lower employment rate than men, with lower average earnings and more work part-time. It was not until the 1980s that significant numbers of women entered the workplace and were potentially able to join workplace pension schemes or earn sufficient income to save for a private pension. It also reflects the fact that many women take time out from employment to have a family or take on other care-based responsibilities and hence, coupled to a lower retirement age, have fewer years in which to earn a pension.

In addition, the State Pension system has tended to assume that females receive their retirement income through their husbands, and assumptions have been made about family structure that are no longer valid. Many married women opted to pay reduced National Insurance contributions which means they do not build up any rights to contribution-based benefits such as Jobseeker's Allowance, and only entitles them to a partial State Pension based on their husband's NI contribution record. On the other hand, women are generally more expensive to pension schemes, as they often retire earlier than men and live longer in retirement. This means that the provision for widows in occupational schemes was important for married women's security in later life. However, by 1971 only one-third of private-sector scheme members were eligible for a widow's annuity for death in service, often because this provision required the male scheme member to give up part of their own entitlement. From 1978 provision for widows' pensions improved due to the requirements for workplace pension schemes wishing to contract out of the state earnings-related scheme. Shortly thereafter the proportion of private-sector schemes providing widows' annuities on death in service rose to 89 per cent and it became the norm for good employers to offer widows' pensions at about half the level of the men's pension (Thane, 2006).

Often pension schemes discriminated against different groups of staff: for example, contract or part-time staff may not have been allowed to join. The Part-Time Workers (Prevention of Less Favourable Treatment) Regulations 2000 came into force on 1 July 2000. While it had already been accepted that differential treatment of part-timers could be grounds for indirect sex discrimination, if it could be demonstrated that the majority of part-time workers were women, the new regulations meant that a provision that discriminates directly against part-timers is in itself actionable. To comply with the regulations, workplace pension schemes must ensure that part-timers are treated no less favourably than full-time members in respect of access to membership of the scheme or in respect of their treatment under the scheme rules. Further to this 'the Preston case' was brought by part-timers claiming indirect sex discrimination on the ground that exclusion of part-timers from workplace pension schemes mainly affected women. In 2001 the European Court of Justice ruled that anyone who has been denied access to a pension scheme in the past as a part-timer and who is still in employment (or who has left within the last six months) is entitled to bring a claim for retrospective membership back to 8 April 1976 (or the start of employment, if later). This led to a substantial cost falling on many DB schemes.

Another way in which equality issues have affected DB pensions is that historically benefits were payable to men and women at different ages. This has led to a number of cases where schemes have had to equalise benefits across male and female members and the majority of schemes have had equal retirement ages since the 1990s, following 'the Barber judgement'. Following the move to a flat rate State Pension, a further equality issue has been raised, regarding Guaranteed Minimum Pensions. On 26 October 2018, the High Court provided long awaited clarity for DB trustees and employers around the issue of inequalities in the treatment of men and women arising from their Guaranteed Minimum Pensions (GMPs). The judgment is relevant to occupational pension schemes that were contracted-out on a salary related basis between 17 May 1990 and 5 April 1997. It sets out a clear obligation on trustees to ensure that there is equality in the pension benefits provided to men and women who participated in a contracted-out scheme between those dates (House of Commons, 2023).

8.11 The major pension scheme benefits

Most pension schemes provide a number of basic benefits. Some are offered by all types of pension scheme and some depend on whether the scheme is DB- or DC-based. Most schemes offer:

- an income in retirement;
- the facility to draw a tax-free lump sum;
- dependants' benefits;
- benefits on death in service and death in retirement.

In addition, DB schemes often offer:

- the ability to enhance a pension through making additional voluntary contributions (AVCs);
- the ability to purchase 'added years' to enhance the final pension;

- benefits on leaving the employer before normal retirement age.
- benefits on serious ill health.

These aspects are described in more detail in what follows next.

8.11.1 Income in retirement

Defined benefit

The major benefit from any pension scheme is the monthly pension amount received by the employee. As explained above, in DB schemes the final sum received will vary according to the number of years the employee has been a member of the scheme and salary level but is generally a monthly amount which is increased annually in line with inflation. DB schemes were obliged under the Pensions Act 1995 to provide increases on pensions in payment of the Retail Prices Index (RPI) or (after 6 April 2005) 2.5 per cent per annum, whichever is the lower. In 2011 the statutory basis for increases changed from the RPI to the Consumer Price Index (CPI) and those funds that automatically used the statutory basis also switched. All pensions in payment are taxable as income.

Defined contribution

Since April 2015 DC members have had more options in retirement if they wish to draw an income from their pension pot. Broadly the income they can receive will depend on the size of the final pension fund, which itself will depend on the amount of contributions paid in, the investment return achieved, and the charges deducted. The main options include purchasing an annuity, keeping their pot invested and drawing down an income directly from their pension pot or taking the whole or part of the pot as cash (an 'uncrystallised funds pensions lump sum' or UFPLS). As with DB schemes any amount in excess of the tax-free cash lump sum is taxable as income including an UFPLS.

8.11.2 Tax-free lump sum

Defined benefit

Instead of taking the whole of their pension as monthly income, scheme members can usually convert part of the final pension sum into a tax-free lump sum. This is known as 'commutation'. There are government-imposed limits on the amount of any lump sum that can be commuted tax-free and this means members may draw up to 25 per cent of the value of their fund (up to the lifetime allowance of £1,073,100 (2023–24)). In public sector (and similar) schemes a lump sum is usually provided as one of the fixed benefits in addition to a lower pension amount.

Defined contribution

DC scheme members can also draw up to 25 per cent of their fund value (up to the lifetime allowance) as a tax-free lump sum. In addition, since April 2015 DC members have other options in relation to drawing cash from their pension pot, as set out above.

8.11.3 *Additional voluntary contributions*

Defined benefit

Most schemes will allow employees to make additional voluntary contributions (AVCs) to increase the value of the final pension benefits. Contributions are usually made into a separate fund provider appointed by the trustees, and the schemes operate in effect as an additional DC or money purchase element of the DB scheme. At retirement the member may have options such as using the pot to buy additional pension in the DB section, taking the AVC fund as tax-free cash, buying an annuity or using the new pension flexibilities to drawdown the fund or take an UFPLS. The options available will depend on when the member took out the AVC policy, what the scheme rules say and what the AVC provider offers so this will differ from scheme to scheme.

Members may also have a free standing AVC policy (FSAVC) which is a policy taken out with a completely separate provider, not connected to the main scheme or the employer.

Defined contribution

Most DC schemes allow members to make additional contributions, but these are generally treated in exactly the same way as main scheme contributions in terms of the way they are invested and the options at retirement.

8.11.4 *Added years*

Defined benefit

Added years are a relatively expensive option for enhancing the pension payable in some DB schemes (especially the public sector schemes). They are often paid through a specific type of AVC contract. They have the advantage that the employee can guarantee to increase the size of the final pension, but are expensive because the employee is normally expected to pay the full cost of the added year (i.e. the employer's contributions as well as their own employee contributions) and all the additional benefits such as death in service and spouse pensions.

Defined contribution

Added years are not applicable to DC schemes.

8.11.5 *Benefits on death*

Defined benefit

The main benefits available if the scheme member dies before reaching retirement age are a death in service lump sum; pensions for spouses (if married); and pensions for children or dependants (if there are any). The death in service lump sum is similar to a life insurance policy and provides a tax-free amount payable directly by fund trustees to the deceased member's estate of between two- and four-times salary (i.e. the scheme self-insures these payments). On death in service, schemes will normally also provide for a pension based on the deceased member's expected pension on retirement, usually half the sum that would have been paid to the member had they lived to normal retirement age. On death as a pensioner, schemes will often 'guarantee' the pension for five years so if the individual dies within five years of retirement the remaining five years' worth of monthly pension instalments is paid to the beneficiaries, as well as a spouse/dependants' pension. Where children are left, the scheme may also provide dependants with an income until they reach adulthood at 18 or sometimes later if the child remains in full time education or has a disability.

Defined contribution

DC schemes do not generally have a specific benefit payable on death, other than the payment of the value of the member's fund at date of death. Some employers provide an additional life policy for employees. This is generally a lump sum only which may be a similar level of benefit to a DB scheme but may have some allowance for a potential spouse benefit.

This has also changed as a result of the implementation of the new pensions flexibilities. Now members can leave their DC pension to be inherited by a beneficiary of their choice and it no longer matters whether or not the member has drawn their pension or not; instead the tax treatment is determined by the age at which the member dies:

- Death before age 75: any payments using the three options (lump sum, drawdown and annuity purchase) will be tax-free (provided that the benefits are designated to the beneficiaries within two years).
- Death after age 75: any payments using the three options (lump sum, drawdown and annuity purchase) will be subject to tax at the beneficiary's marginal rates.

8.11.6 Leaving an employer before retirement

Defined benefit

As discussed above, for employees, one disadvantage of a final salary pension scheme is that it discriminates in favour of those who stay with the same employer for their entire working life. Because the scheme is designed to reward those who remain loyal to the employing organisation, there are usually penalties for those who leave that employer's service before retirement age. Where employees wish to retire early (other than through ill-health), there are often provisions for 'early retirement' whereby the employee can take the pension accrued to date as long as they have reached the minimum pension age. However, under this early retirement arrangement, the pension is normally actuarially reduced to compensate the scheme for the fact that the pension will be paid for a longer period and is based on a shorter period of investment growth. Conversely the scheme may offer a late retirement enhancement if the member retires after normal pension age.

Early retirement has been a very useful device in redundancy or 'downsizing' exercises, allowing workers close to retirement age to leave the organisation and take their pension, often with some form of enhancement to encourage the move. This has happened in both the private and public sectors in the past, but such early retirement options currently appear to be reducing – partly because of the costs involved by the scheme and partly because of the introduction of later pension ages to deal with the demographic changes.

Depending on their length of service, where employees choose to leave their employer's service to move to a new employer, employees can either seek to transfer their accrued pension to the new employer; have a refund of their contributions to date; or defer collection of the pension until they reach retirement age. Transfer is usually much easier to arrange with a DC scheme as the transfer is simply of a fund, not an entitlement to a guaranteed level of pension. As already explained, any deferred DB pension must be increased each year by at least 2.5 per cent or the CPI (whichever is the lower).

Defined contribution

There are generally no adjustments made to a DC pot as a result of the member retiring early or late in relation to their normal pension age. It is possible for an employer to make additional contributions into a DC pot to increase the benefit, but this is expensive and only limited amounts can be paid in before exceeding the annual allowance.

8.11.7 Serious ill-health benefits

Defined benefit

Most DB schemes have a provision that allows for early payment of benefits in cases where the member can medically justify their need to retire early for reasons of serious ill-health. In some cases, this allows the member to draw their pension early, which can be earlier than the minimum pension age. In other cases, the pension may be enhanced: for example, by removing the application of any reduction for early payment or by granting additional years of service.

It can also be possible to convert DB benefits into a lump sum which can be paid out in cases where the member has less than 12 months to live. This is called total commutation.

Defined contribution

DC schemes have limited provision for benefits on ill health, other than drawing the pot that has accumulated to the date of retirement. Some employers do provide additional policies, such as critical illness or income protection which are available at member choice: these may be available through a flexible benefits package, for example.

SELF-ASSESSMENT EXERCISE

What are the major benefits available from a typical workplace pension scheme? Which of these do you think is most valuable for employees? What should employers do to deploy workplace pension benefits as an element of employee engagement?

8.12 The role of HR in pensions

While specialists either employed by the organisation or under contract normally administer pension schemes, the HR department will be the first point of contact for scheme members and will normally manage communications with members. According to the CIPD, the role that HR plays in pensions 'is influenced by a number of factors, including size of employer, financial resources, the reward philosophy of the organisation and the attitude of owner/s towards pensions' (CIPD, 2009b: 4). At one extreme, the role of HR is helping their employer select a workplace pension scheme so as to be compliant with legal requirements. At the other, it is integrating the pension plan into the company's total reward approach to attract and retain talent and to support its business objectives.

It should be remembered that under the Financial Services Act 1986 and the Pensions Act 1995, there are restrictions on who can give financial advice to employees. However, it is to be expected that HR professionals give information on their organisation's workplace pension scheme, including the basic details of the benefits and contributions and the rights of people leaving the organisation's employment, as long as this simply relates to information. Employers can give guidance and information on member options but specific advice on which decision the member should make (e.g. whether or not a member should buy added years) is prohibited. HR professionals may also be involved in pre-retirement planning, and information about pension rights will be a major item on any such programme. A major role for HR is often communicating the details of the pension scheme to individual employees and assisting with the various administrative processes (see CIPD, 2004).

8.13 Reasons for the dramatic shift in workplace pensions provision

Stability around workplace pension provision between the 1960s until the late 1990s has, as described above, given way to major changes in both state and workplace pension provision. From being a somewhat invisible issue, talk of a 'pensions crisis' analysed in research published by Mercer (2010) has made it a matter to the fore of much employment relations activity. As already noted, action against proposed changes by employers to employees' pension entitlements has involved high profile instances of industrial action coordinated by trade unions.

KEY ISSUES IN REWARD MANAGEMENT 8.2

Union to fight changes to Tesco's pension

Threat to defined benefit scheme as retailer faces financial woes

Tesco's plans to scrap its defined benefit pension scheme have moved a step forward as the supermarket chain struggles financially, reports have said.

A letter sent to staff by Ruston Smith, the company's pensions director, said: 'In January we announced our plans to consult on closing our existing pension scheme and replacing it with a new scheme… These proposed changes would allow us to continue to protect any pension you have already built up and allows us to continue to offer a competitive pension for colleagues in the future.'

'We appreciate that this is a significant change, which is why we are committed to listening to your views before any changes are made.'

The Usdaw union said it would work to save the defined benefit scheme and urge management to find other ways to save costs, as the employer faces an estimated £5 billion hole in its finances.

An official consultation between the union and the supermarket started today and is set to run for 90 days.

Pauline Foulkes, Usdaw national officer, said: 'We understand that everyone will be disappointed about the proposed changes to the defined benefit pension scheme. We will be seeking further details… including the business case and rationale for the proposed changes, what can be done to maintain a defined benefit pension scheme and for the defined contribution scheme Tesco is proposing to replace it with.'

She called on staff at the supermarket chain to participate in the consultation process.

(*People Management*, 21 April 2015)

To summarise the issues, since 2000, citing CIPD (2019b) the workplace pension landscape has been shaped by:

- insufficient investment returns and low yields to help fund DB pension pots;
- increased longevity meaning more years in retirement for many people;
- greater flexibility in working patterns;

- the end of the default retirement age for most occupations;
- increasing pension regulation;
- the introduction of auto-enrolment;
- ending the requirement to buy an annuity;
- changes to pension tax relief;
- the increase in the State Pension age;
- ending the 'contracting out' of pensions;
- the new flat-rate State Pension.

Various reasons have been put forward to help in interpreting the forward-facing issues in retirement provision. These include:

- The escalating cost of employer pension scheme contributions due to requirements such as having to provide deferred pensions for employees who have left and statutory increases in deferred pensions and pensions in payment, deterring employers from providing pensions or at least leading to less generous schemes being offered.
- Long-term demographic trends – namely, pensioners living much longer than expected – meant that the pension has had to provide for a much longer period of retirement than had been funded for.
- The removal of the ability for employers to make workplace pension scheme membership compulsory and the introduction of personal pensions which reduced the level of employee participation in DB schemes. It also led to a miss-selling scandal as some employees were advised to leave their employer's DB scheme and join a personal pension or even to transfer their benefits away from their employer's DB scheme altogether when it was often not in their interest to do so, based largely around commission-based sales incentives for the advisers.
- The predicted return on pension fund investments has reduced significantly in recent years, particularly following the financial crisis in 2008 and interest rate decisions by the Bank of England.
- The increasing state regulation of pensions and the increased governance requirements, following the pensions scandals of the 1990s, has deterred employers from establishing or maintaining schemes.
- A decision by the UK Accounting Standards Board in 2000, through Financial Reporting Standard 17, changed the way pension scheme assets are valued. This change, effective from 2005, requires organisations to value pension fund assets and liabilities in annual accounts on a market-related basis, meaning that the fluctuations in fund assets are now shown in the company balance sheet, affecting the perceived value of the company among investors.
- The size of the pensioner population is projected to grow significantly, such that the proportion of the working population paying in to pension schemes will be unable to support the enlarged retired population. The ratio of active to pensioner members is referred to as the 'maturity' of a pension scheme. As a pension scheme matures the level of contributions being paid in falls

relative to the pensions being paid out. This can lead to fund trustees having to sell assets to pay pensions which in turn means that the returns on those assets can no longer be relied on to fund the benefits, thus driving up the cost further.

- One additional issue that has driven up the value of pension liabilities is Quantitative Easing (QE) which led to the Bank of England buying huge quantities of government bonds (gilts) from private sector companies such as banks and insurance companies. The intention behind this was for these companies to invest the additional money and put it back into the economy. However, one of the consequences of QE is that the increase in demand for gilts pushed the cost up and, relative to the cost, the return from gilts, called the 'yield', fell. Most DB pension schemes use gilt yields as the basis for calculating the value of the liabilities they owe (i.e. the cost of paying out all the benefits that are due to scheme members). The scheme actuary needs to estimate the level of future investment return that the assets will achieve and often use gilts to do this. The fall in gilt yields therefore has led to a lower assumption of the predicted return on the assets and the liabilities going up. For example, information from the Pensions Regulator shows that aggregate deficits on a scheme funding basis were £98 billion in 2008 but had risen to £300 billion by 2015 (Bank of England, 2018). A more encouraging picture was reported in 2023, namely that before March 2022, there had been sustained low gilt yields for a long period of time, but they have risen sharply since then. Long-term real gilt yields fell into negative territory in 2014 and had remained there until September 2022 but are now yielding positive yields again. Nominal yields had fallen in the same fashion but have also increased substantially (The Pensions Regulator, 2023). Overall, the changes in market conditions and aggregate pace of schemes' funding plans mean that deficits as at December 2019 and March 2020 are expected to have turned into surpluses as at December 2022 and March 2023 (The Pensions Regulator, 2023).

In order to deal with this important issue of public policy, the government established the Pensions Commission, chaired by Lord Adair Turner. The 'Turner Commission', as it became known, produced three reports, which in turn led to government legislation in 2007.

8.13.1 The Turner reports

Turner's first report (Pensions Commission, 2004) analysed the problems faced and posed four options for the future:

- Pensioners will have to get poorer compared to the rest of society.
- A greater share of taxation will have to be spent on pensions.
- People will have to save more for their retirement.
- People will have to work longer.

The first report's key conclusions were that:

1. Growing life expectancy, coupled to a declining birth rate in the UK, mean that by 2050 the proportion of the population aged 65 and over will have doubled and will continue to increase thereafter. The 'baby boom' of the past 30 years has delayed this effect but will now produce 30 years of very rapid increase in the dependency ratio (the number of pensioners to those of working age).
2. Raising retirement ages and increasing the number of elderly people in employment is one solution, but this is insufficient alone to deal with the problem.
3. The UK State Pension system has been one of the least generous in the developed world. This deficiency, however, has been compensated for by the fact that the UK had the most developed system of voluntary private funded pensions, so that the overall percentage of GDP transferred to pensioners has been comparable to other countries. Government plans to cut back on state provision to deal with the demographic and cost projections, however, required the private sector to develop its provision to offset the state's declining role. The underlying trend in private sector employer contributions had been downwards since the early 1980s, but the outcomes of this trend were not appreciated until the late 1990s. Since then, DB schemes had been closed to new members and replaced by less costly DC schemes. This meant that the underlying level of pension saving was falling rather than rising to meet the new challenges.
4. Given these trends, many employees would face 'inadequate' pensions in retirement, unless they had large non-pensions income or intended to retire much later than current practice. Three-quarters of all DC scheme members had contribution rates below the level required to produce adequate levels of pension.
5. Non-pension savings and housing assets would be insufficient for most people to use in retirement as a replacement income.
6. There were considerable barriers to encouraging more voluntary retirement income provision, but this situation had been made worse by the complexity of the UK pension system, state and private combined. Means testing within the state system had both increased complexity and reduced the incentives to save via pensions.

To achieve adequacy, Turner offered three possible options:

- a major revitalisation of the voluntary system;
- significant changes to the state system; and/or
- an increased level of compulsory private pension saving beyond that already implicit within the UK system.

The first report was followed by a second (Pensions Commission, 2005), which laid out recommendations for change. This report laid out four key dimensions for a future integrated approach. These were:

- Reform the state scheme to deliver a more generous, more universal, less means-tested and simpler State Pension.

- Strong encouragement to individuals to save for earnings-related pensions through automatic enrolment at a national level.
- A modest minimum level of compulsory employer contributions to ensure that savings are beneficial for all savers.
- The creation of a National Pension Savings Scheme, where there is no good employer-sponsored pension provision, with the state taking on the role of organiser of pension savings and bulk buyer of fund management to ensure low costs and hence higher pensions and better incentives to save.

The third and final report (Pensions Commission, 2006) reiterated the recommendations of the second report but provided more detailed proposals on the latter two recommendations – the employer contribution and the size of the National Pension Savings Scheme.

The government responded to the Turner Commission with a white paper outlining a number of proposals based on the Commission's recommendations. Following consultation on this white paper the government introduced new legislation, the Pensions Act 2007, which made major reforms to the State Pension system, including higher pension ages, the introduction of a single, higher basic pension and the ending of the second earnings-related pension and contracting-out from 2016. The Pensions Act 2008 then introduced auto-enrolment and the creation of the state-sponsored DC master trust scheme NEST (National Employers Savings Trust).

8.13.2 Public sector pensions

As indicated above, due to the decline in DB pension schemes being offered by private sector employers, pension provision has been seen as more generous in the public sector and many more employees are members of public sector schemes than those offered in the private sector. Following the election of the UK coalition government in May 2010, Lord John Hutton (previously a Labour Secretary of State for Work and Pensions) was invited to chair an independent Public Service Pensions Commission. The Commission was asked to undertake a fundamental structural review of the various public sector pension schemes and make recommendations by the Budget 2011. The Commission was asked to consider how public sector pensions could be made sustainable and affordable in the long-term, both for the public

Table 8.1 Public sector pension accrual rates

Scheme	CARE accrual rate	CARE revaluation rate
NHS Pension Scheme	1/54th	CPI + 1.5%
Local Government Pension Scheme	1/49th	CPI
Teachers' Pension Scheme	1/57th	CPI + 1.6%
Principal Civil Service Pension Scheme	1/43.1th	CPI
Police Pension Scheme	1/55.3th	CPI + 1.25%
Firefighters' Pension Scheme	1/59.7th	Average Weekly Earnings index

service workforce and the taxpayer, and ensure that they are consistent with the fiscal challenges ahead. An interim report was published in October 2010 (Hutton, 2010) and a final report in 2011 (Hutton, 2011).

Hutton's interim report disputed the commonly held view that public sector pensions were 'gold-plated', pointing out that the average pension paid out was around £7,800 a year and the median £5,600 a year. Nine in ten public sector pensioners received less than £17,000 a year and one in ten received less than £1,000 a year (Hutton, 2010). He also indicated, however, that final salary DB schemes could no longer be afforded and that an alternative calculation method was needed. In terms of a short-term solution to the problem, Hutton recommended that raising employee contribution rates would be the most effective method but that the low paid should be protected under any such move. The report pointed out that employers' contribution rates had increased much faster than employees' rates. As a result, employee contributions increased from April 2012.

The outcome of the Hutton reports was a major renegotiation of public sector schemes. The substantive change was a move away from final salary for future service so that pensions are calculated on a career average revalued earnings (CARE) basis. Service built up before the changes remains calculated in relation to final salary. The new CARE arrangements are different for each of the public service schemes although all saw an increase in the accrual rate from 1/80 of salary per year of service. There are also different rates used to increase the CARE pension each year.

It should be noted that these figures relate to the public service schemes in England and Wales. Those offered in Scotland and Northern Ireland may differ.

In addition, the changes increased Normal Retirement Age in line with State Pension Age but included transitional protection for those within 13.5 years of Normal Retirement Date when the changes were announced in April 2012.

SELF-ASSESSMENT EXERCISE

Is there a moral obligation on employers to provide pensions for their workers? Or should the state be the major provider, as in other European countries, with a consequent increase in taxation on both employers and employees to pay for this scheme? Ask fellow students and others within your network what they think.

8.14 Auto-enrolment

As a result of the Pensions Commission recommendations, from 2012 the government's policy of automatic enrolment into pension schemes was introduced. This means that all employees aged between 22 and State Pension age are automatically enrolled into a qualifying pension scheme, although they have the freedom to opt out. It is important to note that auto-enrolment is not compulsion. The intention is to use the concept of inertia and the likelihood that this will lead to members remaining in pension saving rather than making the conscious decision to opt out. The auto-enrolment duty on employers was phased in according to the size of employer, starting with the largest. By April 2017 all existing employers were to have enrolled their staff, followed by new organisations by February 2018. Contribution levels were also being phased in, increasing to a total minimum contribution of 8 per cent (with at least 3 per cent from the employer) by April 2019. Under auto-enrolment, job holders may be enrolled into an existing workplace pension scheme if it meets or exceeds certain requirements. Alternatively, employers may amend current schemes, set up a new scheme or arrange for enrolment into the National Employment Savings Trust (NEST), which was created by the Department for Work and Pensions specifically to meet the auto-enrolment requirements. In order to ensure that as many workers as possible are automatically enrolled, since October 2015 employers have been required to re-enrol all eligible workers who have subsequently opted-out of the qualifying pension (as long as they have not opted out in the previous 12 months).

For employers, as well as additional cost and administrative complexity, auto-enrolment has often had a direct impact on the benefits packages offered to staff. For example, employers may introduce salary sacrifice of pension contributions to help to mitigate the cost. There are also particular considerations for employers that offer flexible benefits. They may need to restructure their flexible benefits arrangement to account for the compulsory minimum contribution rate and also to ensure it takes account of the Pension Regulators 'safeguarding' obligations which require employers to demonstrate that any benefit options are not acting as an inducement to members to opt out of a qualifying pension scheme.

However, research on auto-enrolment published by the CIPD in November 2014 found that many employers were going above and beyond what was legally required (CIPD, 2014b). Of the 1,080 employers surveyed, 68 per cent had already automatically enrolled eligible staff into a scheme. The average employer contribution to schemes was 5.6 per cent of salary and the average employee contribution 4.7 per cent. Of those who had already gone through automatic enrolment, 22 per cent reported that there were no significant extra costs, while 38 per cent reported that they had been able to absorb the additional expense. By contrast, 14 per cent had restricted or stopped wage growth while 13 per cent scaled back on hiring or reduced staff numbers in response to the pension reforms. The most significant problems with the roll-out appeared to apply to smaller businesses.

A decade on, a UK government report published in October 2022 argues that auto-enrolment has transformed pension saving, with key points informed by data that has been collected as follows:

- participation has increased among private sector eligible employees in every industry and occupation between 2012 and 2021, including those with historically low rates of employees saving into a workplace pension;
- this has been replicated in every region of Great Britain, and in the most common private sector eligible employee jobs within each region; and
- the increases in total annual workplace pension contributions have been replicated across all industries and all occupations, except for the Energy and Water sector.

KEY ISSUES IN REWARD MANAGEMENT 8.3

Pensions whistleblowing

In October 2015 *People Management* reported on a 'surge in employees flagging pensions issues to watchdog', commenting that 'a sharp rise in the number of employees reporting concerns about pensions to the Pensions Regulator suggests staff are increasingly worried their employers are failing to comply with rules'.

In spring 2019, the Pensions Regulator stated that, as a public body, it is legally required to report on the whistleblowing disclosures received from certain workers. Whistleblowing is the term used when someone provides the Regulator with information concerning wrongdoing relating to their workplace pension: a 'whistleblowing disclosure'.

An article on the Pension Regulator's website continues as follows:

- Under the Prescribed Persons (Reports on Disclosure of Information) Regulations 2017 we must report the following information every year:
  - the number of disclosures we received (which met certain criteria);
  - the number of those disclosures where we decided to take further action;
  - a summary of the action we took in relation to the disclosures;
  - a summary of how workers' disclosures have impacted our ability to perform our functions and meet our objectives;
  - an explanation of our functions and objectives.

Number of disclosures 2018–19

We received 6,963 disclosures during the reporting period of 1 April 2018 to 31 March 2019 which fell within the remit of our statutory functions and objectives.

Number of disclosures and summary of actions

We took further action in relation to 794 of the 6,963 qualifying disclosures, with the majority of action taken as a result of disclosures reporting a suspected breach of, or failure to undertake, automatic enrolment duties or pay contributions.

In 196 of the instances where we took further action, we issued a Warning Notice or Unpaid Contribution Notice, Fixed Penalty Notice, Escalating Penalty Notice or Compliance Notice. Other actions we took as a result of disclosures included appointing new trustees, referrals to professional bodies, and supporting schemes to establish robust data improvement plans.

The action we take is consistent with the principles set out in the Regulator's Code. We are a risk-based regulator that must carry out our activities in a way which is proportionate, accountable, consistent, transparent and targeted. In this context, whistleblowing disclosures help us to inform our intelligence and enforcement action and take action where we see it as appropriate.

In instances where we didn't undertake enforcement action due to a disclosure not meeting the qualifying criteria, the information gathered was used to inform our intelligence work, such as our strategic intelligence assessments or compliance validation work.

(**SOURCES:** www.thepensionsregulator.gov.uk/en/document-library/corporate-information/whistleblowing-disclosures; www.thepensionsregulator.gov.uk/en/about-us/how-we-regulate-and-enforce/regulators%27-code-)

8.15 Conclusions and key learning points

In this chapter we have considered the role of pensions, as a deferred element within the overall reward package. In the past, pensions have been a common feature of organisations with strong internal labour markets, playing an integral part in employer recruitment and retention strategies. But there are suggestions that contemporary workforce members may place less value on this benefit than in the past. This even though investing in a pension is one of the most tax-efficient forms of saving and, where the employer contributes, a very valuable benefit for the employee. This may be partly due to a lack of communication to employees of the benefit of pensions by employers, action on which regulatory changes were made in 2022.

The UK State Pension scheme provides a minimum level of entitlement for all citizens who meet certain criteria, but an increasing number of employers also provide private workplace pension schemes, partly because this is now a statutory requirement through auto-enrolment. Recent legislation categorises private pensions into three broad types: defined benefit (DB), defined contribution (DC) and shared risk (or defined ambition) schemes. Each type of scheme has advantages and disadvantages for employers and employees, but the disadvantages of DB schemes appear to be uppermost in most employers' minds today. The withdrawal of DB schemes has led to some major employee relations problems as unions have mobilised their members in defence of such schemes.

There are a number of pressures encouraging employers to either close their DB pension schemes or reduce the benefits from them. At the same time there is an increasing demand, looking ahead with shifting demographics, for adequate retirement incomes. The question of who should pay for these – government taxpayers, the employer or the worker – is an ongoing area of debate. The government is keen to shift the burden of retirement incomes to both employers and employees. Responding to a series of government-commissioned reports on this issue, legislation has been introduced providing for a new state single pension, new obligatory membership by certain categories of workers of a private workplace pension scheme and mandatory minimum contributions from employers. In its role as an employer, the government has made public sector pensions a particular target and major reforms have taken place in these schemes as the government has striven to make significant savings in state expenditures since the 2008–09 financial crisis. Given the sums involved, these trends seem set to continue, with DC or defined ambition workplace pension scheme membership continuing to rise.

Explore further

For the CIPD viewpoint on workplace pensions, see www.cipd.co.uk/knowledge/fundamentals/people/benefits/workplace-pensions-factsheet, 5 May 2023.

For a legal perspective see CMS Pensions Team (2021, 15th edition) *Pensions Law Handbook*, London: Bloomsbury Professional. The main responsibilities of key personnel in the operation and governance of occupational pension schemes are outlined together with statutes, regulations, regulatory guidance and case law.

For qualitative insights into employers' perspectives on pensions auto-enrolment, conducted by the UK government's Department for Work and Pensions, published in October 2022, see www.gov.uk/government/publications/workplace-pensions-and-automatic-enrolment-employers-perspectives-2022/.

Facts and figures on pensions, with an archive of research reports, are accessible via the Pensions Policy Institute, www.pensionspolicyinstitute.org.uk.

09 Non-financial and total reward

CHAPTER LEARNING OUTCOMES

At the end of this chapter, you should understand and be able to explain the following:

- The meaning, constitution and role of non-financial reward within strategic reward management systems.
- Debates in the literature around 'total reward', 'employee engagement', the 'value proposition' and related phenomena in commentary and reported practice.
- The journey a large organisation embarked on, exemplifying design, communication and enactment of a reward strategy laying emphasis on holistic system principles: 'what it's like to be here'.

CIPD STRATEGIC REWARD MANAGEMENT (7HR03) LEARNING OUTCOMES

Learners will be able to:

2.1 Critically evaluate the significance of a total rewards approach including monetary and non-monetary incentives.

2.5 Discuss the significance of non-financial rewards as part of a total rewards approach.

9.1 Introduction

In Chapter 7 we described and appraised elements of the employee reward package comprising non-cash benefits, as summarised in the list in Table 7.1, and grouped into categories in Table 7.2. We also provided commentary on flexible and voluntary benefits as well as benefits communications practices. This chapter is designed to extend thinking and practice around strategic reward management, moving into the interesting, if sometimes unclear and frequently complex, realm of non-financial reward and the evolving concept of 'total reward'.

When Davis commented that it was not that long since 'Compensation was the primary reward' and benefits 'were a separate and seemingly low-cost supplement for employees', total reward, the concept of combining pay, benefits and other non-financial rewards 'to influence employee behavior on the job' (Davis, 2007: 1), was arguably at its height. Up until then, evolution in employment systems may be perceived as having prompted rethinking of the alternatives available when designing and managing the effort–reward bargain, especially when, as hinted in the final part of the quotation above, the intention is to have an influence on how employees behave at work. In a review of a book speculating on 'the future of management', co-authored by 'management guru' Gary Hamel, readers are reminded that while 'human beings were not born to be employees', management orthodoxy during the previous century appears to have been founded on the premise that, to achieve discipline and efficiency, people should be 'enslave[d]... in quasi feudal top-down organisations', with the result that 'human imagination and initiative [have been]... squandered' (Johnson, 2007). In the context of a perceived shift towards 'an intelligence economy', in which 'worthless... [r]aw information... needs to be processed by a thinking and feeling being' to become valuable (Coyle, 2001: 33), the argument has been made that employees are recognised 'as drivers of productivity, rather than as relatively interchangeable cogs in a larger wheel' (Davis, 2007: 2).

Under this scenario, rather than through 'a capacity to labour' for an employer, potential employee contribution is seen as frequently vested in tacit knowledge (e.g. Gururajan and Fink, 2010; Slaughter, Ang and Boh, 2007). Given the perceived 'shift in the economics of value creation... footloose... workers in possession of the most desirable skills...' are making 'more complex and more subtle demands' on the employment relationship – especially if the employer wishes to 'entice' them 'along the extra mile' (Reeves and Knell, 2001: 41). Such 'engaged' input to organisational performance is 'something the employee has to offer: it cannot be "required" as part of the employment contract' (CIPD, 2007b: 1). One response has been development and popularisation of a discourse under the term 'total reward', something we will define and discuss in this chapter.

Employers may choose to apply 'total reward' to balance and complement extrinsic rewards offered to employees with more intrinsically oriented elements, in pursuit of what has been described as an 'engaged' workforce (CIPD, 2023b; MacLeod and Clarke, 2009; Purcell, 2006). It is possible to attribute to the total reward rubric recognition that, amplified by changes not only to types of work and work settings but also to workforce composition, reward management approaches may not have the same effect on all employees, even assuming consistent application.

If complex organisations employ a diversity of people, it follows logically that employees may be responsive to equally heterogeneous HR policies (Kinnie et al,

2005). Specifically, in the case of reward policies, while there may be significant scope to standardise pay administration (Vernon, 2006), as explained in Chapter 7, this is less likely to be the case in relation to non-cash benefits, particularly in relation to institutional factors, such as variation in tax treatment of perks and other benefits between jurisdictions resulting in marked differences in 'value' conveyed to employees.

Moreover, although most organisations' reward practices appear to mimic those of other organisations, and despite the attractions of standardisation to achieve efficiency gains, Gerhart and Rynes (2003: 261) imply that organisations might achieve competitive advantage by being 'as different as legitimately possible'. While other organisations within a perceived competitor group may be able to replicate pay and benefits packages, a more distinctive 'employee value proposition' (Lawler, 2005; Ulrich and Brockbank, 2005) may be desired particularly in tight labour markets. Extending the emphasis to intrinsic rewards, subject to variations in how individuals and groups perceive value, contingent on their varying aspirations, beliefs and needs (Kinnie et al, 2005), consequences at the effort–reward nexus are likely to be even more marked.

More recently, the cost of living and living wage debates have cast 'total reward' as a poor attempt by HR departments to ameliorate or even excuse low pay work with calls for a re-emphasis on tangible compensation as the key to retaining and motivating employees (Brown, 2015) rather than the more nebulous 'employee value proposition'.

Against this background, in this chapter, clarification is offered to help grasp concepts and associated debates in the literature concerned with non-financial (or non-material) reward management, and its potential within wider employment and business systemic contexts. To ground the discussion in practice, an account of a real life 'journey' embarked on a few years ago by a large commercial employer, CaseCo Group, is unfolded throughout the chapter. The Group's corporate management invited customers and employees alike to accompany them. The choice to align marketing and people management held out the prospect of positive consequences for the overall 'employee value proposition'.

9.2 Defining total reward

While the increasingly popular umbrella term 'total reward' may be used to label non-financial reward, its meaning is not straightforward to specify: 'it is easy to see how people can use the term... only to find that they are referring to very different notions' (Davis, 2007: 2). Reflecting on initial definitions on offer, a relationship may be discerned between 'total reward' and ideas such as 'high investment work systems' (Lepak et al, 2007), 'mutual gains' (Bacon and Blyton, 2006) and 'high involvement work practices' (Huselid, 1995); 'employee involvement programmes' (Cox et al, 2006; Marchington and Cox, 2007), notions of 'employee voice' and 'partnership at work' (e.g. Ackers et al, 2003); as well as 'emotionally intelligent' leadership (Brown et al, 2006; Goleman, 2002; Palmer et al, 2001), coupled with attention to 'employee well-being' and the 'psychological contract' (e.g. Guest and Conway, 2004).

Adopting a broad definition, and using it interchangeably with the term 'employee value proposition', or 'total value', total reward 'can expand to encompass everything that is "rewarding" about working for a particular employer or everything employees get as a result of their employment' (Corby and Lindop, 2009; Davis, 2007: 2). In a Factsheet on the topic, the CIPD refers to the concept of total reward encompassing:

> ...all aspects of work that are valued by people, including such aspects as flexible working opportunities, or being rewarded fairly, in addition to the pay and benefits package.
>
> (CIPD, 2023c)

The implication is that, by going beyond the extrinsic elements of the effort–reward bargain, employers will 'actively manage... aspects of the work experience' that may have been 'taken for granted' (Richards and Hogg, 2007: 3). Implicitly consistent with a systems view of the world, employees are being invited to value their offer and the contribution expected of them in return as greater than the sum of its individual parts.

Inherent in the total reward concept here, then, is the expectation of managerial proactivity, with the consequence that 'embedded' managerial attitudes towards effort–reward management and the part they have to play need to be factored into considerations of total reward design and process (Marchington and Cox, 2007). The 'CIPD viewpoint' expressed in its Factsheet is that 'Total reward has implications for cultural change as it can focus in part on employee empowerment', and can help 'create a powerful and unique employer brand' (CIPD, 2023b).

Figure 9.1 An inclusive view of total reward

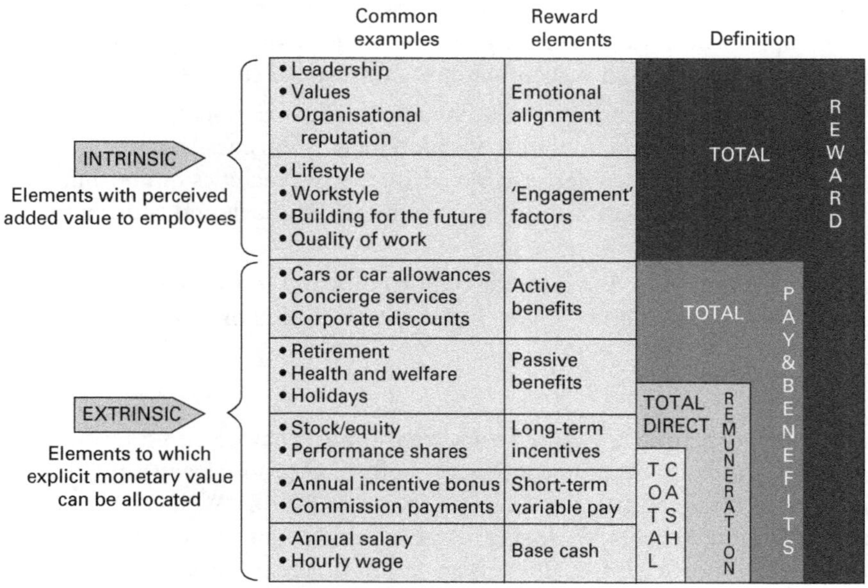

SOURCE: Adapted from Helen Murlis and Clive Wright (personal correspondence)

In the WorldatWork's handbook on total rewards (notice the added 's' in this US label), the emphasis is on employees' perception of value. In short: 'For a total rewards strategy to be successful, employees must perceive monetary and nonmonetary rewards as valuable' (Davis, 2007: 4).

Reward commentators Helen Murlis and Clive Wright, having long careers as consultants and researchers in the field, use a diagram like the one in Figure 9.1 to help communicate visually the types of phenomena the various total reward definitions appear to comprise, depending on breadth of approach adopted. But active management of total reward is not a one-way, employee-centric enterprise. The notion of an effort–reward exchange is emphasised, albeit implicitly, in the WorldatWork definition. In combination, extrinsic and intrinsic rewards are 'provided to employees in exchange for their time, talents, efforts, and results': key elements are 'artfully tailored' into a package intended, on the one hand, to secure and retain talented employees, as well as, on the other hand, to motivate them optimally to achieve business results (Davis, 2007: 4). The components of WorldatWork's evolved total rewards model are summarised as follows.

- **Compensation:** Pay provided by an employer to its employees for services rendered (i.e. time, effort, skill). This includes both fixed and variable pay tied to performance levels.
- **Benefits:** Programmes an employer uses to supplement the cash compensation employees receive. These health, income protection, savings and retirement programmes provide security for employees and their families.
- **Work–life effectiveness:** A specific set of organisational practices, policies and programmes, plus a philosophy that actively supports efforts to help employees achieve success at both work and home.
- **Recognition:** Either formal or informal programmes that acknowledge or give special attention to employee actions, efforts, behaviour or performance and support business strategy by reinforcing behaviours (e.g. extraordinary accomplishments) that contribute to organizational success.
- **Performance management:** The alignment of organisational, team and individual efforts toward the achievement of business goals and organisational success. Performance management includes establishing expectations, skill demonstration, assessment, feedback and continuous improvement.
- **Talent development:** Provides the opportunity and tools for employees to advance their skills and competencies in both their short- and long-term careers.

(WorldatWork, 2019)

A major shift in rhetoric associated with total reward has occurred in the wake of the Covid-19 pandemic and the concept of 'wellbeing' is now frequently included in frameworks of total reward. For example, a recent WorldatWork (2022: 1) report lists compensation, benefits, wellbeing, careers and recognition as effective elements of a total reward portfolio that 'fuel organizations and employees'.

CASE STUDY 9.1

Interpreting total reward in practice

We locate this discussion in the context of the rolling company case we are using to ground discussion of the total reward concept in specific practice, in the words of the former Head of Pay Policy & Market Intelligence at CaseCo Group:

> Historically, we defined reward and talked about our package (internally and to prospective employees) in terms of salary (or 'base pay') alone. However, recognising that people can, and do, receive much more than just base pay, we set the goal of moving understanding along a spectrum.
>
> At the first stage of the journey, we began to talk in terms of the 'total cash' an individual receives each year combining base pay and bonus or other incentive payments. Talking about the 'employment offer' in terms of total cash began to better represent how people are actually rewarded. However, we also invested a considerable amount in non-cash benefits and, in the same way, it was clear that there was a gap between what people received and how we talked about it.

The diagram in Figure 9.2 illustrates the stages in the CaseCo Group total reward journey.

Continuing the narrative explaining the rationale for setting out on the journey:

> We were missing out on a significant part of our 'employment deal'. Partly in terms of the investment, partly in terms of people not being able to calculate the true worth of their package, and partly because there was a range of elements that people might really value but that weren't really 'communicated'. We realised the importance of process, reflecting the dynamism involved: while we might talk about pay and benefits, as though these were static, the real difference was being made through flexibility in how they were applied. As a result, we formed a deliberate plan to move along the spectrum – to talk to our existing people and to

Figure 9.2 CaseCo Group's reward management journey

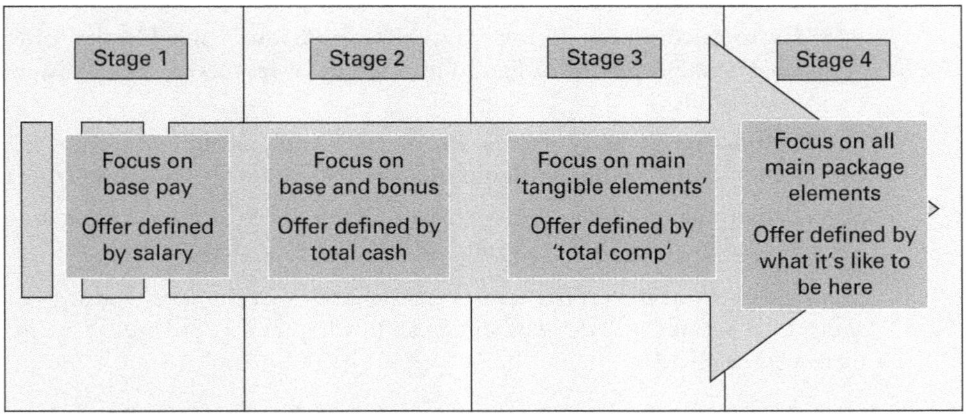

prospective employees in much broader terms about the total package.

This next stage also brought a conscious change of voice. Firstly we moved from communicating to 'marketing' – introducing a new and different colourful employee reward brand. This brand served to create a reward identity: it stimulated 'anchors' and 'hooks' for people. For the first time, we could talk about one element of reward and automatically encourage people to make connections with other elements of the package. The initiative helped us in getting people to take notice of the broader elements of the CaseCo Group reward proposition and over time became a type of self-fulfilling prophecy.

To round off this 'definitional' section of the chapter, an analysis of various models of total reward (Thompson, 2002) may help to establish a sense of the aspirations that may be observed as characterising this area of commentary and reported practice. The review of practice echoes the discourse outlined above, but is usefully expressed below in précis form, finding that total reward combines the following features. It is:

- **Holistic:** with a focus on how employers attract, retain and motivate employees to contribute to organisational success using an array of financial and non-financial rewards.
- **Best fit:** adopting a contingency approach, the advice is that total reward approaches should to be tailored to the organisation's particular culture, structure, work process and business objectives.
- **Integrative:** delivering innovative rewards that are integrated with other human resource management policies and practices.
- **Strategic:** aligning all aspects of reward to business strategy – total reward is driven by business needs and rewards the business activities, employee behaviour and values that support achievement of corporate priorities.
- **People-centred:** recognising that people are a key source of sustainable competitive advantage, the starting-point is a focus on what employees value in the 'total work environment'.
- **Customised:** enabling rewards to be tailored into a 'flexible mix' offering choice and improved design to match employees' needs, their lifestyle and stage of life.
- **Distinctive:** using a complex and diverse 'employment experience' to create an idiosyncratic 'employer brand' to differentiate the organisation from its rivals.
- **Evolutionary:** a long-term approach to effort–reward determination is adopted, based on incremental rather than on radical change.

The strategic and integrative aspects associated with the total reward concept are subjects of specific and detailed attention in Chapter 12, 'Strategic reward management within HRM'.

STUDENT EXERCISE

The scope of total reward

Search online for company annual reports statements and look at the section dealing with 'our people' or for company job pages detailing reward offerings. Two examples we found follow.

Google

Health & wellness

- Medical, dental, and vision insurance for employees and dependents
- Employee assistance programs focused on mental health
- Workplace accommodations for physical or mental health concerns
- Onsite wellness centers
- Access to mental health apps
- Second medical opinion for you and your loved ones
- Medical advocacy program for transgender employees

Financial wellbeing

- Competitive compensation
- Regular bonus and equity refresh opportunities
- Generous 401(k) and regional retirement plans
- Annual cross-company pay equity analysis and adjustments
- Student loan reimbursement
- 1-on-1 financial coaching

Flexibility & time off

- Paid time off, including vacation, bereavement, jury duty, sick leave, parental leave, disability, and holidays
- Hybrid work model with remote work opportunities also available
- Four 'work from anywhere' weeks per year
- Part-time work and job-sharing options

Family support & care

- Fertility and growing family support
- Parental leave and baby bonding leave
- Caregiver leave
- Elder care and support
- Backup childcare
- Survivor income benefit

Community & personal development

- Educational reimbursement
- Googler-to-Googler peer learning and coaching platform
- Donation matching and time off to volunteer
- Employee resource groups
- Internal Googler community groups and local culture clubs

Googley extras

- Inspiring spaces to work, recharge, and collaborate with fellow Googlers
- On-site meals and snacks
- Fitness centers, massage programs, and ergonomic support
- On-demand fitness, wellbeing, and cooking classes
- Art programs, Talks @ Google, legal services… and of course, Dooglers

Please note that while our philosophy is the same in every place Googlers work, benefits may vary by office/country.

(**SOURCE:** careers.google.com/benefits/)

University Hospitals of Leicester NHS Trust

Rewarding @ its best

Caring at its Best Awards

The 'Caring at its Best Awards' are our awards which reward our inspirational staff, those that live our values and deserve recognition for their amazing success and commitment to providing 'Caring at its Best'.

Award winners will be those staff members who demonstrate that they go the extra mile for colleagues and patients. They will be working examples of our values in action and role models of professionalism and courtesy, caring and compassion.

Well-being at Work

Well-being at Work offers discounted and free activities and therapies to all staff employed by Leicester Hospitals to help them achieve a healthier lifestyle.

Activities include exercise classes, badminton, 5-a-side football, cricket, quiz nights, beauty therapists and lots more.

Pay and conditions

We offer a generous annual leave entitlement for all staff who join us of 27 days for a full year. This increases to 29 days after five years' service and 33 days after 10 years.

Access to Occupational Health services

The Trust provides a comprehensive Occupational Health service to all staff. A full range of services can be accessed including pre-employment health assessments, immunisation programmes, health and safety advice, health surveillance and infection control.

NHS Discounts

NHS Discounts is an independent discount resource for NHS employees. Staff can register and get discounts on services and a range of products.

(**SOURCE:** www.leicestershospitals.nhs.uk/aboutus/work-for-us/rewarding-its-best/)

Student activity: Using these examples or others you identify, try to reach a consensus with a group of fellow students on the scope of 'total reward' thinking and the kinds of issues it might address. The criteria included in the definitions section above may guide your judgements. Further questions to consider might include how the internal and external context of organisations influences total reward approaches.

9.3 A high-investment employment experience

In this section, we explore the non-financial aspects of 'total rewards' positioned in terms of deliberate managerial initiatives to align employees and work systems by moving beyond monetary-style 'incentives' to contribute to organisational performance. Relating the practices involved back to the discussion of 'efficiency wage' theory in Chapter 2, the underlying thinking may be viewed as investment- rather than cost-oriented, based on the assumption that 'investment returns' will follow, to be evaluated using 'HR metrics' (Beatty et al, 2007: 364). The ultimate aim for an effective total rewards strategy, therefore, is to produce 'a workforce that has the right people in the right jobs who are motivated and engaged to do the right things – and feel loyal to the organization and its success' (WorldatWork, 2019).

From this perspective, pay on its own is unlikely to be sufficient to achieve corporate goals through the employment relationship. And, although marking a progressive initial step, flexible administration of employee benefits may not go far enough for employers who wish to create a distinctive employment value proposition. Workforce members may regard flexible benefits as 'little more than an extension to the existing salary package and something, therefore, that can be matched by rival companies' (Richards and Hogg, 2007: 2). For maximum effect, in terms of obtaining competitive advantage through sourcing talented people and them achieving profitable high performance, the advice is to align organisational strategy with employee aspirations and needs into something that is hard for others to replicate.

Once organisational alignment with employee aspirations and needs becomes an organisational objective, the necessary question is one of identifying what those needs and aspirations are. By empowering employees to tailor a portfolio of rewards to match preferences that may differ among individuals and groups, and change over time (through the career life-cycle for example (Madhani, 2014)), the employer may be better able to highlight the financial value delivered to employees. So individuals are afforded the flexibility to construct a reward portfolio, making trade-offs between the various elements, and building understanding of the 'benefit' received from both active and passive benefits exemplified in Figure 9.1, comparing themselves with others, and how they are rewarded, inside and outside the organisation.

CASE STUDY 9.2

Customising total reward in practice

Indicative of the learning that takes place at each stage of the CaseCo Group journey, our insider HR specialist observes that:

> Relying on pay to achieve the things we want our line management to do was only abdicating line management to pay. What we found was that, in reality, the impact of pay is limited... unless you get it wrong – in which case it can have a significantly negative impact. Therefore, get pay right; then focus on the things that really do make a difference.
>
> We started to treat people on a much more individualised basis. With some 65,000 people, with a rich diversity of backgrounds and aspirations, it no longer made sense to treat them like one homogeneous group. We undertook detailed investigation into take-up trends across our flexible benefits programme (introduced in 2003). We found that there were some very clear patterns across particular groups of individuals (differentiated, for example, by age, length of service, and income). We cross-matched the data to our customer segmentation model and found that there were five main groupings that could be regarded as distinctive. Specific groups of

people were responding to different things in different ways, in terms of what they valued, where they 'spent their money' and how they liked to be communicated with.

From this it was a small step to conclude that we ought to be talking to key distinctive groups in different ways. Using the expertise developed in the Group's marketing function, under an umbrella brand, we radically changed our communications, tailoring them to the characteristics of each broad segment. The result was a disproportionate increase in take-up within our specifically targeted segments (those where take up had previously been lower than trend).

SELF-ASSESSMENT EXERCISE

In CaseCo Group the recognition of a plurality of different groups in the workforce led to a more individualised approach to communicating the total reward message.

In your organisation, or one with which you are familiar, what sort of groups might exist that have both different communication needs and different reward aspirations? Identify as far as possible what those needs and aspirations might be and consider the implications for the existing approach to reward in the organisation.

9.4 Unpacking the total reward employment experience

While the total reward ethos is holism, given the complex nature of the range of potentially interconnected parts, we will examine in this section of the chapter the total reward factors, namely, recognition; balance (of work and life); career or professional development; workplace environment and culture. Each element will be taken in turn – for description and reflection on accompanying positive and negative argument in the literature – before weighing the argument that the bundle is 'greater than the sum of its parts'.

9.4.1 *Recognition*

In a recent report, CIPD (2022d: 3) define recognition as

> … personal non-monetary rewards given to employees to acknowledge and reinforce their efforts, behaviour or achievements. They are usually set retrospectively, so are unexpected, and are relational and unconditional.

Recognition can encompass a range of different activities from small acts and gestures to all-company recognition awards, for example:

> ... personal compliments, positive feedback or thanks, announcing achievements, or presenting awards. They can be given verbally, via a thank-you card, company newsletters or noticeboards, or even with emojis.
>
> (CIPD, 2022d: 3)

According to the CIPD Reward Management Survey 2019, 38 per cent of UK respondent organisations use individual non-monetary recognition schemes to recognise performance (Marriot and Perkins, 2019). In the United States that figure could be closer to 81 per cent when all recognition schemes, including those for length of service, are included (WorldatWork, 2015). Recognition Professionals International (RPI) attributes 'strategic' status to employee recognition activities (RPI, 2015). Some organisations have indeed invested in developing fairly sophisticated employee recognition schemes that go beyond mere acknowledgment by management representatives of what an employee has done, to include a tangible, non-cash 'award'. A survey of 499 WorldatWork members in 2013 found that the most common tangible recognition award came in the form of a certificate or plaque (77 per cent); followed by gift vouchers (50 per cent); company logo merchandise (47 per cent); food (e.g. a celebratory lunch) (36 per cent); timepieces (32 per cent); and jewellery (31 per cent) (WorldatWork, 2013: 21).

Tracking the return on managerial investment, the same survey found 74 per cent of respondents agreed that their programmes were meeting objectives although only 10 per cent used return on investment (ROI) measures. An earlier assessment of the effects of formalised employee recognition appeared in a report published in the USA in February 2007 by the Institute for Corporate Productivity (i4cp), stating:

> While 73% of recently surveyed companies said that they have an employee recognition program in place... 37% of respondents said they do not know how satisfied their employees are with the program, and more than 15% said their employees are not satisfied at all.
>
> (i4cp, 2007)

A spokesperson for i4cp implied that managerial processes were at fault. Employee recognition was rated a key factor in the motivation of employees, linked to organisational outcomes, but it was argued that a system of checks and balances needed to be in place to make sure formal employee recognition arrangements did what management intended. The implication is that, where employee recognition is formalised, at least, holistic thinking is needed backed up by formal processes so that recognition is firmly located within the overall reward management system.

Hansen et al (2002) sound a cautionary note regarding the assumption that employee recognition can be organised managerially into an administrative procedure. They criticise commentary in which reward and recognition are treated as synonymous, arguing instead that the results of each approach reflect a dualistic impact on human motivation. Hansen et al (2002) ground their argument in theoretical commentary on human motivation, as discussed in Chapter 2 above. Citing

Herzberg's 'two-factor' approach and Maslow's 'needs hierarchy', Hansen et al (2002: 65) draw a distinction between extrinsic and intrinsic motivation stimuli. Relating this to reward and recognition, they argue that rewards should only be viewed instrumentally, as 'means-to-end' for 'doing chores'. This contrasts with the 'appreciating', 'honouring' and 'noticing' that they say should apply to recognition, even if that recognition is perceived managerially as encouraging and supporting an action. This is supported by research by Montani et al (2017) which suggests that manager and co-worker recognition promotes meaningfulness for employees and leads to work engagement and behavioural performance.

Hansen et al (2002) cite Deci's (1972) argument that intrinsic motivation is derived from an individual's changed perception related to competence – intrinsically motivating recognition is thus associated with an emphasis on 'competence feedback'. This compares with actions predicted to decrease intrinsic motivation, which for Hansen et al are those 'administered controllingly'.

> Recognition that is perceived to be superficial or frivolous will be seen as a veiled attempt to manipulate. It will undermine rather than support the intrinsic motivational processes it is designed to support.
>
> (Hansen et al, 2002: 69)

To avoid praise being viewed by an employee as attempted behavioural control, in the way that 'money or threats' may be perceived, so communicating to employees that their response should be similarly instrumental, the process needs to 'provide people with positive information about their self-competence' (Hansen et al, 2002: 66). Hence, following this line of reasoning, the actions that management plan for the various units of total reward need to be organised against the presence of two motivational sub-systems.

Intended employee recognition should be organised in accordance with the intrinsic motivational sub-system, delineated from the other half of the reward–recognition duality associated with extrinsic motivation. Whereas reward programmes that support extrinsic motivation have a finite life and desired behaviours may fall away as the programme degrades over time, Hansen et al (2002) argue that properly handled attention to recognition – whether the behaviours are specifically recognised or not – will ensure that how employees operate at work are continuously motivated 'from the inside out' (Hansen et al, 2002: 72).

Respecting the employee heterogeneity argument by Kinnie et al (2005), active acknowledgement of desired behaviours may offer management an important means by which to build positive relationships with specific employee communities. For example, Bergmann and Gulbinas Scarpello cite research scientists as likely to regard 'aspects of their work [as] more important than money' (2001: 584). The commentators argue that for such an employee group 'freedom to create and to discover' (2001: 584) is likely to encourage commitment to an employing organisation. We will return to these considerations when discussing career/professional development and workplace 'culture' below.

CASE STUDY 9.3

Employee recognition scheme: 'One and All Employee Awards' at Cornwall County Council

The aim of the project

The aim of the project was to deliver a fair and transparent recognition scheme which promotes the new Council behaviours and realises the following benefits:

- help create a positive work environment;
- encourage desired behaviours;
- motivate high performance;
- increase morale;
- support organisation mission/values;
- increase staff retention/decrease staff turnover;
- encourage loyalty;
- support a culture adaptable to change.

Background research or data

Following feedback from the Employee Engagement Group (EEG), issues highlighted from various surveys and best practice research it was identified that the existing scheme was not fit for purpose. Examples being that it was not timely as it was an annual scheme, with only approx. a six-week opportunity to make a nomination, there was no element of choice in terms of the manner in which the recognition was delivered and the award itself.

Best practice recommends that recognition should occur as close to the successful behaviour or achievement as possible, as this helps to reinforce the behaviours, activities and outcomes the employer wants to encourage. They should also be simple, flexible, fair and transparent.

Process followed

- Identify existing recognition processes (corporate and local) and ascertain what does and doesn't work.
- Research (i.e. internet, Investors in People (IIP), Chartered Institute of Personnel Development (CIPD)) best practice.
- Employee consultation such as recognition focus groups (with diverse range of employees in terms of sex, grade, services and locations), communications, surveys and the Council's employee voice group.
- Approval from the People and Workforce Board on the proposed scheme.
- Attend each Directorate Leadership team and Senior Leadership team to explain the scheme, its importance and how they can help make it a success.
- Market the scheme.
- Implement the new scheme in April 2017.

Outcome

The new scheme provides the opportunity for all employees, irrespective of any protected characteristic, role, grade, location, to equally participate in the scheme. The name of the new scheme was derived through an open competition for all employees, with the winning name being the 'One and All' awards. As well as being the motto on the Cornwall Coat of Arms it signifies the awards are open to everyone.

The new scheme provides all aspects of best practice as follows:

- Simple – it is one short simple form that can be completed and submitted online, or hard copy for those without intranet access. External nominations are taken from the compliments system. The categories are that of the council's behaviours as this helps reinforce them.
- Flexible – we can have up to eight winners per month, they don't have to be an even spread of categories or services. We carry out monthly surveys for all those nominated and all that that win in order to continually review the scheme and make changes where necessary.
- Fair and transparent – it is open to all employees and on a monthly basis we monitor the number of nominations per directorate, service and location in order that we can target additional marketing where needed. Judging is undertaken electronically via matrix scoring by a Strategic Director, Service Director and a previous winner (all from different directorates), these judges change each month.
- Provide choice – we provide choice in: how recognition is delivered, what award they would like to receive, whether or not they are happy for us to use their names on internal marketing, if they would like to attend the annual awards ceremony.
- Timely – the scheme is open all year round and within two days maximum of a nomination coming in, the nominee receives a congratulations email which provides the narrative of the reasoning of their nomination. Monthly winners are announced approx. the middle of the following month.

(**SOURCE**: Cornwall County Council, 2017)

The report goes on to say that between April and June 2017, 282 nominations had been received, 72 per cent of nominees surveyed said they felt engaged and encouraged by the nomination and 86 per cent said the nomination made them feel ecstatic or happy.

CASE STUDY QUESTIONS

Taking into consideration arguments outlined above regarding extrinsic and intrinsic motivation and the use of formal recognition schemes, discuss with fellow students:

1. What are the strengths of the 'One and All' Employee Awards as it has been designed and implemented?
2. How sustainable is such a scheme?
3. Are you surprised by the number of nominations and reactions of nominees?

9.4.2 Work–life balance and wellbeing

> Work–life balance is a term associated [on the one hand] with individual choice and responsibility; on the other hand, the term stands accused of obscuring global and interconnected issues that require reciprocal negotiation and changes between men and women, in their families, their workplaces, their communities and wider society.
>
> (Shearn, 2007: 601)

That dichotomy provides a setting for discussion of this element of total reward thinking that has become the subject of extensive commentary.

Notions of 'employee wellbeing', and concomitant managerial initiatives to combat workplace and work–life stress, may also be considered under the 'work–life' rubric, although running the risk of being perceived as little more than 'a clever re-labelling of traditional absence management, occupational health and good management practice' (CIPD, 2007a: 1). A more recent report by the CIPD is less equivocal: 'There is substantial evidence showing that employee health, well-being and engagement are important for organisational success' (CIPD, 2014d: 2). And certainly, the UK government's own research indicates that there is 'a prima facie case for employers to consider investing in the wellbeing of their employees on the basis of the likely performance benefits' (Bryson, Forth and Stokes, 2014). This conclusion is reached on the basis of evidence for a positive association between subjective well-being (SWB) and work performance and 'evidence which indicates that higher levels of SWB may lead to (cause) higher levels of job performance in some circumstances' (Bryson, Forth and Stokes, 2014).

DEFINITIONS

Well-being or wellness policies... are directed at improving the physical and mental health of employees through the provision of information, advice, education and services... Contemporary well-being policies are the modern expression of a long tradition of welfare work within personnel management. They are motivated by a number of concerns, including a desire to be a good employer, responsive to the needs of employees... and a belief that promoting employee well-being can reduce absenteeism and raise productivity.

Work-life balance is the principle that paid employment should be integrated with domestic life and community involvement in the interests of personal and social well-being. The UK government and major employers have endorsed this principle, reflecting growing concern that long hours of work may damage personal relationships and community cohesion.

Work-family integration is a term used by some in preference to the notion of work-life balance. The latter is felt to be unsatisfactory because it implies that work and domestic life are equivalent in terms of their import and priority for individuals. Work-family integration occurs when individuals do not experience work-family conflict and are able to integrate successfully their work and family demands.

Work-family conflict is a form of role conflict, in which the demands of paid employment, particularly those arising from the length and scheduling of working time, prevent the effective performance of family roles as spouse, parent, or carer.

(Heery and Noon, 2017)

At the European level, work–life balance (WLB) has been perceived as a central theme of the EU gender equality framework, although standards vary across member states with different welfare regime traditions (Idil Aybars, 2007). The 2011 WERS findings, however, suggest caution in generalising around managerial attention to balancing the demands of work and other commitments, accounting for firm sector. Indeed, the direction of travel since the previous WERS in 2004 suggests less, rather than more, managerial attention to WLB:

> Workplaces where the manager agreed that it was up to individual employees to balance their work and family responsibilities accounted for 70% of all employees in 2011, compared with 55% in 2004. In 2011, managers in the private sector were more likely to agree that employees were responsible for their work-life balance (78%) than managers in the public sector (67%).
>
> (van Wanrooy et al, 2013: 33)

Messersmith (2007) reviews research findings on 'work–life conflict', which he defines as 'a construct referring to the general interference that work life tends to have on an employee's personal life' (Messersmith, 2007: 430). The construct is 'a more general form of work–family conflict', defined by Greenhaus and Beutell (1985: 77, in Messersmith, 2007: 430) as 'a form of inter-role conflict in which the role pressures from the work and family domains are mutually incompatible in some respect'. An imbalance between work and employees' other activities can be exemplified as intrusions of work into family time and leisure activities. It may also be manifested in a general inability to stop thinking about employment-associated work even when physically moving out of the workplace to the home and personal environment.

While appearing to readily meet Knell's (2000) definition of the 'footloose worker' on whom employers have come to depend in the intelligence economy, peopled by Coyle's (2001) 'thinking feeling beings' whose labour converts the raw information to valuable organisational knowledge, Messersmith (2007) argues that employees in the information technology sector are more prone than most to work–life conflict. Consequently, learning to manage this conflict is posited as an important corporate challenge. The business case for managerial action is expressed in stark cost terms: as the experience of work–life conflict increases, especially among key professional employees, research suggests that both job satisfaction and commitment to organisational objectives decrease, leading to unplanned employee wastage among employees with high 'career mobility' potential (Messersmith, 2007).

One possible management response to work–life conflict within the total rewards portfolio is to establish 'family-friendly' and 'life-friendly' policies. Evaluators publishing lists of 'best place to work' organisations are reported to demand the 'big three' of on-site childcare, flexible work arrangements and 'accommodating' time off policies (Federico, 2007: 110). Social jobs and careers community Glassdoor.com recently released its Top 20 Companies for Work-Life Balance in the UK based on employee feedback alongside survey evidence from job-seekers that indicated WLB was a more important factor in deciding which job to apply for than either company culture or company finances. Characteristic features of WLB and wellbeing included flexible hours, working from home options, family-friendly work environments as well as ease of access to food and fitness amenities. Perhaps most notable was senior leadership's support of work–life balance and role-modelling good work-life practices in many of the companies on the list (Glassdoor, 2018). Policies to enable employees to work 'virtually', enabling employees with children and elder carers to meet calls on their time while working full- or part-time, appear central to achieving WLB. In addition, Messersmith argues (2007: 437–9):

> Virtual work reduces time-based conflict by reducing the number of hours an employee is asked to commute each week. Employees may enjoy significant time-savings in major metropolitan areas, allowing them to engage in more non-work-related activities.

While there appears to be a case in favour of virtual work as a form of 'family flexibility' employment, there are reported downsides. First, if the once-present boundary between work and personal life is severed, virtual work is actually predicted to increase levels of work–life conflict. Secondly, virtual work may not successfully reduce work–life conflict unless accompanied by a willingness on the part of employers to invest in establishing the technical infrastructure to facilitate it at both the organisation and the employee's home. Thirdly, there is a risk that isolation will cause 'virtual workers' to lose touch with informal intra-organisation networks, ultimately leading to a loss of promotion and advancement opportunities (Pinsonneault and Boisvert, 2001, cited in Messersmith, 2007).

Widening the critique still further, Eikhof et al (2007: 325) call for 'analysis that explores the back-story to work–life balance debate as well as the operation of work–life balance policies'. There is little, they argue, in the work–life debate that challenges work per se, especially the over-work phenomenon 'identified as a problem throughout the modern world' (Roberts, 2007: 334); and 'life' is too narrowly perceived, equating it with women's care work, hence the emphasis on 'family-friendly' polices (Eikhof et al, 2007). For Gambles, Lewis and Rapoport (2006, cited by Shearn, 2007: 601) work–life balance is no more than a myth arising from 'three critical tensions: the invasiveness of paid work, the need for time and energy to care about each other, and gender roles'.

As is so often the case, modern technology plays an ambiguous role here. The prevalence of internet-enabled mobile technology enables employees to achieve a level of WLB, allowing them to work virtually anywhere at any time, but because they can work at any time from any place, the expectation to do so increases as does the risk of blurring lines between work and non-work time. Research by Nam

(2014) suggests that using the internet and mobile technologies influences work–life balance experience across four WLB types:

- integration – frequent crossing of boundaries between the two domains 'work' and 'life';
- autonomy – the relaxation of one domain to meet the needs of the other;
- interference – interruption from one domain into the other;
- segmentation – compartmentalisation of competing role demands by operating each domain independently and maintaining boundaries between the two.

Nam (2014) also found that the consequences of using technology on WLB were complex and highly dependent on context. Use of mobile technology could both increase and decrease job satisfaction, job stress and overwork; for example, using the internet for work at home could increase workload and aggravate work-related stress, but using a mobile phone at work for a personal purpose could reduce job stress.

So, in the context of total reward, ensuring WLB practices are designed and implemented with critical appreciation of work-life conflict issues and the extent to which modern working practices can enable both positive integration of work and life or can create undesirable tension between the two.

CASE STUDY 9.4

Work–life balance considerations in practice

In CaseCo Group, WLB policies are seen as 'a critical way of engaging people and harnessing talent', according to our insider:

> Reflecting what I've already said about taking notice of the diversity of wants and needs among the people we employ, the view is that by accommodating these differences it helps us to recruit, retain, and 'engage' the people we need.
>
> We know (for example, from internal surveys of employee opinion, and from option take-up through flexible benefits), that people really do value the opportunity to balance their work and home life – a third of our staff now work reduced hours, and many more work flexibly in various patterns on an informal basis. So, again, if we provide people with the flexibility to create more balance, it is very likely that it will positively impact on their engagement in the organisation. Which, in turn, will ultimately feed through to bottom line results.
>
> If it's managed properly, flexible working is also a clear investment. Giving people the flexibility they need (as long as it's balanced with the needs of the organisation), we find, invariably leads to the individual giving more to the company – through greater flexibility and commitment on the part of the individual, as well as the fact that people tend to work more 'smartly' making much more effective use of time. Many individuals across the organisation will say that, by providing greater flexibility to balance their work and home life, it means they can actually give more to both.

STUDENT EXERCISE

Conduct a quick poll among people you know from your network of professional and wider contacts on what respondents say they understand by the terms 'work–life balance' (and its opposite); wellbeing; and flexibility around working life. Using the range of definitions you assemble, draw up a plan specifying ways in which business needs for committed and 'available' people can be achieved while satisfying employee aspirations.

9.4.3 Career or professional development

Specialist texts on employee resourcing and learning and development will provide a fuller commentary on career and professional development than we intend to here. Such material may, however, be complemented by examining arguments suggesting that the signals and benefits perceived by employees from managerial investment in their career and/or professional development should be positioned within the total reward envelope, while being mindful of Kinnie et al's (2005) caveat on workforce differences. WorldatWork (2017) identify three key areas of 'talent development' that sit within the total reward framework:

- learning opportunities;
- coaching and mentoring;
- advancement opportunities.

Access to learning opportunities – both formalised training and through a range of planned and corporately supported experience – may be perceived among workforce members as a form of 'progression', and so potentially valued as an intrinsic benefit. This is particularly the case where flatter organisational structures, designed to enhance lines of communication and responsiveness to market demands, limit traditional promotion opportunities and accompanying pay 'progression'.

Rather than experiencing work as something mechanical 'within an incomprehensibly huge machine', Kressler (2003: 33) argues that employees will feel 'rewarded' and enabled to attain personal development and self-actualisation if work is experienced 'as [making] a contribution to business objectives, as recognized performance, as… confirmation of personal and professional competence'. Thus, it is argued that work should be managed so as to fulfil the individual's 'desire for personal growth' as well as 'a need for belonging – to a business, a group or a profession, at least to something that imparts a positive value, including status and prestige' (2003: 33).

As a minimum, having a clear understanding of one's role eliminates wasted time and energy spent trying to work out the tasks that need to be completed and the internal and external customers with whom the employee is expected to communicate. This is particularly noteworthy during new employee induction/socialisation processes. Messersmith (2007, citing King et al, 2005) contends that, as a result, workers (particularly those in 'knowledge-intensive' roles) feel less role conflict and therefore are more likely to be committed to the organisation and have higher levels of job satisfaction. Actions may include allocating mentors, so connecting new entrants, for example, to more experienced employees.

A reality check on this upbeat line of argument is offered, however, by Marchington and Wilkinson, who contrast reports of the emergence of 'learning organisations', and 'knowledge management' with the view that 'it remains the case that in many workplaces access to training and development remains inadequate and partial' (2005: 218). Citing Herriot (1998), Marchington and Wilkinson (2005: 34) argue that the foundation of the contemporary 'psychological contract' is based on the principle that employees will offer the organisation 'flexibility, accountability and long hours' in return for provision of 'a good job' (as well as a high salary). A 'good' job is here understood, using criteria outlined by Marchington and Wilkinson (2005), as providing employees with:

- scope to exercise a range of skills and talents;
- a requirement to see an identifiable job through from start to completion;
- a sense of a significant role to perform, measured in terms of impact on others;
- autonomy and discretion in selecting methods and working time; and
- clear feedback on how performance is judged by supervisors.

Maximising these characteristics is expected to result in workforce members:

- experiencing meaningful work;
- having a sense of being responsible for outcomes; and
- gaining knowledge of the results of work activities.

Focusing in particular on high 'growth-need strength' workforce segments, the conclusion is that employees are more likely to secure a positive work experience (assessed in terms of their psychological state) if these principles are in evidence in work design and career management practices (Marchinton and Wilkinson, 2005).

Bergmann and Gulbinas Scarpello (2001) also single out specific workforce segments for attention. Workers in creative sectors and research and development roles are cited as exemplars of employee groups 'for whom aspects of their work are often more important than money'. Thus, a work environment needs to offer a setting – e.g. access to the latest technology, as well as room for autonomy – that will enable these people to create and discover (Bergmann and Gulbinas Scarpello, 2001: 584). Another route by which to 'reward' specialists (creatives and innovators) non-financially is through 'the creation of career paths that recognize members' particular skills' (2001: 584).

This rehearses a long-standing argument whereby standard career ladders are criticised on the ground that they lack the flexibility to accommodate routes to advancement for some workers other than moving into 'management'. Although offering tangible rewards commensurate with equivalent managerial levels, operating 'dual career ladders' permits 'researchers to continue to do what they do best, creating and innovating', something 'often more beneficial to both the researchers and the organization' (Bergmann and Gulbinas Scarpello, 2001: 584).

The general thrust of this argument may apply not just to particular occupational groups but also to public sector workers, noted earlier as actively seeking 'public service' employment because they wish 'to do something worthwhile' (PA Consulting Group, 2007). Another group, possibly emerging in all sectors, is one for whom 'meaningful work' may represent any work considered to be significant by the individual (Monnot and Beehr, 2014) which could include a range of socially or environmentally responsible activities. In the case of innovators, a more tangible recognition may of course be opportunities to share in the success of realisation and commercialisation of their inventiveness, so that patent rights and royalties do not simply pass to the employer, as has traditionally been the case (Bergmann and Gulbinas Scarpello, 2001).

Reflecting a 'resource-based' theoretical stance, Dyer and Ericksen argue that more than 'heavy investments in cutting-edge training and development' (2007: 275) are necessary if organisations are to be 'dynamic', in the sense of being flexible and ready to adapt to constantly changing business environments, and to build capabilities among a 'fluid' workforce that is not only valuable but also hard for competitors to replicate. Following this line of reasoning, one of the actions managements need to take is to 'provide unwavering support for employees who move from opportunity to opportunity in pursuit of smart risks that sometimes pay off in a big way but always result in highly valuable future oriented-learning even when they fail' (2007: 275–76).

Employees likely to succeed in such environments are perceived as expecting to be supported in this way, and to be assigned to roles that are not simply bundles of regular tasks with scope for innovation limited to 'other duties as assigned': instead core tasks are reduced to a minimum, with wide discretion to be constantly on the look-out for new challenges as well as new ways of meeting familiar ones. Creating a mind-set attuned in this way, it is argued, will create an enriched talent pool as well as retaining talented individuals and groups who otherwise might pursue more rewarding job design elsewhere or at best not perform to corporate expectations. Evidence from WERS 2011 appears to bear this reasoning out. Despite employees reporting increased work intensity, the study also found an increase job satisfaction which the authors attribute, at least in art, to a parallel increase in job-based autonomy (van Wanrooy et al, 2013).

'Strategic workforce planning' has been advocated by The Conference Board under the rubric of 'forecasting human capital needs to execute business strategy' (Young, 2006). But Isles (2007: 107) criticises a 'dearth of formal internal succession plans for even senior positions'. He argues that a propensity among talented people to switch organisations, enhanced by 'broadening geographic mobility', among other things, to improve their 'employability and earnings potential' (2007: 107) might help explain the interest in 'talent management'. Here 'talent' is not only a form of trait, 'the sum of a person's abilities'; it is also vested in 'opportunity', 'because talent requires opportunity to be displayed' (2007: 107). Talent management initiatives may not only exist to extract the value of talent for the organisation's benefit; the result may be viewed under the total reward rubric as another way in which to retain key workforce segments who might otherwise depart in response to offers of 'the right culture [providing] self-fulfilment, a sense of accomplishment and emotional attachment in their employment' (2007: 107).

Isles (2007) identifies a combination of talent management practices, including work design initiatives, actions to foster relationships via mentoring and coaching, and encouragement for networking between individuals and their functional areas for mutual benefit. Of course, yet again rehearsing Kinnie et al's (2005) diversity argument, different talent segments (e.g. 'player managers' in financial services, compared with research and development specialists in manufacturing) may need different talent management initiatives to enable them to add value and so feel recognised.

Career and professional development as features within total reward may thus be seen as aligning reward management with employee resourcing policies and practices: one aspect of providing skilled people with the sense that the organisation is an 'engaging' place to be compared with alternatives on offer. While tangible reward in the short run may not be the issue, employees may make connections between actions taken to manage their professional careers that they value immediately while perceiving the link with longer-term higher earnings potential. In a 'letter from the chair' in the CIPD Reward Forum Newsletter, Clive Wright has argued that actively securing connections between employee reward and initiatives like 'strategic workforce planning' helps HR specialists to demonstrate direct 'business' support for the organisation, consequently making it difficult for managers to 'opt out'.

STUDENT EXERCISE

The explicit connections between a range of HR policies and practices, including career and professional development, under the total reward rubric has been discussed in this section of the chapter.

Discuss the ways in which people professionals might help line managers identify initiatives for creating a 'high-investment workplace'.

9.4.4 Workplace environment and culture

A range of commentary under this heading may be found in the employee relations literature, as well as wider HRM writing, discussing managerial style and the contexts in which employees may individually and collectively participate in managerial decision taking at work (e.g. Ackers et al, 2003; Johnstone and Ackers, 2015; Marchington et al, 2001). This non-financial form of 'partnership' differs from, although may complement, employee financial participation, for example, through profit share schemes and employee share option plans, described in Chapter 6. As in the case of career and professional development, the intention is not to replicate specialist material developed elsewhere at greater length, but to briefly consider the ways in which this strand of the total reward framework may be understood, standing in proximity to other organisational and people management activity.

In the UK government-commissioned *Good Work: The Taylor Review of Modern Working Practices* (Taylor, 2017), six high level indicators of 'quality work' were identified based on pan-European QuInnE project research:

- wages;
- employment quality;

- education and training;
- working condition;
- work–life balance;
- consultative participation and collective representation.

There are clearly elements of this framework that overlap with aspects of the total reward rubric already examined in this chapter, but it is working conditions and consultative participation, essentially worker autonomy and voice, that we consider in this section, what Taylor (2017: 15) describes as:

> A greater voice, in the organisational decisions that affect your job can make people feel better about their work. It can also add to a more collegiate environment between management and staff, boosting the feeling of fulfilment and increasing productivity. The Review heard that for many having no say in the way they work had negative impacts on their wellbeing.

Employee voice, and the culture it operates within, have been identified as crucial drivers of employee engagement by the Engage for Success project (MacLeod and Clarke, 2009; Institute for Employment Studies & CIPD, 2014). Research in 2010, with Kingston Business School, found that engagement was driven by a number of factors, the most important being: 'meaningful work, voice, senior management communication style and vision, supportive work environment, person–job fit and line management style' (Alfes et al, 2010).

Marchington and Cox (2007) point to possible problems if line managers do not share the principles adopted by employee communications and involvement policy architects, or lack the skills to handle related procedures and their consequences in terms of employee response. This may help explain why senior management intentions for this aspect of the non-financial rewards bundle may not be precisely translated into practice. Line managers 'act as the interface between the organisation and the employee' and therefore 'can do much to impact on engagement' if their 'potential to be engaging leaders' is maximised (Alfes et al, 2010).

At WorldatWork's Total Rewards 2023 Conference in San Diego, USA, Lora Lawler, Senior Vice President of Total Rewards at Hilton Hotels, spoke about Hilton's initiatives intended to help facilitate a 'culture of belonging' (Christie, 2023). These initiatives included an organisation-wide series of 'Courageous Conversations' in which employees shared personal stories about their struggles to 'navigate issues such as race, mental health and well-being'. She also said that the company's total reward philosophy was built on a culture where employees can answer 'yes' to the following questions:

> Am I welcome here?
>
> Am I healthy?
>
> Can I grow here?
>
> Am I part of something bigger than my job?
>
> (Christie, 2023)

Although it can increase employee commitment and satisfaction levels, creating the conditions for an inclusive workplace environment and a culture in which employees have a voice under the total reward rubric is not without risk (Richards and Hogg, 2007). A significant ideological and practical commitment is required from management at all levels and there are risks for employees too. Messersmith (2007) balances the argument that 'high-involvement work practices' may serve as 'buffering mechanisms' that reduce the negative consequences of work–life conflict with a possible downside:

> Despite the importance of involvement in sustaining job satisfaction and organizational commitment, involvement can have negative consequences [with] several studies linking career identity salience with the number of hours worked and ultimately to work–life conflict.
>
> (Messersmith, 2007: 433)

STUDENT EXERCISE

Discuss perceived priorities and risks in locating workplace culture and environment within the total reward portfolio in fast-paced, knowledge-intensive organisations.

9.5 Total reward: Greater than the sum of its parts?

So, what may be discerned from the unravelling and review of elements attributed to the total reward bundle over the preceding pages of this chapter? Is it reasonable to assume that the whole is greater than the sum of the parts?

Singly, the experience of being recognised, enabled to address work–life conflicts and support personal wellbeing, trained and developed, located in a skills-matched career path, or involved in workplace decision-making may have a functional role. But, taken together, experiencing HR practices may have 'a non-instrumental role in both reflecting and reinforcing organisational climate' (Kinnie et al, 2005: 11). Informed by social exchange theory, the researchers argue that, when positive, these reactions constitute a sensation among employees of a personal commitment to them by the employer, mediated in particular through the relationship with the individual's immediate supervisor. The organisation is rewarded, in turn, by reciprocal 'affective' commitment (Purcell, 2006), that is, the employee shares the organisation's values and is likely to offer discretionary behaviour and task performance helpful to achievement of organisational goals.

CASE STUDY 9.5

Aligning 'business case total reward' strands in practice

Having 'got the basics right', our CaseCo Group insider says, 'we moved on to focus on what really does make a difference' in the relationship between CaseCo Group and people employed across the group company. The 'basics' involved: (1) creating market-informed 'salary zones', balancing internal and external equity; (2) creating a sense of distributive justice by giving people a share in business success with meaningful variable pay, funded by business performance and then distributed according to individual achievement over the relevant performance cycle; and (3) enabling flexible benefits choices.

> Our focus is on the complementary themes of diversity, choice and flexibility. We're making progress in managing total reward through branding, communication, and marketing. At this stage in the journey, total reward is still in the domain of the more tangible elements. Moving further along the spectrum [see Figure 9.2] means having an answer to the question – What's it like to work here? What do we stand for? What does our employment brand comprise?
>
> We tested hypotheses that once pay is managed properly, the drivers of people's performance, motivation, and engagement are much more likely to be founded in the non-pay arena. Our internal research was consistent with this proposition. For example, we talked to people about what they really valued and found that an overwhelming number of people came back stating that they would really value greater flexibility. This was perhaps unsurprising. However, more importantly, behind this, we found that an equally large proportion of our people (some 85 per cent) were also saying that if we gave them more flexibility it would change the way they felt about CaseCo Group for the better. This formed the base for one of the strands of our business case: we have measured the take-up – and the attitudinal change – and shown really positive results.
>
> Also, if you are spending a significant amount of money on benefits (to give an example, £100 million p.a.) and people are only valuing part of this – or may not even be aware of all that is there – then there is a risk of a significant value loss. We tested this with our employees and found out that, on an extrapolated basis, people were only valuing 80 per cent of the true spend. Now, on the one hand, by helping raise people's awareness of the total spend and, on the other hand, making sure that people have access to things that they actually want, we reasoned that closing this gap by just two percentage points offered a saving worth £2 million in otherwise destroyed value.

The summary position is illustrated in Figure 9.3.

Figure 9.3 Business case total reward strands in CaseCo Group

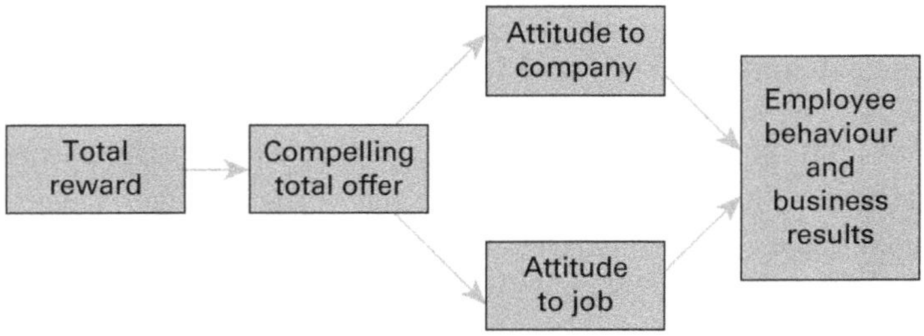

The rhetoric of total reward has come under fire recently for being increasingly meaningless in a post-recessionary environment where downward pressure on pay and economic insecurity are endemic. Brown (2014) argues that the reality in today's organisations is that reward professionals are increasingly isolated and out of touch with employees. Citing an IES report finding that HR has become 'stuck in administrative and cost-reduction-focused, routine processes' and is 'seen as inefficient and powerless' (Hirsh, 2008 cited in Brown, 2014), Brown goes on to claim that:

> Employers have clung to the rhetoric of total reward strategies, claiming for the past two decades to be replacing inflexible, paternalistic, fixed-cost–focused rewards with attractive business and employee-driven, flexible packages. In reality, many were simply following market practice and, in the United Kingdom, looking for tax and national insurance contribution savings in areas such as pension contributions and child care provision.
>
> (Brown, 2014: 48)

Questioning whether total reward is out-dated and 'dead' as a concept (Paton, 2014) may well reflect the scepticism shown towards total reward's popular incarnation as a consultancy staple with little academic underpinning or empirical evidence-base. Ironically, just as its validity is being questioned in the practitioner field, research is emerging to show that, in some areas at least, the principles of non-financial reward can indeed attract the 'footloose' talent required by the knowledge and service economies. Schlechter, Thompson and Bussin (2015) investigated whether the presence of non-financial aspects that would typically make up a total reward package (work–life balance, learning and career advancement) would influence the perceived attractiveness of a job offering. Their findings indicate that this is indeed the case and it is particularly so for women. Certainly, many people professionals appear to support the premise of total reward as the future of reward management. As one participant in Pattnaik and Padhi's (2023: 153) research on the pandemic-driven move toward more compassionate total reward put it, the future of reward is about the move 'from being cash-based and tangibles to experience-based and intangibles'.

This chapter has explored arguments made for managerial proactivity in combining elements on extrinsic and intrinsic, financial and non-financial aspects of the reward package in order to better recognise, reward and motivate employees to perform and behave in organisationally desired ways. In a period of continued economic uncertainty, the attractiveness for organisations of non-financial reward is unlikely to be questioned, but it is being increasingly recognised that the idea of being able to engage and motivate employees through a 'notionally employee-driven, flexible package of 'chocolate box' benefits bundled together under the brand total reward' (Paton, 2014) is unlikely to either satisfy employees nor fulfil organisational expectations for improved performance.

A crucial point is organisations recognising that non-financial reward does not necessarily equate with low investment. Brown (2014: 147) argues for 'smarter' rewards which provide:

> A simpler and clearer focus on a few core values and principles, a stronger basis in evidence and measurement, more emphasis on employee engagement through rewards and improved and more open communications and line management of reward.

SELF-ASSESSMENT EXERCISE

Draw up a total reward 'balance sheet' with 'assets' and 'liabilities'.

What would you include on the side of 'assets'? i.e. what are the 'gains' for the organisation in applying a total reward approach?

What would you include as questions that might feature on the 'liabilities' side of the balance sheet? i.e. what are the total reward 'costs' to the organisation?

Using this balance sheet as a starting point, what sort of business case can you make for a total reward approach in your organisation?

9.6 Conclusions and key learning points

It may be concluded from the foregoing review that non-financial rewards are multi-faceted, and may be interpreted differently depending on the recipient. As such, policy design and application informed by total reward principles are complex, and demand careful reflection as well as a willingness by senior managers and HR specialists to involve employees and the line managers on whom successful practice largely depends. Choices are necessary to commit to investment in non-financial rewards, accepting as a consequence the need for management time allocation to be built into the process – accepting the need to address possible tensions where the priority seems to be a swift response to environmental context beyond the organisation.

In reflecting on non-financial rewards, people professionals will wish to consider the following:

- Evolution in employment systems is reported as creating the conditions under which what is included in the effort–reward bargain needs to be rethought, especially when managements wish to secure discretionary effort and a sense of identification among employees for whom 'pay and benefits' provide only part of the employer's consideration.

- While flexible benefits may go some way to addressing workforce diversity issues, ideas grouped under 'total reward' are promoted by commentators as building blocks for still further customisation, with the prospect of achieving a distinctive employment proposition.
- Definitions of non-financial reward are multi-faceted and often complex, requiring dissection of the elements to facilitate detailed cost–benefit analysis while simultaneously seeking to promote holistic 'employment experience' value greater than the sum of the parts.
- To interpret and evaluate the alternatives and possible consequences of a total rewards approach, it is helpful to apply multidisciplinary theoretical lenses.
- Research findings suggest that senior managers and total rewards policy designers need to pay particular attention to the role of frontline managers if expectations from investment in employee engagement using total rewards are not to be misplaced.
- Unpacking the total reward portfolio may bring tensions to the surface between the reward elements and their management, which managements need to reflect on carefully, to be clear about what may be necessary to mitigate and compromise on before committing to strategic decisions that may be deemed unsuitable for the organisation, its principals and/or workforce members.
- The ethical and moral dimensions of ideological initiatives intended to secure voluntary identification between individual employees and the organisation need to be understood and acted on in framing policy choices and their detailed application.

Explore further

For a comprehensive, but non-critical, guide to creating a total reward approach, see the US-oriented *WorldatWork Handbook* (2021) 2nd edn (edited by Dan Cafaro).

For an evidence-based view of employee engagement strategies and organisational outcomes see Alfes, K, Truss, C, Soane, EC, Rees, C and Gatenb, M (2010) *Creating An Engaged Workforce. Findings From The Kingston Employee Engagement Consortium Project*, London: Chartered Institute of Personnel and Development.

For a critique of total reward approaches, see Brown, D (2014) The future of reward management: from total reward strategies to smart rewards, *Compensation & Benefits Review*, vol. 46, no. 3, pp. 147–51.

PART FOUR

In the three chapters that make up Part Four, specific attention is focused on approaches to rewarding employees who have a direct influence on corporate governance, as well as the reward management implications of organisational expansion requiring transnational knowledge mobilisation. Finally, attention turns specifically to questions around alignment between organisational strategy, HRM and employee reward management as a systemic whole.

10
Rewarding directors and executives

CHAPTER LEARNING OUTCOMES

At the end of this chapter, you should understand and be able to explain the following:

- The constitution of reward for directors and other senior executives and related developments in corporate governance requirements surrounding executive reward management design and practice.
- Detailed design and reporting considerations associated with rewarding directors and other senior executives.
- Argument and evidence to facilitate sober assessment of debates surrounding this high profile, politically sensitive field of employee reward activity.

CIPD STRATEGIC REWARD MANAGEMENT (7HR03) LEARNING OUTCOMES

Learners will be able to:

3.4 Examine the role of remuneration committees in determining and managing executive reward packages.

4.1 Critically discuss the key legal requirements relating to pay and reward and the implications of non-compliance.

10.1 Introduction: Context for rewarding directors and executives

In May 2023, the CEO of the London Stock Exchange, Julia Hoggett, stated that 'The efficacy of London's capital markets ecosystem has been an important topic of discussion recently, but one critical element that has not received enough attention is the UK's approach to executive compensation.' Her argument was that 'attracting and retaining domestic and international talent... to support the creation of globally consequential companies in the UK to drive innovation, jobs and growth in the economy is something that UK listed company boards and their executive leadership teams strive to do every day. ... And yet, very often, this talent objective is hampered by the advice and analysis of the proxy agencies and some asset managers voting against executive pay policies even when those pay levels are significantly below global benchmarks.' The conclusion was: 'It is essential to have a constructive discussion with all stakeholders about a topic that tends to generate emotion and strong views' (Hoggett, 2023).

Four years earlier the *Financial Times* reported a 'blistering attack' by Bill Winters, CEO of Standard Chartered, on investors 'who staged a protest against his pay'. Some 40 per cent of the bank's investors were reported as having 'declined to back the lender's new remuneration policy at its annual meeting' (FT, 2019a). Such cases illustrate a shift among the 'competing interest streams' involved in regulating executive remuneration (Perkins, 2017). 'Outrage' among stakeholders is no longer containable under the guise of 'market pricing'. The remuneration committee (Remco) chair, Christine Hodgson, faced what an institutional investor labelled a 'concerted backlash' at StanChart's 2020 annual general meeting 'if she fails to step up, admit error and act decisively' (FT, 2019a). The controversy was viewed as going to the root of whether UK corporate governance is to be regarded as fit for purpose: 'non-executives must be prepared to stand up against aggressive executives to assert correct procedure and behaviours' (FT, 2019a).

This chapter addresses an area that occupies a significant proportion of the energies of corporate human resource specialists, as well as the decision-makers they advise. CIPD commentary helps us to understand the context for this arguably disproportionate focus on 'top pay'. The report's title demonstrates the way the issue and the role of key institutions associated with executive reward management is being framed:

> Remco Reform: Keeping executive pay in check and governing successful organisations that benefit everyone
>
> (CIPD, 2019d)

Less exercised with the talent management orientation championed by the London Stock Exchange CEO, for the CIPD the focus for governing successful organisations, an issue that became especially prominent in the wake of problems arising internationally in 2008–09, was unacceptable risk-taking:

> The financial crisis has put the issue of executive pay under the spotlight, bringing to prominence the concern that executive compensation arrangements may have

> contributed to excessive risk-taking. This sits alongside a longer-standing concern around the increase in the remuneration of executives relative to other employees.
>
> (Lupton et al, 2015: 30)

In other words, outcomes and processes associated with this aspect of reward management need to be understood as a corporate governance problem; they also relate to socio-economic concerns around equity in the effort bargain extended to different organisational workforce segments. General commentary it seems has now caught up with the analysis offered by Perkins and Hendry (2005), even if practice has not yet extended to taking up their concluding suggestion: '(not entirely whimsically) that the greatest contribution to effective corporate governance in the area of pay that legislation or codes of practice might make is the appointment of a social scientist as an observer to remuneration committees with a brief to report on their functioning' (Perkins and Hendry, 2005: 1465).

A plethora of high level investigations and regulatory pronouncements has set out to rebalance the systemic influences on corporate reward management applicable to company directors and to other executives who Walker (2009), investigating reward practices applicable in banking and financial services, refers to as 'high-end' employees (i.e. individuals potentially earning more than £1m annually). See Key Issue in Reward 10.1 for a brief description of the special status of directors – who may combine the role of officeholder and employee – and Table 10.2 for a tabulated summary of corporate governance initiatives since 1992 impacting on executive reward management.

In the debates around rewarding executives some have used a 'market forces' argument to explain high levels of remuneration and other employment benefits. However, following the financial crisis, in resetting the context for regulation the British government has adopted a more behavioural economics perspective (Samson, 2014): 'Market discipline proved to be an ineffective constraint on risk-taking in financial markets [with] banks' remuneration policies [having] added to the riskiness of the financial system, as they focused too much on short-term profit.' Informed by their empirical research, Perkins and Hendry (2005) anticipate this conclusion, arguing, 'Ordering top pay may prove to be contingent more on 'communication' than performance management considerations' (2005: 1464). They draw attention to reward management as a social, not simply economic process (Perkins and Shortland, 2022). The High Pay Commission similarly has argued that reliance on market forces is to misunderstand how markets work at their best: again accenting communication, a report suggests that developments in pay among high-end groups represent an economic market distortion: executive pay outcomes are 'patently not linked to performance' and send out 'the wrong message... clearly a symptom of a poorly functioning market' (High Pay Commission, 2011: 11; see also Hutton, 2011).

Perkins (2015) reframes the top pay debate comparing and contrasting perspectives that privilege economics, in particular agency theory (Jensen and Meckling, 1976) and optimal contracting theory (Bebchuk and Freid, 2013) with more sociological frames of reference: managerial power theory (Pfeffer and Salancik, 1977) and upper echelon theory (Hambrick and Mason, 1984). These ideas are reviewed further later in the chapter. A further perspective draws on psychological theorising to help understand 'sorting and incentive impacts of pay structures on the propensity [among high-end employees] to take risks' (Pepper and Campbell, 2014: 6). This builds on work by Wright et al (2007) and Wowack and Hambrick (2010), with the latter writers arguing that absent from the theoretical literature is the question of the impact of personal differences among those targeted by executive reward policies and practices.

A key expectation underlying the extensive corporate governance system and its interaction with systems of executive reward management is that, rather than the 'invisible hand' featuring in classical economics theorising, formal **supervision** should be visibly human. The expectation applies especially to stock market listed corporations (underpinned by the UK Corporate Governance Code, 2018, Statutory Instrument No. 1981 Large and Medium Companies Accounts and Reports (Amendment) Regulations 2013 and, in the case of banking and financial services, the Financial Services Act, 2010), but with the net increasingly spread to include not-for-profit organisations. As will be discussed below, ideas from agency theory have been strong drivers in this more 'institutional perspective' (internal, planned systemic drivers of action rather than 'free' market forces) informing regulation and compliance – with the latter concerns arguably having become dominant over the recruit, retain, motivate mantra traditionally associated with reward management applicable to the workforce generally. The role of HR specialists involved in executive reward management has taken on as much a regulatory compliance function as one related to helping shape the effort bargain.

In order to be judged legitimate, decisions about the levels and make-up of executive reward and processes for earning and managing it are expected to be **transparent**. Making public the details of executive reward management – once regarded as privileged information – has been prompted by criticisms about a lack of independent scrutiny of rewards to executive directors, during a period where the gap between those on 'top' and minimum levels of reward from employment has grown, for example, with Hargreaves (2019: 5) arguing that 'in the UK and US those in the top 0.1 per cent of the income scale [are] pocketing nearly six per cent of national income – a level last seen in the 1920s, just before the Great Depression'. Criticism has been compounded by reports of executive reward in both private and public sectors rising faster than that available to median and low earners, where 'CEOs gain at the expense of others' (Hallock, 2012: 4). A lack of evidence of alignment between performance and reward levels has further fuelled media hyperbole – in extreme cases provoking so-called 'rewards for failure' accusations, when executives were shown receiving large payoffs, including enhanced contributions to guaranteed pensions, to step down following inadequate levels of organisational performance.

Within the banking and financial services sector, the transparency imperative has been associated with accusations that a 'bonus culture' played a central role in developments leading up to the financial crisis and its adverse consequences for governments and their citizens (White and Hollingsworth, 2018). A more ethically nuanced factor – **fairness** – has also surfaced where the interconnectedness of the UK's business system and the wider social system have been explicitly spotlighted (Flammer, Hong and Minor, 2019). Author of a UK government commissioned report to investigate 'fair pay in the public services', although in practice serving as a moral benchmark for all sectors, the economist Will Hutton, implicitly adopts an open systems oriented tone when he states (2010a):

> When the economy grew there were fewer concerns about fairness in general and fair pay in particular. Now the economy is under pressure, how fairly society distributes its benefits and burdens has suddenly become more pressing.

With these interconnected systemic issues in mind, we discuss below the need to locate developments and the assessment of outcomes in executive reward and its management within a political rather than purely managerial frame of reference. We then outline and comment on the ways reward for directors and other executives may be approached, in particular the role and accountabilities of 'remuneration committees' (hereafter, Remcos) that, depending on their legal status, boards have to or choose to establish with the aim of bringing independence to setting and monitoring the executive effort-reward bargain, and complying with stakeholder reporting expectations on how these accountabilities have been discharged. Drawing on theory headlined in this introductory section and published research findings, the issues under consideration are weighed to illustrate the kinds of consequences that may follow specific choices in managing executive reward and corporate governance systems, thereby informing HR professionals in selecting their approach.

The generic term 'executive reward' will be used throughout the chapter to cover reward issues at corporate director level as well as related to other senior organisational managers and 'high-end' employees. It should be noted that while company board officeholders share equal legal accountability for oversight of the business, the non-executives elected to the board have, under the contemporary regulatory regime, been charged with playing a professionalised role in governing the reward arrangements applicable to their 'executive' colleagues (Shortland and Perkins, 2023). In addition, regulatory instruments and guidelines have come to emphasise the responsibility on management consultants advising Remcos and to the institutional shareholders the 'principals' to whom their 'agents' on corporate boards primarily account for their behaviour and their organisations' commercial performance, to assure adherence to best practice, respectively, in consulting ethics and stewardship (Dive, 2022; Lozano-Reina and Sánchez-Marín, 2020). See the 'Explore further' section for details.

KEY ISSUES IN REWARD MANAGEMENT 10.1

The company director

A company director is an officer charged with the conduct and management of a company's affairs. A director may be an 'inside' or 'executive' director (a senior management employee who is also an officer of the company, such as the finance director or marketing director) or an 'outside' or non-executive director (sometimes referred to as an 'independent director'). The directors collectively are referred to as a board of directors. In the UK and the USA, a so-called unitary board is constituted, whereas in continental Europe companies' operational and supervisory aspects may be formally separated by the constitution of two-tier board arrangement.

The (normally full-time) executive members of a company board are a special class of company 'employee', with an officeholder's service agreement distinguishing the appointee from other employees contracted to work for the firm. While their obligations were previously subject to common law provisions (in the UK), Part 10 Chapter 2 of the Companies Act 2006 fully implemented in 2009 specifies directors' duties in a statutory statement 'in place of the corresponding equitable and common law rules' (Linklaters, 2006: 1).

The duties of directors include provisions that require them to act in ways likely to promote the company for the benefit of members of the company as a whole; to exercise reasonable care, skill and diligence; to exercise independent judgement; and to avoid conflicts of interest. It is the latter statement that holds relevance in the case of the actions board members take in settling directors' remuneration. Arguably, this places directors – as managers of corporate assets – in a situation where their interests (in achieving employment benefits) may conflict with their duties to promote the benefits of the company and its members, in particular those who have a claim on residual assets. The appointment of an independent remuneration committee (composed exclusively of non-executive members) to oversee and account for the determination of executive directors' rewards, featuring in corporate governance guidelines, is derived specifically from this position.

Individuals may be part of a senior management team established and led by the chief executive whose collective function is to oversee the firm's operations, but these officers may not necessarily be a company director. (In practice this suggests an informal parallel with the two-tier governance structure referred to above.) However, both the UK Corporate Governance Code and the Walker Report indicate that the remit of Remcos includes reward policy applicable to the senior corporate executive team and other senior employees, in the interests of good governance and consistency of approach.

A further point to bear in mind when considering approaches to directors' and other executive-level rewards, compared with other employee groups, is the relative impact on organisational performance attributable to executives. Dive (2002) explains that, while all work in organisations will have an 'operational' side, towards the top of the hierarchy, the emphasis is on 'strategic' action; that is where discretion over decision-taking and attendant resource allocation is such that attainment of corporate purpose may be significantly influenced. Trade-offs are determined here, based on interpretation of opportunities and threats to the organisation's overall future health. And at executive level the average time necessary to complete the portfolio of tasks for which the individual is accountable is relatively greater than at subordinate levels, providing a rationale for performance incentives similarly targeted over the longer term. Although the question of what constitutes 'long-term' in relation to executive reward outcomes has become a debating point, with recent regulatory requirements proposing a controversial period over which even when earned, money can be clawed back from individuals if subsequent corporate performance falls short of expectations (Pyzoha and Jenkins, 2019).

The *Financial Times* reported in June 2015 that the UK's Prudential Regulation Authority and Financial Conduct Authority had announced plans to let banks take back bonuses from senior managers for up to 10 years in the event of misconduct or risk management failures. The period extended to a maximum of seven years if staff were 'material risk takers'. Long-term incentive rewards are expected to have a comparatively external rather than inwardly focused orientation, relevant to ways in which behaviour and decision-making by high-end employees can positively or negatively impact on the value of financial investors' stakes in the business. A practical illustration appears later in the chapter (Table 10.3), an example of a typical FTSE 100 executive remuneration framework which contains a section intended to illustrate the nature and timeframe over which executive performance, aligned with incentive plans, is tracked.

STUDENT EXERCISE

Comparative reward management, culture and organisational systems

Orlagh Hunt, HR director of a large British insurance company, RSA, was quoted during the consultation phase on proposed regulations on banking and other financial services sector organisations as cautioning the Financial Services Authority (FSA) against a singular focus on curbing pay levels. Implicitly adopting a more systemic starting point for reform, she argued for attention to organisational structures and culture in the sector, to understand and correct behaviours associated with excessive risk taking. As the *Economist* (2010) puts it, even if an organisation can show itself to tick all the boxes to demonstrate compliance with corporate governance standards, this 'cannot make up for a toxic corporate culture'. As one way of making executive reward management 'more ethical', CIPD research and policy adviser Charles Cotton (2018) calls for recognition that 'business success is a collective endeavour. Too often, corporate achievement is ascribed to the efforts of those at the top and that is where pay is concentrated.' To address this, he calls on HR professionals 'to ensure that there is more alignment through the organisation over how individuals are rewarded relative to their contribution'.

For Hunt the organisational problem has been the relative influence corporately of large business units compared with the risk management function. The implication is that voices arguing for prudential behaviour were ignored or overlooked. Hunt is quoted as agreeing with the then City minister Lord Myners that 'there must be an end to short-term bonus cultures' (Churchard, 2009: 6). However, proposals then being floated to impose caps on base pay levels were judged as likely to carry detrimental consequences in the form of a 'flight of talent' to financial centres in jurisdictions with lighter regulatory regimes. Hunt argues that such a move could drive even more risk taking. The problem is that 'some of what drives those ridiculous bonuses is that base pay is relatively small in comparison with the package' making up financial services executives' rewards (Churchard, 2009: 6).

In the UK government's 'mini-budget' in autumn 2022, a proposal was introduced to scrap the cap on bankers' bonuses. Despite the change of Chancellor and reversal of most of that budget's proposals, that proposal was retained. The rationale was 'to boost growth through a post-Brexit shake-up of the rules covering the financial sector' (Race, 2022):

> City bosses have long complained about the EU-wide bonus rules which cap bonuses at twice an employee's salary, arguing they lead to higher base pay that pushes up banks' fixed costs.
>
> Unlike bonuses, those costs cannot be adjusted in line with the firm's financial performance, they add, making the UK a less attractive place to locate their business than the US or Asia.
>
> (Race, 2022)

Criticising the move the TUC General Secretary, Frances O'Grady, argued: 'Everyone who works for a living deserves to earn a decent living, but ministers are holding down the pay of millions of key workers, while lining the pockets of City financiers' (Race, 2022). The union body cited findings that bonuses in the financial sector were at their highest ever recorded level, worth around £20,000 pa on average.

Consider and discuss the following propositions:

- Capping salaries for banking and financial sector employees risks encouraging 'talent flight' out of the country to more lightly regulated jurisdictions.
- An absence of 'sensible base pay' leads to risk taking among financial sector executives.
- Excessive bonus payments to financial sector executives are the product of an imbalance in the influence of risk management specialists compared with operational executives.
- The primary focus for financial services regulatory attention is on cultural issues.

10.2 What do executives earn, how does it compare with other employees, and what are the arguments for and against?

A few years ago Vicky Wright, a CIPD Past President, was reported as stating that discovering the details of executive reward 'is a bit of a forensic exercise... Oddly enough, there is a view that directors make more than they actually do' (Newing, 2007). Tyson (2005) advises looking to data residing in surveys such as those produced by large management consultancies to help answer the questions.

Help is at hand in the form of a joint study by the CIPD and High Pay Centre (2019), which found that Median FTSE 100 CEO pay (including salary, bonus, long-term incentive plan, benefits and pension contributions) for the financial year ending 2018 was £3.46 million (compared with £3.97 million in 2017). Almost half of CEO pay was found to be made up of long-term incentive plans, which can vary from year to year due to several factors, some of which might be outside the control of the CEO, such as government policy or stock market volatility. The same study showed median FTSE 100 chief executive pay to be 117 times higher than that of the median UK full-time worker. Among the CEOs whose reward was reviewed for the study, only six were female, and they were found to be paid 32 per cent less than their male counterparts. Four years on, the High Pay Centre (2023) reports that chief executive officer (CEO) median pay in the Financial Times Stock Exchange 100 Index (FTSE 100) as £3.41 million (a 39 per cent increase on January 2022 pay levels). This is 103 times the £33,000 median full-time worker's pay (increased over the same period by 6 per cent). FTSE 100 CEOs only had to work for around 30 hours (until 2pm on 5 January 2023) to overtake median pay for the UK full-time worker. The top 100 CEOs had to work nine hours less to achieve this than in the previous year, underscoring the upward trend in CEO pay and widening pay differentials.

To give a historical perspective, the High Pay Commission reported in 2011 that compared to the position some 30 years earlier the share of GDP going to the general workforce had shrunk to 12 per cent (2008 data). Examples were offered by the High Pay Commission of company 'lead executive' total earnings in 2009–11, including BP £4.5m, Barclays £4.4m, and GKN £1.5m, contrasting with a director's pay in the year 1979–80 of £140,000, £87,000 and £81,000 respectively. Pointing to the degree to which a gap had opened over the reporting timeframe between executive reward and average employee earnings, the percentages for 2009–11 were 63 per cent (BP), 75 per cent (Barclays) and 50 per cent (GKN), up from 16.5 per cent, 14.5 per cent and 15 per cent for the same three companies respectively in 1979–80. A graphic illustration of how the general workforce has fared across multiple decades is given in Figure 1.1 (Chapter 1), where the IMF tracks the share of national income across advanced and emerging market economies.

Interpreting executive reward data is controversial, however. Peter Boreham of management consultancy Hay Group criticises the way he claims the average pay increase quoted by Incomes Data Services in an autumn 2010 analysis of Financial Times Stock Exchange-listed (FTSE) top 350 directors is 'skewed by a small number of large increases in high-performing companies'. If the median were used instead, he says, the increase reported by IDS of 45 per cent drops to 23 per cent. Compounding the complaint, Mr Boreham argues that the method used by IDS to value 'pay' allows for share price movements, 'including paper gains on share options that may yet be reversed'. That's not to say that this commentator, writing to the *Telegraph* newspaper on 1 November 2010, is uncritical of developments in executive reward in the UK: 'the real concern [he argues] is the significant increases in annual bonuses, which were not, in general, underpinned by improvements to corporate earnings'.

Tyson (2005: 21) comments that UK executive pay levels 'may seem beyond the dreams of most ordinary working people'. Setting aside for now debate around the drivers of the gap in rewards between high-end and other employees, the scale is even greater in the USA. Caulkin (2010) reports 'the pay ratio [over the past three decades] from chief executive to average worker has ballooned from 30–40 to 300–400'. Citing data published by *Forbes* magazine cataloguing the pay awarded to a list of 'top ten earners', Tyson (2005: 22) notes that 'The lowest... was Seibel System's CEO on $88 million.'

Figure 10.1 Year on year comparison of components of FTSE 100 single figure pay

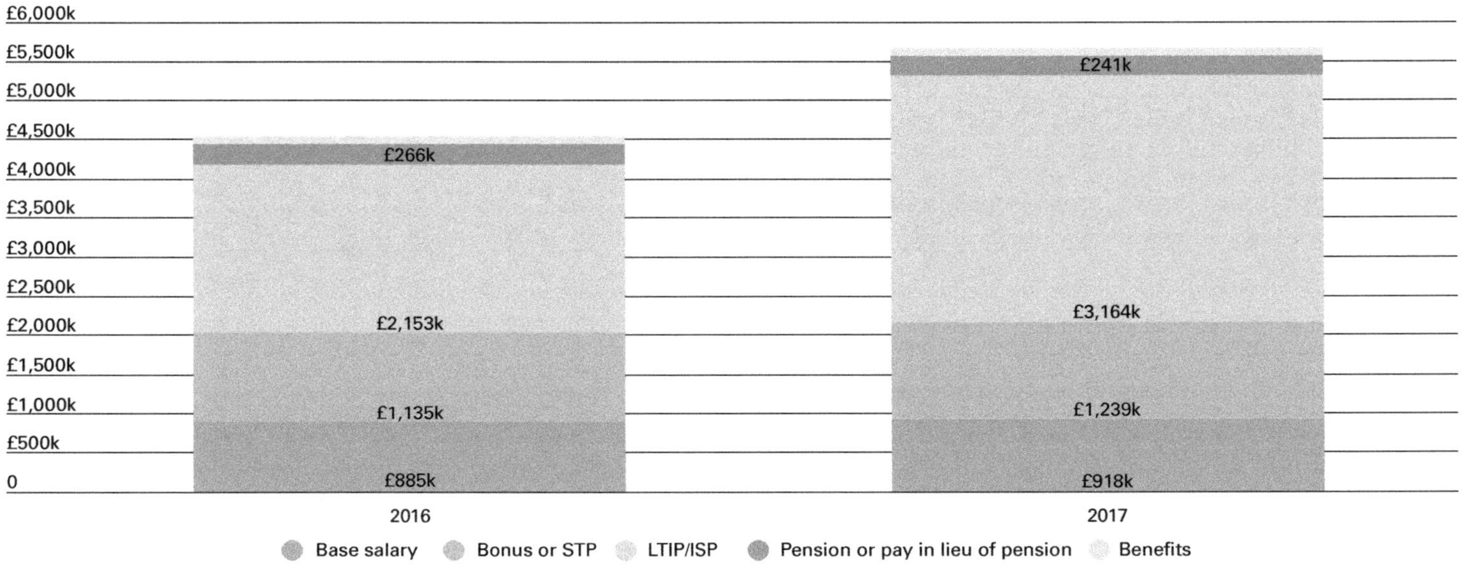

SOURCE: CIPD (2018d)

Conyon and Murphy (2000) report that, controlling for size, sector and other firm and executive characteristics, CEOs in the USA earn 46 per cent higher direct cash remuneration and 190 per cent higher total reward (accounting for 'package' elements such as share options) than their UK counterparts. And, in a similar vein to the High Pay Centre findings above, comparing pay at the top of US corporations with wage levels among other workers, Anderson et al (2007: 5) sum up the position across Fortune 500 companies as follows:

> CEOs of large U.S. companies last year made as much money from just one day on the job as average workers made over the entire year.

10.2.1 Arguments against executive reward levels

Starting with a chapter titled 'Who wants to be a millionaire?', Hargreaves (2019) opens her book asking the omnibus question: 'Are chief executives overpaid?' Representatives of British workers answer in the affirmative. For example, former TUC General Secretary Brendan Barber (2006) comments on executive pay trends as follows:

> It is hard not to conclude that this further huge rise in executive pay is more about greed than performance. No one should now have any illusions that executive remuneration has been brought under control. Giving shareholders a vote on boardroom pay has failed to rein in excess, as remuneration committees have simply found new ways to keep pushing up pay. The stratospheric levels of directors' pay compared to average wages mean that executives now live in a class apart, even from employees in their own companies. It is not just socially divisive, but bad for the economy.

The 'talk of top talent tends to be a smokescreen for increasing rewards', Hargreaves (2019: 22–23) argues, drawing on evidence from the Fortune Global 500 companies list that shows 'just four' out of 489 CEO appointments across the world were recruited by another company overseas while already working as a CEO. Her analysis is that international moves are made at lower levels in the organisational hierarchy, whereas top level executives tend to be older with families that need to be accommodated when managing their own career trajectory. Hargreaves places the onus on decision-makers, suggesting that Remco members tend to have similar backgrounds to the directors whose rewards they are setting. 'That makes them comfortable with big figures and happy to justify top pay awards. It also reduces the challenge over excessive remuneration since there are few who speak out or even see a problem' (Hargreaves, 2019: 25).

10.2.2 The alternative case

Drawing on his testimony to the US House of Representatives Committee on Financial Services, Kaplan (2007) answers with an unequivocal 'no' to the question 'Are CEOs overpaid?' Resting his case on the 'market forces' argument referenced in the introduction – although not specifically furnishing evidence that the talent represented by high-end employees is actively traded between the various sectors – Kaplan contends that 'while CEOs earn a great deal, they are not unique... the increase in pay at the top seems to be systemic' (2007: 23). The peer-level comparison ('other groups with similar talents and backgrounds' (2007: 23)) is used to defend a view that rather than causing general increases in economic inequality, executive reward escalation is merely being carried along as part of the trend. Rather than reward inflating consultancy advice and self-serving board relationships, as he says critics have suggested, Kaplan believes that CEO reward is 'bid up' as firms get larger, and the size of returns to the employer increases as a function of hiring a more productive CEO.

To substantiate the claimed benefits to investors derived from paying more for stewardship of the firms in which they have placed finance capital, using 'average' data illustrations, Kaplan contends that since 1980 the market values of large US firms have increased 'by a factor of four to seven times' (2007: 28). And, as 'the CEO job has become increasingly difficult and less pleasant', as well as 'riskier today than it has been in the past' (2007: 23), if 'compensation' is not pitched high, then temptations for stock market listed company leaders to defect, for example, to high-paying private equity-owned firms freed from public scrutiny, may be acted on.

Kaplan concludes: 'Rather than being "irrationally exuberant" [a term used by Alan Greenspan, when head of the US Federal Reserve], the US stock market and US companies have benefited from unexpectedly good productivity growth'. And 'while pay abuses have occurred, those examples are not typical and are likely to become less common' (2007: 36). Note the pre-financial crisis date of this commentary.

We may surmise from the material in this section that debates around the substance of executive reward are far from concluded. The most recent regulatory developments, discussed below, being applied in the UK as well as across mainland Europe, have been designed to make the 'say on pay' at the top more rigorous still.

10.3 So much for substance: What about the process?

While the comparative data summarised above are important, it is easy to become ensnared in 'the numbers' surrounding executive reward management, possibly losing sight of the processes involved. Lawler and Finegold (2007: 38) observe that discussion of CEO remuneration tends to revolve not just around the question of whether the levels are too high. Echoing commentary cited above that stands contrary to Kaplan (2007), Lawler (2009) cites the ongoing survey of US board company board members he has been conducting with executive search consultancy Heidrick & Struggles: 'Board members do acknowledge that CEO compensation is frequently too high. For the last 10 years more than 25 per cent of board members have said it is generally too high, and 50 per cent agreed that it is too rich in some high-profile cases.' As already noted, understanding executive reward management needs locating alongside concerns summarised under the rubric of 'corporate governance' (Jensen et al, 2004, Perkins and Shortland, 2022). Lawler (2009) expresses support for European regulators' action requiring stewardship behaviours on the part of shareholders. He believes that non-executive directors' ability to discipline chief executives is insufficient: 'Because shareholders are "the boss", they are the logical ones to determine CEO compensation.' That view has characterised developments in UK regulatory initiatives during the current decade. From October 2013, reforms published by the UK government Department for Business, Innovation and Skills included giving shareholders a binding vote on a resolution to approve the directors' remuneration policy in stock market listed companies (BIS, 2013). The 'say-on-pay' initiative has been extended to other countries, including the Netherlands (2004), Australia (2005), the United States (US) (2011), Italy (2011), Spain (2011), Belgium (2012) and France (2014) (Lozano-Reina and Sánchez-Marín, 2020).

10.3.1 Corporate governance and executive reward management standards

While there is no single model of the company – and thus how it should be governed – in the Anglo-American tradition, the relationship between the company and its shareholders is a proprietary one. Shareholders, deemed to be part-owners of a business in which they have invested finance capital, are entitled to expect the company to be governed exclusively in their interests (Parkinson, 2003). This argument is used 'to defend the fundamentals of the current [Anglo-American] governance structure', under which shareholders-as-owners elect directors 'to run the business on their behalf and hold them accountable for its progress' (Parkinson, 2003: 482). In the UK, corporate governance is encapsulated in the form of Acts of Parliament (regulation) and the UK Corporate Governance Code (best practice)

While subject to critical debate – and alternative traditions, for example, in mainland European countries – it is fair to say that these sentiments form the basis on which both mainstream analysis and policy interventions related to directors/executive employment contracts and concomitant reward determination are constituted. It is probably the case that the UK has led thinking worldwide over much of the past two decades regarding corporate governance and executive reward management (see the evolution of corporate governance regulation summarised in Table 10.2).

A seminal report from a committee chaired by Sir Adrian Cadbury, published in 1992, contains guidance regarded as 'highly influential in the UK and abroad' (Point, 2005: 61), and this initiative was followed in 1995 by a second committee of enquiry chaired by another then-serving large public limited company (plc) chairman, Sir Richard Greenbury. While Cadbury had plenty to say about executive pay as a feature of corporate governance, Greenbury focused even more specifically on tackling what by the mid-1990s had become a subject of sustained popular concern (at least as represented in media and political circles where 'almost frenzied attention' (Tyson, 2005: 20) had been visible. But this issue does not seem to have been targeted at the substantive level: prominent voices calling for intervention were not proposing a general reduction in what executives receive as appointees and employees of large stock market-listed firms. The exercise was 'theoretically designed to… make high pay levels acceptable' (Point, 2005: 61).

Perkins (2017) traces the evolution of executive reward management under a corporate governance rubric, based on the premise that the process is a socially constructed one; not something that can be deemed objective even when notionally independent decision-makers in Remcos are involved. In codifying the basis for regulating executive reward, account needs to be taken of the people taking the lead in doing so. The problem may stem from the fact that what legal firm Pinsent Masons colourfully label corporate 'grandees' (from Sir Adrian Cadbury onwards) have predominated 'attempts to shape and legitimise' the basis on which executive reward is regulated (Perkins, 2017: 81). However, public pressure to address accusations of greed rather than reward such as that earlier attributed to Brenden Barber (TUC, 2006) has over the past few years brought under scrutiny not just the outcomes of corporate decision-making but the monopoly of agenda setting until now held by corporate grandees who have led the various commissions informing the UK Corporate Governance Code (FRC, 2018). A review of the current Code commenced in 2022, with consultation on any proposed revisions beginning in the first quarter of 2023, and a revised Code is due for publication in 2024 (FRC, 2022).

In the light of criticism regarding the perceived influence of various forms of incentive plans to address the performance-risk-sustainability equation (High Pay Commission, 2011; Walker, 2009), the question of the fairness of relative pay levels has been under the spotlight for over a decade (e.g. Hallock, 2012). Hutton (2010a: 99) cautions those concerned with setting pay for senior employees in the UK public sector against the transfer of private sector reward management arrangements, observing that private sector 'pay arrangements and corporate governance have not delivered proportionality in pay'.

In the final report of his 'Review of Fair Pay', Hutton (2011) proposed the development of a Fair Pay Code, or 'framework for fairness in senior remuneration'. The rationale is to achieve pay proportional to an individual's contribution to an organisation, supported by a fair process, with the accent on transparent reporting. Only in this way can the public be assured, he argued, that high pay for public servants has been deserved, in the face of pay dispersion increases not only in private sector environments but also in public service bodies such as the NHS, local government, extra-government agencies and quangos. Unnecessary pay inflation in the public sector is attributed to restricted labour markets for senior positions – interaction between labour resource and reward systems is thus indicated in this analysis of the 'fair pay' problem. Hutton's recommendation is to apply fair pay principles 'also in the wider private sector', creating social norms whereby high-end private sector employees face some 'downside risk' rather than perpetuating what he regards as giving executives too much remuneration in too undemanding a way (2011: 5). Given the outsourcing of large portions of public services activity, Hutton (2011) also contends that applying fair pay principles generally across the economy would enable governments to protect themselves against charges that they are turning over large parts of public service provision to profiteering private businesses. Such allegations flared up again under the spotlight consequent on the Covid-19 pandemic.

Hutton (2010b) criticises what he calls a 'two-tier' British economy, made up on the one hand of a 'wheeler-dealer' 'Big Finance' segment where any restraint on payment of large bonuses is attacked by vested interests as anti-competitive and a trigger to an exodus from London. On the other hand there is the 'real economy' where structural impediments to jobs-based growth are a cause for concern. Here resides the public sector, which according to calculations by the Work Foundation has been the source of more than 70 per cent of all net new job creation outside London.

Hutton (2010b) states that introducing a 'pay multiple' governing the gap between reward for senior and lower level public service employees has prompted a mixed response. He sets out to develop an 'optimum ratio', acknowledging the difficulty likely to be encountered in doing so, and ruling out ratios based on either the UK national minimum wage or mean salary levels.

Hutton's analysis received criticism. Unsurprisingly, given its neoclassical orientation, the Institute of Economic Affairs (a think-tank) published commentary arguing that mandating public sector workforce pay multiples between top and bottom, an approach consistent with an institutional perspective, 'will create perverse incentives and lead to systematic gaming of the rules, with damaging effects, particularly for low paid public sector workers' (Davies, 2010). The expectation is that the lowest level paid work will be eliminated or outsourced to enable preservation of the status quo at the top while conforming to a forecast 20 to 1 ratio. And concerns about putting downward pressure on pay for senior public servants were evidenced in an article in *People Management* magazine published in September 2010, using local government pay and performance data collected by polling firm Ipsos Mori. This indicated a correlation between the highest-paid council chief executives and the best-performing local authorities. In the same report, a senior HR specialist at Buckinghamshire County Council, Gillian Hibbard, was quoted as saying that it was important to put into context reports of 9,000 public sector employees earning over £100,000 a year. This number is only a fraction of a huge public sector workforce, she said. In systems terms the argument here is that focusing exclusively on the reward system neglects its interconnection with the resource management system, and the dynamics of the environment in which recruitment to leadership and management positions is situated. The head of reward at Kent County Council, Colin Miller, was quoted by *People Management* as warning that even if a standard were adopted where 20 to 1 is the maximum ratio between highest and lowest paid this 'should not prevent employers offering an additional market premium to secure talented individuals for difficult to fill roles'. In practical terms, the Hutton recommendations seem to have influenced expectations about the transparency of executive pay and requirement for pay ratio reporting, to highlight disparities and associated ongoing trends.

Increasingly, institutional investors – particularly in the UK – are using their capacity to censure what is viewed as excessive executive reward management outcomes. A 2019 study by a business law academic reported by the *Financial Times* found from a study of voting patterns that among investors in FTSE 350 companies there had been an increase from 1.7 to almost 3.0 per cent 2013–17 among large asset managers against management recommendations in this area. While it may seem small, Surain Gomstain from University of Leeds Law School is quoted in the *FT* article saying that given the routine nature of asset manager voting at company AGMs such a shift can be regarded as significant. There is, it is suggested, a link between attention in the media, parliament and the public and this greater willingness to buck a tradition of 'siding with management' given long-standing criticism that executive pay is 'out of control' (*FT*, 2019b). Recent research by Perkins and Shortland (2023) uncovered views among institutional investors about their stewardship accountability. They expressed concern about what they perceive as siloed thinking among Remcos in their interpretation of codified corporate governance standards. Reliance on external comparisons, rather than deep knowledge about the specifics of the organisation when determining executive pay, risks homogenised rather than customised outcomes justified by corporate performance.

10.3.2 Executive reward variables

Consistent with prevailing interest in aligning employee reward directly with performance contribution, the details of which are discussed in Chapters 4 and 7, a balancing corporate argument has been made by commentators. While 'market forces' under globalisation may require high rewards to assist organisations competing in what has become known as the 'war-for-talent', overall reward levels should be defensible by reference to measures that shareholders at least, and possibly other organisation stakeholders, would recognise as appropriate. Academic researchers have been challenged to demonstrate objectively cause and effect. To that end a 'legion of academic articles' (Baden-Fuller, 2000: 475), written by economists, in particular, has surfaced, especially in the USA, in which sophisticated models are described and tested in an attempt not only to catalogue executive reward trends, but also to explain what consequences follow the choice of executive reward management techniques adopted to regulate the effort–reward bargain among these occupational groups.

One sustained focus has been on discovering economic relationships between top management pay, firm size and corporate performance (Veliyath, 1999). CEO remuneration has also been studied in relation to organisational strategy (Balkin and Gomez-Mejia, 1990; Kline and Brown, 2019); length of tenure (Hill and Phan, 1991); the structure of internal incentives (Lambert, Larcker and Weigelt, 1993); the dimensions of board structure and control (Conyon, 1997); and information disclosure (Conyon, Mallin and Sadler, 2002; Conyon and Sadler, 2001; Pyzoha and Jenkins, 2019). In spite of all this industry, prominent writers such as Martin Conyon have suggested that attention be paid to a richer set of social and political explanations' of the problems that have been articulated (Conyon and Peck, 1998a: 146). However, there is relatively little analysis that examines the processes of executive reward management: see Bender and Moir (2006); McNulty and Pettigrew (1999); Perkins and Hendry (2005), Perkins (2017); Perkins and Shortland (2022); Pye (2001); Roberts et al (2005).

SELF-ASSESSMENT EXERCISE

Time for banking shareholders to step in?

An article in the *Economist* argued that evidence of prioritising employees over shareholders in allocating trading profits suggested that investment banks continue to suffer poor management. This despite the fallout from the 2008–09 financial crisis when the UK government injected £37 billion into a number of large banks judged 'too big to fail', managing these assets through an arms-length agency created for the purpose, and the subsequent reviews of governance across the banking and finance sector generally to tackle perceived excess risk taking where reward loomed large in the criticism of a 'toxic bonus culture'.

Describing the unfolding scenario, the *Economist* laid out the background in stark terms:

> It is a year since the investment-banking industry committed reputational suicide by paying bumper bonuses just a few months after the worst financial crisis in living memory... [Payments] were made from profits buoyed from public subsidies [and] at the expense of rebuilding capital buffers. In 2009 the typical firm's wage bill was equivalent to between a quarter and half of its core capital. Investment banks, it seemed, were not being run in the interests of the economy or even of their owners, but for their staff. It was financial mutiny.

The *Economist* cited a report by lobbying group the Institute of International Finance and consultancy Oliver Wyman, in which three-quarters of the firms they asked said that risk was now taken into account in when calculating bonus payments and almost 40 per cent of aggregate bonus pools were in the form of deferred stock-based compensation. For the *Economist* (2010) this was a moot point: 'Managers at Lehman Brothers and Bear Stearns owned lots of shares, just as the corporate-governance policy said they should, yet ran their firms aground.'

While regulators had answered 'the subordinate question (how should bankers be paid?)', they had ignored the one that matters to most people: 'how much should they be paid?' (*Economist*, 2010).

Despite expectations among financial services sector observers of a fall in revenues of up to a fifth in 2010, and greater reported volatility in revenues making it more important that pay is controlled, according to the *Economist*, even in really big firms profits are 'barely acceptable' but still employees are being paid 'a lot'.

Regulators' grounds to intervene on pay are limited to circumstances where 'banks cannot make enough money, or attract new equity, to raise their capital ratios to the required level'.

In another unintended consequence of the regulatory changes in European jurisdictions, the *Financial Times* reported in December 2010 that the world's biggest investment banks intended to revise pay structures to differentiate between 'high-end' employees based in Europe and those based elsewhere. A senior European banker is quoted as describing politicians as naive if they expected non-EU banks to apply the new rules voluntarily across their global operations. The report states that US and Swiss banks were in many cases considering paying higher salaries and lower bonuses to their 'high-end' employees mostly based in London, to ensure compliance with regulations being introduced by the Committee of European Banking Supervisors, the pan-European regulator, limiting cash pay-outs.

The European banking respondent is quoted as observing that 'the ironic effect will be another hike in salaries, which is a fixed cost, which rather makes nonsense of the idea of pay for performance' (Jenkins, 2010). A report on top executive compensation in Europe 2010 published by the Hay Group addresses this issue, stating an expectation that some Remcos will increase fixed pay and long term incentive (LTI) payments given the regulatory requirements to defer short-term bonuses and include clawback provisions. In the case of LTIs, it is noted that not only is it hard to predict the impact of these awards due to volatile share prices, particularly in a recovering market; it is also challenging in extending LTI use to establish appropriate links between pay and performance, despite the imperative to 'display a coherent connection between corporate strategy and remuneration policy' (Jenkins, 2010: 4).

Five years on, in 2015 the *Financial Times* reported that 'in a year when 40 per cent of JP Morgan shareholders voted against the bank's pay plan' its CEO was the world's best-paid bank chief executive, having 'topped the table in three of the past five years' (FT, 2015). His reported combined annual earnings amounted to $27.6m.

The *Economist*'s (2010) view is stark:

> During the boom, banks' shareholders showed all the resistance of a doormat on pay. But now they have lots of capital tied up in a mature, even declining, industry that cannot control its costs properly, it is time for them to take command.

QUESTIONS

- Why do you think the banks' action over pay can be described in the way the *Economist* does in the article cited above?
- What counter-arguments could you put forward justifying the remuneration decisions observed across the banking sector?
- What would you include in a brief to the board remuneration committee of an investment bank to inform discussion and decision taking on bonus payments and related remuneration planning mindful of the regulatory regime, and wider environmental influences that might interact with the reward management system?

Table 10.1 Corporate governance regulation 1992–2023

Initiative	Emphasis
Cadbury Committee, 1992	Separation of chair and CEO role. Standing committees for matters such as audit and directors' remuneration.
Greenbury Committee, 1995	Specification of best practice in determining and publicly accounting for directors' remuneration. Remuneration committee independence. Decision-makers to weigh merits of alternative forms of long-term incentive to stock options: LTIPs 'subject to challenging performance criteria'. Shareholder votes on new schemes.
Hampel Committee, 1998 (set up to review implementation of Cadbury and Greenbury recommendations)	Promoting 'principles' in place of 'the more detailed guidelines of the Cadbury and Greenbury codes': Remuneration committee reports on behalf of unitary board (not 'independently'). Less prescription on LTIPS – judgement by remuneration committee regarding best fit and explanation to shareholders. More gradual shift to one-year director notice periods/ calculation for loss of office payments, given existing contractual norms. Accrued pension rights reporting as value of company liability, not element in individual's total remuneration. Shareholder voting on remuneration committee report at company discretion.
Turnbull Report, 1999 (Flint Report, 2004)	Specification of best practice on embedding internal control and risk management for UK listed companies to safeguard shareholders' funds and corporate assets. Guidance on avoiding unnecessary financial risks and exposing fraud and reporting on actions taken to shareholders annually. Includes monitoring the board and its committees to assess effectiveness of controls. In July 2004, the FRC set up a group chaired by Douglas Flint (Group Finance Director, HSBC Holdings plc) to review the guidance and update it where necessary, in the light of experience in implementing the guidance and developments in the UK and internationally since 1999.

(continued)

Table 10.1 (Continued)

Initiative	Emphasis
Myners Report, 2001	Reviewing UK institutional investment practice to encourage active engagement of shareholders in monitoring and communicating with directors of companies in which they hold shares, including exercising votes on governance-related issues (consistent with the various guidance listed in this table). The Institutional Shareholder Committee (ISC) published 'Principles' setting out strengthened responsibilities on the part of institutional shareholders and fund managers in respect of publishing policies on how they will actively engage with the companies in which they place capital funds, evaluating and reporting to clients or beneficiaries on the effectiveness of practice – including intervening where necessary where they are concerned about managerial actions. The UK Stewardship Code 2020 formalises the position.
Directors' Remuneration Report Regulations 2002 Statutory Instrument No. 1986	Obliging directors of a quoted company to prepare a directors' remuneration report for each financial year, containing specific information including details of remuneration committee, policy on directors' remuneration, and its detailed application to individuals. Updated as DRRR 2008 (part of implementation of Companies Act 2006) to include a requirement to report information enabling comparison of directors' and employees' pay.
Higgs Report, 2003 (published simultaneously with the Smith Report on audit committees) Tyson Report, 2003	**Higgs** Review of appointment, role, remuneration and effectiveness of non-executive directors. Identification of a senior independent director to be available to shareholders for discussion of corporate governance-related concerns. Broaden pool of candidates for non-executive appointments. Minimum three non-executives on remuneration committee. Delegated responsibility for setting chairman and executive directors rewards, plus level and structure for (other) senior executives. No single non-executive to sit on the three principal board committees: audit, nomination and remuneration.

(continued)

Table 10.1 (Continued)

Initiative	Emphasis
	Chief executive not to become chairman of the same company (so as to be judged 'independent'); board to agree separated chair/CEO role statements. **Tyson** Intended to complement Higgs, with a specific focus on enhancing board effectiveness via a range of different backgrounds and experiences among board members, exploring how a broader range of non-executive directors can be identified and recruited (incl. internationally).
DTI Report: 'Building Better Boards', 2004	Product of discussions with academia, business and executive search consultants. Best-practice guide to help companies improve recruitment and performance in the boardroom and to make a business case for effective diversity and better practices in the boardroom.
Walker Report, 2009	Sets the threshold for best managerial practice to reflect lessons learned from the October 2008 financial crisis and ensuing recession. Key areas considered include functioning of the board and evaluation of performance, governance of risk and remuneration.
The UK Corporate Governance Code, 2014 building on the totality of corporate governance guidance evolving since Cadbury, initially enshrined in the Combined Code which came into force in 2003	Setting out standards of good practice in relation to issues such as board composition, annual re-election of directors, and the diversity and balance of skill sets. Director development and time devoted to performance of directors' offices are also covered. Specific requirements on boards are detailed in terms of how remuneration is governed, including a requirement for criteria for performance related pay for directors not to be limited to purely financial aspects, and to relate to the company's long-term interests, risks and systems. Standards are also specified relating to audit, the requirement for constructive challenge by non-executive directors, the chair's responsibility for leading the board, and relations with shareholders. And now stipulating accountability on Remco chairs to disclose both the policy on directors' remuneration and its implementation by their company's board. The Code draws on each of the various corporate governance exercises undertaken since 1992.

(continued)

Table 10.1 (Continued)

Initiative	Emphasis
	All companies incorporated in the UK and listed on the main market of the London Stock Exchange are required under the Listing Rules to report on how they have applied the Code's provisions in their annual report and accounts.
The Companies Act 2006, fully implemented on a phased basis by October 2009, revises and consolidates UK company law, following the recommendations of the Company Law Review, which reported on the modernisation of UK company law in 2001	Among the key areas covered by the Act are: Description of directors' duties (including corporate social responsibility expectations), allowing companies to indemnify directors, and providing for corporate governance rules implementing EU directives. Overriding reported aim: to 'enhance shareholder engagement and a long-term investment culture'.
EU Recommendation on Executive Remuneration and EU Recommendation on Remuneration of Risk-taking Staff in Financial Institutions 2009	Specifies an 'appropriate' remuneration policy to ensure pay for performance and stimulate directors to ensure sustainability of the enterprise, providing guidance on remuneration structure, and enjoining shareholders in supervision. In the case of financial services sector risk-taking staff recommendations are provided on structuring remuneration policies to be consistent with and promote 'sound and effective risk management'. Makes provision for payment of 'the major part' of bonuses to be deferred and clawed back 'where data [on performance] has been proven to be manifestly misstated'.
The UK Stewardship Code published in June 2010, and revised in 2012 and again in 2020, setting out the principles of effective stewardship by investors; the specification intended to assist institutional investors better to exercise their stewardship responsibilities in relation to stock market companies, but equally setting best practice standards for 'principals' in discharging their responsibilities in all areas of corporate governance	The Financial Reporting Council charged with regulating UK corporate governance has promoted the Stewardship Code as complementary to the UK Corporate Governance Code, with an aim of improving long-term returns to shareholders by active steps by institutional investors (e.g. investment trusts and pension funds) to increase the quality of strategy, performance and risk management in the companies they invest in. Specific recommendations apply in relation to managing conflicts of interest relevant to the protection and enhancement of shareholder value.

(continued)

Table 10.1 (Continued)

Initiative	Emphasis
Committee of European Banking Supervisors (CEBS) Instructions on remuneration, July 2010 (amending the Capital Requirements Directive, 2007) and UK Financial Services Authority Final Code on Banker's Pay, December 2010 applicable to the 2,700 institutions regulated by the FSA effective as at 1 January 2011	The European instructions empower national bank and financial regulatory authorities to take action against any financial institution that fails to comply with provisions judged 'far stricter' than applying in other financial centres. 'High end' employees bonuses are capped at 30 per cent of the total award (20 per cent for 'large bonuses') with at least 40 per cent of variable remuneration paid in share awards deferred for three to five years, with a clawback provision if the individual's performance turns out to be weaker than predicted. Scope to pay 'guaranteed bonuses' - the promise of a fixed sum irrespective of performance by the individual or firm has been removed with the exception of 'golden hello' payments to new recruits.
The Large and Medium-sized Companies and Groups (Accounts and Reports) (Amendment) Regulations 2013 (SI 2013/1981)	The Amendment is to the 2008 version of the regulations and revises provisions related to the remuneration report, covering directors in quoted companies. Information to be included in the report is a single total remuneration figure table in respect of each individual who was a director during the relevant financial year under report. This is subject to external auditing requiring auditors to declare whether or not the section has been prepared in accordance with legislative requirements.
European Commission Capital Requirements Directive (CRR IV) (Directive 2013/36/EU): Articles 92-95; Capital Requirements Regulation (CRR) (Regulation 575/2013): Article 450, amending the so-called Basel Accord, known as Basel III	Designed to cover certain prescribed employees (effectively high end employees in banking and finance with a material impact on corporate risk profiles) requiring approaches to and disclosure of remuneration to avoid excessive risk taking. Setting out rules governing the variable (or bonus) element of reward and the fixed (salary) element.

(continued)

Table 10.1 (Continued)

Initiative	Emphasis
2018 Companies (Miscellaneous Reporting) Regulations and the revised UK Corporate Governance Code, applicable from 1 January 2019. In its introduction to the Code, the Financial Reporting Council specifies that in addition to its application to 'premium' listed companies, for parent companies with a premium listing, the board should ensure that there is adequate co-operation within the group to enable it to discharge its governance responsibilities under the Code. This includes the communication of the parent company's purpose, values and strategy. Externally managed investment companies (which typically have a different board and company structure that may affect the relevance of particular corporate governance principles) are directed to the Association of Investment Companies' Corporate Governance Code to meet their obligations under the Code. In addition, there is a version of the Code for mutual insurers to use produced by the Association of Financial Mutuals.	Mandate more detailed reporting of how company directors have fulfilled their responsibilities under the 2006 Companies Act. Section 172 of the Act says that directors should act in the interests of the company's 'members' (that is, shareholders), but should also have regard for other stakeholder groups including workers, customers or wider society. There are possible implications for thinking about how pay is distributed throughout the organisation. When setting executive pay, reasons must be given as to why pay policies are appropriate using internal and external measures. This is complemented by the requirement to publish intra-company pay ratios between the CEO and their median UK employee. In addition, remuneration committees must report on what engagement with the workforce has taken place to explain how executive remuneration aligns with wider company pay policy. Companies must adopt specific mechanisms to incorporate stakeholder voice into corporate governance structures.

(continued)

Table 10.1 (Continued)

Initiative	Emphasis
The Companies (Directors' Remuneration Policy and Directors' Remuneration Report) Regulations 2019	Building on the 2013 regulations, these are intended to encourage long-term shareholder engagement, the regulations implement the executive pay aspects of the revised Shareholder Rights Directive. The regulations give shareholders further information to assess how rewards to directors are matched by performance and to compare the annual change in directors' remuneration to the annual change in average employee pay over a rolling five-year period. In force from 10 June 2019, the regulations implement a requirement in certain companies that the remuneration of the Chief Executive Officer and any Deputy Chief Executive Officer must be reported even if they are not a director on the board of the company. Previously under UK law, only the remuneration of the directors on the board were required to be reported.
Westminster Government Mini Budget 2022	In the autumn of 2022 then-Chancellor of the Exchequer Kwasi Kwarteng announced government plans to scrap the so-called bankers' bonus cap. The decision was one of a handful retained by Jeremy Hunt, appointed Chancellor following the removal of Kwarteng, and positioned as part of a drive to reaffirm the UK's status as a global financial services centre.
Corporate Governance Code Consultation 2023 (Revised Code expected to apply to accounting years on or after 1 January 2025)	Following the 2022 consultation on Restoring Trust in Audit and Corporate Governance, the FRC was asked by the Government to strengthen the UK Corporate Governance Code in specific areas. In May 2023 a public consultation on the proposed revision to the Code took place, described by the FRC as a limited revision to enhance the Code's effectiveness in promoting good corporate governance. Among the changes are proposals for: • a stronger basis for reporting on and evidencing the effectiveness of controls; • improving the functioning of comply-or-explain; • revisions to reflect the responsibilities of the board and audit committee for sustainability and Environmental, Social and Governance (ESG) reporting; • ensuring the Code aligns with changes to legal and regulatory requirements called for by the Government including strengthening reporting on malus and clawback processes.

See also the Financial Reporting Council's graphic detailing the evolution of the UK Corporate Governance Code, www.frc.org.uk/directors/corporate-governance#how-did-the-corporate-governance-code-evolve.

10.4 Institutional and regulatory controls on executive reward

Placing reward issues in the foreground, 'shareholder activists' Robert Monks and Allen Sykes argue that corporate governance problems on both sides of the Atlantic have become so acute as to represent a systemic problem (Monks and Sykes; 2002, Sykes, 2002).

As well as having an appreciation of the debates surrounding executive reward practice, then, HR 'thinking performers' need to be aware of the successive waves of regulatory initiatives by national and supranational states mindful of the contention surrounding this aspect of organisational affairs. Rather than passively accepting the logic of regulation, however, specialists need to be aware of entrenched positions adopted by interested parties (Sánchez-Marín et al, 2022). While governments may feel obliged to act for political reasons, those like Kaplan (2007) advise against legislation (such as that, he says, colloquially referred to as 'say on pay') given the potential he believes such policy intervention may have to impose cost on companies and boards, where it is possible to 'imagine politically oriented shareholders attempting to make political statements' when enfranchised to vote on executive pay decisions, rather than remaining bounded by economic considerations.

The UK government has acted directly to regulate, or else co-opted policy-related initiatives by institutions such as the London Stock Exchange and representative bodies such as the Association of British Insurers (ABI), the National Association of Pension Funds (NAPF), etc. Corporate governance regulations from Cadbury onwards enshrine the principle that executive reward should contain 'strong incentives for executives to act in shareholder interests' (Ogden and Watson, 2004: 35). UK government representatives have in the past emphasised, however, that '... directors deserve high rewards for good performance' (Patricia Hewitt, then Secretary of State for Trade and Industry, recorded in Hansard, 2004: 51–52 WS).

While the tenor may have changed to some extent qualitatively with amendments to a European Directive applicable to the financial services sector, governance prescriptions 'were never intended specifically to hold down pay levels' (Ogden and Watson, 2004: 35), but to ensure that executive reward determination complies with sanctioned governance standards, or else decision-making is accompanied by detailed explanation for departures from 'best practice'. A statement of principles exemplifying core values and expectations surrounding executive reward, expressed on behalf of the finance capital investment community, appears in Key Issues in Reward Management 10.2, extracted from guidelines published in 2006 by the ABI. The simple phrase 'comply or explain', enshrined in the UK Corporate Governance Code, carries significant meaning that corporate managers and their advisers need to be mindful of in discharging their accountabilities.

Also there has been a material shift in the way executive reward management is expected to apply to reflect good corporate governance illustrated in a rewording of a key section in the 2014 iteration of the UK Corporate Governance Code. Whereas earlier versions signalled that, in common with rewarding employees generally, executive reward should be sufficient to attract, motivate and retain directors, while 'avoiding paying too much', wording describing that approach was expressly deleted in a document the Financial Reporting Council issued as part of consultation on updating that version of the Code. Instead directors are to be rewarded on the basis of an expectation that they will 'promote the long term success of the company' (FRC, 2014: 10).

Two lines of scrutiny are expected to assure desired outcomes. Rather than rely on board executive directors to regulate their own reward against the governance principles, first, remuneration committees of company boards are expected to be populated exclusively by 'independent' (or non-executive) directors, charged with designing performance-based reward systems covering their executive colleagues, and accounting for their decisions to shareholders. (Non-executives are not only 'governance scrutineers', however; they are expected to work hand in hand with the executive team to set corporate strategy, a possible source of tension.) Secondly, in turn, shareholders have for several years been called on to challenge 'situations where directors enjoy rich rewards whilst companies perform poorly and shareholders and employees suffer' (Hansard, 2004: 51–52 WS, UK Corporate Governance Code, 2010).

KEY ISSUES IN REWARD MANAGEMENT 10.2

Principles of executive reward

Boards are responsible for adopting remuneration policies and practices that promote the success of companies in creating value for shareholders over the longer term. The policies and practices should be demonstrably aligned with the corporate objectives and business strategy and reviewed regularly.

Remuneration Committees should be established in accordance with the provisions of the Corporate Governance Code. They should comprise independent directors who bring independent thought and scrutiny to all aspects of remuneration. It is important to maintain a constructive and timely dialogue between boards and shareholders regarding remuneration policies and practices.

Executive remuneration should be set based on selection and interpretation of appropriate benchmarks. Such benchmarks should be used with caution, in view of the risk of an upward ratchet of remuneration levels with no corresponding improvement in performance.

Executive remuneration should be linked to individual and corporate performance through graduated targets that align the interests of executives with those of shareholders. The resulting arrangements should be clear and readily understandable.

Shareholders will not support arrangements which entitle executives to reward when this is not justified by performance. Remuneration Committees should ensure that service contracts contain provisions that are consistent with this principle.

(**SOURCE:** Extract from ABI guidelines on executive remuneration policies and practices. For detailed information on the guidelines refer to the ABI Principles of Remuneration published in November 2013, www.ivis.co.uk/media/5887/ABI-Principles-of-Remuneration-2013-final.pdf)

Although the regulatory environment has stiffened considerably, alleged historical laxity in Remcos' oversight has been subject to criticism. Reilly and Scott (2005) give as an example situations in which executives have been authorised to exercise large grants of stock option awards just prior to a share price collapse, when the losses experienced by shareholders may be perceived as the fault of poor performance by the executive(s) concerned. Such behaviour stands in stark contrast, for example, to the Association of British Insurers (ABI) guidelines, as summarised in Key Issues in Reward Management 10.2.

Publicly expressed disquiet over 'rewards for failure', especially when these involve 'severance' terms when an executive is being removed from office, is rooted in the view that 'such payments reflect an inappropriate culture at the top of organisations and can have a strong influence in wider society, making the issue one in the public interest' (ACCA, 2005). Compensation granted to underperforming executives at the time of departure seen to be over-generous might, it was felt, damage the image and reputation of British business as a whole, in the words used in UK government consultation undertaken 20 years ago.

To try to remedy problems encountered in the past, regulatory guidance is premised on an expectation that Remcos (working in association with the board 'nominations' committee) will take steps at the time executives are initially contracted to the organisation to ensure that terms and conditions connected with possible future severance are seen to be fair and reasonable. If a situation arises, the logic is that termination will be capable of resolution transparently and satisfactorily (ACCA, 2005). Prompted in particular by the 2008–09 financial crisis the two-pronged governance strategy adopted by legislators expecting to see 'increased activism by institutional investors, and the promotion of best practice' to remedy the situation, rather than add further to regulatory instruments (Hewitt, 2004), has given way to additional legislation.

Applicable to companies with premium listed shares traded on the UK stock exchange, incorporated in the UK or elsewhere, the latest version of the Corporate Governance Code applies to accounting periods beginning 1 January 2019 or later. In respect of directors' remuneration, a key facet is the information companies are required to publish that will form the basis on which shareholders are expected to take a view, voting at annual general meetings. The Code includes a requirement that company boards establish a remuneration committee comprised of non-executive members, the chair of which needs to have prior experience of serving on a remuneration committee. In the company's annual report, a description of the Remco's work is to be provided with the following coverage:

- an explanation of the strategic rationale for executive directors' remuneration policies, structures and any performance metrics;
- reasons why the remuneration is appropriate using internal and external measures, including pay ratios and pay gaps;
- a description, with examples, of how the remuneration committee has addressed factors intended to assure stakeholders that remuneration policy applicable to executive directors is clear, simple, risk-managed, leads to outcomes within predictable limits, is proportionate in terms of performance achieved and aligns with corporate culture;

- whether the remuneration policy operated as intended in terms of company performance and quantum, and, if not, what changes are necessary;
- what engagement has taken place with shareholders and the impact this has had on remuneration policy and outcomes;
- what engagement with the workforce has taken place to explain how executive remuneration aligns with wider company pay policy; and
- to what extent discretion has been applied to remuneration outcomes and the reasons why.

(SOURCE: FRC, 2018: 15)

Despite the further tightening of corporate governance regulations applicable to executive reward, in spring 2019 a UK Parliamentary Select Committee published a report calling for the regulatory regime to go further still. It cited public disquiet at the huge 'endemic differentials' between FTSE 100 executives and other employees, blaming remuneration committees for inadequate oversight of reward levels including over over-generous and ever more opaque incentive packages (BEIS, 2019b). As evidence for this criticism, the report also pointed to 'shaming' pay decisions such as the 2017 payment of a £75m bonus to the former CEO of housebuilder Persimmon where it had been revealed that a taxpayer-funded help-to-buy scheme was a key influence on the corporate performance that had been recorded, undermining the idea that this was due to the application of top executive skills and effort. Another example cited was where 70 per cent of shareholders had in 2018 voted against payment of a £5.8m 'golden hello' to the incoming Royal Mail CEO. The headline recommended action to address the problem was for Remcos to be obliged to enforce an absolute cap on total pay for executives in any one year, coupled with a requirement to add at least one employee representative to the committee. The range of companies to be covered by reporting requirements, the report recommended, should be widened to include FTSE 250 plcs; and an effort should be made to make greater use of reward schemes that share profits more evenly throughout those working for a company.

The government's response was that the Committee's proposals were a useful contribution to the continuing public debate on high levels of executive reward. But rather than accepting them, its 'immediate priority was to focus on the effective implementation and assessment of the recent reforms', then due to be first fully reported on by companies in 2020. A briefing note by professional services firm KPMG says that the government, therefore, has no immediate plans to make further changes to the reporting and disclosure of executive pay. In particular, the government rejected calls to require:

- an employee representative on the remuneration committee;
- an absolute cap on executive director pay; and
- CEO pay reporting to be extended to all companies (not just quoted companies) with 250 or more employees.

However, the government was clear in its response to the consultation on its Corporate Governance Reform Green Paper in 2017 that it would monitor the impact of the reforms and would consider further action at a future point unless there is clear evidence that companies are taking active and effective steps to respond to significant shareholder concerns about executive pay outcomes (KPMG, 2019).

And as noted earlier, the Financial Reporting Council has been tasked by the government to undertake consultation on further revisions, leading to an updated Code scheduled for release in 2024.

10.5 Theorising executive reward: Contested terrain

Alongside the legislative and regulatory commentary emerging over the past quarter century, comprehensive reviews of the extensive, still-growing academic literature have been compiled over the period from the late 1990s. Notable examples include Gomez-Mejia and Wiseman (1997), Devers et al (2007), Finkelstein et al (2009), Pepper and Campbell (2014) and Li (2020). Inspiration from these and other sources is applied in this section to understand the debates around ways in which academic commentators have tried and struggled to make sense of trends in rewarding directors and executives.

10.5.1 Markets

Commentary in the academic and related literature attempting to theorise executive pay and the contingencies against which it is determined reveals a range of views. On the one hand, consistent with classical macro-economic theory 'market forces' have been cited by those offering a defensive rationale for executive reward management practice (e.g. Kaplan, 2007). And the viewpoint is not an exclusively 'academic' one. Stiles and Taylor (2002: 76) report on discussions with company directors in which the latter judge 'market factors' as 'very important in determining executive pay', constituting 'a central factor in recruitment, retention and motivation'.

Pepper (2006: 15) cites an even more unequivocal remark by a large UK stock market-listed company CEO made in response to a question at a shareholders' meeting. The individual apparently declared: 'My remuneration is determined by market forces.'

Using more measured terms, the report of the committee on governance chaired by Sir Ronald Hampel states that to attract business executives 'of the required calibre' their remuneration will be 'largely determined by the market' (1998: 4.3, emphasis added). The predecessor Greenbury Committee also referred to market forces, but acknowledged 'imperfections' so that:

> While market forces set a broad framework... remuneration committees for the most part have quite a wide range of discretion in setting levels and forms of remuneration.
>
> (Greenbury, 1995: 6.4)

Explaining 'why the market doesn't work' in relation to executive reward determination, Pepper (2006: 15) argues that 'practically none' of the conditions for a perfect economic market to operate are visible. Rather than free market entry and exit, there are limitations on the numbers of executive jobs open and suitable candidates to fill them at any one time. Executives are not homogeneous commodities: no two individuals are the same. The same difficulty applies to systematic comparative evaluation of 'unique' executive roles to be filled (Dive, 2019; Hijazi and Bhatti, 2007; Perkins and Hendry, 2006).

Moreover, 'despite claims that high levels of boardroom pay are essential to prevent a management brain drain... only a handful of top companies in continental Europe and the US are led by UK executives' (Milner and Seager, 2007: 26). Citing the author of a study into management practices at 4,000 companies, a question mark was raised as to 'whether British executives could cut it overseas if... disenchanted with pay levels in Britain'. According to the director of the Centre for Economic Performance, Professor John Van Reenen, who co-authored the report:

> UK management is not in the premier league. Management aspires to pay as well as the US, but our study finds that average management quality in the US far outstrips that in the UK. Only one in every 50 American firms in our sample can be described as 'very badly managed', compared with roughly 1 in 12 in the UK.
>
> (Milner and Seager, 2007: 26)

Finally, even if the market position were to be accepted, while (proxy) market comparisons have been encouraged by more comprehensive disclosure of total executive rewards, information on how to 'price' executive experience and skills is far from perfect. A sample of FTSE 100 remuneration committee members interviewed by Perkins and Hendry (2005) voiced barriers to calibrating price-value norms objectively: idiosyncrasies arise between executives and the roles they are asked to undertake that require 'artful' assessments (Noldeke and Samuelson, 1996). The price-value placed on a specific executive may depend more on the characteristics and preferences of the recruiter than on the 'talent' (perceived capability and potential to perform) being acquired. In conceptualising executive reward outcomes, therefore, it seems that HR specialists must give consideration to institutional factors and socially contextualised decision-taking as much as to economic factors (Perkins and Shortland, 2022).

10.5.2 Performance

Given the very mixed views regarding a 'market forces' justification for executive reward regulation, to what extent is the faith regulators have vested in performance contingencies well placed? The adequacy of alignment between the executive reward levels and 'corporate performance' (e.g. 'total shareholder return' – i.e. share price appreciation and dividend yield) has been 'a central theme within the UK debate' (Conyon and Sadler, 2001: 141). Kaplan's (2007) macro-economic assessment again faces a challenge in the face of a wide-ranging review of evidence from a series of studies in both the UK and USA which conclude that, even where a statistical link is identifiable between executives' direct rewards (salary and cash bonuses) and the stock market performance of their firms, this is small.

Conyon (1998) finds a more robust correlation between company size and pay level. Conyon and Sadler examine evidence from studies since the end of the 1990s that reflect the changing composition of executive reward packages shifting the balance away from 'current cash compensation' to emphasise non-cash (share-based-related) incentives (2001: 146), consistent with the Hay Group (2010) survey findings on top executive rewards in Europe. Conyon and Sadler conclude that taking account of a reward portfolio calibrated in favour of 'changes in the value of the stock and equity options held by the CEO... the pay–performance link may be becoming stronger' (2001: 151).

Jensen et al (2004) attack equity-based reward policies currently in operation, however. The commentators argue that the latter types of performance-based executive reward initiatives compound a problem of overvalued corporate equity. When executives recognise that the position is not sustainable, the risk is that they attempt to artificially manipulate short-term equity prices. The worst-case scenario is an Enron-style corporate scandal. Even in less high-profile cases, however, shareholder capital suffers 'value destruction' over the long run. Li (2020) comments on practices affecting Chinese companies compared with those related to executives in American and European companies highlighting the role mergers and acquisitions can play influencing upward executive remuneration trends, especially in relation to what he terms financial related executives in private versus state-owned firms.

Jensen et al (2004) do not limit their criticism to executives and Remcos. They also adopt a negative attitude towards financial investment market managers, who 'are not acting as shareowners' (2004: 239). In the UK, as observed above, state policy-makers have called on institutional shareholders to play a more 'engaged' role. The 2001 government-commissioned Myners Report explicitly sought to encourage greater 'shareholder activism' – especially in the stance taken towards underperforming companies, 'exercising their votes in a considered way' (Mallin, 2004: 239), with the Stewardship Code an attempt to institutionalise this supervisory accountability. This is something that has been vociferously advocated by long-standing activists representing the beneficial owners of company shares, such as Monks and Sykes (2002). Reinforced in the Corporate Governance Code of Practice (FRC, 2018) and related Companies (Directors' Remuneration Policy and Directors' Remuneration Report) Regulations 2019 (see Table 10.1).

10.5.3 Socio-political interaction

If 'thinking performers' using this text are not satisfied with economic market explanations for executive reward decision-taking or attempts to find an unequivocal reward–performance link, calls for control to be exercised suggests attention may be needed towards socio-political phenomena (Perkins, 2009, 2017; Perkins and Hendry, 2005; Perkins and Shortland, 2022). The nature of relations between the parties to executive effort-reward contracting comes to the fore. A major strand of the theoretical literature on executive reward focuses on debates around the value of 'agency' considerations (Jensen and Mecklin, 1976; Jensen et al, 2004). The notion of 'power-dependency' (Pfeffer and Salancik, 2003; Wright and McMahan, 1992) also surfaces when considering interpersonal and intra-organisational relationships, as does the role of 'tournament'-based interaction between actors close to the top of corporate hierarchies (Conyon, Peck and Sadler, 2001; Conyon and Sadler, 2001). And social constructionist accounts provide another conceptual lens through which to view relations between executive agents and their 'principals' (Perkins, 2017; Roberts, 2001). We briefly review this commentary next.

10.5.4 Agency theory

Analysis of corporate governance has been significantly influenced for over 30 years by Jensen and Mecklin's (1976) theorisation of the firm, its management and managers' relationship with the firm's 'owners', using the concept of 'principal–agency' relations (Arrowsmith et al, 2010; Buck et al, 1998; Safriliana et al, 2019). An agency relationship is defined as a contract: a principal (ultimately, the beneficial owner(s) of shares in productive capital) engages an agent to perform some service on the principal's behalf. The 'shareholders are seen as the focal group whose interests are furthered through crafting executive pay arrangements that cause a top management team motivated by self-interest to maximise shareholder value' (Bruce et al, 2005: 1493).

Agency problems may arise for shareholders when evaluating whether they are getting the best value return from the executives to whom corporate management is delegated. If it were easy to ensure alignment between payments (inputs) to executives and performance (outputs), shareholders could simply pay their executives a fixed salary (in effect, a form of insurance payment), and then assess whether that agent is supplying optimal effort in the shareholder's interest (Perkins, 2015; Perkins and Hendry, 2005). Jensen et al (2004) contend that the agency problem cannot be eliminated, only mitigated. And if inappropriate, there is a risk that reward arrangements will actively give rise to agency problems, leading to value-destroying agency on the part of executives entrusted with the running of the firm (Evans and McIver, 2009; Jensen et al, 2004; Perkins and Shortland, 2023).

The mediated agency relationship is a further source of disquiet. Sykes (2002: 256) alleges 'widespread conflicts of interest', derived from the complicated sets of interrelations involving institutional investment managers concerned with widely dispersed share portfolios managed on behalf of beneficiaries and non-executive directors. Sykes's (2002: 256) criticism is aimed at 'largely passive shareholders' and 'complacent and ineffective non-executive directors'.

There is executives' own role too. Members of a unitary board of directors, although formally delegating administration to the board's Remco, ultimately sanction their own reward and may influence the way it is accounted for. The issue to which regulatory interventions have been especially targeted is that, in the final analysis, 'directors have power to influence their own rewards and to affect the performance of their firms, probably to a greater extent than other employees, at lower levels' (Tyson and Bournois, 2005: 7).

In her written introduction to the consultative document on directors' remuneration, then Secretary of State for Industry Patricia Hewitt observed that this is 'the issue above all others, on which directors face a conflict of interest' (DTI, 2001: 4). This view explains the legal obligation placed on UK publicly traded companies under the Directors' Remuneration Report Regulations, 2002, updated in the Companies (Directors' Remuneration Policy and Directors' Remuneration Report) Regulations, 2019, not only to require extensive disclosure in a remuneration committee report accompanying company annual reports and accounts. The report must also be submitted for approval at the annual general meeting, with the ambition of locating executives as stakeholders in the firm and its fortunes alongside other interested parties (Lozano-Reina and Sánchez-Marín, 2020).

10.5.4 Power-dependency theory

Pfeffer and Salancik (2003) draw attention specifically to the impact of power in relations between organisational actors, arguing that, if organisations are to be controlled and managed (as well as understood), account needs to be taken of the actions of 'core' interest groups. Emphasising context, they argue that academic literature tends to overlook – or take as a given in modelling economic transactions – that behaviour in organisations is environmentally adaptive behaviour. Senior managers are not just acted on by institutions – they are themselves actors with intentions and wants as they seek to 'orchestrate the affairs of the corporation' (Tyson, 2005: 16). Using the language of agency theory, principals must acquire and maintain the resources necessary to develop and enact strategy and operations. And the more the principal depends on the resources the more leverage that resource (agent) may exercise in the transaction around whether or not and to what extent to perceive their interests as aligned with those of the principal interest-holders.

'No one stakeholder can speak with unchallenged authority for the corporate interest' (Tyson, 2005): managers require delegated authority to take initiatives based on information they have access to (unlike shareholders, or indeed employee groups lacking corporate oversight) in order to be able to act on opportunities and avoid being ensnared by operational difficulties. However, this latitude includes the freedom for managers 'to align [their] interests with the "interests" of the corporation' (2005: 16), or not to do so. Sykes (2002: 257–8) perceives consequential problems such as Remcos lacking independence; management choosing the consultants to advise on their pay setting; managerial action motivated by pressures to produce value over impossibly short time periods – and stock option gains to be made.

Managerial agents 'control' the capability (experience and skills) necessary for value-creating activity. And they need to be induced voluntarily to put it to work for the principal. The relative power of principals and their agents in determining the effort–reward contract, for example, may be perceived as derived from mutually dependent relations (Molm et al, 1999). Festing et al (2007) argue that the extent to which behavioural adaptation occurs, with outcomes that more or less favour principals or agents, is therefore moderated by existing power relationships within the firm (Kornelakis and Gospel, 2022). Consequently, the relationship between the parties to corporate governance relationships may be theorised as 'the product of ongoing interaction and discussion' (Roberts, 2001: 1549). While Conyon (1998) finds that the threat of dismissal may discipline young CEOs, Bebchuck and Fried argue that executives may be able to mobilise embedded power resources to 'entrench themselves in their positions, making it difficult to oust them when they perform poorly' (2003: 72).

10.5.5 Tournament theory

Rosenbaum (1989: 336) defines tournaments as 'systems for selecting the most talented individuals by a series of progressively more selective competitions', in which the declared winners of each tournament are allowed to climb the career ladder and later compete in a new tournament for the next higher career position.

The so-called tournament effect has been cited as an explanation of why a significant gap exists between CEO and other executives' reward levels, restricting the ultimate economic 'prize' to the incumbent CEO (Perkins, 2015).

O'Connell (2006) notes arguments that CEOs receive the highest relative reward owing to the increased level of responsibility they shoulder, with demand for CEOs outstripping supply. As noted earlier, arguments have also been put forward that changes in corporate performance and executive reward increases may be matched (Kaplan, 2007). However, when examining published data from FTSE companies over the period 1990–2004, O'Connell (2006) finds no strong case to suggest that responsibility at CEO level has become relatively greater over that timeframe. Moreover, he can offer no obvious reason why fewer CEO candidates are available to fill the job slots. And from this data series, when looking at performance alignment it seems that the rate of increase in CEO cash reward has continued to run ahead of increases in corporate performance.

Under tournament theory, the prediction is that locating a distinctive 'prize' at the top of the organisation motivates agents in contention for CEO positions, for example, to compete by out-performing fellow executives, with the result that the organisation and its principals benefit from the sum of individual contributions. However, once there are 'no tomorrow aspects of the final stage of the game' (Rosen, 1986, cited by Conyon and Sadler, 2001), the predicted benefits may not be sustained. O'Connell's (2006) analysis also finds no obvious evidence that, compared with other board-level executives, CEO pay is more strongly a reflection of performance.

Greater transparency not only in terms of rewards obtained but also levels of performance makes pay–performance alignment easier to observe in non-business settings, in which the majority of testing predictions derived from tournament theory has taken place, such as among racing drivers, jockeys or professional golfers (Conyon and Sadler, 2001). Conyon et al (2001) test tournament predictions using data on 100 large stock market companies, and find 'some confirmatory evidence' that 'the ratio of pay increases as one moves up the hierarchical level' (2001: 155). They also observe a positive relationship between the CEO reward premium and the number of tournament contenders. However, empirical work informed by the tournament approach specifically focused on business and related organisations is limited; caution is required, therefore, before drawing general conclusions.

10.5.6 An alternative orientation (stakeholder agency theory)

Calling for a return to first principles, Roberts (2001) challenges the dominant agency orientation in corporate governance literature and policy. Agency theory, he argues, is predicated on an essentialist perspective of human nature: accordingly, employment relationships are no more than a series of implicit and explicit socio-economic contracts with associated rights.

A more relativist perspective, on the other hand, introduces the possibility of learned and reinforced trust. Buck et al (1998), for example, extend agency theory beyond its 'traditional financial version' to propose a Stakeholder Agency Theory (SAT). As an heuristic for structuring enquiry into corporate governance complexities in more volatile environments (such as immediately post-Soviet Russia), SAT draws attention to the possible existence of organisational cultures in which trusting relationships encourage stakeholders to suspend opportunistic actions in favour of an ethic of co-operation (Buck et al, 1998).

Hambrick and Mason (1984) introduce theorising relevant to executive reward related to the effects of social stratification: what they describe as an 'upper echelon' perspective. Managers as social actors interpret so as to act on – and in – the corporate world; such subjective interpretations being influenced by the individuals' socialisation. Managers filter the information they receive about the socio-economic environment in which they operate using their particular values and experience as members of upper echelons in society, interacting within that community, forming and enacting roles bounded by the particular norms of their distinctive social group. In turn, conditioning the managers' agency as members of corporate teams, interacting with the manner and nature of their rewards, feeding through into corporate performance. Cadsby et al (2007) observe a sorting effect whereby organisations attract and repel different individuals as a result of policies that put reward significantly 'at risk'. Upper echelon theorising has been developed to suggest that pay incentives to encourage risk taking may not in practice directly influence behaviour, instead serving a subtler role, acting to mute or accentuate the attributes of individuals working together as corporate management teams, influenced by their demographic characteristics, as well as value-driven propensity to engage in risk taking (Wowak and Hambrick, 2010).

Remco members, also upper echelon corporate actors, have become increasingly exposed to 'social outrage' effects arising from 'say on pay' regulatory initiatives (Bebchuck and Freid; 2003; Perkins and Shortland, 2022). Illustrations were offered in the preceding section where, encouraged by government ministers, shareholders are exercising their voice when asked to accept high-end employee remuneration reports. As described above, the UK Corporate Governance Code (FRC, 2018) and Companies (Directors' Remuneration Policy and Directors' Remuneration Report) Regulations, 2019, require Remcos to explain in some detail not only the 'facts' but also the committee members' underlying judgments around the flexible application of remuneration policy, and how this relates to reward management across the organisation. Attention is required to discretion exercised in setting reward packages to attract particular individuals to accept executive management appointments. Remcos are required to forecast the degree to which such investments will enhance shareholder value, within a specific timescale. Reports have to offer evidence linking business strategy to outcomes from executive reward management interventions to enable shareholders to grasp and evaluate what the organisation is trying to do and why particular performance measures have been put in place to achieve these outcomes (BIS, 2013).

In summary, there is a lack of consensus across the academic community justifying the quantum of executive reward, absolutely and relatively; how it should be set; and who should take the lead role in controlling this corporate governance aspect. Each of these factors may be perceived as creating a context, in open systems terms, within which executive reward may be observed, interpreted and appraised.

KEY ISSUES IN REWARD MANAGEMENT 10.3

Discourses in corporate social responsibility and shareholder value

In considering the context for executive reward determination, attention might be paid to debating contrasting notions of 'corporate social responsibility' (CSR), on the one hand, and 'shareholder value', on the other hand. 'The rational economic notion of "shareholder value" [locates] the interests of the shareholder as paramount and encourages managers to privilege only those strategies and decisions that directly benefit shareholders in the short term' (Michelson and Wailes, 2006: 239). Simultaneously, CSR 'speaks of a range of legitimate claims on the organisation and suggests social, ethical and moral considerations ought to play a more significant role in corporate strategic planning and decision-making' (Michelson and Wailes, 2006: 239).

Kessler (2007) observes that for some years 'strategic' reward management has been advocated as the overriding concern of progressive human resource management, but draws attention to the argument that this does not imply a binary alternative to more traditional concerns around the effort–reward bargain to do with equity and fairness. Consequently, it may be proposed that 'effective' executive performance and reward management, aligned with more corporately responsible organisational stewardship, may imply consideration of factors that go beyond the shareholder value dimension. It is to this argument that the proposed development of a 'framework for fairness in senior remuneration' speaks (Hutton, 2011).

Emphasising the need to pay attention to the dynamics of power in organisational affairs, Michelson and Wailes (2006) argue, however, that in the struggle for dominance between what they term the 'meta-discourses' of CSR and shareholder value, the power shift to those whose priority is shareholder value results in 'bounded rationality' on the part of executive management such that, even when nominally pursuing CSR-inclined policies and practices, the 'effectiveness' benchmark ultimately will be: is this 'good for the business' measured relative to those whose capital stake is financial?

Michelson and Wailes (2006) chart changes beginning in the late 1970s in the purpose attributed to organisations and their management, which the analysts attribute to a shift in socio-economic power. They argue that the changes constitute a reaction to the governance of organisations observable in the mid-20th century against principles sometimes referred to as 'managerial capitalism' (Jacoby, 2006). That is, the senior managers of corporations 'owned' by shareholders in western economies were able to accumulate power to secure their status relative to shareholders who during that period were dispersed, providing managers with a dispositional advantage in power-dependency terms (Pfeffer and Salancik, 2003). Corporate managers could engage in so-called 'empire building', accumulating business units that reduced the firms' competitive exposure, but allegedly at the cost of delivering returns rightly due to financial investors. It also enabled managers allegedly to transfer a higher than justified share of retained earnings to increase their own remuneration.

However, during the final decades of the 20th century, increased concentration of shareholdings under fund managers – for example, major insurance and/or retirement funds – reduced the room for managerial manoeuvre, and increased the leverage that shareholders (or institutional managers acting on the part of beneficial interest holders) could apply. While initially adopting a defensive stance towards the challenge to their autonomy, a new generation of corporate managers during the 1980s and 1990s appeared to make common cause with the 'shareholder value' ideology, as initiatives derived from principal–agency-based theorising on the relationship between investors and management took hold, with its prospect of wealth accumulation opportunities for individual executives, via stock options and other forms of long-term incentive payments (Jacoby, 2006).

Michelson and Wailes describe the scope for dysfunctional behaviour on the part of executives to arise consequent on following a shareholder value orientation and concomitant reward strategy, for example the collapse of energy company Enron where, until the company filed for bankruptcy in 2001, a public face was conveyed by the corporate leadership, for example, in a letter sent to shareholders by the chief executive in 2000, 'portraying the organisation as perfect in every way' (2006: 257). Similar judgements have been made regarding the circumstances in banking and financial services leading up to the 2008–09 financial crisis and its aftermath.

The same analysts contend that those concerned with regulation of corporate governance and executive behaviour have taken 'the wrong lesson' (2006: 257) from corporate scandals such as this. Rather than judging the problem as systemic – that is, an inevitable consequence of 'shareholder value'-based management – opening the way for a less bounded CSR discourse to take root, Enron's failure was presented 'as the outcome of a series of unfortunate and complex events… "special" or "unusual" circumstances' (Michelson and Wailes, 2006: 257). Beck-Krala et al (2022) call on decision-takers to come up with more socially responsible reward in the interests of corporate sustainability.

STUDENT EXERCISE

Working in groups, discuss the comparative merits of the corporate social responsibility and shareholder value discourses. What actions are open to HR specialists to navigate the tensions outlined in the literature reviewed in this chapter? Are you able to reach a 'professional' consensus view comparing different groups' conclusions?

10.6 Designing and reporting on executive reward

We have reviewed debates around the substance and process of the executive reward management system, including the corporate governance context, and associated theoretical orientations shaping interpretation and analysis. Attention now turns to the fabric of the executive effort-reward bargain, the make-up of a 'reward portfolio' and how this is communicated among stakeholders.

Veliyath (1999: 124) arranges the primary variables as follows: '(1) fixed compensation independent of firm performance, versus variable reward [tied to a performance measure], and (2) current compensation accruing at the end of the year, versus deferred compensation accruing in later years.' When considering executive reward design and administration attention is required also to account for choices made and consequences flowing from them. Beyond the bargain agreed between the employer (represented by appointments and remuneration committees) and employee (executive/director), increased public scrutiny of executive reward arrangements accompanying corporate governance regulatory developments requires companies to report on how corporate governance standards have been met – or, as noted earlier, to explain departures from the Code. The features of executive reward design, administration and reporting are described below with that basic architecture in mind, drawing on current published evidence.

10.6.1 The agent's interest

It is important also not to overlook the executive's own viewpoint when interpreting executive reward determination. Individuals are likely to evaluate the worth of pay and benefits offered under the rubric of an executive employment relationship, measured against their own perceptions of an acceptable return on the investment of human capital (i.e. the experience and skills the individual brings to the employment relationship in addition to a willingness to apply these on the employer's behalf). Whether or not the executive's assessment is warranted by the Remco, and in turn shareholder representatives, depends on the criteria applied (and wider systems factors such as the power-dependency balance). It may be unwise to assume uncritically that the positions may be objectively verified – the indeterminate nature of the effort–reward bargain introduces subjective factors that are difficult to control for. It may be argued, therefore, that designing and rationalising executive reward portfolios represents an artful as much as a scientific process.

The search for an executive employment relationship to satisfy the aims of both employer (or 'principal') and employee (or 'agent'), as well as to comply with standards of public reporting, have led to the establishment of executive reward 'package' norms. Three principal elements may be observed payable either directly in cash or ultimately convertible to cash: the salary traditionally afforded to a 'staff' employee (someone whom it is assumed the employer anticipates can have an impact on the organisation beyond the hour or the day of hire); a 'bonus' payment for meeting short-term performance requirements beyond contributing attendance and capability to perform; and forms of deferred reward, specifically long-term incentives for meeting objectives of strategic significance over an extended period (generally beyond one year), and a company-funded retirement pension. An additional element of the executive reward package may comprise perks and other non-cash benefits such as insured benefits, company-funded cars, etc.

10.6.2 Executive reward portfolios

Qualifying conditions (Buck et al, 2003) for including items in executive reward portfolios (or packages) to satisfy the multiplicity of goals and interests involved, as well as contextual dynamics, introduce limits on the discretion of decision-makers. The executive reward management system interacts with external influences: in particular, the combined pressure of 'competition for scarce talent in an international market' (House of Commons Trade and Industry Committee, 2003: 17), and the corporate governance regulatory developments summarised in Table 10.1. As we have already seen, these phenomena are each subject to robust debate in the literature.

Payment of a salary may continue to anchor the executive reward package, but its relative position has been subordinated as 'good practice' guidelines have shifted the focus increasingly towards 'at risk' reward, intended as an incentive for executive agents to perceive their interests aligned with shareholder principals – sharing the risk and potential reward (Norris, 2005; Pepper, 2006). This has been further refined so that executive reward should combine not only incentives to perform individually in making a short-term contribution to the profitable organisation. In addition, a longer-term element has been factored in: to retain executives in post, and to focus their attention on value-creating agency over the longer term. While it is true to say that at-risk (or incentive) elements have become increasingly common across all employee groups, in the case of executives, the logic articulated is that as the group most able to impact positively or negatively on corporate success, the bias in the guaranteed (basic) elements of their pay should be shifted towards the variable (incentive) elements. That said, as noted above, more recent pressure to defer bonus payments and to introduce clawback provisions has led to the prospect of a shift of emphasis back to salary to shore up total reward to meet financial services 'high-end' employee expectations, judged as potentially resulting in perverse outcomes in terms of fixed reward costs.

Pepper (2006: 14) posits 'a strong prima facie case' for keeping the three elements of salary, short-term bonus payments and deferred incentives in balance. The conclusion to be drawn is that, at least in theory, decision-makers anticipate that the reward amalgam will motivate behaviour on the part of executives acting together to represent shareholder interests, and sometimes those of wider stakeholders (Jensen et al, 2004), beyond the separate effects of the elements comprising the package taken singly. As we have seen, analysis within the empirical literature as to whether or not this aim is achieved in practice remains inconclusive.

10.7 Executive reward compliance/disclosure issues

Expectation and prescription has given rise to complexity in executive reward design, administration and reporting: producing compliance statements for inclusion in publicly listed company (plc) annual reports is a resource-intensive activity. Remco reports have become a sizeable part of the documentation plcs now regularly produce for reporting purposes, running to several pages in length, with cross-references to other parts of the annual report, to make explicit connections between executive reward and corporate commercial performance, and between executive reward and the arrangements applicable to all other employees.

Table 10.2 is derived from part of a Remco report included in a FTSE 100 company's annual report and accounts, detailing the reward portfolio applicable to directors. Actual reported values will of course vary from firm to firm. In addition to describing the substance of executive rewards, to meet regulatory standards an account is provided also of what the board intends to reward executive directors for, assessed against a variety of reward contingencies. The report itself further contains detailed (audited) information on the pay levels and other employment benefits received by named individuals covered by these arrangements. This includes details of the timing of exercise of outstanding share options, share grant values, individual shareholdings and trading in company shares.

The detailed account may be perceived as carefully crafted to 'tell the story' behind actions taken to order the relationship between the agents and principals in corporate governance and employment relations, enshrined in reward content and processes. Underscored by a statement of guiding principles, the aim may be understood as an attempt to demonstrate how gains from employment received by executives, financed from resources that might otherwise pass to shareholders, represent a legitimate share in the value created by the individual and collective action of the executives on behalf of shareholders.

Detailed statements on executive reward – and indeed Remcos – would historically have been an exceptional feature of companies' annual reports and accounts. Deloitte (2004: 19) note that shareholder representatives consulted by them report that the requirement in the Directors' Remuneration Report Regulations (2002) to vote on whether or not to accept the remuneration committee report had a 'very significant impact upon [shareholder] attitudes and behaviours'. More comprehensive disclosure is perceived as playing a vital role in assuring the means for informed supervision of activity in an area where a whole range of socio-economic systems collide. As noted earlier, the degree of detail required to be covered in the remuneration reports presented to shareholders by Remco chairs continues to expand. The

Table 10.2 Large UK stock market listed company executive reward framework

Reward component	Purpose	Award description	Policy application
Salary	To attract and retain the best talent.	Payable monthly in cash and counted as salary for pension accumulation purposes.	Subject to review annually and fixed for 12 months. In determining levels, the Remuneration Committee considers the Group as a whole and also the packages received by similar individuals at the Company's peers in the sector and other companies of comparable market capitalisation. Individual salary level is positioned against the relevant comparator group for each role, accounting for the level of skill, experience and scope of responsibility. Attention is paid also to business performance, scarcity of talent, economic climate and market conditions.
Annual Bonus/ Short-term Incentive Plan	To drive behaviour and communicate key priorities for the year To incentivise delivery of performance over the one-year operating cycle.	A performance-related cash payment awarded annually; [normally] not counted for pension accumulation purposes. Informed by metrics designed both to: • drive growth strategies while improving operating efficiencies; and • ensure focus on customer experience.	On target bonus paid when a director's performance is in line with plan; this normally results in a payment worth 100% of salary. At maximum performance, the payment is worth 200% of salary.

(continued)

Table 10.2 (Continued)

Reward component	Purpose	Award description	Policy application
Long-Term Incentive Plan (LTIP)	To incentivise achievement of sustained performance over the long term [ie not less than three years]. At the same time to encourage alignment with shareholder interests through a high level of share ownership. Total shareholder return (TSR) is combined with free cash flow to balance the need for discipline in making capital investment decisions combined with rigorous cash management (crucial to maintaining a 'going concern' business) with thinking about sustained value creation, as a shareholder is expected to do. [TSR is assessed by combining share price movements and dividend payments.]	Performance shares are granted annually. The value of awards is highly variable owing to the vesting schedule over which ownership of the shares is confirmed. Awards under the LTIP scheme are not pensionable. [LTIPs became popular following the 1995 Greenbury Report intended to offer a performance incentive over the long term – the 'long term' has been redefined over the ensuing period especially with the demise of Executive Share Option Schemes, but with pay-out timing shifting from five to 10 years to three years.]	Award levels and the framework for determining vesting are determined by the Remco mindful of the link with corporate strategy delivery. Awards vest not less than three years after the award based on an assessment of corporate level operational performance and external performance in terms of the returns to shareholders. Dividend equivalents are paid to individuals holding vested shares in cash after the vesting date (ie once the director owns the shares).
Pension	To provide competitive post-retirement reward.	Pension is counted as deferred income, which is payable on retirement in the form of a monthly pension with the option to receive part as a lump sum.	Directors may choose to participate in the company's defined contribution scheme or to receive a cash allowance in lieu of pension. The pension contribution or cash payment is equal to 24% of annual gross salary.

(continued)

Table 10.2 (Continued)

Reward component	Purpose	Award description	Policy application
Benefits	To aid retention and remain competitive in the marketplace.	Benefits include: • company car or cash allowance, fuel and in certain circumstances access to a chauffeur; • private medical, death in service and disability insurance, plus annual health checks; • relocation allowances if the company asks the individual to move home; • legal fees if appropriate; • other benefits in line with those offered to employees generally.	Benefits are provided with reference to practice in the relevant market where the individual is employed. While the expectation is that benefits will remain at a constant level, the value may fluctuate depending on personal situation as well as external factors including insurance premiums.

time required of Remco members and their specialist internal advisors and those outside the organisation, incurs a significant corporate cost so as to comply with the Companies (Directors' Remuneration Policy and Directors' Remuneration Report) Regulations, 2019.

10.8 Behind what is in the portfolio

In order to meet the requirements specified in the regulations, Directors' Remuneration Reports contain information that describes policies and their application overall and as this applies to individuals covered by the reporting requirements. The latter audited section details the specific values of remuneration awarded to individuals. In a narrative accompanying the numbers, information on the chair and membership of the Remco is set out, along with statements evidencing members' independence from the group company's executive directors. The number of Remco meetings over the year may be confirmed along with a register of members present and absent. The UK Corporate Governance Code, in combination with the Reporting Regulations, tends to be referenced as guiding the basis for policy on executive reward management, and the aim of the policy is set out. A statement is made that the elements of the reward portfolio are considered together and judged competitive but not excessive in each individual director's case.

> An example of a Directors' Remuneration (Remco) Report – running to 22 pages within the company annual report and accounts documents – is that published in 2023 by Vodaphone. The information includes an introduction titled a 'letter' from the Remco chair, describing application of the policy on its directors' remuneration that had been approved by the company's 2020 Annual General Meeting of shareholders. The report sets out in detail how the shareholder-approved policy has been applied during the fiscal year and planned application for the year ahead. A copy can be viewed at the company's website at the time of going to press at: investors.vodafone.com/sites/vodafone-ir/files/2023-05/vodafone-fy23-annual-report.pdf – pp. 85–106. There is also a link to a video in which the Remco chair speaks about her role.

Remco reports tend to offer the committee's stated position on their approach to executive reward management, and its fit with the corporate and market context as well as in relation to reward management across the organisation as a whole. Statements are likely to include claims such as those signed on 16 May 2023 by Valerie Gooding, Vodaphone's Remco chair:

> Our current Policy Report was approved at the July 2020 AGM, with a vote in favour of over 96%. Following the policy entering its third year of operation without amendment, the Committee has been reviewing our remuneration structures ahead of the regulatory requirement for a new policy to be submitted to shareholders at the 2023 AGM.
>
> The Committee is clear that consistency and flexibility should be maintained within the new policy and in the event material revisions are required before the end of its three-year regulatory lifecycle then the Committee will re-engage with shareholders.
>
> Following its review of the current arrangements, which the Committee is satisfied remain appropriate and operating as intended, and having made a significant number of best practice changes when the policy was last renewed, the Committee is not proposing to make any material changes at this time.
>
> Instead, some refinements to our framework and the implementation of our structures are proposed. These include the review of our short-term incentive to more fully support our priorities of Growth and Customers... The Committee is also strengthening our clawback policy with the current list of trigger events expanded to include a breach of an executive's restrictive or confidentiality covenants, reflecting the importance in our industry of retaining and protecting key talent and intellectual property. Clawback time frames are also being revised to ensure compliance with the recently announced SEC requirements, the vast majority of which our current arrangements already complied with.

> The implementation of our long-term incentive plan is subject to the Global Incentive Plan Rules which were last approved by shareholders at the 2014 AGM. In line with UK regulations, the Rules need to be approved by shareholders at least every 10 years and will be submitted for approval at the 2023 AGM. The Committee, with its external legal advisers, has reviewed the Rules to ensure they reflect latest market practice.

Reviewing this against the Corporate Governance Code (FRC, 2018), the statement may be seen to match against its core principles, namely:

- Reward policies and practices designed to support strategy and promote long-term sustainable success. Executive remuneration aligned to company purpose and values and clearly linked to the successful delivery of the company's long-term strategy.
- A formal and transparent procedure for developing policy on executive reward and determining director and senior management remuneration, with no director involved in deciding their own remuneration outcome.
- The exercise of independent judgement and discretion by directors acting as a Remco when authorising remuneration outcomes, taking account of company and individual performance, and wider circumstances.

Changes have been particularly in the nature of long-term incentive arrangements among stock market-listed companies (Deloitte, 2004; IDS, 2006d). In 2006 IDS reported a rise in incentive scheme potential payments at the maximum, justified in terms of action to align directors' and shareholders' interests, leading to a shift in the balance between fixed and variable pay towards performance-related remuneration, although no corresponding reduction in salary increase levels is reported. As noted earlier, these continue to rise above the general average in the employment system.

There is a range of potential outcomes from operation of an executive reward framework such as the one illustrated in Table 10.2, taking account of the combination of fixed and variable elements intended to cohere as the basis for recognising against stated criteria how senior executives create value for shareholders over the short- and longer-term. In setting levels of reward, Remco reports will tend to include statements that members have considered the total remuneration packages paid in what they consider to be relevant comparator companies. The statements usually express a judgement in the appropriateness of positioning total remuneration between the median and upper quartile of this group, given the group company's size and complexity, including on an international scale.

Complex calculations often attach to the estimated value arising from awards to be made to executives in accordance with incentive plans, forming part of the information companies are expected to disclose in accordance with good practice. With LTIPs, mathematical models (e.g. 'Black Scholes' or 'Binomial') may be used to indicate future outcomes. While the principles of shareholder-aligned performance may be theoretically sound, in practice wide deviations between the estimates and eventual outcomes are reported. And declaration of performance targets against which executives are to be assessed is further complicated by corporate concern regarding making public details of operating plans that may be commercially sensitive. Despite this, regulators have been encouraging greater simplification in the overall determination of executive reward, in particular, performance incentives.

The following examples help illustrate ways in which regulating and reporting on executive reward management has been evolving, informed by an Executive Remuneration Database, looking at large UK stock market listed companies (e-Reward, 2019):

- Severn Trent opted for a new type of remuneration report replete with large sections on workforce, engagement, social purpose and fairness.
- Marks & Spencer included significant information regarding alignment with culture and direct feedback from its 'business involvement group', the staff representative body.
- Following a large shareholder vote against its remuneration policy Royal Mail responded by implementing an 'independent investor perception' survey to ascertain their views and objections.
- Vodafone invited a Reward Director from another FTSE 30 company to meet with its committee to share views/experiences which will become an annual event.

SELF-ASSESSMENT EXERCISE

Source a recent FTSE 100 plc annual report and turn to the Remco report section. Study the content and see if you can work out how the 'comply or explain' principles underlying current UK corporate governance regulations have been interpreted.

Table 10.3 Selected UK banking groups use of ESG factors in incentive plans

	No.	Minimum	Lower quartile	Median	Average	Upper quartile	Maximum
FTSE 100	7	25.0	43.0	76.0	73.3	99.6	127.0
Mid-250	8	9.3	22.5	36.0	33.1	42.5	55.0

SOURCE: e-Reward (2023)

Environmental, social and governance (ESG) measures have become more and more prominent within UK remuneration policies applied to executive directors. In their Executive Remuneration Database, e-Reward record 24 different performance measure categories, and the list of ESG targets includes those that may be themed as:

- safety-related;
- customer-related;
- employee-related;
- other ESG targets – environment, climate, diversity, culture, etc.

Illustrating the application of these categories, drawing on remuneration reports by large UK banks published in late 2022, e-Reward (2023) tabulate the measures used in each bank's annual bonus and long-term incentive plans, as reproduced in Table 10.3.

10.9 The reward specialist's role in executive reward management

Developments surrounding design, management and accounting for executive reward have given rise to specific consequences for the part the HR specialist may play in this complex and politically sensitive organisational sphere. Conversations with leading corporate reward specialists indicate that the role has shifted over the past 20 years so that more than a reward technician's skills are deemed necessary. Knowledge of a range of disciplines – actuarial, finance, legal – in addition to reward management know-how is required, as well as a capacity to play the part of skilled diplomat or 'go-between' in relation to members of Remcos and senior corporate executives (Perkins and Shortland, 2023). Effective liaison may also be called for in dealings with consultants appointed not only by the specialists' employer but also by the Remco, and with other external parties such as the ABI and NAPF, as well as the FCA, whose guidance and instructions non-executive directors are wary of contradicting, given risks to individuals' reputation as competent corporate supervisors acting on the shareholders' behalf in their dealings with management.

Attention to detail in the preparation of Remco papers and in the records of decisions is important. As one reward director put it: 'With so many moving parts it's easy to overlook something that may have consequences later.' The instance was given of where, during a significant organisational change, the need to consult shareholders concerning an aspect of an already existing long-term incentive plan was recognised at a late stage, having been overlooked to that point by external advisors. Project management skills are thus called for to ensure that the process runs to time and cost: given the sheer range of activity demanded, the latter can be significant.

The reward specialist may also need to draw on other skill sets with further resource consequences internally – for example, to obtain support from colleagues (e.g. in the finance function) to undertake complex financial modelling to meet Remco demands for systematic evaluation of projected outcomes from applying certain performance measures with goal-setting and computation of executive bonus and related incentive awards. Given the scale and complexity of disclosure reporting annually in the directors' remuneration report, excellent drafting skills are necessary, as well as awareness of the latest regulatory developments requiring compliance action, most likely working in co-operation with the company secretariat and finance function.

Competence in communicating, accurately and diplomatically, orally as well as in writing is viewed as a prerequisite. Non-executive directors do not expect to be 'lectured' by a specialist operating below their peer level, but offered a précis briefing on an issue to be debated or in response to a question to inform their decision-making. The view has been put forward by seasoned specialists consulted that an employment relations background – building experience in understanding the views of the parties and engaging in negotiating outcomes – as well as in representing the organisation in determining terms and conditions related to individual senior appointments may be useful developmental experience to prepare an aspirant future head of reward for exposure to Remco activity.

While addressing corporate expectations, ensuring that the individual's professional integrity is safeguarded has also been noted as critical: in the politically sensitive arena of contemporary executive reward management the answer may not always be 'yes'. Thus, in summary, the role of the contemporary senior-level corporate reward specialist has become one of skilful expert across a range of interconnected disciplines: efficient and effective project manager and corporate governance steward; accomplished communicator; and social diplomat able to preserve personal and professional integrity.

10.10 Executive reward in the public sector

Discussion in this chapter is primarily informed by commentary regarding executive reward determination in for-profit enterprises. However, a 'new management' ethos directed towards the public/not-for-profit sector of the economy (Perkins and White, 2010) means we should not neglect to mention the implications for executive-level reward. Cahan, Chua and Nyamori (2005: 441) argue: 'the purpose of public sector reforms is to make public sector entities more like private sector firms, including the use of private sector-style boards as the primary internal corporate governance mechanism'. However, in terms of reward management in the absence of an externally determined share price, determining changes in the public entity's value is more difficult, complicating attempts to apply traditional agency-based reward systems to align executive incentives with the interests of owners (i.e. the state and ultimately citizens) and managers (Cahan, Chua and Nyamori, 2005).

The same researchers report 'limited, if any, empirical research examining, for example, the relationship between CEO compensation and board structure in the public sector' (2005: 441). They argue that public sector board effectiveness is particularly important given the reduced substitute control mechanisms compared with the private sector (i.e. 'market monitoring'). Although the gap between executive pay and lower levels in 'liberal market economy' private sectors, most notably in the USA, is not open to replication on a similar scale in an environment where 'wealth accumulation' instruments like stock options are not available, then, the position is noteworthy where a new generation of public sector executives may be instrumentally inclined to embrace a more contingent approach to reward, given potential to manage it in their favour.

For example, Brickley et al (2003, cited by Cahan, Chua and Nyamori, 2005) researched a sample of just over 300 not-for-profit hospitals in the USA, examining the relation between chief executive reward and board structure. The researchers found, first, higher levels of chief executive reward when the chief executive was a voting member of the board; and, secondly, some evidence that chief executive reward was positively related to board size and the percentage of 'inside' (or executive) directors.

The situation is not confined to the size or rate of increase in reward levels: the so-called 'rewards for failure' debate in the media received a fillip in the UK, surrounding the fate of Paul Gray, former chairman of HM Revenue and Customs, who resigned in November 2007 over an 'extremely serious failure' of security, but reportedly would retain his entitlement to final earnings-linked pension benefits (Gilmore and O'Connor, 2007). And as already noted an investigation was commissioned by the UK coalition government to review 'fair pay' in the public sector (Hutton, 2010a). Following publication of the report of the review, next steps included use of a code of practice drafted by the Senior Salaries Review Body as a starting point from which to construct a 'fair pay framework'. Its key components were to develop a pay multiple (currently posited at 20:1) for application as a benchmark on a dispersion between pay at the most senior and most junior levels of public servant judged fair irrespective of the kinds of organisation and different regions within which people may be employed. The Review also promised to examine ways in which pay for performance may form part of fair pay, as well as suggesting ways in which the public sector could make better use of alternative performance pay systems, and developing understanding of labour market issues and the interplay between reward systems and those covering recruitment and retention, talent management and related issues. Progress may be halting; in its 44th report, styling its approach as consistent with that taken by large private sector organisations, where an executive remuneration committee or similar body exists, the Senior Salaries Review Body put it bluntly:

> We continue to emphasise the need for a more strategic approach to reward and the importance of focusing on outcomes. The Government has endorsed this approach but has done little to translate its support into concrete action.
>
> (Read, 2022: 3)

Commenting on dilemmas arising in the face of efforts to address pay dispersion grounded in notions of fairness, Read (2022: 1) adds:

> Depressing senior pay over very long periods damages motivation and morale and lowers the attractiveness of leadership positions. Moreover, some senior managers are now paid less than those they are responsible for, which is a particular problem in parts of the senior civil service. This can deter applicants from feeder groups from applying for promotion. The cumulative effect of restraining senior pay over long periods distorts incentives at all levels of an organisation.

10.11 Conclusions and key learning points

In this chapter, a range of contemporary literature has been drawn on to inform reflection and understanding regarding the alternatives and consequences associated with executive reward and its management, as well as the systemic context in which executive reward systems interact dynamically between elements and actors within and outside the organisation. One conclusion is that executive reward design and management may be interpreted as combining to delineate a distinctive employment relationship between an organisation and those to whom leadership and management is entrusted by those with a beneficial stake in its effective governance.

With reference to stock market companies, in a strictly legal sense within Anglo-American business systems the beneficiaries are limited to shareholders. However, although commentators may disagree on the merits of widening the zone of interests to be served by corporate leaders, regulation has expanded with the intention that stakeholders more generally see their interests served in corporate organisation, as reflected in forms of incentive and recognition afforded to organisational stewards. This may be especially the case as public service and voluntary sector organisations are brought into consideration. As has been illustrated using the literature reviewed for this chapter, the position is complex and controversial – and may be subject to contradiction (Perkins, 2009). The ever increasing raft of European and UK corporate governance legislation emphasises the supervisory responsibilities falling to institutional shareholders in particular, implicitly taking into account wider 'public interest' considerations especially following reactions to the need to divert taxpayers' funds to avoid a threatened collapse in the financial system during the financial crisis more than a decade ago. And with a new interest in 'fairness', that began with a formal review of pay dispersion in public service organisations but with the author signalling an intention that new benchmarks should form the basis for judging the legitimacy of pay levels in for-profit enterprises as well, ongoing scrutiny and debate around what represents acceptable practice is expected to further intensify. While the 2019 Select Committee report fell victim at least in part to the overriding government focus on Brexit, pressure for structural change in the regulation of executive reward is unlikely to dissipate as the FRC's consultation completes leading to a further revised UK Corporate Governance Code in 2024.

HR specialists may wish to approach executive reward bearing in mind the need to accommodate the requirement to align it with business strategy; to be able to demonstrate this achievement to the extent required by corporate governance codes of practice, ensuring that practice is fully compliant with transparency and disclosure standards. Simultaneously, it is necessary to design and operate reward arrangements for executives that are aligned with trends in appropriate employment markets, bearing in mind the possible influence of international considerations, and that the substance and processes involved act to clearly communicate the priorities for corporately desired outcomes and behaviours. Adding to systemically interacting factors around executive reward management what WorldatWork (2007) labels 'community concerns', designers and decision-takers may wish to consider:

- the internal environment unique to each organisation – not only the enterprise and its aims but also its human capital resources to achieve them, including people's expectations, and the philosophy to guide action to address these phenomena;
- the range of stakeholders with both financial and social interests in the organisation, its governance and consequences;
- the external environment (domestic and international economic trends, industry sector developments, impact of government and special interest groups, etc) that is likely to comprise factors outside the control of the organisation and its management, but which need to be accounted for when designing executive reward arrangements;
- disclosure and transparency, and how forms of socio-political regulation interact with the organisation's values and priorities and strategy for engaging with economic threats and opportunities, impacting on the extent to which the organisation provides complete and comprehensible information – or explains exceptions to compliance provisions.

Explore further

For a discussion of arguments around executive reward management in a historical context see chapters 27 and 28 in *The Routledge Companion to Reward Management* (2022) edited by Perkins, SJ, London: Routledge. The first, by Brian Dive, critiques the notion of 'market' arguments for 40 years of escalating executive rewards; the second, by Andreas Komelakis and Howard Gospel, locates executive reward management within the theoretical notion of 'corporate financialization'.

For discussion using a four-part typology to inform critical engagement with thinking around practical considerations, see Perkins, SJ (2015) Perspectives on problems in managing managers' remuneration, in Wilkinson, A (ed.) *Handbook of Research on Managing Managers*, Cheltenham: Edward Elgar.

For a summary review of academic literature published between 2007 and 2013, see Pepper, A and Campbell, R (2014) *Executive Reward: A review of the drivers and consequences*. London: CIPD, www.cipd.org/en/knowledge/reports/reward-executive-report/. Bringing the issues further up to date, see the report prepared for the FRC by researchers at the University of Portsmouth: Abdelfattah, T, Aboud, A, Khaled Hussainey, K and McBride, K (2021) *Changes in Remuneration Reporting Following the UK Corporate Governance Code 2018*, London: Financial Reporting Council, www.frc.org.uk/getattachment/c9347fef-ac65-41f7-85e5-43723c71e448/FRC-UoP_Remuneration-Research-Report_May-2021.pdf.

A CIPD resource for members is *Role of the Remco: How to achieve good governance of pay, people and culture: Roadmap for HR leaders seeking to broaden the remit of remuneration committees* (published in July 2021), www.cipd.org/en/knowledge/reports/reforming-remuneration-policy/.

For those interested in public services contexts, see the following House of Commons Public Administration Select Committee report, 'Executive Pay in the Public Sector, a volume of submissions by interested parties to inform an Inquiry', www.parliament.uk/globalassets/documents/upload/Memosforweb271009.pdf.

11 International reward management

CHAPTER LEARNING OUTCOMES

At the end of this chapter, you should understand and be able to explain the following:

- The contexts multinational employers encounter influencing their aims and choices in determining employee reward across international operations.
- The various types of employees for whom employee reward strategies, policies and processes need to be designed and administered.
- The use of theory and knowledge derived from empirical research in weighing opportunities and problems in rewarding employees in an international context.

CIPD STRATEGIC REWARD MANAGEMENT (7HR03) LEARNING OUTCOMES

Learners will be able to:

3.5 Examine a range of factors that impact on international remuneration decisions.

11.1 Introduction

The United Nations Conference on Trade and Development's 2023 World Investment Report (UNCTAD, 2023) illustrates the significance of transnational organisational activity as a context for international reward management. While global overlapping global crises (the war in Ukraine, high food and energy prices, and soaring public debt) led to a 12 per cent decline compared with the previous year, UNCTAD reports the flow of foreign direct investment (FDI) globally amounted to $1.3 trillion in 2022. Over 350,000 companies employed 250 or more people worldwide in 2021 and a few years earlier UNCTAD estimated almost 76 million people being employed in multinational enterprises' (MNEs') 'foreign affiliates', recorded as up from 28.5m in 1990 (UNCTAD, 2019).

Whole texts are devoted to managing people across international contexts. And we have contributed to this specialist literature – for example a discussion of pay for performance in Europe (Sahakiants et al, 2016). In this chapter, the focus will be on the reward management issues associated with mobilising resources to support organisational operations around the world. Sometimes this involves the transfer of individuals on expatriate assignments of various types/durations. Sometimes it involves the employment, retention and motivation of employees drawn from countries playing host to MNE operations to perform in accordance with employers' priorities. Reward management is a complex endeavour wherever it is carried out. Undertaking reward management internationally, mindful of cultural and institutional considerations, adds a further layer of complexity for managers to address (Briscoe and Schuler, 2004; Sahakiants et al, 2016).

11.2 Rewarding expatriation – rewarding multi-local talent

The HR specialist faces problems to be solved, first, in supporting a MNE's wish to employ 'parent country nationals' (PCNs) not only in the organisation's country of origin, drawing from domestic employment sources. PCNs may be expatriated to work in other countries to resource business development and operations there. And these transfers may be more than an isolated 'out-return' cycle but require multiple assignments over time as the MNE and its strategy-structure arrangements evolve (Shortland and Perkins, 2019). The assignments may vary in terms of duration, as well as giving rise to different considerations around the effort–reward bargain, bearing in mind that the employee's circumstances, like those of the organisation, are unlikely to remain static.

Secondly, there is the question of employing individuals sourced from the 'host' country where the MNE sets up operations, to support the enterprise in that jurisdiction. If 'host country nationals' (HCNs) are working alongside PCNs – possibly occupying positions of superiority in leading regional operations – according to the equal pay for work of equal value principle, it may be hypothesised that they should be subject to PCN reward management terms and conditions. While local contextual considerations may be factored-in, such as the value of pay to individuals in terms of purchasing power, remuneration versus payments to 'keep expatriates whole' (discussed below), clarity on policy and its communication to all employees affected is essential.

Thirdly, as MNEs increase their presence, and develop confidence in the potential of talented employees in countries around the world to transfer corporate practice embedded in their experience and knowledge beyond their country of origin, corporate management may choose to widen the source from which to assign managers and specialists transnationally. These 'third country nationals' (TCNs) may have been recruited and rewarded on terms embedded in their country of origin employment system. But if they are expected to contribute to corporate performance, working transnationally, in the same way as PCNs, again, is there a case that their reward should be synchronised with that of the PCNs?

11.3 Convergent transnational capital power – divergent business systems

Prevailing wisdom may be to theorise a convergence between employment systems worldwide – even if this involves two capitalist 'varieties' (Hall and Soskice, 2001): a deregulated 'liberal market'-oriented variant, on the one hand, and a more politically 'co-ordinated' type, on the other hand.

In liberal market economies, the tendency is for active stock market regulation of business, with unitary boards and decentralised industrial relations: typical examples cited are the UK and USA. In co-ordinated (sometimes 'social') market economies, stock markets may be balanced by direct engagement in business governance by banks and other long-term-oriented financial interests. Industrial relations tend to be centralised, with legislation on occupational categorisation sometimes specifying a hierarchy of pay rates; and trade unions may sit on the supervisory part of a two-tier board structure along with capital investors, overseeing top management appointments and strategy. Typical examples cited include Germany, Japan and the Scandinavian countries (albeit with variation between them, just as there are between the UK and USA, in terms of detailed business system characteristics – e.g. in Japan, industrial relations tends to be highly decentralised). These are very simplified descriptions, and the reader is directed to classic sources such as Hall and Soskice (2001) for a more comprehensive specification.

From the point of view of the MNE management wishing simply to follow a common recipe for rewarding workforce members irrespective of the operating environment, however, as Brookes et al (2005) argue, diverse 'business systems constitute mechanisms and structures for regulating market relations. While, at least partially, they may be backed up by coercive power, they are most visible in shaping, moulding and making possible everyday exchange relationships through imitation and network ties' (2005: 406–7). The MNE's dispositional advantage as the source of FDI capital may suggest potential on the part of the inward investor to mobilise coercive power. But although 'use of coercion as a means of backing up and enforcing practices' is feasible, this constitutes 'a relatively inefficient and resource-intensive mechanism that is unlikely to deployed in day-to-day social transactions' (2005: 407). Observable underlying cultural and institutional factors continue to vary (Sparrow, 1999, 2000), reflecting differences in tax and social insurance regulations, as well as social considerations affecting work orientations that, in practice, enable and constrain reward management choices in the multinational organisation (Bloom et al, 2003).

The growing significance of major 'developing' and 'transforming' economies such as China and India, coupled with the recent economic crises originating in the finance sectors of both liberal- and coordinated-market variants, raises questions around a potentially shifting centre of economic and political gravity. Empirical research in countries that are former members of the Soviet Union has indicated that in the transition economies important specificities in the remuneration systems can be accounted for by reference to their 'socialist past', implying that what is referred to as 'path dependence' needs to be borne in mind (Sahakiants et al, 2016).

11.4 Not for profits alone

While much of the literature (and therefore its discussion in this chapter) reports on developments in profit-seeking enterprises, many of the considerations around employee reward and its management apply equally to not-for-profit organisations, such as transnational and supranational government institutions and voluntary sector bodies. Such organisations also operate across a variety of international locations and compete for talented people to run them – both indigenous and expatriate.

Moreover, not-for-profit enterprises face employee reward management issues just as, if not more, pressing than those encountered by commercial trading entities. While people may be perceived as joining voluntary or regulatory organisations for reasons different from those attributed to people recruited to profit-centred business firms, it is easy for these assumptions to cloud the universal problem of getting scarce people resources into place – when often those places not only demand highly skilful capabilities; they may also represent especially challenging environments in which to deploy people.

11.5 Multinational contexts for employee reward management

In the case of commercially governed businesses (although much the same could be argued to apply to other forms of organisation), operations in countries outside the MNE's country of origin are reported to have become increasingly significant as the balance of commercial emphasis has shifted, compared with domestic activities (Farashashi, Hasi and Molz, 2005). Revenue streams from devolved manufacturing and/or trading across the MNE, once limited compared with domestic country operations, have taken on 'strategic importance', as the UNCTAD (2023) evidence cited earlier indicates. Geppert (2005: 1) reports staged multinational development involving decisions 'to move from the early internationalisation concerned with exporting, licensing and franchising towards foreign direct investment strategies [towards]... the establishment of host country subsidiaries... as driven [mainly] by economic calculations to improve [a MNE's] profitability, cost efficiency and innovativeness'.

Non-domestic activities now command an increasingly large proportion of corporate resources that all need to be deployed so that the MNE can compete profitably on a global scale.

> Specifically, corporate management teams are to focus on 'the generation and transfer of knowledge across national settings, organizations and *networks*'.
>
> (Goodherham and Nordhaug, 2003: 1, emphasis added)

The reference to networks is significant: 'a MNE's ability merely to enable the flow of knowledge from its headquarters to its national subsidiary units no longer represents a sufficient competitive advantage' (Nohria and Ghoshal, 1997: 1–2). Traditional scale economies have been eroded, it is argued, and competitors are no longer limited to domestic firms. MNEs face other giant-sized multinational corporations in 'head-to-head' competition for profitable revenues. Accordingly, MNEs have been encouraged to migrate from HQ-led and hierarchical organisation structures to the 'multi-headed' (Morgan and Whitley, 2003), or 'transnational' (Ghoshal and Bartlett, 1998) or 'differentiated network' (Nohria and Ghoshal, 1997) structure. This model is consistent with the shift from an emphasis on exploiting sources of cheap labour to one of tapping tacit knowledge, embedded in new strategic assets around the globe, such as multi-local industry districts, with the accent on what Nohria and Ghoshal (1997) describe as 'prolific innovation'.

Offering a reality check to this strategy discourse, however, Edwards et al (2005: 1261) observe that, while ideas about the networked transfusion of knowledge may appear as corporate imperatives, 'there is little evidence on this phenomenon'. In fact, bringing our focus back to people management, what Edwards et al (2005) describe as 'reverse transfusion' of employment practices to support multi-headed organisation may be inhibited by the difficulties of dislodging institutional structures and practices. This implies that, for example, people in internationally facing roles located at corporate HQ may experience difficulty in changing, undermining the basic premise of the model.

Illustrating this in practice, Perkins (2006) reports evidence at the European regional level of a large, well-known information technology (IT) company. In the past, scope had existed to influence, and possibly reinterpret reward policies to meet transnational operating conditions, where lessons learned were fed back to HQ in the USA to enrich corporate policy. Now the US-based 'central hub' exclusively undertook development of reward management programmes and governance processes: activity in the regions had shifted to enabling the corporately mandated framework to work effectively across the various countries involved. Regional specialists said they accepted the logic behind the drive for centralisation and rationalisation, in response to the problem of remaining profitable in a tight globally competitive market. But they felt the new strategy of 'minimising differences' required a 'mindset change' at the corporate level. And this is not an isolated case. Perkins (2006) reports evidence suggesting efforts more generally on the part of multinational corporate reward designers to 'reduce differences', contrasting with trends discernible half a decade earlier that implied 'dispersed network' theory was being acted on in practice (Perkins and Hendry, 2001).

Edwards et al (2005) argue that, contrary to its ascribed flexibility as a liberal market economy, institutional legacies in the US employment system may inhibit innovation when co-ordinating activities at the multinational level. They specifically cite the example of businesses, like the IT case above, which started out under the direct management of founders with a paternalistic managerial style. One emphasis was on keeping trade unions out, translating among other things to relatively generous reward levels – consistent with the principles of efficiency wage theory described in Chapter 2. While, as in the case outlined, a fundamental break with legacy employment conditions may occur, necessitated by changing commercial conditions, the institutionally embedded mindset of 'the way we do things around here' may prevail among US corporate HQ members, influencing their dealings with other parts of the MNE, undermining the notion of a 'networked structure'.

SELF-ASSESSMENT EXERCISE

Consider the division of labour and policy-based authority among HR specialists in a large MNE with a network of regionally located operations. To what extent should members of HR specialist teams working from regional offices around the world defer to HQ in the detailed interpretation and application of reward policies and practices in support of their line management 'business partners'? What might be ways of sharing experience in working with corporate reward strategies across the network? What would be the prerequisites in terms of working relationships between line and senior corporate management and between HR specialists possibly working to a matrix reporting line?

11.6 Choices for multinational management and their reward consequences

The role, organisation and priorities of MNEs and associated people management has important consequences for employee reward considerations, especially bearing in mind a perceived ongoing tension between globalisation and localisation of reward systems (Drape et al, 2010).

First, use of the term 'international reward', as it has appeared in the HRM literature, may need to be revisited when considering treatment of employee segments subject to management in the contemporary international context (Perkins and Hendry, 2001). Secondly, the ascription of a strategic role for international operations and to the profitable generation and networked transfer of knowledge may be interpreted as requiring more corporate managerial attention to employee reward across the enterprise than may have been the case previously. While, on the one hand, acknowledging diversity in the character of the multinational population, giving rise to segmented employment administration issues, on the other hand, the emphasis in the corporate strategy literature on transnationally networked resource management implies a requirement for more integrated policymaking.

If a MNE's human resource strategy shifts from one of exploiting cheap labour sources, to securing '[t]acit knowledge of local markets [as] perhaps the ultimate source of value and... the basis for developing unique competitive strategies' (Harvey et al, 2002: 285), reward management choices will need to avoid consequences the actors perceive as unfair and so divisive, undermining multi-headed team structures working to a common set of aims. This is consistent with Kessler's (2007) argument that reward designs should not be informed by business strategy in isolation from considerations of internal and external equity. If the people to be employed and managed internationally are counted as 'strategic' resources (thereby demanding top corporate management attention), then it follows logically that purposeful, co-ordinated and context-sensitive employee reward policy and practice interventions will be required.

Cuervo-Cazurra et al (2007) argue that a lack of complementary resources required to operate abroad, that is people and their interaction with other corporate resources including operating systems and processes, represents an important inhibitor to internationalisation in search of new and profitable revenues. And even if corporate management seek to achieve a balance between global strategy and local sensitivity the design and application of 'employee engagement' approaches to facilitate profitable knowledge mobilisation does not occur in a vacuum.

Other MNEs will be seeking to acquire, retain and align these 'strategic capabilities' also. Assuming individuals will be aware of the demand for their particular skills and willingness to put them to work, talented people are likely to bring expectations to the kind of employment relationship – and its terms – on offer for their voluntary co-operation with a corporate project that also demands accommodation within international reward design. Mamman et al (1996) advocate that, despite surprisingly few studies investigating the issue, MNE managements pay attention to employees' preferred criteria for pay systems to which they will be subjected, accounting for cultural factors, demographics and industry type.

Aleweld et al (2015: 5) set out a set of strategic questions or prompts against which managers of MNEs can reflect on the choices and consequences in context of their approach to 'global reward governance', summarised as follows:

- How far along the centralisation-decentralisation continuum for reward management decision taking does the organisation intend to be?
- What results from explicitly reflecting on the organisation's headquarters' and subsidiaries' perspectives on global rewards?
- What account do reward designers take of the various hierarchical levels (senior managers, middle managers, operational employees) in analysing and making decisions around reward management globally?
- What degree of centralisation versus decentralisation applies to management of the various elements of reward globally (salary, variable pay, financial and non-cash employment-related benefits)?
- To what extent are reward practices similar in application across the MNE's headquarters and subsidiaries?

- What organisational as well as country-specific factors set the context for global reward management and what impact do they have?
- How effective is the balance between centralised and decentralised reward management practices, in terms of achieving organisational objectives?

Among the findings from research Aleweld et al (2015) conducted against the above framework they discovered that variable pay and specifically the pay of senior managers is managed more centrally; that the degree of centralisation correlates with company size as is where the headquarters is located (US more centralised, Germany less so, for example). Added to these findings, the researchers discovered that the more 'culturally distant' headquarters and subsidiaries are the more decentralised reward management becomes, in particular related to forms of variable pay. And corporate strategy is the driving force behind centralised reward management, with local law (or institutional requirements) associated with localised approaches. In terms of effectiveness, when HR respondents were questioned headquarters representatives favoured centralised practices with subsidiary representatives arguing for the opposite.

Based on responses from 158 reward managers located at the headquarters or subsidiaries of MNEs, Tekieli et al (2018) analysed the relationship between the centralisation of reward management decision-making and its perceived effectiveness in MNEs. The researchers found that headquarters managers perceive a centralised approach as being more effective, while for subsidiary managers this relationship is moderated by the manager's role identity. The study informs the debate around standardisation versus localisation, encouraging attention to psychological processes. The importance of in-group favouritism in headquarters and the influence of subsidiary managers' role identities on reward management decision-making is highlighted.

STUDENT EXERCISE

Working in groups, identify multinational organisations known to you and share ideas on what their approach to 'doing business abroad' seems to be. It may be helpful to prepare for this exercise by looking on the internet for marketing material, corporate governance reporting information and/or other documents released into the public domain on initiatives to develop and win support from shareholders, donors, customers and other sources of capital and revenue.

How extensive do operations appear to be worldwide? Is the organisation 'mature' internationally or at an earlier stage of development? Where is the 'home' country? What are the implications of what you find out and synthesise in your discussion? List the top three priorities for setting terms and conditions for employing people globally consequent on your conclusions.

11.7 Factors and trends in rewarding *expatriated* knowledge mobilisation

Following Harvery et al's (2002) suggestions, the idea of mobilising key capabilities to achieve organisational goals is a promising one to focus consideration of approaches to international employee reward. If we go along with the proposition that active reward management offers employers one route by which to communicate what they value (Lawler, 1995), then there is a role in getting the message across about prioritising mobilisation of employees' knowledge so as to put it to work in situations (and places) where this can create profitable outcomes.

As a first step, the types of 'mobilisation' involved within MNEs need to be identified. This may help in thinking about the implications for reward design and practice specifically applicable to the various categories of employee making up the global workforce. It may also assist in clarifying what is meant by 'international reward' for the organisation pursuing a strategy of purposeful knowledge mobilisation.

Lowe et al (2002) are critical of the 'expatriate myopia' in literature concerned with managing people in international contexts. As indicated above, when addressing reward system issues MNEs are being encouraged to pay greater attention to how they build relationships with all the people they employ, with a strategic focus on organising them across globally integrated networks. So, when discussing international reward and recognition, a tendency in some international HRM commentary to equate 'global reward' design with considerations pertaining to the terms and conditions applicable to expatriate assignments (e.g. Watson and Singh, 2005) needs to be regarded critically. In practice, multinational reward considerations encompass the terms and conditions applicable to the three principal employee categories referred to earlier: HCNs, PCNs and TCNs. Commonalities and interactions between the categories in pursuit of alignment deserve attention, but there are also reasons to unscramble international reward management approaches applied in each case.

Special considerations arise in the case of expatriated PCNs and TCNs, taking account of the fact that a prevalent approach MNEs adopt to mobilise the knowledge capabilities they offer is by relocating employees (possibly accompanied by family members) across national borders. Issues follow specific to the act of relocation between employment (and residential) systems not applicable in the case of HCNs. For this reason, policies and practices specific to expatriate mobilisation have evolved, giving rise to issues that differentiate geographically mobile employees from those retained in the territory and employment system where they were recruited. Such arrangements – and accompanying costs and complexity – are not easily set aside. But the focus in corporate strategy prescription on networking knowledge implies that reward practices that have in the past isolated expatriates from co-workers, inhibiting knowledge networking, may be part of the 'complementary resourcing' difficulties implied by Cuervo-Cazurra et al (2007). Thus, not only is proper attention desirable to reward management of the entire multinational workforce, but even when specifically addressing expatriate reward management, account must be taken of the corporate goal of integration if the distributed network model of international organisation is pursued. Rewards for expatriate employees are discussed next, after which trends in international employee reward generally are reviewed.

11.8 Defining expatriates

A preliminary task in considering expatriate employees is to clarify who these people are; we will then describe the forms and durations over which they are deployed beyond their country of origin.

PCN expatriates have been defined as 'experts and managers' who are citizens of the country in which the MNE's corporate headquarters is located, assigned to work in a foreign country, tasked with transplanting corporate culture, competence and strategy to local units (Harris et al, 2003; Moore, 2006; Phillips and Fox, 2003). In turn, TCNs may be defined as 'citizens of a country other than the headquarters or host country' (Phillips and Fox, 2003: 466). TCNs represent a 'hybrid' choice for managing international subsidiaries, residing between PCNs and HCNs. TCNs 'combine the advantages and disadvantages of the use of expatriates and host country nationals' (Tan and Mahoney, 2006: 480). In theory, TCNs may have more local knowledge than PCNs and yet have less local knowledge than HCNs. And TCNs may have a deeper understanding of corporate policies than HCNs but may be less familiar with the parent organisation's 'culture, competence, and strategy' than expatriates from the corporate centre. Resourcing decisions to populate transnational operations are therefore strategic in nature, with clear consequences for the capabilities and likely performance outcomes being invested in.

But is there evidence not only of an increased demand for managers with international experience as more organisations join the multinational marketplace? Has the character of international employee mobilisation become more strategic, calling for fresh thinking about the models applied to expatriate reward management with an increased focus on performance in return for the significant financial investments MNEs make in resourcing their trans-national affiliates (Festing and Perkins, 2008)? Martin and Bartol (2003) answer in the affirmative, citing an argument by Gregersen et al (1998) that leadership experiences obtained from completing international assignments have been recognised as impacting positively on longer-term senior executive career development. Calls for more systematic management of expatriate performance imply consequences for the ways in which this is rewarded and recognised, paying attention to issues around short- and long-term incentive rewards (reviewed in Chapter 6).

11.9 Expatriate assignments

The typical expatriate assignment lasts two or three years (Harris and Dickmann, 2005), generally with a five-year limit (Briscoe and Schuler, 2004). Survey evidence suggests that over the past two to three decades alternatives have emerged, including permanent migration, short-term assignments, cross-border job swaps or membership of multicultural project teams (Forster, 2000). Energy multinational Shell spent some two years exploring the definition of international mobility applied across the business (Perkins, 2006), concluding that rather than polarise notions of expatriation, policy-makers might find it more helpful, given the changing nature of international organisation and the accompanying developments in expatriation, to think about employee mobility in terms of a continuum, as illustrated in Figure 11.1.

Figure 11.1 The international mobility continuum

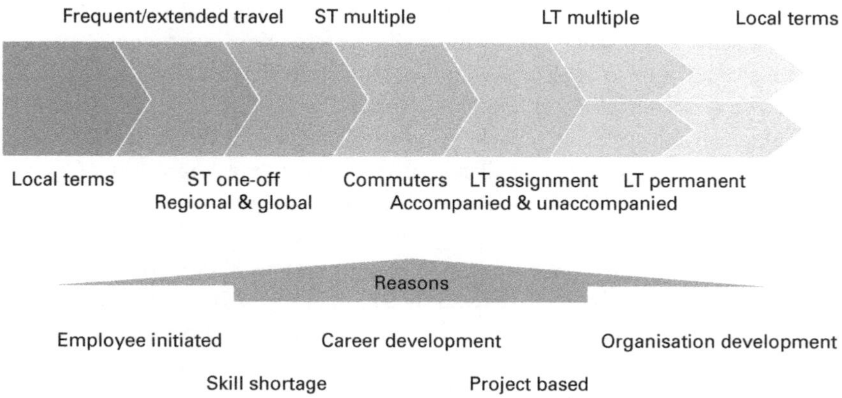

SOURCE: Perkins (2006)

NOTE: Based on a review undertaken by Shell

Here the variety of reasons for requiring expatriation could be set against assignment duration, facilitating a match in turn to appropriate expatriate policy terms.

A survey of policies for employees on short-term expatriate assignments, typically lasting between three and 12 months, indicates that short-term assignments are becoming more popular. Just over 60 per cent of respondents surveyed by Organization Resource Counselors Inc. (ORC) signalled an increase in short-term expatriation in their organisations (ORC, 2006). The same survey findings contrast short-term expatriate assignments with 'commuter assignments', popular where home and host location are close. Companies like Unilever may appoint an individual to work weekly in London, while retaining a family home in, say, Geneva to which the assignee returns each weekend. One reason offered for why the variety of expatriate assignments has been widening is reluctance on the part of individuals to accept assignments over the traditional duration in view of dual-career commitments where both partners are following professional careers, or when children's schooling or eldercare mean that long-term absences from the country where an employee has social ties would be unacceptable (ORC, 2004).

Short-term assignments enable knowledge mobilisation across geographies, without unsettling the individual's core lifestyle and relationships. There may, however, be hidden costs beyond the provision of serviced accommodation and supplemental travel and subsistence reimbursements, where the transnational commuter experiences even more barriers to becoming embedded in the local business environment, reinforcing the 'outsider' stereotype with attendant barriers to integrated performance referred to earlier. (For a detailed discussion, see the technical appendix to chapter 5 of Perkins and Shortland, 2006).

Table 11.1 Trajectory of an increasingly complex international assignment landscape

SOURCE: Mercer (2023)

Management consultancy Mercer (2023) argue that a new international assignment landscape is challenging traditional compensation approaches:

> For many years, expatriate compensation has been focused on a dilemma: having assignees on expensive home-based expatriate package versus localisation – which is about replacing expatriates with locals or at least transition expatriates from an expatriate package to a local salary. Many predicted that the traditional home-based balance sheet approach would gradually disappear. The predictions of the demise of the typical expatriate approach have been greatly exaggerated. We are witnessing the emergence of new compensation challenges instead, due to the complexity of having to manage multiple types of assignments and assignee categories.
>
> The home-based approach still retains its utility for certain kinds of moves (eg business-critical assignments or moves to hardship locations). Local strategies are becoming more common but, due to the difficulty of applying them consistently in all transfer destinations, they are used only in some cases (moves between similar countries, developmental moves) and take multiple forms as 'purely local' or local-plus approaches. Additional approaches like international compensation structures have emerged to address issues of global nomads. The challenge for HR managers is, therefore, not so much to find the best approach applicable for all assignments as to deal with individual assignment complexity, envisage greater mobility policy segmentation and, if relevant for the company, map each compensation approach to a particular assignment in a consistent way.
>
> (Mercer, 2023)

11.10 Accounting for expatriation reward management

Bonache (2006) points to the multifaceted purpose of expatriation reward management, summarised as follows:

- attract people to participate in expatriate assignments;
- be cost-effective for the employer;
- be fair in relation to host country employees and/or other expatriates from the same or a different home country;
- facilitate repatriation;
- support the organisation's international development plans.

So, the traditional 'recruit, retain, motivate' trinity of reward management drivers is augmented by reference to these wider considerations. The specific focus on growing and sustaining a business in competitive international markets adds a further layer for the reward management professional to consider and factor-in to policy recommendations and their interpretation when considering corporate reward strategy.

Figure 11.2 Example of an expatriate 'salary build-up' or 'balance sheet' plan

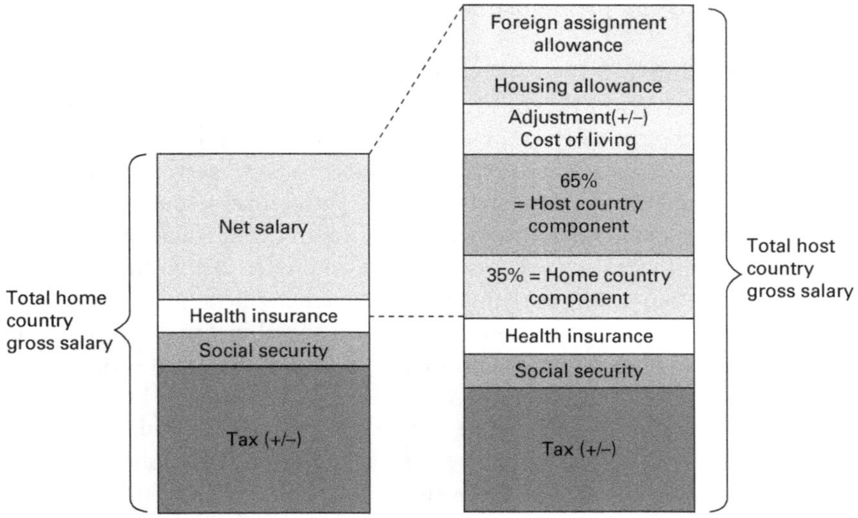

SOURCE: Festing and Perkins (2008)

One principle – 'keeping the expatriate whole' (Phillips and Fox, 2003: 470) – has governed reported thinking and practice on expatriate reward design. It is not merely a case of semantics to argue that this line of reasoning has downplayed the 'reward' aspect in favour of providing 'compensation' for accepting 'changes in life-style, enduring 'hardship', etc.' (Perkins and Shortland, 2006: 185). The sense of an 'exchange relationship' (we introduced this notion in Chapter 1) is still in focus, but the underlying rationale appears to veer away from the tradition of an 'effort bargain'.

This change of orientation is expressed, first, in terms of pay package design intended to preserve existing relativities with PCN peers, or at least to preserve consistency with reward levels for the employee's occupational group and level in their country of origin in the case of TCNs. Secondly, the express ambition is to maintain 'purchasing parity' – so that the expatriate may enjoy the same living standards as at home (Dowling et al, 2013; Fenwick, 2004).

The approach aligned to this policy orientation, known as the 'home-based/salary build-up', or 'balance sheet' (ORC, 2004), augments basic pay with a 'foreign service premium' (Dowling, Festing and Engle, 2013), as well as cash supplements to compensate for 'hardships' (e.g. working in remote or politically unstable locations, or those with limited social infrastructure). Housing and children's education costs are reimbursed, extending the 'kept whole' principle to the employee's family members. In addition to salary adjustments to neutralise cost of living differences, other allowances may include home leave, relocation, spouse assistance/dual career allowances and so on (Fenwick, 2004; Perkins and Shortland, 2006).

Adding complexity to expatriate 'compensation' administration, accompanying this traditional 'build-up' plan, consistent with the kept-whole principle, 'tax equalisation' generally accompanies balance sheet expatriate compensation. What this means is that the value of tax and social insurance contributions the employee would hypothetically have paid at home is deducted from the home base pay to arrive at a 'net' salary. Allowances and premiums are then added to that amount, and the organisation pays any tax falling due within host jurisdiction on the compensation package total amount.

An illustrative example of such an expatriate compensation scheme, sourced from a German MNE, is set out in Figure 11.2. The total salary payable in the host country is built up from the net salary that would have been payable for the same job in the individual's home country. The net 'home country salary' serves as the comparative base line for calculating the expatriate salary. Differences in cost of living, living standards and housing standards are incorporated into the calculation.

In the case of the illustrative organisation, the employee is guaranteed the calculated net expatriate salary, subject to an annual exchange rate adjustment converting between home and host currency values. A tax and social insurance 'grossing-up' is undertaken and the host organisation unit pays the taxes and social insurance in the host country.

The **cost-of-living adjustment**, undertaken based on a home country 'basket' of items and the currency exchange rate used for the salary calculation, is designed to balance differences in cost of living between the home country and the host country. The intention of applying this cost-of-living index is to allow the consumption of goods and services in the host country of the same type, quality and amount as would apply at home. In this MNE, the cost-of-living allowance is applied to 65 per cent of the comparative net domestic salary. This percentage corresponds to a statistical value of the typical proportion of income required for daily expenses.

The cost-of-living allowance (COLA) has been reported as a source of dissatisfaction among expatriates (Suutari and Tornikoski, 2001). To determine a rate regarded as independent, MNE managements may use the services of consultants who specialise in providing regularly updated COLA information on a global basis to their clients (Festing and Perkins, 2008).

The **housing allowance** means that the host organisation either settles rental costs directly or authorises a host rental budget, which the expatriate receives in the expatriate salary calculation. In return, an amount equivalent to the normal housing cost in the home country may be deducted as part of the expatriate salary calculation. In some cases, for example in developing countries where infrastructure is not in line with western expectations, the organisation may own a 'township' associated with operational facilities, supplying company-provided housing. In other cases, a fixed allowance for accommodation may be paid or an assessment made based on a portion of income, out of which actual housing costs are paid. 'Housing issues are often addressed on a case-by-case basis, but as a firm internationalizes, formal policies become more necessary and efficient' (Dowling, Festing and Engle, 2013).

The **foreign assignment allowance** is an incentive for an employee to accept assignment requiring international mobility, and may also recognise intangible difficulties as well as material hardships, where individuals and family members experience a lifestyle different from that enjoyed in the home country, not accounted for in the COLA payment. Issues intentionally covered by what may be termed a 'hardship' payment, such as personal safety, distance, language, cultural and climatic differences, economic conditions as well as the political and social environment are included in this element.

11.10.1 Prevalence of the expatriate balance sheet

According to one large-scale survey, some 70 per cent of European MNEs continue to favour the balance sheet approach to expatriate compensation; in the USA and Japan the percentage rises to 85–95 per cent (ORC, 2002). There are reports, however, that MNEs find funding expatriate balance sheet packages incompatible with corporate cost containment goals (Shortland and Perkins, 2022a; Wentland, 2003). Those experimenting with movement away from 'topping up' home-based compensation without any reference to local market conditions may attempt destination-based expatriate reward planning, using host country market benchmarks instead. This may be judged especially appropriate in 'developed' countries; in 'developing' countries, expatriates at middle and senior executive levels still tend to expect some compensation for 'hardship'.

Among a newer generation of globally mobile professionals, even in the latter territories a more 'bare-bones' approach may be tried, especially where there is agreement between the parties that the assignment has a more 'developmental' focus, as part of longer-term career management for corporate executives (Perkins and Shortland, 2006). In its purest form 'host-benchmarked' expatriates are rewarded at the same rates as their local counterparts. Although this approach may be used for permanent transfers (so-called 'localisation'), on the whole the use of pure host-based approaches is rare. As Perkins and Shortland (2006: 187) explain:

> ... net to net comparisons need to be calculated to determine the feasibility of this approach and the rationale for the assignment needs to be considered carefully. Even if the net to net calculation provides the basis for this approach to succeed (in host reward policy terms), international assignees who are expected to return home or move on to another location are likely to have issues that set them apart from locals – most notably housing and schooling. They are also likely to require some assistance with home leave to maintain home country ties and ease repatriation. International assignees may wish to retain home country housing (assuming they are homeowners) and, with the exception of very young children, are most likely to wish to keep their children in either a school of their own nationality or an international school, so that children's education is not compromised. In addition, assignees are likely to require assistance with taxation – from the very basics of completing tax returns in the foreign jurisdiction to ensuring that additional tax liabilities are met.

Region-based arrangements represent a variant of this 'destination-' rather than 'home'-facing orientation (Fenwick, 2004). Here the equity benchmark is between the assignee and local/regional peers, with the emphasis on integration (Watson and Singh, 2005), although if the location is in a low-pay country, the MNE usually supplements base pay with additional benefits and payments (Perkins and Shortland, 2006). Hybrid systems, combining elements of home and host approaches, as well as individually tailored packages, apply in some MNEs (Suutari and Torkowski, 2001).

Short-term assignment terms are generally intended to be less complex, and less expensive, than arrangements applied to long-term expatriation, although there is evidence that militates against generalising in this regard (Festing and Perkins, 2008). While those assigned for six months or less tend to receive reduced terms compared with long-term assignees, for those abroad for between six months and a year (after which long-term assignment terms generally apply), 'services, incentives, hardship compensation, housing, transportation, relocation allowances [and] trips home' continue to be provided to assignees (ORC, 2006: 12).

In their 2009 survey, ORC reported that short-term assignments were increasing among almost half of the MNEs surveyed. Cost reduction is not given as the primary driving force for the change. Instead, reasons listed are as follows (ORC, 2009):

- transferring knowledge and data (74.7 per cent);
- setting up a new business or operation (55.5 per cent);
- filling a skill gap (48.1 per cent);
- compensating for a resource shortage (46.1 per cent)

The overriding challenge for HR professionals and overseas subsidiary managers is assuring that the length of the assignment does not go over that specified at the outset. Otherwise, all sorts of complications can ensue concerned with tax compliance, immigration status, home leaves and family visits, housing, etc.

Commuter assignments, which Mayerhofer et al (2004) label 'flexpatriation', tend to fall outside the traditional policy categories covering expatriate reward. Commuters' international mobility tends to involve stays of weekly (or monthly) intervals, or some other duration, leaving family members at home. Expenditure will be less on household provisions and in situ transportation but more on restaurant meals and home/host/home round trips. Commuter packages therefore tend to be home-based and contain elements primarily relating to reimbursement of travel (air fares paid) and serviced accommodation costs.

While simplifying international mobilisation, on the one hand, complications in taxation (as well as visa issues) may arise in administering policies applicable to this group of international workers (Perkins and Shortland, 2006). And the trend may militate against 'transnational' organisational designs, signalling a return to ethnocentric management that inhibits expatriate enculturation into host environments (Phillips and Fox, 2003) and the concomitant sense of interdependency between expatriate and key local employees.

International assignments are important investments for MNEs. Brewster et al (2001) estimate that the costs of sending someone on an expatriate assignment are at least three times higher than those of domestic appointments. A PricewaterhouseCoopers (PwC, 2006) study states that, on average, costs per annum for an expatriate amount to $311,000. This includes direct pay and benefits costs and the costs to the organisation of managing the international assignments programme. The latter accounted for 7 per cent of the total assignment costs ($22,378).

Specifically, the direct costs of employee salaries, taxes, housing, shipment of household goods, children's education, (sometimes) spouse support, cross-cultural training, goods and service allowances, repatriation logistics and reassignment costs are further inflated by the administrative costs of running an international assignment programme. Administrative aspects include home-based HR support (assignment planning, selection and reward management, assignment location- or host-based HR support, post-assignment placement costs as well as post-assignment career tracking costs (Festing and Perkins, 2008). Furthermore, intangible factors such as 'adjustment' costs of the expatriates must be accounted for. Added to this, managing non-domestic operations through the medium of expatriates exposes MNEs to risk attributable not only due to direct and indirect costs associated with assignment reward packages: 'Indirect costs of a failed assignment may include loss of market share and damage to international customer relationships' (Brewster et al, 2001: 27).

It is therefore not surprising that more and more organisations claim to be interested in measuring a return on investment in international assignment; however, to date there is evidence that only 14 per cent are addressing this complex task, mainly looking at the definition and respective fulfilment of assignment objectives (GMAC, 2006).

Despite the controversy surrounding expatriate reward debates, an argument can still be made, informed by institutional economics theory, that expatriation remains a cost-effective solution (Bonache and Fernández, 2005). In short, corporate management may be unwilling to entrust safeguarding the value of the corporate brand to individuals recruited from local external labour markets, where attitudes to corporate governance and wider cultural values may contrast with corporate governance and trading imperatives. And if the organisation is pursuing a strategy that requires skill sets fully conversant with distinctive corporate knowledge and ways of applying it beyond the country of origin, corporate management may regard appointment of an individual long socialised into the corporate culture as a prerequisite.

The transaction costs associated with expatriate compensation packages may thus be equivalent to or even lower than those accompanying an external hire (Bonache and Fernández, 2005). The time and other resources consumed in integrating a manager recruited from one of the local economies in which subsidiary operations are located may be incompatible with the need to achieve early returns on the investment in subsidiary operations. As noted earlier, the halfway-house TCN, with a balance of global/local know-how, offers MNEs scope to meet resourcing demands while not compromising core values, at least until such time as mutual confidence and trust has been established between all parties to a differentiated network operation.

11.11 HR role: Scope for tension with the line

Risks around expatriation-dependent multinational management may bring corporate HR specialists and line managers into potential conflict in meeting expectations around their respective roles (Perkins and Daste, 2007). Tensions may arise between an aim to achieve successful transnational performance across knowledge networks, limiting differences under competitive trading conditions, and the traditional principle of 'keeping expatriates whole'. Those carrying devolved responsibility for supervising expatriate managers unsurprisingly are likely to wish to smooth assignment conditions so that failure risks – that may have adverse consequences for supervisors' own reputations as well as for expatriates themselves – are minimised.

While corporate HR specialists may adopt the role of 'corporate policy integrity guardian', supervising managers in a direct line relationship may feel less constrained by what may be labelled 'personnel' issues, relying on 'the business case' to vary policy to accommodate individual expatriates' demands. We can theorise this problem using commentary on social situations giving rise to 'strategic contingency' in organisations (Pfeffer and Salancik, 1977). Supervisors in MNEs must achieve results but they depend on others (expatriates) to do so. The result is that the 'doers' accrue power to influence the terms of the relationship (see the parallels with the 'agency' and 'power-dependency' arguments discussed generally in Chapter 2, and, in relation to executive reward, in Chapter 10). The greater the dependency, the greater leverage may accrue to expatriates in bargaining around the terms of their co-operation (effort–reward).

HR specialists *depend* on expatriate supervisors to apply corporate policy consistently and cost-effectively in managing expatriate managers – their influence may be limited to *guiding* expatriate supervisors' action. Pfeffer and Davies-Blake (1987) argue that an individual's salary (and by extension other employment terms) is contingent not only on the role they occupy but is also how this 'resource' is embedded in the organisation (i.e. the operational context). An expatriate supervisor may be influenced to interpret corporate policy on expatriation biased towards satisfying an expatriate manager's expectations of a package that will suitably 'compensate' their willingness to accept an assignment abroad.

This practical imperative may stand in tension with HR specialists' ambition to satisfy corporate priorities around rationalisation and standardisation of employment terms and conditions, including expatriation packages, to contain costs accumulated corporately across the expatriate managerial population. Despite a common goal, in principle, of serving corporate interests, reflection on the problem of expatriating managers, informed by analysis of empirical evidence gathered among a sample of large western MNEs leads Perkins and Daste (2007) to predict tensions comparing influences on expatriate supervisors, in contrast to the viewpoint corporate HR specialists project in describing their feelings towards line management receptiveness to 'professional' advocacy.

One consequence may be that a more critical reading of the expatriation literature, moving beyond a simple focus on the administrative aspects, to account for political interaction between interested organisational actors, is necessary to assist HR specialists in diagnosing this strategic issue (Shortland and Perkins, 2022a). It is one with significant implications for their credibility with expatriates, their supervisors and corporate top management, as corporate policy quality assurance guardians. The HR team in a global banking and financial services corporation sum up the problem by reference to a traditional culture of individual 'deals', accompanying active steps to migrate towards more 'mature' expatriate reward management practices (Perkins, 2006).

Nurney (2001) argues that MNEs should 'stop negotiating individual packages for international assignees' when a MNE's transnational presence increases, and with it the diversity of nationalities (country start-through-and-end points) becomes significant. At this time, core reward management factors need to be weighed in formulating and applying policy that go beyond getting someone to accept a foreign posting. The message needs skilful communication, supported by the HR function, but underlined by top management, so that expatriates, their supervisors and fellow workforce members alike understand key principles surrounding mobilisation of individual 'knowledge carriers', requiring cross-border postings. If policy development, refinement, review and learning-based adaptation processes involve these key stakeholders then policy legitimisation may be enhanced too.

Practical considerations of numbers, types, duration, as well as cost-effectiveness of expatriate assignments need to be balanced against socio-political factors including trust and equity considerations (Nurney, 2001). However, interpreting standardisation in ways that imply rigidity is inconsistent with the need for nimbleness to meet competitive demands, as Baruch (2004: 220) observes '... while general guidelines should lead to a "fair" and constructive system, situational factors will force companies to be inventive and flexible in setting and managing the remuneration system across borders.'

While complicated by cross-cultural and varying institutional contexts, fairness in relation to comparisons expatriates make, and co-workers make with them, can be seen as a significant issue. Given the period expatriate managers can take to adjust and thus become a fully effective member of the workplace to which they have been deployed, local peers or even subordinates may become resentful not just around salary-related variances between expatriates and locals (or even expatriates and expatriates from different home locations). While 'bankable' benefits may not be visible, other factors where the multinational employer funds a lifestyle intended to preserve the expatriate family way of life which may be at odds with locals' ability to live similarly are clearly transparent. This carries envy risks unless clearly shown and accepted as merited in terms of the unique value added by a particular expatriate manager (Harvey, 1993).

There are also expectations of the expatriate manager's household who may expect the reward and related support from a multinational employer to evolve positively in terms of its benefit to the expatriate as the individual's career in the location moves upwards. Recent research reveals the importance of accounting for a gendered dimension here too (Shortland and Perkins, 2016; Shortland and Perkins, 2022b). The question is whether or not an employer who has adopted, say, a global approach to expatriate reward, applying common terms irrespective of the host location, will consider the package already generous and thus in turn expect the expatriate to absorb additional accountabilities on the job – perhaps only offering some straight salary-related enhancement, while the employee anticipates 'total reward' adjusted upwards.

And then there is the perennial problem which Harvey and Moeller (2009) report of expatriates when debriefed following assignments. Namely, one of disappointment when being repatriated to the home location that the role does not reflect the status and accompanying reward they have become used to in the host location relative to other employees there. Or that expectations of career and accompanying reward progression do not materialise given changes in the home organisation that were unanticipated at the start of an assignment, possibly several years beforehand. Moreover, the lifestyle of an expatriation where additional support services raising above home standards the sense of self-worth of an employee may be dented, leading to a sense of demotivation when the expatriate returns to the home setting, with the lifestyle context that they left prior to the assignment but perhaps have forgotten.

Expatriates have been recorded expressing a view that a suitable repatriation programme ought to have been scoped out at the beginning of the assignment – a time when in the excitement and stress to commence, without a clear corporate policy, may lead to issues being overlooked or ignored (Harvey and Moeller, 2009). Issues that only come back to impact negatively on expatriate commitment to the employer and motivation to stay and apply what has been learned while on assignment following its conclusion without an effective 'returns' infrastructure.

The implication for HR specialists of the issues sketched above is not simply to hold up the standard of what 'should be', but to be capable to participate in what Festing and Perkins (2008) describe as social exchange negotiations around expatriation, informed by theoretical as well as situated empirical reflection. The social exchange involves not only resolving issues around material considerations, but also clarifying the kind of 'psychological contract' on offer (see Chapters 2 and 9). Care is needed before generalisation, but it may be tentatively suggested that 'relational' contracts that enable expatriates to locate assignments within a longer-term career plan may encourage the behaviours favourable to distributed network organisations, requiring give and take between all the members wherever they may be located.

If a more 'transactional' relationship is enshrined in the expatriate 'deal' then specialists and line managers should not be surprised if employees adopt a more insular and instrumental orientation to the organisation and their peers across the multinational network. In short, when approaching expatriation reward: 'Attention is required to examining not only the "how" (primary approaches) but also the "why" (salient contextual or situation factors) firms should consider when determining how to assemble an appropriate package' (Sims and Schraeder, 2005: 107).

KEY ISSUES IN REWARD MANAGEMENT 11.1

An international assignment policy for regional expansion

Group exercise

Taipei-headquartered Taiwanese MNE Hiqual-locost Automotives aims to build a worldwide assembly manufacturing and trading presence. An initial target was a successful trans-European operation, establishing a regional office in Frankfurt and operating facilities in cities in France, Italy and the UK, before extending further into Central and Eastern Europe. The Frankfurt office has responsibility for contributing towards the company's corporate performance and people resourcing within the region. While seconding senior Taiwanese managers from headquarters, a managerial cadre of Western Europeans has been groomed, not only to succeed to regional leadership roles, as the Taiwanese expatriates complete what are regarded as costly assignments. High-potential European managers are to be mobilised to work in the first two regional expansions beyond Western Europe: new manufacturing plans in Bulgaria and Romania.

Having socialised these key recruits into corporate ways of managing the enterprise, it is felt that they will be well equipped, as TCN expatriates, to transplant this knowledge to support the further international expansion. In addition, as part of PCN succession arrangements some mobility is planned between the existing European offices to fill positions requiring expertise that has emerged concentrated in particular countries. Corporate HR have advised the board that a policy will be developed to underpin these further expatriations – with the proviso that significant cost savings will be made over those anticipated if a further HQ assignment were countenanced.

The Frankfurt-based HR team has been charged with advising the HQ function on considerations to be considered in designing the new pan-European assignment policy to address these four types of international assignments. Based on what you have learned so far in this chapter, flesh out the details of the brief to the Frankfurt HR team, including the kinds of information needed to guide corporate policymaking. List and justify the individuals and groups who should be invited to take part in the exercise.

11.12 Factors and trends in rewarding *non-expatriated* knowledge mobilisation

11.12.1 Considerations at the expatriate–local interface

By way of a bridge between the 'big but narrow' topic of expatriate compensation and discussion of international reward issues applicable to the vast majority of the MNE core headcount (Festing and Tekieli, 2022), let us briefly consider what the research literature reports regarding issues to be accounted for in reward design sensitive to interaction between PCNs, TCNs and HCNs:

> As multinational companies operate across nations and continents at vastly different levels of economic development, disparity in employee compensation is unavoidable. The disparity is most salient in the remarkable gap between the compensation received by the local employees of international joint ventures in developing countries and foreign expatriates from developed countries.
>
> (Chen et al, 2002: 807)

On average, the compensation delivered to western expatriates, deemed necessary to get individuals to work in nations where pay and living conditions are significantly lower, has been estimated to be not only considerably above that received by their home country counterparts; it is a great deal more than that received by the local nationals in the developing countries (Reynolds, 1997). Adding a further twist to this inequality issue, it has been reported that international joint ventures (IJVs) pay more to locals than do domestic enterprises in the countries where the IJVs are established, and reward may be 'packaged' in different ways too (Chen et al, 2002). However, there is evidence to support a case that, while needing careful handling, straight expatriate–local comparisons are not always problematic. Again, we turn to theory to seek clarification.

Equity theorists indicate that people are egocentric – they make judgements about equity based on how favourable the outcome is to them. Judgements are based on social referents. Following this line of reasoning, the question becomes: how do locals compare themselves with expatriates? Chen et al (2002) argue that people compare themselves against 'similar others' – this may be people undertaking similar work tasks at a similar organisational level. It may also depend on factors such as age, gender, race and tenure. The question for corporate reward policy designers becomes: are the expatriates so different from their local counterparts that they are not meaningful social referents for one another?

Chen et al (2002) conducted a study of IJV employment practices in China and found that comparisons between local national employees in IJVs and those of other IJVs were an important source of moderating feelings of injustice between their own reward levels and those of expatriates. Building an understanding of local comparators, investigating employee preferences, sensitive to culture and industry, as Mamman et al (1996) advocate, and adopting a 'premium' pay posture (an 'efficiency wage' orientation – see Chapter 2) relative to the market for local recruits may, therefore, assist efforts by MNE managements to build team-cohesion between locals and expatriates, even where the latter receive higher absolute levels of reward.

Chen et al (2002) found that the mitigation effect was the same irrespective of the level of disparity between the expatriates and locals. The effect was *offsetting*, not just moderation of a negative effect. Local elite status counts, then. The ability to set premium pay will depend on the level of investment (and anticipated profitability) of the local subsidiary, and of the local human capital influence over open market rates – dependency theory signals that employee leverage will accrue based on managerial perceptions of how much these people are needed. Chen et al (2002) emphasise the importance for HR specialists of developing reasonable explanations and justifications for the inequities – as well as offering alternative non-financial recognition such as fast-track management development for key locals. Demonstrating a caring and sensitive attitude itself may have positive benefits, showing local core workforce members the extent to which corporate management are interested in their feelings and general welfare, as valued members of the organisation seeking competitive success in local markets and delivering returns for other stakeholders. While attention to cultural considerations, as surfaced in Chapter 1, is important the more salient issue may be overcoming economic disparities mindful of *relative* equity considerations (Shortland and Perkins, 2022b).

The issue may go beyond horizontal alignment of HR–reward practices, however, bearing in mind vertical influences flowing between employment relations management and corporate strategy. Based on the knowledge mobilisation imperative, attempted shifts to the multi-headed transnational organisation may trigger a chain of events that further alter the context for assessing reward relativities across the MNE. Milkovich and Bloom (1998) argue that the organisational goal should be to rethink international reward to develop 'global mindsets' across all the workforce members, one outcome of which could be to shrink perceived social differences between the expatriate and local population. 'A global work environment may… stimulate social comparisons with otherwise dissimilar co-workers when employees from diverse social backgrounds interact with each other to perform joint tasks' (Chen et al, 2002: 808).

SELF-ASSESSMENT EXERCISE

Managing employee reward in a multinational context is a highly complex endeavour. The perennial issue is balancing corporate ambition to conjoin knowledge where it produces profitable outcomes – however 'profitable' may be defined, depending on the sector involved. Identify and prioritise the steps thinking performers in HR specialist roles may take to use theoretical frameworks, complemented by reported empirical experience among MNEs, to manage this complexity and diversity of ideas and expectations. What are the opportunities and risks for MNEs, and how may the latter be minimised?

11.13 Strategy, dominant logic and opportunism

Vernon argues that the pay element of international reward has more 'standardisation' potential than other aspects of HRM, owing to 'the relative simplicity of administering pay across national borders' (2006: 217). This raises the prospect of opportunities to use pay 'strategically' in MNEs, or, as Gomez-Mejia and Balkin (1992: 4) puts it, 'as an essential integrating and signalling mechanism to achieve overarching business objectives'. While highlighting its strategic potential, Vernon (2006) counsels that unthinking ethnocentric application of western normative reward management principles is to be avoided, however. Factors applicable across multi-local settings at least need to be systematically appraised and 'managed' before applying universalistic reward 'solutions' (Prince and Prince, 2022). In other words, while avoiding the trap of stereotyping, attention to culture (Sparrow, 1999, 2000) as well as institutional values and traditions between business systems (Perkins and Vartiainen, 2010; Whitley, 2000) is necessary.

Referring to contexts for employment relations such as Germany, where on the face of it managerial prerogative is constrained by institutional practice whereby, for example, structures of employee representation are codified to a greater extent than in, say, the UK and USA, Edwards et al (2005: 1283) argue that 'practices negotiated through this route may be received with less scepticism by employees than those that are imposed'. Also, as considered earlier by reference to the IT case organisation, while administratively it may be possible to enact changes initiated by the corporate centre, vertically aligned with revisions to business strategy, reorienting workforce expectations – horizontally aligning reward decision-taking with related processes such as employee communications – offers a more complex managerial challenge (Festing and Tekieli, 2022).

Bloom et al (2003) argue that the 'dominant logic' for managing the reward system adopted by MNEs may vary across several recognisable types, reflecting competing pressures for consistency of approach in pursuit of global alignment with organisational aims and local conformance pressures. What Bloom et al (2003) term 'export oriented' reward strategies aim to transfer wholesale the parent firm's reward system to the overseas affiliates, in pursuit of a 'common mindset', driven by headquarters thinking. An 'adapter' group, by contrast, chooses practices designed to match as closely as possible the conditions of the local context. Within these extremes, 'integrationists' may attempt what at worst may be little more than a cobbling together of a diverse array of practices, but at best suggests efforts to craft a coherent and comprehensive transnational reward management regime mindful of the mutually interdependent nature of the MNE management and workforce members. In keeping with the 'distributed network' proposed by Nohria and Ghoshal (1997), policies may flow as easily between subsidiaries and from subsidiaries to headquarters, as from headquarters 'down' and outwards to operations located worldwide (Festing and Tekieli, 2022).

In practice, Bloom et al (2003) suggest that MNEs tend to be opportunistic across their international operations in the adoption of practices that reflect one or more of the approaches described theoretically. They identify three complementary features that may reflect or influence MNE reward strategies derived from their operating contexts. First, the weight of institutionally generated pressures to conform to the conditions of local jurisdictions and markets may be deemed overwhelming – representing an 'investment cost' of choosing to trade in a particular economy. Secondly, MNE managements may identify scope to avoid or forestall acquiescence with local conformance pressures – where the application of regulatory and market practices is lax, for example. Thirdly, if the MNE is bringing investment capital that host governments regard as significant, active resistance to local conformance pressures may be initiated, mediated through attempts to challenge or change (at least in some way to influence) factors in the host context, using access to legislators and other key opinion formers. The framework is usefully summarised as a matrix (Table 11.2)

Again, then, the situation is dynamic and universal prescriptions require cautious interpretation (Brookes et al, 2005). As Perkins (2006: 11) observes:

> The insight from the analysis is that the degree of variation in contextual factors – between and within – local host contexts rather than just the type of host contexts (cultural norms, economic conditions, regulatory pressures, etc.) may be what matters most when multinational managements consider how to balance corporate versus host influences on reward strategy design.

An investigation by Lowe et al (2002), measuring the position on various reward management approaches in ten countries around the world (although notably excluding Europe), supplemented by managerial perspectives on what practices 'should' be applied, indicated a degree of consistency that the researchers found surprising given the range of cultural and institutional contexts surveyed (from China to the USA).

Table 11.2 Context-related multinational reward management factors

	Conform	Avoid	Resist
Adapters	Generally	Where possible	Rarely
Exporters	Rarely	Generally	If cost-effective
Globalisers	If necessary	Sometimes	Where feasible

SOURCE: Perkins (2006), summarising Bloom et al (2003)

In terms of managerial perceptions of the extent to which reward practices were related to the employment of high performers, satisfied employees and an effective organisation:

> Collectively, these findings suggest that there is a high degree of cross-cultural consistency in the perceived utility of compensation plans as a method for achieving organisational effectiveness. However, the mix of appropriate compensation practices is likely to vary across these same countries.
>
> (Lowe et al, 2002: 69)

In the case of future focused preferences, the researchers argued that the data set indicated thoughtful item-by-item responses by managers surveyed, rather than any 'within-country scale-anchor preferences' (Lowe et al, 2002: 71). Managers generally expressed a bias in favour of increasing the incidence of incentives, benefits and long-term pay focus compared with the current practice. Consistent lines between the results of 'cultural programming' variances across countries and regions and the practice and preferences of organisational managers are not in evidence from this research, therefore. The implication is that systematic 'due diligence' analysis on the part of MNE corporate reward policy architects to match reward and recognition plans for employees in countries around the world may be a worthwhile investment, when expanding their overseas operations (Prince and Prince, 2022). The discussion of contingency theory in Chapter 2 may be helpful in thinking through this proposition. Lowe et al (2002) contend that, by enhancing understanding of 'best practices' in other countries, their findings serve to challenge the extreme positions reported by Bloom et al (2003), whether ethnocentric exportation of reward management designs or 'locally responsive' adoption of the status quo in a given locale.

SELF-ASSESSMENT EXERCISE

Sparrow (1999) lists five groups of factors that may be influenced by national culture with possible consequences for how employees respond to reward management: (1) attitudes to what makes an 'effective' employee; (2) orientations to giving and receiving work performance feedback; (3) career anchor preferences – e.g. seniority versus performance; (4) expectations of manager–subordinate relationships; and (5) conceptions of what makes 'socially healthy' pay distribution between individuals and groups.

Based on the research findings referenced above regarding organisational aspirations to achieve transnational work team cohesion, some measure of pay system standardisation and the factors employees appear to deploy when making comparisons horizontally and vertically about equitable reward treatment, what priorities would you emphasise in counselling a new transnational team leader about their role?

Brown and Perkins (2007) report on CIPD survey findings, where HR specialists in MNEs were asked to define the level of influence that proactive components of the business strategy, such as increasing total shareholder returns and customer satisfaction, actually had on reward practices in their organisation. Respondents were also asked to rate the influence of external and less controllable factors on rewards, such as the rates of price and wage inflation, external labour markets and the activities of their competitors for staff, as well as trade unions.

According to the results obtained, a more reactive (traditional personnel administration-style) approach appears to feature in more of the organisations than those claiming to be proactive. When asked about the influence of parent country reward principles compared with local differentiators, and in turn compared with a mix-and-match approach of the kind Bloom et al reported, the picture was almost evenly balanced 33:33:33 between responses obtained. The inference may be one of 'good old muddling through' or, by reflecting more deeply on these findings, one of sophisticated opportunity management recognising that global–local balancing will be a constant challenge to be addressed, requiring skilful handling.

The findings reported imply that multinational reward decision-takers are not simply reading from a common template at the level of specific practice. Using more in-depth interview data, Perkins (2006) reported that large MNEs appeared to be attempting to increase the degree of co-ordination in transnational reward management. The first case below illustrates the action long-established MNEs may take to restructure business operations in ways that use employee reward interventions to emphasise accountability, beyond membership of a federation of geographically situated units to corporate brand development opportunities. Some MNEs have made a significant investment in new information technology-based infrastructure to rationalise and standardise reward management practice across the enterprise (for details, see the Honeywell case study in Perkins, 2006: Part Three). While no doubt these shifts will be the subject of debate among organisational members, the explicit commercial focus means the new focus has a logic that most will acknowledge.

This contrasts with the issues corporate management have encountered in the second case below, where a voluntary sector organisation has taken steps to increase the common focus on performance by introducing a pay-related recognition element. A diversity of voices – right up to the highest policy-making levels – has engaged in a debate on whether, despite an economic logic, the approach 'fits' what the organisation stands for and how it goes about meeting corporate aims and objectives.

CASE STUDY 11.1

Branded goods MNE Unilever employs 234,000 people in around 100 countries. A restructuring operation under a new group chief executive, bringing with it a change in management style, anticipated important consequences for reward management processes applied to junior managerial jobholders and above.

The new corporate strategy design was to capitalise more effectively on corporate brands than may have been the case since Unilever's formation in 1930. Group-wide influence on explicit 'reward management' is constrained, according to corporate specialists, in the case of the 200,000 people around the world occupying roles such as plantation workers, manufacturing workers, salespeople, etc, whose employment terms and conditions are often subject to collective bargaining.

In the case of managers, however, the orientation to employee reward has shifted. While the trinity of attracting and retaining and motivating these employees remains, the focus is on finding ways in which reward management may be used more explicitly to align with corporate governance goals what people do, and the way their contribution is recognised,

Accenting transnational integration, the HR function itself has been reorganised, combining reward management policymaking within a single corporate unit with activities focused also on 'talent management', 'organisational effectiveness' and 'learning'. Thus, an aspiration may be discerned to integrate people management at both the vertical level (with corporate strategy and governance) and horizontally across the HR function.

The reward system architecture was not to be altered as such under the new regime: instead, the emphasis was on improving its execution, aligned with the new corporate strategic priorities. The challenge was seen as one of articulating the idea of 'corporate value creation' as something that Unilever people see as 'relevant' to them, while accommodating diversity in economic conditions affecting regionally dispersed operations. On the one hand, helping the company to benefit from emerging market growth opportunities had to be recognised without inflating results, taking account of fluctuation in currency values. On the other hand, in the 'mature' economies, such as those of Western Europe and the USA, the managerial task was perceived as achieving targets associated with retaining profitable market share.

A 'talent management listing process' intended to integrate the identification of high-potential employees was implemented with actions to increase what the system architects referred to as 'performance accountability'. The incentive reward management system was to be operated in ways that differentiate the distribution of extrinsic rewards: while differentiation might be anticipated as a self-evident feature of individual incentive reward arrangements, past practice was to emphasise consistency in applying market-leading levels of reward. Instead, the plan was 'to ensure at least some of our money goes to where it is supposed to', according to the head of reward who participated in the new scheme design.

The importance of 'accountability' in 'One Unilever', as the CEO termed it, was to remove barriers to the networking of knowledge between the MNE's branded 'lines of business' and geographical regions, to support the corporate value-creation priority. Initiatives were launched to address unnecessary 'complexity and intellectualism' that risks resource inefficiencies through duplication of effort across business operations (e.g. in managing product development or marketing activity).

Clarifying accountability across corporate networks, on the one hand, was expected to reduce misalignment with corporate policy and cost-effective mobilisation of skill sets. On the other hand, there was an attempt to make people management more than reading-off detailed rules from functionally policed templates.

In reward management terms, detailed decisions about policy application in individual cases were devolved to line managers, to increase transparency. This was perceived as a culture change accompanying the new accountability, requiring local managerial judgement within the performance-oriented corporate principles. 'Managers are no longer asked to just fill in a spreadsheet box only for corporate HR to change the numbers afterwards,' the researcher was told.

(**SOURCE:** Perkins, 2006)

CASE STUDY 11.2

Explicit pay for performance management remains controversial, especially beyond the commercial sector. The charity HelpAge International is a very diverse organisation, with 'over 70 nationalities employed right up to senior management level', according to the head of HR interviewed for the CIPD international reward and recognition research. Trustees are similarly diverse – the board is 'incredibly diverse', with a majority of members female and from developing countries. There is an emphasis on building up local capacity, employing people from the regions concerned, reducing a reliance on expatriates and keeping the London head office slim.

The guiding principles for reward management are 'consistency and fairness within and across the organisation'. Modest changes have been made to the reward system but have been the subject of 'hot debate' among management decision-makers. Limited performance contribution recognition had been introduced over a two-year period, at the time of annual salary reviews. In addition to the across-the-board inflation-linked salary increases, two additional employee assessment categories were introduced to determine increase levels for 'good' and 'exceptional' contributors.

The scheme was not a (forward-calibrated) formal incentive programme. It was a (retrospective) recognition arrangement, intended to signal acknowledgement of particular contribution levels (see Chapter 6). It was recognised that the levels involved were not likely to act as a retention device in the case of people leaving for higher material rewards elsewhere.

While top management's intention was to communicate a positive message, there was some negative reaction. Dissatisfaction centred on things like who is included and why and, at an individual level, debate on issues such as 'why rate me *only* "good" not "exceptional"?' Some senior management team members voiced anxieties about differentiation: pay-for-performance may run counter to the overriding principles considered typical of not-for-profit MNEs.

(**SOURCE:** Perkins, 2006)

11.14 Conclusions and key learning points

International reward and its management may be approached from a variety of angles, as the chapter has illustrated. If Ghoshal and Bartlett's (1998) 'transnational solution' to multinational business strategy is adopted, reward may be viewed as an important managerial resource for profitable knowledge mobilisation supported by an effort to encourage a shared 'global mindset' across the workforce (Milkovich and Bloom, 1998). While aspiration may be voiced, we have seen that although administratively reward may offer scope for consistent practice, reverse diffusion of learning may be inhibited, less for technical reasons than political (Festing and Tekieli, 2022).

Consistent with our open systems conceptual framework, we have considered rewards for the international workforce segmented between expatriates and others, on the one hand, in order that nuances of expatriate 'compensation' administration may be appreciated. On the other hand, we have drawn attention to the need for policy design mindful of the interaction between the segments that, as Chen et al (2002) and Aleweld et al (2015) have stressed, does not break down simply in terms of an expat–local dichotomy, but demands local–local and globally oriented governance too.

With a reported accent on standardisation to support an incentivised performance orientation (Prince and Prince, 2022), MNE reward architects also need to draw on theoretical and empirical knowledge of practices that may be discovered in the generic reward literature, which commentators such as Perkins and Vartiainen (2010) suggest managers are reflecting on rather than reading from a template or at least are approaching 'strategically', accounting for in-country as well as transnational enablers and constraints to 'best practice' (Aleweld et al, 2015; Bloom et al, 2003; Brown and Perkins, 2007).

The competitive context has amplified the problems for MNEs, but reward system design may still be usefully informed by some overriding principles articulated three decades ago (Carey and Howes, 1993), interpreted and slightly extended, in summary form, below:

- As companies establish themselves globally, corporate strategies are called for that can accommodate both unity and diversity: this surfaces issues such as how to allocate rewards and how to tie reward outcomes to corporate goals.
- Specifically, MNEs need to develop reward system characteristics that fit with overall corporate strategy but are tailored to the needs not only of business operations but also of employees in specific locations. Flexibility not only regarding the quantum but also in terms of how employees receive their material rewards may be increasingly expected. This may apply not just in home markets and other developed country settings but also across discerning knowledgeable 'global talent' populations. On the other hand, where socio-economic infrastructure remains limited, some substantive guarantees may remain a priority expectation.
- Purchasing power parity (the rate of exchange at which general price levels are equalised) may work more effectively than the more volatile spot rates for currency conversion when setting long-term pay levels.

- Reward comparator groups may need to comprise a combination of both other MNEs in the same industrial sector and other industry groupings. Account needs to be taken also of local–local comparisons that HCNs may make when recruited to international joint ventures as well as organisations wholly funded by foreign direct investment sources.
- When creating a global reward regime, the total pay and benefits mix in various countries requires measured evaluation: decisions are required here as to the role allocated to salaries, short-term bonuses, long-term incentives and other material benefits, and to whether these should be measured in pre-tax or post-tax terms. Given pressures to reduce tax burdens, jurisdictions have been cutting back government-provided benefits, raising the question of the extent to which these should be factored-in to 'total reward' calculations (see Chapters 7, 8 and 9 for detailed consideration of these issues).
- While enabling choice may appear contrary to standardisation and unifying initiatives through reward management, allowing choice when migrating from multi-local to a more globally integrated system may support communication, education and understanding building among transnational workforce members, as well as facilitating acceptance and ownership of new corporately branded frameworks.

Explore further

A review of relevant theory summarised in a heuristic model to help interpret approaches to expatriate reward management appears in Festing, M and Perkins, SJ (2008) Rewards for internationally mobile employees, in Brewster, C, Sparrow, P and Dickmann, M (eds.) *International HRM: Contemporary issues in Europe*, 2nd edn, London, Routledge.

Approaches to theorising expatriation are critically reviewed in Shortland, S and Perkins, SJ (2022a) Segmenting international assignments: theorising expatriate reward, in Perkins, SJ (ed.) *The Routledge Companion to Reward Management*, London: Routledge, pp. 191–99.

The discussion is related to the theme of performance related reward management across European business systems in Shakiants, I, Festing, M and Perkins, SJ (2016) Paying for performance in Europe, in Dickmann, M, Brewster, C and Sparrow, P (eds.) *International HRM: Contemporary issues in Europe*, 3rd edn, London, Routledge.

Companies are managing more diverse work forces, and pay systems must be designed to attract, retain and motivate these employees who may have very different pay preferences from employees of previous decades. A study by Scott et al (2015) examines how employee characteristics (i.e. gender, age, education, work experience, annual pay and number of dependents) are related to pay preferences. Developing the diversity and expatriation theme, see Shortland, S and Perkins, SJ (2022b) What do we know about diversity, intersectionality and inclusion in organisationally-assigned expatriation? A review of relocation management company/consultancy practitioner research, *Career Development International*, vol. 27, no. 2, pp. 274–97.

CIPD-commissioned research on trends in international reward among MNEs (primarily large mature companies but also considering the challenges faced by voluntary sector organisations operating across national borders) is published in Perkins, SJ (2006) *International Reward and Recognition*, Research Report, London: Chartered Institute of Personnel and Development.

For a collection of articles reviewing debates surrounding the idea of regional convergence in reward systems see the special issue Reward management in Europe, *Thunderbird International Business Review*, vol. 52, no. 3 (2010), pp. 175–87, edited by Perkins, SJ and Vartianinen, M.

12 Strategic reward management within HRM

CHAPTER LEARNING OUTCOMES

At the end of this chapter, you should understand and be able to explain the following:

- Ideas grouped under the rubric of 'HRM' and their interaction with thinking about employee reward design and management.
- Critical appraisal of HRM/strategy/reward commentary, as one recipe for managing the employment relationship, located in open systems contexts.
- Implications of adopting a strategic reward or 'new pay' orientation for roles and competency requirements among line managers and specialists.

CIPD STRATEGIC REWARD MANAGEMENT (7HR03) LEARNING OUTCOMES

Learners will be able to:

1.1 Examine the key factors influencing the design of reward strategy and policy frameworks.

1.2 Discuss the importance of aligning the reward framework to the wider organisational context and strategy.

1.4 Critically evaluate the impact of organisational reward strategies to attract, motivate and retain talent.

12.1 Introduction

If we situate reward management as a sub-system within an organisation's human resource management system and, in turn, its corporate strategic management system, it follows that choosing to act in accordance with ideas about human resource management – and the concept of 'HRM' in particular – will have consequences for how employee reward and its management is approached. In this chapter we discuss the ways in which commentators have defined 'HRM' and how this set of ideas about people management may be seen interacting with developments in thinking about rewarding employees.

Of course, thinking about reward management is not limited to 'HRM': the latter concept may be viewed critically from perspectives that do not limit the focus to the firm and its management, but recognise their systemic interaction with other political economic institutions (see Chapter 3 for a discussion of contextual issues). Drawing from perspectives emerging both under the 'HRM' rubric and those with wider conceptual roots, systemic interaction between HRM and employee reward may, however, be framed for critical appraisal. In the course of such consideration the implications for parties to reward management determination (HR specialists, line managers, individual employees and collective employee institutions, as well as regulators in particular jurisdictions) may be subjected to review.

12.2 Defining HRM

Ideologically presented as 'the alternative to pluralistic employee relations' and 'how employees ought to be managed' (Keenoy, 1999: 2, emphasis in original), HRM adopts the principles of strategy from the business management literature (Marchington and Wilkinson, 2016). HRM is contrasted with what may be positioned as more 'passive' people management (perhaps labelled as personnel management/administration). Organisational strategy, defined in terms of choices about where and how resources are to be deployed in pursuit of corporate aims relative to competitors (Zeckhauser, 1991), is, however, contested terrain and competing perspectives on 'strategy' will be discussed below.

For Storey (2007), HRM is one among several alternatives for the management of the employment relationship and one which is debated and challenged. 'HRM-ism' (Keenoy, 1997, 1999) has been branded an attempt to manage meaning between the members of work organisations (Storey, 2007). Initiatives such as 'changing the organisation's culture' may be cited as one illustration of this argument – in reward terms, for example, shifting expectations on pay progression from a fixed increments system based on seniority to a performance-contingent regime, as though the latter were an obvious choice rather than one based on debatable principles reflecting particular interests and socio-economic goals. These HRM 'rhetorics' contrast with a 'reality' (Legge, 1995) in which 'high-commitment' or 'high involvement' employment practices were slow to be adopted by British workplaces (Cully et al, 1999). The most recent large-scale WERS survey shows a rise in the proportion of employees feeling committed and engaged with their workplace and yet less than half of the employee population are satisfied with their level of involvement in decision-making (van Wanrooy et al, 2013) suggesting that reality does not yet reflect the HRM rhetoric.

Ideas prompting debates around HRM as a strategic approach to people management may be traced back to commentary emerging in the USA at the end of the 1970s. Two strands of argument have been identified as characterising the initial phase of HRM development. A 'matching model' of HRM (Fombrun et al, 1984) encourages managers to 'read off' choices about managing people at work directly from the organisation's strategic objectives. Depending on the corporate emphasis, it is reasoned that there will be one right way of workforce management.

For example, Delery and Doty (1996) present evidence from the banking industry in the USA, which they argue indicates a universal logic for implementing employee profit-sharing arrangements to secure high-performance outcomes. Their premise, explicitly underlined by agency theory, is that, 'by definition all banks strive for profit' and 'by tying individual compensation to organizational profit, the organization is rewarding behavior that is consistent with its overall performance' (1996: 826).

In addition to matching HRM to business strategy, for organisational effectiveness to be secured, it has been argued that alignment is required between the various elements that comprise the HRM 'bundle' (Purcell, 1999). Hence attention is required to the 'fit' between component parts of reward management and its attendant processes.

A second foundational approach, known as the 'Harvard model' (Beer et al, 1984), encourages attention not only to strategy: implying more 'open systems' thinking, greater account is to be taken also of the interaction between organisational strategy and factors from outside the individual firm. Rather than perceiving HRM as determined exclusively by organisational structure, practices are tailored contingent on factors such as management's leadership philosophy, and interpretation of workforce characteristics, as well as external factors such as labour market circumstances. Compromises and trade-offs may be necessary as management seeks to balance owner interests with those of other stakeholders (including employees and society at large).

This more pluralistic orientation is in contrast to the apparent assumption by Fombrun et al (1984) of unity among organisational interests: that is, what is good for owners will also benefit other stakeholders. Under the Harvard approach, matching HRM practices to the specificities of each organisation is more nuanced. The scope for strategic choice informed by ideological considerations alluded to by Beer et al (1984) also factors in the likely outcomes and longer-term consequences of managerial policy and practice. The Harvard model's 'feedback loop' again appears to reflect assumed interaction between organisational systems and external systemic features – for example, the political economy and employment system – which may enable fine-tuning and adaptation by decision-makers as the context changes during strategy implementation, that is, a more emergent approach.

The case study below illustrates the proactive investment strategy reportedly adopted by one organisation, Pentland Brands, to align HRM policies and practices with what the business aims to achieve, derived from predictions about how, in turn, people management and development should inform the business strategy. The case further illustrates actions that may be taken along the lines advocated by Delery and Doty (1996) to synchronise elements of people management and development so that, for example, commercial brand promotion interconnects with employee engagement and efforts to motivate employees giving them a voice in the brand-building linked to personal development and associated rewards.

CASE STUDY 12.1

Aligning HRM and business strategies

Pentland Brands plc is the sports, outdoor and fashion group which owns Berghaus, Speedo, Red or Dead and Boxfresh. Their brands are positioned for quality and long-term sustainability and they seek to become 'category leaders – not always the biggest but aiming to be the best' (Pentland, 2015a). In business strategy terms they might be categorised using Porter's generic business strategy model (1985) as following a differentiation strategy based on both quality and niche consumer demand (clothing for a specific sport for example).

Despite employing over 1,200 people in the UK, the private company's HR strategy appears to be founded on retaining the authentic values of what is still a family-owned business: 'supporting… people while giving them the freedom to innovate and become the best they can be in their work' (Pentland, 2015b). This approach has led to a level of external recognition. Pentland were listed as one of the UK's top 10 best large workplaces in 2014 (Great Places to Work, 2014); in addition they won the CIPD People Management Awards 2014 'Best Employee Engagement Initiative' as well as the accolade of overall winner 2014.

In their summation, CIPD judges explicitly highlighted the 'connection of employees to business strategy' within the organisation and praised the 'articulation of the right balance between financial results, long-term global brand building and people-centredness' (Pentland, 2015c)

A subsequent report in *People Management* magazine explains how HRM practices at

Pentland have been designed to underpin business objectives:

> With too many silos and not enough understanding of the Pentland brand, an HR-led programme was rolled out to explain a new, coherent strategy in face-to-face workshops driven by senior leaders and backed by a new 'SMART' way of working.
>
> A sculpture in reception at head office demonstrates just how committed employees now are to the bigger picture: it's constructed from hundreds of Lego bricks, on each of which a staff member has written a personal pledge. The latest staff survey found that 98 per cent understand the company's vision.
>
> It's all been possible because Pointer [Tim Pointer, HR Director] and his team utilised the marketing skills already inherent in the business, crunching data to understand what staff really wanted in the same way Pentland's marketers get to grips with customers' needs. But it's also about being close to the business, he says: 'We challenge ourselves about talent and capability in my team just as much as in the rest of the company. If we don't have a real understanding of our [internal] customers and our brands, we're not fit for purpose.'
>
> 'We have a real sense of everyone coming together to build something that's bigger than the sum of the individual parts. But that doesn't just happen on its own. It's about creating an incredible sense of momentum across the business.' (Jeffery, 2014)

The company website further details the reward proposition offered by Pentland Brands reflecting a mix of intrinsic development-oriented and extrinsic rewards; pentlandbrands.com/careers/.

STUDENT EXERCISE

The Pentland Brands case is an example of an organisation apparently pursuing a commitment-oriented HRM approach based on alignment with a quality and values driven business strategy. Based on your reading of the case study, consider the following questions:

1. What type of employee reward policies and practices would you expect to encounter in this type of organisation?
2. Would these policies and practices be universally applied irrespective of where employees are located and the jobs they hold?
3. To what extent does Pentland's approach to HRM imply the need for company leaders to be sensitive to external systemic factors (e.g. economic climate, political changes and labour market conditions)?
4. How would you expect this integrated approach to enable Pentland Brands to navigate through the continued uncertainties of a slow economic recovery?

Paauwe (2004) reports an explosion of interest in HRM during the 1990s after a seminal 1995 paper by American HRM commentator, Mark Huselid, making a claim for a link between what Huselid (1995) terms 'high-performance work practices' and high organisational performance. Paauwe (2004) notes the readiness of practitioners to embrace this apparent link, but with limited consideration as to what 'performance' implies. In fact, since its inception, HRM commentary has been subject to criticism for being under-theorised (Martín-Alcázar et al, 2005): located in a longer-established strand of social science commentary, writers such as Guest (1987) initially framed the debate in terms of 'human resource management and industrial relations'. Guest's stated aim was to overcome the alleged looseness with which the term had been applied, by defining HRM so as 'to differentiate it from traditional personnel management' (1987: 503), to aid development of testable hypotheses about its impact (see WERS 1998 findings above). Guest remained undecided a decade and a half later, however, as to 'whether [HRM] theory is sufficiently precise to point to the kind of empirical testing that results in convincing support or refutation' (2001: 1094).

Hatch (2006) argues that it is useful to bear in mind the stage of social development when different ideas about organisation and organising emerge. Paauwe (2004) argues that HRM as a 'high-performance work system' recipe is a product of its time and place. Again, attention to context helps to avoid the deterministic 'closed system' trap. Unprecedented mid-1990s stock market growth, following in the wake of the managerial 'excellence' movement of the 1980s (e.g. Peters and Waterman's 1982 book on 'lessons from America's best-run companies'), putting the USA 'back on top' in comparative political economy terms, following the Japanese threat to global competitive dominance. Neo-liberalism was the era's received wisdom – the 'dot com' crash and corporate scandals were yet to emerge.

Paauwe (2004) concludes: so why would one debate the meaning of performance? It followed axiomatically from the contemporary corporate governance paradigm and ('Anglo-Saxon') managerial priorities. Rather than accept uncritically an HRM reflective of its place and time of inception, however, Paauwe (2004) advocates greater pluralism in specifying 'performance' to include indicators that may sit more comfortably with a social market economy variant of capitalism (Hall and Soskice, 2001). Emphasising that his position is not anti-profit, Paauwe (2004) argues that paying attention to a wider stakeholder base is required to promote sustainable organisational success reflecting performance through people.

Boxall and Purcell (2003) also emphasise that if sustainable organisational effectiveness is the desired goal of strategic HRM, the social legitimacy of managerial actions needs to be placed alongside workforce productivity and organisational flexibility.

In a similar vein, Bach (2005) perceives a 'new HRM', where preoccupations with competing 'managerialist' models within idealised closed systems have been moderated, recognising that, while HRM may constitute a management-oriented perspective on regulation of the employment relationship, choices and consequences will always be conditioned by the structural, institutional and ideological context. This more open systems approach may help overcome criticism of an overly rationalised and static HRM, accounting for mediating values (Martín-Alcázar et al, 2005).

First, Bach (2005) argues, globalisation and information and communications technology have combined to enable multinational organisations to devolve production to employment systems where costs are perceived to be lower, as well as to match goods and services to the demands of diverse multi-local consumers. ICT may also be used to enable surveillance of local operators from a central vantage point. Technological 'hardware' operates alongside the 'software' of performance management systems and processes. We further discuss these trends and their implications for employee reward in Chapter 11.

Secondly, Bach (2005) argues, in liberal market economies such as the UK (Hall and Soskice, 2001), there has been some political 're-regulation', admitting a role for trade unions – not as champions of social justice, but as 'partners' in securing organisation effectiveness fit to compete in the 'globalised' world economy. State policy-making has also sought to discipline employers – especially those in small and medium-sized enterprises – to invest in human capital, not just 'sweat' labour commodities.

Thirdly, rapid and continual corporate restructuring, shifting organisational boundaries, has changed the nature of 1980s debates around 'core–periphery' workforce members, with the new accent on who 'owns' the workforce and deserves its commitment. This evolving context for and character of HRM raises interesting issues for reward management if the intention remains to align the organisation's people and strategy vertically and horizontally – in particular, the extent to which it is logical to privilege 'strategic' managerial priorities over employee concerns for equitable treatment (Kessler, 2007).

This evolution in the conceptualisation of HRM continues as it interacts with the environment in which it is operated. Presumably in response to the reflections on global corporate and financial systems that brought the world's economies to the brink of collapse from 2007 onwards, there have been a number of calls for business practices generally, and HRM practices more specifically, to adopt an alternative approach. Wright and McMahan (2011) claim that the 'human' aspects of HRM had been neglected and a greater emphasis on human capital is needed. Kramar (2014) examines the features of an emerging approach to challenge the dominance of strategic HRM. Sustainable HRM 'acknowledges organisational outcomes, which are broader than financial outcomes' and emphasises 'the importance of human and social outcomes'. In a departure from previous HRM incarnations, this approach 'explicitly identifies the negative as well as the positive effects of HRM on a variety of stakeholders… [taking] an explicit moral position about the desired outcomes of organisational practices in the short term and the long term (Kramar, 2014: 1069).

In many ways, the emergence of a more people-oriented approach in HRM, which does not prize performance and profit for shareholders as the only goal for organisations, brings us full circle to the more stakeholder-oriented 'Harvard model' of HRM discussed above. Indeed, Beer, Boselie and Brewster (2015: 431) argue that in the 30 years since its original emergence 'HRM [has] colluded with managers and ignored the wider stakeholder perspective' implicit in their conceptualisation of HRM in the 1980s. They 're-advocate' a multi-stakeholder perspective for developing HRM theory where 'complex objectives are seen as central to the way the business operates, perhaps foreshadowing the development of "not-*just*-for-profit" businesses' (Beer et al, 2015: 435, emphasis in original).

12.3 Strategy perspectives and employee reward choices

If, however, HRM is synonymous with (proactively defined) strategy, it appears to be a logical progression that, consequent on choosing a 'HRM approach' to people management, there will be a 'strategic' approach to reward as an HRM sub-system. As Kessler (2007) observes, advocacy for a strategically driven reward approach was in evidence over a decade and a half ago (e.g. Gomez-Mejia and Balkin, 1992). Placing the foregoing contextual concerns to one side, an obvious question, then, is to ask whether widespread take-up may be evidenced. Looking at recent studies the indication seems to be that some form of strategically aligned reward management may well be in evidence, at least in the UK.

Results from the CIPD Reward Management Survey 2012 indicate 'that private sector firms using different business strategies in their chosen product / service sectors have adopted markedly different reward management practices' (Jones et al, 2012: 6).

The research looks for differences in approach to reward management according to their strategic orientation using Miles and Snow's (1984) competitive business strategy typologies, 'Defender' and 'Prospector':

- Defenders operate in relatively stable markets for their products and/ or services; they offer a narrow range of products and/or services and invest in maximising efficiency in existing operations. Process engineering, cost control and functional structures are characteristic in Defender-oriented organisations.
- Prospectors on the other hand are market leaders, continually looking for product and market opportunities, often in completely unrelated fields. The emphasis on experimentation and innovation means Prospectors may not always be efficient. Prospector characteristics include a divisionalised structure and attention to market research, research and development.

Findings indicate that Defenders and Prospectors do adopt different reward management approaches suggesting some support for the strategic reward hypothesis. Table 12.1 details these differences and also indicates where adopting certain strategies may result in better HR outcomes.

The report concludes that:

> Many UK-based organisations are choosing actively to manage rewards, using base and incentive pay in ways their corporate focus would imply, influenced not only by sectoral 'big picture' factors, but also by the characteristics of the workforces particular employers may assemble. And there is clear evidence from what survey respondents have told us suggesting that careful reward management does make a difference – in some respects surprisingly so – in terms of creating a positive climate of relationships between employer and employees, reducing reward related disquiet, and retaining talent.
>
> (Jones et al, 2012: 30)

It would seem then that there is some limited evidence that UK organisations are aligning their reward strategies vertically with their business strategies. However, the

Table 12.1 Business strategies, reward practices and HR outcomes

	In organisations with a prospector strategy... (that is, continuous product/ service diversification in pursuit of high returns)	**In organisations with a defender strategy... (that is, cost- and/or quality- based competitive defence in a preferred core product/service market)**
Reward practices		
Market positioning of reward	Reward levels are likely to be positioned in the top 10% of the market versus competitors	
Base pay structures	Pay structures are likely to be used for managing base pay rather than individualised pay systems	
	Broad-banding is likely to be used for management/professional employees (includes senior managers, middle and front-line managers, professional, technical and scientific employees)	
Base pay level determination	Ability to pay is not likely to be considered as the most important factor in determining pay levels	Ability to pay is likely to be considered the most important factor in determining pay levels
	Market rates (with job evaluation) are likely to be considered the most important factor in determining pay levels	
Base pay progression	Competencies and skills are likely to be used as pay progression criteria	Length of service is likely to be used as pay progression criteria for management/professional employees
	Length of service is not likely to be used as pay progression criteria for non-management employees (includes administrative support, trades and production workers as well as customer service and sales staff)	
Base pay review factors	Movement in market rates was likely to have been considered an important factor in general pay award decisions in 2011	Shareholder views were likely to have been considered an important factor in general pay award decisions in 2011
		Ability to pay was not likely to have been considered an important factor in general pay award decisions in 2011
Performance-related reward, incentive and recognition	Performance-related reward, incentive and recognition schemes are likely to be in operation	Performance-related reward, incentive and recognition schemes are not likely to be in operation

(continued)

Table 12.1 (Continued)

	In organisations with a prospector strategy... (that is, continuous product/service diversification in pursuit of high returns)	In organisations with a defender strategy... (that is, cost- and/or quality- based competitive defence in a preferred core product/service market)
HR outcomes		
Employee relations climate	There is likely to be a very good employee relations climate	
Labour productivity	There is likely to be far better labour productivity in comparison with competitors It is likely that labour productivity has increased considerably in the past three years	It is likely that labour productivity has decreased in the past three years
Pay discontent	It is not likely that discontent related to pay has been raised by employees in the past 12 months	

SOURCE: CIPD Annual Survey Report Supplement: Aligning Strategy and Pay (Jones et al, 2012)

research is limited to date and there are suggestions within the report that reward management approaches are more nuanced than the prescriptive literature may suggest, when we take account of contextual factors (capability, culture, institutional factors, etc). Indeed, research by Trevor and Brown (2014: 573), largely based on the previous empirical work of Trevor (2010), concludes that institutional and social factors create 'unavoidable obstacles to the ability of management to implement pay systems aligned to strategic goals' indicating that strategic applications of pay in UK organisations will be fundamentally limited. Despite these limitations, however, the implications emerging from the data for HR and reward practitioners could well be profound:

> These findings offer people professionals an evidence base from which to engage their managerial colleagues in a dialogue for the purpose of systematically weighing choices of how best to apply scarce resources matched to an understanding not only of what the business wishes to achieve, but also the circumstances within which to organise proactively.
>
> (Jones et al, 2012: 30)

SELF-ASSESSMENT EXERCISE

1 Consider the business strategy of your firm (or one with which you are familiar). Can you classify the organisation according to Miles and Snow's (1984) Defender/Prospector typology? Are the findings from the CIPD Annual Survey

Report Supplement detailed in Table 12.1 consistent with reward practices in your organisation? What other contextual factors influence the reward approaches adopted?

2 Based on these findings and your answers to the questions above, prepare what you would say to senior colleagues when asked for your opinion on the best reward approaches to support business objectives in your organisation.

12.4 Strategy contested

Of course, as Wright (2005: 1:1) observes, 'The term "strategy" is much abused throughout organisations. It is often used when what people are really talking about is a series of programmes or a set of objectives.' And, just like HRM, notions of strategy as 'proactive management' are contested: deliberate managerial choices are located at one end of a spectrum, with 'emergent' strategy at the other (Whittington, 2001). Rather than perceiving strategy as an objective phenomenon, it may be regarded as a social construction, as such reflecting and encapsulating a range of influential factors (Marchington and Wilkinson, 2016). Moving beyond economic determinism, the astute HR professional may ask: if strategy is emergent and socially constructed, does this render problematic the idea of unitary relations between the social actors involved, or is it necessary to account for a plurality of interests in dynamic interaction around the effort–reward bargain?

Moving beyond simply defining strategy, Whittington (2001) asks whether strategy matters. It does matter, he argues, given that different commentators attach different levels of importance to what managers attempt to do in organising competitively. Some ascribe to management a planning role, to comprehend and master the external environment. The task is to gather information about economic market conditions and apply techniques in a rational and calculative way, so positioning the organisation to achieve competitive advantage. Managers as 'strategic planners' must master the organisation's environment as well as the organisation itself: the environment is seen as pliable, and the strategist knows how to handle it.

The rational approach may be viewed in the manner of some early institutionalist approaches discussed in Chapter 2, where, for example, efficiency wage theory is adopted to drive reward investment, possibly delivered using mediums that seek to balance intrinsic with extrinsic reward in pursuit of an internalised market relationship with employees intended to insulate both the organisation and its core workforce from external market vagaries. Applying such techniques, it is predicted, will secure the goodwill and high performance from the workforce on the assumption that they will perceive a unity of interest with managerial goals.

In other words, the aim is to achieve closed system conditions at least to some extent separate from open (economic/employment) system pressures derived from the application of universal 'best practice' from a central location (irrespective of cultural and institutional influences beyond the enterprise). Commentary specifically advocating 'strategic reward' interventions is likely to share these assumptions, as discussed below.

Whittington (2001) contrasts what he labels this 'rational' approach to strategy, which tends to occupy the mainstream of managerial literature, with three other broad classifications of how strategy and its role significance may be understood: the 'fatalistic', 'pragmatic' and 'relativist' perspectives. While each approach can offer a plausible rationale for managers to act in certain ways, the prescriptions are fundamentally opposed to one another.

The **fatalist** school regards organisational survival and prosperity in economic markets as simply a matter of chance or luck. The environment, not managerial action, is what will select out winners and losers – the best the manager can do is hope to hit on a profit-maximising strategy that will enable the organisation to survive the ruthless process of 'natural selection'. Impersonal markets, not managers, make the important choices – and, as indicated in Chapter 2, adopting this theoretical stance implies a limited role for active reward management beyond environmental scanning, which may enable the strategist to spot the patterns that if imitated may aid survival (Hatch, 2006).

The prescription for management is to attempt to match market supply and demand considerations (both in terms of product and service offerings), and in securing labour with the accent on efficiency: the rationale for offering work organised under an employment contract is to optimise the transaction costs, which are expected to be higher if the choice is to get work done by self-employed contract workers, involving a series of trading exchanges. Economies of scale can be made through avoiding the need for continual renegotiation of terms, while shared knowledge about expectations between the parties is expected to speed up output delivery times – that is, getting the work done without needing repeated socialisation into the specifics of an organisation's operations.

The reward contingency in this instance might relate to the example of a firm with a single-product strategy in which the design and management of employee reward would be paternalistic and unsystematic (Marchington and Wilkinson, 2005: 4). In contrast, for a diversified firm following the more rationalist orientation, 'best practice' could be to rely on large bonus payments based on profitability and subjective assessments about contribution to company performance.

Pragmatic strategy commentators agree with fatalists that rational-type long-range planning is largely futile. However, the viewpoint is less pessimistic and more politically sensitised. Organisational settings are imprecise and 'sticky' – despite rationalist advocacy, organisational managers have too little knowledge and too limited a capacity to deploy it proactively to make a difference. Managers and their competitors in economic markets are too careless and inattentive to plans to optimise their execution – things change as time progresses. Market selection processes are just as sub-optimal: no one knows what the optimal strategy is, and if they did they would be too lax to stick to it. Consequently, sub-optimal strategic planning and execution is unlikely to be fatal in terms of competitive advantage.

Here approaches such as power-dependency theory may help understand reward management outcomes – those who gain episodic advantage around politically contested organisational control frontiers (Edwards, 1990), including having knowledge that organisation managers have come to depend on them until such time as they can substitute people with alternative technologies, can expect to negotiate individually oriented reward 'deals'. In Chapter 11, we exemplify the way this line of reasoning may play out in practice when discussing approaches associated with employment terms in some forms of expatriation.

In common with rationalists, the **relativist** school of thought, as characterised by Whittington (2001), regards strategy as important and something managers should be concerned with. However, whereas rationalists – in common with mainstream HRM ideas – anticipate a unitary interest among the parties to organisation, relativist theory draws attention to the embeddedness of organisational action and hence to the need to understand organisations – and their leaders – as products of the social as well as economic contexts in which they are situated.

This chimes with the viewpoint expressed by Boxall and Purcell (2016), and Paauwe (2004), as well as in Bach's (2005) 'new HRM', outlined above. The world is viewed as a social construction, and hence open to reconstruction: not only profit maximisation to benefit finance capital shareholders under neoliberal market conditions may be prioritised: trade-offs and compromises may be required in recognition of pluralistic interests in organisation. Thus attention is needed to the social system in which strategy is to be formed and enacted: it also implies that universalistic approaches and the attempted transplantation of 'strategic' or 'best' practice between socio-economic settings is problematic.

Perhaps disguised, a rational approach is nonetheless the driving force: so a willingness exists to adapt not only the content but also the delivery mechanisms associated with employee reward, to accommodate variety in what will be regarded as an equitable distribution and forms of value, for example, among organisational stakeholders.

In summary, strategy and HRM may be considered from multiple angles, each chosen path implying a set of predicted consequences, and HRM as an ideology carrying with it the character of the context(s) from which it emerged. Armed with these insights, we may examine the ways in which, in parallel with HRM discourse, ideas about approaches to employee reward may be described and subjected to appraisal.

12.5 Strategic reward ('the new pay'): Advocates and critics

Kessler (2007) observes that early 'strategic reward' commentary privileged reward among HRM initiatives as the means by which corporate performance was to deliver competitive 'success'. He points out, citing Gomez-Mejia and Balkin (1992: 4) that, under this managerial orientation, 'issues of internal equity and external equity are viewed as secondary to the firm's need to use pay as an essential integrating and signalling mechanism to achieve overarching business objectives'. As will be noted below, in considering criticism of the strategic reward discourse, Kessler (2007) questions the plausibility of a statement that views equity and business strategy as competing principles in employee reward determination, arguing that the view has been overtaken by a perspective that regards them as closely related.

In 1992 a book was published in the USA entitled *The New Pay*, a label that University of Southern California academic Edward E. Lawler III had coined (Lawler, 1984) to underscore the terms of 'a strategic approach' to reward management. The authors of the 1992 publication, management consultants Jay R Schuster and Patricia K Zingheim, set out to popularise Lawler's thinking. Their challenge was stark: 'To survive, American industry must have a new view of the future' – a future in which 'the responsibility and rewards for success' would be shared between organisations and employees (1992: 4).

Heery (1996) notes that the new pay architects specified the problem by reference to a perceived dichotomy. Arrangements applied to manage the employment relationship, including the effort–reward bargain, functional in stable environments and organisations designed around hierarchy and scientific mass production systems informed by the 'scientific management' principles that an earlier consultant, Frederick W Taylor, had advocated early in the 20th century (Taylor, 1911), had to give way to a new regime. New pay, demanded by the new employee–organisation relationship, matched the more fluid organisational form applicable under a less certain environment, demanding modification of 'attitudes, plans and approaches to both how we work and how we are paid' (Schuster and Zingheim, 1992: 4).

In keeping with the rationalistic principles associated with mainstream HRM ideas, Lawler explains that the ideas he and his associates outline are intended to integrate work and employee reward arrangements with each other and with business priorities so that individuals will engage in 'the kind of performance that contributes to overall organizational effectiveness rather than simply making the individual look good' (1996: 196). Under this 'new logic' organisational design and management style flow from the business strategy, and both drive reward systems. 'New pay' is not an alternative form of pay nor a set of techniques (e.g. broad bands, pay-for-performance), but a different way of thinking about the role of reward systems in complex organisations (Lawler, 1995).

Six foundational factors support Lawler's (1995) 'strategic' reward management recipe:

First, an emphasis on attracting people whose expressed and actual behaviour is congruent with the kinds of attributes specified in describing the human resource aspects of the business strategy. This idea does, of course, imply that characteristics can be specified and that individuals can have fixed traits that can be deployed in ways that match organisational demands.

Second, attention is drawn to the role reward systems can play in employee motivation. Lawler uses expectancy theory to stress the need for a 'line of sight' matching reward to the conditions applicable to the individual targeted and its delivery. The assumption is that employees' 'mental maps' enable them to orient their assessment of signals from organisations and to reach conclusions as to how they will respond. There is an onus on management to offer reward giving off signals to which employees are likely to respond positively, given the context and their priorities from the employment relationship.

Third, the reward system is to be directed in ways that reinforce employees' tendency to learn from experience and to turn that learning into skills the organisation wishes to pay for. Some organisations have therefore implemented skills-based pay – that is, pay increases for skills acquisition. The issue is akin to motivating employees to perform, but this time the emphasis is on ongoing development of the employee's capacity to be valuable to the organisation. Rewards need to be packaged so as to encourage employees to develop skills and competencies the organisation's strategy has specified as necessary to its successful achievement.

A fourth element in strategic reward architecture is culture. Carrying the implication that managers can act on it by direct intervention, culture, as an objective phenomenon, is to be shaped using reward forms and processes to promote behaviour types that become dominant patterns of behaviour in the organisation and influence employee perceptions of what the organisation believes in, stands for and values. Given the old/new change imperative, the assumption is that how the organisation develops and administers its reward system can communicate a cultural offering that is different from the culture the reward system practices create in another organisational setting. The employer branding initiative sketched earlier in the case study exercise may be one indication of how 'culture management' may be approached as a central strategic reward tenet.

Fifth, strategic reward commentary stresses that reward systems reinforce and define organisation structure, something Lawler (1995) claims few executives recognise during reward system design. The impact may be significant even if not intentional. The reward system can reinforce hierarchy and impact on decision-making structures. And integration among workforce members can be positively or negatively affected by reward structure and delivery modes. Differentiation in rewarding employees requires careful handling. It may be counterproductive if unity between organisation members is the goal.

Sixth, reward system designers are exhorted to factor in to their thinking how much the proposed reward system and its relative components will cost, and to review the extent to which costs should be fixed or varied with the organisation's ability to meet them. Lawler (1995) argues that one indicator of a well-designed reward system is that it leads to cost increases when the firm can afford it and containment when it cannot.

Zingheim and Schuster (2000) extrapolate from these foundations six principles to ensure the organisation will 'pay people right!' These are:

1. Create a 'positive and natural' reward experience: employees are to be involved and 'educated' as to the reasons and shared benefits for changing reward systems, guidance that assumes unitary interests between employer and workforce, or at least the basis on which rational management can 're-educate' individuals and groups who may not perceive interest overlap.
2. Align rewards with business goals to create 'a win-win partnership': clear managerial direction is to be provided that individual employees must continue to 'add value', in ways that the company will then recognise with rewards.
3. Extend people's line of sight: managers are to encourage all workforce members to become 'knowledgeable stakeholders', showing how an individual's efforts impact on the team, business unit and company, including the need to adapt to customer needs.
4. Integrate rewards: each reward tool is to be used for what it does best, integrating each element of total reward to offer a customised 'deal'.

5 Reward individual ongoing value with 'base pay', applying three elements: employee salary is to reflect increases in competencies the firm finds useful; consistent performance over time; and the individual's value in the external labour market.

6 Reward results with variable pay: it is uncritically accepted that the firm must 'meet shareholder expectations' (reasonableness is not discussed) and 'provide a compelling future'; variable pay is deemed suitable as part of the total reward offer to recognise these 'results' (as well as enjoining employees in the corporate project).

The consultants argue that 'total reward strategies are becoming more global and less industry-specific', as 'global talent can migrate from company to company because of their success in global business, rather than industry-specific success' (2000: 334). Convergence on a universalistic set of reward management norms, read off from corporate managerial strategy predilections, appears the logical outcome, for which reward designers must prepare.

Heery (1996: 58) acknowledges the potential value of the 'new pay' model. But he also looks critically at the consequences of its application, and specifically the assumption on the part of strategic reward commentators that linking pay and performance is axiomatic, carrying with this choice 'the intention to increase employee risk'. Under the 'new pay' reasoning, the proportion of guaranteed pay and benefits is reduced in favour of 'at risk' payments – commissions, merit pay and bonuses, which may not be consolidated into permanent, let alone pensionable total remuneration.

Not only variable performance pay, but also basic pay progression over time follows the logic of employee compliance with corporate strategy. And what Heery (1996) refers to as 'soft' measures of performance may be applied managerially to determine contingent reward outcomes; measures that may not be directly controlled by employees (in the way, for example, piece-rate pay/production is calibrated).

Tying reward outcomes to team contribution, or group/business unit performance, customer satisfaction ratings or financial measures (which may be subject to managerial fine-tuning for other purposes over specific time periods not set by employees) generates uncertainty for workforce members. The indicators may be subjective or susceptible to influences outside an individual's sphere of influence in the workplace.

Moreover, so-called 'nimble reward management' processes (Ledford, 1995), where line managers are called to make 'rapid but necessarily rough and ready judgements about employee entitlement to reward' (Heery, 1996: 59) may combine with the substance of 'new pay' in ways that harm employee wellbeing, standing in contradiction to employees' needs for stable and secure income from selling their labour. (Refer to Chapter 9 for discussion on employee wellbeing and total reward.)

Under conditions where employment systems have been deregulated and trade unions' capability to support resistance to injustice severely weakened (Heery, 1996), the transfer of risk from employer (to secure performance returns on investment in labour) to employee through variable and contingent forms of reward represents an issue carrying potentially negative consequences when evaluated on ethical and moral grounds.

Heery (1996) warns about more explicit forms of injustice arising from the scope inherent in 'strategic', business-aligned reward management for inconsistent treatment of employees, in contradiction to 'equal pay' principles designed to avoid direct and indirect discrimination on grounds related to demography. Issues arise here when considering the relative capacity of line managers and HR specialists to govern reward management in ways that do not contravene regulatory provisions and/or good practice in relation to fair treatment and human dignity at work.

As part of his critique, Heery points to 'the attachment of new pay writers to the principle of employee involvement in the management of pay' so as to secure not only understanding but also 'acceptance of the system' (1996: 61). Lawler himself (1996) argues that, when building 'from the ground up', an organisation's strategic reward choices may fall on stony ground if it fails to account for the propensity of the workforce to feel similarly positive about the approach.

Employees have exercised a strategic choice in selecting an organisation to work for on criteria such as reward arrangements. Heery cites 'evidence that employees have separate and opposing interests regarding remuneration to those of employers' (1996: 61), which he feels may best be channelled through collective representation. Accepting a shift of onus to secure pay based on their performance as judged by managers, rather than on managers to secure performance in return for guaranteed pay, may run contradictory to the basic interests Heery (1996) describes for income stability and security.

There is thus scope for employee–employer conflict around the enduring bases of pay systems long ago juxtaposed by Gowler and Lupton (1969) – pay for time (reporting for work) versus pay for performance (what happens when at work). While the assumption of unitary interests between employers and employees sits at the core of HRM ideology, a more pluralistically oriented perspective suggests that the interface of strategic choices between the parties to the effort–reward bargain needs to be considered.

Another core feature of the 'new pay' recipe is the requirement for managerially led change, to adjust to the 'new logic' of organisation (Lawler, 1996). The assumption that managers know best is challenged in remarks by Marc Thompson expressed during a debate about the interaction of reward management with notions of trust between employees and organisational leaders, where the latter hope to combine trust in 'a virtuous trinity' with commitment-building and employee motivation to work productively.

Thompson's suggestion was that perhaps organisations should go with the grain of employees' thinking around work practices and interrelationships rather than engaging in perennial attempts to change that thinking. Instead of assuming that the onus is on managers to lead the educational process, he argued, '[i]n future organisations may have to re-educate themselves to get the performance they want' (Perkins and Sandringham, 1998: 6).

Heery (1996: 63) proposes an alternative 'new pay' prescription aimed at creating a situation of 'acceptable risk', in which the interest of the employer in contingent and variable pay is balanced against the interest of the employee in reasonably stable and predictable income. Principles he believes could secure that balance are as follows:

- the use of variable pay as a supplement and not a replacement for a 'fair' base salary;
- commitment to maintaining the value of employee benefits and particularly those that provide for economic security;

- basing contingent pay systems on rigorous measures of performance that are subject to employee control;
- regulation of management decision-making about pay, supported through training, strict guidelines and review;
- transparency and full communication of pay system rules;
- regular monitoring and periodic audit of pay systems to ensure consistency of application and an absence of discrimination;
- effective 'due process' mechanisms for employees to appeal against management judgements;
- full involvement of employee representatives in the design, application and review of payment systems.

(SOURCE: Heery, 1996: 63)

Judging the content of his list as running contrary to the dominant trends in mid-1990s reward management practice, Heery anticipated that 'very few organizations are likely to adopt it' (1996: 63), recommending recourse to legislation to enshrine the right of employees to bargain for their reward.

Pursuing a different line of critique, just over a decade on, Kessler (2007) takes the 'strategic reward' prescriptions to task on the grounds of an underlying assumption that what have been labelled 'contribution based pay' practices (Brown and Armstrong, 1999), perceived as 'second generation' strategies for aligning reward and performance management, will generate the necessary worker attitudes and behaviours in a mechanistic and unproblematic way, so that any concern with equity, which might affect such employee responses, becomes incidental. It is only when attempts are made to theorise the relationship between pay and the achievement of business goals that issues of equity, process and meaning re-emerge as important, Kessler (2007) argues. If a holistic systems mindset is adopted this is of course logical.

Thinking about the importance of equity may be developed paying attention to externally oriented equity benchmarks as well as those that may be identified between employees inside the organisation. Kessler (2007) cites reported evidence over recent years where, especially in industrial sectors such as finance, reward systems have been affected combining payment of performance-related sums with 'premium rates' in response to tight markets for certain kinds of employees to acquire the skills needed to meet organisational goals. Rather than the clinical distinction in the Gowler and Lupton (1969) pay-for-performance versus pay-for-time dualism, hybrid reward 'solutions' are being selected. Resource dependence theory (Pfeffer and Salancik, 2003) may help in interpreting these kinds of trends where, as Festing et al (2007: 123) explain, resources that are 'scarce or controlled by a few actors... may affect strategic organisational behaviour [and] the stronger the dependencies the more power the focus actor has in terms of influencing organisational behaviour'.

Paying attention to peer reward comparisons beyond the organisation may be strategically astute not only at private industry flashpoints involving specialist labour market segments. Kessler (2007) shows that, for example, uneven external labour market pressures have influenced public sector pay-setting, leading to the award of pay supplements tied not only to occupation types but also to regional geography. External equity considerations are further observed in employer actions to establish grading structures and 'job families' that clarify and enhance employee 'total reward' progression opportunities. Kessler sees such moves as an echo of the development of internal labour markets (discussed in Chapter 2 above), originally designed as a hedge against competitive pressures in tight labour market circumstances.

Turning to internal reward comparisons, the re-regulation impacting on HRM that Bach (2005) refers to impacts on the equity between employees within the same organisation. Kessler (2007) notes that the UK government has enacted legislation intended to regulate reward management outcomes to narrow differentials between employees at the extremes of the labour market. As discussed in Chapter 3, the National Minimum Wage provisions have been designed to secure a minimum protective floor, on the one hand, while not detrimentally affecting competitiveness, productivity, employment levels or wage inflation, on the other hand. In the case of 'top pay', as discussed in Chapter 10, the government has intervened to increase transparency related to directors' and executives' reward – not necessarily to modify outcomes, but to assure the justifiability of high payouts based on a demonstrable link to corporate performance. And, Pepper, Gosling and Gore (2015) have found evidence that 'fairness considerations are salient to senior executives', and that while prevalent views of executive pay emphasise incentives, they 'underestimate the role and significance of fairness' because they are dominated by agency theory and related concepts (Pepper et al, 2015: 1308).

A further significant public policy concern that Kessler (2007) highlights is the particular issue of equality of treatment between women and men. Pressure on the government and employers to address this issue from a range of interest groups has been observable – exacerbated by evidence that despite the elapse of over four and a half decades since the Equal Pay Act 1970, the gap between male and female employees remains stubbornly wide. As noted in Chapter 3, provisions of the Equality Act 2010 have sought to address this and other inequities in work and society. Accounting not only for the substance of employee reward determination but also issues of process, paying attention to procedural justice and psychological contract considerations, Kessler (2007) concludes that, contrary to early 1990s commentary, equity factors, far from being alternatives to strategic imperatives in reward management, may be central to whether or not strategic goals are achievable in practice.

STUDENT EXERCISE

Informed by the 'new pay' advocacy and critique detailed in this section, consider the following questions for discussion in groups:

1. How far are the 'new pay' principles expounded by Lawler (1995) and others compatible with issues of fairness and equity in organisations given the claims of Heery (1996) that new pay practices have the potential: to harm employee wellbeing; to remove economic stability and security for individuals; and to undermine 'equal pay' principles?
2. Reflect on your organisation's reward practices (or reward practices of an organisation with which you are familiar). Would you describe them as conforming to 'new pay' principles? If so, how does this impact fairness, consistency and equity?

12.6 Actors and their roles in reward management under the HRM rubric

Elevating HRM and with it reward management policy and practice to the level of corporate strategy implies changes not only in thinking but also a shift in the roles played by specialists and line managers in administering the reward system. If recent arguments have salience, emphasising the crucial role of process, so as to avoid undermining strategic aspirations, education of management as much as workforce members assumes importance.

Storey (1995) argues that the impetus for HRM (and, one might reason, by extension 'strategic reward') came not from the welfare-oriented or IR-oriented specialists but from line managers. The latter wanted to focus attention on business – as noted above, reflecting the 'enterprise culture' and growing managerialist confidence that emerged in the 1980s. They were impatient with proceduralism around the employment relationship and wished to force the pace of change, acting over the heads of traditional trade union and personnel specialists alike.

Under this change imperative, HRM is not some idealised human relations paradigm. HR practitioners may thus need to weigh the nature of expectations about people and the role expected and tolerance for procedure or ambiguity when advising specific organisation managements. On the other hand, even in the most hard-edged individualised contexts, line management aspirations willing pluralism to go away in relations with employees may not be enough.

An exhortation to 'help managers to be strategic' (Dalziel and Strange, 2007: 45) recognising that, at first-line level in particular, there is a 'vital' role to play in managing the effort–reward bargain (Purcell and Hutchinson, 2007) prompts reflection on HR specialists' role as well. Dalziel and Strange counsel HR specialists to take opportunities to help both 'the senior team' and line managers at the organisation–workforce interface.

In the case of top-down strategy, the assistance may be mapping the strategy process to facilitate its communication to others in ways that enable them to see the relevance of their job in achieving it. Where strategy 'emerges from lower levels', the HR specialist should 'find ways to get the key information to the people at the top' (Dalziel and Strange, 2007: 45).

The implication is that HR practitioners need to move beyond traditional concerns with designing and administering pay structures and/or incentive arrangements, salary market survey and review planning, in reaction to internal or external stimuli, to a more proactive engagement in strategy development synchronised with people management at the organisation-wide level. As mentioned in Chapter 11, in some cases organisations are making significant investments in information technology-enabled transnational employee reward administration, to enable self-service among line managers.

But although this may permit HR specialists to raise their sights, external regulatory compliance stipulations, as well as pressure to assure return on corporate investment in increasingly complex reward 'portfolios' matched to organisation and employee preferences, necessitate attention to setting, communicating and auditing line management performance against clear corporate standards, and supporting their interpretation in given circumstances.

In the case of line managers, Brown and Purcell (2007) note the burgeoning levels of responsibility over the past ten years to appraise employee performance, determine pay and bonus adjustments, and explain flexible benefits plans, while fewer, more distant HR specialists are available to support them. In spite of this evidence suggesting the crucial role to be played, front-line managers are perceived as constituting the 'Achilles heel' at the level of strategy implementation.

Brown and Purcell draw on CIPD research indicating that while one consequence of HR functional restructuring is further devolution of more pay and people management responsibilities to the line, 'HR does not seem to be devoting enough resources to training and equipping line managers to handle these responsibilities, despite the increasingly rapid rates of change in reward methods and the spread of more sophisticated and complex scheme designs' (2007: 30–1).

These research findings inform a recommendation that HR specialists should do more to involve line managers in reward management system design and modification, for example, in the way that one retail organisation named in the research report successfully implemented a new competency-based reward framework following a focus group programme during the development phase. People reportedly like the new system because, citing a senior manager in the case organisation, 'it uses our language' (Brown and Purcell, 2007: 32).

A second recommendation relates to the support line managers receive to help them shoulder their reward management accountability – at the most practical level, a willingness to invest corporate resources in assuring competence in ways that are visible to workforce members, imbuing them with confidence in the proficiency of their supervisor to act in a manner that combines organisational efficiency and justice prerequisites. The example is given of an insurance company that accompanied introduction of a new pay-for-performance programme covering call centre operatives with provision of a minimum of two days' training and practice in its operation. Line managers were viewed by the corporate HR functional leadership as needing 'to live and breathe [the pay system]... to own it and realise how important it is to the business strategy to make it work' (Brown and Purcell, 2007: 32).

12.7 Conclusions and key learning points

In this chapter, the interplay between reward management and the ideas and practices that have become associated with HRM has been considered. Debates around HRM, reaching back to the early 1980s, have been reviewed, to identify the ways the concept has been defined and the expectations that have been raised concerning active alignment between organisational strategy along one dimension and between the variables in the HRM bundle along the other. Having emphasised the 'strategy' factor, attention has been paid to the multiple perspectives available to approach this concept and in turn to shape HRM thinking.

A 'strategic HRM' approach is neither simple nor self-evident, once it is recognised that a multiplicity of choices exists in this aspect of people management, each imbued with assumptions regarding the location of managerial action within systemic contexts, and each accompanied by sets of consequences for organisational outcomes, members and wider stakeholders. These foundations have been deployed to assist in considering 'strategic' commentary directed at employee reward – both advocacy for the merits of 'new pay' and caution regarding accepting the universal application of such prescription uncritically.

In summary:

- HRM can be understood as ideology as much as a set of people management practices, and empirical evidence indicates that while the term may have mainstream discourse status, comprehensive application remains quite rare.
- HRM prescriptions may be understood as reflecting the time and place in which the concept originated, and as such need to be weighed against specific situational factors encountered by contemporary practitioners.
- Not only HRM ideas but also orientation to strategy are contested, and so require the exercise of caution, accounting for the complexity of socio-economic relations around organisation, and the shifting influences on interactive outcomes, before choosing to apply universal HRM recipes in particular contexts.
- Strategic reward management commentary carries the marks of the wider HRM and strategy debates. In evaluating advocates' claims, attention to arguments drawing on a wider social science literature, including ethical considerations, would be beneficial.
- Application of strategy when designing and implementing employee reward policies and practices at the least demands attention to the character of the workforce concerned and to the managers required to take the lead role. A significant role opens up for HR professionals to take the lead in addressing the organisational needs diagnosed for attention.

Explore further

To gain a full appreciation of their tripartite HRM strategy as efficiency, organisational-flexibility and legitimacy model, see Boxall, P and Purcell, J (2016) *Strategy and Human Resource Management*, 4th edn, Basingstoke: Palgrave Macmillan.

For a provocative look at the reasons why HRM has faced criticism through the ages and how its activities are tied irrevocably to wider economic contextual factors, see Cappelli, P (2015) Why we love to hate HR... and what HR can do about it, *Harvard Business Review*, July–August Issue.

For contrasting statements for and in critique of 'the new pay', see (1) Lawler, EE (1995) The New Pay: A strategic approach, *Compensation & Benefits Review*, 27 July–August, pp. 14–22; and (2) Heery, E (1996) Risk, representation and the new pay, *Personnel Review*, vol. 25, no. 6, pp. 54–65.

CIPD commissioned empirical research on the relative reward management roles attributable to HR specialists and line managers is presented in Purcell, J and Hutchinson, S (2007) *Rewarding Work: The vital role of front line managers*, Change Agenda, London: Chartered Institute of Personnel and Development.

REFERENCES

Abercrombie, N, Hill, S and Turner, BS (2000) *Penguin Dictionary of Sociology*, 4th edn. London: Penguin

Acas (2014a) *Job Evaluation: Considerations and risks*. London: Acas

Acas (2023a) *Equal Pay and the Law*, www.acas.org.uk/equal-pay/equal-pay-law (archived at https://perma.cc/MJT4-5KD9)

Acas (2023b) 5 years of gender pay reporting: how much further until we close the gap, www.acas.org.uk/5-years-of-gender-pay-reporting-how-much-further-until-we-close-the-gap (archived at https://perma.cc/4BLA-KMRJ)

ACCA (2005) Executive pay, *Policy Briefing Paper*, June. London: ACCA

Ackers, P, Marchington, M, Wilkinson, A and Dundon, T (2003) *Partnership and Voice, with or without Trade Unions: changing UK management approaches to organisational participation*. Research Series Paper 2003: 4. Loughborough University Business School

Adams, L, Hall, P and Schafer, S (2008) *Equal Pay Reviews Survey 2008*. IFF Research. Research report 2. Equality and Human Rights Commission

Albert, M (1993) *Capitalism Against Capitalism*. London: Whurr

Aleweld, T, Festing, M and Teklell, M (2015) *European Reward Governance Survey*. Berlin: Aon Hewitt, ESCP Europe

Alfes, K, Truss, C, Soane, EC, Rees, C and Gatenb, M (2010) Creating An Engaged Workforce. Findings From The Kingston Employee Engagement Consortium Project. London

Allison, N, Brett, S and Hatchett, A (2002) A square deal, *People Management*, July

Allport, GW (1954) The historical background of modern social psychology, in Lindzey, G (ed.) *The Handbook of Social Psychology*, vol. 1. Reading, MA: Addison-Wesley, pp. 3–56

Altman, M (2020) Inside the black box of the firm: 'Why choice, power and preferences matter for productivity and efficiency', in M. Altman (ed.) *Smart Economic Decision-Making in a Complex World*. London: Academic Press, pp. 147–87, https://www.sciencedirect.com/science/article/abs/pii/B9780128114612000079?via%3Dihub (archived at https://perma.cc/A8L2-H95Z)

Anakwe, UP (2002) Human resource management practices in Nigeria: challenges and insights, *International Journal of Human Resource Management*, vol. 13, no.7, pp. 1042–59

Anderson, S, Cavanagh, J, Collins, C, Pizzigati, S and Lapham, M (2007) *Executive Excess 2007: The Staggering Social Cost of U.S. Business Leadership, 14th Annual CEO Compensation Survey*. Washington, DC: Institute for Policy Studies and Boston, MA: United for a Fair Economy

Anglin, AH, Kincaid, PA, Short, JC and Allen, DG (2022) Role theory perspectives: past, present, and future applications of role theories in management research, *Journal of Management*, vol. 48, no. 6, pp. 1469–502, doi.org/10.1177/01492063221081442 (archived at https://perma.cc/B2MT-LV8L)

Antoni, C (2022) Psychological perspectives on reward management, in Perkins, SJ (ed.) *The Routledge Companion to Reward Management*. London: Routledge, pp. 16–24

Armstrong, M (2002) *Employee Reward*, 3rd edn. London: Chartered Institute of Personnel and Development

Armstrong, M (2012) *Armstrong's Handbook of Reward Management Practice: Improving performance through reward*. London: Kogan Page

Armstrong, M (2019) *Armstrong's Handbook of Reward Management Practice: Improving performance through reward*, 6th edn. London: Kogan Page

Armstrong, M and Baron, A (1995) *The Job Evaluation Handbook*. London: IPD

Armstrong, M and Brown, D (1999) *Paying for Contribution*. London: Kogan Page

Armstrong, M and Murlis, H (2007) *Reward Management. A handbook of remuneration strategy and practice*, 5th edn. London: Kogan Page

Armstrong, M and Stephens, T (2005) *A Handbook of Employee Reward Management and Practice*. London: Kogan Page

Armstrong, M, Cummins, A, Hastings, S and Wood, W (2003) *Job Evaluation. A guide to achieving equal pay*. London: Kogan Page

Arnault, EJ, Gordon, L, Joines, DH and Phillips, GM (2001) An experimental study of job evaluation and comparable worth, *Industrial and Labor Relations Review*, vol. 54, no. 4 July, pp. 806–15

Arrowsmith, J, Nicholaisen, H, Bechter, B and Nonell, R (2010) The management of variable pay in European banking, *International Journal of Human Resource Management*, vol. 21, no. 15, pp. 2716–40

Arrowsmith, J and Sisson, K (1999) Pay and working time: towards organisation-based systems?, *British Journal of Industrial Relations*, vol. 37, no. 1, pp. 51–75

Atkinson, J (1984) Manpower strategies for flexible organisations, *Personnel Management*, vol. 16, no. 8, pp. 28–31

Atkinson, JW (1964) *An Introduction to Motivation*. Princeton, NJ: Van Nostrand

Attwood, S (2015) *Bonus practices across UK organisations*, www.xperthr.co.uk/survey-analysis/bonus-practices-across-uk-organisations/155267/?t=215 (archived at https://perma.cc/BZ3S-K8CK)

Attwood, S (2019) *Bonus payments for professional staff: 2019 survey*, www.xperthr.co.uk/survey-analysis/bonus-payments-for-professional-staff-2019-survey/164071/ (archived at https://perma.cc/RRH9-XSD4)

Bach, S (2005) *Managing Human Resources: Personnel management in transition*, 4th edn. Blackwell: Oxford

Bach, S (2010) Public sector industrial relations: The challenge of modernisation, in Colling, T and Terry, M (eds.) *Industrial Relations: Theory and Practice*, 3rd edn. Chichester: John Wiley and Sons

Bach, S (2013) Performance management, in Bach, S and Edwards, MR (eds.) *Managing Human Resources*, 5th edn. Chichester: John Wiley and Sons Ltd

Bacon, N and Blyton, P (2006) Union co-operation in a context of job insecurity: negotiated outcomes from teamworking, *British Journal of Industrial Relations*, vol. 44, no. 2, pp. 215–37

Baden-Fuller, C (2000) Editorial: executive compensation in Europe, *Long Range Planning*, vol. 33, pp. 475–77

Bajorek, Z and Bevan, S (2015) Performance-related-pay in the UK public sector, *Journal of Organizational Effectiveness: People and Performance*, vol. 2, no. 2, pp. 94–109

Baldmus, W (1961) *Efficiency and Effort*. London: Tavistock

Balkin, DB and Gomez-Mejia, R (1990) Matching compensation and organizational strategies, *Strategic Management Journal*, vol. 11, pp. 153–69

Balkin, DB and Werner, S (2013) Theorizing the relationship between discretionary employee benefits and individual performance, *Human Resource Management Review*, vol. 33, no. 1

Bank of England (2018) Staff Working Paper No. 714

Barney, J, Wright, M. and Ketchen, DJ (2001) The resource-based view of the firm: ten years after 1991, *Journal of Management*, vol. 27, no. 6, pp. 625–41, doi.org/10.1177/014920630102700601 (archived at https://perma.cc/HR45-NYKH)

Baruch, Y (2004) *Managing Careers: Theory and Practice*. London: FT-Prentice Hall

Barringer, M and Milkovich, G (1998) A theoretical exploration of the adoption and design of flexible benefit plans: a case of human resource innovation, *Academy of Management Review*, vol. 23, no. 2 (April), pp. 305–24

Baska, M (2018) Businesses 'throwing money down the drain' by not communicating employee benefits, *People Management*, 27 July, www.peoplemanagement.co.uk/news/articles/businesses-throwing-money-down-drain-not-communicating-employee-benefits (archived at https://perma.cc/4HQD-YD78)

Beatty, RW, Huselid, MA and Schneier, CE (2007) New HR metrics: scoring on the business scorecard, in Schuler, RS and Jackson, SE (eds.) *Strategic Human Resource Management*, 2nd edn. Oxford, Blackwell, pp. 352–65

Beaumont, P and Hunter, L (2000) Labour economies, competition and compensation, in Thorpe, R and Homan, G (eds.) *Strategic Reward Systems*. London: FT/Prentice Hall, pp. 45–62

Bebchuck, LA and Fried, JM (2003) Executive compensation as an agency problem, *Journal of Economic Perspectives*, vol. 17, no. 3, pp. 71–92

Becker, GS (1957) *The Economics of Discrimination*. Chicago: University of Chicago Press

Beck-Krala, E, Scott, D and Klimkiewcz, K (2022) Socially responsible and sustainable reward programmes, in Perkins, SJ (ed.) *The Routledge Companion to Reward Management*. London: Routledge, pp. 97–111

Beer, M, Boselie, P and Brewster, C (2015) Back to the future: implications for the field of HRM of the multistakeholder perspective proposed 30 years ago, *Human Resource Management*, vol. 54, no. 3, pp. 427–38

Beer, M, Spencer, B, Lawrence, P, Mills, Q and Walton, R (1984) *Managing Human Assets*. New York: Free Press

Behrend, H (1957) The effort bargain, *Industrial and Labour Relations Review*, vol. 10, no. 4, pp. 505–15

BEIS (2019a) Trade Union Statistics 2018, www.gov.uk/government/statistics/trade-union-statistics-2018 (archived at https://perma.cc/32ZV-TBPZ)

BEIS (2022) Trade Union Statistics 2021, www.gov.uk/government/statistics/trade-union-statistics-2021 (archived at https://perma.cc/DZ3M-WT67)

Belle, N (2015) Performance-related pay and the crowding out of motivation in the public sector: a randomized field experiment, *Public Administration Review*, vol. 75, no. 2, pp. 230–41

Bender, R and Moir, L (2006) Does 'best practice' in setting executive pay in the UK encourage 'good behaviour'?, *Journal of Business Ethics*, vol. 67, no. 1, pp. 75–91

Benson, J (1995) Future employment and the internal labour market, *British Journal of Industrial Relations*, vol. 33. no. 4 (December), p. 38

Bergmann, TJ and Gulbinas Scarpello, V (2001) *Compensation Decision Making*, 4th edn. Orlando, FL: Harcourt College Publishers

Berrocal, F, García, A, Miguel A and Ramírez-Vielma, R (2018) Influence on the type of methods on the results of job evaluation, *Universia Business Review*, 3rd Quarter, Issue 59, pp. 114–29

Bichard, M (1999) *Performance Management. Civil Service Reform – A Report to the Meeting of Permanent Heads of Departments, Sunningdale. 30 September–1 October 1999*. London: Cabinet Office

BIS (2013) *Directors' Remuneration Reforms: Frequently Asked Questions*. London: Department for Business, Innovation and Skills

BIS (2014) Business and Enterprise Guidance – Employee, www.gov.uk/guidance/employee-shareholders (archived at https://perma.cc/FN4W-9X86)

Black, J (2002) *Oxford Dictionary of Economics*, 2nd edn. Oxford: OUP

Blanchflower, DG and Bryson, A (2010) The wage impact of trade unions in the UK public and private sectors, *Economica*, vol. 77, pp. 92–109, DOI:10.1111/j.1468-0335.2008.00726.x (archived at https://perma.cc/9Z8D-6ZX5)

Blanchflower, DG and Oswald, A (1987) *Profit Sharing – can it work?* LSE Discussion Paper 255. London: London School of Economics

Blanchflower, DG and Oswald, AJ (1988) Profit-related pay: prose discovered, *Economic Journal,* vol. 98, pp. 720–30

Blanco, J, Drenik, A and Moser, C and Zaratiegui, E (2022) A Theory of Non-Coasean Labor Markets (30 December), SSRN, papers.ssrn.com/sol3/papers.cfm?abstract_id=4124811 (archived at https://perma.cc/FFN3-48WA)

Blasi, J, Freeman, R and Kruse, D (2016) Do broad-based employee ownership, profit sharing and stock options help the best firms do even better?', *British Journal of Industrial Relations*, vol. 54, no. 1, pp. 55–82

Blau, F (1996) *Where Are We in the Economics of Gender?* NBER Working Paper 5664, July. Cambridge, MA: National Bureau of Economic Research

Bloom, M, Milkovich, G and Mitra, A (2003) International compensation: learning from how managers respond to variations in local host contexts, *International Journal of Human Resource Management*, vol. 14, no. 8, pp. 1350–67

Bonache, J and Fernández, Z (2005) International compensation: costs and benefits of international assignments, in Scullion, J and Linehan, M (eds.) *International Human Resource Management: A critical text.* London: Palgrave, pp. 114–30

Bonache, J (2006) The compensation of expatriates: a review and a future research agenda, in Stahl, GK and Bjoerkman, I (eds.) *Handbook of Research in International Human Resource Management.* Cheltenham: Edward Elgar, pp. 158–96

Boreham, P (2010) Incomes Data Services' contention that FTSE 100 executive directors have received 55 per cent pay rises is a misrepresentation of the facts, Letters, *The Telegraph*, 1 November, p. 38

Boswell, WR and Boudreau, JW (2000) Employee satisfaction with performance appraisals and appraisers: The role of perceived appraisal use, *Human Resource Development Quarterly*, vol. 11, no. 3 (Autumn), pp. 283–99

Bowey, A and Thorpe, R (2000) Motivation, in Thorpe, R and Homan, G (eds.) *Strategic Reward Systems.* London: FT Prentice Hall, pp. 81–100

Boxall, P and Purcell, J (2003) *Strategy and Human Resource Management.* Basingstoke: Palgrave Macmillan

Boyatzis, R (1982) *The Competent Manager. Model for effective performance.* Hoboken, NJ: Wiley

Braverman, H (1997) *Labor and Monopoly Capital. The degradation of work in the twentieth century.* New York: Monthly Review Press

Brewster, C, Harris, H and Sparrow, P (2001) *Globalising HR.* London: Chartered Institute of Personnel and Development

Briscoe, DR and Schuler, RS (2004) *International Human Resource Management*, 2nd edn. New York: Routledge

Brookes, M, Brewster, C and Wood, G (2005) Social relations, firms and societies: a study of institutional embeddedness, *International Sociology*, vol. 20, no. 4, pp. 403–26

Brown, D (2001) *Reward Strategies: From intent to impact.* London: Chartered Institute of Personnel and Development

Brown, D (2014) The future of reward management: from total reward strategies to smart rewards, *Compensation & Benefits Review*, vol. 46, no. 3, pp. 147–51

Brown, D (2015), Want to motivate staff on low wages? Pay more', *People Management*, 13 April

Brown, D and Armstrong, M (1999) *Paying for Contribution. Real performance-related pay strategies.* London: Kogan Page

Brown, D and Perkins, SJ (2007) Reward strategy: making it happen, *WorldatWork Journal*, vol. 16, no. 2, pp. 82–93

Brown, D and Purcell, J (2007) Reward management: on the line, *Compensation & Benefits Review*, vol. 39 (May–June), pp. 28–34

Brown, D and Rickard, C (2019) Gender pay gaps and solutions: what can governments and employers do to deliver equal pay – what works?, in Perkins, SJ (ed.) *The Routledge Companion to Reward Management*. London: Routledge, pp. 125–46

Brown, FW, Bryant, SE and Reilly, MD (2006) Does emotional intelligence – as measured by the EQI – influence transformational leadership and/or desirable outcomes?, *Leadership & Organization Development Journal*, vol. 27, no. 5, pp. 330–51

Brown, L (2019) Only 5 per cent of businesses have considered their ethnicity pay gap, www.peoplemanagement.co.uk/news/articles/only-five-per-cent-businesses-considered-ethnicity-pay-gap (archived at https://perma.cc/2A7A-GAMJ)

Brown, W (1989) Managing remuneration in the UK, in Sisson, K (ed.) *Personnel Management in Britain*. Oxford: Blackwell

Brown, W, Bryson, A and Forth, J (2009) Competition and the Retreat from Collective Bargaining, in Brown, W; Bryson, A, Forth, J and Whitfield, K (eds.) *The Evolution of the Modern Workplace*. Cambridge: Cambridge University Press

Bruce, A, Buck, T and Main, BGM (2005) Top executive remuneration: A view from Europe, *Journal of Management Studies*, vol. 42, no. 7, pp. 1493–506

Bryson, A, Forth, J and Stokes, L (2014) *Does Worker Wellbeing Affect Workplace Performance?* London: Department for Business, Innovation and Skills

Bryson, A, Forth, J and Stokes, L (2017) How much performance pay is there in the public sector and what are its effects?, *Human Resource Management Journal*, vol. 27, no. 4 (November), pp. 581–97

Buck, T, Filatotchev, I and Wright, M (1998) Agents, stakeholders and corporate governance in Russian firms, *Journal of Management Studies*, vol. 35, no. 1, pp. 81–89

Burgess, S, Propper, C, Ratto, M and Tominey, E (2004) *Incentives in the Public Sector: Evidence from a government agency*. CMPO Working Paper Series 04/103. Bristol: University of Bristol, Centre for Market and Public Organisation

Burrell, G and Morgan, G (1979) *Sociological Paradigms and Organisational Analysis*. London: Heinemann

Cadsby, CB, Song, F and Tapon, F (2007) Sorting and incentive effects of pay-for-performance: an experimental investigation, *Academy of Management Journal*, vol. 50, no. 2, pp. 387–405

Cahan, SF, Chua, F and Nyamori, RO (2005) Board structure and executive compensation in the public sector: New Zealand evidence, *Financial Accountability & Management*, vol. 21, no. 4, pp. 437–65

Caldwell, R (2006) *Agency and Change*. London: Routledge

Calmfors, L and Driffill, K (1988) Centralisation of wage bargaining and macroeconomic performance, *Economic Policy*, vol. 6, pp. 13–61

Cappelli, P (1995) Rethinking employment, *British Journal of Industrial Relations*, vol. 33, no. 4, pp. 563–602

Cappelli, P and Tavis, A (2016) The Performance Management Revolution, *Harvard Business Review*, October 2016, hbr.org/2016/10/the-performance-management-revolution (archived at https://perma.cc/TNR6-YVEA)

Carey, DJ and Howes, PD (1993) Developing a global pay program, *Compensation & Benefits Review*, vol. 25 (July–August), p. 78

Casey, B, Lakey, J, Cooper, H and Elliott, J (1991) Payment systems: A look at current practice, *Employment Gazette*, August, pp. 53–8

Caulkin, S (2010) On management: cheques and balances, *FT Business Education*, 6 December, www.ft.com/cms/s/2/48d31e72-fe0a-11df-853b-00144feab49a.html#axzz19Utc9cFC (archived at https://perma.cc/4EWR-77GA)

CBI (2011) *A view from the top. The CBI 2011 pensions survey*. Confederation of British Industry

Chen, CC, Choi, J and Chi, S-C (2002) Making justice sense of local-expatriate compensation disparity: mitigation by local referents, ideological explanations, and interpersonal sensitivity in China-foreign joint ventures, *Academy of Management Journal*, vol. 45, no. 4, pp. 807–17

Child, J (1975) Managerial and organizational factors associated with company performance, part 2: a contingency analysis, *Journal of Management Studies*, vol. 12, no. 1, pp. 12–27

Child, J (1984) *Organization. A guide to problems and practice*, 2nd edn. London: Harper & Row

Christen, A (2018) How does gender pay gap reporting affect transgender employees?, *Personnel Today*, 13 July, www.personneltoday.com/hr/how-does-gender-pay-gap-reporting-affect-transgender-or-non-binary-employees/ (archived at https://perma.cc/B2NL-TDY7)

Christie, B (2023) Utilizing data to personalize Total Rewards, WorldatWork, 14 June, worldatwork.org/resources/publications/workspan-daily/utilizing-data-to-personalize-total-rewards (archived at https://perma.cc/DJ8F-HFH6)

Churchard, C (2009) City pay caps are not the answer to bonus culture, *People Management*, 10 September, p. 6

CIPD (2001) *Reward Determination in the UK*. Research Report. London: Chartered Institute of Personnel and Development

CIPD (2003) *The psychological contract, CIPD Factsheet*. London: CIPD

CIPD (2004) *Pension communications: Realising the Value*. London: Chartered Institute of Personnel and Development

CIPD (2006) *Pay and reward: an overview, CIPD Factsheet*. London: Chartered Institute of Personnel and Development

CIPD (2007a) *Flexible Benefits Factsheet*. London: Chartered Institute of Personnel and Development

CIPD (2007b) *What's Happening with Well-being at Work?* Change Agenda. London: Chartered Institute of Personnel and Development

CIPD (2009a) *Performance Management in Action: Current Trends and Practice*. London: Chartered Institute of Personnel and Development

CIPD (2009b) *Research Synopsis. The Business Case for Pensions*. London: Chartered Institute of Personnel and Development

CIPD (2014a) *Pay Progression: Understanding the barriers for the lowest paid*. Policy report. October 2014. London: CIPD/John Lewis Partnership/Tooley Street Research

CIPD (2014b) *Labour Market Outlook: Focus on pension auto-enrolment 2014*. November. London: Chartered Institute of Personnel and Development

CIPD (2014c) *Research Insight: Developing managers to manage sustainable employee engagement, health and well-being*. London: Chartered Institute of Personnel and Development

CIPD (2015) *Pay Progression: Understanding the Barriers for the Lowest Paid*. Policy report. London: Chartered Institute of Personnel and Development

CIPD (2016) *Could Do Better? Assessing what works in performance management. Research Report*, December 2016, www.cipd.co.uk/Images/could-do-better_2016-assessing-what-works-in-performance-management_tcm18-16874.pdf (archived at https://perma.cc/WV73-NCBJ)

CIPD (2018a) *Getting Started with People Analytics: a Practitioner's Guide*. London: Chartered Institute of Personnel and Development.

CIPD (2018b) Bonuses and incentives. Factsheet, www.cipd.co.uk/knowledge/fundamentals/people/pay/bonuses-factsheet (archived at https://perma.cc/8BWP-V3NP)

CIPD (2018c) Flexible and voluntary benefits, *CIPD Factsheet*. London: Chartered Institute of Personnel and Development

CIPD (2019a) Workplace Pensions, www.cipd.co.uk/knowledge/fundamentals/people/benefits/workplace-pensions-factsheet (archived at https://perma.cc/BU7C-MLTQ)

CIPD (2019b) Remco Reform: Governing successful organisations that benefit everyone. London: Chartered Institute of Personnel and Development

CIPD (2021a) Ethnicity Pay Gap Reporting: A guide for employers, www.cipd.co.uk/Images/cipd-ethnicity-pay-reporting-guide_tcm18-100551.pdf (archived at https://perma.cc/XU49-2RE8)

CIPD (2021b) Reward Management Survey: Reward fairness, www.cipd.org/globalassets/media/knowledge/knowledge-hub/reports/2021-pdfs/reward-management-fairness_tcm18-91389.pdf (archived at https://perma.cc/2ZMQ-RGWG)

CIPD (2022a) Pay structures and pay progression, www.cipd.co.uk/knowledge/fundamentals/people/pay/structures-factsheet (archived at https://perma.cc/KJC4-3LUF)

CIPD (2022b) Job evaluation and market pricing, www.cipd.org/uk/knowledge/factsheets/market-pricing-factsheet/#paydata (archived at https://perma.cc/H2TR-AGB7)

CIPD (2022c) *Incentives and recognition: an evidence review*, www.cipd.org/globalassets/media/knowledge/knowledge-hub/evidence-reviews/incentives-recognition-practice-summary_tcm18-105466.pdf (archived at https://perma.cc/QS2M-B6Q6)

CIPD (2023a) *Employee benefits: An introduction*, prod.cipd.co.uk/en/knowledge/factsheets/benefits-factsheet/ (archived at https://perma.cc/7TQK-6LLR

CIPD (2023b) *Employee Engagement and Motivation*, www.cipd.org/uk/knowledge/factsheets/engagement-factsheet/ (archived at https://perma.cc/3AK4-PQBK)

CIPD (2023c) *Strategic reward and total reward*, www.cipd.org/uk/knowledge/factsheets/strategic-total-factsheet/ (archived at https://perma.cc/JJN4-K3LU)

CIPD-High Pay Centre (2019) *Executive Pay in the FTSE 100: Is Everyone Getting a Fair Slice of the Cake?* London: Chartered Institute of Personnel and Development

Coates, D (2000) *Models of Capitalism: Growth and Stagnation in the Modern Era*. Cambridge: Polity Press

Cockburn, C (1991) *Brothers. Male dominance and technological change*. London: Pluto Press

Cole, N and Flint, D (2003) Perceptions of distributive and procedural justice in employee benefits: flexible versus traditional plans, *Journal of Managerial Psychology*, vol. 19, no. 1, pp. 19–40

Collins, A (2019) Employers confident contract deal will end NHS pay drift, *HSJ*, www.hsj.co.uk/workforce/employers-confident-contract-deal-will-end-nhs-pay-drift/7022001.article (archived at https://perma.cc/PG8F-NWVX)

Conroy, SA and Gupta N (2015) Team pay-for-performance: the devil is in the details, *Group and Organization Management*, vol. 41, no. 1, pp. 32–65

Conyon, MJ (1997) Corporate governance and executive compensation, *International Journal of Industrial Organization*, vol. 15, no. 4, pp. 493–509

Conyon, MJ (1998) Directors' pay and turnover: An application to a sample of large UK firms, *Oxford Bulletin of Economics and Statistics*, vol. 60, no. 4, pp. 485–507

Conyon, MJ, Mallin, C and Sadler, G (2002) The disclosure of directors' share option information in UK companies, *Applied Financial Economics*, vol. 12, no. 2, pp. 95–103

Conyon, MJ and Murphy, KJ (2000) The prince and the pauper? CEO pay in the US and UK, *Economic Journal*, vol. 110, pp. 640–71

Conyon, MJ and Peck, SI (1998a) Board control, remuneration committees and top management compensation, *Academy of Management Journal*, vol. 41, no. 2, pp. 146–57

Conyon, MJ and Peck, SI (1998b) Corporate tournaments and executive compensation: UK evidence, *Warwick Business School Working Paper* (EIASM workshop)

Conyon, MJ, Peck, SI and Sadler, GV (2001) Corporate tournaments and executive compensation: Evidence from the U.K., *Strategic Management Journal*, vol. 22, no. 8, pp. 805–15

Conyon, MJ and Sadler, GV (2001) Executive pay, tournaments and corporate performance in UK firms, *International Journal of Management Reviews*, vol. 3, no. 2, pp. 141–68

Corby, S and Lindop, E (2009) Drawing the threads together, in Corby, S, Palmer, S and Lindop, E (eds.) *Rethinking Reward*. Basingstoke: Palgrave Macmillan, pp. 247–56

Cornwall County Council (2017) Case study 15: Employee Recognition scheme, www.cornwall.gov.uk/media/31110581/case-study-15-recognition-scheme.pdf

Costa Dias, M, Joyce, R and Parodi, F (2018) *The gender pay gap in the UK: children and experience in work*, ifs.org.uk/publications/gender-pay-gap-uk-children-and-experience-work (archived at https://perma.cc/6UMN-D9H5)

Cotton, C (2018) Pay for the UK's top bosses nudges higher, *CIPD Voice*, no. 15, www.cipd.co.uk/news-views/cipd-voice/issue-15/exec-pay-nudges-higher (archived at https://perma.cc/8H6Z-Z7AW)

Cotton, C, Marriott, E and Perkins, SJ (2021) *Findings: From the 2020 CIPD Annual Reward Survey: Focus on Reward and Covid-19*. London: Chartered Institute of Personnel and Development

Cotton, C, Marriott, E and Perkins, SJ (2022) *Findings: From the 2021 CIPD Annual Reward Survey: Focus on Employee Benefits*. London: Chartered Institute of Personnel and Development, www.cipd.org/en/knowledge/reports/reward-surveys/ (archived at https://perma.cc/D9CJ-QRXJ)

Cox, A, Zagelmeyer, S and Marchington, M (2006) Embedding employee involvement and participation at work, *Human Resource Management Journal*, vol. 16, no. 3, pp. 250–67

Cox, AL (2004) Managing variable pay systems in smaller workplaces: the significance of employee perceptions of organisational justice', in *Employment Relations in SMEs*. London: Routledge

Coyle, D (2001) *Power to the People*, in *The Future of Reward*. Executive Briefing. London: Chartered Institute of Personnel and Development, pp. 33–7

Coyle-Shapiro, J, Morrow, PC and Richardson, R (2002) Using profit sharing to enhance employee attitudes: a longitudinal examination of the effects on trust and commitment, *Human Resource Management*, vol. 41, no. 4 (Winter), pp. 423–39

Criscuolo, C, Haramboure, A, Hijzen, A, Koelle, M and Schwellnus, C (2022) 4. The role of firm performance and wage-setting practices in wage inequality, *OECD Employment Outlook 2022: Building Back More Inclusive Labour Markets*. OECD iLibrary, www.oecd-ilibrary.org/employment/oecd-employment-outlook-2022_1bb305a6-en (archived at https://perma.cc/353F-3QJR)

Cuervo-Cazurra, A, Maloney, MM and Manrakhan, S (2007) Causes of the difficulties in internationalization, *Journal of International Business Studies*, vol. 38, no. 5, pp. 709–25

Cully, M, Woodland, S, O'Reilly, A and Dix, G (1999*) Britain at Work: As Depicted by the 1998 Workplace Employee Relations Survey*. London: Routledge

Daft, RL and Marcic, D (2020) Systems theory and the study of organizations, in Daft, RL, *Organization Theory and Design*. Boston, MA: South-Western Centage Learning, pp. 12–32

Dale-Olsen, H (2005) *Using linked employer-employee data to analyse fringe benefit policies, Norwegian experiences*. Institute for Social Research Norway. Paper presented to Policy Studies Institute seminar, July

Dalingwater, L (2018) *Can mandatory gender pay gap reporting deliver true opportunity for women?*, eprints.lse.ac.uk/88466/1/politicsandpolicy-mandator-gender.pdf (archived at https://perma.cc/ZD6S-DCXK)

Dalziel, S and Strange, J (2007) How to become strategic, *People Management*, vol. 13, no. 5, pp. 44–5

Dastin, J (2018) Amazon scraps secret AI recruiting tool that showed bias against women, Reuters, 11 October, www.reuters.com/article/us-amazon-com-jobs-automation-insight/amazon-scraps-secret-ai-recruiting-tool-that-showed-bias-against-women-idUSKCN1MK08G (archived at https://perma.cc/5U2W-7M3C)

Davies, S (2010) Will Hutton's pay proposals may increase the scope for cronyism, IEA, www.iea.org.uk/blog/will-hutton's-pay-proposals-may-increase-the-scope-for-cronyism (archived at https://perma.cc/BZL5-VYQ8)

Davis, ML (ed.) (2007) Total Rewards: *Everything* that employees value in the employment relationship, in *WorldatWork Handbook of Compensation, Benefits, and Total Rewards*. New York: John Wiley and Sons, pp. 1–13

Deci, EL (1972) The effects of contingent and non-contingent rewards and controls on intrinsic motivation, *Organisational Behaviour and Human Performance*, vol. 8, pp. 217–29

de la Torre-Ruiz, JM et al (2017) Benefit flexibility and benefit satisfaction: does employee's personality matter?, *Personnel Review*, vol. 46, no. 1, pp. 2–16

Delery, JE and Doty, DH (1996) Modes of theorizing in strategic human resource management: test of universalistic contingency, and configurational performance predictions, *Academy of Management Journal*, vol. 39, no. 4, pp. 802–35

Deloitte (2004) Report on the Impact of the Directors' Remuneration Regulations: A Report for the Department of Trade and Industry. London: Deloitte & Touch LLP

Devers, CE, Cannella, AA, Gregory, JR, Reilly, P and Yoder, ME (2007) Executive compensation: a multidisciplinary review of recent developments, *Journal of Management*, vol. 33, pp. 1016–72

Dhami, S, Wei, M and al-Nowaihi, A (2023) Classical and belief-based gift exchange models: Theory and evidence, *Games and Economic Behavior*, vol. 138, pp. 171–96

Dickinson, J (2006) Employees' preferences for the bases of pay differentials, *Employee Relations*, vol. 28, no. 2, pp. 164–83

Dive, B (2002) *The Healthy Organization: A Revolutionary Approach to People and Management*. London: Kogan Page

Dive, BJ (2019) The market – what market?, London's Big Bang consequences, myths and reality, in Perkins, SJ (ed.) *The Routledge Companion to Reward Management*. Routledge, London, pp. 288–97

Doeringer, P and Piore, M (1971) *Internal Labour Markets and Manpower Analysis*. Lexington, MA: D. C. Heath

Donaldson, L (2003) Organization theory as a positive science, in Tsoukas, H and Knudsen, C (eds.) *The Oxford Handbook of Organization Theory: Meta-Theoretical Perspectives*. Oxford: Oxford University Press, pp. 39–62

Dowling, PJ, Festing, M and Engle, AD (2013) *International Human Resource Management: Managing people in a multinational context*, 5th edn. London: Thomson

Drape, T, Quintanilla, J and Green, SG (2010) Individual pay for performance in Spain: cognitive sociology and the subsidiary insider perspective, *Thunderbird International Business Review*, vol. 52, no. 3, pp. 217–30

Druker, J (2000) Wages and low pay, in White, G and Druker, J (eds.) *Reward Management: A critical text*. London: Routledge

Druker, J (2009) Wages and low pay, in White, G and Druker, J (eds.) *Reward Management: A critical text*. 2nd edn. Abingdon: Routledge

DTI (2001) *Directors' Remuneration: A Consultative Document*, URN 01/1400, December. London: Department for Business Enterprise and Regulatory Reform

DWP (2016) *The Charge Cap: Guidance for trustees and managers of occupational schemes*. London: HMG Department for Work and Pensions

DWP (2018) Benefits and pension rates 2019-20, Department for Work and Pensions, www.gov.uk/government/publications/benefit-and-pension-rates-2019-to-2020 (archived at https://perma.cc/MRH7-DAWN)

Dyer, L and Ericksen, J (2007) *Workforce Alignment and Fluidity May Yield a Competitive Advantage*. ILR Impact Brief 22. Cornell University

Economist, The (2010) Mutiny over the bounty: Investment banks have cut pay a bit but shareholders are still getting a raw deal, 4 November, www.economist.com/finance-and-economics/2010/11/04/mutiny-over-the-bounty (archived at https://perma.cc/6C3M-4D44)

Edwards, PK (1986) *Conflict at Work*. Oxford: Blackwell

Edwards, PK (1990) Understanding conflict in the labour process: the logic and autonomy of struggle, in Knights, D and Willmott, H (eds.) *Labour Process Theory*. Basingstoke: Macmillan, 125–52

Edwards, PK (2003) The employment relationship, in Edwards, P (ed.) *Industrial Relations: Theory and practice*, 2nd edn. Oxford: Blackwell, 1–36

Edwards, T, Almond, P, Clark, I, Colling, T and Ferner, A (2005) Reverse diffusion in US multinationals: barriers from the American business system, *Journal of Management Studies*, vol. 42, no. 6, pp. 1261–86

EHRC (2014) *Gender-Neutral Job Evaluation Schemes: An introductory guide*. London: Equality and Human Rights Commission

EHRC (2016) *Equal Pay: Statutory Code of Practice*, www.equalityhumanrights.com/en/publication-download/equal-pay-statutory-code-practice (archived at https://perma.cc/DMY8-RCZ4)

Eichenwald, K (2012) Microsoft's Lost Decade, *Vanity Fair*, 8 July

Eikhof, DR, Warhurst, C and Haunschild, A (2007) 'What work? What life? What balance? Critical reflections on the work–life balance debate, *Employee Relations*, vol. 29, no. 4, pp. 325–33

Employee Benefits/Towers Watson (2014) *Flexible Benefits Research 2014*, www.employeebenefits.co.uk/benefits/flexible-benefits/employee-benefits-/-towers-watson-flexible-benefits-research-2014/104459.article (archived at https://perma.cc/53T5-3ENK)

Employee Ownership Association (2022) Purcell – Our EO Story: 'Community of many voices' strengthened and empowered, employeeownership.co.uk/success-stories/purcell-our-eo-story-community-of-many-voices-strengthened-and-empowered/ (archived at https://perma.cc/6F43-5LRE)

Employee Ownership Association (2023) What is Employee Ownership?, employeeownership.co.uk/what-is-employee-ownership/ (archived at https://perma.cc/BD7Z-DUAF)

e-Reward (2014) *Performance Management: Part 2. E-Reward Survey*. Stockport: E-Reward

e-Reward (2019) Executive Pay: Boardroom Remuneration Database; www.e-reward.co.uk/executive-pay?utm (archived at https://perma.cc/3CX8-F693)

e-Reward (2023) E-Reward Bites 621, email.firstinternet.co.uk/t/r-e-ttllijty-l-l/ (archived at https://perma.cc/A2XR-N5ZX)

Evan, W and MacPherson, D (1996) Employer size and labour turnover: the role of pensions, *Industrial Relations and Labor Review*, vol. 49, no. 4, pp. 707–29

Evans, S and McIver, C (2009) Credit crunched: executive pay across Europe, *Cross-border Quarterly*, January–March, pp. 25–32

Fang, M and Gerhart, B (2012) Does pay for performance diminish intrinsic interest? *International Journal of Human Resource Management*, vol. 23, no. 6, pp. 1176–96

Faragher, J (2019) Court of Appeal: Asda workers can proceed with equal pay claims, www.personneltoday.com/hr/court-of-appeal-asda-workers-can-proceed-with-equal-pay-claims/

Farashashi, M, Hasi, T and Molz, R (2005) Institutionalized norms of conducting research and social realities: a research synthesis of empirical works from 1989 to 2002, *International Journal of Management Reviews*, vol. 7 no. 1, pp. 1–24

Fawcett Society (2015) The gender pay gap, www.fawcettsociety.org.uk/pages/news/category/gender-pay-gap (archived at https://perma.cc/68BV-TCRF)

Federico, RF (2007) The work–life impact: A best list retrospective, *Workspan*, vol. 50, no. 1, pp. 109–12

Fenwick, M (2004) International compensation and performance management, in Harzing, A-W. and Van Ruysseveldt, J (eds.) *International Human Resource Management*, 2nd edn. London: Sage, pp. 307–32

Festing, M and Perkins, SJ (2008) Rewards for internationally mobile employees, in Brewster, C, Sparrow, P and Dickmann, M (eds.) *International HRM: Contemporary Issues in Europe*, 2nd edn. London: Routledge

Festing, M, Eidems, J and Royer, S (2007) Strategic issues and local constraints in transnational compensation strategies. An analysis of cultural, institutional and political influences, *European Management Journal*, vol. 25, no. 2, pp. 118–31

Festing, M and Tekieli, M (2022) Global reward management, in Perkins, SJ (ed.) *The Routledge Companion to Reward Management*. London: Routledge, pp. 209–21

Figart, DM (2001) Wage-setting under Fordism: the rise of job evaluation and ideology of equal pay, *Review of Political Economy*, vol. 13, no. 4, pp. 405–25

Finkelstein, S, Hambrick, DC and Cannella, AA (2009) *Strategic Leadership: Theory and research on executives, top management and boards*. Oxford: Oxford University Press

Fish, A (2022) Revisiting Maslow: enhancing staff psychological health for staff engagement through eupsychic reward management, in Perkins, SJ (ed.) *The Routledge Companion to Reward Management*. London: Routledge, pp. 72–81

Flammer, C, Hong, B and Minor, D (2019) Corporate governance and the rise of integrating corporate social responsibility criteria in executive compensation: Effectiveness and implications for firm outcomes, *Strategic Management Journal*, vol. 40, no. 7, pp. 1097–122

Flannery, TP, Hofrichter, DA and Platten, PE (1996) *People, Performance and Pay: Dynamic compensation for changing organizations*. New York: Free Press

Folger, R and Cropanzano, R (1998) *Organisational Justice and Human Resource Management*. Thousand Oaks, CA: Sage

Fombrun, C, Tichy, N and Devanna, MA (1984) *Strategic Human Resource Management*. New York: Wiley and Sons

Forster, N (2000) The myth of the 'international' manager, *International Journal of Human Resource Management*, vol. 1, no. 1, pp. 126–42

Forth, J, Bryson, A and Stokes, L (2014) *Are Firms Paying More for Performance?* Centre for Economic Performance Discussion Paper 1272, LSE. ISSN 2042-2695

Forth, J and Millward, N (2000) *The Determinants of Pay Levels and Fringe Benefit Provision in Britain*. Discussion Paper 171. London, National Institute of Economic and Social Research

Fox, A (1974) *Beyond Contract: Work, Power and Trust Relations*. London: Faber and Faber

Frank, RH and Cook, PJ (1995) *The Winner-Take-All Society*. New York: Free Press

Franklin, D (2006) *The World in 2006*. London: Economist

FRC (2014) *The UK Corporate Governance Code*. London: Financial Reporting Council

FRC (2018) *The UK Corporate Governance Code*. London: Financial Reporting Council

FRC (2022) *A Review of Corporate Governance Reporting*. London: Financial Reporting Council

Friedman, AL (1977) *Industry and Labour: Class Struggle at Work and Monopoly Capitalism*. London: Macmillan

Friedman, AL (1984) Management strategies, market conditions and the labour process, in Stephen, FH (ed.) *Firms, Organization and Labour*. London: Macmillan, pp. 176–200

FT (2015) JPMorgan and Morgan Stanley chiefs top banker pay league table, *Financial Times*, 3 July

FT (2019a) Bill Winters has undermined good corporate governance, *Financial Times*, 24 July 24, www.ft.com/content/f85fbb88-3109-3771-8074-dfdb5044e890 (archived at https://perma.cc/9L6R-QRPD)

FT (2019b) Big asset managers take boards to task over pay, *Financial Times*, 28 July, www.ft.com/content/dc219490-9f9b-3220-81a7-b28ce9a34662 (archived at https://perma.cc/77NT-TVXQ)

Furåker, B (2005) *Sociological Perspectives on Labor Markets*. London: Palgrave Macmillan

Gallie, D, Zhou, Y, Felstead, A and Green, F (2012) Team-work, skill development and employee welfare, *British Journal of Industrial Relations*, vol. 50, no. 1, pp. 23–46

Gennard, J and Judge, G (2002) *Employee Relations*, 3rd edn. London: Chartered Institute of Personnel and Development

Gennard, J, Judge, G, Bennett, T and Saundry, R (2016) *Managing Employment Relations*, 6th edn. London: Chartered Institute of Personnel and Development

Geppert, M (2005) The local–global dilemma in MNCs revisited: institutionalist contributions, Summary of Presentation at the Research Seminar of the School of Management and Organizational Psychology at Birkbeck, University of London, 16 June

Gerhart, B and Fang, M (2014) Pay for (individual) performance: issues, claims, evidence and the role of sorting effects, *Human Resource Management Review*, vol. 24, no. 1, pp. 41–52

Gerhart, B and Milkovich, G (1990) Organisational differences in managerial compensation and financial performance, *Academy of Management Journal*, vol. 33, pp. 663–90

Gerhart, B and Rynes, SL (2003) *Compensation: Theory, Evidence and Strategic Implications*. London: Sage

Gerhart, B, Rynes, SL and Fulmer, IS (2009) 'Pay and performance: individuals, groups and executives', *The Academy of Management Annals*, vol. 3, no. 1, pp. 251–15

Gharajedaghi, J (1999) *Systems Thinking: Managing Chaos and Complexity*. London: Butterworth Heinemann

Ghoshal, S and Bartlett, CA (1998) *Managing Across Borders: the transnational solution*. London: Random House

Gilbert, D and Abosch, KS (1996) *Improving Organisational Effectiveness Through Broadbanding*. Scottsdale, AZ: American Compensation Association

Gilbert, K (2005) The role of job evaluation in determining equal value in tribunals. Tool, weapon or cloaking device?, *Employee Relations*, vol. 27, no.1, pp. 7–19

Gilbert, K (2012) Promises and practices: job evaluation and equal pay forty years on, *Industrial Relations Journal*, vol. 43, no. 2 (March), pp. 137–51

Giles, C (2022) UK strikes: are pay review bodies fit for purpose?, *Financial Times*, 20 December, www.ft.com/content/0953587e-6a20-40d4-8459-d4d7a2aa4d27 (archived at https://perma.cc/2D83-UUF6)

Gilmore, G and O'Connor, R (2007) Paul Gray: family, football and sheep give comfort to 'a really affable guy', *Times*, 21 November

Glassdoor (2018) *Energy Business #1 in Glassdoor's 20 Highest Rated Companies for Work-Life Balance 2018*, www.glassdoor.co.uk/blog/energy-company-1-in-glassdoors-20-highest-rated-companies-for-work-life-balance-2018/ (archived at https://perma.cc/PM6R-2PCE)

GMAC (2006) *GMAC global relocation trends: 2005 survey report*. Global Relocation Services in conjunction with US National Foreign Trade Council Inc and SHRM Global Forum

Goleman, D (2002), Leaders with impact, *Strategic HR Review*, vol. 1, no. 6, p. 3

Gomez-Mejia, L and Balkin, D (1992) *Compensation, Organizational Strategy and Firm Performance*. San Francisco: Southwestern

Gomez-Mejia, LR and Wiseman, RM (1997) Reframing executive compensation: an assessment and outlook, *Journal of Management*, vol. 23, no. 3, pp. 291–374

Goodherham, PN and Nordhaug, O (2003) *International Management: Cross-boundary challenges*. Oxford, Blackwell

Gospel, H (1992) *Markets, Firms and the Management of Labour in Modern Britain.* Cambridge: Cambridge University Press

Gov.uk (2019a) Tax and Employee Share schemes: Share Incentive Plans (SIPs), www.gov.uk/tax-employee-share-schemes/share-incentive-plans-sips (archived at https://perma.cc/ACC7-Y9D4)

Gov.uk (2019b) Tax and Employee Share schemes: Enterprise Management Incentives (EMIs), www.gov.uk/tax-employee-share-schemes/enterprise-management-incentives-emis (archived at https://perma.cc/8TCZ-YVR7)

Gov.uk (2019c) Tax and Employee Share schemes: Company Share Option , www.gov.uk/tax-employee-share-schemes/company-share-option-plan (archived at https://perma.cc/T5J5-MEWF)

Gov.uk (2023) Ethnicity pay reporting: guidance for employers, www.gov.uk/government/publications/ethnicity-pay-reporting-guidance-for-employers (archived at https://perma.cc/9SSY-XTM8)

Government Actuary's Department (2006) *Occupational Pension Schemes: the 13th survey by the Government Actuary*. London: GAD

Government Equalities Office (2011) *Think, Act, Report Framework*. London: Home Office

Gowler, D and Lupton, T (1969) *Selecting a Wage Payment System*. Littlehampton: Littlehampton Book Services

Green, F, Hadjimatheou, G and Smail, R (1985) Fringe benefits and distribution in Britain, *British Journal of Industrial Relations*, vol. 23, no. 2, pp. 261–80

Greenbury, Sir R (1995) *Report of the Study Group on Directors' Remuneration*. London: Gee Publishing

Gregersen, HB, Morrison, AJ and Black, JS (1998) Developing leaders for the global frontier, *MIT Sloan Management Review*, Fall Issue, sloanreview.mit.edu/article/developing-leaders-for-the-global-frontier/ (archived at https://perma.cc/NGL2-CG4S)

Guest, D E (1987) Human resource management and industrial relations, *Journal of Management Studies*, vol. 24, no. 5, pp. 503–21

Guest, DE (1997) Human resource management and performance: a review and research agenda, *International Journal of Human Resource Management*, vol. 8, no. 3, pp. 263–67

Guest, DE (2001) Human resource management: when research confronts theory, *International Journal of Human Resource Management*, vol. 12, no. 1, pp. 1092–106.

Guest, DE (2004) The psychology of the employment relationship: An analysis based on the psychological contract, *Applied Psychology: An International Review*, vol. 53, no. 4, pp. 541–55

Guest, DE (2007) Don't shoot the messenger: a wake-up call for academics, *Academy of Management Journal*, vol. 50, no. 5, pp. 1020–26

Guest, DE and Conway, N (2004) CIPD Research Report: *Employee Well-Being and the Psychological Contract.* London: Chartered Institute of Personnel and Development

Gururajan, V and Fink, D (2010) Attitudes towards knowledge transfer in an environment to perform, *Journal of Knowledge Management*, vol. 14, no. 6, pp. 828–40

Haines, SG (1998) *The Manager's Pocket Guide to Systems Thinking and Learning.* Amherst, MA: HRD Press

Hales, C and Gough, O (2002) Employee evaluations of company occupational pensions. HR implications, *Personnel Review*, vol. 32, no. 3, pp. 319–40

Hall, P and Soskice, D (2001) *Varieties of Capitalism: The Institutional Foundations of Comparative Advantage*. Oxford: Oxford University Press

Hallock, KF (2012) *Pay: Why people earn what they earn and what you can do now to make more.* Cambridge: Cambridge University Press

Hambly, K, Kumar, RV, Harcourt, M, Lam, H and Wood, G (2017) Profit-sharing as an incentive, *International Journal of Human Resource Management*, DOI:10.1080/09585192.2017.1334149 (archived at https://perma.cc/DDU5-FF2Y)

Hambrick, DC and Mason, P (1984) Upper echelons: the organization as a reflection of its top managers, *Academy of Management Review*, vol. 9, pp. 193–206

Hampel, Sir R (1998) *Committee on Corporate Governance: Final Report*. London: Gee Publishing

Hansen, F, Smith, M and Hansen, RB (2002) Rewards and recognition in employee motivation, *Compensation & Benefits Review*, vol. 34, no. 5, pp. 64–72

Hargreaves, D (2019) *Are Chief Executives Overpaid?* London: Policy Press

Harkness, S, Borkowska, M and Pelikh, A (2019) *Employment pathways and occupational change after childbirth*. London: Government Equalities Office, assets.publishing.service.gov.uk/government/uploads/system/uploads/attachment_data/file/840062/Bristol_Final_Report_1610.pdf (archived at https://perma.cc/V9VB-SRR7)

Harris, H and Dickmann, M (2005) *Guide to International Management Development*. London: Chartered Institute of Personnel and Development

Harris, H, Brewster, C and Sparrow, P (2003) *International Human Resource Management*. London: Chartered Institute of Personnel and Development

Harvey, M (1993) Designing a global compensation system: the logic and a model, *Columbia Journal of World Business*, vol. 28, no. 4, pp. 57–72

Harvey, M and Moeller, M (2009) Expatriate managers: a historical review, *International Journal of Management Reviews*, vol. 11 no. 3, pp. 275–96

Harvey, M, Spier, C and Novicevic, M (2002) The evolution of strategic human resource systems and their application in a foreign subsidiary context, *Asia Pacific Journal of Human Resources*, vol. 40, no. 3, pp. 284–305

Hastings, S (2009) Grading systems and estimating value, in White, G and Druker, J (eds.) *Reward Management: A critical text*, 2nd edn. London: Routledge

Hatch, M-J (2006) *Organization Theory: Modern, symbolic, and postmodern perspectives*. Oxford: Oxford University Press

Hays (2023) Recruiting Trends; Benefits and Hybrid Working, www.hays.co.uk/salary-guide (archived at https://perma.cc/823Z-3Q8B)

Hayter, S (2015) Unions and collective bargaining, in Berg, J (ed.) *Labour Markets, Institutions and Inequality: Building just societies in the 21st century*. Cheltenham: Edward Elgar Publishing, pp. 95–122

Heery, E (1996) Risk, representation and the new pay, *Personnel Review*, vol. 25, no. 6, pp. 54–65

Heery, E (1998) A return to contract? Performance-related pay in a public service, *Work, Employment and Society*, vol. 21, no. 1, pp. 73–95

Heery, E (2000a) Trade unions and he management of reward, in White, G and Druker, J (eds.) *Reward Management: A Critical Text*. London: Routledge, pp. 54–83

Heery, E (2000b) The new pay: risk and representation at work, in Winstanley, D and Woodall, J (eds.) *Ethical Issues in Contemporary Human Resource Management*. Basingstoke: Macmillan Business

Heery, E and Noon, M (2017) *A Dictionary of Human Resource Management,* 3rd edn. Oxford: Oxford University Press

Hendry, C (2003) Applying employment systems theory to the analysis of national models of HRM, *International Journal of Human Resource Management*, vol. 14, no. 8, pp. 1430–42

Henehan, K and Rose, H (2018) *Opportunities Knocked? Exploring pay penalties among the UK's ethnic minorities*, www.resolutionfoundation.org/app/uploads/2018/07/Opportunities-Knocked.pdf (archived at https://perma.cc/DD9L-L9CZ)

Heneman, RL (1992) *Merit Pay. Linking pay increases to performance ratings*. Reading, MA: Addison Wesley

Heneman, RL and von Hippel, C (1995) Balancing group and individual rewards: rewarding individual contributions to the team, *Compensation and Benefits Review*, vol. 27, no. 4, pp. 63–68

Herriot and Pemberton (1995) *New Deals: The Revolution in Managerial Careers*. Chichester: Wiley

Hewitt, P (2004) Trade and industry statement on directors' remuneration, contracts, performance and severance, *Hansard*. 25 February, cols 51–2 WS

High Pay Centre (2023) High pay hour, 5 January, highpaycentre.org/high-pay-hour-how-quickly-ceos-earn-the-uk-median-wage/ (archived at https://perma.cc/4D6A-GZHG)

High Pay Commission (2011*) Cheques with Balances: Why tackling high pay is in the national interest*. London: High Pay Centre

Hijazi, ST and Bhatti, KK (2007) Determinants of executive compensation and its impact on organizational performance, *Compensation and Benefits Review*, March–April, pp. 58–68

Hill, CWL and Phan, P (1991) CEO tenure as a determinant of CEO pay, *Academy of Management Journal*, vol. 34, pp. 707–17

Hills, FS (1989) Internal pay relationships, in Gomez-Mejia, LR (ed.) *Compensation and Benefits*. ASPA-BNA Series 3. Washington, DC: Bureau of National Affairs

Hirsch, D (2016) *London Weighting and London costs – a fresh approach?*, Trust for London, www.trustforlondon.org.uk/publications/london-weighting-and-london-costs-fresh-approach/ (archived at https://perma.cc/C6Y3-EBAW)

HMRC (2015) Pensions Tax Manual, www.hmrc.gov.uk/manuals/ptmanual/ptm022000.htm (archived at https://perma.cc/YST2-QUQW)

HMRC (2022) Employee Share Schemes statistics: commentary, www.gov.uk/government/statistics/employee-share-scheme-statistics/employee-share-schemes-statistics-commentary#commentary (archived at https://perma.cc/Q8RD-3BTW)

Hoggett, J (2023) We need a constructive discussion on the UK's approach to executive compensation, www.lseg.com/en/insights/julia-hoggett-ceo-uk-approach-executive-compensation (archived at https://perma.cc/U5VG-VJ27)

Holmwood, J (2006) Social systems theory, in Turner, BS (ed.) *The Cambridge Dictionary of Sociology*. Cambridge: Cambridge University Press, pp. 587–88

House of Commons Library (2023) Guaranteed Minimum Pension (GMP) equalisation, commonslibrary.parliament.uk/research-briefings/cbp-8427/ (archived at https://perma.cc/U7KJ-72TL)

House of Commons Trade and Industry Committee (2003) *Rewards for Failure: Sixteenth Report of Session 2002–2003*. London: The Stationery Office

Hsu, AW and Liao, C (2013) Earnings quality and pay-performance sensitivity: Evidence from employee profit-sharing bonus in Taiwan, *Asia Pacific Management Review*, vol. 18, pp. 277–82

Hull, CL (1952) *A Behavior System: An Introduction to Behavior Theory Concerning the Individual Organism*. New Haven, CT: Yale University Press

Hume, DA (1995) *Reward Management: Employee performance, motivation and pay*. Oxford: Blackwell

Huselid, MA (1995) The impact of human resource management practices on turnover, productivity, and corporate financial performance, *Academy of Management Journal*, vol. 38, no. 3, pp. 635–72

Hutton, J (2010) *Interim Report*. Independent Public Service Pensions Commission

Hutton, J (2011) *Final Report*. Independent Public Service Pensions Commission

Hutton, W (2010a) *Hutton Review of Fair Pay in the Public Sector. Interim Report*. London: Stationery Office

Hutton, W (2010b) If we don't rein in Big Finance the economy will never recover, *The Observer*, 19 December

Hyman, J (2000) Financial participation schemes, in White, G and Druker, J (eds.) *Reward Management: A critical text*. London: Routledge, pp. 177–93
Hyman, J (2009) Financial participation schemes, in White, G and Druker, J (eds.) *Reward Management: A critical text*, 2nd edn. London: Routledge
i4cp (2007) Organizations struggle with employee recognition programs. Institute for Corporate Productivity Knowledge Center, www.i4cp.com (archived at https://perma.cc/258C-J4VZ)
Idil Aybars, A (2007) Work–life balance in the EU and leave arrangements across welfare regimes, *Industrial Relations Journal*, vol. 38, no. 6, pp. 569–90
IDS (2004) *Understanding Reward. The pros and cons of market-related pay*. IDS Pay Report 907 June: 8–9. London: Incomes Data Services
IDS (2006a) *Pay in the Public Services*. London: Incomes Data Services
IDS (2006b) *Job Families*. IDS Study 814. London: Incomes Data Services
IDS (2006c) *An Assessment of the Causes of Pay Drift in UK Organisations*. Research Report for the Office of Manpower Economics. December. London: Incomes Data Services
IDS (2006d) *Directors' Pay Report 2006*. London: Incomes Data Services
IDS (2007a) *Job Evaluation + guide to suppliers*. IDS HR Studies Plus 837. London: Incomes Data Services
IDS (2007b) *Performance Management*. IDS HR Studies 839. February. London: Incomes Data Services
IDS (2007c) *Pay and Conditions in Engineering 2006/7*. London: Incomes Data Services
IDS (2007d) *Bonus Schemes*. IDS HR Studies 843. April. London: Incomes Data Services
IDS (2010a) *Pay progression*. IDS HR Study 929. November. London: Incomes Data Services
IDS (2010b) *London Allowances*. IDS HR Study 930. November. London: Incomes Data Services
IDS (2010c) *Bonus Schemes*. IDS HR Study 911. February. London: Income Data Services
IDS (2010d) *Employee Benefits*. IDS HR study 915. April. London: Incomes Data Services
IDS (2012) *Job Families*. HR Studies 972. August. London: Incomes Data Services
IDS (2013a) Building blocks of reward: job evaluation. *IDS Pay Report* 1114, July. London: Incomes Data Services
IDS (2013b) Building blocks of reward: salary surveys and pay clubs. *IDS Pay Report 1113*. June. London: Incomes Data Services
Institute of Risk Management (2002) *The Risk Management Standard*. London: IRM
IPD (1997) *The IPD Guide on Broadbanding*. London: IPD
IPD (2000) *Study of Broad-banded and Job Family Structures*. IPD Survey Report. January. London: IPD
Ipsos Mori (2008) *Enterprise Management Incentives (EMI) Evaluation Survey : Use of EMI and its perceived impact*. HMRC Report 41
IRS (2000a) *Pay Prospects for 2001 – a survey of the private sector*. Pay and Benefits Bulletin 510. December. London: Industrial Relations Services
IRS (2000b) *The Truth about Merit Pay. Pay and Benefits Bulletin 501*. August. London: Industrial Relations Services
IRS (2011) *Bonus schemes 2011: Providing an incentive*, www.xperthr.co.uk/survey-analysis/bonus-schemes-2011-providing-an-incentive/111390/?t=215 (archived at https://perma.cc/76DD-KE7K)
Isles, P (2007) Employee resourcing and talent management, in Storey, J (ed.) *Human Resource Management: A critical text*, 3rd edn. Andover: Thompson Learning
Jacoby, SM (2006) Corporate governance and employees in the United States, in Gospel, H and Pendleton, A (eds.) *Corporate Governance and Labour Management*. Oxford: Oxford University Press, pp. 33–58

Jacques, E (1964) *Time Span Handbook*. London: Heinemann

Jeffery, R (2014) 'We're building something bigger than the sum of its parts', *People Management*, www.cipd.co.uk/pm/peoplemanagement/b/weblog/archive/2014/10/24/we-re-building-something-bigger-than-the-sum-of-its-parts.aspx

Jeffery, R (2019) How much should you pay them?, *People Management*, July–August, pp. 34–38

Jenkins, P (2010) Banks to overhaul global pay structures, *Financial Times*, 20 December

Jensen, M and Murphy, K (1990) CEO incentives – 'It's not how much you pay, but how', *Harvard Business Review*, May–June

Jensen, M, Murphy, KJ and Wruck, EG (2004) Remuneration: where we've been, how we got to here, what are the problems, and how to fix them', *ECGI Working Paper No. 44/2004*. Social Science Research Network Electronic Paper Collection, ssrn.com/abstract=561305 (archived at https://perma.cc/6XLL-6V8L)

Jensen, MC and Meckling, WH (1976) Theory of the firm: Managerial behavior, agency costs and ownership structure, *Journal of Financial Economics*, vol. 3, no. 4, pp. 305–60

Johnson, R (2007) Why passion and humanity are the keys to unlocking innovation, *People Management*, vol. 13, no. 22, November, p. 48

Johnstone, S and Ackers, P (2015) *Finding a Voice at Work? New perspectives on employee relations*. Oxford: Oxford University Press

Jones, SE, Marriott, E, Brown, M, Perkins, SJ, Shields, J (2012) *Reward Management Survey Report 2012 Supplement: Aligning Strategy and Pay*. London: Chartered Institute of Personnel and Development

Jones, SE, Marriott, E, Brown, M, Perkins, SJ and Shields, J (2013b) *Reward Management Survey Report 2013 Supplement: Aligning Strategy and Benefits*. London: Chartered Institute of Personnel and Development

Jones, SE, Marriott, E, Perkins, SJ, Shortland, S and Shields, J (2015) *Reward Management Survey Report 2014–15*. London: Chartered Institute of Personnel and Development

Jones, SE and White, G (2021) Reward strategy and managing performance, in Rees, G and Smith, P (eds.) *Strategic Human Resource Management: An international perspective*, 3rd edn. London: Sage Publications Ltd

Kalleberg, AL (2003) Flexible firms and labor market segmentation: effects of workplace restructuring on jobs and workers, *Work and Occupations*, vol. 30, no. 2, pp. 154–75

Kaplan. SN (2007) Are CEOs overpaid?, *WorldatWork Journal*, vol. 16, no. 3, pp. 22–37

Katz, HC and Darbishire, O (2000) *Converging Divergences: Worldwide Changes in Employment Systems*. London: Cornell University Press

Keenoy, T (1997) HRMism and the languages of re-presentation, *Journal of Management Studies*, vol. 34, no. 5, pp. 825–41

Keenoy, T (1999) HRM as hologram: a polemic, *Journal of Management Studies*, vol. 36, no. 1, pp. 1–23

Kerr, C, Dunlop, JT, Harbinson, FH and Myers, CA (1964,) *Industrialism and Industrial Man*, 2nd edn. Oxford: Oxford University Press

Kerr, C and Tate, C (2008) *Evaluation of Tax-advantaged All-employee Share Schemes*. HMRC Research Report, September

Kersley, B, Alpin, C, Forth, J, Bryson, A, Bewley, H, Dix, G and Oxenbridge, S (2006) *Inside the Workplace: findings from the 2004 Workplace Employment Relations Survey*. London: Routledge

Kessler, I (2000) Remuneration systems, in Bach, S and Sisson, K (eds.) *Personnel Management in Britain: a comprehensive guide to theory and practice*, 3rd edn. Oxford: Blackwell

Kessler, I (2001) Reward systems choices, in Storey, J (ed.) *Human Resource Management: A Critical Text*, 2nd edn. London: Thomson, pp. 206–31

Kessler, I (2005) Remuneration systems, in Bach, S (ed.) *Managing Human Resources: Personnel Management in Transition*. Oxford: Blackwell Publishing, pp. 317–345

Kessler, I (2007) Reward choices: strategy and equity, in Storey, J (ed.) *HRM: A Critical Text*, 3rd edn. London: Thomson Learning, pp. 159–76

Kessler, I (2013) Remuneration systems, in Bach, S and Edwards, MR (eds.) *Managing Human Resources*, 5th edn. Chichester: John Wiley and Sons Ltd

Kessler, I and Purcell, J (1992) Performance-related pay: objectives and applications, *Human Resource Management Journal*, vol. 2, no. 3, pp. 34–59

Kinnie, N, Hutchinson, S and Purcell, J (1998) *Getting Fit, Staying Fit: developing lean and responsive organisations*. London: Chartered Institute of Personnel and Development

Kinnie, N, Hutchinson, S, Purcell, J, Rayton, B and Swart, J (2005) Satisfaction with HR practices and commitment to the organisation: Why one size does not fit all, *Human Resource Management Journal*, vol. 15, no. 4, pp. 9–29

Kleinginna, PR Jr. and Kleinginna, AM (1981) A categorized list of motivation definitions, with a suggestion for a consensual definition, *Motivation and Emotion*, vol. 5, no. 3, pp. 263–91

Kline, WA and Brown, RS (2019) Merger and acquisition targets: the role of moral hazard and acquiring firm executive compensation, *Journal of Managerial Issues*, vol. 31, no. 2, pp. 119–36

Knell, J (2000) *Most Wanted: The quiet birth of the free worker*. London: The Industrial Society

Knights, D and McCabe, D (2000) 'Ain't misbehavin': opportunities for resistance under new forms of 'quality' management, *Sociology*, vol. 34, no. 3, pp. 241–36

Ko, J and Hur, S (2014) The impacts of employee benefits, procedural justice, and managerial trustworthiness on work attitudes: integrated understanding based on social exchange theory, *Public Administration Review*, vol. 74, no. 2, pp. 176–87

Kohn, A (1993a) *Punished by Rewards: The Trouble with Gold Stars, Incentive Plans, A's, Praise and other Bribes*. Boston, MA: Houghton Mifflin

Kohn, A (1993b) Why incentive plans cannot work, *Harvard Business Review*, September–October, pp. 54–63

Kornelakis, A and Gospel, H (2022) CEO pay and corporate financialization: the UK in comparative perspective, in Perkins, SJ (ed.) *The Routledge Companion to Reward Management*. London: Routledge, pp. 298–308

Koskinen Sandberg, P (2017) Intertwining gender inequalities and gender-neutral legitimacy in job evaluation and performance-related pay, *Gender, Work and Organization*, vol. 24, no. 2, pp. 156–70

Kozenkow, J (2013) 'New institutional economics: foundations and latest trends', *Society and Economy*, vol. 35, no. 1 (March), pp. 87–101

KPMG (2013) *Guide to Directors' Remuneration Reporting – Quoted companies*. London: KPMG

Kramar, R (2014) Beyond strategic human resource management: is sustainable human resource management the next approach?, *Journal of International Human Resource Management*, vol. 25, no. 8, pp. 1069–89

Kressler, HW (2003) *Motivate and Reward: Performance appraisal and incentive systems for business success*. Basingstoke: Palgrave Macmillan

Kulik, C (2001) Book review on *Compensation in Organizations by Rynes and Gerhart. Academy of Management Review*, vol. 26, no. 1, p. 28

Lambert, RA, Larcker, DF and Weigelt, K (1993) The structure of organizational incentives, *Administrative Science Quarterly*, vol. 38, pp. 438–61

Lambert, S (2000) Added benefits: the link between work-life benefits and organizational citizenship behavior, *Academy of Management Journal*, vol. 43, no. 5, pp. 801–15

Lawler, EE (1984) *The New Pay*. CEO publication G84-7(55), Los Angeles, CA: Center for Effective Organisations, University of Southern California

Lawler, EE (1995) The New Pay: a strategic approach, *Compensation & Benefits Review*, vol. 27 July–August, pp. 14–22

Lawler, EE (1996) *From the Ground Up: Six principles for building the New Logic Corporation*. San Francisco: Jossey-Bass

Lawler, EE (1996) Competencies: a poor foundation for the new pay, *Compensation and Benefits Review*, November–December

Lawler, EE (2000) *Rewarding Excellence: Pay strategies for the new economy*. San Francisco, CA: Jossey-Bass

Lawler, EE (2005) Creating high performance organizations, *Asia Pacific Journal of Human Resources*, vol. 43, no. 1, pp. 10–17

Lawler, EE (2009) Fixing executive compensation excesses, *Business Week*, 5 February

Lawler, EE and Finegold, D (2007) CEO compensation: what board members think', *WorldatWork Journal*, vol. 16, no. 3, pp. 38–47

Lawter, L, Kopelman, RE and Prottas, DJ (2015) McGregor's Theory X/Y and Job Performance: A Multilevel, Multi-source Analysis, *Journal of Managerial Issues*, vol. 27, no. 1/4, pp. 84–101

Lazear, EP (1995) *Personnel Economics*. Cambridge, MA: MIT Press

Lazear, EP (1999) Personnel economics: past lessons and future directions, *Journal of Labor Economics*, vol. 17, no. 2, pp. 199–236

Leblanc, PV (1992) Banding: the new pay structure for the transformed organisation, *Journal of Compensation and Benefits*, January-February, 34–38

Ledford, GE (1995) Designing nimble reward systems, *Compensation & Benefits Review*, July–August, pp. 46–54

Legge, K (1995) *Human Resource Management: Rhetorics and realities*. Basingstoke: Macmillan

Legislation.gov.uk (2023a) *Employment Rights Act 1996, Section 1 (1)*, www.legislation.gov.uk/ukpga/1996/18/section/1 (archived at https://perma.cc/5PXJ-UFVD)

Legislation.gov.uk (2023b) *Employment Rights Act 1996, Section 27 (1) (a)*, www.legislation.gov.uk/ukpga/1996/18/section/27 (archived at https://perma.cc/L4B9-CJ7C)

Leigh Day (2019) Asda workers in Employment Tribunal for second stage of the UK's largest equal pay claim, www.leighday.co.uk/News/2019/May-2019/Asda-workers-in-Employment-Tribunal-for-second-sta (archived at https://perma.cc/AN9N-LZQ5)

Lengnick-Hall, ML and Bereman, NA (1994) A conceptual framework for the study of employee benefits, *Human Resource Management Review*, vol. 4, no. 2, pp. 101–5

Lepak, DP, Taylor, MS, Tekleab, AG, Marrone, JA and Cohen, DJ (2007) An examination of the use of high-investment human resource systems for core and support employees, *Human Resource Management*, vol. 46, no. 2, pp. 223–46

Levinson, H, Price, CR, Munden, KJ and Solley, CM (1962) *Men, Management and Mental Health*. Cambridge, MA: Harvard University Press

Lewis, D (2017) Is this the end of employee benefits?, *People Management*, 27 April, www.peoplemanagement.co.uk/long-reads/articles/end-employee-benefits (archived at https://perma.cc/DJ9F-66DD)

Lewis, D and Sergeant, M (2017) *Essentials of Employment Law*, 14th edn. London: Chartered Institute of Personnel and Development

Lewis, G (2015) Employee benefits 'wasted' if not tailored to gender and age, *People Management*, www.peoplemanagement.co.uk/article/1744156/benefits-tailored-gender-age (archived at https://perma.cc/S6P3-MUV5)

Lewis, P (1998) Managing performance-related pay based on evidence from the financial services sector, *Human Resource Management Journal*, vol. 8, no. 2, pp. 66–77

Li, X (2020) Literature review of executive compensation, *Journal of Service Science and Management*, vol. 13, pp. 153–67

Lips, HM (2013) The gender pay gap: challenging the rationalizations. perceived equity, discrimination, and the limits of human capital models, *Sex Roles*, vol. 68, no. 3–4, 169–85, doi.org/10.1007/s11199-012-0165-z (archived at https://perma.cc/CG4A-L5LH)

Linklaters (2006) *The Matrix: An Overview of Corporate Governance*. London: Linklaters LLP

Living Wage Foundation (2016) *Closing the Gap: A living wage that means families don't go short*, www.livingwage.org.uk/calculation (archived at https://perma.cc/A7UN-EPXY)

Livy, B (2020) *Job Evaluation: A critical review*. London: Taylor and Francis

Locke, EA, Shaw, KN, Saari, LM and Latham, GP (1981) Goal setting and task performance: 1961–1980, *Psychological Bulletin*, vol. 90, no. 1, 125–52

Lockey, S, Graham, L and Zhou, Q (2017) *Evidence for Performance-Related and Skills-Based: Pay Implications for Policing*. Centre for Leadership and Followership Policing Research Unit, Durham University

Loretto, W, White, P and Duncan, C (1999) 'Thatcher's children' pensions and retirement. Some survey evidence, *Personnel Review*, vol. 30, no. 4, pp. 386–403

Low Pay Commission (2019) *20 years of the National Minimum Wage: A history of the UK minimum wage and its effects*, assets.publishing.service.gov.uk/government/uploads/system/uploads/attachment_data/file/790910/20_years_of_the_National_Minimum_Wage_-_ a_history_of_the_UK_minimum_wage_and_its_effects.pdf (archived at https://perma.cc/P3VM-PKVC)

Low Pay Commission (2021) *Non-compliance and enforcement of the National Minimum Wage*, www.gov.uk/government/publications/minimum-wage-underpayment-in-2021/non-compliance-and-enforcement-of-the-national-minimum-wage-a-report-by-the-low-pay-commission (archived at https://perma.cc/G9LF-55NG)

Lowe, K, Milliman, J, DeCieri, H and Dowling, P (2002) International compensation practices: a ten-country comparative analysis, *Human Resource Management*, vol. 41, no. 1, pp. 45–66

Lozano-Reina, G and Sánchez-Marín, G (2020) Say on pay and executive compensation: A systematic review and suggestions for developing the field, *Human Resource Management Review*, vol. 30, no. 2

Lupton, B, Rowe, A and Whittle, R (2015) *Show me the money! The behavioural science of reward*. Research Report. London: Chartered Institute of Personnel and Development

Mabey, C, Salaman, G and Storey, J (1998) *Human Resource Management: A Strategic Introduction*, 2nd edn. Oxford: Blackwell

Machin, S (1999) Wage inequality in the 1970s, 1980s and 1990s, in Gregg, P and Wadsworth, J (eds.) *The State of Working Britain*. Manchester, Manchester University Press

MacLeod, D and Clarke, N (2009) *Engaging for Success: Enhancing Employee Performance Through Employee Engagement*. London: Department for Business, Skills and Innovation

MacQueen, R (2022) What is happening with UK wages?, www.economicsobservatory.com/what-is-happening-with-UK-wages (archived at https://perma.cc/39XB-5T9U)

Madhani, PM (2014) Managing sales compensation: career life cycle approach, *Journal of Indian Management*, Jul-Sept, pp. 5–15

Madigan, RM and Hoover, DJ (1986) Effects of alternative job evaluation methods on decisions involving pay equity, *Academy of Management Journal*, vol. 29, no. 1, pp. 84–100

Mahoney, TA (1989) Employment compensation and strategy, in Gomez-Mejia, LR (ed.) *Compensation and Benefits*. ASPA-BNA Series (3) Washington, DC: Bureau of National Affairs

Mahoney, TA (1992) Multiple pay contingencies: strategic design of compensation, in Salamon, G (ed.) *Human Resource Strategies*. London, Sage

Makinson, J (2000) *Incentives for Change. Rewarding performance in national government networks*. Public Service Productivity Panel. HM Treasury. London: HMSO

Mamman, A, Sulaiman, M and Fadel, A (1996) Attitudes to pay systems: an exploratory study within and across cultures, *International Journal of Human Resource Management*, vol. 7, no. 1, pp. 101–212

Marchington, M and Cox, A (2007) Employee involvement and participation: structures, processes and outcomes, in Storey, J (ed.) *Human Resource Management: A critical text*, 3rd edn. London: Thomson, pp. 177–94

Marchington, M and Wilkinson, A (2005) *Human Resource Management at Work: People Management and Development*, 3rd edn. London, Chartered Institute of Personnel and Development

Marchington, M and Wilkinson, A (2016) *Human Resource Management at Work: People management and development*, 6th edn. London: Chartered Institute of Personnel and Development

Marchington, M, Wilkinson, A, Ackers, P and Dundon, A (2001) *Management Choice and Employee Voice*. London: Chartered Institute of Personnel and Development

Marriot, LM and Perkins, SJ (2018) *CIPD Annual Reward Survey: Focus on Benefits*. London: Chartered Institute of Personnel and Development

Marriot, LM and Perkins, SJ (2019) *CIPD Annual Reward Survey: Focus on Pay*. London: Chartered Institute of Personnel and Development

Marsden, D (1999) *A Theory of Employment Systems: Micro-Foundations of Societal Diversity*. Oxford: Oxford University Press

Marsden, D (2004) The role of performance related pay in renegotiating the 'effort bargain': the case of the British public service, *Industrial and Labor Relations Review*, vol. 57, no. 3, pp. 350–70

Marsden, D (2007) Pay and rewards in public services: fairness and equity, in Dibben, P, James, P, Roper, I and Wood, G (eds.) *Modernising Work in Public Services. Redefining roles and relationships in Britain's changing workplace*. Basingstoke: Palgrave Macmillan

Marsden, D and French, S (1998) *What a Performance: Performance-related pay in the public services*. London: Centre for Economic Performance

Marsden, D and Richardson, R (1994) Performance pay? The effects of merit pay on motivation in the public services, *British Journal of Industrial Relations*, vol. 32, no. 2, pp. 243–61

Martín-Alcázar, F, Romero-Fernández, PM and Sánchez-Gardey, G (2005) Strategic human resource management: integrating the universalistic, contingent, configurational and contextual perspectives, *International Journal of Human Resource Management*, vol. 16, no. 5, pp. 633–59

Martin, DC and Bartol, KM (2003) Factors influencing expatriate performance appraisal system success: an organizational perspective, *Journal of International Management*, vol. 9, no. 2, pp. 115–32

Martins, PS (2021), Internal Labor Market Dimensions and Labor Productivity, in Polachek, SW, Tatsiramos, K, Russo, G and van Houten, G (eds.) *Workplace Productivity and Management Practices* (Research in Labor Economics, vol. 49). Bingley: Emerald Publishing Limited, pp. 107–37

Maslow, A.H (1954) *Motivation and Personality*. New York: Harper and Row

Mayerhofer, H, Hartmann, L, Michelitsch-Riedl, G and Kollinger, I (2004) Flexpatriate assignments: A neglected issue in global staffing, *International Journal of Human Resource Management*, vol. 15, no. 8, pp. 1371–89

Mayhew, K and Keep, E (1999) The assessment: knowledge, skills and competitiveness, *Oxford Review of Economic Policy*, vol. 15, no. 1, pp. 1–16
Mayo, E (1945) *The Social Problems of Industrial Civilization*. London: Routledge
McHugh, P, Cutcher-Gershenfeld, J and Bridge, D (2005) 'Examining structure and process in ESOP firms'. *Personnel Review*, vol. 34, no. 3, pp. 277–93
McNabb, R and Whitfield, K (2001) Job evaluation and high performance work practices: compatible or conflictual?, *Journal of Management Studies*, vol. 38, no. 2 (March), pp. 293–312
McNulty, T and Pettigrew, A (1999) Strategists on the board, *Organization Studies*, vol. 20, no. 1, pp. 47–74
Mercer (2010) *Mercer Scheme Design Survey*. Mercer Benefits
Mercer (2023) Managing International Assignments: Compensation Approaches, mobilityexchange.mercer.com/insights/article/managing-international-assignments-compensation-approaches (archived at https://perma.cc/4M5V-Z29S)
Messersmith, J (2007) Managing work–life conflict among information technology workers, *Human Resource Management*, vol. 46, no. 3, pp. 429–51
Michelson, G and Wailes, N (2006) Shareholder value and corporate social responsibility in work organisations, in Hearn, M and Michelson, G (eds.) *Rethinking Work: Time, Space, and Discourse*. Cambridge: Cambridge University Press, pp. 239–62
Miles, RE (1965) Human relations or human resources? *Harvard Business Review*, vol. 43, no. 4, pp. 148–63
Miles, RE and Snow, CC (1984) Designing strategic human resources systems, *Organizational Dynamics*, vol. 13, no. 1, pp. 36–52
Milkovich, G and Newman, JM (2004) *Compensation*, 8th edn. New York: McGraw Hill
Milkovich, G and Newman, JM (2008) *Compensation*, 9th edn. Boston, MA: McGraw-Hill International Edition
Milkovich, G, Newman, J and Gerhart, B (2014) *Compensation*, 11th edn. Boston, MA: McGraw-Hill International Edition
Milkovich, GT and Bloom, M (1998) Rethinking international compensation, *Compensation & Benefits Review*, vol. 30, no. 1, pp. 15–23
Milner, M and Seager, A (2007) Executive pay: UK bosses: are they worth the money?: Evidence scant that big salaries stop brain drain, *Guardian*, 31 August, p. 26
Mincer, J and Polacheck, S (1974) Family investments in human capital: earnings of women, *Journal of Political Economy*, vol. 82, no. 2, Part 2, S76–S108
Mitchell, DJB, Lewin, D and Lawler, EE (1990) Alternative pay systems, firm performance and productivity, in Blinder, AS (ed.) *Paying for Productivity: A look at the evidence*. Washington, DC: Brookings Institution
Mitchell, O (1982) Fringe benefits and labor mobility, *Journal of Human Resources*, vol. 17, no. 92, pp. 286–98
Mitchell, O (1983) Fringe benefits and the cost of changing jobs, *Industrial Relations and Labor Review*, vol. 37, no. 1, pp. 70–78
Mitra, A, Gupta, N and Shaw, JD (2011) A comparative examination of traditional and skill-based pay plans, *Journal of Managerial Psychology*, vol. 26, no. 4, pp. 278–96
Molm, LD (2010) The structure of reciprocity, *Social Psychology Quarterly*, vol. 73, no. 2, pp. 119–31
Molm, LD, Peterson, G and Takashini, N (1999) Power in negotiated and reciprocal exchange, *American Sociological Review*, vol. 64, no. 6, pp. 876–90
Monks, R and Sykes, A (2002) *Capitalism Without Owners will Fail: A policymaker's guide to reform*. London: CSFI Publications
Monnot, MJ and Beehr, TA (2014) Subjective well-being at work: disentangling source effects of stress and support on enthusiasm, contentment, and meaningfulness, *Journal of Vocational Behavior*, vol. 85, no. 2, pp. 204–18

Montani, F, Boudrias, J and Pigeon, M (2017) Employee recognition, meaningfulness and behavioural involvement: test of a moderated mediation model, *International Journal of Human Resource Management*, DOI:10.1080/09585192.2017.1288153 (archived at https://perma.cc/6DRJ-5GVS)

Moore, F (2006) 'Recruitment and selection of international managers, in Edwards, T and Rees, C (eds.) *International Human Resource Management: Globalization, national systems and multinational companies*. London: FT-Prentice Hall, pp. 195–216

Morgan, G and Whitley, R (2003) Introduction to special edition on multinational companies, *Journal of Management Studies*, vol. 40, no. 3, pp. 609–16

Morrison, EW and Robinson, SL (1997) When employees feel betrayed: A model of how psychological contract violation develops, *Academy of Management Review*, vol. 22, no. 1, pp. 226–56

Moss, R (2015) Employee-shareholder contracts rarely used, *Personnel Today*, 9 March, www.personneltoday.com/hr/employee-shareholder-contracts-rarely-used/ (archived at https://perma.cc/MP9F-Y99R)

Nam, T (2014) Technology use and work-life balance, *Applied Research in Quality of Life*, vol. 9, no. 4, pp. 1017–40

NAPF (2007) *Workplace Pensions in Demand*. Press Release, 25 May. London: National Association of Pension Funds

NAPF (2010) *NAPF Workplace Pensions Survey*. London: National Association of Pension Funds

Naylor, S (2014) Has flexible benefits had its day? *Employee Benefits*, 26 November

Newing, R (2007) Executive remuneration: quality over quantity, *Financial Times*, 12 October

Nohria, N and Ghoshal, S (1997) *The Differentiated Network: organizing multinational corporations for value creation*. San Francisco: Jossey-Bass Wiley

Noldeke, G and Samuelson, L (1996) A dynamic model of equilibrium selection in signaling markets, ELSE working papers 038, ESRC Centre on Economics Learning and Social Evolution, econwpa.wustl.edu:8089/eps/game/papers/9410/9410001.pdf

Norris, P (2005) Shareholders' attitudes to directors' pay, in Tyson, S and Bournois, F (eds.) *Top Pay and Performance: International and Strategic Approach*. London: Elsevier, pp. 29–56

Nurney, SP (2001) When to stop negotiating individual packages for international assignees, *Compensation & Benefits Review*, vol. 33 (July–August), pp. 62–7

Nyberg, A (2010) Retaining your high performers: moderators of the performance-job satisfaction-voluntary turnover relationship, *Journal of Applied Psychology*, vol. 95, no. 3, pp. 440–53

Nyberg, A, Maltarich, MA, Abdulsalam, D, Essman, SM and Cragun, O (2018) Collective pay for performance: a cross-disciplinary review and meta-analysis, *Journal of Management*, vol. 44, no. 6, pp. 2433–72

O'Connell, V (2006) The CEO's share of total directors' cash compensation: U.K. evidence, *Compensation and Benefits Review*, vol. 38, September/October, pp. 28–34

OECD (2011) *Divided We Stand: Why Inequality Keeps Rising*. Paris: OECD

OECD (2017) *Trade unions, employer organisations, and collective bargaining in OECD countries*, www.oecd.org/els/emp/Flyer-Collective%20bargaining.pdf (archived at https://perma.cc/M9L7-ABCK)

OECD (2019), *OECD Employment Outlook 2019: The Future of Work*, OECD Publishing, Paris, doi.org/10.1787/9ee00155-en (archived at https://perma.cc/H3GW-ZZRW)

Ogden, S and Watson, R (2004) Remuneration committees and CEO pay in the UK privatized water industry, *Socio-Economic Review*, vol. 2, no. 1, pp. 33–63

Olkkonen, M-E and Lipponen, J (2006) Relationships between organizational justice, identification with organization and work unit, and group-related outcomes, *Organizational Behaviour and Human Decision Processes*, vol. 100, no. 2, pp. 202–15

Olsen, WK and Walby, S (2004) *Modelling Gender Pay Gaps*. Manchester: Equal Opportunities Commission

Olsen, W, Gash, V, Vandecasteele, L, Walthery, P and Heuvelman, H (2010) The gender pay gap in the UK 1995–2007: research report number 1. UK: Government Equalities Office

OME (2006) *Developments in Occupational Pay Differentiation*. Research report for the Office for Manpower Economics. London: OME

OME (2014) *A review of the evidence on the impact, effectiveness and value for money of performance-related pay in the public sector*. The Work Foundation. 1 December 2014. London: Office of Manpower Economics, www.gov.uk/government/publications/a-review-of-the-evidence-on-the-impact-effectiveness-and-value-for-money-of-performance-related-pay-in-the-public-sector (archived at https://perma.cc/3WUE-Z7AS)

ONS (2006) *Labour Force Survey. Quarter 2*. London: Office for National Statistics

ONS (2015) *Life expectancy at birth and at age 65 by local areas in England and Wales, 2012 to 2014*, www.ons.gov.uk/ons/dcp171778_422285.pdf (archived at https://perma.cc/8WZV-7G4M)

ONS (2017) Annual Survey of Hours and Earnings (ASHE) – Proportion of all employee jobs with weekly, fortnightly, four-weekly and monthly pay periods, UK, April 2017, www.ons.gov.uk/employmentandlabourmarket/peopleinwork/earningsandworkinghours/adhocs/007746annual survey of hoursand earning sa she proportion of all employee jobs with weekly fortnightly four weekly and monthly pay period suk april2017 (archived at https://perma.cc/2BZJ-86A5)

ONS (2018) *Annual Survey of Hours and Earnings time series of selected estimates*, release date October 2018, www.ons.gov.uk/employmentandlabourmarket/peopleinwork/earningsandworkinghours/datasets/ashe1997to2015selectedestimates (archived at https://perma.cc/8QNP-CAU2)

ONS (2019a) Employee workplace pensions in the UK: 2018 provisional and 2017 revised results, www.ons.gov.uk/employmentandlabourmarket/peopleinwork/workplacepensions/bulletins/annualsurveyofhoursandearningspensiontables/2018provisionaland2017revisedresults (archived at https://perma.cc/9488-MM23)

ONS (2019b) Occupational Pension Schemes Survey 2018, www.ons.gov.uk/peoplepopulationandcommunity/personalandhouseholdfinances/pensionssavingsandinvestments/bulletins/occupationalpensionschemessurvey/2018 (archived at https://perma.cc/6DRD-U27B)

ONS (2020) Employee workplace pensions in the UK: 2021 provisional and 2020 final results, www.ons.gov.uk/employmentandlabourmarket/peopleinwork/workplacepensions/bulletins/annualsurveyofhoursandearningspensiontables/2021provisionaland2020finalresults (archived at https://perma.cc/VE8B-T5XX)

ONS (2022) Employee workplace pensions in the UK: 2021 provisional and 2020 final results. London: Office for National Statistics, www.ons.gov.uk/employmentandlabourmarket/peopleinwork/workplacepensions/bulletins/annualsurveyofhoursandearningspensiontables/2021provisionaland2020finalresults (archived at https://perma.cc/VE8B-T5XX)

ONS (2023a) Household income inequality, UK: financial year ending 2022, statistical bulletin, www.ons.gov.uk/peoplepopulationandcommunity/personalandhouseholdfinances/incomeandwealth/bulletins/householdincomeinequalityfinancial/financialyearending2022 (archived at https://perma.cc/3DYV-HL6C)

ONS (2023b) The impact of strikes in the UK: June 2022 to February 2023, www.ons.gov.uk/employmentandlabourmarket/peopleinwork/workplacedisputesandworkingconditions/articles/theimpactofstrikesintheuk/

ORC (2002) *Worldwide Survey of International Assignment Policies and Practices*. New York: Organization Resource Counselors Inc.

ORC (2004) *2004 Worldwide Survey of International Assignment Policies and Practices*. New York: Organization Resource Counselors Inc.
ORC (2006) *Survey of International Short-term Assignment Policies*. New York: Organization Resource Counselors Inc.
ORC (2009) *Survey of Short-term International Assignment Policies*. London: ORC Worldwide
Osborne, H (2016) Asda faces £100m equal pay battle with shopfloor staff, www.theguardian.com/business/2016/oct/14/asda-equal-pay-shopfloor-staff-women (archived at https://perma.cc/4NUZ-KU6W)
PA Consulting Group (2007) *Practices in Assessing Employee Quality, Report Commissioned by the Office of Manpower Economics*. London: OME
Paauwe, J (2004) *HRM and Performance: Achieving long term viability*. Oxford, Oxford University Press
Palmer, B, Walls, M, Burgess, Z and Stough, C (2001) Emotional intelligence and effective leadership, *Leadership & Organization Development Journal*, vol. 22, no. 1, pp. 5–10
Park, R and Kim, J (2022) Differential effects of autonomy on employee satisfaction and organizational performance depending on the type of financial incentives: evidence from a four-wave panel of Korean companies, *International Journal of Human Resource Management* [Online] 1–31
Parkinson, J (2003) The company and the employment relationship, *British Journal of Industrial Relations*, vol. 41, no. 3, pp. 481–509
Paton, N (2014) Is total reward dead?, *Employee Benefits*, 12 October
Pattnaik, S and Padhi, M (2023) Towards compassionate total rewards: COVID-19's clarion call for a paradigmatic shift, *South Asian Journal of Human Resources Management*, vol. 10, no. 1, pp. 152–62
Pendleton, A (1997) Characteristics of workplaces with financial participation: evidence from the Workplace Industrial Relations Survey, *Industrial Relations Journal*, vol. 28, pp. 103–19
Pendleton, A, Whitfield, K and Bryson, A (2009) The changing use of contingent pay at the modern British workplace, in Brown, W, Bryson, A, Forth, J and Whitfield, K (eds.) *The Evolution of the Modern British Workplace*. Cambridge: Cambridge University Press
Pensions Commission (2004) *Pensions: Challenges and Choices. The First Report of the Pensions Commission*. London: The Stationery Office
Pensions Commission (2005) *A New Pension Settlement for the Twenty-First Century. The Second Report of the Pensions Commission*. London: The Stationery Office
Pensions Commission (2006) *Implementing an Integrated Package of Pension Reforms. The Final Report of the Pensions Commission*. London: The Stationery Office
Pentland (2015a) Our brands, pentlandbrands.com/our-brands/ (archived at https://perma.cc/W9FB-9Z65)
Pentland (2015b) Working for us, www.pentland.com/working-for-us (archived at https://perma.cc/9BJN-HGLA)
Pentland (2015c) Pentland Brands receives top prize at 2014 CIPD/People Management Awards, pentlandbrands.com/pentland-brands-receives-top-prize-at-2014-cipd-people-management-awards/ (archived at https://perma.cc/M3CD-BCTG)
Pepper, A and Campbell, R (2014) *Executive Reward: A review of the drivers and consequences*. London: Chartered Institute of Personnel and Development
Pepper, A. Gosling, T and Gore, J (2015) Fairness, envy, guilt and greed: building equity considerations into agency theory, *Human Relations*, vol. 68, no. 8, pp. 1291–314
Pepper, S (2006) *Senior Executive Reward: Key models and practices*. Aldershot: Gower
Perkins, SJ (1998) Communication and the reward strategy agenda, *Croner Pay and Benefits Briefing*, vol. 151, October. Kingston-upon-Thames: Croner Publications

Perkins, SJ (2000) Losing our most creative employees: why and how do we stop it?, *Croner Pay & Benefits Briefing*, 20 July

Perkins, SJ (2006) *CIPD Guide to International Reward and Recognition*. London: Chartered Institute of Personnel and Development

Perkins, SJ (2009) Executive reward: Complexity, controversy, and contradiction, in White, G and Durcker, J (eds.) *Reward Management: A critical text*, 2nd edn. London: Routledge, pp. 148–73

Perkins, SJ (2015) Perspectives on problems in managing managers' remuneration, in Wilkinson, A (ed.) *Management of Managers*. Cheltenham: Edward Elgar, pp. 36–61

Perkins, SJ (2017) The social construction of executive remuneration in the UK: Elite competition around codification and legitimation, *Journal of Organizational Effectiveness: People and Performance*, vol. 4, no. 1, pp. 76–88

Perkins, SJ (ed.) (2019) *The Routledge Companion to Reward Management*. London: Routledge

Perkins, SJ and Daste, R (2007) Pluralistic tensions in expatriating managers, *Journal of European Industrial Training*, vol. 31, no. 7, pp. 550–69

Perkins, SJ and Hendry, C (2001) Global champions: who's paying attention?, *Thunderbird International Business Review*, vol. 43, no. 1, pp. 53–75

Perkins, SJ and Hendry, C (2005) Ordering top pay: interpreting the signals, *Journal of Management Studies*, vol. 42, no. 7, pp. 1443–68

Perkins, SJ, Marriott, E and Cotton, C (2019) *Focus on Pay: Findings from the 2019 Annual Reward Survey.* London: Chartered Institute of Personnel and Development

Perkins, SJ and Sandringham, St J (eds.) (1998) *Trust, Motivation and Commitment: A reader*. Faringdon: SRRC

Perkins, SJ and Shortland, S (2006) *Strategic International Human Resource Management*. London: Kogan Page

Perkins, SJ and Shortland, S (2022) The social construction of executive pay: governance processes and institutional isomorphism, *Journal of Organizational Effectiveness: People and Performance*, vol. 9, no. 4, pp. 610–36

Perkins, SJ and Shortland, S (2023) Do executive remuneration decision-makers know what's going on? The gap between independence and institutional contexts, *Journal of Organizational Effectiveness: People and Performance*, January, DOI:10.1108/JOEPP-08-2022-0219 (archived at https://perma.cc/9MDK-BSUZ)

Perkins, SJ and Vartiainen, M (2010) European reward management? Introducing the special issue' [co- editors' introduction to the Special Issue: Reward Management in Europe], *Thunderbird International Business Review*, vol. 52, no. 3, pp. 175–87

Perkins, SJ and White, G (2010) Modernising pay in the UK public services: trends and implications, *Human Resource Management Journal*, vol. 20, no. 3 (July), 244–57

Perry, JL, Trent, AE and So, YJ (2009) Back to the future? Performance-related pay, empirical research, and the perils of persistence, *Public Administration Review*, January/February, pp. 39–51

Peters, TJ and Waterman, RH Jr (1982) *In Search of Excellence: Lessons from America's best-run companies*. New York: Harper & Row

Pfeffer, J (1998a) Six dangerous myths about pay. *Harvard Business Review,* 76 May–June: 108–19

Pfeffer, J (1998b) *The Human Equation. Building profits by putting people first*. Boston, MA: Harvard Business Press

Pfeffer, J and Davies-Blake, A (1987) Understanding organizational wage structures: a resource dependence approach, *Academy of Management Journal*, vol. 30 (September), pp. 437–55

Pfeffer, J and Salancik, GR (1977) Who gets power – and how they hold on to it: a strategic contingency model of power, *Organizational Dynamics*, Winter, pp. 3–21

Pfeffer, J and Salancik, GR (2003) *The External Control of Organizations: A Resource Dependence Perspective*. Stanford: Stanford University Press

Phillips, L and Fox, M (2003) Compensation strategy in transnational corporations, *Management Decision*, vol. 41, no. 5, pp. 465–76

Pinder, CC (1987) Valence-instrumentality-expectancy theory, in Steers, RM and Porter, LW (eds.) *Motivation and Work Behavior*, 4th edn. San Francisco: McGraw-Hill, pp. 69–89

Pink, D (2009) *Drive: The surprising truth about what motivates us*. New York: Free Press

Pirsig, RM (1991) *Zen and the Art of Motorcycle Maintenance: An inquiry into values*. London: Vintage Books

PLSA (2019) Breaking the barriers to pensions understanding, blog posting by George Currie, www.plsa.co.uk/Blog/Article/Breaking-the-barriers-to-pensions-understanding (archived at https://perma.cc/XTF2-PVAZ)

Point, S (2005) Accountability, transparency and performance: comparing annual report disclosures on CEO pay across Europe, in Tyson, S and Bournois, F (eds.) *Top Pay and Performance: International and strategic approach*. London: Elsevier, pp. 57–84

Poole, M and Jenkins, G (1990) Human resource management and profit sharing: employee attitudes and a national survey, *International Journal of Human Resource Management*, vol. 1, no. 3 (December), pp. 289–328

Porter, M (1985) *Competitive Advantage: Creating and Sustaining Competitive Advantage*. New York: Free Press

Price, L and Price, R (1994) Change and continuity in the status divide, in Sisson, K (ed.) *Personnel Management: A comprehensive guide to theory and practice in Britain*, 2nd edn. Oxford: Blackwell

Prince, NR and Prince, JB (2022) Adapting to a global world, in Perkins, SJ (ed.) *The Routledge Companion to Reward Management*. London: Routledge, pp. 200–08

Pritchard, D and Murlis, H (1993) *Jobs, Roles and People. The new world of job evaluation*. London: Nicholas Brearley

Purcell, J (1999) Best fit and best practice: chimera or cul-de-sac?, *Human Resource Management Journal*, vol. 9, no. 3, pp. 26–41

Purcell, J (2006) Building better organisations, in *Reflections on Employee Engagement*. Change Agenda. London: Chartered Institute of Personnel and Development, pp. 3–4

Purcell, J and Ahlstrand, B (1994) *Human Resource Management in the Multi-divisional Company*. Oxford: Oxford University Press

Purcell, J and Hutchinson, S (2007) *Rewarding work: The vital role of front line managers*. Change Agenda. London, Chartered Institute of Personnel and Development

PwC (2006) *Measuring the value of international assignments*. London: PricewaterhouseCoopers

PWC (2022) *Mandatory UK Gender Pay Reporting: Managing the Transition to Global Reporting on Fairness*, www.pwc.co.uk/human-resource-services/assets/pdfs/year-5-gender-pay-gap-report-2021-2022.pdf (archived at https://perma.cc/DUE6-MRBQ)

Pye, A (2001) Corporate boards, investors and their relationships: accounts of accountability and corporate governance in action, *Corporate Governance An International Review*, vol. 9, no. 3, pp. 186–95

Pyzoha, JS and Jenkins, JG (2019) The influence of auditor quality and executive compensation structure on financial reporting executives' restatement decisions in a clawback environment, *Current Issues in Auditing*, vol. 13, no. 1, pp. 28–36

Quaid, M (1993) Job evaluation as institutional myth, *Journal of Management Studies*, vol. 30, no. 2 (March), pp. 239–60

Race, M (2022) Cap on bankers' bonuses will still be lifted, BBC News, 17 October, www.bbc.co.uk/news/business-63290169 (archived at https://perma.cc/ZD72-VYYR)

Randle, K (1997) Rewarding failure: operating a performance-related pay system in pharmaceutical research, *Personnel Review*, vol. 26, no. 3, pp. 187–200

Read, M (2022) *Fortieth Annual Report on Senior Salaries* (report no. 94) assets.publishing.service.gov.uk/government/uploads/system/uploads/attachment_data/file/1092289/SSRB_44th_AR2022_accessible.pdf (archived at https://perma.cc/8YKQ-8XMH)

Recardo, RJ and Pricone, D (1996) Is skill-based pay for you?, *SAM Advanced Management Journal*, vol. 6, no. 4 (Fall), pp. 16–22

Rees, A (1973) *The Economics of Work and Pay*. New York: Harper & Row

Reeves, R and Knell, J (2001) All these futures are yours, in *The Future of Reward*. Executive Briefing. London: Chartered Institute of Personnel and Development, pp. 39–46

Reilly, M and Scott, D (2005) An inside look at compensation committees, *WorldatWork Journal*, second quarter, pp. 34–40

Reynolds, C (1997) Expatriate compensation in historical perspective, *Journal of World Business*, vol. 32, no. 2, pp. 118–32

Richards, J and Hogg, C (2007) *Total Reward*. Factsheet. London: Chartered Institute of Personnel and Development

Rickard, C, Reilly, P and Mercer, M (2012) *Case Studies on Pay Progression. Final report*. Brighton: Institute for Employment Studies

Roberts, J (2001) Trust and control in Anglo-American systems of corporate governance: The individualizing and socializing effects of processes of accountability, *Human Relations*, vol. 54, no. 12, pp. 1547–72

Roberts, JD, McNulty, T and Stiles, P (2005) Beyond agency conceptions of the work of the non-executive director: Creating accountability in the boardroom, *British Journal of Management*, vol. 16(S1), S5–S26

Roberts, K (2007) Work–life balance – the sources of the contemporary problem and the probable outcomes: a review and interpretation of the evidence, *Employee Relations*, vol. 29, no. 4, pp. 334–51

Robinson, A and Hudson, R (2008) From fringe to mainstream? A portrait of employee benefit provision in Britain, in Vartiainen, M, Antoni, C, Baeten, X, Hakonen, N, Lucas, R and Thierry, H (eds.) *Reward Management – Facts and trends in Europe*. Lengerich, Germany: Pabst Science Publishers

Roe, MJ (2003) *Political Determinants of Corporate Governance: Political Context, Corporate Impact*. Oxford: Oxford University Press

Rosenbaum, JE (1989) Organization career systems and employee misperceptions, in Arthur, MB, Hall, DT and Lawrence, BS (eds.) *Handbook of Career Theory*. New York: Cambridge University Press, pp. 329–53

Rousseau, D and Tijoriwala, S (1998) Assessing psychological contracts: issues, alternatives and measures, *Journal of Organizational Behaviour*, vol. 19, no. 7, pp. 679–95

Rousseau, DM (1995) *Psychological Contracts in Organizations: Understanding Written and Unwritten Agreements*. Thousand Oaks, CA: Sage

Rousseau, DM (2006) Is there such a thing as 'evidence-based management', *Academy of Management Review*, vol. 31, no. 2, pp. 256–69

Rousseau, DM and Greller, MM (1994) Human resource practices: Administrative contract makers. *Human Resource Management*, vol. 33, no. 3, 385–401

(RPI) Recognition Professionals International (2015), About, www.recognition.org/?page=about_rpi (archived at https://perma.cc/Y8FA-FHJ6)

Rubery, G and Grimshaw, D (2003) *The Organization of Employment: An International Perspective*. Basingstoke: Palgrave Macmillan

Rubery, G (1997) Wages and the labour market, *British Journal of Industrial Relations*, vol. 35, no. 3, pp. 337–66

Russell, A (1998) *The Harmonisation of Employment Conditions in Britain. The changing workplace divide since 1950 and the implications for social structure*. Basingstoke: Macmillan Press

Rynes, SL and Gerhart, B (2000) *Compensation in Organizations. Current Research and Practice*. San Francisco: Jossey-Bass

Safriliana, RM, Subroto, B, Subekti, I and Rahman, AF (2019) Overviews of contracting theory & agency theory: determinants public accounting firms switching on voluntary, *International Journal of Organizational Innovation*, vol. 1, no. 3, pp. 10–21

Sahakiants, I, Festing, M and Perkins, SJ (2016) Pay for Performance in Europe, in Dickmann, M, Brewster, C and Sparrow, P (eds.) *Contemporary HR Issues in Europe*, 3rd edn. London: Routledge, pp. 355–74

Samson, A (ed.) (2014) *The Behavioral Economics Guide 2014*, www.behavioraleconomics.com (archived at https://perma.cc/ZE8Z-36K7)

Sánchez-Marín, G, Lucas-Pérez, ME, Baixauli-Soler, S, Main, BGM and Mínguez-Vera, A (2022) Excess executive compensation and corporate governance in the United Kingdom and Spain: A comparative analysis, *Managerial and Decision Economics*, vol. 43, pp. 2817–37

Schein, EH (1965) *Organizational Psychology*. Englewood Cliffs, NJ: Prentice Hall

Schifferes, S (2005) Pension reform: What other countries do, BBC News, 24 November, news.bbc.co.uk/go/pr/fr/-/1/hi/business/4462404.stm (archived at https://perma.cc/GX45-ZW6U)

Schiller, B and Weiss, R (1979) The impact of private pensions on firm attachment, *Review of Economics and Statistics*, vol. 61, no. 3, pp. 369–80

Schlechter, A, Thompson, NC and Bussin, M (2015) Attractiveness of non-financial rewards for prospective knowledge workers, *Employee Relations*, vol. 37, no. 3, pp. 274–95

Schuster, JR and Zingheim, P (1992) *The New Pay: Linking Employee and Organizational Performance*. New York: Lexington Books

Scott, D, Browne, M, Shields, J, Long, R, Antoni, C, Beck-Krala, E, Lucia Casademunt, AM and Perkins, SJ (2015) A global study of pay preferences and employee characteristics, *Compensation and Benefits Journal*, vol. 47, no. 2, pp. 60–70

Shaw, JD, Dineen, BR, Fang, R and Vellella, RF (2009) Employee-organization exchange relationships, HRM practices, and quit rates of good and poor performers, *Academy of Management Journal*, vol. 52, no. 5, pp. 1016–33

Shaw, JD and Gupta, N (2007) Pay system characteristics and quit patterns of good, average, and poor performers, *Personnel Psychology*, vol. 60, no. 4, pp. 903–28

Shaw, JD and Gupta, N (2015) Let the evidence speak again! Financial incentives are more effective than we thought, *Human Resource Management Journal*, vol. 25, no. 3 (July), pp. 281–93

Shearn, M (2007) Book Review: *The Myth of Work–Life Balance: The Challenge of Our Time for Men, Women and Societies*, *Work, Employment and Society*, vol. 21, no. 3, pp. 601–2

Shields, J (2007) *Managing Employee Performance and Reward: Concepts, Practices, Strategies*. Cambridge: Cambridge University Press

Shields, J (2015) *Managing Employee Performance and Reward: Concepts, practices, strategies*, 2nd edn. Cambridge: Cambridge University Press

Shields, J, Brown, M, Kaine, S, Dolle-Samuel, C, North-Samaradzic, A, McLean, P, Johns, R, O'Leary, P, Plimmer, G and Robinson, J (2021) *Managing Employee Performance and Reward: Concepts, Practices, Strategies*. Cambridge: Cambridge University Press

Shortland, S and Perkins, SJ (2016) Long-term assignment reward (dis)satisfaction outcomes: hearing women's voices, *Journal of Global Mobility*, vol. 4, no. 2, pp. 1–27

Shortland, S and Perkins, SJ (2019) Great expectations? Female expatriates' perceptions of organisational performance and development reviews in supporting access to international assignments', *Career Development International*, vol. 24, no. 2, pp. 110–26

Shortland, S and Perkins, SJ (2022a) Segmenting international assignments: theorising expatriate reward, in Perkins, SJ (ed.) *The Routledge Companion to Reward Management*. London: Routledge, pp. 191–99

Shortland, S and Perkins, SJ (2022b) What do we know about diversity, intersectionality and inclusion in organisationally-assigned expatriation? A review of relocation management company/consultancy practitioner research, *Career Development International*, vol. 27, no. 2, pp. 274–97

Shortland, S and Perkins, SJ (2023) Resourcing remuneration committees: in the dark or on the dark side of professionalisation?, *Employee Relations*, vol. 45, no. 2, pp. 402–20

Silverman, M, Kerrin, M and Carter, A (2005) *360-Degree Feedback: Beyond the spin*. Brighton: Institute for Employment Studies

Sims, RH and Schraeder, M (2005) Expatriate compensation: an exploratory review of salient contextual factors and common practices, *Career Development International*, vol. 10, no. 2, pp. 98–108

Skinner, BF (1953) *Science and Human Behavior*. New York: Macmillan

Slaughter, SA, Ang, S and Boh, WF (2007) Firm-specific human capital and compensation-organizational tenure profiles: an archival analysis of salary data for IT professionals, *Human Resource Management*, vol. 46, no. 3, pp. 373–94

Smith, A (1776) *The Wealth of Nations*. London, Penguin Books [1970 edn]

Smith, I (1983) *The Management of Remuneration: Paying for effectiveness*. London: IPD

Smith, I (1989) *Incentive Schemes: People and Profits*. London: Croner

Smith, I (2000) Benefits in White, G and Druker, J (eds.) *Reward Management: A critical text*. London: Routledge, pp. 151–75

Smith, I (2005) Pay, motivation and a re-think, Croner, *Pay and Benefits Briefing*, no. 293, pp. 4–6

Sparrow, P (1996) Too good to be true, *People Management*, 5 December, pp. 22–7

Sparrow, P (1999) International reward systems: to converge or not converge?, in Brewster, C and Harris, H (eds.) *International HRM: Contemporary Issues in Europe*. London: Routledge, pp. 102–119

Sparrow, P (2000) International reward management, in White, G and Drucker, J (eds.) *Reward Management: A critical text*. London, Routledge, pp. 196–214

Steers, RM and Porter, LW (1987) *Motivation and Work Behavior*, 4th edn. San Francisco: McGraw-Hill

Stiles, P and Taylor, B (2002) *Boards at Work: How Directors View their Roles and Responsibilities*. Oxford: Oxford University Press

Stockhammer, E (2013) *Why Have Wage Shares Fallen? A panel analysis of the determinants of functional income distribution*. Conditions of Work and Employment Series no. 35. Geneva: International Labour Organization

Storey, J (ed.) (1995) *Human Resource Management: A critical text*. London: Routledge

Storey, J (ed.) (2007) *Human Resource Management: A critical text*, 3rd edn. London: Thomson

Strebler, M, Thompson, M and Heron, P (1997*) Skills, Competencies and Gender: Issues for pay and training*. Report 333. Brighton: Institute of Employment Studies

Suutari, V and Tornikoski, C (2001) The challenge of expatriate compensation: the sources of satisfaction and dissatisfaction among expatriates, *International Journal of Human Resource Management*, vol. 12, no. 3, pp. 389–404

Sweney, M (2023) BT to axe up to 55,000 jobs by 2030 as it pushes into AI, *The Guardian*, www.theguardian.com/business/2023/may/18/bt-cut-jobs-telecoms-group-workforce (archived at https://perma.cc/G5HK-TUCY)

Sykes, A (2002) Overcoming poor value executive remuneration: resolving the manifest conflicts of interest, *Corporate Governance*, vol. 10, no. 4, pp. 256–60

Tan, D and Mahoney, JT (2006) Why a multinational firm chooses expatriates: integrating resource-based, agency and transaction cost perspectives, *Journal of Management Studies*, vol. 43, no. 3, pp. 457–84

Taylor, FW (1911) *The Principles of Scientific Management*. New York: Harper Bros

Taylor, M (2017) *Good work: the Taylor review of modern working practices*, www.gov.uk/government/publications/good-work-the-taylor-review-of-modern-working-practices (archived at https://perma.cc/4R2S-SQTG)

Taylor, S (2009) Pensions, in White, G and Druker, J (eds.) *Reward Management: A critical text*, 2nd edn. London: Routledge, pp. 192–211

Tekieli, M, Festing, M and Baeten, X (2018) Centralization and effectiveness of reward management in multinational enterprises, *Journal of Personnel Psychology*, vol. 17, no. 2, pp. 55–65

Tepper, B, Duffy, MK, Henle, CA and Schurer Lambert, L (2006) Procedural injustice, victim precipitation and abusive supervision, *Personnel Psychology*, vol. 59, no. 1, pp. 101–23

Thane, P (2006) The 'scandal' of women's pensions in Britain: how did it come about?, History and Policy Paper, www.historyandpolicy.org/policy-papers/papers/the-scandal-of-womens-pensions-in-britain-how-did-it-come-about (archived at https://perma.cc/Q2XN-ZU99)

The Pensions Regulator (2023) Annual Funding Statement Analysis 2023, www.thepensionsregulator.gov.uk/en/document-library/statements/annual-funding-statement-analysis-2023 (archived at https://perma.cc/F7TU-B8KL)

Thompson, M (1993) *Pay and Performance: The employee experience*. IMS Report 258. Brighton: Institute of Manpower Studies

Thompson, M (1995) *Team Working and Pay*. Brighton: Institute of Employment Studies

Thompson, M (2000) Salary progression systems, in White, G and Druker, J (eds.) *Reward Management: A critical text*. London: Routledge, pp. 125–49

Thompson, M (2009) Salary progression systems, in White, G and Druker, J (eds.) *Reward Management: A critical text*, 2nd edn. London: Routledge

Thompson, P (2002) *Total Reward*. London: CIPD

Thurow, L (1975) *Generating Inequality*. London: Macmillan

Towers Perrin (1997) *Learning from the Past: Changing for the future*. London: Towers Perrin

Thursfield, D (2015) Resistance to teamworking in a UK research and development laboratory, *Work, Employment and Society*, vol. 29, no. 6, pp. 989–1006

Transparency International UK (2016) *Incentivising Ethics: Managing Incentives to encourage good and deter bad behaviour*, www.transparency.org.uk/publications/incentivising-ethics-managing-incentives-to-encourage-good-and-deter-bad-behaviour/ (archived at https://perma.cc/SW8V-W5GK)

Tregaskis, O and Brewster, C (2006) Converging or diverging? A comparative analysis of trends in contingent employment practice across Europe over a decade, *Journal of International Business Studies*, vol. 37, no. 1, pp. 111–126

Trevor, CO, Gerhart, B and Boudreau, JW (1997) Voluntary turnover and job performance: curvilinearity and the moderating influences of salary growth and promotions', *Journal of Applied Psychology*, vol. 82, no. 1, pp. 144–93

Trevor, J (2010) *Can Pay be Strategic? A Critical Exploration of Strategic Pay in Practice*. Basingstoke: Palgrave MacMillan

Trevor, J and Brown, W (2014) The limits on pay as a strategic tool: obstacles to alignment in non-union environments, *British Journal of Industrial Relations*, vol. 52, pp. 553–78

TUC (2006) *Press release: Reaction to IDS Directors' Pay Report 2006*, 3 November. London: Trades Union Congress

Tyson, S (2005) Fat cat pay, in Tyson, S and Bournois, F (eds.) *Top Pay and Performance: International and Strategic Approach*. London: Elsevier, pp. 12–28

Tyson, S and Bournois, F (2005) Introduction, in *Top Pay and Performance: International and Strategic Approach*. London: Elsevier, pp. 1–11

Ulrich, D (1997) *Human Resource Champions: The Next Agenda for Adding Value and Delivering Results*. Boston, MA: HBS Press

Ulrich, D and Brockbank, W (2005) *The HR Value Proposition*. Boston, MA,: Harvard Business School Press

UNCTAD (2019) *World Investment Report 2019: Special Economic Zones*. New York: United Nations Publications

UNCTAD (2023) United Nations Conference on Trade and Development 2023 World Investment Report, unctad.org/publication/world-investment-report-2023 (archived at https://perma.cc/BN7H-V8MS)

University of Kent (2008) Equal Pay Report, media. www.kent.ac.uk/se/17733/equal_pay_audit.pdf (archived at https://perma.cc/358B-H9BD)

Van Wanrooy, B, Bewley, H, Bryson, A, Forth, J, Freeth, S, Stokes, L and Wood, S (2013) *Employment Relations in the Shadow of Recession. Findings from the 2011 Workplace Employment relations Study*. Basingstoke: Palgrave Macmillan

Vaughan-Whitehead, D (2015) *The European Social Model in Crisis: Is Europe losing its soul?* London: Edward Elgar/International Labor Organisation

Veliyath, R (1999) Top management compensation and shareholder returns: Unravelling different models of the relationship, *Journal of Management Studies*, vol. 36, no. 1, pp. 123–43

Vernon, G (2006) International pay and reward, in Edwards, T and Rees, C (eds.) *International Human Resource Management: Globalization, national systems and multinational companies*. London: Prentice Hall, pp. 217–41

von Bertalanffy, L (1969) *General System Theory: Foundations, Developments, Applications*. New York: George Braziller

Vroom, VH (1964) *Work and Motivation*. New York: John Wiley

Walby, S and Olsen, W (2002) *The Impact of Women's Position in the Labour Market on Pay and Implications for UK Productivity*. Women and Equality Unit, London. Department of Trade and Industry

Walker, D (2009) *A Review of Corporate Governance in UK Banks and other Financial Industry Entities: Final recommendations*. London: The Walker Review Secretariat

Wallerstein, I (1983) *Historical Capitalism with Capitalist Civilization*. London: Verso

Watson, BW Jr and Singh, G (2005) Global pay systems: compensation in support of a multinational strategy, *Compensation & Benefits Review*, vol. 37, January/February, pp. 33–6

Watson, M (2005) *Foundations of International Political Economy*. Basingstoke: Palgrave-Macmillan

Weitzman, ML (1984) *The Share Economy: Conquering stagflation*. Cambridge, MA: Harvard University Press

Wentland, DM (2003) A new practical guide for determining expatriate compensation: the comprehensive model, *Compensation & Benefits Review*, vol. 35, no. 3, pp. 45–50

Wheatley, MJ (2020) *Leadership and the New Science: Discovering Order in a Chaotic World*. Oakland, CA: Berrett-Koehler Publishers

White, G (2000) The Pay Review Body system: its development and impact, *Historical Studies in Industrial Relations*, vol. 9 (Spring), pp. 71–100

White, G (2009) Determining pay, in White, G and Druker, J (eds.) *Reward Management: A critical text*, 2nd edn. London: Routledge, pp. 23–48

White, RS and Hollingsworth, KG (2018) How can we pay to get out of this? executive compensation and bank risk during the financial crisis, *Banking & Finance Review*, vol. 10, no. 1, pp. 19–34

Whitley, R (2000) *Divergent Capitalisms: The Social Structuring and Change of Business Systems*. Oxford: Oxford University Pres

Whittington, R (2001) *What is Strategy and Does it Matter?*, 2nd edn. London, Thomson Learning

Williamson, O (1975) *Markets and Hierarchies*. New York, Free Press

Wilson, F and Bowey, AM (1989) Profit- and performance-based systems, in Bowey, AM (ed.) *Managing Salary and Wage Systems*. Aldershot: Gower

Woodruffe, C (1991) Competent by any other name, *Personnel Management*, September, pp. 30–3

Woodworth, RS (1918) *Dynamic Psychology*. New York: Columbia University Press

WorldatWork (2007) *Executive Rewards Questionary*. Scottsdale AZ: World@Work

WorldatWork (2013) Trends in Employee Recognition 2013, www.worldatwork.org/waw/adimLink?id=72689 (archived at https://perma.cc/C77P-F25H)

WorldatWork (2015) Total rewards programs and Practices: A survey of what is in use today, worldatwork.org/media/CDN/dist/CDN2/documents/pdf/resources/research/2015_Total-Rewards-Inventory-Survey.pdf (archived at https://perma.cc/X4DA-5CLZ)

WorldatWork (2017) Total rewards inventory, www.worldatwork.org/docs/marketing/2017_BRO_TRinventChecklist_J5674_FNL_web.pdf (archived at https://perma.cc/HP8V-NUAK)

WorldatWork (2019) What Is Total Rewards, worldatwork.org/content-topics/total-rewards (archived at https://perma.cc/6KXZ-P7NP)

Wowak, AJ and Hambrick, DC (2010) A model of person-pay interaction: how executives vary in their responses to compensation arrangement, *Strategic Management Journal*, vol. 31, pp. 803–21

Wright, A (2004) *Reward Management in Context*. London: Chartered Institute of Personnel and Development

Wright, A (2009) Flexible benefits: shaping the way ahead?, in Corby, S, Palmer, S and Lindop, E (eds.) *Rethinking Reward*. Basingstoke: Palgrave Macmillan, pp. 247–56

Wright, C (2005) Reward strategy in context, in (Childs, M, consultant ed.) *CIPD Reward Management* (loose-leaf publication). London: CIPD, section 1.2

Wright, P, Kroll, M, Krug, J and Pettus, M (2007) Influences of top management team incentives on firm risk taking, *Strategic Management Journal*, vol. 28, no. 1, pp. 81–9

Wright, PM and McMahan, GC (1992) Theoretical perspectives for strategic human resource management, *Journal of Management*, vol. 18, no. 2, pp. 295–320

Wright, PM and McMahan, GC (2011) Exploring human capital: Putting 'human' back into strategic human resource management, *Human Resource Management Journal*, vol. 21, no. 2, pp 93–104

XpertHR (2012) *Using market-pay comparisons: The 2012 XpertHR survey*. London: XpertHR

XpertHR (2013) *Location pay and allowances: 2013 XpertHR survey*. London: XpertHR

XpertHR (2014a) *Employers' Use of Competencies*. London: XpertHR

XpertHR (2014b) *Maternity pay and leave: XpertHR survey 2014*, www.xperthr.co.uk/survey-analysis/maternity-pay-and-leave-xperthr-survey/2014/153301 (archived at https://perma.cc/GK33-K4FK)

XpertHR (2014c) *Paternity pay and leave: XpertHR survey 2014*, www.xperthr.co.uk/survey-analysis/paternity-pay-and-leave-xperthr-survey/2014/ 153305 (archived at https://perma.cc/9R6A-KK3G)

XpertHR (2015a) *Annual Leave: 2015 XpertHR survey of employer practice*, www.xperthr.co.uk/sur ve y-analysis/annual-leave-2015-xpert hr -survey-of-employer-practice/154102 (archived at https://perma.cc/THL6-7UG2)

XpertHR (2015b) *Occupational Sick Pay scheme survey 2015: Rates of pay offered by organisations*, www.xperthr.co.uk/survey-analysis/xperthr-survey-analysis/occupational-sick-pay-schemes-survey-2015-rates-of-pay-offered-by-organisations/155891/ (archived at https://perma.cc/2KUB-HJGJ)

XpertHR (2019) *XpertHR benefits and allowances survey 2019*, www.xperthr.co.uk/survey-analysis/xperthr-benefits-and-allowances-survey-2019-overview/164457/ (archived at https://perma.cc/E5MW-PEW8)

Young, MB (2006) *Strategic Workforce Planning: forecasting human capital needs to execute business strategy*. The Conference Board Report R-1391-06-WG

Zeckhauser, RJ (ed.) (1991) *The Strategy of Choice*. Cambridge, MA: MIT Press

Zingheim, PK and Schuster, JR (2000) *Pay People Right! Breakthrough reward strategies to create great companies*. San Francisco, Jossey-Bass

Zondo, RWD (2018) The impact of gainsharing in the automotive parts manufacturing industry of South Africa, *South African Journal of Economic and Management Sciences*, vol. 21, no. 1, E1–E8

Zweimüller, J and Barth, E (1992) Bargaining structure, wage determination and wage dispersion in six OECD countries, Institute of Industrial Relations Working Paper Series, University of California, Berkeley

INDEX

NB: page numbers in *italic* indicate figures or tables